FARINA

Denise —
What a pleasure to have you in "Farina"!
Thank you for dining with us.
Enjoy the lifelong adventure of
good food, family & friends!

2023

Buon Appetito!

FARINA

MICHAEL SMITH

PHOTOGRAPHY BY JENNY WHEAT

FARINA
Copyright © 2022 by Michael Smith
Photographs copyright © 2022 by Jenny Wheat

ISBN: 978-1-7376046-2-4

Library of Congress Cataloging in Publication data
available upon request.

All rights reserved. Except for review purposes, no portion of this book may be reproduced in any form without the express written permission of Michael Smith and Story Farm.

Published in the United States by Story Farm
www.story-farm.com

Editorial director	Bo Morris
Art director	Jason Farmand
Production director	Tina Dahl
Copy editor	Karen Cakebread
Proofreader	Anja Schmidt
Recipe tester	Nancy Boyce
Indexer	Amy Hall

Printed in China by Crash Paper of Playa Del Rey, California

First printing, November 2022
10 9 8 7 6 5 4 3 2 1

Cover image by Jenny Wheat
www.wheatphoto.com

THIS BOOK IS DEDICATED TO the women who shaped my life. I love you all. To my mother Donna and my sister Nathelle. To my wife Nancy, thank you for following the path with me and guiding my boundless energy. To Misha and Sophie, you are on your own paths now. Have fun and be happy!

CONTENTS

FOREWORD 9

INTRODUCTION 11

FARINA WINE SERVICE 18

PIATTINI, INSALATA & SOUPS 24

PASTA 80

ENTRÉES 144

COCKTAILS 182

DESSERT 200

THE MODERN PANTRY 226

ACKNOWLEDGMENTS 278

INDEX 280

Amur Ossetra Caviar

Plymouth Champagne Massachusetts

Wellf[leet] Cape Massach[usetts]

Bill and Peggy Lyons

FOREWORD

I AM A READER. I will give just about anything a shot, and if the subject matter or style doesn't grab me, I move on. So, I remember well, in 2000, when I picked up Anthony Bourdain's breakthrough book, *Kitchen Confidential*, and read it straight through. Even though I had no connection to the restaurant business, Bourdain's humorous, fast-paced and occasionally raunchy insider's look at life in the kitchen was wildly entertaining and educational.

His description of *owning* a restaurant was particularly memorable: the low odds of success; the skinny (or nonexistent) margins; the "transient and unstable" workforce. He compared owning a restaurant to "standing on the tracks, watching the lights of the oncoming locomotive, knowing full well it will eventually run [you] over."

It wasn't too long after this that a colleague dropped a rough business plan on my desk and suggested I take a look. He knew I liked food and wine. He knew I appreciated creative people and enterprises. He assumed I could take a reasonable financial risk.

It was, of course, the first draft of Michael Smith's business plan for 40 Sardines, a new restaurant concept to be built from scratch. Michael had decided to leave The American Restaurant, Kansas City's finest at the time, where he had recently won the prestigious James Beard Award as the best chef in the Midwest. He had worked all over the world in notable restaurants and was ready to be his own boss.

Twenty-four years and four restaurants later, I can report that my decision to ignore Bourdain's scary advice about restaurant ownership was an excellent one. While the potential pitfalls were all as advertised—including some, like a global pandemic, that came out of nowhere—there were several things that made this ownership experience decidedly different.

First, Michael is a true entrepreneur. His upbringing was simple, often hard, and he learned how to make do with what he had to overcome challenges. Like most entrepreneurs, he works crazy hours and draws on a well of energy that most people simply don't have. His ever-present ponytail is always on the move. His work ethic is second to none.

Second, Michael is both a learner and a teacher. His cooking style has pivoted from French to "New American" to Mediterranean and now, to contemporary Italian. It has evolved from refined and somewhat presentation-centric to something more relaxed and higher up the "comfort" scale. Creative reinvention is the key to longevity in the restaurant business, and Michael's craft is never static. As his experience in the food business has grown into perspective, and his perspective has grown into wisdom, he has shared his knowledge with a cadre of young chefs who have gone off to start their own successful establishments. He has created an ecosystem of food-centered success.

Third, Michael is simply a people person. If the kitchen is short-staffed, he will happily jump in as a line cook for the night to keep things moving, but he is happiest when he can work the front of the house, greeting regulars (whom he often calls "cool cats") and new customers, hopping from table to table, sometimes sitting down for a brief conversation. He understands that people come together over a meal to enjoy each other's company and good conversation, and his food is the vehicle for that. I have never seen a chef who is so genuinely pleased to greet, chat with and thank his customers.

I am delighted that Michael is now able to present this beautiful book about the food, drink and inspiration of Farina. I am proud that he convinced previous investors and me to support his abundant creativity as it has evolved over the decades. Farina is a lively and welcoming restaurant, housed in a carefully restored, 100-year-old brick building in the heart of one of Kansas City's historic neighborhoods. It is a gem.

Enjoy Michael's recipes. Enjoy his restaurant. Be a cool cat.

BILL LYONS
OWNER, FARINA RISTORANTE & OYSTER BAR

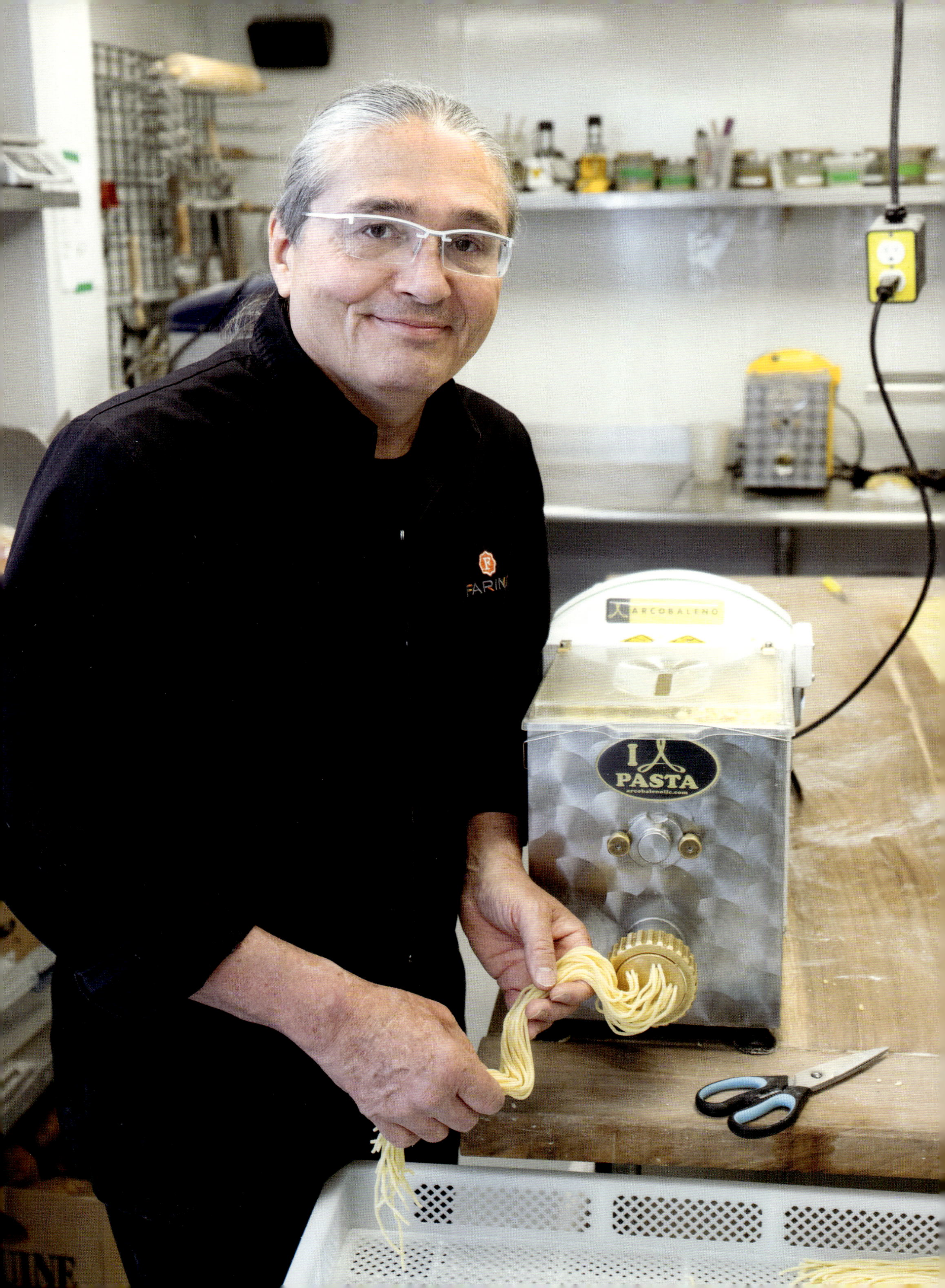
ARCOBALENO
I PASTA
arcobalenollc.com

INTRODUCTION

THE ROAD TO FARINA

It all started with a pasta machine.

Not just any pasta machine. But an Arcobaleno AEX10, the "Lola" model, a stainless steel beauty weighing in at 43 pounds and capable of punching out 13 pounds of dough an hour with more than 40 different shapes. This was a few years after I had opened Michael Smith Restaurant with my wife, Nancy. The place was doing well. It had won widespread acclaim. Hell, Mick Jagger once ate dinner there. But like all restaurateurs we kept a very close eye on the bottom line. And Lovely Lola put a $6,500 dent in the company credit card—an admittedly questionable purchase since I was, after all, a French-trained chef not exactly known for his pasta.

But I am known for being a restless kind of guy. Always eager to learn something new, try something different. Buying Lola was me looking for a way to refresh our menu at the restaurant. It was also me looking for a way to keep the kitchen staff excited about dragging themselves into work each day. A bored crew is not a crew that cooks well.

Lola proved to be an inspiration to us all. Before long we were experimenting with everything from bigoli and gemelli to orecchiette and spaccatelli, with plenty of screwups along the way. We learned a lot. We had fun. We got to eat our mistakes.

And eight years later, with hard-won confidence in our pasta-making chops, the backing of our wonderful business partners, and a whole lot of luck, we opened the doors of Farina.

Thanks, Lola.

FROM BUSBOY TO GRILL GUY

Folks often ask what inspired me to become a chef. The answer is simple: I *love* to eat.

Not that I grew up with anything even approaching a refined palate, unless that includes deep knowledge of TV dinners. I was born in Gettysburg, South Dakota (population: 1,152), about 15 miles east of the Missouri River. My mother Donna was a good cook, but we were really poor for a few years during my childhood, and at mealtime she had to get creative. Her specialty was Southern-Midwestern fare—pan-fried beef liver, fried okra, fried gizzards, casseroles, mashed potatoes. Finding time to cook? That was the hard part. My mother worked long hours and struggled to raise my older sister Nathelle and me by herself. After moving us to Texas and through a succession of Panhandle towns, we were living in a trailer park outside of Lubbock when my mother signed on as a manager for Zuider Zee, a chain of family restaurants once popular throughout Texas and the Southwest. She excelled at her job, turning around underperforming restaurants and making them profitable. How did Zuider Zee reward my mother? By relocating her from one town to another. When it was time for our family dinners, my mother was usually at work.

So, yeah. TV dinners. My mother used to buy them twenty at a time. We would save the aluminum trays and when all the dinners were gone my mother would find her way to the kitchen and cook something from her standard repertoire. Then she would refill the trays, freeze them, and we'd have homemade TV dinners for the days ahead.

From the time I was 12, my sister and I worked at Zuider Zee every day that my mother worked. We peeled potatoes, peeled shrimp, made salad dressings, cleaned restrooms and vacuumed dining rooms. I fell in love with the kitchen lingo: "86 the fried clams!" "Order in!" "Fire!" "Pick up!" "Corner!" It was like learning an exotic new language.

My first home-cooking experience came when I was 13 or 14. It was nothing simple like beans 'n' weenies. We had gone out to dinner at a semi-fancy restaurant—a rare treat—where we ordered whole, steamed artichokes. I'd never eaten anything like that and decided to try making them at home. They were freaking delicious. Pretty cool, I thought. I like doing this.

By the time I was in junior high school we had moved to Denver, and my mother was working for Mr. Steak, a larger chain that at one time had nearly 300 locations. I enrolled in a work-study program that allowed me to leave school at 11:30 a.m. to bus tables and wash dishes at Mr. Steak. I gotta say, I was awesome at busing tables. I loved moving through the restaurant, straightening things, making sure everything was in order. I still love doing that. When you visit Farina, if I'm not in the kitchen you'll most likely see me in motion on the floor, chatting up customers, shaving truffles and popping oysters at the oyster bar. I learned it working for my mother at Mr. Steak.

After Mr. Steak transferred her to Pueblo, Colorado, my mother hired me as a server for a few months until a cook's job opened up. For the record, she soon fired me because, well, I was a 17-year-old turd, an annoying know-it-all kid telling her how to run a restaurant. I wound up working the grill at a Western Sizzlin steakhouse before entering the University of Southern Colorado (now Colorado State University Pueblo) and landing a kitchen job at La Renaissance, which was Pueblo's best restaurant even though everything, even the potatoes, came out of big #10 cans.

Officially, I was studying psychology in college, but I was really studying pasta. Every day after finishing class and before starting my shift at La Renaissance, I ate a one-pound package of spaghetti slathered with cheap bottled sauce. I knew nothing about real Italian cooking. But I liked spaghetti and needed the carbs to power me through the long days. I kept this up for years. When I think about it now, I cringe.

And I consider our pasta program at Farina my official apology to the food gods for eating hundreds of jars of Ragú.

CHASING THE FOOD DREAM

The owners of La Renaissance, brothers Bob and Jim Fredregill, first planted the idea of me going to culinary school. At the time, I didn't know there even was such a thing. All I knew was that after finishing four years at La Renaissance and four years of college, the last thing I wanted was to go back to school.

So, after graduation I spent the summer backpacking through Europe, from England to Greece. It changed my life. I knew I wanted to do two things—travel and eat. And I mean, *really fucking eat*. No more recycled TV dinners. No more packaged spaghetti and lousy sauce. I wanted good food every day. The only problem was, upon returning to the States, I had no clue how I was going to make my food dreams happen.

One day I spotted an ad in the *Denver Post* that read: "Fine French restaurant looking for cooks." No name. Just a phone number. I called and set up an interview with Chef Jean-Pierre Lelievre of Chateau Pyrenees, a landmark Denver restaurant, since closed, known for its whimsical, sandcastle-like design. So intimidated was I by the thought of being grilled by a real French chef that I bought a copy of the Culinary Institute of America (CIA) cookbook and read it from cover to cover. When I showed up for the interview, my head was ready to explode. The first question Chef Jean-Pierre asked me was: "When can you start?" He didn't ask me a single thing about cooking. I told him my only experience was at steakhouses. "It's OK," he said. "I'll teach you." I signed on for seven dollars an hour.

Soon I was whipping up baked Alaska, filleting salmon, cleaning lamb racks and feeling so cocky about my growing chef skills that I applied to the CIA and got accepted. Chef

Jean-Pierre urged me not to leave. "Stay here and learn from me," he said. I don't know what he saw in me. Just a kid who was hungry and didn't mind hard work and long hours—the basic requirements for being a chef. So, I stayed. And I've never once regretted that decision, even though not long after I turned my back on the CIA, Chef Jean-Pierre decided to return to France to open a traiteur and charcuterie shop in Nice. I was devastated, but his successor, Chef George Mavrothalassitis, proved to be a generous teacher too. Chef Mavro, as everyone calls him, had left his restaurant in Cassis, France, to come to America and run Chateau Pyrenees. I worked as Chef Mavro's sous chef for a year and then left for France. Mavro suggested to his ex-wife, who continued to operate his former restaurant in Cassis, that I would be a good hire in the kitchen and so I spent a nine-month season in their restaurant, La Presqu'île. Perched along the Mediterranean with killer views of the Calanques, the rocky cliffs and bays that stretch between Cassis and Marseilles, La Presqu'île is still there today. Working there was a great gig. I made squid ink pasta every day, dove for sea urchins in waters surrounding the restaurant and discovered habanero peppers for the first time. The other cooks were all young, single guys like me. We lived above the restaurant, woke up each morning to a gorgeous view of the sea, got two meals a day and worked our butts off. It was heaven.

When I decided to head home in 1987, that experience helped me secure a job with Charlie Trotter, who had just opened his first namesake restaurant in Chicago. I quickly made my way up to sous chef, working with Charlie for a couple of years before returning to France one more time, as chef de cuisine for Jean-Pierre at Restaurant Albion. After more than two years in Nice it was back to Chicago, where I served as executive chef at Gordon Sinclair's eponymous contemporary restaurant Gordon.

Travel. Eat. Cook. Repeat.

I was living the dream alright. But somewhere in the back of my head I was thinking maybe it was time to settle down.

FINDING HOME

It was an act of God that brought me to Kansas City. Namely, the Great Flood of 1993, which wreaked havoc throughout the Midwest.

There was a big fundraiser in Chicago for the flood victims and I took part in it. Jim Ackard, executive chef of The American Restaurant at the time, attended the event. His food station was crazy busy, and I ended up helping him most of the night. A year and a half later, Ackard resigned from The American. He pulled my name out of a stack of resumes and recommended me to my soon-to-be boss, Tom Johnson.

I didn't know much about Kansas City other than it wasn't on my list of places with "real restaurant cultures." A nice place, but one most famous for barbecue and the blues. I figured I would be in Kansas for a couple of years before moving along. But after settling in at The American and getting my first James Beard nomination in 1997 for "Best Chef: Midwest," Kansas City had begun to feel like home. We had also launched an annual James Beard Foundation fundraising event that over a seven-year period brought in more than a hundred of America's finest chefs. It helped elevate the city's culinary profile and proved a great training ground for young chefs throughout the region.

Having won the James Beard Award in 1999, I left The American two years later and, after a lot of pavement-pounding and fundraising, started my own restaurant, 40 Sardines. It won a James Beard Award for "Best Restaurant Graphics" in 2003 and was a finalist for "Best New Restaurant."

While all the accolades and laurels were gratifying, I wasn't ready to rest on them. The next stop was Kansas City's emerging Crossroads Art District, where in 2007 Nancy and I opened Michael Smith Restaurant and Extra Virgin, our Spanish tapas restaurant. We were also traveling whenever we could. The trip that changed everything was in 2012, when we ate our way through Italy's Piedmont region, including memorable meals at Chef Ugo Alciati's famed restaurant, Guido.

I loved Italian food before that trip—I mean, who doesn't?—but after returning to Kansas City, I found myself not just loving it, but craving it. I wanted to cook and eat Italian all the time. I like to joke that I needed to get the French out of me, but that's truly what it amounted to. That's when I bought Lola, the $6,500 pasta machine. After I and the rest of the kitchen crew were finally ready to show off our skills, we began shifting gears with the menu at Michael Smith Restaurant. First came weekly "Big Night" dinners paying homage to the great 1996 film starring Stanley Tucci. Next up was a full-on pivot to an Italian menu we called "Finding Guido," a tribute to our favorite Piedmont restaurant and a takeoff on that popular animated film featuring a young clownfish who goes missing from his family. The Michael Smith name and logo was plastered on the building and I didn't know how to position the concept change with a new name. Close friends on our Piedmont trip, Brad and Teresa, suggested I name it "Michael Smith Finding Guido." Although it sounded a bit corny because of the movie, I justified it in my mind because I was *finding my inner Guido!*

Then one Saturday night in 2018, during the middle service at Michael Smith Restaurant, I got a phone call from Bill Lyons. This was surprising, since Bill and Peggy Lyons, our partners, would never have called during prime time in the kitchen. But what Bill had to tell me was well worth the interruption.

"You know that Italian restaurant we've been talking about?" Bill said. "The space next door to Michael Smith just became available. But we only have 24 hours to move on it."

And move we did.

WELCOME TO FARINA

Sitting at a table in the sleek, modern comfort of Farina, it's hard to imagine that prior to the space being home Kansas City's first White Castle, an art gallery, and a dental equipment dealer, it was a Montgomery Ward auto center. Indeed, our bar sits right where grease monkeys used to rotate tires and perform oil changes.

I love the location and the people who pass through here. For the first time in 30 years, you can look out on the corner of Baltimore and 19th Street with views of the 85-year-old Town Topic burger joint. Our oyster bar looks directly onto 19th Street, and our guests love looking at the busy street scene that was once desolate, now filled with people from all walks of life cruising through the Crossroads. There's a real sense of place.

We've helped lead the revitalization of one of Kansas City's most dynamic neighborhoods. Where empty lots and dilapidated buildings once stood, hotels and swanky apartments are popping up, served by a full array of breweries, boutiques, restaurants and coffee shops. The vibe is definitely that of a transformative place. And I like to think our menu at Farina reflects that. Just as our building has transformed over the years, so have my interests as a chef.

While our name might be taken from the Italian word for flour, our offerings go far beyond pasta, as the pages that follow will show. These are some of our favorite dishes.

I am proud to share the recipes with you.

Salame del
Contadino
1x € 7,50
2x € 14,00

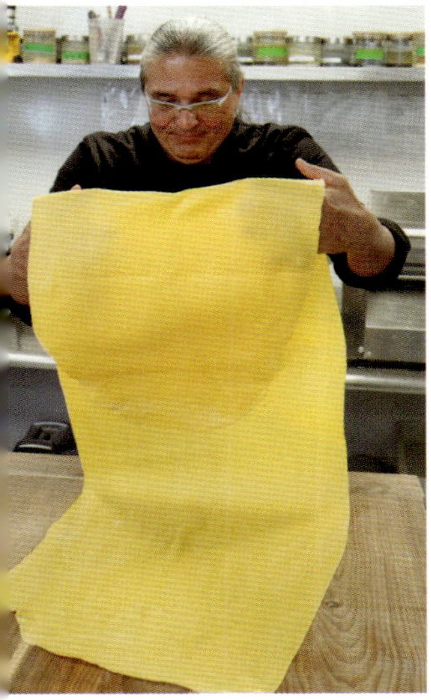

BRUNELLO
DI MONTALCINO
2016
POGGIO LANDI

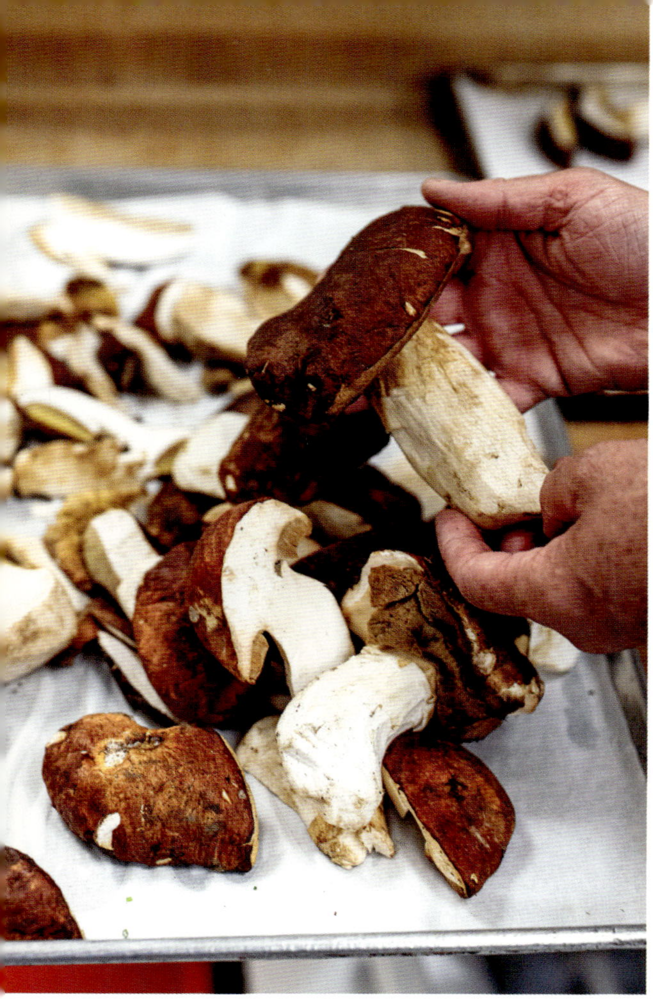
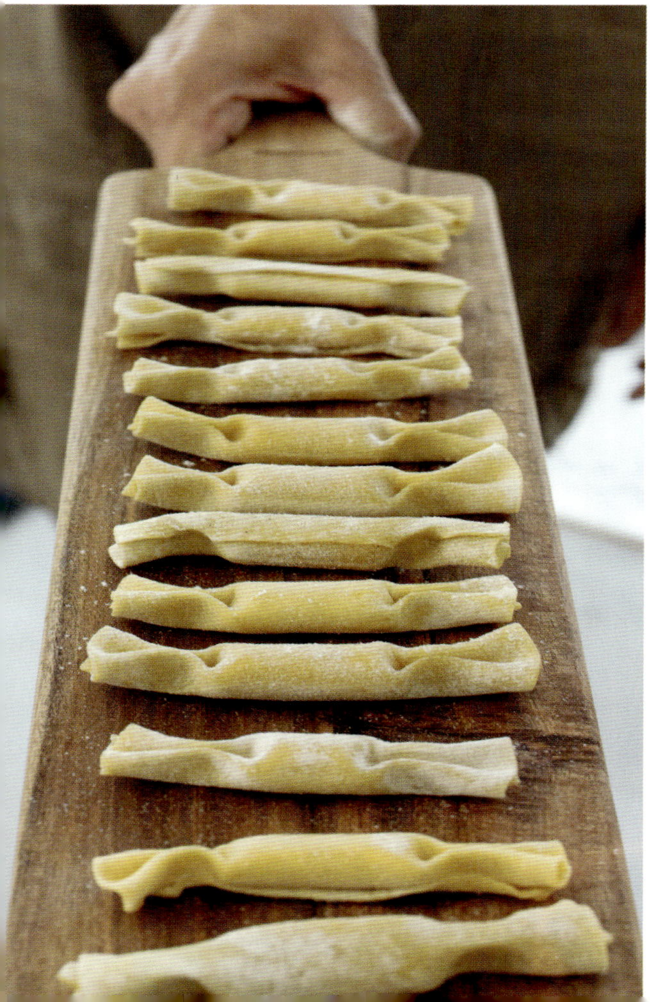
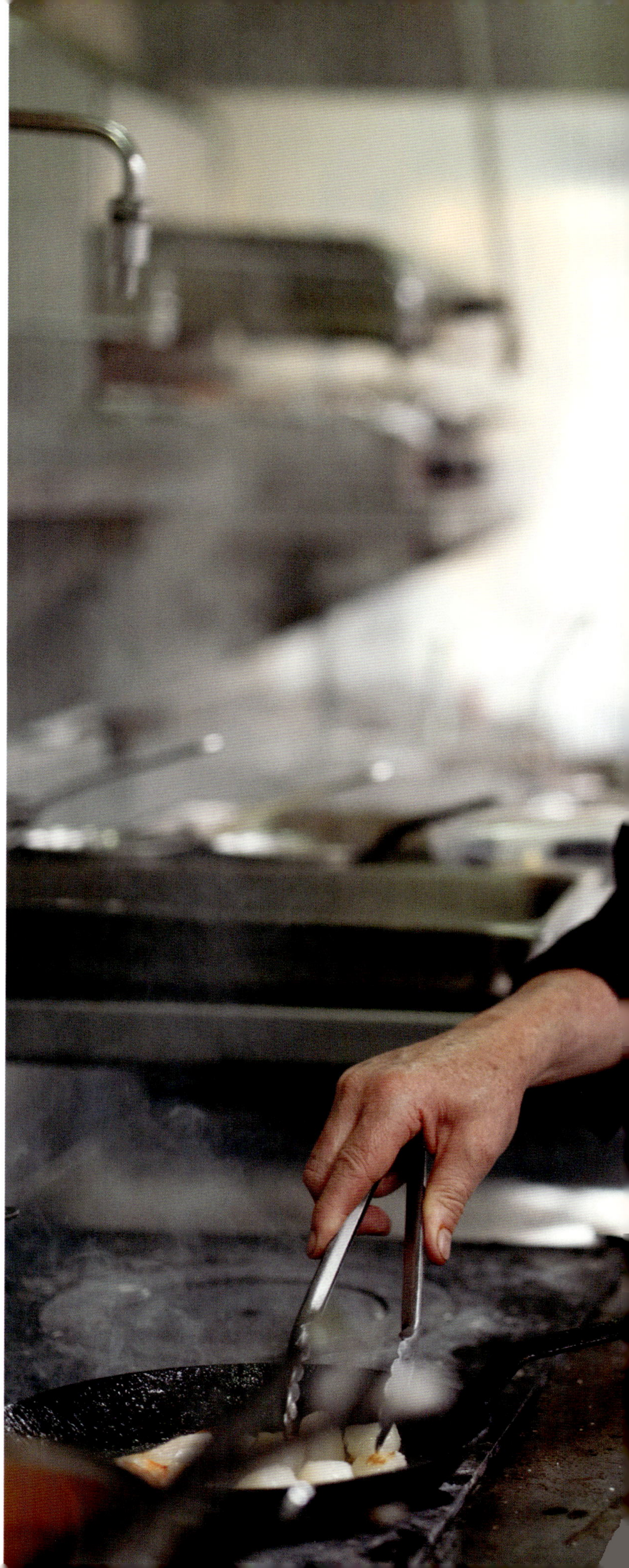

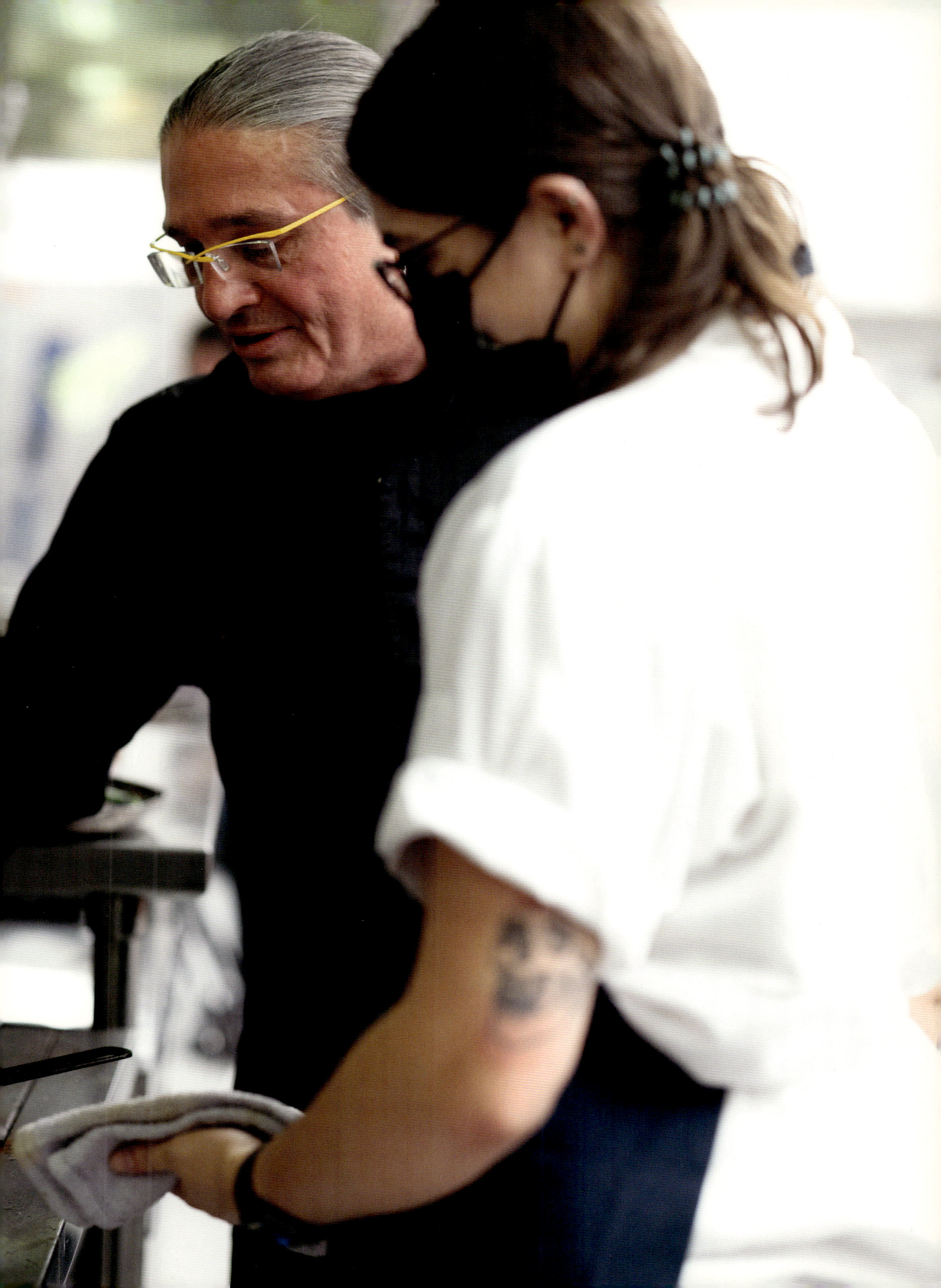

FARINA WINE SERVICE

One question we often get asked at Farina is: "What's your favorite wine?" It's like being asked to pick your favorite child. There's no way to answer it. There are too many factors that go into tasting, liking and understanding wine to pick a single favorite. The season, the food, the weather, the mood, the company, the type of celebration (or commiseration)—all influence the best choice of wine for a particular occasion.

Nancy works the floor nightly at Farina greeting guests, checking in on tables and coordinating the dining room and kitchen service teams. But mostly she sells wine. She is a first-level sommelier and that is essentially her function, but she prefers to be recognized as a wine steward. She doesn't have any awards or an abundance of certificates, but she knows a hell of a lot about wine. Most important, she knows what our guests like to drink. And if they don't know what they like, she is great at listening and learning about their preferences. Listening to our guests is the most important part of Nancy's job. She loves discussing and tasting wines with experienced wine drinkers and novices both. When approaching a table to discuss wine, a few things she always asks are:
1. What do you normally like to drink?
2. What are you having to eat tonight?
3. Tell me what you don't like? Butter? Oak? Leather? Tar? Sweet wine? Dry wine?

We have an extensive wine list that covers a lot of territory and price ranges. We're confident we can find something you like. And if it turns out you don't like the wine, we will find you something else. It's simply not a big deal. You won't hurt our feelings. We want you to enjoy the experience of drinking wine at Farina.

Years ago, at Michael Smith restaurant, our main focus was to pair wines with tasting menus, starting with something light and easy then moving to fuller taste profiles as the dishes became more involved and intense. When we opened Farina in 2019, we switched gears and created an Italian food menu. Nancy tasted a lot of Italian wine and familiarized herself with the varietals from Tuscany, Piedmont, Sicily, Alto Adige and so on. She was already familiar with drinking Italian wine but needed to study it and immerse herself in its history and regions, knowing full well guests would rely on her to pair wines with their dinner. Kansas City wine drinkers are pretty damn sophisticated, and our guests travel all over the world. They like to experience good food and wine, and that makes us happy.

If a guest is not sure they want to commit to a glass or a bottle, Nancy will ask, "How about a half glass of that rosé we discussed? And while you're enjoying that, we can choose a bottle of red and give it time to open." Our guests don't need to commit to a full glass. We want them to feel comfortable tasting and experiencing wine no matter the circumstances. For a quality wine program, it is important to serve wines at the correct temperature, and we make certain to have the correct refrigeration for all our wines at Farina. The wines are stored properly and kept at the right temperature, and that improves the chances that the guests will enjoy what we recommend for them. If they don't like the wine, we will take it off the table. If the wine is not compromised in any way, we're confident we can sell it by the glass. Some restaurants make drinking wine such a chore—too serious and imposing. That's never the case at Farina.

Pairing wine with foods is a fun part of the job, especially if a guest is feeling adventurous and we can tweak the direction toward something a little funky or unconventional. There is never one right answer, either. We feel comfortable suggesting an unoaked Chardonnay from Alto Adige and a Piedmont Nebbiolo with bucatini carbonara on the same table. Why? Because guests that are white wine lovers and red wine lovers are often at the same table and they want to share food. We don't discourage it and it lets Nancy explain how wine works, like the crispness of an unoaked Chardonnay brightening up the creamy egg yolk, and how the acidity of the Chardonnay complements the acidity of the cheese. Meanwhile, the charred character of the pancetta and the power of black pepper work perfectly with the leather and meatiness of Barolo. Bucatini carbona can have several friends. Our next suggestion? Top it with shaved Alba black truffles!

As an Italian restaurant, our focus is Italian wines, but we understand that not everyone loves Italian wine. Kansas City loves Napa Cabernets and good-quality Pinot Noir, and we're okay with that. Some of our favorite wines in the world are Napa Cabs and Pinots. Half bottles are an interesting part of our list, but in general, half-bottle selections gain and wane in popularity through the years. What about the guests that want to drink Riesling, Malbec or Sancerre? Answer: half bottles. We try to cover other popular regions and varietals with half-bottle selections so that everyone can enjoy a glass or two of their favorite wines without feeling pressure to buy a whole bottle. Along those same lines, many guests simply want to drink by the glass, so we keep a vibrant wine-by-the-glass program that is seasonally focused.

Another crucial aspect of our wine service is the ability to tell a story connecting us (or our guests) to a vineyard or a winemaker. Guests want to know and hear about interesting places, and we love to share our travel and wine-tasting history with them because they've tasted and visited some great places too. Often a story can be the clincher to a wine decision. Perhaps a guest can't decide, and when we relate a personal story, they are intrigued and want to have the chance to drink that juice too.

We try to cover a lot of bases on the Farina wine list, from heavy hitters to very affordable varietals. We want to select a wine that will spark conversation and be enjoyed by our guests. Drinking wine makes memories and when it's outstanding, you won't soon forget it or where you had it. At Farina, we are here to help you create wonderful memories. We strive to do that through our food, wine and cocktails. That's what we do, and you are why we do it.

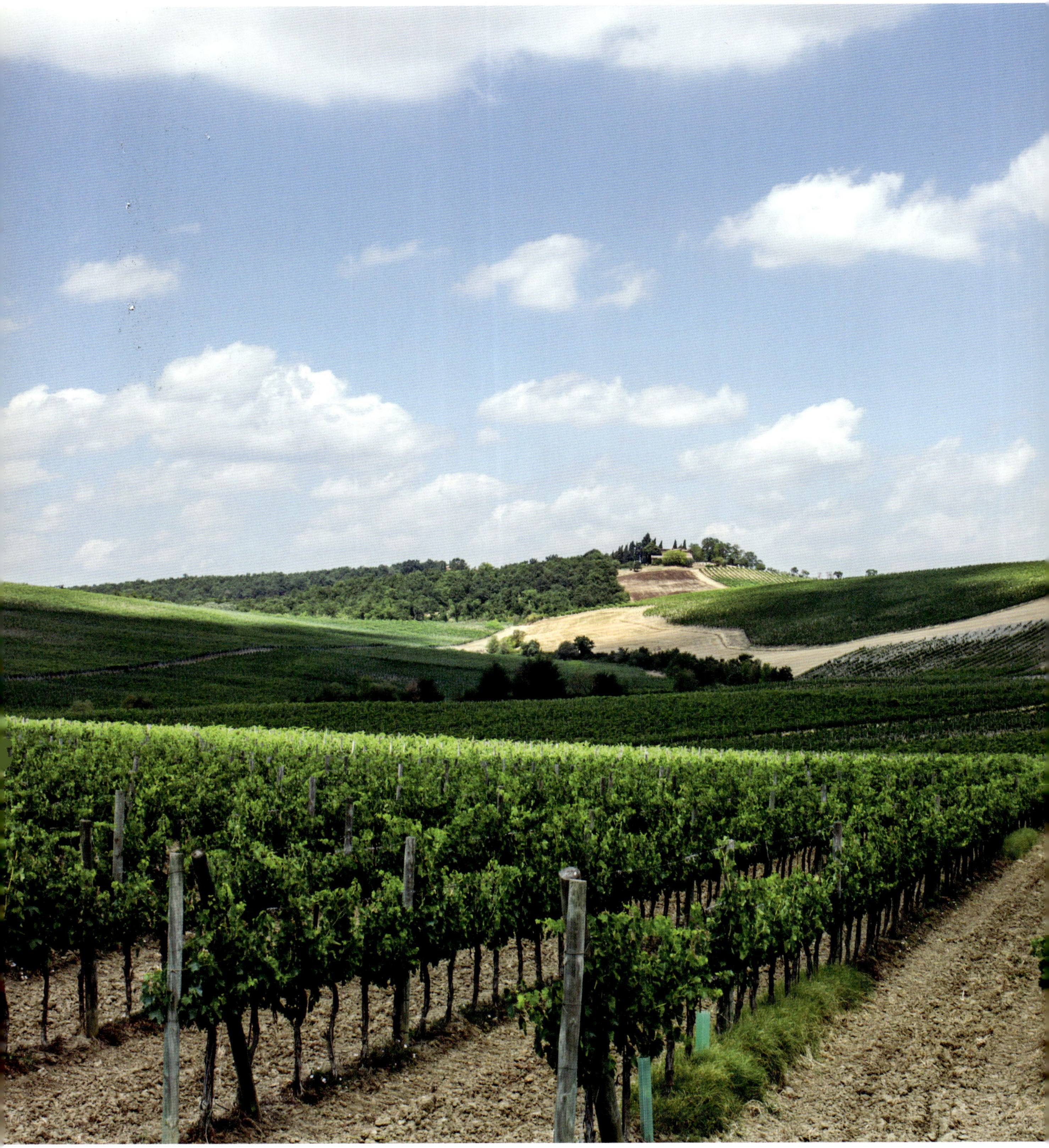

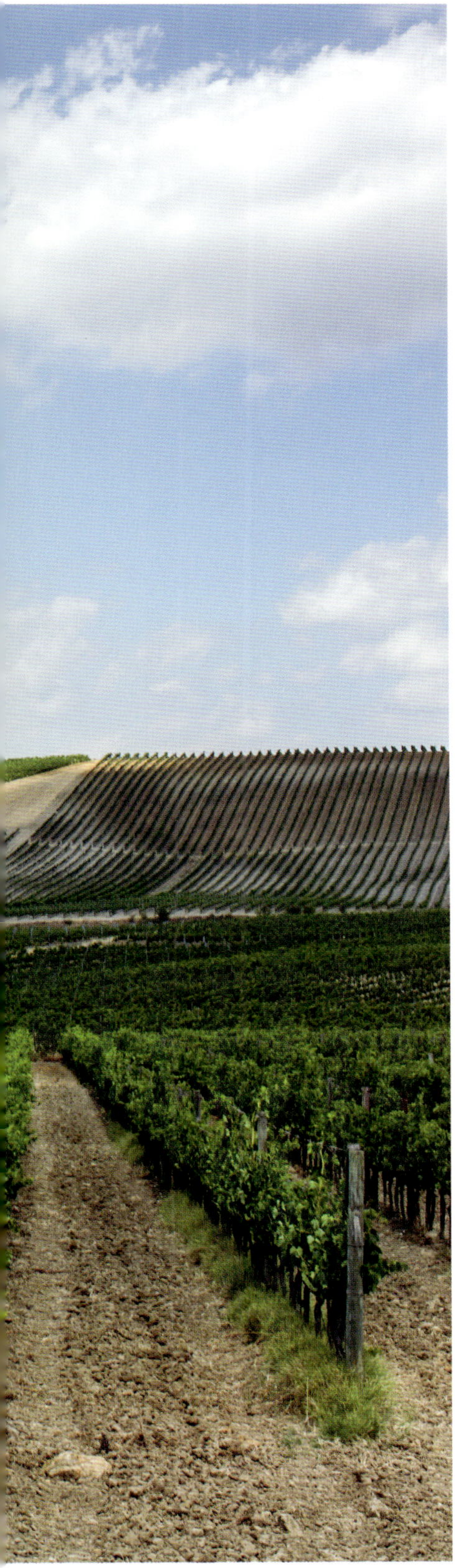
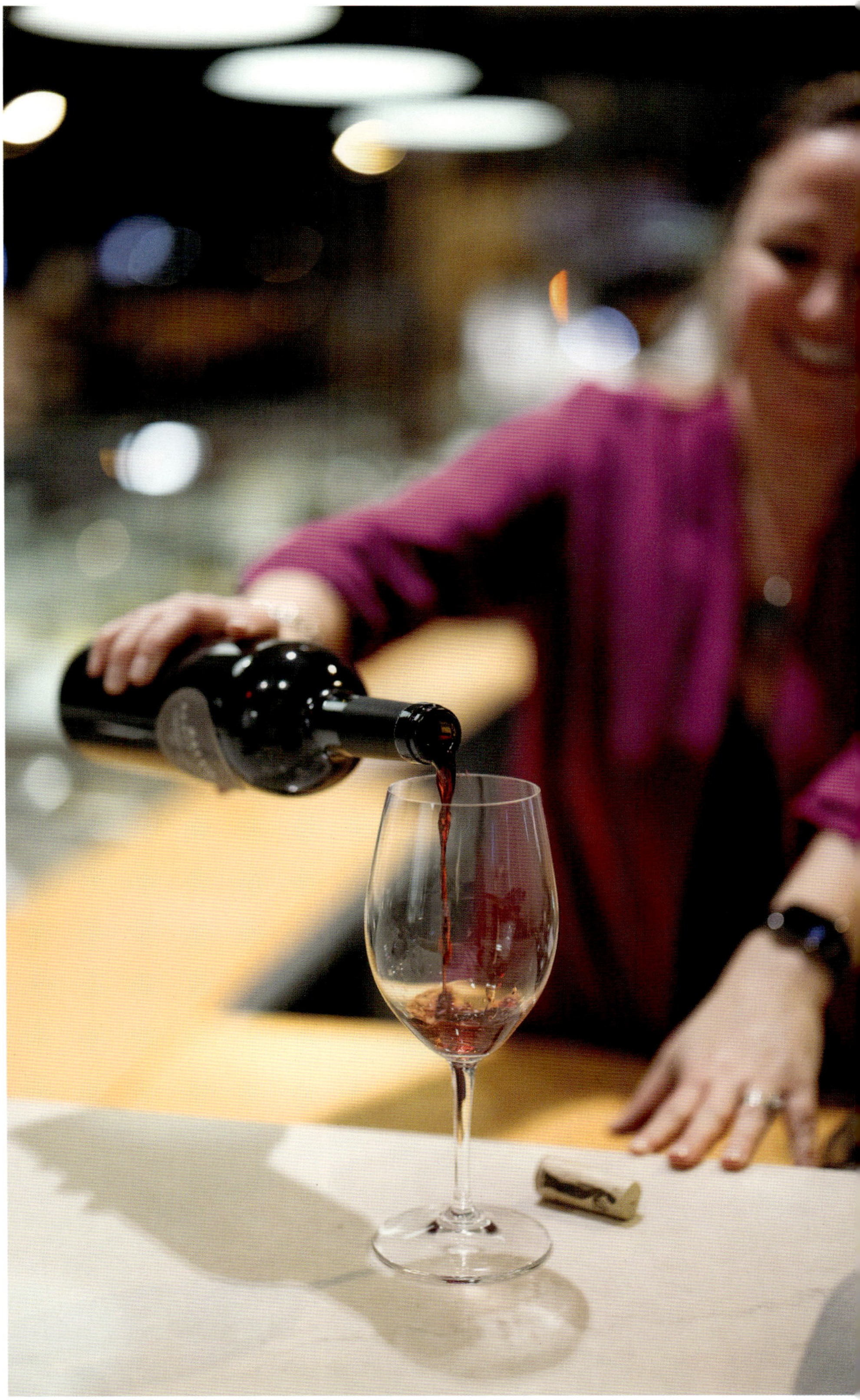

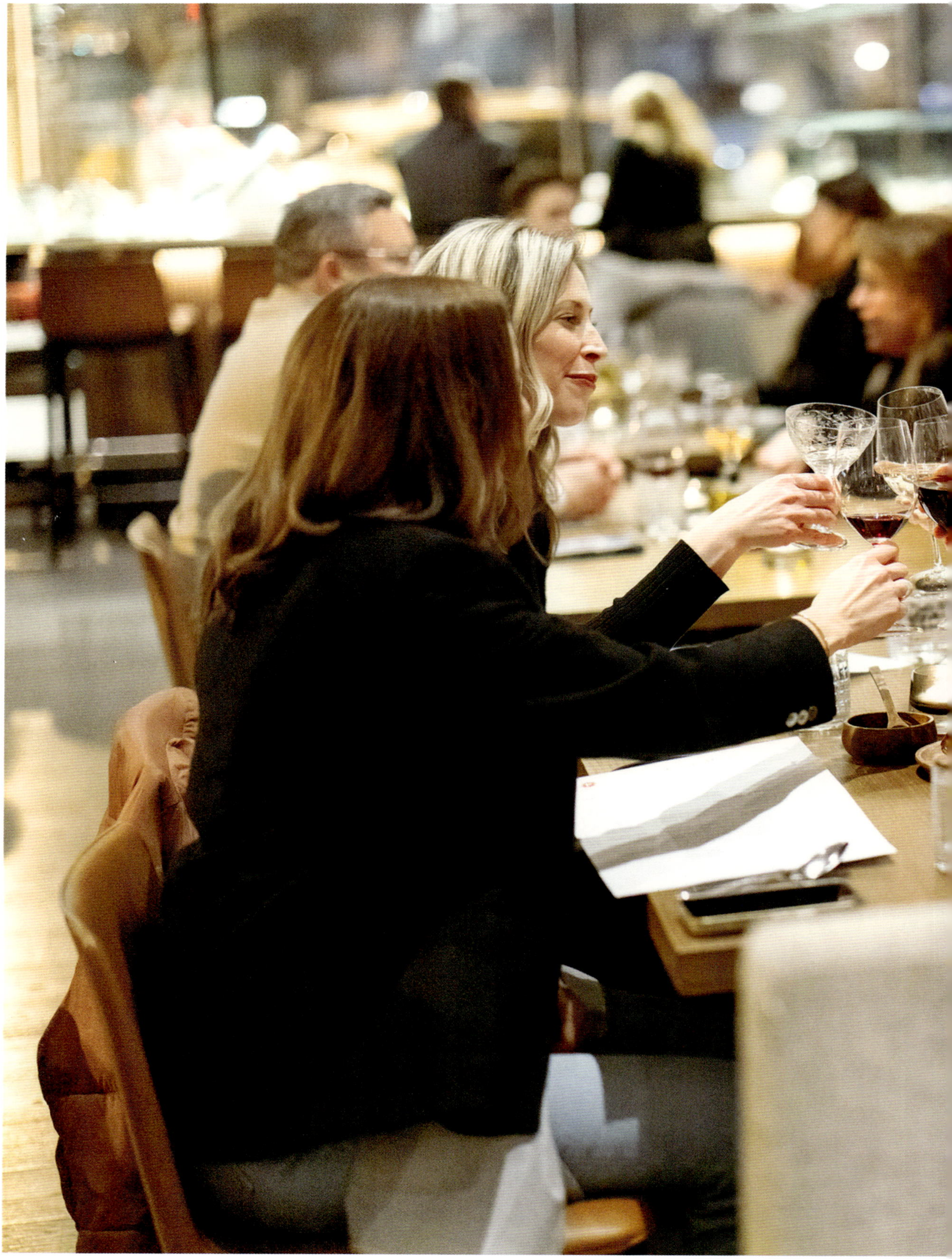

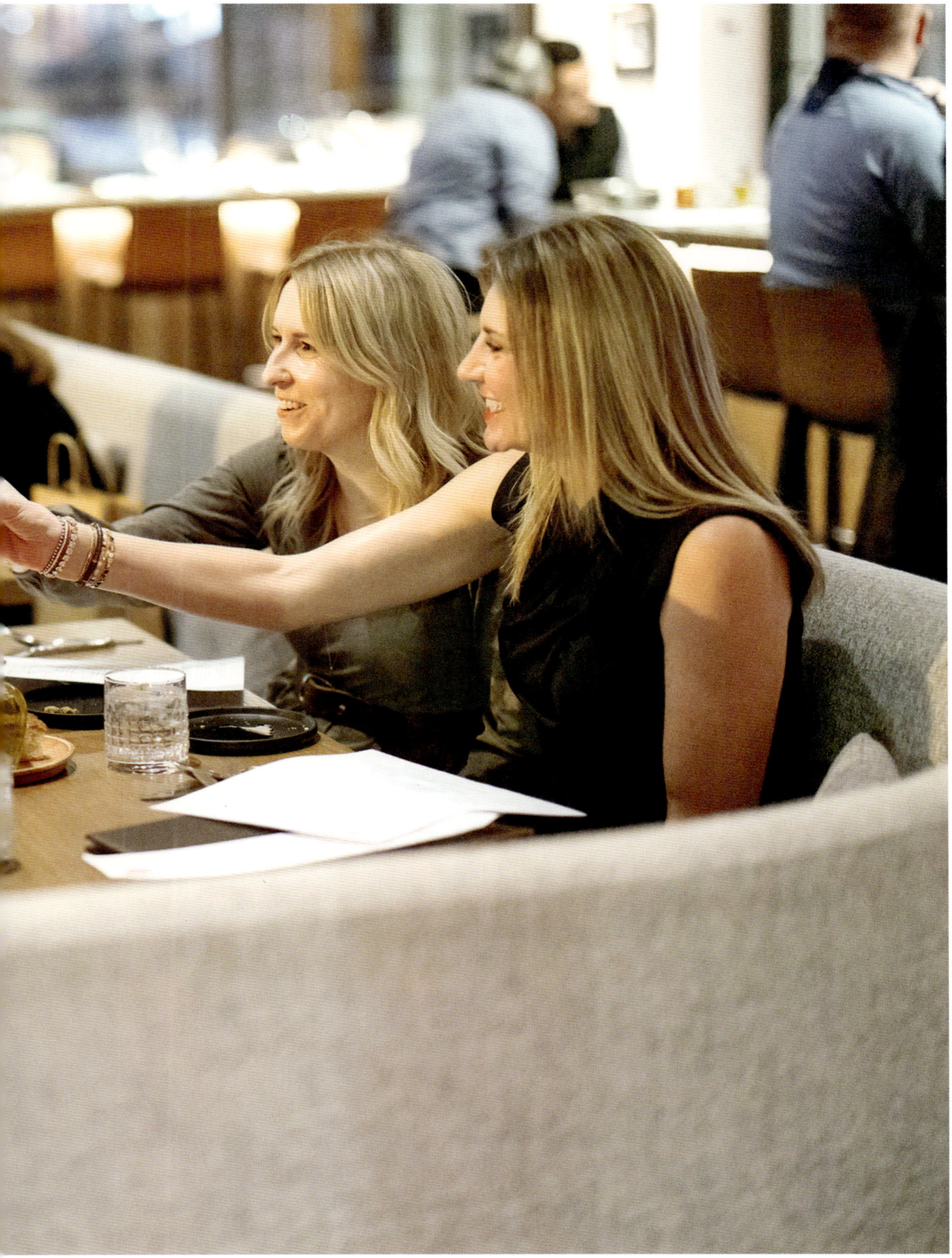

1

PIATTINI, INSALATA & SOUPS

When the delivery guys bring food products into our kitchens each day, the comment I hear time and again is, "It sure smells good in here!" First impressions make all the difference.

That's certainly the case when it comes to the small plates and appetizers at Farina. As the appetizers arrive at the table—whether warm duck meatballs, glistening icy trays of fresh shucked oysters, or our Sardinian black rice—the presentation sets the expectation for the remainder of the evening. Amid the glow and vibrant hum of the dining room, the appetizer course is where our guests, with cocktails in hand, begin to experience the vibe we have created at Farina. It's an introduction that reveals the quality of our food and the professionalism of our staff.

Most of the recipes in this chapter are simple to prepare, while some require slightly more work, and a few require a significant investment (like purchasing truffles and caviar). Some of these dishes have become iconic within the Farina world. There would be an uproar if we took them off the menu, and I'm always gratified when guests develop cravings for these starters.

CAVIAR

DELICIOUS INDULGENCE

Caviar is the Lamborghini of culinary ingredients. It is undeniably expensive but not nearly as pricey as it once was. In 2005, after overfishing caught up with the Russian caviar industry, critically endangering wild sturgeons, a series of bans and trade embargoes made it illegal to import wild Russian or Iranian Caviar to the United States. As a result, caviar farms have popped up all over the world, from Italy, China and the Middle East to Madagascar and the U.S.

Most connoisseurs recognize beluga caviar as the highest quality. It comes from the largest and rarest of the sturgeon varieties, fish that can live up to 80 years. But the osetra sturgeon, which can live up to 50 or 60 years, is renowned among caviar lovers for producing the most balanced notes of ocean brine. The osetra eggs are rarely black, ranging in color from bronze and shiny gold to greenish brown. While the eggs are slightly smaller than beluga, the long, buttery finish of osetra caviar is so sublime you want it to last forever.

With the price of sturgeon caviar dropping so dramatically in recent years, I have taken advantage of this happy circumstance at Farina. We have served more than 250 pounds of Amur osetra caviar since we opened in 2019. We offer a traditional caviar service, along with a caviar sandwich, burrata and caviar, caviar beggar's purses, and caviar spaghetti. I want people to enjoy caviar regularly and not just for special occasions. Because it's fun. And utterly delicious.

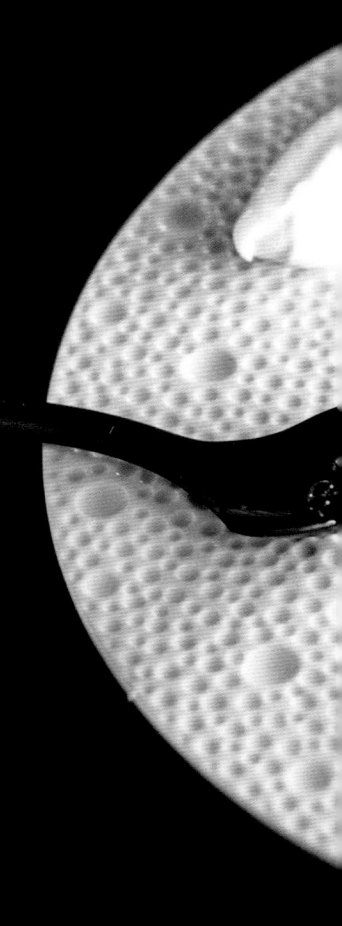

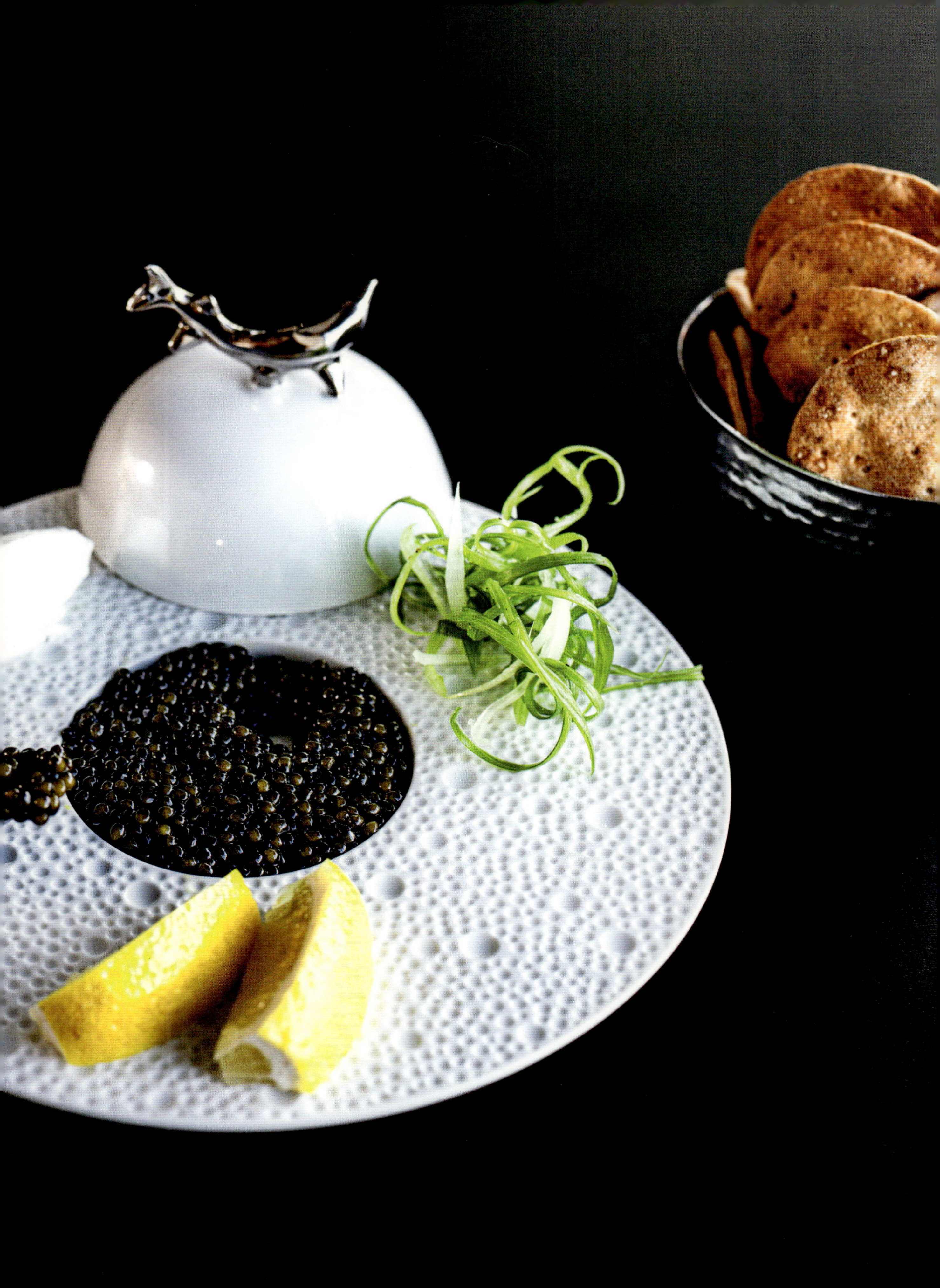

CAVIAR BEGGAR'S PURSES

CREPES

Makes 12 crepes (freeze any leftover crepes)

2 large eggs

1¼ cups whole milk

1 cup all-purpose flour

5 tablespoons canola oil, divided

1 teaspoon kosher salt

BEGGAR'S PURSES

2 crepes

1 tablespoon crème fraîche (or substitute sour cream)

2 ounces osetra caviar

2 long fresh chives, blanched for 2 seconds in boiling water

A celebrated New York restaurant, the Quilted Giraffe, made these popular back in the 1980s. Chef/owner Barry Wine would serve them on candelabras in the dining room. It was a great presentation and a fun interaction with the guests. In 1993, I was a visiting chef in Charlie Trotter's kitchen for a special event with Barry and the Quilted Giraffe. Charlie tasked me with making 120 Caviar Beggar's Purses for the evening's amuse-bouche. It took me all day, but they were awesome! When I was creating the opening menu for Farina, I wanted to sell caviar in any way, shape or form. So I put these on the oyster bar menu and served them on octopus-shaped candelabras. // MAKES 2 PURSES

MAKE CREPES

Combine eggs, milk, flour, 2 tablespoons oil and salt in a medium mixing bowl. Whisk constantly until mixture is smooth, then pass the batter through a fine strainer.

Heat a 10-inch nonstick sauté pan over medium heat for 2 minutes. Soak a triple-folded paper towel in remaining canola oil and wipe the bottom of the pan, leaving just a residue of cooking oil. Hold the handle in one hand and pour in 4 tablespoons of crepe batter, swirling and tilting the pan immediately to spread batter in a thin, even layer over the bottom of the pan.

Let crepe cook on medium heat until the top side looks dry, about 20 seconds. Using a thin metal (or plastic) offset spatula, lift one edge of the crepe and flip it over. Cook on the second side for 10 seconds, then transfer to a plate. Repeat with remaining batter until all the crepes are made.

MAKE BEGGAR'S PURSES

Lay 2 crepes out on a flat work surface and, with a spoon, smear a thin splotch of crème fraîche in the center of each. Clean the spoon and place 1 ounce of caviar on top of crème fraîche.

Pull the crepe together to form a little purse, pressing the gathered center together. Tie the gathered portion of the purse with one of the blanched chives to hold it in place. The top will flair out a bit and drape over the filled portion of the purse. Refrigerate until ready to eat.

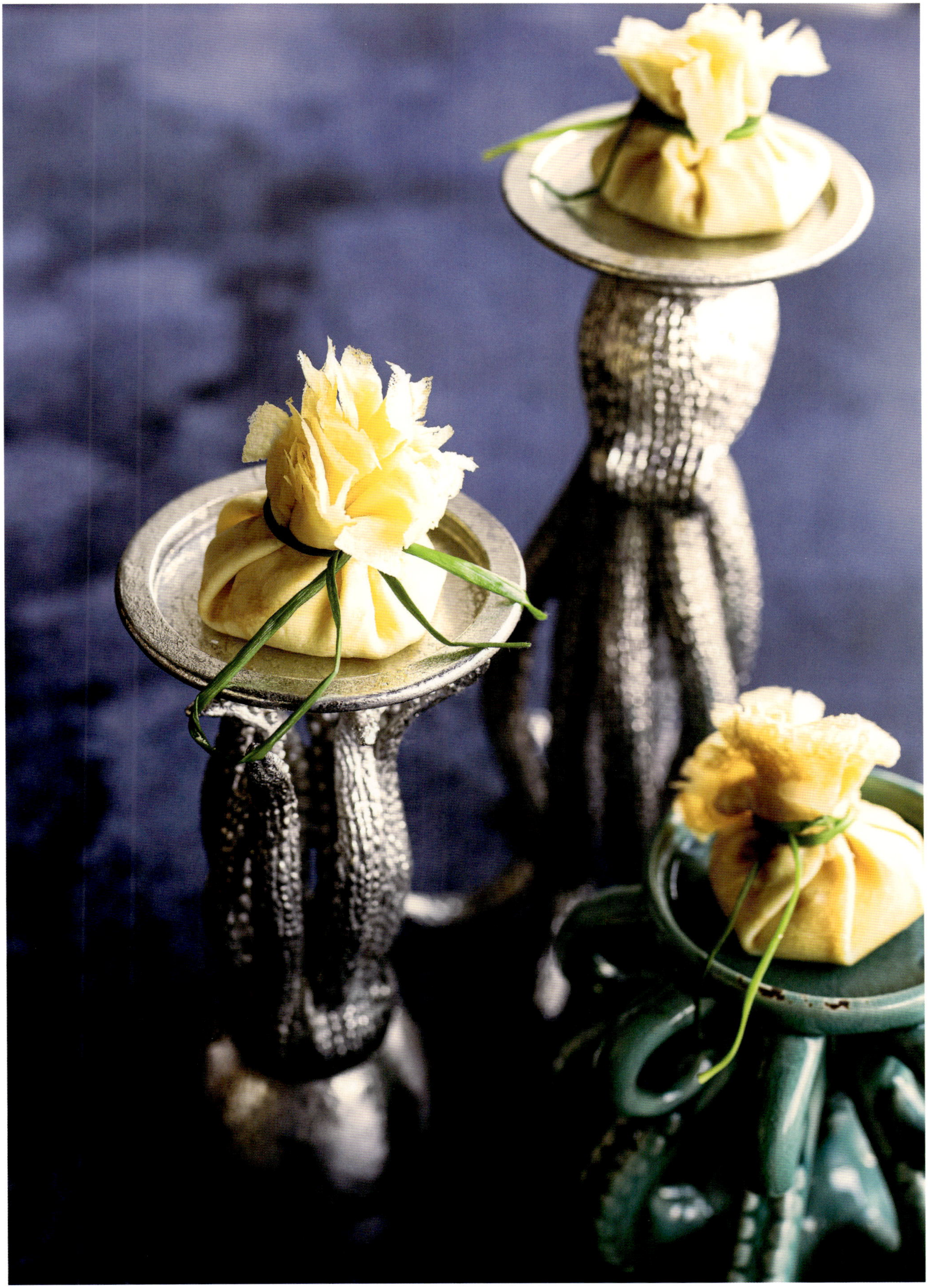

PIATTINI

CAVIAR SANDWICH

4 slices Pepperidge Farm thin wheat bread

1 tablespoon crème fraîche (or substitute sour cream)

2 ounces osetra caviar

1 tablespoon fresh chives, minced

My daily morning ritual consists of arriving at Farina around 9 a.m., then beelining it to the espresso machine. In the winter months, a caviar sandwich often accompanies my morning java. A peculiar pairing perhaps, but it's all part of my master plan to make caviar an affordable everyday enjoyment. A caviar sandwich can be served any time of the day and certainly doesn't have to be coupled with coffee. Try this recipe as an hors d'oeuvre before an intimate dinner party with close friends. It's sure to impress.

// **MAKES 4 SANDWICHES**

Place bread slices in a toaster and toast until golden brown. Lay 4 toast slices flat on a work surface and, using a spoon, spread crème fraîche fully on 2 slices. Clean the spoon and spread 1 ounce caviar on each of the other 2 slices of toast. Sprinkle chives on caviar.

Use a knife to cut all four toasts diagonally, then put them together to form 4 triangle-shaped sandwiches. Refrigerate until ready to eat.

> Cutting the single toasts separately, instead of cutting the assembled sandwiches, keeps the caviar from squishing out.

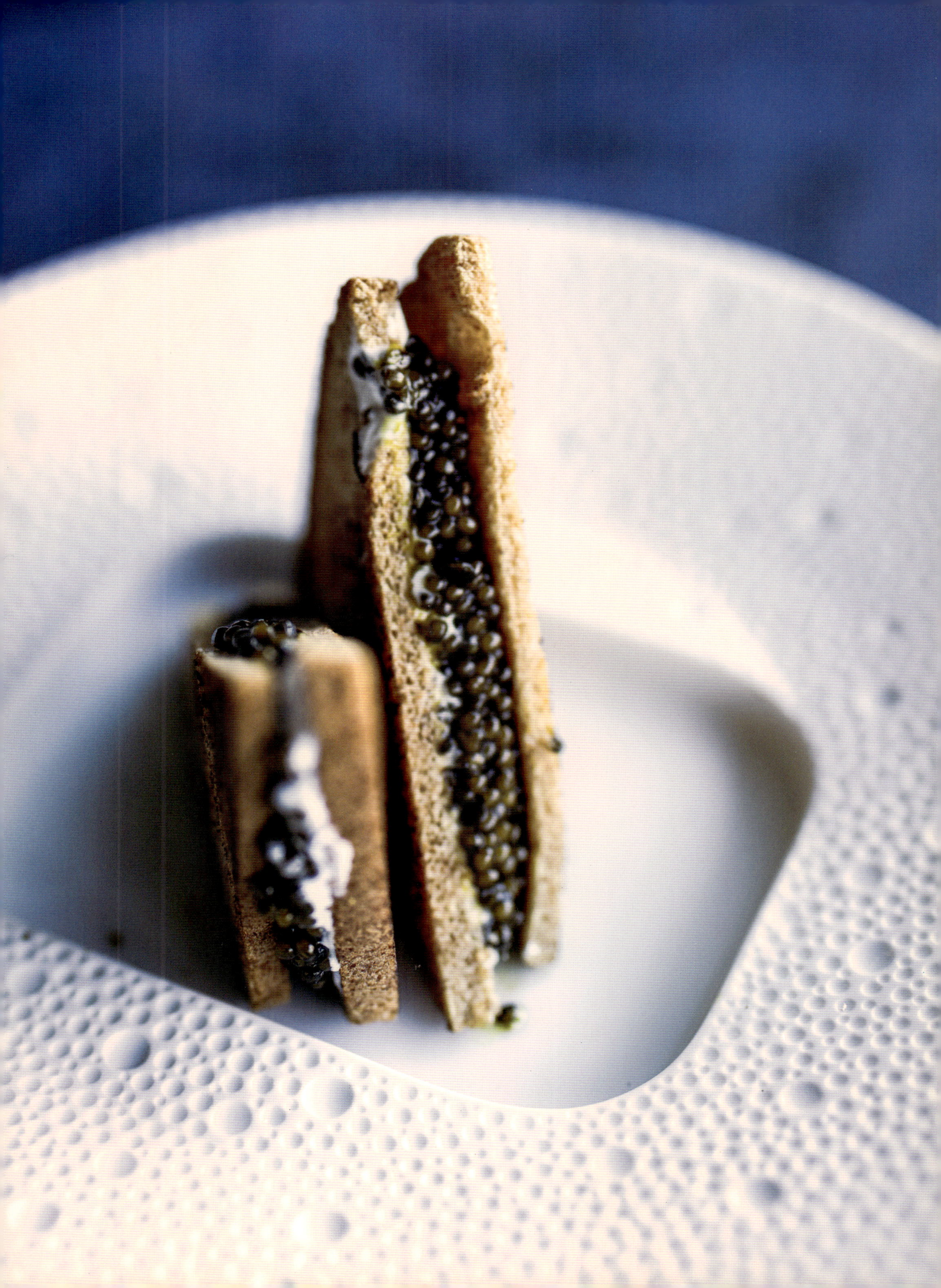

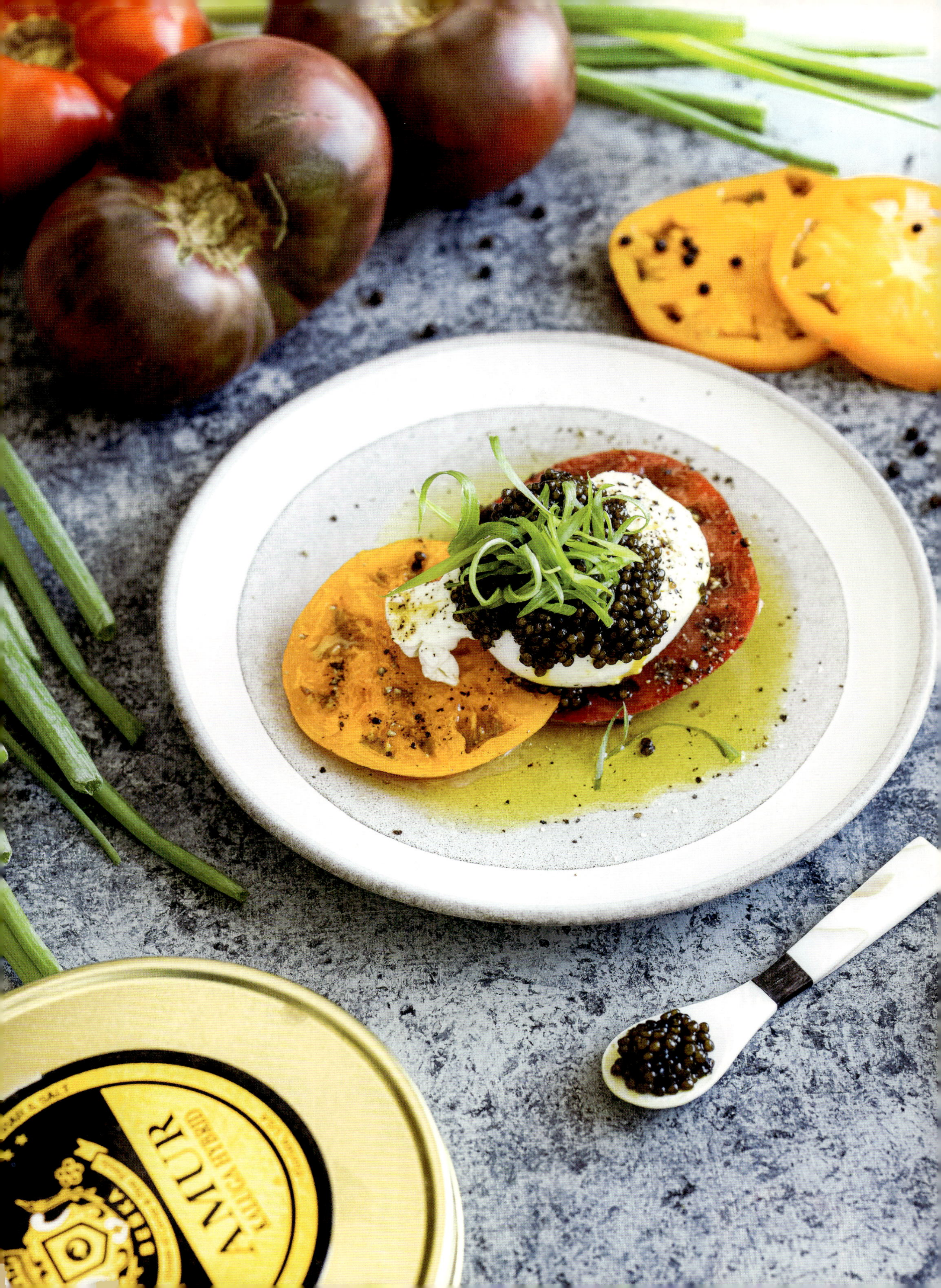
AMUR
KALUGA HYBRID

BURRATA *and* OSETRA CAVIAR

1 large ripe heirloom tomato

1 teaspoon fleur de sel (or any quality garnishing salt), divided

1 2-ounce burrata boule

1 to 2 ounces osetra caviar (or splurge on what you can afford)

1 tablespoon fresh chives, minced

High-quality extra-virgin olive oil, for drizzling

In France, Champagne makers have advocated for years that it's not just for special occasions, that it is delicious and affordable enough to drink just as regularly as any wine. I have the same opinion about caviar: It is not just for special occasions! The sweet acidity of summer heirloom tomatoes is a great foil for the salty and nutty caviar. And the extra virgin olive oil is the icing on the cake! // **SERVES 2**

Remove tomato stem and discard. Cut 2 half-inch-thick slices from the tomato. Place tomato slices in the center of an appetizer plate and sprinkle with half of the fleur de sel.

Drain burrata on a paper towel and discard the whey water. Cut burrata in half and put each piece on a tomato slice, cut side up. Sprinkle with remaining fleur de sel. Spoon a dollop of caviar onto the center of each burrata half. Sprinkle top with chives and drizzle generously with extra-virgin olive oil. Serve immediately.

> Choose a colorful heirloom tomato and don't discard what remains of it after you plate this dish. The rest of the tomato will undoubtedly find another salad to enhance.

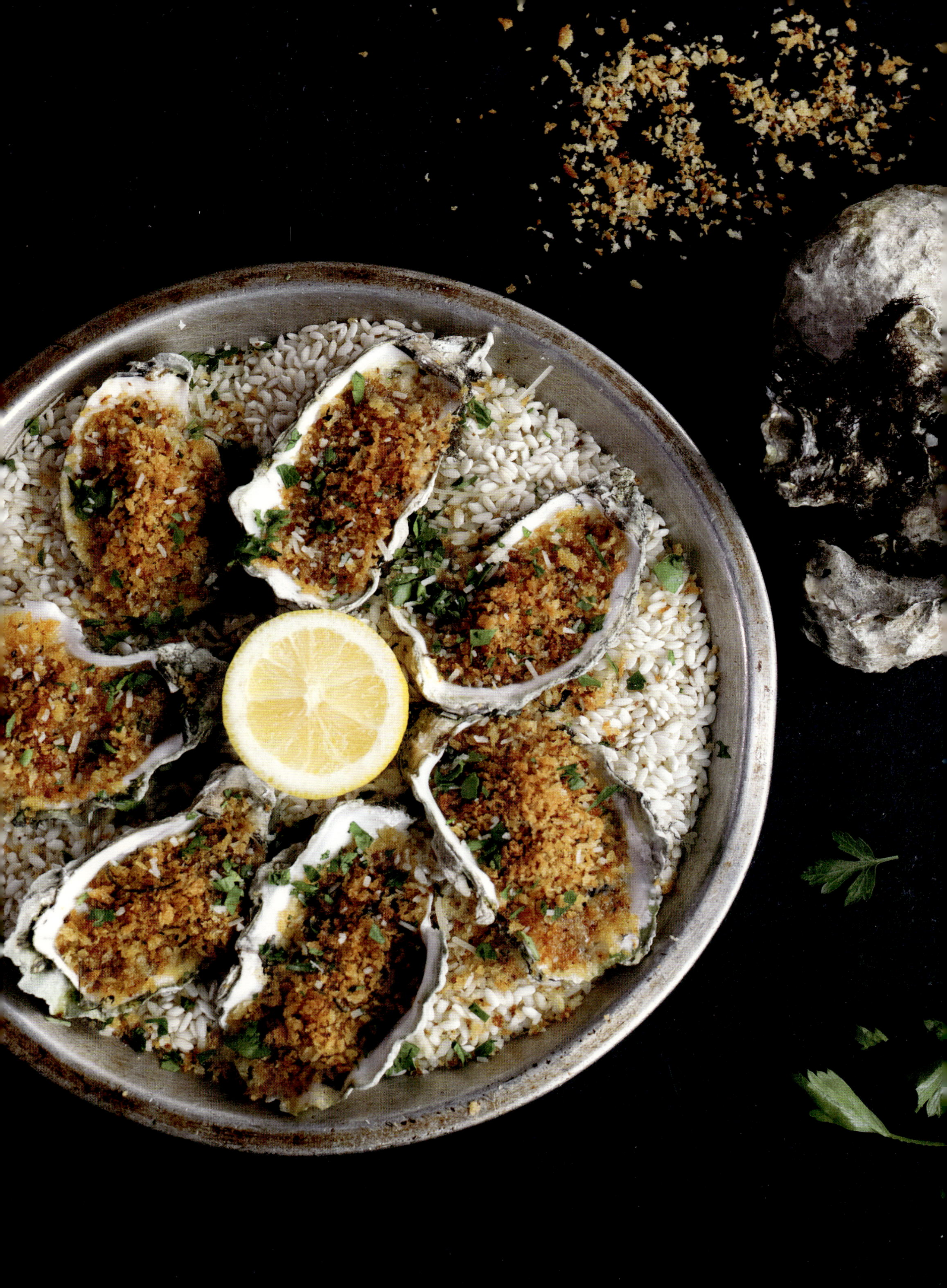

BROILED COTUIT OYSTERS

12 freshly shucked Cotuit oysters, on the half shell

½ cup Seafood Broiling Butter, softened (page 259)

1 cup Pangrattato (page 267)

¼ cup grated Grana Padano cheese

¼ cup fresh parsley, chopped

4 lemon wedges

Cotuit oysters from Nantucket Sound are some of the prettiest I've seen. They are plump and large enough for a broiled preparation. They are also extraordinarily delicious raw, but their brininess helps them stand up to garlic butter, lemon and breadcrumbs. You can substitute any of your favorite oysters, but large oysters work best because they shrink during cooking.

// **MAKES 1 DOZEN**

Heat oven to 400°F.

Place oysters on a baking sheet and use a spoon to smear a thick dollop of seafood butter on each oyster. Sprinkle pangrattato generously on top of butter. Place baking sheet on the middle rack in the oven for 6 minutes. Turn oven to broil and move baking sheet 8 inches from the heating element. Broil oysters until deeply golden, about 1 to 2 minutes.

Remove baking sheet from the oven. (If you've had two martinis, then slurp the oysters right off the hot tray.) Otherwise, transfer broiled oysters to a serving platter. Sprinkle with Grana Padano and chopped parsley. Squeeze fresh lemon over the top and enjoy.

PIATTINI

KING CRAB *and* ASPARAGUS BRUSCHETTA

4 slices Farina Focaccia (page 264)

2 tablespoons kosher salt (plus more for seasoning)

12 pieces pencil-thin green asparagus, with 1 inch cut off the ends

6 pieces fresh white asparagus (optional), peeled, with 1 inch cut off the ends

2 tablespoons fresh chives, cut 1 inch long, divided

4 tablespoons Farina Italian Dressing (page 233), divided

12 ounces king crabmeat, cleaned from shell

1 avocado, cut in half and pitted

2 tablespoons fresh lemon juice

Lemon zest, for garnish

High-quality extra-virgin olive oil

King crab and asparagus are a great springtime combination, and I like putting them to work on a warm, toasted piece of bruschetta. The avocado spread acts like glue to hold the ingredients in place. Add a tangy drizzle of dressing plus plenty of fresh herbs and you have one delicious snack. // **SERVES 4**

Toast focaccia under the broiler until golden brown. Set aside.

Heat 2 quarts water with 2 tablespoons salt in a large soup pot and bring to a boil over high heat. Prepare an ice bath for the blanched asparagus. Blanch green asparagus for 4 minutes (same for white asparagus if using). Transfer cooked asparagus to the ice bath to halt cooking. Drain and dry cooked asparagus on a kitchen towel or paper towels. On a cutting board, cut asparagus spears into 1½-inch pieces on a bias. Transfer cut asparagus to a small bowl and add half the cut chives and 2 tablespoons Italian dressing. Toss to mix well. Set aside.

Break up king crab into bite-size pieces and place in small a prep bowl. Add remaining 2 tablespoons Italian dressing and remaining cut chives to the bowl and mix gently. Set aside.

Scoop avocado out of shell into a small bowl and crush with a fork. Add lemon juice and a pinch of salt, and mix well.

Place the 4 bruschetta slices flat on a work surface. Spread the top of the bruschetta with crushed avocado puree, then scatter and spread asparagus on the bruschetta, then crabmeat. Grate lemon zest over all 4 finished bruschetta and drizzle with olive oil.

> Fresh white asparagus is delicious in the spring, and it's great in this recipe if available. However, white asparagus stalks always need to be peeled from just past the tips down to the ends, or they will be chewy and woody. I also recommended peeling thick green asparagus, but the pencil-thin stalks are tender enough to eat as is.

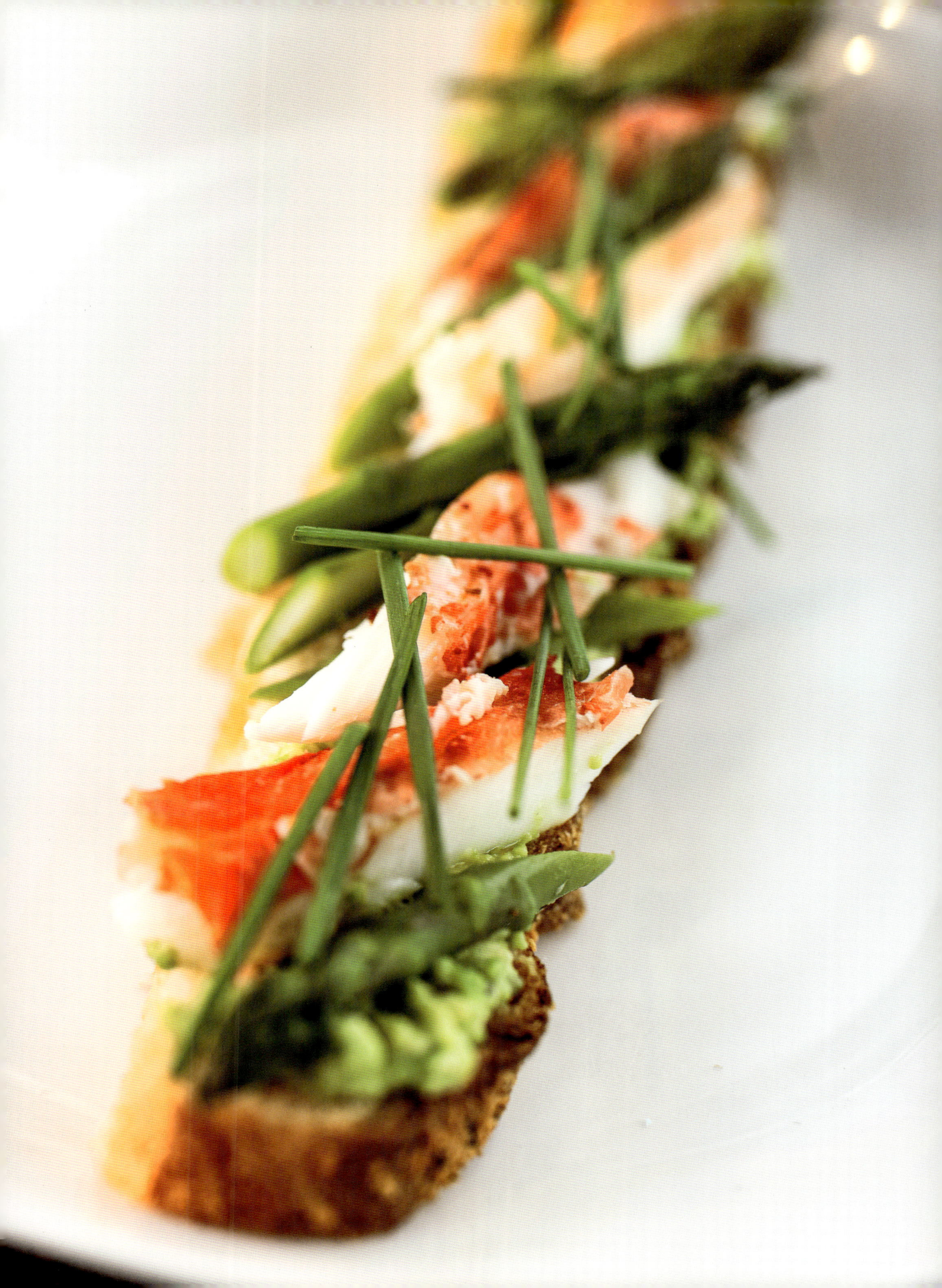

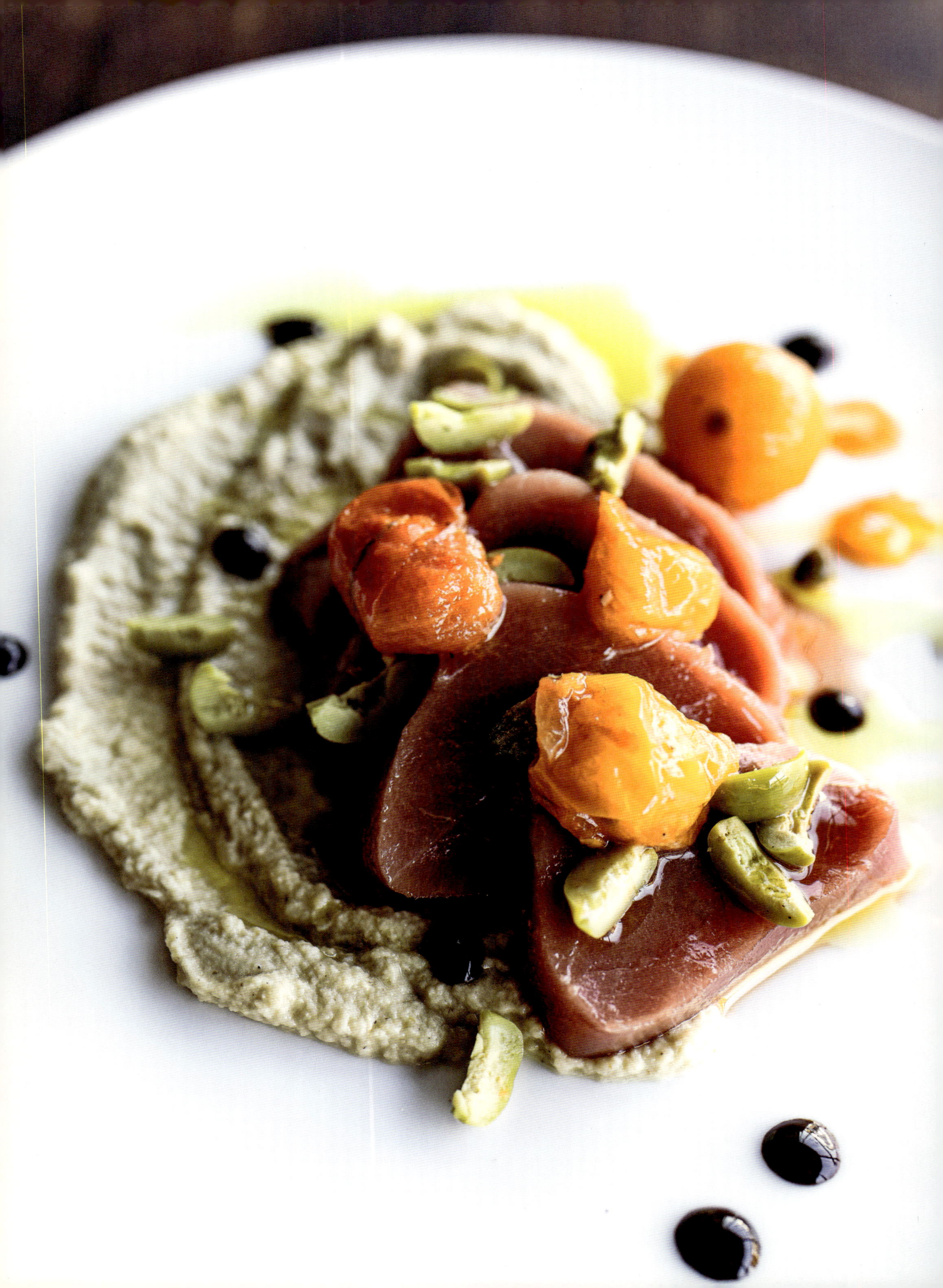

TUNA CRUDO
with EGGPLANT, BLISTERED TOMATOES, LEMON and BASIL

2 medium purple eggplants

½ cup extra-virgin olive oil

⅓ cup fresh lemon juice, divided

Kosher salt

1 pound sushi-grade ahi tuna loin, cut into 20 thin slices

½ cup Blistered Cherry Tomatoes (page 243), cut in half

8 pitted Castelvetrano olives, cut into thin wedges

1 tablespoon fresh basil, diced

High-quality extra-virgin olive oil, for drizzling

The first time I ate raw fish was in 1984 in Denver, while I was working under Chef George Mavrothalassitis. We received the biggest loin of fresh, burgundy-colored tuna that I had ever seen. Chef "Mavro" was slicing small chunks and eating it right off his knife. I was standing there looking at him in bewilderment when he offered me a piece. It was shimmering and beautiful from the coating of olive oil and the natural tuna color. While I didn't automatically love the texture, I didn't dislike it either. I simply found it fascinating. In the years since, sushi, fish carpaccio, crudos and ceviches have expanded our notions of what the seafood world can offer us to eat. Fresh raw fish, sliced thin with great olive oil, spice and acid is just so simple and satisfying and very Sicilian... *Manciàri!* // **SERVES 4**

Prepare an outdoor grill or preheat oven to 400°F.

Grill eggplants whole or bake in oven on a baking sheet until they are completely soft in the middle, approximately 30 minutes. If using a grill, transfer cooked eggplants to a baking sheet and let cool for 20 minutes. If baking in the oven, remove the baking sheet and let eggplants cool for 20 minutes.

Slice eggplants in half and use a spoon to scrape the pulp into a food processor. Add olive oil, three-quarters of the lemon juice and 2 teaspoons salt to the food processor. Pulse on high speed for 30 to 40 seconds, creating a smooth eggplant puree.

Spread 3 tablespoons eggplant puree in a long oval shape on the center of 4 plates.

Shingle 5 slices tuna onto one edge of the eggplant puree to showcase both the bright red tuna and silky eggplant puree. Season tuna with a pinch of kosher salt and a drizzle of lemon juice.

Scatter blistered cherry tomatoes and olives on and around tuna. Sprinkle basil on top and finish with a drizzle of extra-virgin olive oil.

PIATTINI

CLAM TOAST

1 Italian bread loaf, cut in ¾-inch slices

1 cup of Clam Butter (page 260)

½ cup Parmesan cheese

Extra-virgin olive oil, for drizzling

I added Clam Toast to the menu at Farina as a nod to Jersey-style Italian-American cooking. I thought it would stay for a few months and we'd move on. But I can't take it off now, it's too popular. Having a pantry (fridge) full of quick and easy food sources allows you to create a snack or appetizer on a minute's notice. I like to broil these pretty dark and then drizzle the caramelized toasts with really good extra-virgin olive oil. They make a great Sunday afternoon football snack!

// MAKES ABOUT 4 TO 6 TOASTS

Preheat oven to 350°F. Bake bread slices on a baking sheet until lightly dried out and golden brown, about 15 minutes. Remove from the oven and let cool.

Set oven to broil and position rack 4 to 6 inches away from the broiler element.

Spread ½ inch of clam butter evenly on bread slices. Arrange covered clam toasts evenly on a baking sheet. Sprinkle each toast evenly with Parmesan cheese. Place baking sheet under broiler for 3 to 4 minutes, until golden brown. Remove from oven, drizzle with olive oil and serve immediately.

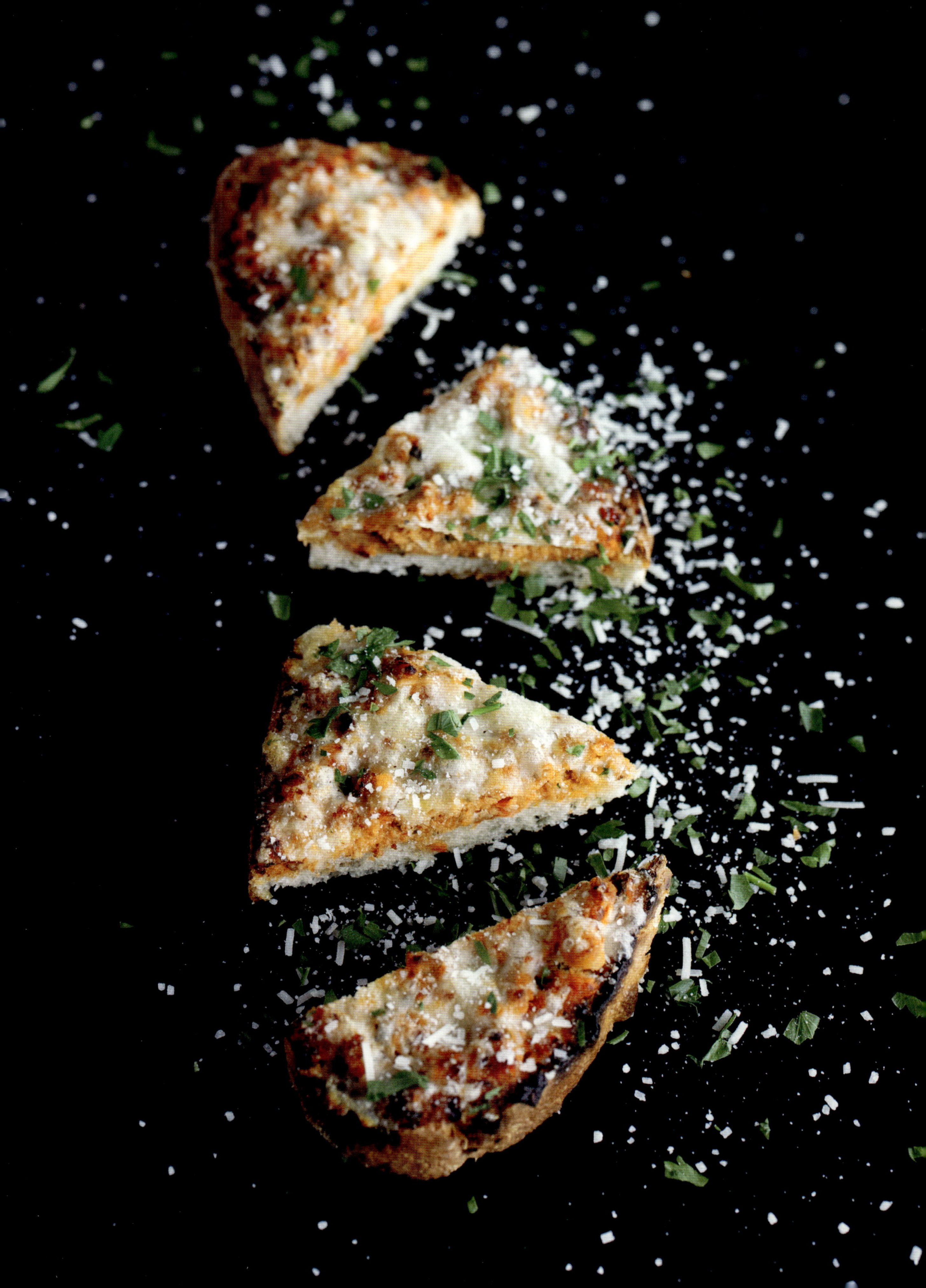

DUCK MEATBALLS

MEATBALLS

2 single duck breasts (approximately 18 ounces), skin removed and cut into 1-inch cubes

6 ice cubes

1 pound ground beef

2 large eggs

2 cups dry breadcrumbs

⅔ cup whole milk

2 tablespoons chopped fresh basil

1 teaspoon fresh thyme leaves

1 teaspoon fresh oregano leaves

2 cloves garlic, minced

1 teaspoon red pepper flakes

2 teaspoons kosher salt

1 teaspoon ground black pepper

½ teaspoon ground allspice

½ teaspoon ground cloves

FOR SERVING

2 quarts Farina Meatball Sauce (page 255)

½ cup grated Grana Padano cheese

3 tablespoons chopped fresh parsley

Meatballs are so prevalent on the menus at Italian restaurants that it's almost cliché. And I'll be damned if they aren't on the menu at Farina too. I choose duck as the driving influence for ours because the sweet cooking spices offer a different flavor profile than the garlic pile driver found in most meatball recipes. Without fail, these meatballs are ordered at almost every table every night at Farina. // **MAKES 30 MEATBALLS**

Spread duck cubes evenly on a baking sheet and place in freezer for 30 minutes.

Transfer duck cubes and ice cubes to a food processor and pulse on high speed until duck meat is coarsely pureed. Transfer duck to a large stainless steel prep bowl and add remaining meatball ingredients. Knead the meatball mixture by hand, or in the bowl of a stand mixer, until all ingredients are well combined, about 4 minutes.

Preheat oven to 400°F.

With your hands, or using a small ice cream scoop, form 30 meatballs that are approximately 1½ inches in diameter. Set each meatball on a baking sheet a half inch apart, then bake for 15 minutes.

After baking, transfer meatballs to a skillet with Farina meatball sauce. Cook meatballs at a gentle simmer for 5 minutes.

To serve, transfer meatballs to a large platter. Sprinkle with grated Grana Padano cheese and chopped parsley.

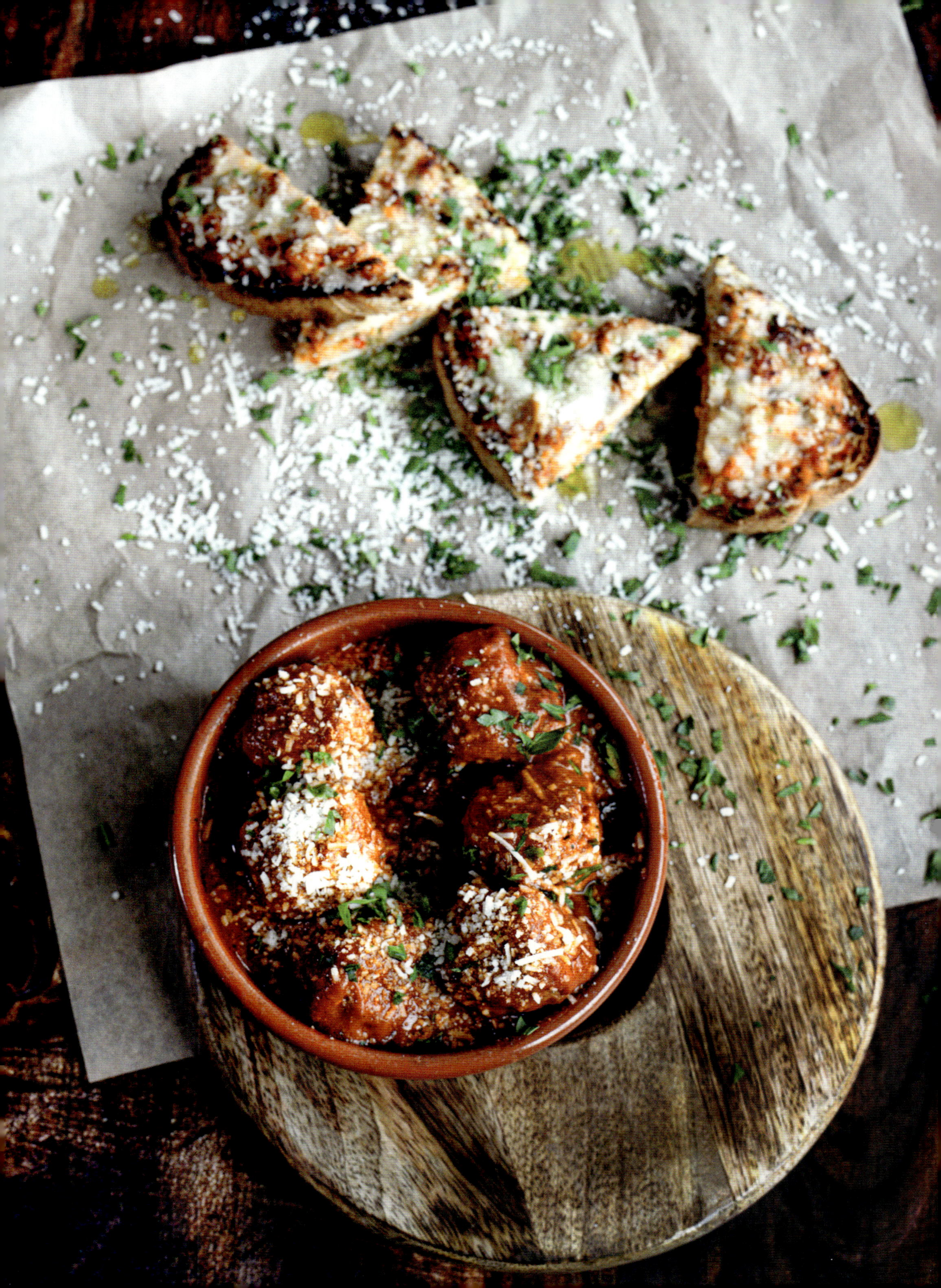

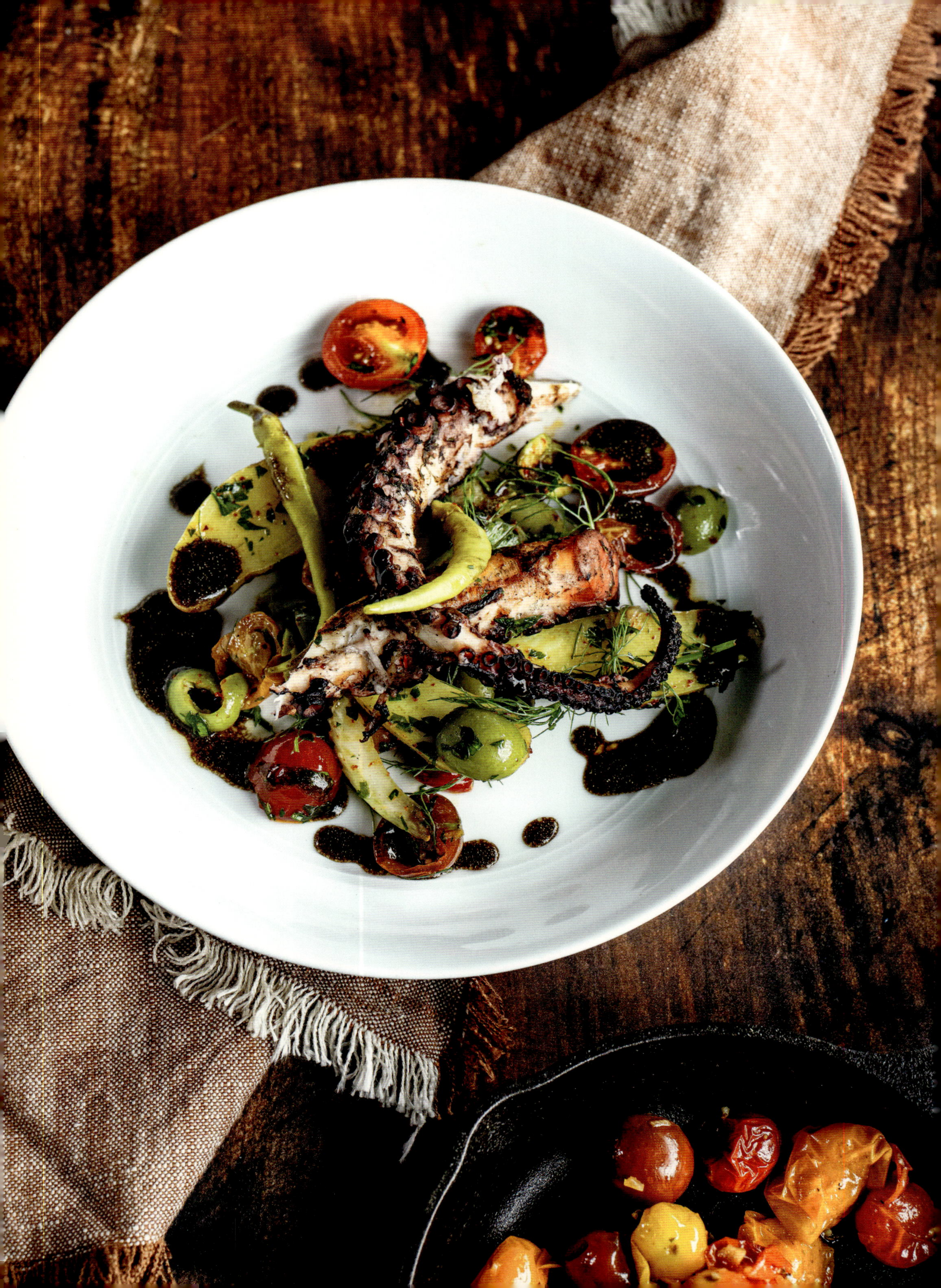

GRILLED OCTOPUS
with POTATOES and BLISTERED TOMATOES

4 large, cooked octopus legs (or whole raw octopus)

2 tablespoons kosher salt (divided)

2 bay leaves

3 sprigs fresh thyme

2 teaspoons red pepper flakes

6 cloves garlic, mashed

1 Spanish onion, sliced thick

3 tablespoons extra-virgin olive oil

12 multicolored marble or new potatoes, boiled until soft

1 cup Blistered Cherry Tomatoes (page 243)

1 bulb fresh fennel, thinly sliced on a mandoline

2 Persian cucumbers, sliced ⅛-inch thick on a bias

16 medium fresh basil leaves

3 sprigs fresh oregano

5 tablespoons Farina Italian Dressing (page 233)

4 tablespoons Romesco Sauce (page 250)

⅓ cup Pangrattato (page 267)

I wrote this recipe for precooked octopus legs, which are widely available in Asian markets, because you can buy them portioned and separated from the body. They are a little easier to work with, but you can certainly cook a whole raw octopus with this recipe too. For that, you'll need to increase the cook time to about 3 hours, or until the legs are tender. // SERVES 4

Place cooked octopus legs in a large stockpot with 1 tablespoon salt, bay leaves, thyme, pepper flakes, garlic and onion. Bring to a boil, then simmer slowly for 1 hour, uncovered. Remove pot from stove and let octopus cool in the cooking liquid for 30 minutes. Remove the legs and dry them on paper towels. Store in the refrigerator for up to 4 days if not using right away.

Prepare an outdoor grill. Pour olive oil into a medium prep bowl and add cooked octopus legs. Sear octopus legs on the grill (careful with fire flare-ups) and char heavily on all sides, for about 5 minutes, or until warm through the interior. Transfer octopus to a baking sheet and keep warm.

In a large prep bowl, combine potatoes, tomatoes, fennel, cucumbers, basil, oregano, 1 tablespoon salt and Italian dressing and toss to mix well. Set aside.

Use a soup spoon to spread romesco sauce in the middle of 4 salad plates. Divide potato-tomato salad between the plates, landing on the sauce. Add grilled octopus legs to the remaining dressing in the empty salad bowl to coat, then set 1 leg on top of each salad. Sprinkle each salad with pangrattato.

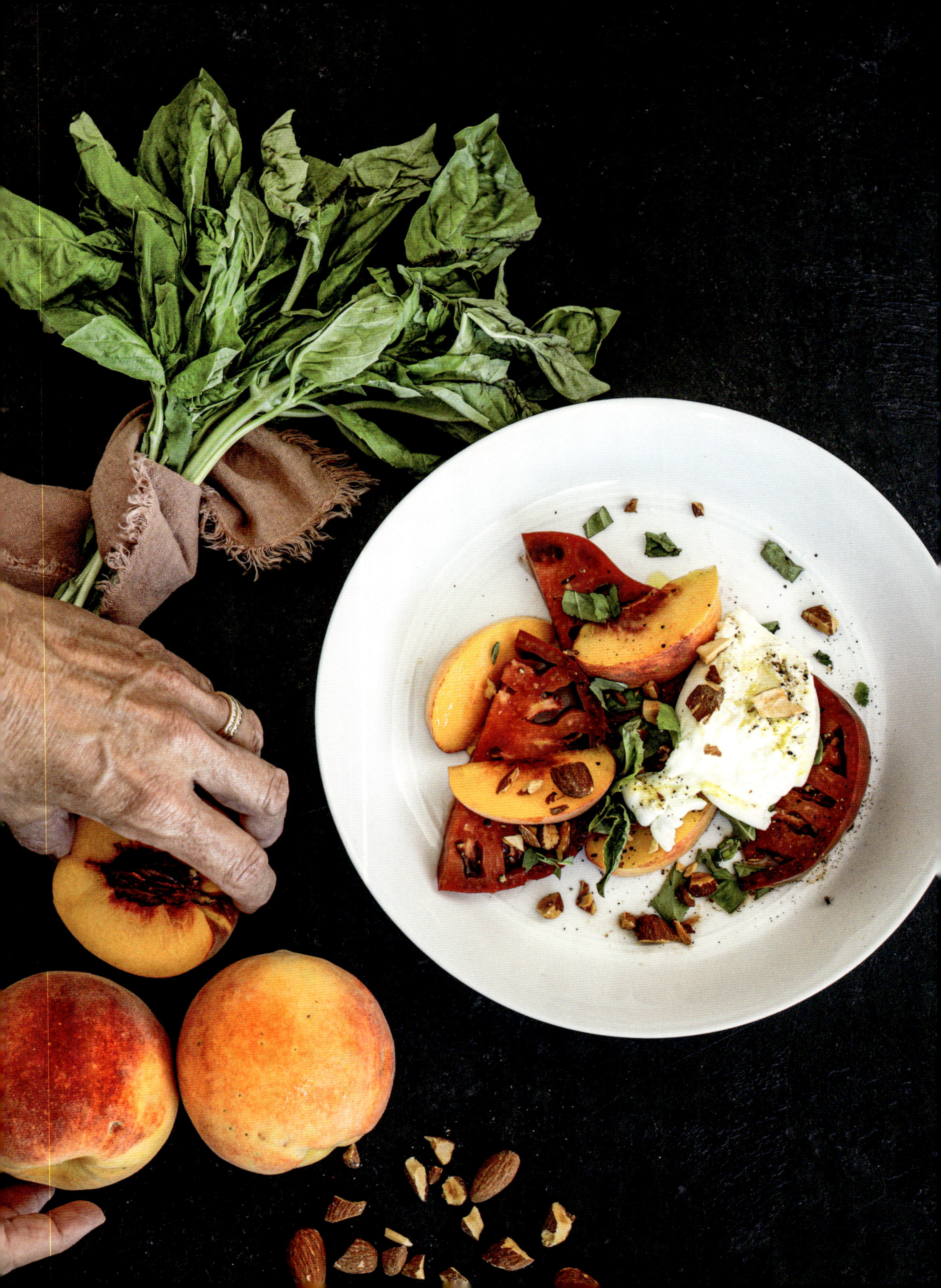

INSALATA

HEIRLOOM TOMATO *and* MISSOURI PEACH SALAD
with BUFFALO MOZZARELLA *and* POMEGRANATE VINAIGRETTE

3 large multicolored ripe heirloom tomatoes

2 ripe summer peaches

2 teaspoons kosher salt

12 pieces ciliegini buffalo mozzarella balls (or regular fresh mozzarella)

8 to 10 leaves fresh basil, snipped roughly into ½-inch squares

¼ cup toasted pistachios, crushed into pebble size

Pomegranate Vinaigrette (page 233)

2 teaspoons freshly cracked black pepper

This salad stars two of Missouri's most delicious summer crops: tomatoes and peaches. I have been pairing summer tomatoes with fruit for a long time—watermelon, peaches and plums are my go-to combinations. Our summer heirloom tomatoes come from Liz and Sky at Kurlbaum Farm and I buy my peaches every week at the Overland Park Farmers' Market. Most types of cheese will work in this salad, and substitute your favorite nuts or seeds . . . I do! One year it is pistachios and the next it might be pepita seeds. The components of the salad can be prepped several hours in advance. Just brush the peaches with a bit of the dressing to keep them from oxidizing, then leave at room temperature until you're ready to serve the salad. **// SERVES 4**

Slice tomatoes and peaches into wedges of various sizes to maximize the visual texture on the plate. Set aside.

To plate the salad, combine peaches and tomatoes in a medium stainless mixing bowl. Add salt and toss gently. Arrange tomatoes and peaches on 4 plates. Tuck in mozzarella balls and sprinkle snipped basil and crushed pistachios over the top. Drizzle a few tablespoons of pomegranate dressing in and around the finished salad. Finish with freshly cracked black pepper.

INSALATA

ROASTED CARROT *and* BEET SALAD

15 young, slender carrots, unpeeled

2 large shallots, peeled and sliced into ¼-inch rings

¼ cup olive oil

3 sprigs fresh thyme

2 teaspoons kosher salt

1 teaspoon ground black pepper

1 cup fresh parsley leaves

½ cup Dijon Red Wine Dressing (page 232), divided

4 small beets (canned, packaged or cooked), quartered lengthwise

2 ounces crumbled Humboldt Fog goat cheese (or any creamy, ripe goat cheese)

¼ cup hazelnuts, skinned, toasted and lightly crushed

Slender, young baby rainbow carrots are best for this dish, and the variety of colors makes for a beautifully presented fall salad. If baby carrots are unavailable, the longer ones will work too; just halve them lengthwise, then cut crosswise on the bias. // **SERVES 4**

Preheat oven to 375°F.

Remove and discard carrot tops and wash carrots well. Halve them lengthwise, and if they are very long, cut crosswise on the bias.

Combine carrots, shallots, olive oil, thyme, salt and pepper in a large, shallow stainless steel mixing bowl and mix well. Spread the mixture evenly on a baking sheet, and roast until carrots are tender, approximately 20 minutes. Transfer carrots and shallots to a clean mixing bowl.

Add parsley leaves to the carrots, along with half the vinaigrette. Toss well to coat and add a pinch more salt if necessary. Use tongs to lift the carrots and parsley from the bowl, piling them evenly onto 4 salad plates. Toss beets with the dressing left in the bowl and arrange beet wedges around the carrots. Sprinkle with goat cheese and hazelnuts. Drizzle a bit of remaining vinaigrette over each salad if desired.

Transfer any leftover dressing to an airtight container and refrigerate for up to 5 days.

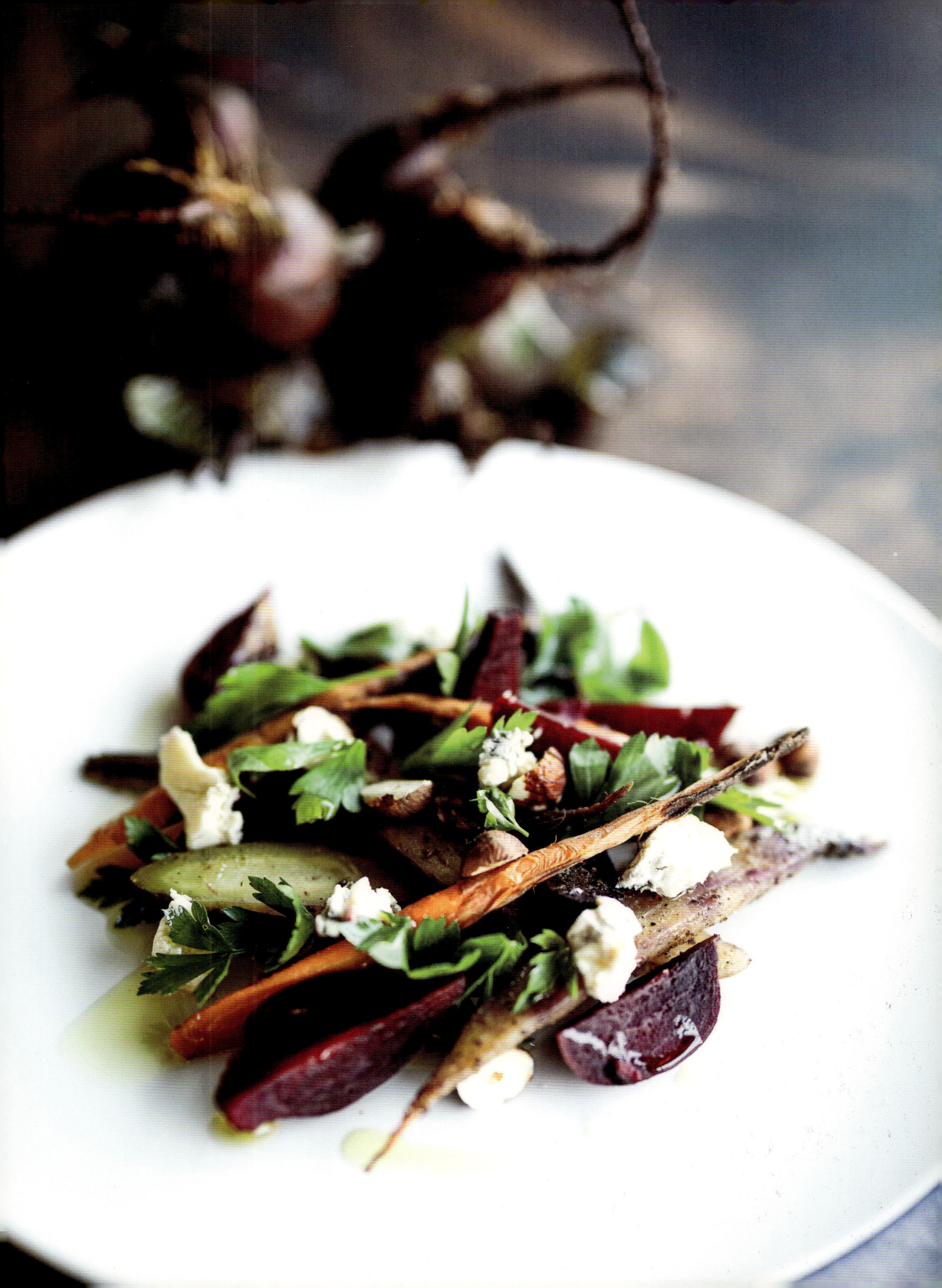

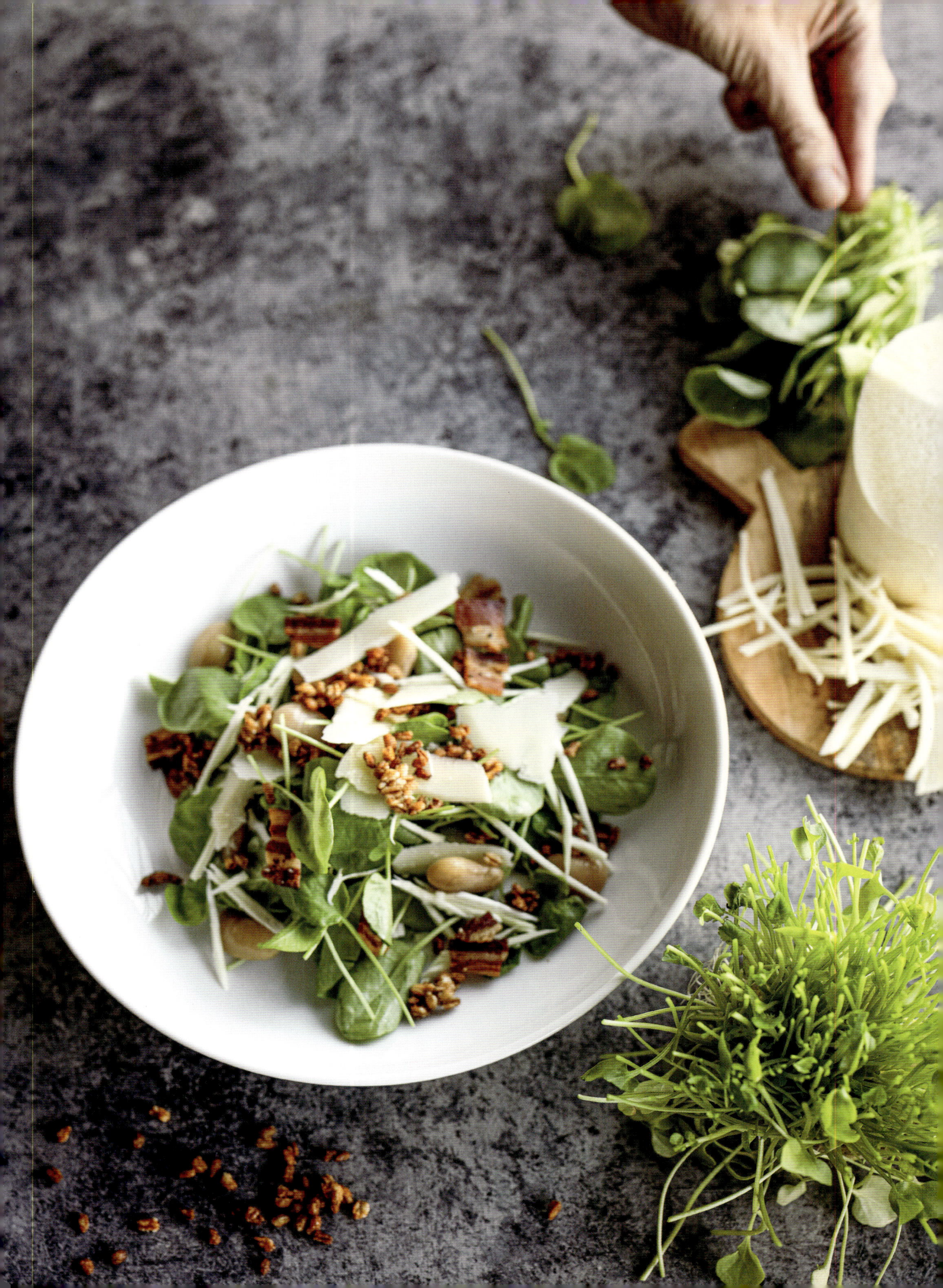

INSALATA

WATERCRESS, HEARTS OF PALM *and* CRISPY FARRO SALAD

1 cup dry gigante beans (or substitute canned borlotti or corona beans)

1 bay leaf

2 sprigs fresh thyme

2 garlic cloves, smashed

1 tablespoon kosher salt

1 3-inch piece fresh heart of palm

1 cup raw pancetta, diced

3 bunches watercress, roots trimmed

⅓ cup Dijon Red Wine Dressing (page 232)

2 tablespoons Crispy Farro (page 262)

½ cup shaved Grana Padano cheese

This is a nice year-round salad developed by Daniel Erhardt, our former chef de cuisine. The farro gives it crunch and the mustard vinaigrette provides just the right amount of zest. Guests often ask me, "How do you know that ingredients will go together?" To which I reply, "Decades of tasting all sorts of foods." A few of the ingredients in this salad marry particularly well—beans, Grana Padano and pancetta, watercress and mustard and so on. Daniel was able to chef-up the salad by adding fresh hearts of palm and the crispy element of fried farro to make an all-around delicious dish.
// SERVES 4

Place gigante beans in a quart-size container and fill with 3 cups water, then let soak overnight.

Drain beans and transfer to a large soup pot. Add 5 cups water, bay leaf, thyme and garlic. Bring to a boil, then reduce to a gentle simmer for 2 hours. If at any time the water dips below the beans, add enough water to cover. When beans are tender, remove from heat, add salt, and allow beans to cool in the broth. When cool, strain beans and save the liquid for soups or other recipes.

Julienne heart of palm on a mandoline and set aside.

Place diced pancetta in a small skillet over medium-high heat. Cook, stirring often, until the pancetta is crispy and deep golden brown. Scoop out cooked pancetta with a slotted spoon onto a towel-lined baking sheet and let cool.

To make the salad, gently toss watercress and hearts of palm in a large salad bowl with pancetta, gigante beans and Dijon dressing; mix well. Divide salad between 4 plates. Sprinkle salads with crispy farro and shaved Grana Padano.

INSALATA

PERSIMMON SALAD
with CARROTS, POMEGRANATE SEEDS and KUMQUATS

1 medium carrot, peeled and sliced lengthwise (on a mandoline if available) to the thickness of a business card

Kosher salt

4 ripe Fuyu persimmons

1 fresh pomegranate

2 cups arugula

6 kumquats, thinly sliced

⅓ cup Pomegranate Vinaigrette (page 233)

Freshly ground black pepper

2 boules buratta (2 ounces each), cut in half

Don't wear white when tapping out the pomegranate seeds! Also, sometimes you can find little cups of the seeds at Costco—for large parties at Farina, I buy them like that. Salting the carrots will season them, but more important, it will "cook them," turning them limp and pliable but remaining crunchy. The flexibility of the shaved carrots helps make the presentation, as the carrots weave in and around the other salad ingredients.

Persimmon is a fascinating fruit, having leapt from relative obscurity to mass-market stardom in recent years. There are two main varieties: the Hachiya is palatable only when completely ripe and mushy; the Fuyu variety is the one that has led the current charge to our plates. Fuyu persimmons are sweet when ripe, and they retain a firm shape, making them easy to slice for salads or for searing to garnish wild game preparations. // **SERVES 4**

Place sliced carrots in a medium prep bowl and sprinkle with a pinch of salt. Gently toss to coat, then let sit for 20 minutes.

Remove stems from persimmons and peel them with a sharp paring knife. Slice each peeled persimmon in half straight down as it normally sits, then cut each half into 4 equal-size wedges. Sprinkle with a pinch of salt and set aside.

Cut pomegranate in half horizontally. Hold one half pomegranate, cut side down, in one hand over a prep bowl and tap it firmly with the back of a spoon, lightly squeezing the fruit at the same time. Repeat this technique multiple times until all the seeds fall into the bowl (along with some juice). Repeat with the other half, then pick out any white interior pith that falls into the bowl along with the seeds. Set aside.

In a large salad bowl, combine arugula, persimmons, kumquats and carrots. Swirl in pomegranate vinaigrette and gently mix all the ingredients well. Add salt and pepper to taste and toss again.

To serve, divide salad between 4 plates. Bend and curl the carrots around the other ingredients to give some visual texture to the plated salad. Sprinkle salads with pomegranate seeds and place half a burrata on each salad. Sprinkle burrata with salt and pepper.

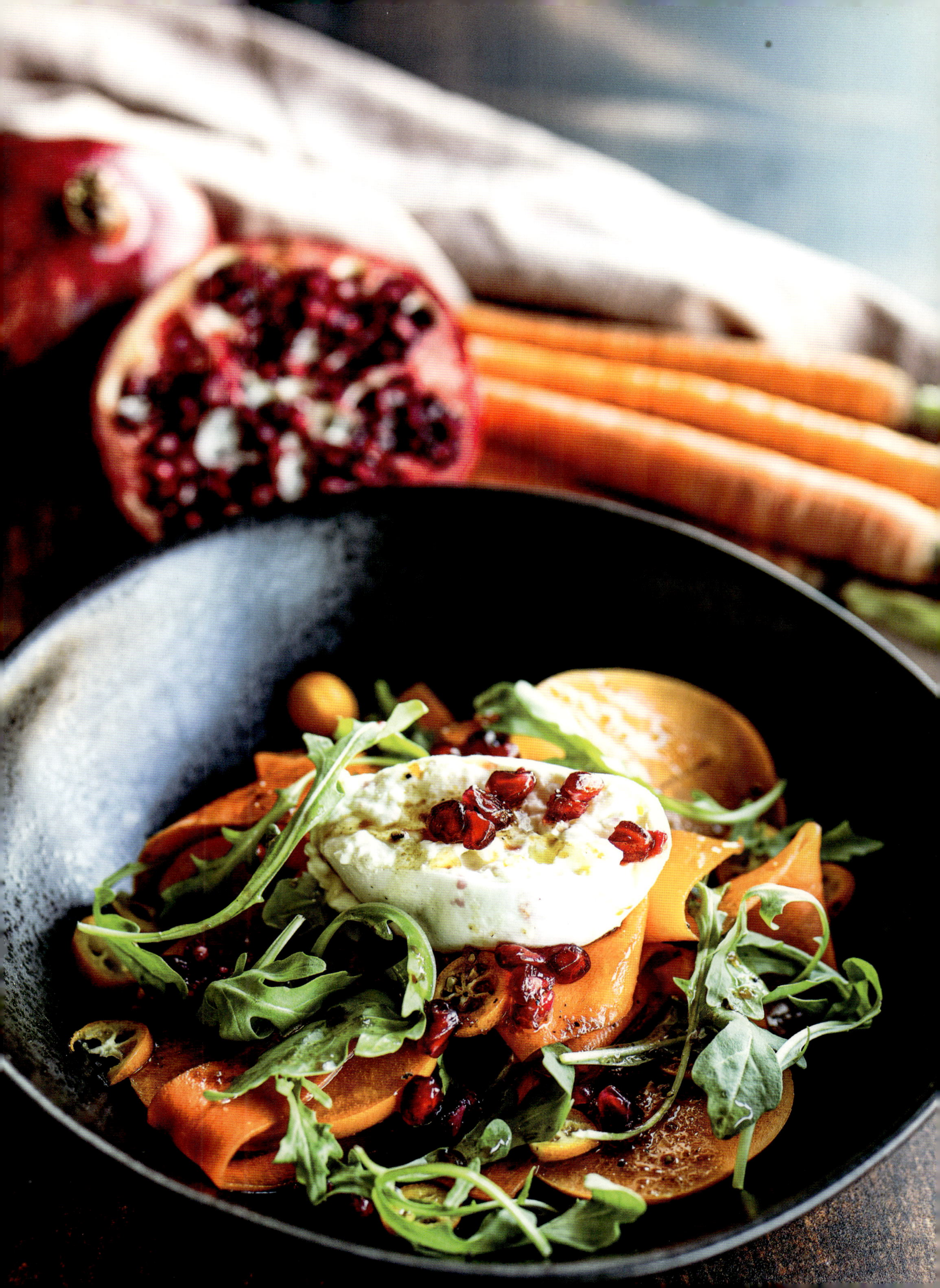

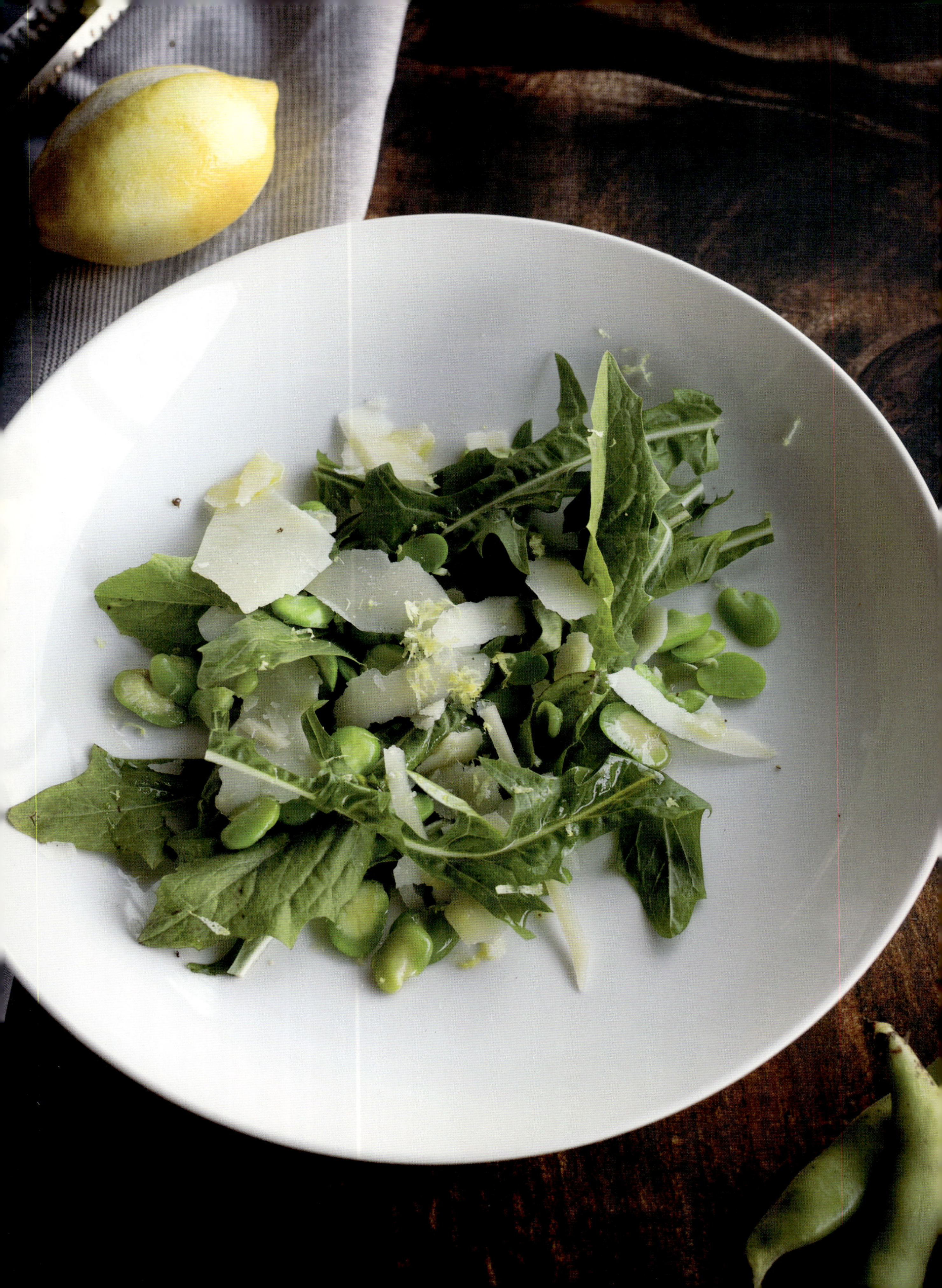

FAVA BEAN *and* DANDELION SALAD
with LEMON DRESSING

- 1 bunch frisée lettuce
- 1 bunch dandelion leaves
- 3 tablespoons extra-virgin olive oil (for croutons)
- ¼ French baguette, torn into ¾-inch pieces
- Kosher salt and freshly ground black pepper
- 4 tablespoons fresh lemon juice
- ⅓ cup extra-virgin olive oil (for dressing)
- 1½ cups fresh fava beans, shucked from pods and skins removed (or substitute frozen soybeans)
- 1 tablespoon fresh tarragon leaves
- ½ cup shaved Grana Padano cheese

> I usually cut frisée at 1- to 2-inch intervals. The long, frizzy salad fronds are difficult to eat, so shorter is better.

Greens of the dandelion—which takes its name from the French *dent de lion* (tooth of the lion) for its jagged leaves—are becoming more common in vegetable markets. They are a good source of vitamin C and make an excellent salad. A tangy lemon dressing helps soften their natural bitterness. The Italians and French have been eating salads like this forever, and in America, we are doing our best to catch up! // **SERVES 4**

With the frisée lettuce core intact, cut 1 inch off the ends if needed (they tend to be wilted and discolored). Hold the core end of the frisée head with one hand and cut across the lettuce at 2-inch intervals until you reach the core, then cut the core off and discard it. Soak frisée in a large bowl of ice water for 15 minutes. Use a salad spinner to spin the frisée fronds dry. Transfer to a large prep bowl and set aside.

Cut off the root end of the dandelion greens and separate the firmest, greenest leaves (you may have to discard some outer leaves). If the greens need to be washed, then rinse the leaves under cold water and use a salad spinner to spin dry. Add cleaned and dried leaves to the frisée prep bowl and set aside.

MAKE CROUTONS

Heat 3 tablespoons olive oil in a skillet over medium heat until oil is shimmering. Add torn bread and a pinch of salt and stir well to evenly coat in olive oil. Reduce heat to medium-low and cook, stirring occasionally, until golden brown and mostly crisp, approximately 4 minutes. Season with salt and pepper to taste, and transfer to a small baking sheet to cool.

MAKE LEMON DRESSING AND ASSEMBLE SALAD

Measure lemon juice and ½ teaspoon kosher salt into a small bowl and stir to dissolve; let sit for 2 minutes. Whisk in ⅓ cup olive oil and ½ teaspoon freshly ground black pepper and set aside.

Add fava beans, tarragon and croutons to the greens in the prep bowl. Add lemon dressing and a pinch of salt and pepper, then toss well to coat.

Divide salad between 4 plates and sprinkle with shaved Grana Padano cheese.

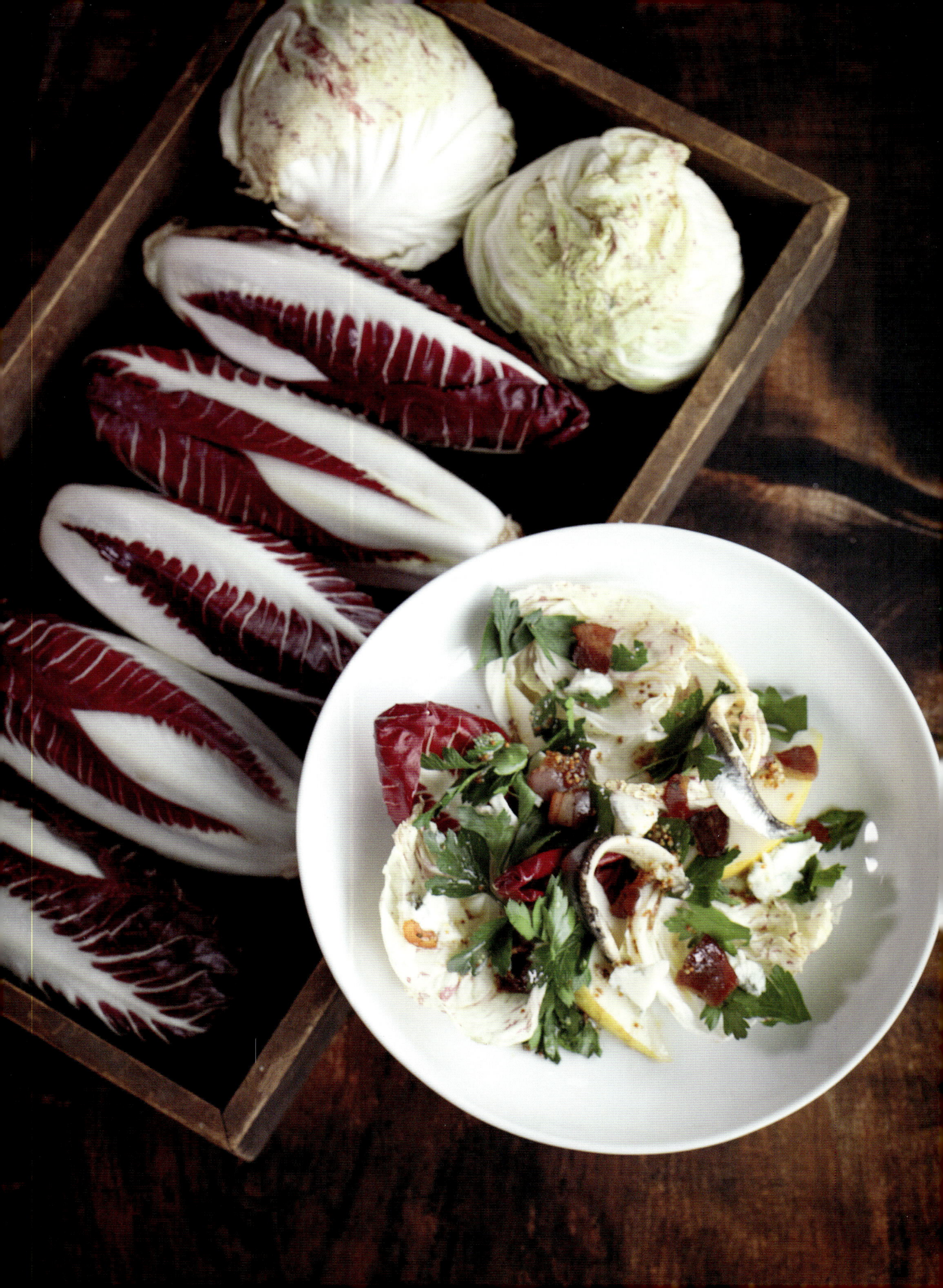

INSALATA

TREVISO *and* BARTLETT PEAR SALAD
with GORGONZOLA

1 head Italian Treviso lettuce, core end and any bruised leaves removed (or substitute radicchio)

1 head Castelfranco lettuce, core end and any bruised leaves removed

2 cups parsley leaves, soaked in ice water

2 ripe Bartlett pears, skin on, halved lengthwise and cored

1 cup pancetta lardons, diced and fried (or substitute bacon)

½ teaspoon cracked black pepper

⅓ cup Orange-Fennel Pollen Dressing (page 234)

6 Spanish white pickled anchovies, cut in half lengthwise

2 to 3 ounces sweet Gorgonzola cheese

> I omit salt from this salad because several elements of it are already highly seasoned (anchovies, pancetta and Gorgonzola).

Treviso is part of the chicory family and native to the Northern Italian region of Veneto, specifically the city of Treviso. Chicory has been cultivated there since the 1500s, and in the early 1900s Treviso was granted an IGP (Indication of Geographic Protection), which is a specific mark of quality and location. I have been using Castelfranco, the other lettuce in this salad, for many years, and when I first put it on the menu at Extra Virgin, guests would send the salad back to the kitchen thinking the radicchio was spoiled. Castelfranco is a chicory lettuce with yellowish white leaves and burgundy streaks running through it. Most people recognize radicchio as bright burgundy in color with white streaks. I've always found pride in introducing new and different products to Kansas City, and this was one of them. **// MAKES 4 SALADS**

Pull apart the leaves of each head of lettuce. Leave the slender Treviso leaves whole (they make a beautiful presentation on the salad plate). Tear Castelfranco leaves into smaller pieces about 3 inches in diameter. Toss Castelfranco leaves in a large salad bowl with drained parsley leaves. Set aside. Cut each pear half into 4 long wedges and set aside.

When ready to finish the salad, add crispy pancetta and pepper to the salad bowl along with dressing. Toss gently but coat leaves well with dressing. Place 2 long leaves of Treviso lettuce on each of 4 salad plates. Divide Castelfranco salad between the 4 plates. Tuck wedges of pear into each mound of salad so that each plate has 4 slices. Add 3 slivers of white anchovies to the top of each salad and finish by sprinkling teaspoon-size dollops of Gorgonzola in and around the Castelfranco leaves.

INSALATA

CUCUMBER SALAD

6 Persian cucumbers, each sliced into 4 pieces on a long bias

Kosher salt

2 ripe avocados, halved and pitted

½ cup Tzatziki (page 235)

¼ cup crispy fried shallots (available at Asian grocery stores)

1 teaspoon nigella seeds

1 teaspoon Burnt Onion Ash (page 249)

Unlike in America, where lettuce is synonymous with salad, throughout the Mediterranean any vegetable, relish, pickle or dip is often referred to as a salad. In this recipe, compact and juicy Persian cucumbers play nicely with creamy avocados. Tzatziki provides a cool contrast—I simply thin out what would be a tasty dip to make it a pleasant salad dressing. // **SERVES 4**

Place sliced cucumbers in a prep bowl and sprinkle with salt. Set aside.

Slice each avocado half into 6 wedges. Sprinkle avocado slices with salt.

To serve, divide cucumbers evenly between 4 salad plates. Arrange 6 slices of avocado on each plate. Drizzle each salad with 2 tablespoons tzatziki. Sprinkle each salad with fried shallots, nigella seeds and a light dusting of burnt onion ash.

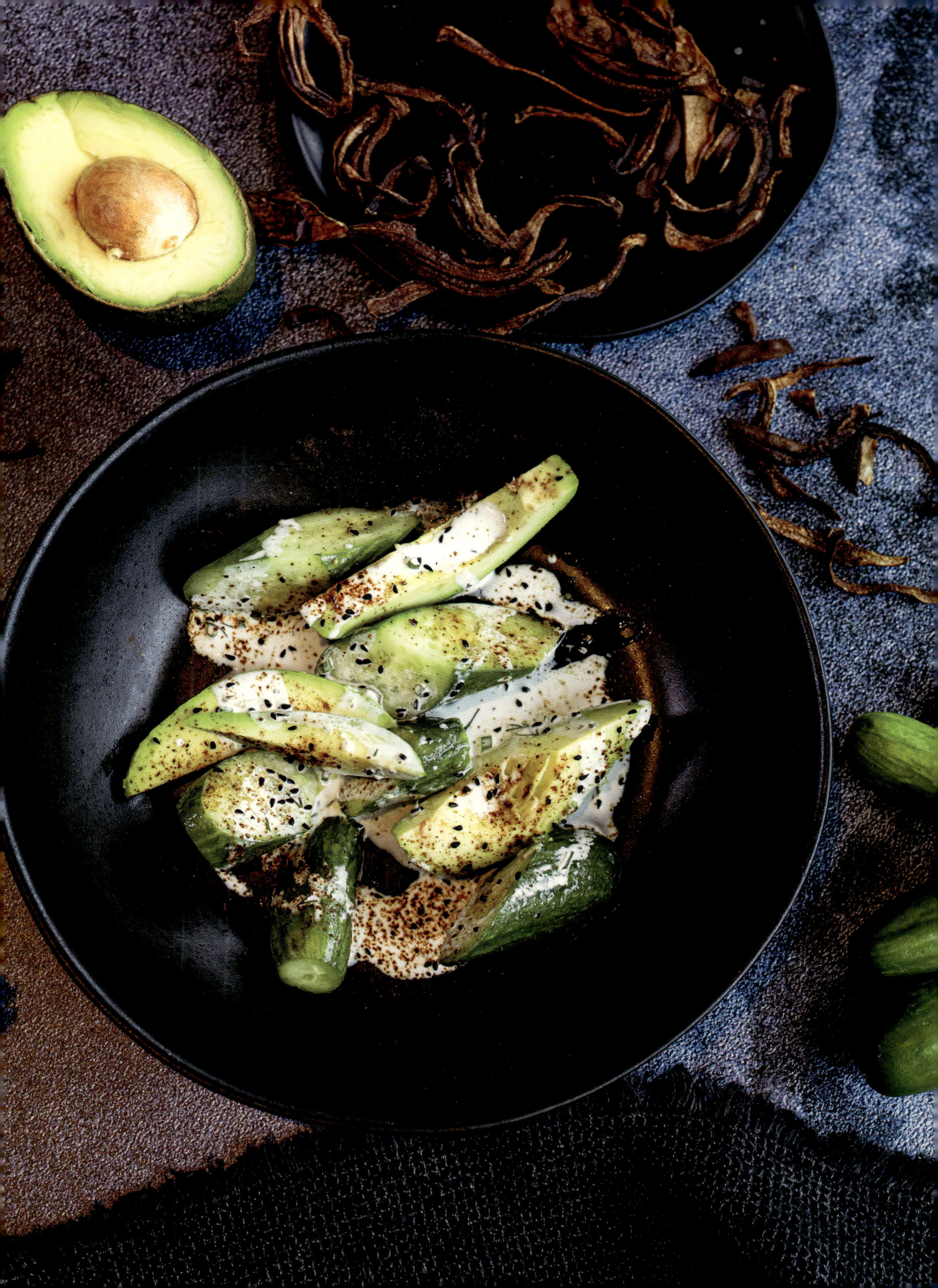

PISTOU
(PAGE 65)

MINESTRONE
(PAGE 61)

**SUMMER
TOMATO
GAZPACHO**
(PAGE 62)

**PROVENÇAL
PISTOU SOUP**
(PAGE 64)

MINESTRONE

MINESTRONE

1 cup dry great Northern white beans (or substitute 28 ounces canned beans, rinsed)

1½ cups diced pancetta (or prosciutto scraps)

1 cup diced yellow onion

4 garlic cloves, thinly sliced

12-ounce can tomato paste

2 tablespoons fresh oregano, chopped

1 tablespoon fresh thyme leaves

1 bay leaf

4 quarts Poultry Broth (page 237)

1 cup Parmesan or Grana Padano cheese rinds

1 teaspoon red pepper flakes

3 cups ripe red tomatoes, diced (or canned diced tomatoes)

1 cup Idaho or Yukon gold potatoes, peeled and diced

1 cup butternut or kabocha squash, peeled and diced

1 cup carrots, peeled and diced

1 cup celery, diced

1 cup diced fennel

1 teaspoon fennel pollen

SOUP GARNISH

1 pound ditalini pasta, cooked al dente according to package directions and lightly oiled

½ cup fresh basil, chopped

Freshly cracked black pepper

Grated Grana Padano cheese, for sprinkling

Crusty artisanal bread, for serving

A few years ago, on a trip to Alba, I met one of the hardest-working winemakers I've ever encountered—Fabio Oberto. He was passionate about everything—the land, the vines, the grapes and, most of all, the winery he and his father built. When I tasted the oh-so glorious Barbera d'Alba, I wanted to hug him. It was like Fabio was welcoming me into his family. I feel the same way about a tasty bowl of minestrone, you just want to savor each spoonful! Cozy up to a fireplace with my version of minestrone and a glass of Barbera d'Alba. Just remember to add the precooked pasta to the soup when you're ready to eat so it will be chewy and toothsome. // **MAKES 5 QUARTS**

Soak dry white beans in 4 cups cold water for at least 2 hours or overnight. Strain and set aside.

Place pancetta and onions in a large soup pot over medium heat. Cook until pancetta starts releasing its fat, 3 to 4 minutes. Add garlic and cook another minute, being careful not to burn garlic. Stir in tomato paste, oregano, thyme and bay leaf. Cook 3 minutes. Add broth, beans, cheese rinds and pepper flakes. (If using soaked beans, bring to a boil, then adjust heat to low and simmer gently until beans are almost cooked through, about 45 minutes, stirring often from the bottom of the pot to keep cheese rinds from sticking. For canned beans, continue to next step without the simmer.)

Add tomatoes, potatoes, squash, carrots, celery and fennel. Continue to simmer until vegetables and beans are cooked but not mushy, 20 to 30 minutes. Remove cheese rinds and stir in fennel pollen.

To serve, add approximately ½ cup cooked ditalini to each soup bowl and ladle 2 cups minestrone over the pasta. Garnish with a sprinkle of fresh basil, cracked black pepper and Grana Padano cheese. Serve with crusty artisanal bread.

Transfer soup and pasta to separate airtight containers and refrigerate for up to 5 days or freeze for up to 6 months.

SOUPS

SUMMER TOMATO GAZPACHO
(SALMOREJO)

4 slices rustic bread (ciabatta or French baguette), sliced 1 inch thick

3 pounds overripe heirloom tomatoes, cored and cut into 1-inch chunks

1 cucumber, peeled and cut into 1-inch chunks

1 cup canned roasted red bell peppers, drained and cut into 1-inch pieces

3 shallots, cut into 1-inch chunks

4 garlic cloves

1 cup tomato paste, divided

¾ cup extra-virgin olive oil, divided

3 tablespoons sherry vinegar

1 tablespoon kosher salt

1 teaspoon ground black pepper

Optional garnishes: freshly snipped chives, basil, fresh goat cheese, crispy croutons and a drizzle of high-quality extra-virgin olive oil

In Spain they call gazpacho by another name—salmorejo. When I first tasted this soup, I loved it immediately! I generally like the soup we call gazpacho in the U.S.; you know, the one with diced raw vegetables and a tart tomato broth. Except, I simply cannot eat raw bell peppers. I don't like them. And I never allow *green* bell peppers in my restaurants . . . ever! At any rate, once I tasted the smooth richness of salmorejo, drizzled with olive oil and perked up with sherry vinegar, well, that was it. Now, it's the only kind I make in the summer. There are a couple secrets to success for this recipe. First, the sherry vinegar gives the soup a crucial jolt of acid, and second, the better the blender, the better the soup. We use a Vitamix at Farina, which yields a smooth, creamy gazpacho without the addition of any cream. // **MAKES 3½ QUARTS**

Place a large, fine-mesh strainer over a deep bowl with at least a 4-quart capacity. Set aside.

Place bread slices in a shallow bowl and cover with 2 cups water. Let stand until saturated but not falling apart, about 10 minutes. Squeeze out and discard water, reserving bread.

Working in 3 batches, combine one-third of the vegetables and one-third of the bread, garlic and tomato paste in a blender and blend on low speed for 30 seconds. Increase speed to high. With the machine running, drizzle in 1 cup water and ¼ cup olive oil and blend for 30 seconds, or until the mixture looks creamy and emulsified. Pour the soup through the strainer and repeat with the remaining ingredients in 2 more batches.

Add sherry vinegar, salt and pepper to the bowl, and whisk vigorously to blend all the batches together. If the soup is too thick, whisk in more water, a little at a time, and season to taste.

Serve as is or with any of the suggested garnishes.

Store the ungarnished soup in an airtight container for up to 5 days in the refrigerator or freezer for up to 6 months.

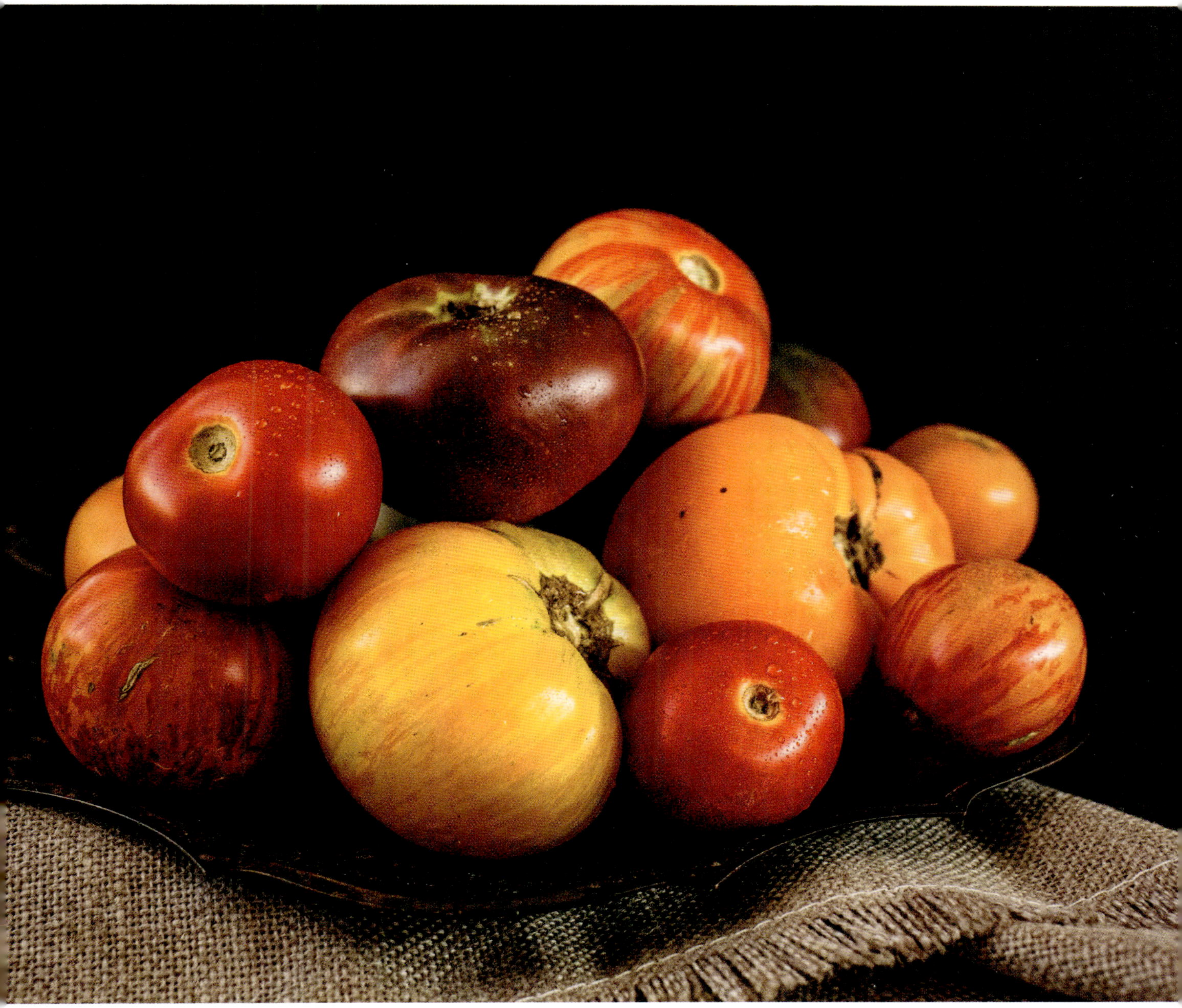

SOUPS

PROVENÇAL PISTOU SOUP

This is a nostalgic soup for me and was a weekly meal when I was working in Nice on the Côte d'Azur in 1985. Many people think Nice was once Italian. It kind of was, and kind of wasn't! In fact, Nice was part of the House of Savoy (Piedmont) until 1860, when Italy reluctantly gave her up to repay France for helping defend Italy from the Austrians. There is a lot more to the story, but we're talking about a recipe here. Pistou is like pesto but without the pine nuts and is a common condiment in the Provence region of France, most often associated with *soupe au pistou*, a clear, brothy version of minestrone. The pistou is incorporated into the soup just before serving. In Nice, Gruyère cheese is sprinkled on the soup as an additional garnish. // **MAKES 3 QUARTS**

SOUPS

PISTOU

2 cups fresh basil leaves

¾ cup freshly grated Grana Padano cheese

¼ cup extra-virgin olive oil

2 cloves garlic

SOUP

1 cup dried cannellini beans (or 28 ounces canned beans, rinsed)

1 teaspoon plus 1 tablespoon kosher salt, divided

1 tablespoon olive oil

½ cup diced leek, white part only

½ cup diced onion

½ cup diced fennel

½ cup diced carrot

½ cup peeled and diced butternut squash

2 quarts Poultry Broth (page 237; or substitute vegetable broth)

1 sprig fresh thyme

1 bay leaf

½ cup green beans, cut into ½-inch pieces

1 teaspoon freshly ground black pepper

1 cup medium-diced gold zucchini (or substitute green zucchini or summer squash)

½ cup medium-diced ripe red tomatoes (or canned diced tomatoes)

1½ cups cooked ditalini or mini bowtie pasta (cooked according to package instructions)

4 tablespoons pistou

Toasted crostini, for garnish (page 247)

Grated Gruyère cheese, for garnish

MAKE PISTOU

Combine basil, cheese, olive oil and garlic in a food processor. Process until garlic and basil are thoroughly combined, 1 to 2 minutes.

MAKE SOUP

Soak white beans in 4 cups cold water for at least 2 hours or overnight.

Strain beans and place in a 2-quart saucepan. Cover with 4 cups cold water and add 1 teaspoon salt. Bring to a boil, then adjust heat so water simmers until beans are soft and cooked through, about 1 hour. Drain well and set aside.

Heat olive oil in a 4-quart stainless steel pot over medium-high heat. Add leek, onion, fennel, carrot and butternut squash and sauté until onions soften, 4 to 5 minutes. Add broth, thyme and bay leaf and bring to a boil. Reduce heat to a simmer and cook for 5 minutes. Add green beans, black pepper and remaining 1 tablespoon salt; continue to simmer until vegetables are tender, 5 to 10 minutes more.

Add zucchini and tomatoes and simmer 5 minutes, then stir in beans. Season to taste with salt and pepper, keeping in mind that pistou will add saltiness from the cheese.

Stir the pasta and a generous helping of pistou into the soup pot and serve family style. Or, ladle soup into individual soup bowls, add pasta, and let your friends stir in their own amount of pistou. Garnish with toasted crostini and a sprinkling of Gruyère.

To store, transfer soup and pasta to separate airtight containers and refrigerate for up to 5 days or freeze for up to 6 months.

> What grows together, goes together. The wines of Provence are beautiful, just like the vineyards and the cuisine. Provence is the benchmark for rosé, so let's drink pink! Try Domaine Aix, a Farina favorite that's as delicious as it is affordable.

TRUFFLES

CONFESSIONS
of a
TRUFFLE KNIGHT

I'm proud to boast that I am a Truffle Knight. Yes, there really is such a thing. And I was officially granted knighthood on November 8, 2019, in the Castle of Grinzane Cavour in Alba, Italy, by the Order of Knights of the Truffle and Wines of Alba. There were 25 of us from all over the world who were knighted that day and charged with the responsibility to "defend and promote the genuine foods and wines of Alba," a solemn task that I enthusiastically accepted. My nomination for knighthood came from Stefano Gagliardo, of the renowned Italian winery Poderi Gianni Gagliardo, who visited Kansas City to serve his family's wines at a winter truffle dinner Nancy and I hosted. Impressed by my vigorous method of slicing white or black truffles on every dish, Gagliardo suggested I become a knight. Truth is, I thought he might have consumed a bit too much of his own wine. But eight months later, there I was in Alba.

Over the years, I have been on numerous truffle hunts. I have eaten whole black truffles baked in puff pastry, been served thick piles of sliced truffles on platters, eaten mashed potatoes so dense with crushed truffles that they turned black. I have purchased tens of thousands of dollars' worth of truffles. While I am a Knight of the Truffle, I am no truffle expert. Still, I do have opinions.

Case in point: truffle oil. I don't use the stuff. That's because commercial truffle oil is not made from real truffles. It's created in laboratories by mixing olive oil with one or more chemical compounds like 2,4-dithiapentane. The essential flavor of real truffles is evanescent, almost otherworldly. It's impossible to capture in an oil.

These days, many people are first introduced to truffles by way of the ubiquitous truffle fries. There are no real truffles on truffle fries, but the truffle oil creates an aroma of truffles that delivers a big bang for the buck. Many chefs use too much of it in their recipes, trying to create over-the-top flavors. It's a far cry from the subtle woodsy and musky nuances of a genuine truffle dug from the earth. And as a Knight of the Order of the Truffle I am sworn to uphold and defend the real deal.

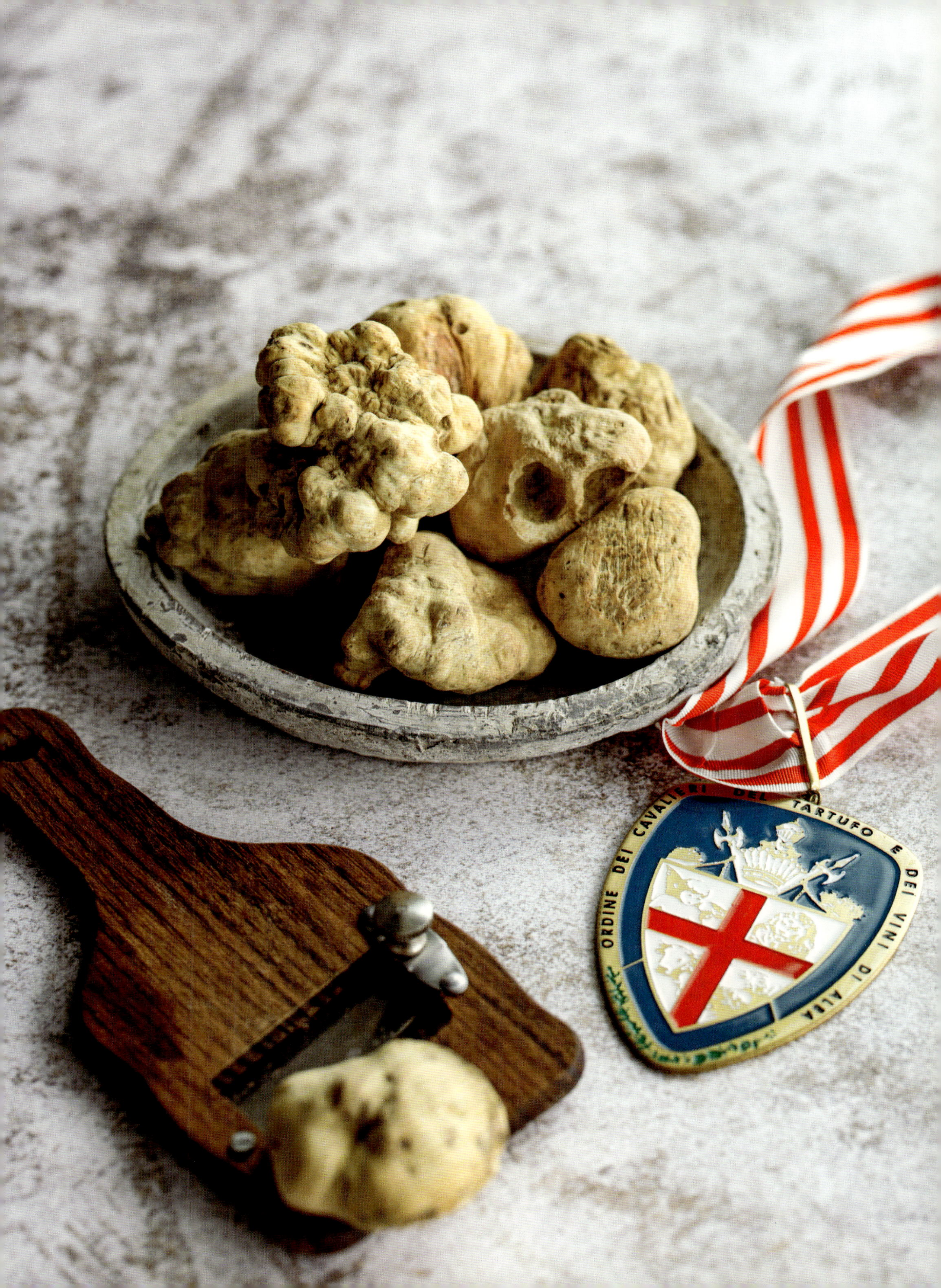
ORDINE DEI CAVALIERI DEL TARTUFO E DEI VINI DI ALBA

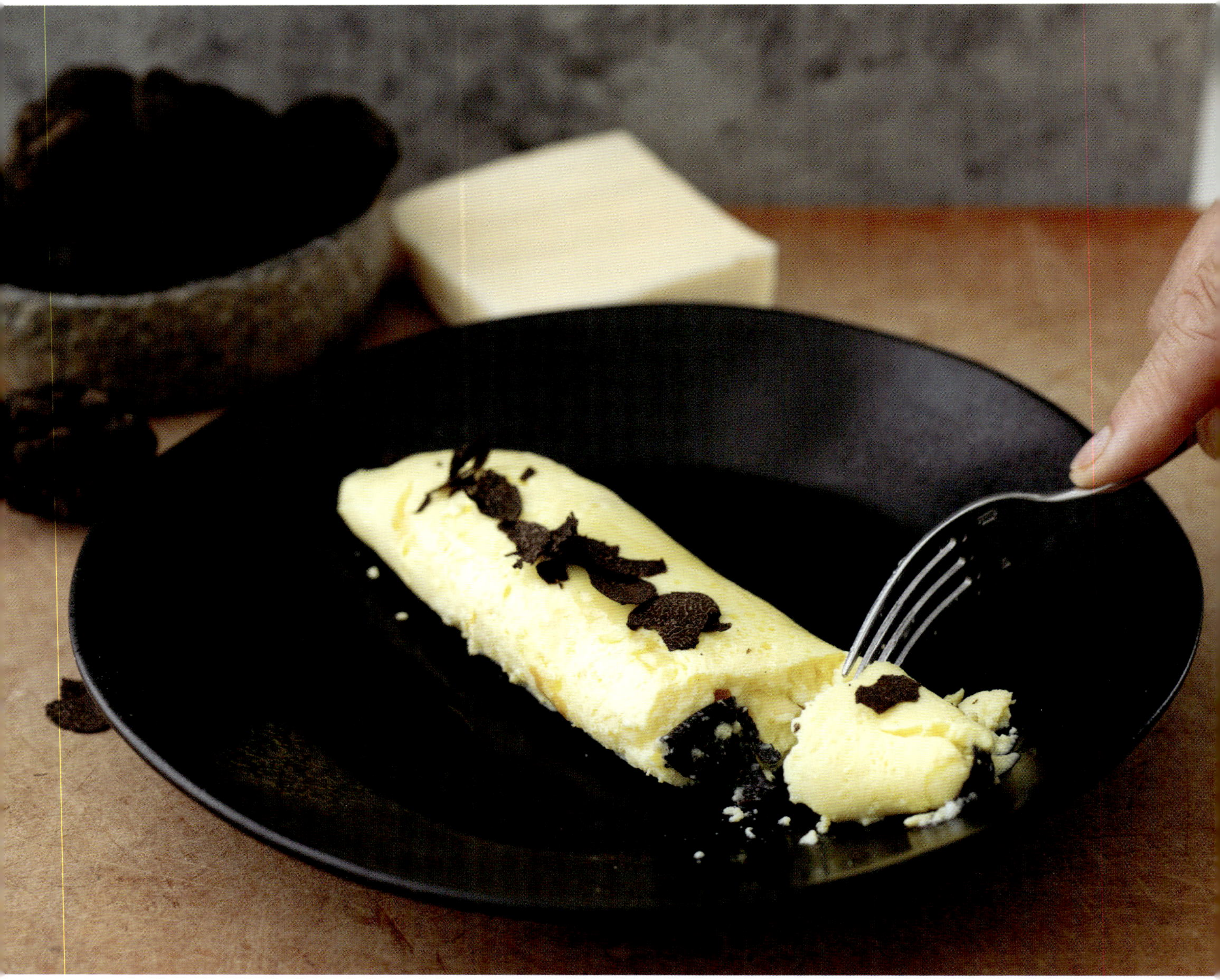

BLACK TRUFFLE OMELET

2 large eggs

1 teaspoon kosher salt

1 pinch ground white pepper

2 tablespoons soft unsalted butter, divided

1 tablespoon fresh black truffle, cut into ⅛-inch batons

1 tablespoon minced fresh chives

I've never been much of an egg eater, which explains why my omelet-making skills were lacking for a long time. That all changed when I experienced the magic created when the venerable black truffle marries an omelet. It immediately forced me to up my egg game. The trick with this recipe is to cook the omelet over low heat and be patient. French chefs are known to rub soft butter onto the finished omelet to make it glossy, but that's optional.

// **MAKES 1 OMELET**

Whisk eggs, salt and pepper in a medium bowl until combined, approximately 30 seconds. Strain through a fine-mesh sieve into a small bowl.

Heat 1 tablespoon butter in an 8-inch nonstick sauté pan over low heat. When butter begins to foam, swirl in eggs with a rubber spatula, stirring eggs in a figure-8 pattern while moving the pan around the burner in a circular motion. Scrape down the sides of the pan as needed. The eggs will thicken as they cook, in approximately 2 minutes. Continue stirring and moving the pan in a circular motion until eggs are cooked through on the bottom but still runny on top. Remove pan from heat and let sit 1 minute. This lets the omelet relax and loosen from the pan. The bottom of the omelet should be smooth and not browned.

Spread the remaining tablespoon of butter on the inside of the omelet. Lay truffle batons down the center of the omelet and sprinkle with minced chives. Hold the sauté pan handle with one hand and slightly tilt it. With your other hand, use a rubber spatula to push the omelet edge closest to the handle toward the center. Repeat this technique from the other side, rolling the cooked egg onto itself and forming a cylinder with the black truffles running down the middle.

Roll omelet out of the pan and onto a plate.

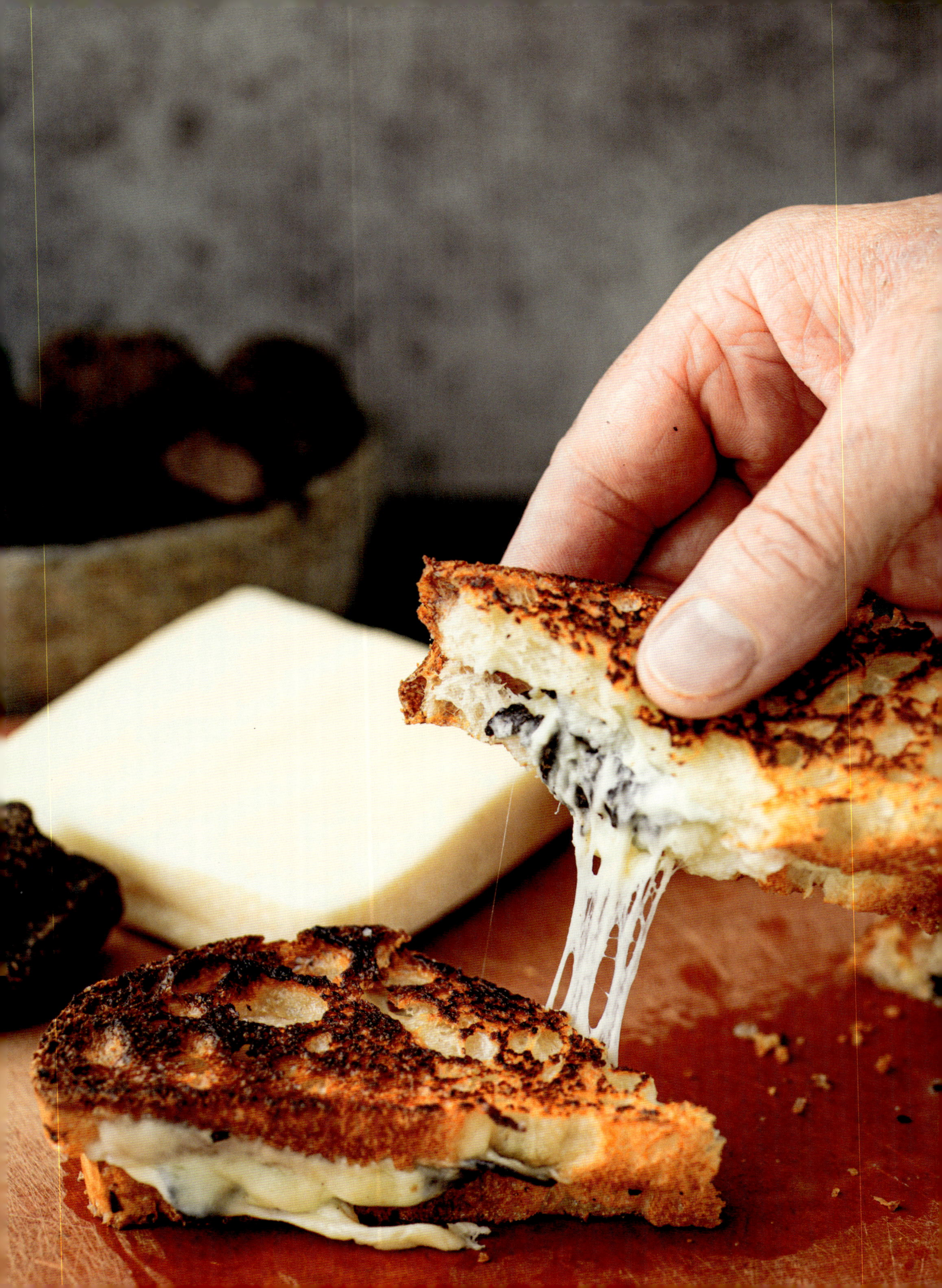

ITALIAN BLACK TRUFFLE *and* CHEESE SANDWICH

1 tablespoon soft butter

4 long slices focaccia bread (or substitute ½-inch-thick slices of artisanal sourdough loaf)

½ cup Crescenza or Stracchino cheese

1 ounce fresh black truffles

4 slices young soft fontina cheese

4 slices Swiss or Havarti cheese

Kosher salt

The grilled cheese sandwich is in everyone's cooking repertoire, but enhancing it with sliced fresh black truffles adds a self-indulgent, or perhaps even wicked, dimension. My chef friend at La Toque in Napa Valley, Ken Frank, taught me to wrap truffle sandwiches in plastic to infuse them for 24 to 48 hours before serving. It's hard to wait that long to devour one, but it's worth it, and I have borrowed his idea. Thank you, Ken!

// MAKES 2 SANDWICHES

Spread soft butter on one side of each of the 4 slices of bread. Flip slices over and use a spoon to spread Crescenza cheese on the unbuttered side of 2 pieces only. Set the other 2 buttered bread slices aside.

Slice truffles very thin with a truffle slicer or mandolin and transfer to a small bowl. Sprinkle truffle slices with a pinch of salt and fluff lightly with a fork. Spread sliced truffles over Crescenza cheese along the length of the bread. Cut fontina and Swiss cheese slices in half (rectangles). Shingle 4 cut slices of each type onto the truffled bread. Put the 2 reserved bread slices on top of the finished slices. Wrap both sandwiches tightly in plastic wrap and refrigerate for 24 hours.

Preheat oven to 375°F.

Heat a large skillet over medium heat and lay the sandwiches in the pan. Cook until they are deep golden brown, then flip them over and do the same on the other side.

Transfer sandwiches to a baking sheet and bake in the oven for 5 minutes, until cheese is melted.

> Truffles are expensive, and you don't want any to go to waste. For this recipe, you are essentially locking the truffle slices into the sandwich with melted cheese on each side. I never worry about the cheese melting while the sandwiches are cooking in the pan. I simply want to get the desired color on the bread and then I'll finish in the oven (or microwave, depending on how hungry I am).

CHAMPAGNE *and* BLACK TRUFFLE RISOTTO

- 3 tablespoons butter, divided
- 2 shallots, minced
- 3 cups arborio rice
- 2 teaspoons kosher salt
- 1 cup champagne
- 2 quarts Poultry Broth (page 237), brought to a boil and set aside
- 2 tablespoons fresh black truffles, chopped
- 8 ounces fresh chanterelle mushrooms, cleaned, thinly sliced and sautéed
- 1 cup grated Grana Padano cheese, divided
- High-quality extra-virgin olive oil, for drizzling

Yep, champagne and truffles! I'm sorry that sounds so cliché. New Year's Eve is a perfect night to make this dish. It's winter and the truffles are in their full glory. Use just enough champagne to deglaze the rice and drink the rest! // **SERVES 4**

Heat a wide, heavy-bottomed saucepan over medium heat. Add 1½ tablespoons butter and shallots, then sweat for 3 minutes without browning. Add rice and stir for 3 to 4 minutes, letting rice lightly toast to a light golden color. Add salt and champagne to the rice, stirring until champagne is nearly evaporated. Add just enough hot poultry broth to cover the rice. Continuously stir until most of the broth is absorbed into the rice and the risotto starts to thicken and dry out, approximately 8 to 10 minutes. Repeat by adding more broth as risotto thickens and absorbs the broth, stirring continuously until the rice is cooked through but al dente, approximately 30 minutes. If you need more liquid, add hot water or more broth.

When risotto is ready to serve, stir in truffles, precooked chanterelle mushrooms, half of the Grana Padano cheese and remaining butter. Serve family-style from the saucepan at the table or divide risotto among 4 warm bowls. Garnish with remaining Grana Padano and drizzle with extra-virgin olive oil.

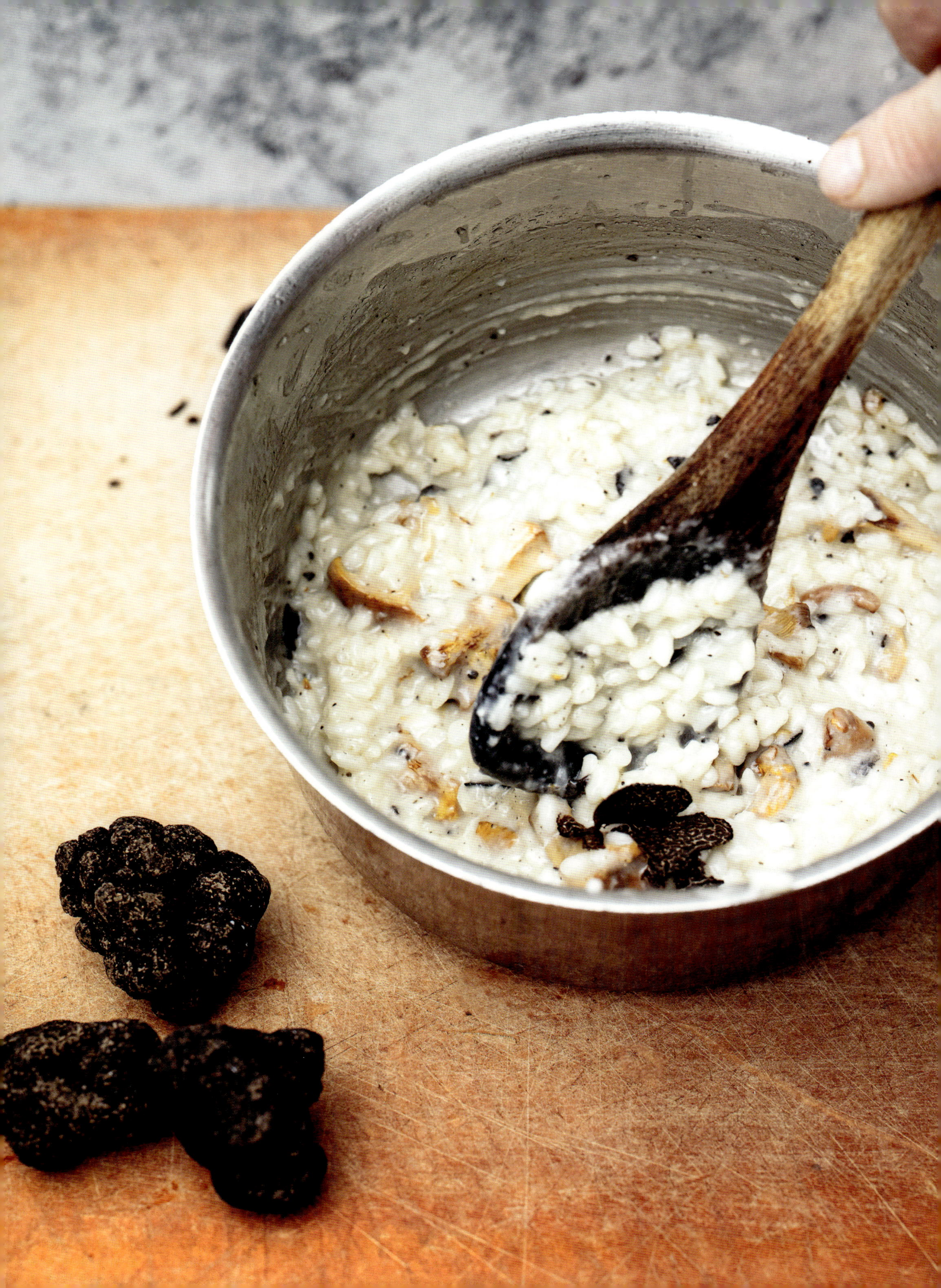

TRUFFLES

CRESPELLE *and* BLACK WINTER TRUFFLES

I learned about this dish from my friend Tony Mantuano of Spiaggia in Chicago, an amazing chef whose knowledge of Italian cooking is beyond reproach. He came to Kansas City for a wine dinner at 40 Sardines in 2004 and this was one of his contributions. I love serving it on special menus because it is so simple and wonderfully delicious. When truffle season rolls around every winter, I get to prepare this dish. // SERVES 4

1 ounce fresh black truffles

Kosher salt

6 ounces good Stracchino cheese, like Crescenza, Robiola or Brie

Egg Pasta Dough (page 90)

1 cup grated Grana Padano cheese

High-quality extra-virgin olive oil, for drizzling

Slice truffles very thinly, using a mandoline or truffle slicer. Place sliced truffles in a small bowl and season lightly with salt. Set aside.

To prepare cheese filling for the crespelle, use your hands or a spoon to mold 4 3-inch cheese coins that are about ¼ inch thick. Set aside.

PREPARE DOUGH SHEETS

Prepare egg pasta dough and follow the directions for rolling and sheeting (page 86). Only roll enough pasta sheets to produce 4 square pieces of dough that are 8 x 8 inches. Cover with plastic wrap and set aside.

Preheat oven to 350°F.

Prepare an ice bath for the blanched pasta sheets. Bring 4 quarts water and 2 tablespoons salt to a rolling boil. Drop the 4 pasta sheets into the water one at a time so they don't stick to each other. Cook for 30 seconds. Drain pasta sheets and dunk them in the ice water. Remove the sheets from ice water and dry on a kitchen towel laid on the work surface.

Shingle 2 slices of truffle in the center of each pasta sheet. Next, place a cheese coin on top of the truffles. Fold the edges of the pasta sheets tightly onto the cheese coin to form a square shape about 4 inches on all sides. Set each crespelle on a baking sheet lined with parchment paper. (These can be made up to 8 hours in advance. Cover and refrigerate if so.)

When ready to cook crespelle, pour a very thin layer of water and a drizzle of olive oil into the bottom of a shallow baking dish. Use a spatula to lift crespelle to the baking pan. Cover with aluminum foil and bake for about 10 minutes or until crespelle swell with steam and cheese is melted.

TO SERVE

Remove crespelle from oven. Use a spoon to scoop a small pile of Grana Padano onto 4 appetizer plates. With a spatula, place 1 crespelle on each pile of cheese. Sprinkle with more Grana Padano cheese, the remaining sliced truffles and a good drizzle of olive oil.

TRUFFLES

SORPRESINE
with POULTRY BROTH and BLACK TRUFFLES

Egg Pasta Dough (page 90), for 24 pieces sorpresine pasta

3 cups Poultry Broth (page 237)

½ teaspoon kosher salt

½ teaspoon hon dashi granules (optional)

1 ounce fresh black truffle

High-quality extra-virgin olive oil, to drizzle

Special equipment:
1 truffle slicer

This is a delicate pasta shape that's very easy to make by hand and looks so elegant floating in a light broth. Whatever broth you choose—mushroom, tomato, saffron, pesto—it will be *delicioso*! Here I've paired the sorpresine with a deeply flavorful poultry broth and shaved black truffles. // SERVES 2

MAKE SORPRESINE

Prepare egg dough recipe and follow directions for rolling and sheeting (page 86). Cut the rolled pasta sheets into perfect 1½-inch squares. (Gather the irregular pieces from cutting the squares and save them for a rustic pasta called maltagliati.)

To shape the sorpresine, arrange a pasta square as a diamond on the work surface. Fold 1 corner across to create a triangle and seal only the small area of dough where the 2 corners meet. Keep the center hollow and do not press the sides together. Use your index finger to gently push the middle of the folded edge, forcing the 2 shorter sides to bend. Bring these 2 corners together and seal them with your finger and thumb. Set each shaped sorpresine on a floured baking sheet. Repeat the shaping process until you have as many sorpresine as you need (this recipe uses 24). Let them dry for 30 minutes, then they are ready to cook. They can also be frozen individually and stored in an airtight container for up to 6 months.

PREPARE DISH

Pour poultry broth into a medium-size soup pot and bring it to a boil over medium-high heat. Add salt and hon dashi to the pot, then add sorpresine to the broth and cook for 2 minutes. Remove broth from the stove and divide into 2 bowls. Use truffle slicer to shave a generous amount of black truffle over each bowl and drizzle olive oil over everything as a final exclamation point.

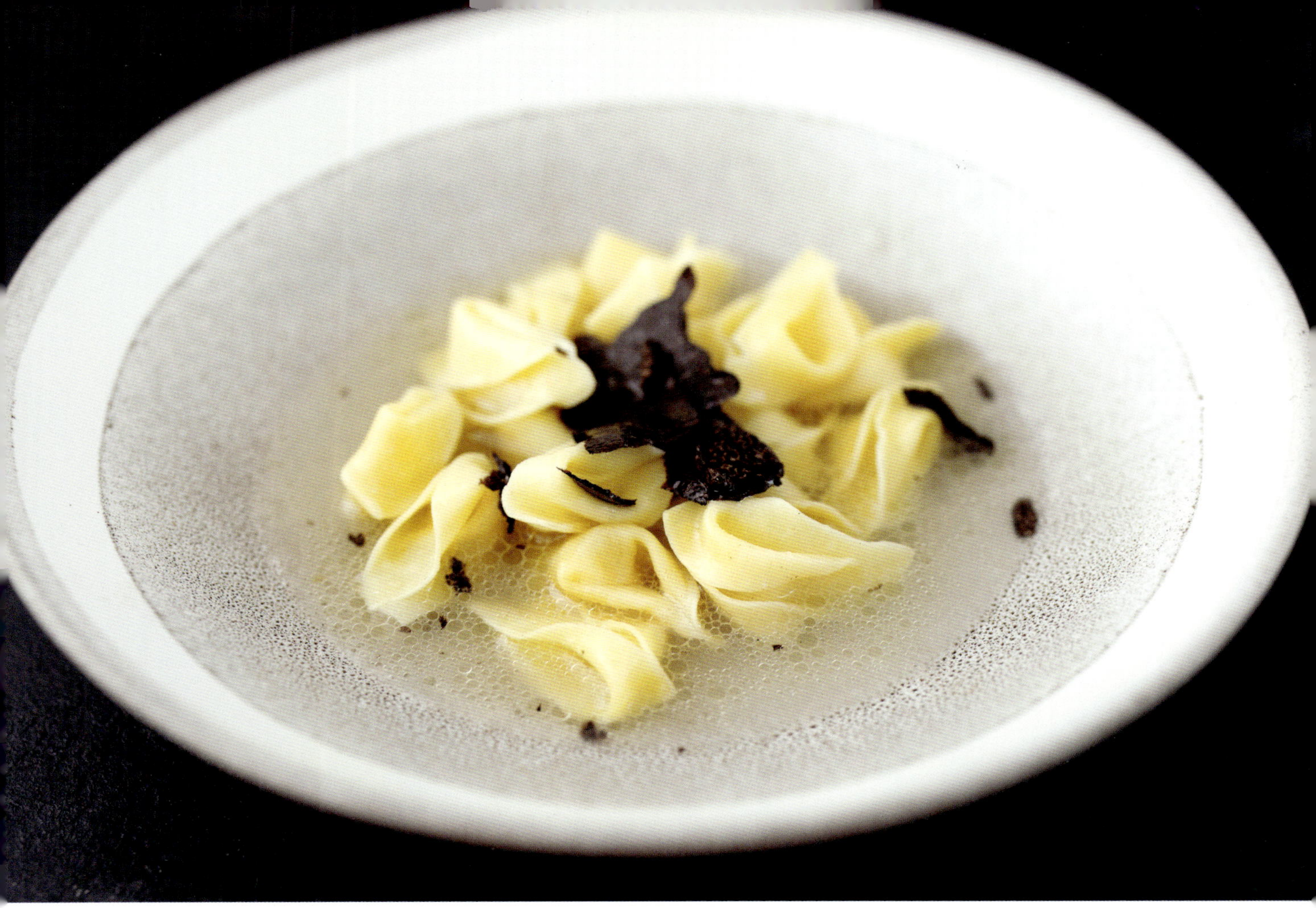

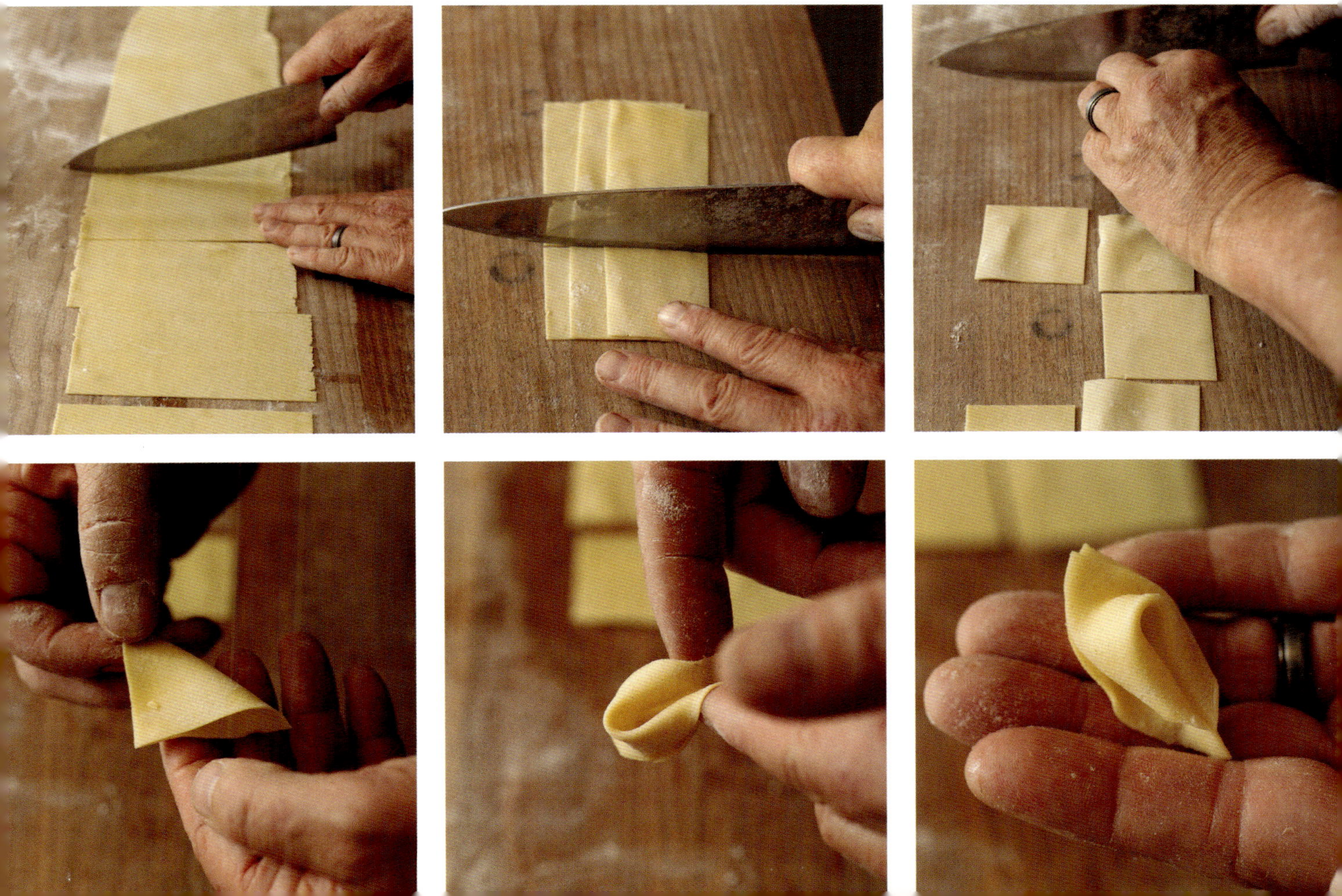

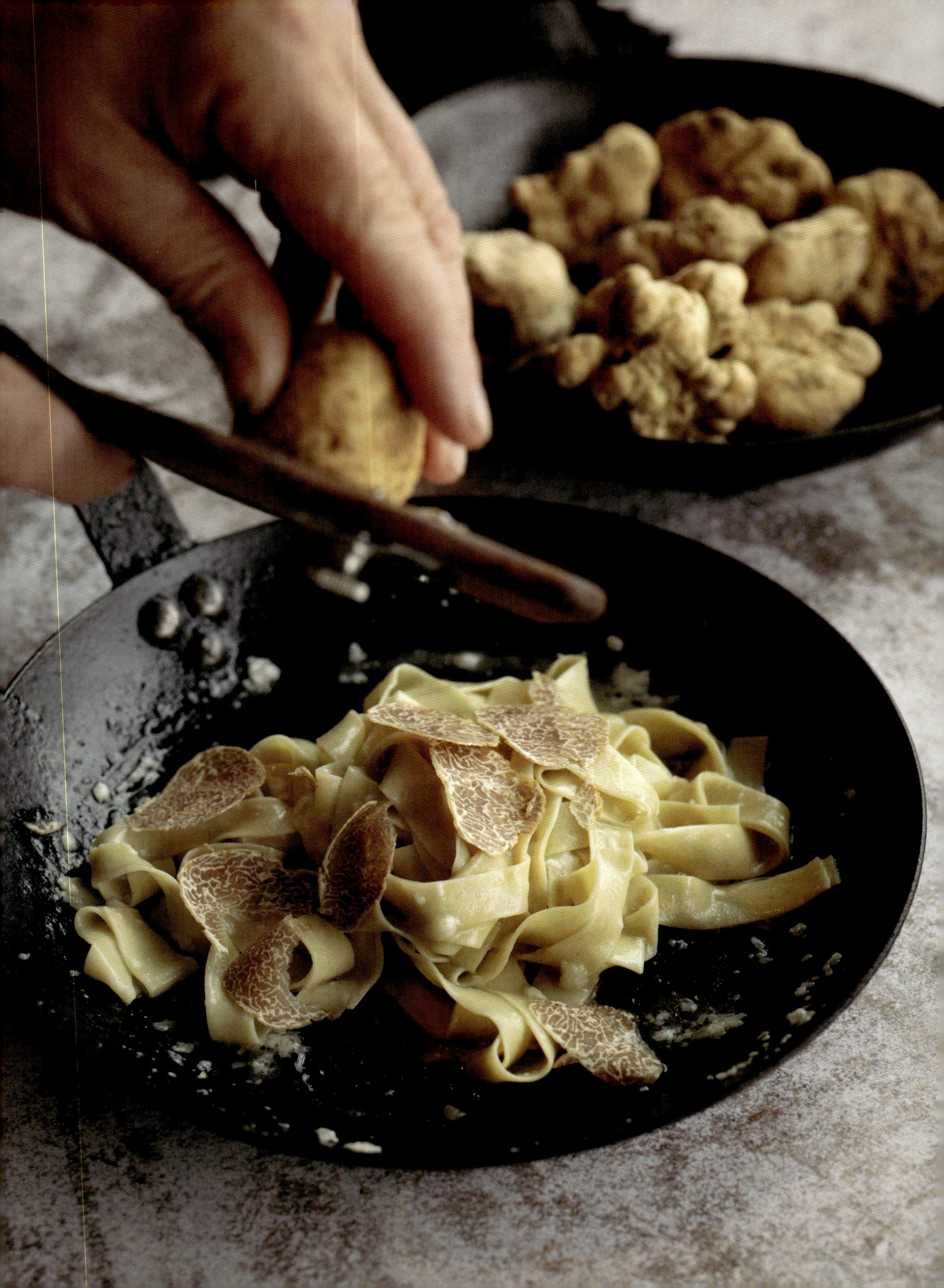

TRUFFLES

TAGLIATELLE
with ITALIAN WHITE TRUFFLES

Egg Pasta Dough (page 90) at room temperature

1 cup all-purpose flour, for dusting

Kosher salt

2 tablespoons unsalted butter

1-ounce nugget fresh white truffle

High-quality extra-virgin olive oil, for drizzling

4 tablespoons grated Grana Padano cheese

Special equipment:
1 truffle slicer

While saffron is often called the world's most expensive cooking ingredient, I think the white truffle from Alba, Italy, probably earns that dubious crown. But it is undoubtedly one of the most incredible ingredients to cook with and eat. I have been using white truffles since my sous chef days for Charlie Trotter in Chicago. A little goes a long way. They are available online, but you can always buy them from me at Farina every November and December. It may be intimidating at first because of the expense, but you are not cooking anything but the pasta in this recipe. All you need to do is shave the truffle (not your finger)! // **SERVES 4**

Prepare egg dough recipe and follow directions for rolling and sheeting (page 86).

Lay finished pasta sheets on a lightly floured work surface. Lightly dust all the sheets with flour and let them sit flat on the work surface to dry for 15 minutes. They won't be dry enough to crumble and break, but dry enough to run through the machine cutter and not stick together. Cut pasta sheets crosswise into shorter, more manageable sheets about 8 inches long. Then run the sheets through the tagliatelle (fettuccine) cutter on your machine, dusting with flour if necessary to prevent sticking. Lay each portion of cut pasta on a floured baking sheet and cover with a damp towel.

Bring 4 quarts water and 2 tablespoons salt to a boil in a large stockpot. When water is boiling, add tagliatelle and stir well to prevent sticking. Cook for 1 minute or until al dente. Reserve 1 cup pasta water, then drain tagliatelle into a strainer and toss it back into the stockpot. Add butter and 1 teaspoon salt. Use tongs or a fork to coat pasta with melted butter.

Divide tagliatelle between 4 pasta bowls. Use truffle slicer to shave paper-thin slices of white truffle over pasta. Drizzle each bowl with olive oil and sprinkle with Grana Padano.

2
PASTA

Every pasta book worth its salt will tell you about the magic that happens when flour and water come together to make pasta. Italians wax poetically about marrying pasta and sauce. Pasta is ONE thing, not two separate things. It's not PASTA and SAUCE. It's PASTA!

I'm not a pasta expert by any stretch of the imagination. I'm always learning new things, and as I learn, I teach my cooks and spread my knowledge. I often tell them that certain pairs of ingredients are "lovers or best friends." By this I mean the two items need each other, intimately, to be their best versions and flourish as equal partners in a harmonized interplay of texture and flavor. Examples of these holy matrimonies include: tomatoes and salt, red cabbage and apples, lemongrass and ginger, raw tuna and ponzu, raspberry and chocolate.

The eternal bond between flour and water is sacred. These two legendary lovers will forever be among my most revered culinary combos. It is hard to describe the addictive aroma of cooked wheat in a steaming pile of freshly strained noodles. I love pinching a small clump of hot, naked spaghetti and shoving it in my mouth, enjoying the slither of long noodles down my throat, and luxuriating in the comfort as I bite into pasta that has achieved perfect chewiness. So simple, yet so delicious. If you can surrender to this moment, then you can understand the wrath Italians have for the American habit of drowning pure noodles in sauce.

The best pasta in the world comes from Italy. Italians do not compromise their pasta with careless cooking, over-saucing, poor ingredients or throwing the kitchen sink at it. Italian cuisine is about subtraction rather than addition: what can you leave out, not what can you add. Therein lies the secret to well-prepared pasta and, not just Italian cooking, but good cooking in general.

There are so many shapes and varieties of pasta in Italy, hundreds perhaps. Some villages may have their own shape that doesn't exist 10 kilometers down the road in another village. Some Italian pasta shapes are so famous the entire world recognizes them. When you have decided what pasta shape to make then you will decide what sauce will accompany that particular shape. Italians are clever and have thought deeply (over the millennia) about which *condimento* or sauce will be the best "lover" for a specific shape. In fact, you'll hear Italian cooks talk about the marriage of pasta and sauce as the final dish comes together. For most Italians, shape and sauce pairings are not debatable. At Farina, we take a few liberties and chalk it up as modernism. But generally, we try to stay in the vicinity of what is correct as chronicled by Italy's long and storied love affair with pasta.

COME ON, MAN!

We take pasta seriously at Farina. The pasta section of this book has more recipes and photos than any other. But this book is not meant to be a pasta bible. I share ideas and techniques. I don't go into all the different components of well-made pasta, such as flours and grains, moisture percentage and humidity. There are some incredibly well-written books on the market that will inspire you to take a deep dive into that hole, if you want to go there. In these pages, I aim to share my favorite pastas and the favorites of my Farina guests. I'm not insisting on perfection. These recipes include dishes that we have served over the years and offer tips on how to work with pasta and make delicious pasta at home.

Indeed, making pasta from scratch can be a little daunting. If you plan ahead and break the preparation into manageable steps, you will reduce your frustration and succeed where once you failed or didn't bother to try. Keep in mind that you'll need to be aware of recipe variables, like weight measurements, heat level of your stove, the quality of ingredients and the time you want to invest in the project. Recreating these recipes and good cooking, in general, requires you to use all your senses to see, feel, taste and hear the food working. What I love about cooking as I've grown older is that I can hear the differences in how certain foods hit sauté pans or smell the aroma of something permeating from the kitchen all the way into the office where I'm working. I can see and smell whether there is salt in blanching water. I can tell the doneness of many foods just by looking at them, even from a distance. That is experience talking to me. As a home cook you may not have acquired this perceptiveness. But by staying aware of your environment while cooking, and using careful technique, you'll achieve your best results.

PASTA TECHNIQUES

In case you haven't made the connection, Farina is the Italian word for flour. We gave the restaurant that name as an homage to the essential ingredient for making pasta, which would be the star of our menu. Nothing brings a bowl of pasta to life quite like using homemade dough. There are as many recipes for pasta dough as there are cooks and Italian mothers. It comes down to flour and eggs (and water on occasion) bound together, first as a tousled mess, but with additional mixing it merges to form a tight mass of dough. The dough texture should be sturdy to knead, not too wet. Your first inclination will be to cut the kneading process short because it's hard and it takes a good 10 to 15 minutes and your arms will tire easily. But if you take the time to knead the dough properly, you will not regret it. If the dough is properly hydrated—meaning it is firm, smooth and not too soft or sticky—you won't need to dry the pasta strands on broom handles randomly balanced all over your dining room chairs. You can simply cut the pasta shape, portion the amount per person and lay it a on a floured tray, ready to cook.

When it comes to sauces, you will want to serve hearty ragùs with hearty shapes that can be short, long or twisty, like pappardelle, rigatoni, bucatini and fusilli. Long, thin pasta shapes, like spaghetti, linguini and angel hair, need delicate condimentos such as pesto, vegetables, herbs or simple marinara. The matrix of pasta shape to condimento is intense and almost inexhaustible.

MAKING FRESH PASTA DOUGH

We use my Egg Pasta Dough recipe (page 90) for all our raviolis, agnolotti, cut shapes and stuffed shapes. You'll notice that the basic ratios stay the same for the other flavored doughs in the book. In Piedmont, they use about 30 yolks per 2.2 pounds of flour and that's the ratio we use in the restaurant. I've adjusted the ratio in this book for a smaller dough ball that's appropriate for home cooking.

I like making dough by hand because I like the tactile sensation of ingredients and food. And I'm a chef—I need to touch food. I dislike wearing latex gloves in the kitchen, so I wash my hands a hundred times a day. (Nancy buys me a lot of lotion!) Anyway, you can certainly use a stand mixer to make the dough. It doesn't make you an inferior cook. Absolutely use a machine if you are going big and want to double the recipes. The part that you'll love about a machine is the kneading, which is an important part of the pasta-making process that lets the flour absorb the moisture (eggs) and smooth out. Extended kneading develops the glutens in the flour, and gluten is what gives the noodles their structure and helps them hold their shape. The more time you spend on this step (patience), the easier your pasta will roll out into sheets and the better your pasta will taste and chew. Kneading the dough by hand is much harder, takes longer and delivers a great arm and shoulder workout! On the other hand, it's probably the part most likely to make you chuck the dough in the trash and buy some dry spaghetti.

Not all the pasta recipes in the book use freshly made dough. Some call for dry pasta that you can easily buy from your local grocer. There are also some great artisanal pasta shapes and flavors available online from specialty retail stores. In the directions for each pasta recipe, if it calls for fresh pasta dough, refer to these pages for the basic directions and techniques.

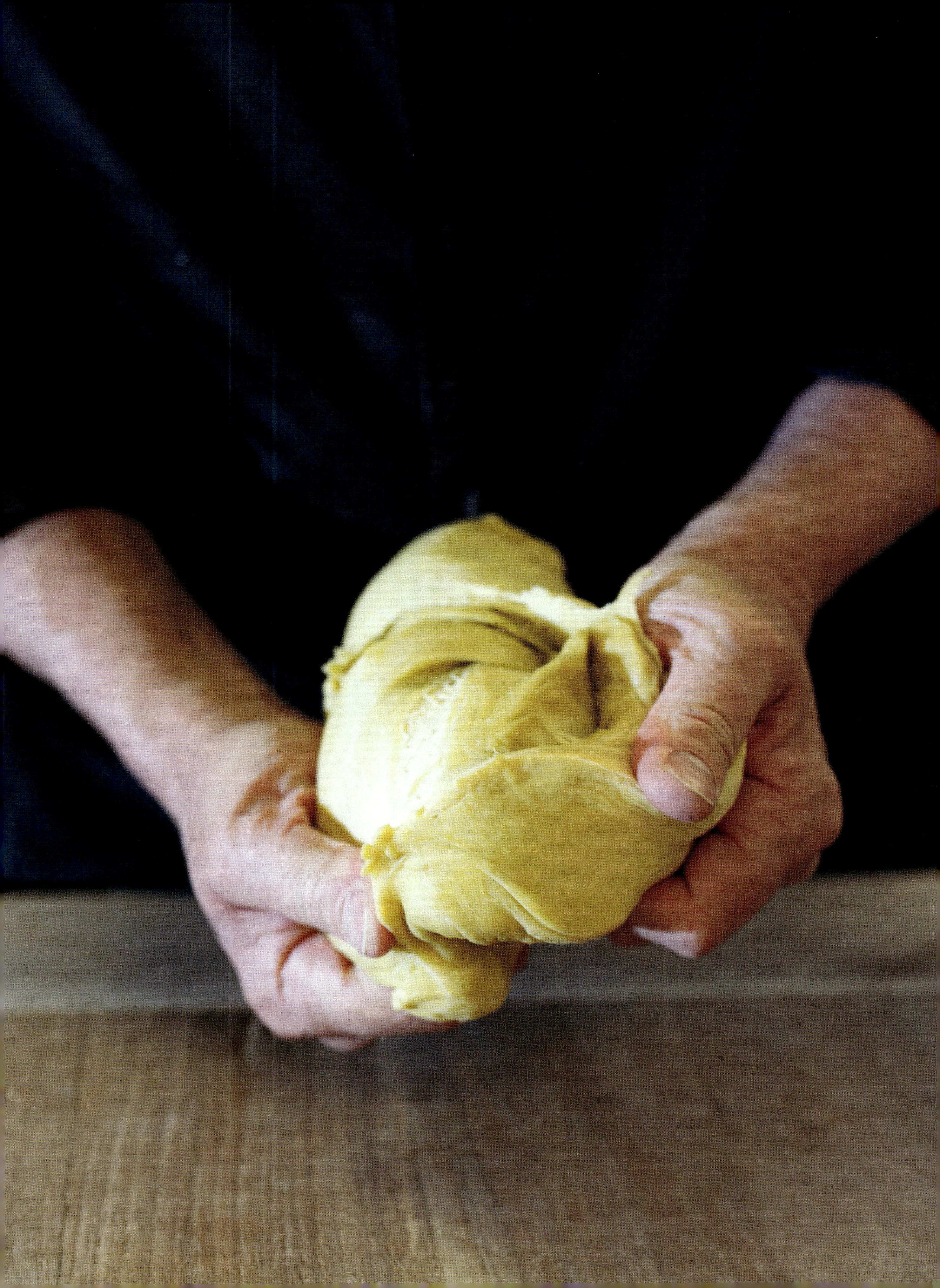

BY HAND

Sift the flour onto the work surface, then make a well in the middle, with the surface visible and the flour high enough to contain the eggs. Pour the beaten eggs in the center of the well.

Working from the middle of the well and using a fork, twirl in a circle to consistently bring flour into the egg. Keep twirling the egg and flour mixture with the fork until it resembles a thick cake batter. Next, use a bench scraper to finish bringing the remaining flour into the egg mixture. Scrape, fold and cut the floury mass as you would when making biscuits or scones. Continue to work until a shaggy dough ball forms.

With both hands, knead the dough ball. Pull the far end of the dough away from you, then fold it back onto the dough and push forward with the heels of your palms. Repeat this technique multiple times while rotating the dough between kneads. The kneading process takes about 15 minutes. The dough will be slightly tacky. Shape it into a smooth, compact ball. Cover the ball in plastic wrap and let it rest at room temperature for 30 minutes.

BY MACHINE

Alternatively, put the flour in the bowl of a stand mixer fitted with a hook attachment. With the machine running on medium speed, add the beaten eggs slowly until the ingredients come together in a tacky ball. Turn the mixer down a notch and continue to knead the dough for about 5 minutes. The dough ball will start to appear silky and develop a sheen.

Turn the dough out onto a work surface. Knead a few minutes with your hands as directed above. Add more flour if the dough is too tacky. Shape the dough into a ball, then flatten it into a disk. It's much easier to roll out when flattened a bit to start. Cover the ball in plastic wrap and let it rest at room temperature for 30 minutes. The dough is ready if it pulls back into place when you gently stretch it with your fingers.

LAMINATING

For most of the hand-shaped and cut pasta shapes in this book, you will follow these directions for rolling out the pasta sheets. Some of you will use a manual pasta machine and maybe some of you will use a KitchenAid attachment or other motorized sheeter. In either case, the process of transforming a dough ball into a thin pasta sheet is the same. It is easier to use a motorized sheeter if you have one. I've had many friends tell me that they are good quality and very useful. Of course, the shape of pasta you intend to make will determine the thickness of your pasta sheet. I use the thickness of five Post-It notes on most rolled and shaped pasta in this book.

Set up your pasta machine, clamping it to a table or countertop. Turn the dial to the widest setting. Divide the pasta dough into 4 pieces, rewrapping the other pieces in plastic to set aside. Working with the first piece, use a rolling pin to flatten it into a general rectangle. Starting with the shorter side of the rectangle, feed it through the rollers. Once the dough has come out of the other end, fold one side of the piece into the middle, then fold the other side over that to form three layers, then press lightly on the top of the dough to seal it.

Starting with one of the open sides of the folded dough, feed the pasta through the machine at the widest setting. Repeat the technique on the widest setting for a total of 4 times. This is called *laminating* and it is basically the process of folding each sheet onto itself while feeding it back into the rolling machine. Repeating this multiple times creates lamination. The main argument for laminating has to do with smoothing out the dough and generating firm texture and bite. It's also a great way to patch up small tears.

Repeat these steps 4 times to complete the laminating process.

ROLLING

When you've finished laminating the dough, then you can begin rolling it thinner. Start on the widest setting and roll or feed the dough through twice. Turn the dial to the next narrowest setting and roll the dough through again, feeding with one hand and catching it with the other hand. As the sheet gets longer, you don't want to pull the end with your hand; rather, lift the sheet off the table, with the sheet resting on the back of your hand. The heat from your finger can tear the ends as you pull. Go slowly through the roller settings at first so you get familiar with the way the dough squeezes through the rollers. While guiding the dough, it will sometimes veer unevenly, bunch up and potentially tear. You can reroll the dough sheet but not too many times, as the dough structure will get too dry. Repeat this technique and keep reducing the roller settings until the dough is as thin as five Post-It notes.

REROLLING EXCESS DOUGH SCRAPS

You can reroll most excess trimmed dough. Discard the tiny half circle cut-outs from round raviolis and likewise discard any pasta scraps that are dirty with fillings. The most efficient way is to stack 4 or 5 similar-sized scraps together instead of wadding up the dough. You may need to lightly brush water between the layers, so they stick together better. Once you have rerolled the scraps through once or twice and it looks as if the pasta sheet will resemble the look of a fresh pasta sheet, continue with regular rolling instructions.

CUTTING AND SHAPING

Some pastas will be cut by a knife or pastry cutter, like maltagliati, sorpresine, crespelle, cappelletti and pappardelle. Some of the pastas can be cut on your machine, most likely tagliatelle, spaghetti and linguini, depending on your machine. To cut tagliatelle or linguini by knife, lay your finished pasta sheet on a cutting board. If you are certain you will cut the pasta by knife, then your pasta sheet needs to be at least 30 inches long in order to avoid excessive waste. Cut each sheet into 10-inch lengths. Dust the sheet lightly with flour, and starting on one end, fold it onto itself about 2 inches deep. Continue folding (rolling) it this way until the end of the sheet. Place the bundles of pasta close to you and use a sharp knife to cut the pasta to the desired width. Generally, linguini will be 3/16 of an inch wide, tagliatelle about 3/8 of an inch wide, and 1 inch wide for pappardelle.

Remember that these are my suggestions and guidelines. You can cut your pasta sheets any width you want. Experiment with different shapes and lengths. It's not supposed to be a chore. Have some fun with pasta while you are learning at the same time.

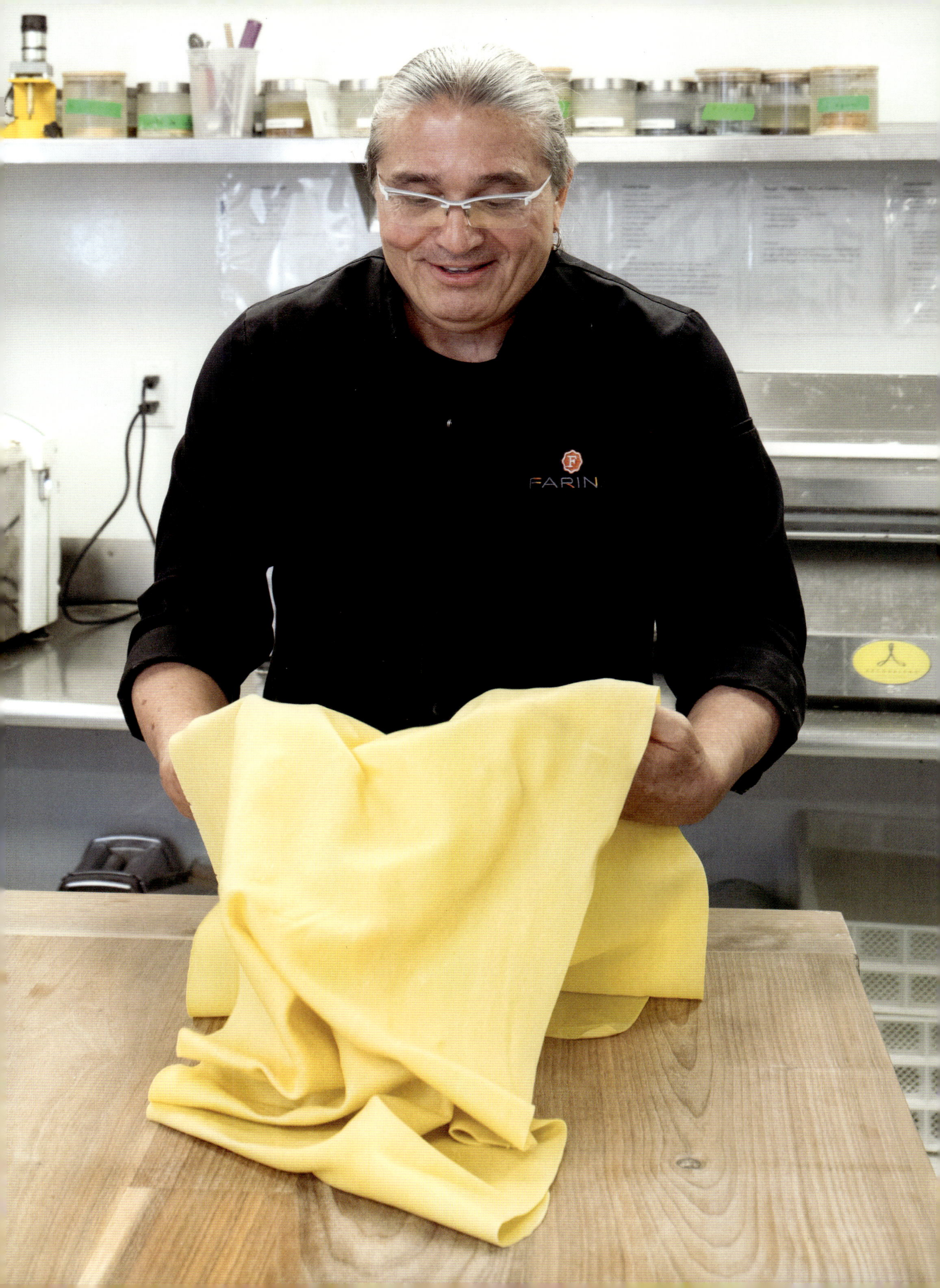
FARIN

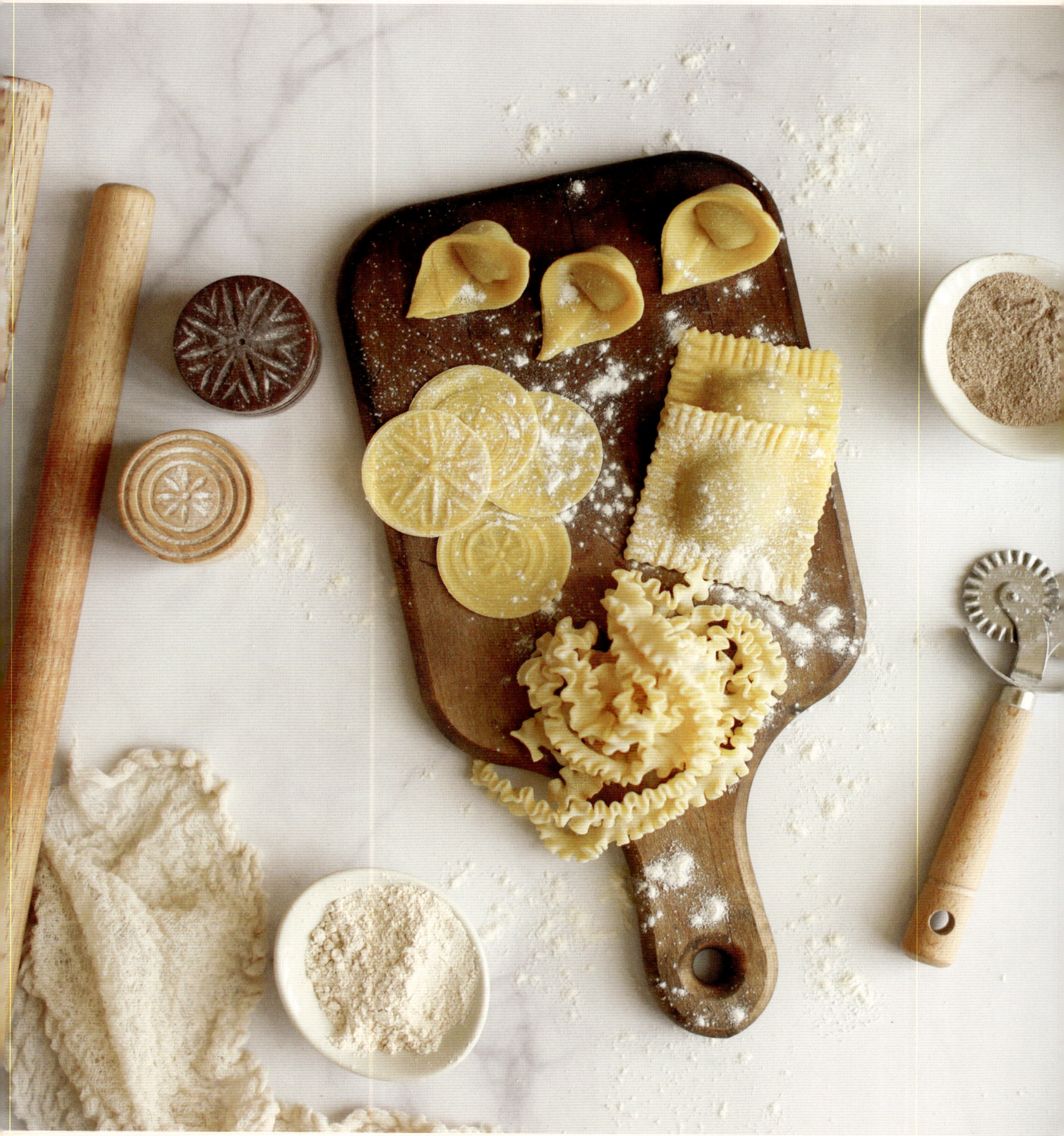

PASTA ATIPICA

This is the section of the menu at Farina where we tend to be a little more creative. I usually stay in my lane with most pasta dishes, but our Pasta Atipica offerings have a high regard for seasonal ingredients. Occasionally, guests will look at our menu and ask, "Are you cooking regional Italian, Michael?" My answer is, "Sort of . . . not really." Italy is a country of widely diverse foods and I like to explore all of them. We follow the seasons of the Midwest and that directs us along the culinary roads of Italy.

AUTUMN: We serve Italian dishes evocative of Tuscany, Umbria and Emilia-Romagna. Mushrooms and beans, darker sauces, last of the season tomatoes and first of the season hard squash. We also start to see apples, pears, persimmons and pomegranates.

WINTER: This time of year brings us to Piemonte, Lombardy and Valle d'Aosta. Our menus manifest in hearty meat braises, bolder sauces, stronger meats like wild boar, and root vegetables like turnips, beets, celery root and salsify.

SPRING: In my opinion, these food ingredients can be found growing anywhere in Italy or the world. Shoots, greens, herbs and vines all begin to emerge, awakened from their winter slumber. On any seasonal restaurant menu, if you can craft dishes using peas, ramps, fava beans, sorrel, asparagus, spring onions, young potatoes, spring radishes, morels, porcinis and nettle, you've got a great spring menu base to work with. Just add meat or seafood. Do no damage! This is how we work.

SUMMER: This is my favorite time of year! We visit Southern Italy south of Rome, from Naples to Puglia and Sardinia to Sicily. Red, yellow and heirloom tomatoes are everywhere on my menus, along with stone fruits, berries, summer squashes, fennel, mushrooms, eggplant, basil and cucumbers. The list of available summer vegetables is long. I first experienced eating these essential summer foods at different times in my life, and those tasting experiences are where I first truly understood umami. Think of the inherently yummy juices dribbling down your chin and the intense flavor properties of anything field ripe!

All of the places and foods I have mentioned above are pillars to lean on for creating a pasta dish or complete menu in a restaurant or at home. We use the same ideology and sources to create our seasonal pasta menus. Just remember to keep the ingredients in your pastas few and the process simple.

EGG PASTA DOUGH

16 ounces 00 flour (or all-purpose flour), plus more for dusting

1½ cups well-beaten egg yolks (16-18 largeegg yolks)

MAKES 6 SERVINGS

Follow the directions in Techniques for Making Dough, page 84.

SPINACH PASTA DOUGH

3 cups stemmed, torn and lightly packed fresh spinach

1½ cups well-beaten egg yolks (16-18 large egg yolks)

16 ounces 00 flour (or all-purpose flour), plus more for dusting

MAKES 6 SERVINGS

Combine spinach and eggs in a blender and process on high until finely pureed, smooth and uniformly green.

Continue as directed in Techniques for Making Dough (page 84), substituting the spinach-egg mixture for plain eggs.

BURNT ONION PASTA DOUGH

3 tablespoons Burnt Onion Ash (page 249)

1½ cups well-beaten egg yolks (16-18 large egg yolks)

16 ounces 00 flour (or all-purpose flour), plus more for dusting

MAKES 6 SERVINGS

Combine burnt onion ash and eggs in a blender and process on high until finely pureed and smooth.

Continue as directed in Techniques for Making Dough (page 84), substituting the burnt onion ash–egg mixture for plain eggs.

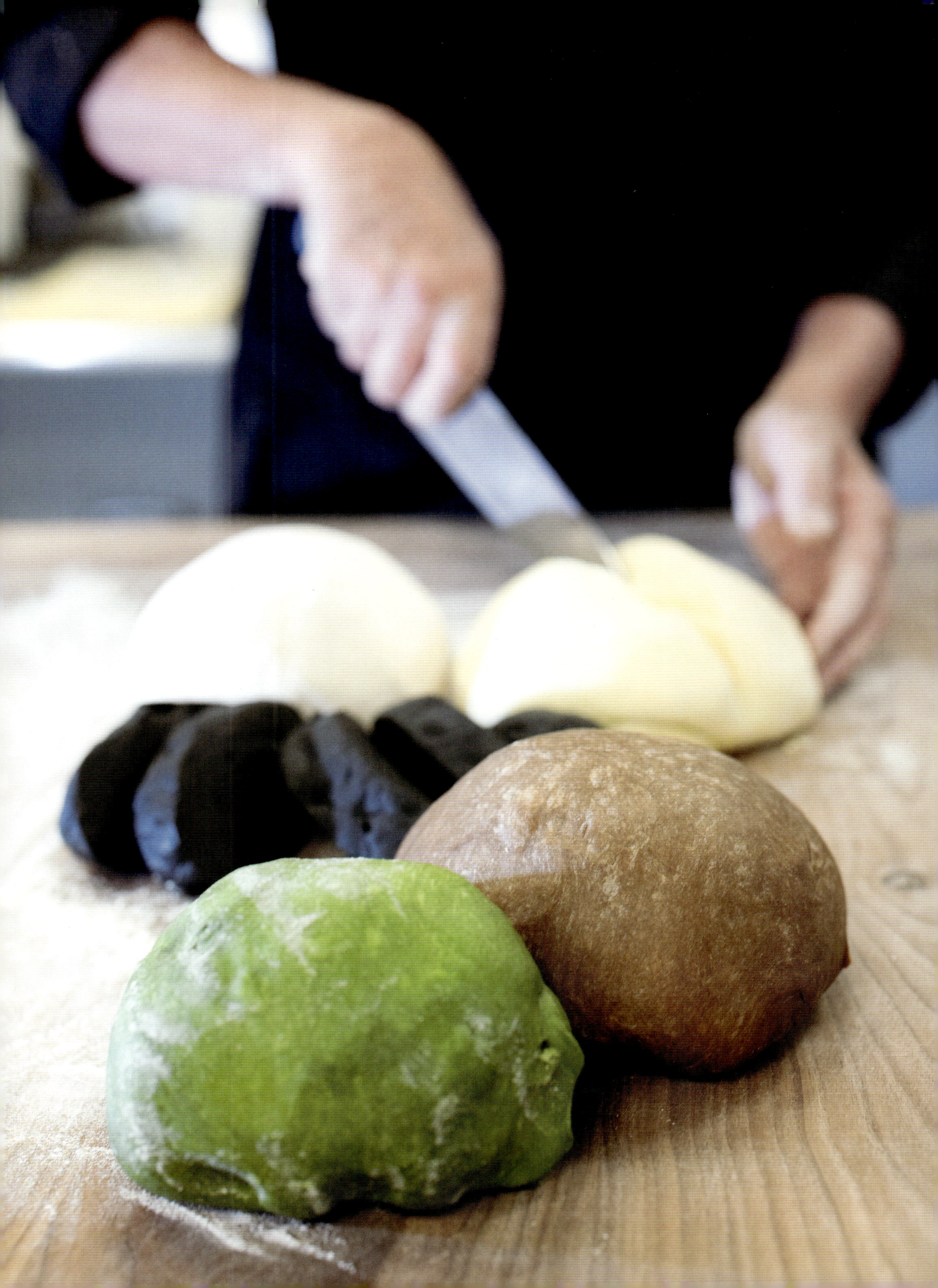

PASTA

SQUID INK PASTA DOUGH

NOTE: Squid ink may stain. Be sure to work on an appropriate surface, and consider wearing disposable gloves while kneading.

1½ cups well-beaten egg yolks (16–18 large egg yolks)

1 heaping tablespoon squid ink

16 ounces 00 flour (or all-purpose flour), plus more for dusting

MAKES 6 SERVINGS

Combine eggs and squid ink in a blender and process on high until mixture is thoroughly pureed, smooth and black, 10 to 15 seconds.

Continue as directed in Techniques for Making Dough (page 84), substituting the egg–squid ink mixture for plain eggs.

SEMOLINA PASTA DOUGH

1¼ cups very warm water

1 teaspoon kosher salt

16 ounces Antimo Caputo Semola semolina flour (not Bob's Red Mill No. 1 Durum Wheat semolina flour for pasta)

MAKES 1 POUND

Combine water and salt in a glass measuring cup, stirring until salt dissolves.

Place flour in the bowl of a stand mixer fitted with a dough hook. With the mixer on low speed, gradually drizzle in 1 cup salted water. Add as much of the remaining water as needed, about a tablespoon at a time, until a soft dough forms. Once dough comes together, continue to knead with the dough hook on low speed for about 10 minutes. The dough ball will be smooth, pliable and soft, not overly firm like other pasta doughs. Transfer the dough to a work surface to rest, covered with a damp towel or plastic wrap, for 20 minutes before shaping.

The dough will keep, tightly covered and refrigerated, for 3 to 5 days, or frozen for up to 3 months.

POTATO GNOCCHI

3 pounds Idaho potatoes
(4 to 6 potatoes)

2 cups 00 flour

1 egg yolk

1 tablespoon kosher salt

The key to these pillowy dumplings—don't overwork the dough. It shouldn't stick to your hands and should come together in about 4 to 5 minutes. // SERVES 6

Preheat the oven to 400 °F.

Bake potatoes in oven until soft, approximately 1 hour. Remove and let cool for 10 minutes or until they are cool enough to handle but still very warm.

Peel potatoes, discarding skins. Put potato flesh through a fine food mill or potato press. Spread it evenly on a lightly floured surface and sift flour over the top of the riced potatoes. Sprinkle salt over potatoes. Stir egg yolk with a fork and pour over potatoes.

Knead potatoes and flour into a soft dough. Flatten dough into a square about 1 to 2 inches thick and keep it lightly floured. Cover and let rest for 15 minutes. In the meantime, heat a large pot of salted water to a boil. Reduce heat while the gnocchi are cut.

Cut the flattened dough into 1-inch-wide slices. Then separate each slice and roll into a long rope using the palms of both hands. Once the ropes are rolled out, cut into individual 1-inch gnocchi. Leave them as is (shaped like a pillow) or press and roll over the tines of a fork for a more traditional look.

Return water to boil and coat a baking sheet with olive oil. Poach the gnocchi (approximately 20 at a time) in the boiling water. The water does not need to be vigorously boiling. Let them cook and eventually float to the top. The gnocchi need to continue cooking for at least 1 minute after rising to the top since it's a thick dough that needs to cook through.

Use a long-handled strainer to scoop out cooked gnocchi and transfer to baking sheet. Repeat with remaining gnocchi. Let cool at room temperature. When all gnocchi are poached and cooled, coat them well in olive oil and store in a covered container in the refrigerator. They will keep well for 4 to 5 days. Store in an airtight container in the freezer for up to 3 months.

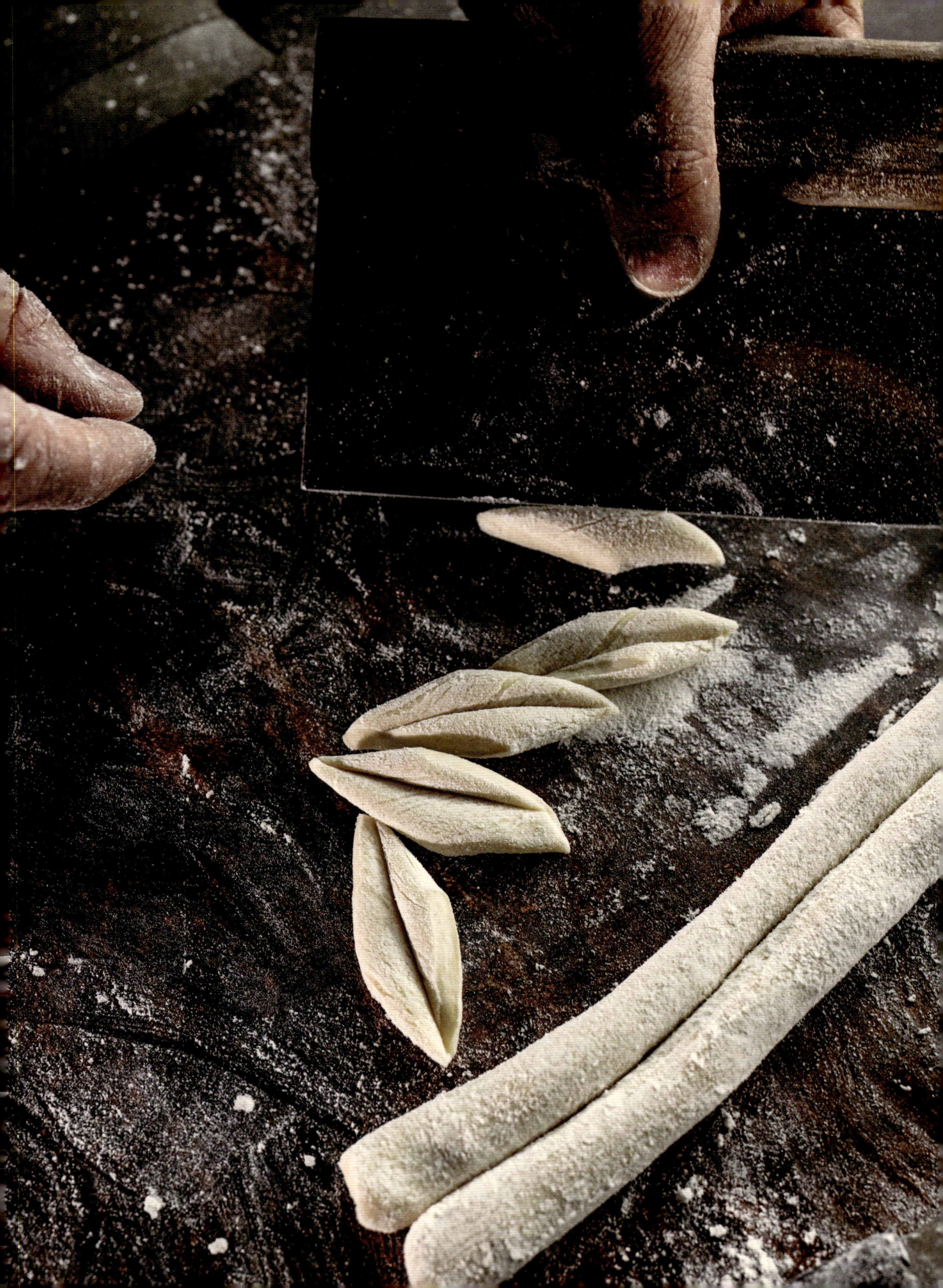

PINCENELLE PASTA DOUGH

1½ cups 00 flour (or all-purpose flour), plus more for dusting

1½ cups ricotta cheese

1 large egg, beaten well

1 teaspoon plus 2 tablespoons kosher salt, divided

3 tablespoons extra-virgin olive oil

This pasta dough is simple to prepare and, when cut and shaped, is essentially a light dumpling that can be paired with a variety of sauces, both light and hearty. My chef friend Ken Vedrinski introduced me to this shape in 2018 during our annual tomato dinner at Michael Smith Restaurant. Practice makes perfect when shaping pincenelle. If you're having trouble handling the dough ball, dust it with additional flour. // MAKES ABOUT 100 PINCENELLE

Combine flour, cheese, egg and 1 teaspoon salt in the bowl of a stand mixer fitted with a dough hook. Mix on low speed until dough comes together in a sticky ball. Continue to knead with the dough hook for 4 minutes. Transfer dough to a lightly floured work surface and dust with flour. Shape into a flat round disk about 1 inch thick. Cover with a damp towel or plastic wrap and let rest for 20 minutes (or up to 3 days).

Fill an 8-quart pasta pot with 6 quarts water and remaining 2 tablespoons salt. Bring to a boil. Prepare a "landing pan" for the cooked pincenelle by spreading a baking sheet with a thin layer of olive oil.

Cut a strip about an inch wide from the disk of dough. Using the palms of both hands, roll the strip back and forth on the work surface to form a ½-inch-thick log, dusting with flour as needed. Cut the log at 1-inch intervals on a sharp angle. Repeat until all the dough is rolled into logs and the sections are cut. Cover with a damp towel or plastic wrap.

Place a piece of cut log on the work surface with one point positioned at 11 o'clock. Holding a dough scraper at a 45-degree angle to the work surface, press the edge of the blade lightly into the center of the dough and flick the blade to the right, so the left side of the dough curls up on the blade. With practice, the action will flick the dough piece to the right of the scraper, and the curled pasta will have a deep crease in the center for catching sauce. Repeat until all the dough has been shaped into pincenelle. Transfer to a clean, parchment-lined baking sheet.

Carefully lift the parchment over the pot and slide the pincenelle into the boiling water. Use a long spoon to gently stir up from the bottom of the pot to loosen any pieces that stick; they will float when done. Use the skimmer to pull a piece out and taste it; it should be cooked al dente. Drain and transfer the cooked pincenelle to the landing pan, and lightly toss and roll them in the oil to coat well. Let cool, then refrigerate.

Poached pincenelle will keep, tightly covered and refrigerated, for 5 days, or frozen for up to 6 months.

HOW TO COOK PASTA

WATER ～～～ SALT ～～～ OLIVE OIL ～～～ SAUCE

WATER

Pasta needs a lot of water to cook properly. I recommend 6 quarts of water for every pound of pasta. Pasta also requires room to move around. During the cooking process you want to swirl it around with a long spoon or tongs. Stir it, move it, swirl it!

Maintaining a rolling boil is also key for well-cooked noodles. Fresh pasta cooks much differently than commercial dry noodles. A hard boil on the water is very important when cooking fresh noodles because the boiling water sets the texture. Fresh noodles cook so quickly that if you put them in water that is not quite boiling they will taste gluey when they're done cooking. You won't achieve the definitive toothsome chew that you recognize as a splendidly cooked noodle. Jumping the gun when cooking dried commercial noodles is more forgiving, and it won't make a significant difference (that you'll notice) because they can take 10 to 12 minutes to cook, as opposed to only 3 to 4 minutes.

SALT

No salt equals no flavor. It's that simple. So unless you have health issues that require less salt intake, I recommend 2 tablespoons of salt per 6 quarts of water. We almost always use kosher salt, but coarse sea salt is a good alternative.

OLIVE OIL

There is an old wives' tale that says you must add oil to the pasta water. That's simply not true. You should never add olive oil to your pasta water on the premise that it will keep the pasta from sticking. This is nonsense. The noodles stick together because you didn't stir them soon enough or often enough. When cooked pasta is slick with oil, the beautiful sauce that you have prepared won't be properly absorbed. Ideally, the pasta should be removed from the water a minute before it's done, then drained and added to the saucepan. The pasta can then finish cooking in the sauce, absorbing all the wonderful flavors. Essentially, you are marrying the two elements and they are becoming one. It's not sauce and noodles, but PASTA!

SAUCE

Does the sauce matter? YES, it matters to Italians. They care and they care a lot! And they might judge you and will argue mightily about which sauce is for which noodle. Meanwhile, you . . . you don't care! But you can care. You can go down that rabbit hole if you want. And if you do, you will be rewarded, and you'll be satisfied that you understand the Italian pasta repertoire a little bit better. In general, however, most people get hungry for certain iconic shapes, and they put that shape with whatever sauce they happen to be hungry for at that time. And that's okay. Just try to keep the ingredients limited to 3 or 4 items. Less is more, as the Italians say.

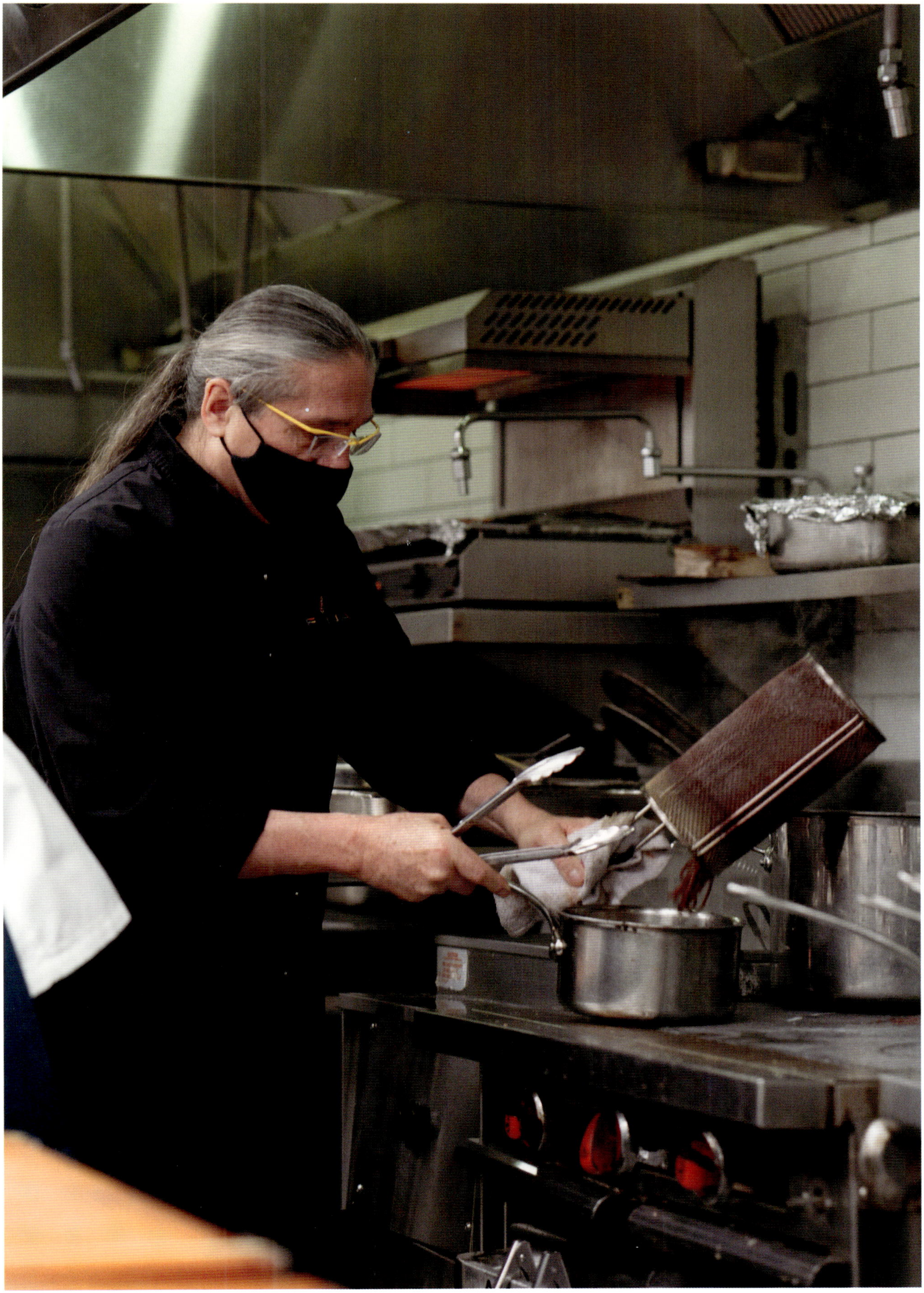

The FOUR KINGS of ROME

In 2018, as the Farina menu was coming into focus, I knew I wanted to feature a small collection of classic pasta mainstays. Unlike our Pasta Atipica, these would be available daily and not be dependent on seasonal ingredients. So I bit the bullet and allowed canned tomatoes in my kitchen. San Marzanos, of course.

That summer I came across *Pasta, Pane, Vino: Deep Travels Through Italy's Food Culture* by Matt Goulding. I discovered a reference to the "Four Kings of Rome" in a passage discussing iconic Roman pastas. Suddenly it dawned on me that I had to have a menu section at Farina dedicated to these four delicious pastas: carbonara, cacio e pepe, amatriciana and gricia.

After some menu tinkering in the early days of Farina, we opted to go with another iconic Italian pasta, tagliatelle al ragù Bolognese, as a replacement for gricia in the pantheon of the Four Kings because I thought that the gricia pasta would be difficult to sell consistently. It's fatty and pretty simple and it made me nervous. Most Kansas Citians (and Americans) don't love gricia because it's too simple (and fatty). I also figured very few guests would question me on the authenticity of a Bolognese pasta in that category, and tagliatelle Bolognese is undoubtedly one of America's favorite Italian pasta dishes.

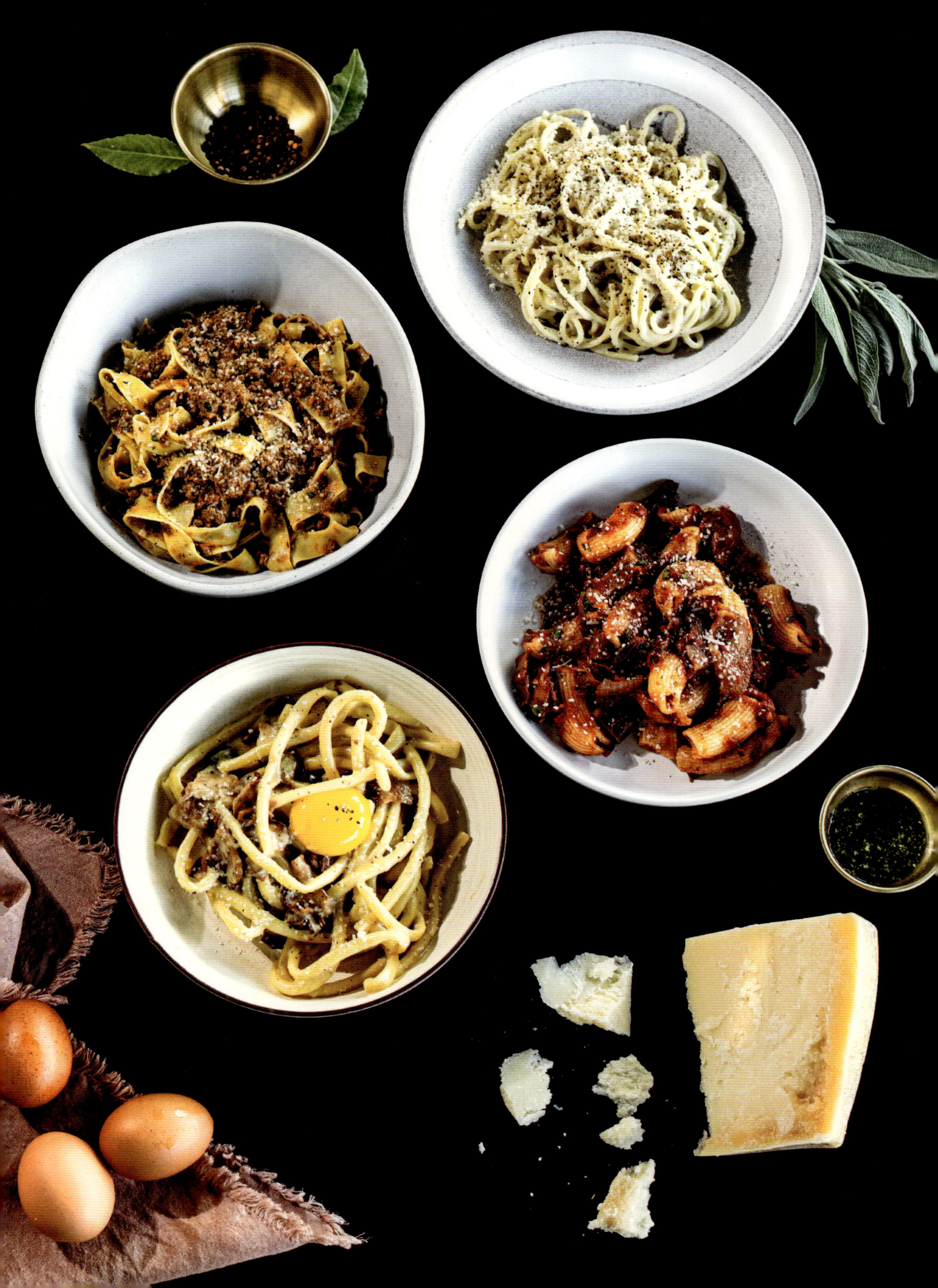

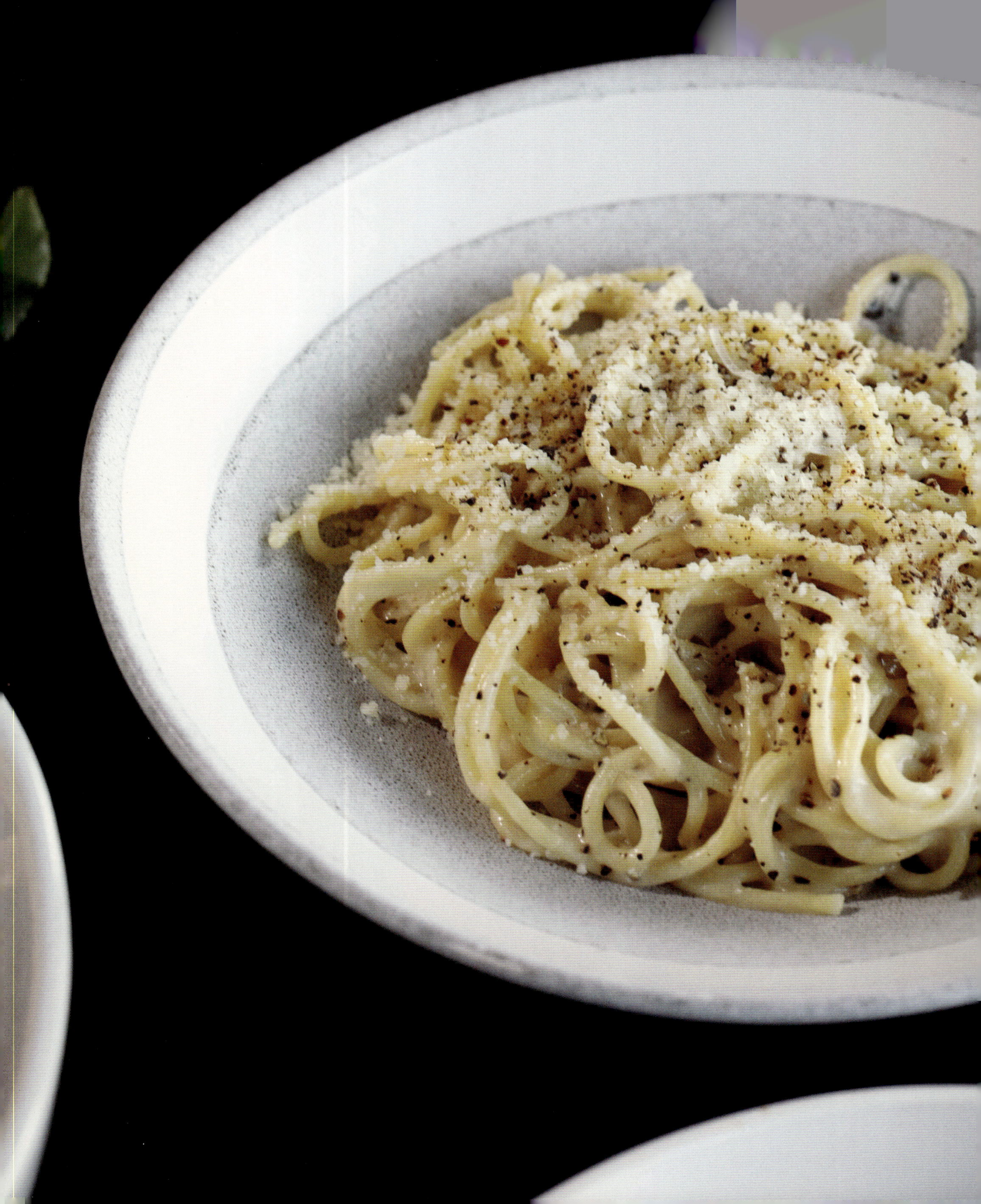

CACIO e PEPE

- 4 cups Grana Padano Cheese Broth (page 238)
- 2 tablespoons semolina
- 1 cup grated Grana Padano cheese, plus extra for garnish
- 1 cup grated Pecorino Romano cheese
- 1 tablespoon unsalted butter
- 2 teaspoons cornstarch
- 1 teaspoon kosher salt
- 1 pound spaghetti
- 2 tablespoons freshly cracked black pepper

From kale salad to chicharrones and spaetzle to vegetable dip, the cacio e pepe combination has splashed across the food world through robust experimentation. And for the most part, Roman chefs have stayed true to history. The pasta is simple in theory but harder to master than it looks. Three ingredients—pasta, cheese and pepper—coalesce to create a perfect umami bomb. It's one of the best-selling pastas at Farina, and to meet the demand for it we make the sauce ahead of time using a cheese rind broth from leftover Grana Padano. It's classic, simple and damn delicious.

// SERVES 4

Combine cheese broth and semolina in a small saucepan and bring to a boil. Turn off heat and let sit for 10 minutes. Return to a boil when ready to use.

Place cheeses, butter, cornstarch and 1 teaspoon salt in a blender. Reheat cheese-semolina broth if necessary, give it a good stir, and add 3 cups to the blender (refrigerate or freeze remaining cheese-semolina broth for another use). Pulse at low speed intermittently to blend the water and cheeses, then increase to high speed for 30 to 40 seconds. Pour the contents from the blender into a saucepan. Bring cheese sauce to a boil over medium-high heat, whisking constantly to prevent burning. Boil for 3 minutes, then reduce heat to simmer for 1 minute. The sauce should be emulsified and slightly thickened. Remove from heat.

Cook spaghetti al dente, according to package directions. Drain well.

Set a large skillet over medium heat. Add cracked black pepper and toast for approximately 30 seconds. Add 2 cups of warm cheese sauce. Add the well-drained spaghetti, stirring and tossing over medium heat until pasta is well coated. Add more cheese sauce if necessary to coat the noodles, and season to taste adding more salt, if desired. Serve immediately, with additional grated cheese as a garnish.

The sauce will keep refrigerated in an airtight container for up to 5 days.

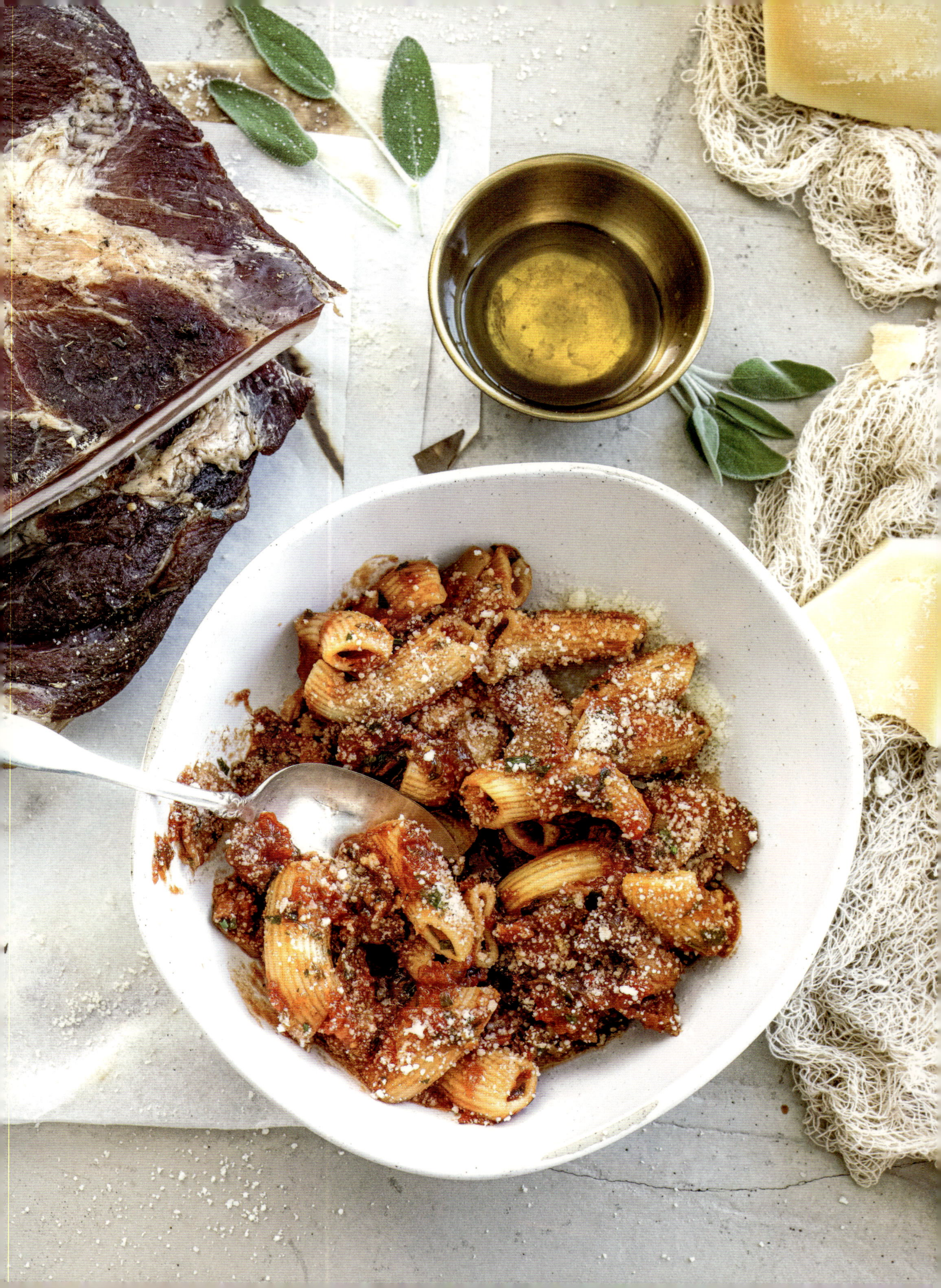

RIGATONI ALL'AMATRICIANA

- 2 tablespoons kosher salt
- 1 pound thinly sliced guanciale, pancetta or high-quality bacon, chopped into 1-inch pieces
- 1 red onion, cut into 1-inch squares
- 2 garlic cloves, thinly sliced
- 1 tablespoon tomato paste
- 5 cups San Marzano ground or crushed tomatoes
- ¼ cup extra-virgin olive oil, plus 2 tablespoons for final simmering
- ½ teaspoon red pepper flakes, or more to taste
- 1 teaspoon ground black pepper
- 1 pound ridged rigatoni
- 1 cup freshly grated Grana Padano cheese

The lone red sauce among the Four Kings of Rome pastas, this dish didn't originate in the Eternal City. First served in Amatrice, a mountainous village that borders Lazio and Abruzzo, variants of the sauce are now staples at nearly every restaurant in Rome. At Farina we serve it with rigatoni, although in Italy it is traditionally served with bucatini. Either pasta shape is a perfect companion for the sauce. We opt for rigatoni to differentiate the dish from our Bucatini Carbonara. Our extruded rigatoni is thick and hearty with a good, satisfying chew. And since we already broke the rules by adding garlic, you can increase the spice level to your liking by adding extra red pepper flakes. // SERVES 4

Bring 6 quarts water and 2 tablespoons of kosher salt to a boil, then cook pasta as directed on the package.

Place guanciale in a 6-quart braising pan over medium heat. Cook until it has rendered its fat and is starting to crisp but has not darkened in color, 8 to 10 minutes. Use a slotted spoon to transfer guanciale to a small bowl and pour off all but 2 tablespoons of fat, reserving it for future use. Add onions to the pan and cook over medium heat until lightly caramelized, 5 to 7 minutes. When onions are nearly done, add garlic and guanciale, and cook for 1 minute. Add tomato paste and stir for 1 more minute.

Add tomatoes, olive oil, red pepper flakes and black pepper. Stir well with a wooden spoon. Adjust heat to simmer and cook for 15 minutes. Add a small amount of water if necessary to keep sauce from getting too thick.

While sauce simmers, cook rigatoni according to package directions until al dente. Reserve ½ cup pasta water for finishing sauce (as needed), then drain pasta. Add pasta and 2 tablespoons olive oil into the simmering sauce; stir well for several minutes. Divide pasta among 4 heated bowls and serve immediately. Garnish with freshly grated Grana Padano cheese.

PASTA

BUCATINI CARBONARA

EGG SAUCE
Makes 7 cups

1 pound pancetta, cut into 1-inch dice

4 cups Grana Padano Cheese Broth (page 238) or water

2 tablespoons semolina

½ cup Grana Padano cheese

12 egg yolks

2 tablespoons pancetta fat (or substitute bacon fat)

1½ teaspoons kosher salt

2 teaspoons coarsely ground black pepper

BUCATINI CARBONARA

6 quarts water

2 tablespoons kosher salt

1 pound dry bucatini pasta

2 heaping cups Egg Sauce

½ teaspoon freshly ground black pepper

4 large egg yolks (optional)

Grana Padano cheese, for serving

The secret to this recipe is our "Egg Sauce," because it provides a method for consistently preparing 30 to 40 orders of carbonara nightly at Farina. For traditional carbonara, you need to toss the hot pasta with egg yolks exactly long enough so the yolks cook ever so slightly and coat the pasta with a rich and decadent sauce. This is incredibly hard to do consistently in large quantities. And in the restaurant business, consistent execution is the key to success. The best thing about Egg Sauce is that it can be ready in the time it takes to cook the pasta. // **SERVES 4**

MAKE EGG SAUCE

Combine pancetta and 4 cups water in a small saucepan and bring to a boil. Remove from heat and immediately drain pancetta through a fine-mesh strainer, discarding the water.

Place pancetta in a large skillet over medium-high heat. Cook, stirring occasionally, until it caramelizes to a dark golden brown, 4 to 5 minutes. Scrape pancetta into a strainer set over a bowl, reserving the fat for the Egg Sauce. Return pancetta to the skillet and set aside for the Bucatini Carbonara.

Combine cheese broth or water and semolina in a small saucepan and bring to a boil. Turn off heat and let sit for 10 minutes. Set aside but keep warm.

Combine cheese, egg yolks, pancetta fat, salt and pepper in a blender. Return semolina water to a boil, remove from heat and add to the blender, processing until cheese is melted and batter is smooth, about 30 seconds. The sauce should thicken smoothly and coat your finger or a spoon.

The sauce will keep, tightly covered and refrigerated, for up to 5 days or frozen for 2 months.

> Imported pancetta can often be too salty. So we bring it to a boil from a cold water and then strain it, discarding the water and saving the pancetta. Then caramelize the pancetta as needed for any recipe.

MAKE BUCATINI CARBONARA

Bring 6 quarts water and salt to a boil. Cook bucatini al dente, according to package directions.

While pasta is cooking, add 2 cups egg sauce, pepper and crispy pancetta to a wide, deep saucepan. Place the pan over very low heat to warm it, stirring occasionally. If steam starts to form or the sauce starts to stick to the pan, turn off the heat.

When bucatini is ready, ladle out and reserve 1 cup of pasta water, then drain pasta.

Add hot bucatini to the pan of egg sauce and begin briskly stirring and folding the pasta around in the sauce. If the sauce does not start to thicken and coat the pasta almost immediately, turn the heat up slightly until it does. Keep tossing and turning bucatini to ensure all of it is well coated in creamy, pale yellow sauce. If sauce gets too thick, turn off the heat and stir in pasta water, ¼ cup at a time, to loosen it.

To serve, divide pasta equally among 4 bowls or transfer to a large serving platter. Garnish each portion with a raw egg yolk, if desired, and sprinkle with Grana Padano cheese.

RAGÙ ALLA BOLOGNESE

3 shallots, thickly sliced

1 medium carrot, roughly chopped

1 celery rib, roughly chopped

3 garlic cloves

6 ice cubes, divided

8 ounces pancetta, medium dice

8 ounces mortadella, medium dice

2 pounds ground beef

1 pound ground pork, preferably pork butt

2 tablespoons pancetta fat or bacon fat

3 sprigs fresh oregano

3 sprigs fresh thyme

1 bay leaf

6 cups bone broth (page 236), divided

1 heaping tablespoon tomato paste

1 cup heavy cream

Kosher salt

Freshly ground black pepper

When visiting Bologna, it is not uncommon to overhear locals bickering about the city's namesake sauce. "A proper ragù should be made with half pork and half beef." "No, please! One-quarter pork and the rest beef." "Pork has a deeper fat flavor, so don't use pork and pancetta. It'll be too much pork!" "Tomato? Where did that come from? I don't use any tomato!" "Use tomato only in the summer!" Such debates are daily events in Bologna's restaurants and homes. After a while, you realize the most important ingredient to a good ragù Bolognese is the love with which you make it. And there is certainly no shortage of that in Bologna. // MAKES 2 QUARTS

Place a fine-mesh strainer over a bowl and set aside.

In a food processor, place half amounts of the shallots, carrot, celery and garlic, and 3 ice cubes. Pulse until vegetables are finely minced, 30 to 40 seconds, scraping down the food processor bowl as needed. Scrape minced vegetables into a strainer and repeat with remaining vegetables and ice. Lightly press on vegetables to extract water and juice. Set aside.

Add pancetta and mortadella to the processor bowl, and process until meats are finely minced. Scrape into a large bowl and add ground beef and pork. Mix lightly, using a large spatula or clean hands, until thoroughly blended.

Heat pancetta fat in a large, heavy-bottomed pot over high heat. Add half the meat mixture to the pan and don't move it for 1 minute, allowing meat to caramelize in the fat. Next, stir meat and continue to brown for 8 to 10 minutes. The meat will release liquid and essentially be sweating out its juices. The juices will evaporate, and meat will begin to sizzle. When the batch is browned, transfer to a bowl and repeat with remaining meat mixture.

When the second batch is browned, return first batch of browned meat to the pot, and continue to let juices on the bottom of the pan stick and caramelize into a stuck layer of bits and residue. Adjust heat as necessary so residue does not burn. Add minced vegetables, oregano, thyme and bay leaf and stir well to distribute. The vegetables will sweat out their juices as they cook. Continue to stir, loosening as much of the stuck brown residue as you can and folding it back into the ragù.

PASTA

> When Italian chefs make sugo and ragú (meat sauces) they refer to "bottom up cooking," which means caramelizing the meat and vegetable scraps on the bottom of a heavy pot or braising pan and then deglazing with liquid. Italian chefs repeat this technique up to 4 times. Each time the meat caramelizes and gets scraped up and folded back into the sugo, it develops another deep layer of flavor.

Let liquids evaporate again, sizzling and creating more residue in the pan, for about 20 minutes. Adjust heat as necessary, so it is high enough that residue will form, but low enough that it does not burn.

Deglaze with 1 cup bone broth and use a metal spatula to scrape up and loosen residue. It should take about 10 minutes for broth to reduce and caramelize in the bottom of the pan, creating another layer of residue. Repeat deglazing step again with another cup of broth, and when broth has evaporated and formed another layer of residue, stir in tomato paste. Add remaining 4 cups bone broth to cover meat. Stir well and reduce heat so ragù simmers gently for 1 hour, stirring occasionally from bottom of pan.

After 1 hour, stir in heavy cream and return to a simmer. Cook until cream darkens and a rich sauce forms, about 30 minutes. Remove from heat to cool. Remove herb stems and bay leaf. Adjust final seasoning to taste with salt and pepper.

The ragù will keep, tightly covered and refrigerated, for at least a week, or frozen for up to 3 months.

FARINA

SPAGHETTI AGLIO e OLIO

¼ cup kosher salt

8 ounces dry spaghetti

½ cup high-quality extra-virgin olive oil

4 garlic cloves, minced

1 tablespoon finely chopped Italian parsley

1 tablespoon red pepper flakes

1 cup grated pecorino cheese or Grana Padano

We get a lot of requests for this dish at Farina. I don't put it on our menu because of its simplicity but I will always make it upon request. The recipe relies on top-shelf extra-virgin olive oil for its flavor, so make sure to use the best available. People often think the sauce is broken when it's oily, but when using high-quality olive oil, that's how it's supposed to look. // **SERVES 4**

Bring 4 quarts of water and salt to a rolling boil in a large pot. Cook spaghetti according to package directions until al dente. When pasta is just about finished cooking, ladle out 1 cup pasta water and reserve. Drain pasta.

While spaghetti is cooking, add olive oil to a large, deep-sided skillet over medium-high heat. Add garlic and slowly toast in oil until barely golden, 4 to 5 minutes, stirring occasionally. The garlic should not brown before spaghetti is finished cooking; if it starts to darken, take the pan off heat. Add parsley and red pepper flakes to oil.

Add hot, drained spaghetti to the pan of garlic and oil over medium heat. Use a pair of tongs or a 2-pronged meat fork to stir and fold garlicky oil into spaghetti. Off the heat, slowly sprinkle in ½ cup cheese, a small amount at a time, continuing to stir and fold. If necessary, add a bit of reserved pasta water if mixture is dry. The combination of stirring in cheese and adding pasta water will create an emulsified "sauce" (stir in a small scoop of soft butter if needed). Season with salt.

Divide pasta evenly among 4 warm bowls. Garnish with remaining cheese.

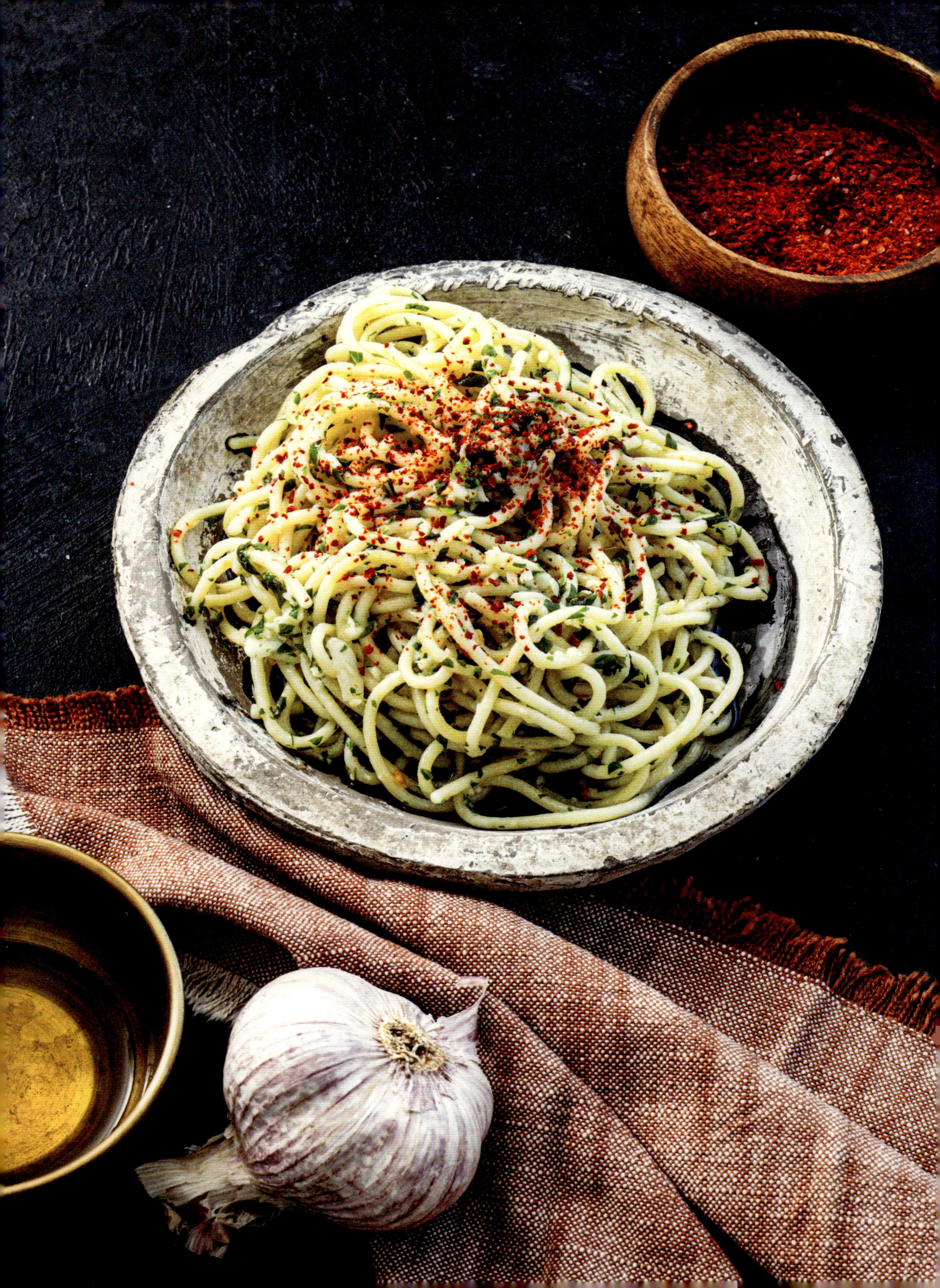

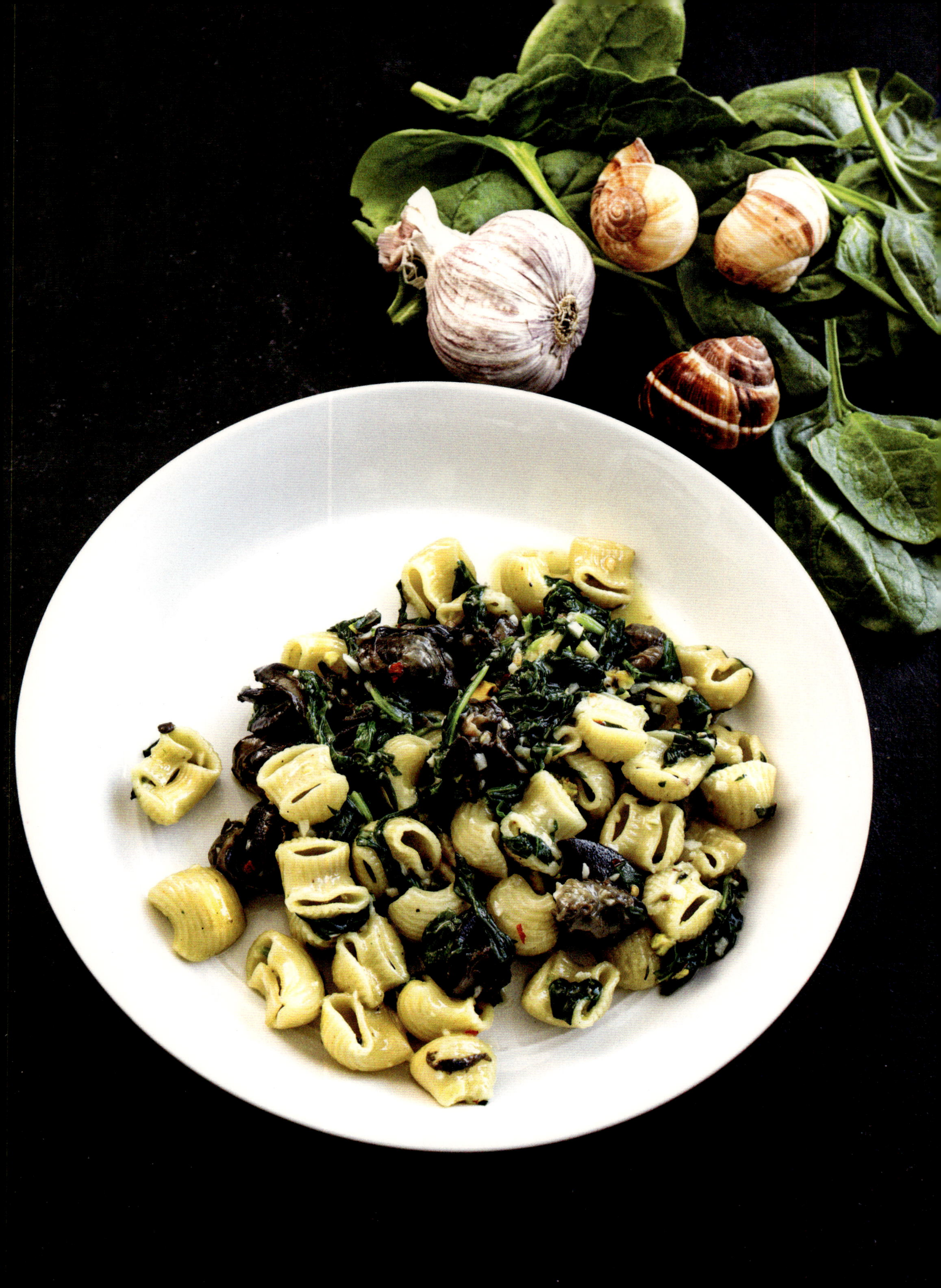

PASTA

LUMACHE
with SPINACH, GARLIC and ESCARGOTS

2 tablespoons plus 1 teaspoon kosher salt, divided

4 tablespoons extra-virgin olive oil, divided

6 cups raw spinach

3 garlic cloves, minced

14-ounce can escargots, drained and rinsed (about 2 cups snails)

½ teaspoon red pepper flakes, or more to taste

16-ounce package dry lumache pasta shells (or substitute fusilli or rigatoni)

3 tablespoons unsalted butter, softened

1 tablespoon fresh lemon juice

6 tablespoons grated Grana Padano, divided

4 tablespoons Pangrattato (page 267)

High-quality extra-virgin olive oil, for drizzling

I created this dish as part of my never-ending quest to introduce people to uncommon ingredients that are different, yet delicious. Snails are certainly common on menus, and we all love Burgundy escargots, but people can still be squeamish about them. Chefs are always pairing an unloved ingredient with a very common ingredient, with hopes that people will give it a try. At Farina, we extrude this pasta shape with pureed spinach so it's bright green, then we add more spinach to the final dish. Don't forget to use the pangrattato (Italian breadcrumbs) as a final garnish. Once you taste the crunchy texture, you'll use them more often in your pasta recipes. // SERVES 4 to 6

In a large stockpot, bring 6 quarts water and 2 tablespoons salt to a boil. While water is heating, swirl 1 tablespoon olive oil in a large, deep-sided skillet over medium heat. Add spinach and cook just until wilted. Transfer cooked spinach to a colander to cool for 15 minutes. Wipe out the skillet and return the pan to medium heat. Add remaining olive oil and garlic, and cook until lightly golden, approximately 1 minute. Add escargots, pepper flakes and remaining 1 teaspoon salt and mix well. Remove pan from heat and set aside.

Cook lumache al dente, according to package directions. Before draining cooked pasta, reserve 1 cup cooking water and set aside.

While pasta is cooking, squeeze excess water from spinach with your hands, and roughly chop. Add spinach to escargot in the skillet.

Drain pasta and add to the skillet. Return pan to medium-high heat and add reserved pasta water, butter and lemon juice. Use tongs or a wooden spoon to toss and mix ingredients well. Add 2 tablespoons Grana Padano cheese and keep tossing and mixing until sauce looks emulsified.

Divide pasta among 4 shallow bowls and sprinkle each with pangrattato and remaining Grana Padano. Finish pasta with a generous drizzle of high-quality extra-virgin olive oil.

SPINACH CAPPELLETTI
FILLED *with* SPRING PEAS

1½ cups fresh green peas (or substitute frozen peas, thawed)

½ cup whole-milk ricotta cheese

1 tablespoon fresh tarragon leaves

3 tablespoons kosher salt, divided

2 tablespoons extra-virgin olive oil

1 recipe spinach pasta dough (page 90), room temperature

All-purpose flour (for dusting)

4 cups Poultry Broth (page 237)

1 tablespoon minced chives

High-quality extra-virgin olive oil, for drizzling

Grated Grana Padano cheese, for sprinkling (optional)

Special Equipment: 4-inch round pastry cutter, spray bottle filled with water, disposable plastic piping bag (substitute a small spoon) and long-handled skimmer

This is Nancy's favorite pasta, with one of her favorite vegetables. We serve it only in the spring, when peas are the sweetest. First, we make a bright green spinach pasta dough and then fill it with a puree of fresh spring peas. Serve it in a light prosciutto cream sauce or float them in a warm penetrating meat broth like we do at Farina. // **SERVES 4 to 6**

To make the filling, combine peas, ricotta, tarragon, 1 teaspoon salt and olive oil in the bowl of a food processor and pulse a few times to blend. Process until mixture forms a homogenous, green puree; it can be slightly coarse in texture. Scrape filling into a disposable piping bag and refrigerate until ready to use.

To shape the cappelletti, follow directions for rolling and sheeting pasta dough (page 86). Place the sheets of dough on a work surface lightly dusted with flour as they are done, and cover with plastic wrap or a damp towel.

Dust a large baking sheet with flour and set aside.

On a lightly floured work surface, cut as many 4-inch circles as possible from the rolled pasta sheets. Shingle the circles on the floured baking sheet and cover with a damp towel or plastic wrap.

Working with 4 to 6 pieces at a time, lay the circles out on the work surface. Cut a ½-inch hole off the end of the piping bag and pipe a generous teaspoonful of filling in the center of each pasta circle. (Alternatively, use a measuring teaspoon to place the filling on the dough.)

Lightly mist the circles using a water bottle. One at a time, fold each circle in half, pressing to seal with the rounded edge facing you. Holding a pointed end in each hand, bring the corners together and press firmly to bind, sealing with water if necessary. (The filling should push up into a plump little mound, the finished shape resembling the Pope's hat.) Set the cappelletti on the floured baking sheet. Repeat with remaining pasta circles, being careful that the finished cappelletti are not touching on the baking sheet. Refrigerate until ready to use, up to 4 hours.

In a large stockpot, bring 6 quarts water and 2 tablespoons salt to a boil. In a separate, small stockpot, bring poultry broth and remaining 2 teaspoons salt to a boil; remove from heat and keep warm.

When the water boils, add cappelletti to the water and cook al dente, about 10 minutes; pull one out to start tasting for doneness at about the 6-minute mark. Scoop cappelletti out with a long-handled skimmer and divide among 4 warm pasta bowls. Pour hot poultry broth evenly into each bowl and sprinkle with chives. Drizzle the bowls with extra-virgin olive oil. Sprinkle with grated cheese, if desired.

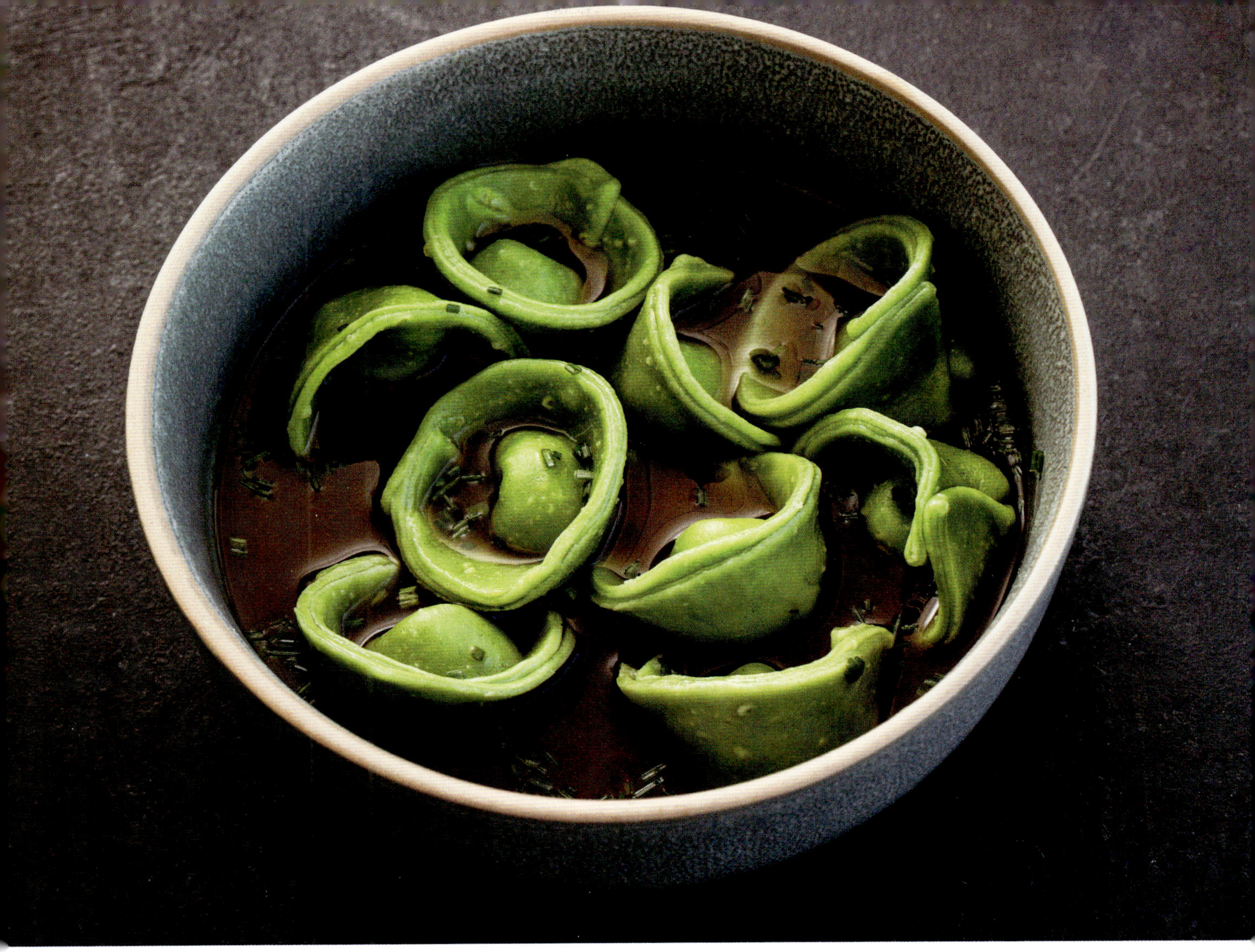
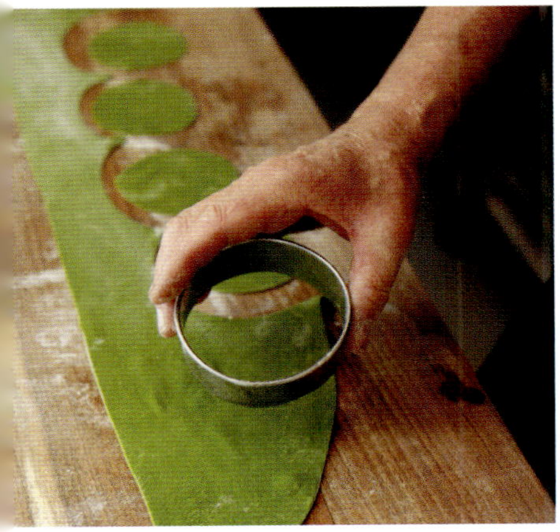
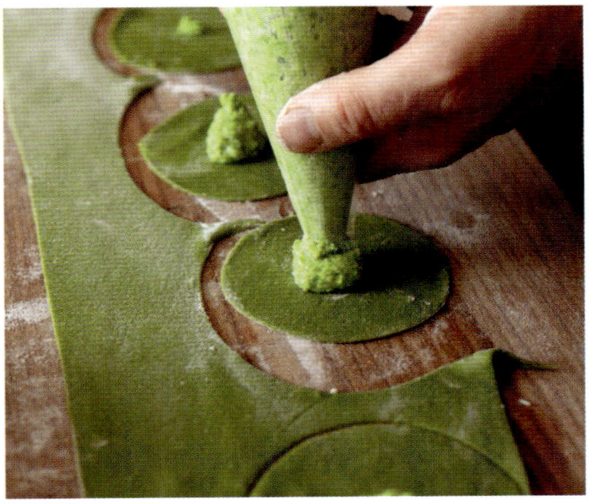
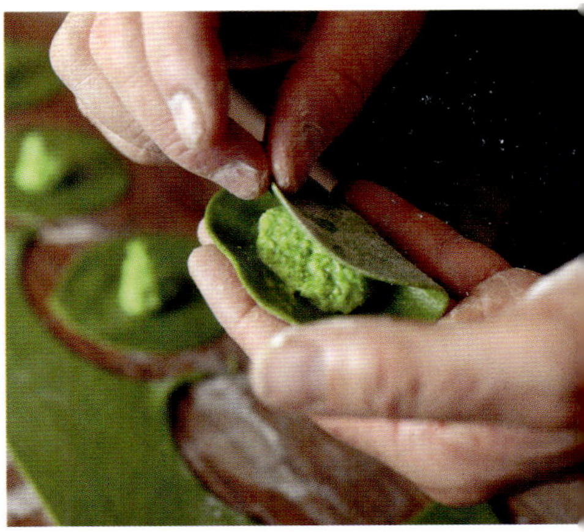
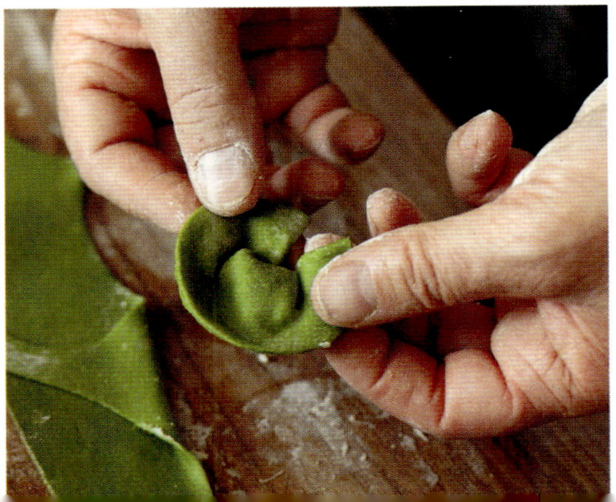
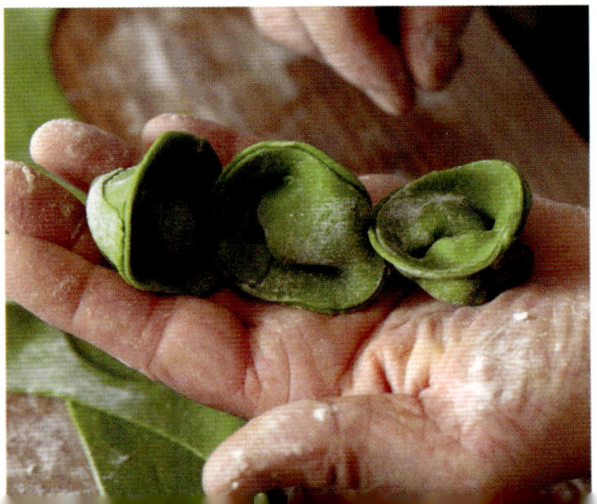

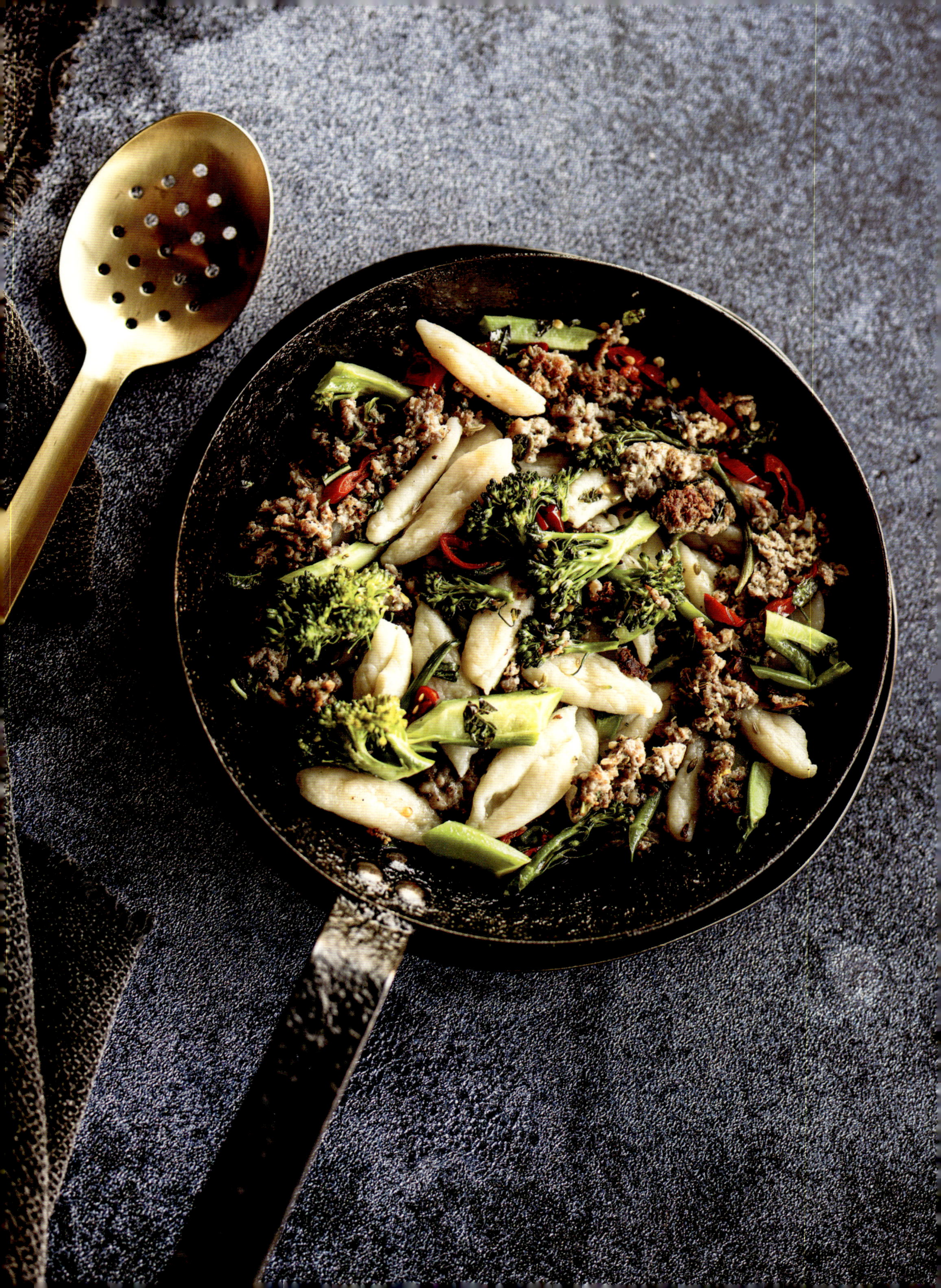

RICOTTA PINCENELLE
with SAUSAGE and BROCCOLI

1 tablespoon plus 1 teaspoon kosher salt, divided

6 ounces (about 8) broccolini stalks, cut crosswise into 1-inch chunks

8 ounces bulk mild Italian sausage

3 Calabrian chili peppers from a jar, drained and sliced (or substitute 2 pickled hot cherry peppers, roughly chopped)

½ cup Castelvetrano olives, roughly chopped and pitted

1½ cups poultry broth (page 237)

80 pieces poached pincenelle (page 95; or substitute 12 ounces dried pasta such as cavatelli or gemelli cooked al dente)

¼ cup Italian parsley, roughly chopped

¼ cup fresh basil, chopped

3 fresh oregano sprigs, leaves picked and roughly chopped

1 cup grated Grana Padano cheese, divided

3 tablespoons unsalted butter, cut in 6 pieces

Kosher salt and freshly ground black pepper

Extra-virgin olive oil, for finishing

I learned about the pincenelle pasta shape from my chef friend Ken Vedrinski. His restaurant, Trattoria Lucca, was a cozy little storefront in downtown Charleston serving Tuscan-inspired dishes. Although the dough does not have potato in the recipe, it has a similar texture to gnocchi. The starchy pasta, chewy sausage and tender broccoli play well together in this recipe. If you're short on time and unable to commit to the homemade pincenelle, substitute a dried pasta such as cavatelli or gemelli for a quicker, but still delicious, variation. // SERVES 4

Bring 2 quarts water and 1 tablespoon salt to a rolling boil in a large pot. Blanch broccolini for 3 minutes. Drain well and set aside. (If using dried pasta, use 6 quarts water and 2 tablespoons salt. Blanch the broccolini, scoop it out and cook pasta in the same water.)

Brown sausage in a large, deep skillet over high heat, stirring and mashing to break it into evenly sized pieces. Add chilies and cook for 1 minute, then add broccolini, olives and 1 teaspoon salt; mix well. Add broth, reduce heat to medium and simmer for about 3 minutes.

Add pincenelle to the pan along with parsley, basil and oregano, gently stirring and folding ingredients together. Turn heat to low and add ¾ cup cheese and butter. Continue folding and turning pasta in the pan. The butter and broth will emulsify, giving the pincenelle a glossy sheen. Season to taste with salt and pepper.

Divide finished pasta among 4 bowls. Garnish with remaining cheese and a drizzle of high-quality extra-virgin olive oil.

PASTA

BUCATINI ALL'UBRIACO
with BROCCOLINI and WALNUTS

2 (750 ml) bottles Ruffino Chianti, or other Chianti of your choice

2 tablespoons sugar

3 garlic cloves, peeled and smashed with the side of a knife

1 tablespoon whole black peppercorns

1 bay leaf

2 fresh thyme sprigs

3 tablespoons kosher salt, divided

10 ounces broccolini (approximately 8 stalks)

½ cup walnut halves

16 ounces dry bucatini (or spaghetti)

4 tablespoons soft unsalted butter, divided

1 clove garlic, minced

½ teaspoon red pepper flakes (or more to taste)

4 tablespoons fresh ricotta cheese, for serving

High-quality extra-virgin olive oil, for drizzling

Ubriaco means "drunk" in Italian, and this pasta calls for the bucatini to be cooked directly in red wine. It is a little unorthodox, but it is delicious! When I was younger and didn't know what kind of cocktails to order in nice bars, a friend suggested a Campari and soda. Some people don't like bitter drinks or bitter foods, but I liked it immediately. I think the tanginess of this pasta follows along those same lines. // **SERVES 4 to 6**

Preheat oven to 350°F.

Combine Chianti, 2 cups water, sugar, smashed garlic cloves, peppercorns, bay leaf, thyme and 2 tablespoons salt in a stockpot. Bring to a gentle boil, then adjust heat so liquid is barely moving, and steep for 10 minutes. Remove from heat and allow to cool for 30 minutes.

Meanwhile, bring 2 quarts water and remaining tablespoon salt to a rolling boil in a saucepan. Add broccolini and cook for 4 minutes. Drain well, and when cool enough to handle, cut on the bias into 1-inch pieces. Set aside.

Spread walnuts on a small baking sheet and toast in the oven until fragrant and just starting to color, 5 to 8 minutes. When cool, lightly crush walnuts and set aside.

Strain the cooled, seasoned wine into another pot large enough to cook the pasta and bring to a boil. Add bucatini and cook al dente according to package directions, approximately 8 minutes. Before draining, reserve 1 cup cooking liquid and set aside.

While pasta is cooking, heat a large skillet over medium-low heat and swirl in 1 tablespoon butter. Add minced garlic and pepper flakes and cook gently without allowing garlic to color for 1 minute; stir in broccolini. Turn off heat and set aside.

Drain pasta and add to the pan of broccolini. Stir and fold the bucatini to mix the ingredients well. Add crushed walnuts, reserved cooking liquid and the remaining 3 tablespoons butter. Gently swirl the pan and fold the pasta to create an emulsified sauce.

Divide the finished pasta equally into bowls and top with a spoonful of ricotta. Drizzle with extra-virgin olive oil.

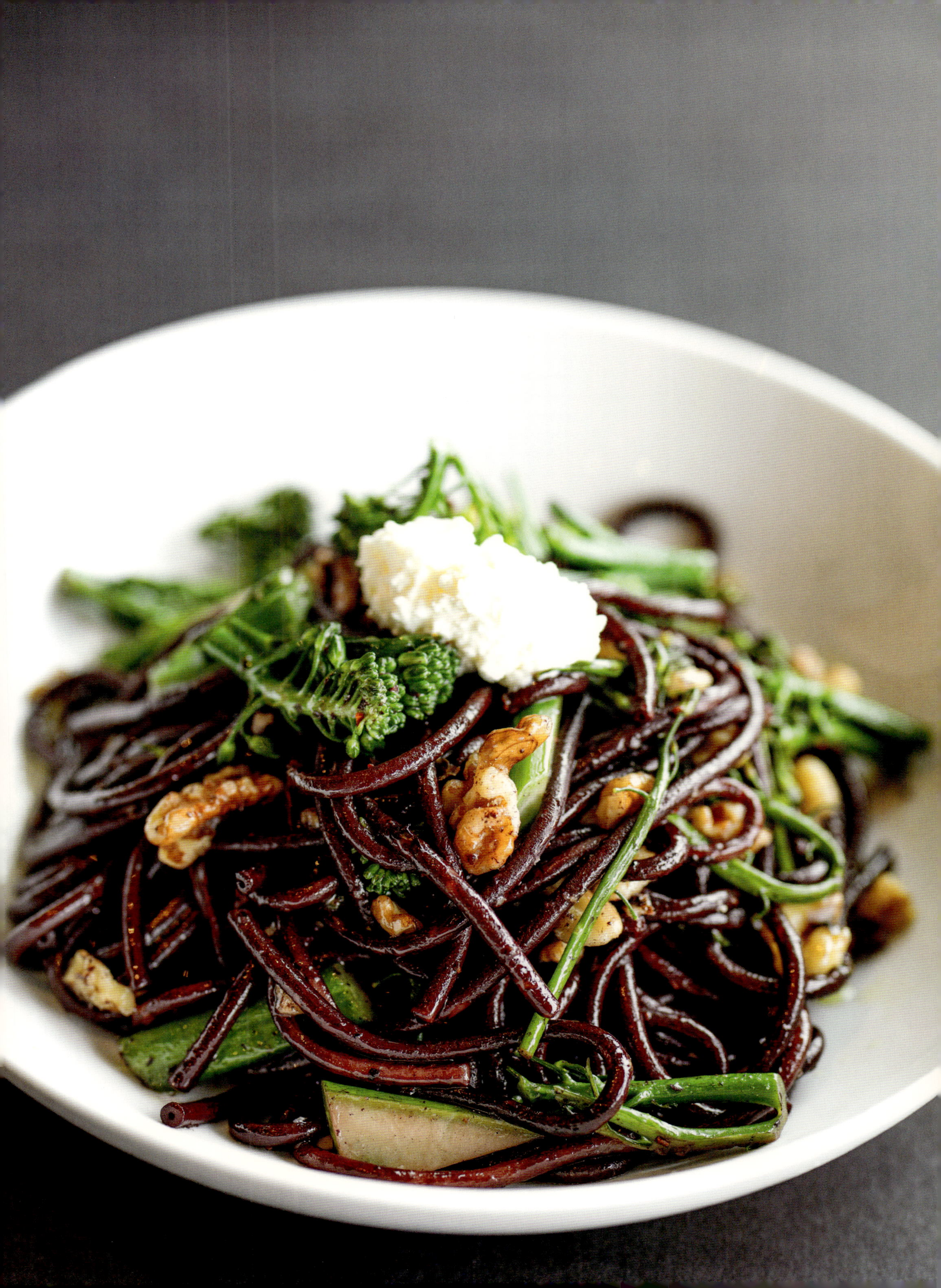

PASTA

BURNT ONION LINGUINI
with SHAVED TUNA HEART and EGG YOLK

1 pound Burnt Onion Pasta Dough (page 90), room temperature

1 cup all-purpose flour, for dusting

2 tablespoons plus 1 teaspoon kosher salt, divided

½ cup extra-virgin olive oil

1 cup roughly chopped fresh parsley

1 tablespoon minced garlic

1 teaspoon red pepper flakes

1 cured tuna heart (available online at Caviar Star)

4 to 6 egg yolks, returned to their individual shells (1 per serving)

¼ cup grated Grana Padano cheese

High-quality extra-virgin olive oil, for drizzling

Shaved tuna heart is an unusual ingredient to most Americans. I discovered it in San Francisco around 2006. Chef Chris Cosentino served Nancy and me this dish at Incanto, his former restaurant in Noe Valley. I was totally enamored with it, stole the idea, and have been serving my version of it since then. Thank you, Chris! Cured tuna hearts are common in Sicily and Sardinia, and the taste is somewhat like bottarga, which is more common in the States. The flavor is strong and needs to stand front and center in any recipe, therefore simple presentations are best. The cured tuna hearts may seem a little too far out there, but a little goes a long way and easily keeps in the freezer for when you want to make this again. Step out on a limb and try this recipe; you might be surprised at how delicious it is. // SERVES 4 to 6

Follow directions for rolling and sheeting pasta dough (page 86). Working with one-fourth of the dough at a time, try to form sheets at least 3 inches wide by about 3 feet long. Place the sheets of dough on a work surface lightly dusted with all-purpose flour as they are done, and allow them to dry for 15 minutes or just long enough so pasta strands will not stick together when cut.

Dust a large baking sheet with all-purpose flour and set aside.

Use a knife or bench scraper to square off the ends of the dough sheets, reserving trim. Cut each pasta sheet crosswise into thirds. (Stack the trimmed pieces and repeat the rolling process to make a final sheet of dough.) Run the sheets through the linguini cutter on your machine, dusting with all-purpose flour if necessary to prevent sticking. Lay each portion of cut pasta on the floured baking sheet and cover with a damp towel.

In a large stockpot, bring 6 quarts water and 2 tablespoons salt to boil. While water is heating, swirl olive oil in a large skillet over medium-low heat. Add parsley, garlic and red pepper flakes and cook for 1 minute. Turn heat off and keep warm.

Drop pasta into the boiling water and stir to prevent sticking. Cook for about 2 to 4 minutes, until al dente. Before draining cooked pasta, reserve 1½ cups cooking water and set aside.

Drain linguini and add to the skillet over medium heat. Add remaining 1 teaspoon salt and reserved pasta water and use tongs or a fork to mix linguini thoroughly with garlic and pepper flakes.

Working quickly, divide linguini among 4 pasta bowls. Using a microplane, grate 2 generous tablespoons of tuna heart over each bowl of pasta. Drop an egg yolk in the center of each dish and sprinkle with grated Grana Padano. To finish, drizzle the bowls with extra-virgin olive oil.

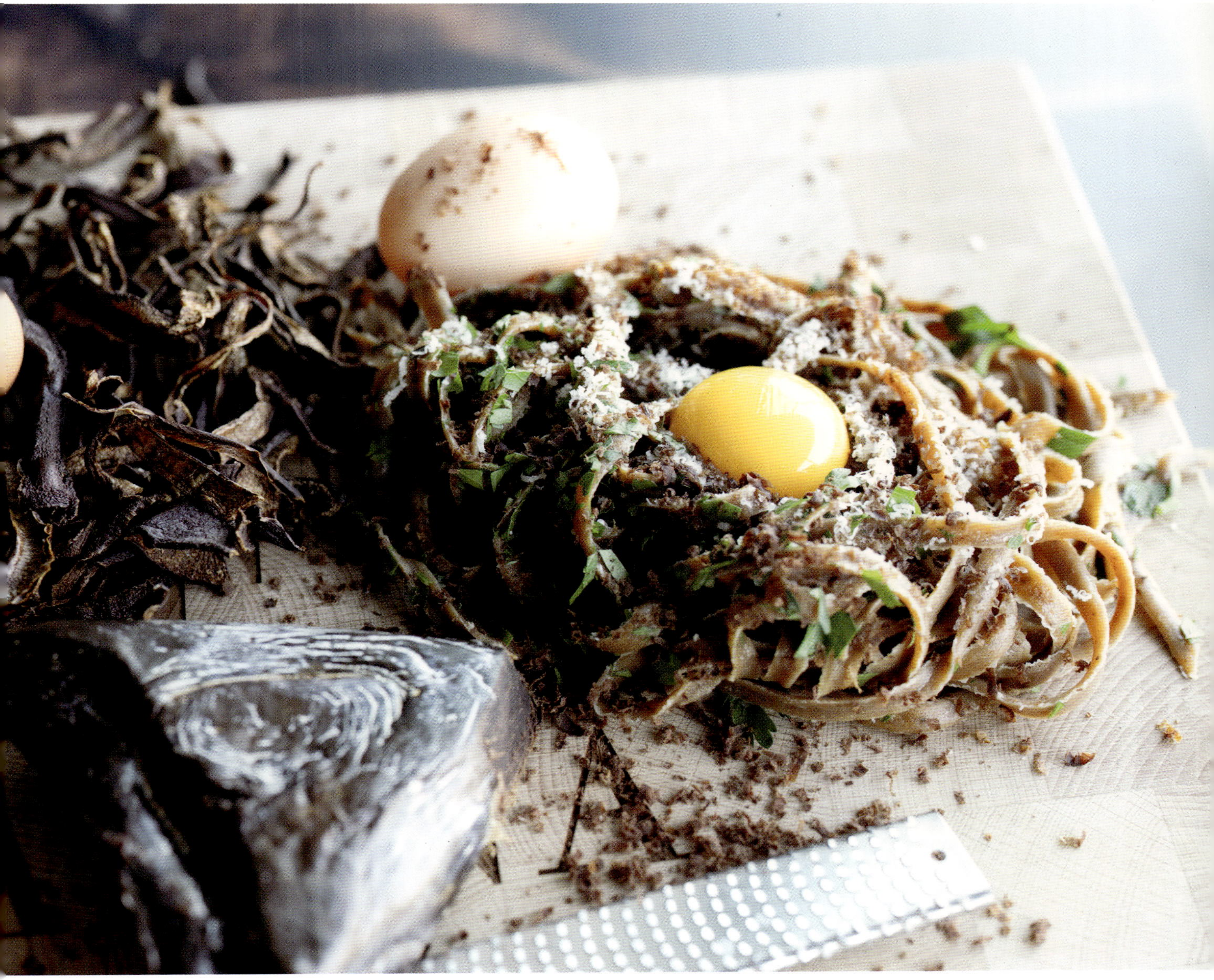

PASTA

SARDINIAN LORIGHITTAS
with MUSSELS, SAFFRON and BLISTERED TOMATOES

½ cup all-purpose flour, for dusting

1 recipe Semolina Pasta Dough (page 92), room temperature

2 tablespoons plus 1 teaspoon kosher salt, divided

4 pounds whole black mussels

½ cup dry white wine

1 shallot, sliced

1 garlic clove, minced

1 sprig fresh thyme

1 teaspoon saffron threads

1½ cups Blistered Cherry Tomatoes (page 243)

3 tablespoons unsalted butter, softened

2 tablespoons roughly chopped basil

High-quality extra-virgin olive oil, for drizzling

Lorighittas are a specialty pasta found in Morgongiori, a village of 800 people at the foot of Monte Arci in western Sardinia. They are recognized as a traditional food and carry PAT certification in Italy for quality historical products. The technique of preparing lorighittas is a generational skill that has been handed down by the women of the village for centuries. This special Sardinian pasta is tricky to make but with a little practice, you'll get it. It's a great dish to share with the whole family. // SERVES 4 to 6

Dust a large baking sheet with flour and set aside.

Pinch off a golf ball–size portion of pasta dough and cover the remaining dough with a damp towel to prevent it from drying out.

Flatten the dough ball into a log. Using the palms of both hands, roll the log back and forth on the work surface to form a very thin string, about ⅛ inch in diameter and about 14 inches long. (This requires a bit of traction; it may be helpful to wipe the work surface and your palms with a damp towel from time to time as you work.)

To form the lorighittas, hold out your left hand with the thumb pointed up and all 4 fingers pointed straight out and pressed together. With your right hand, pick up one end of the dough string, and wrap it twice around your outstretched fingers to make 2 loops. (You can hold the end of the string in place with your left thumb, if necessary. Reverse these directions if you are left-handed.) Seal the 2 loose ends together with water, if needed, and pinch off any excess dough.

Working gently, slide the double loop of dough off your left hand and hold it between your thumbs and index fingers. Weave the loose loops through each other to form a single braided ring. Pull the ring into an oval and place it on the floured baking sheet. Repeat with the remaining dough, making sure the finished lorighittas are not touching each other on the baking sheet.

continues on page 122

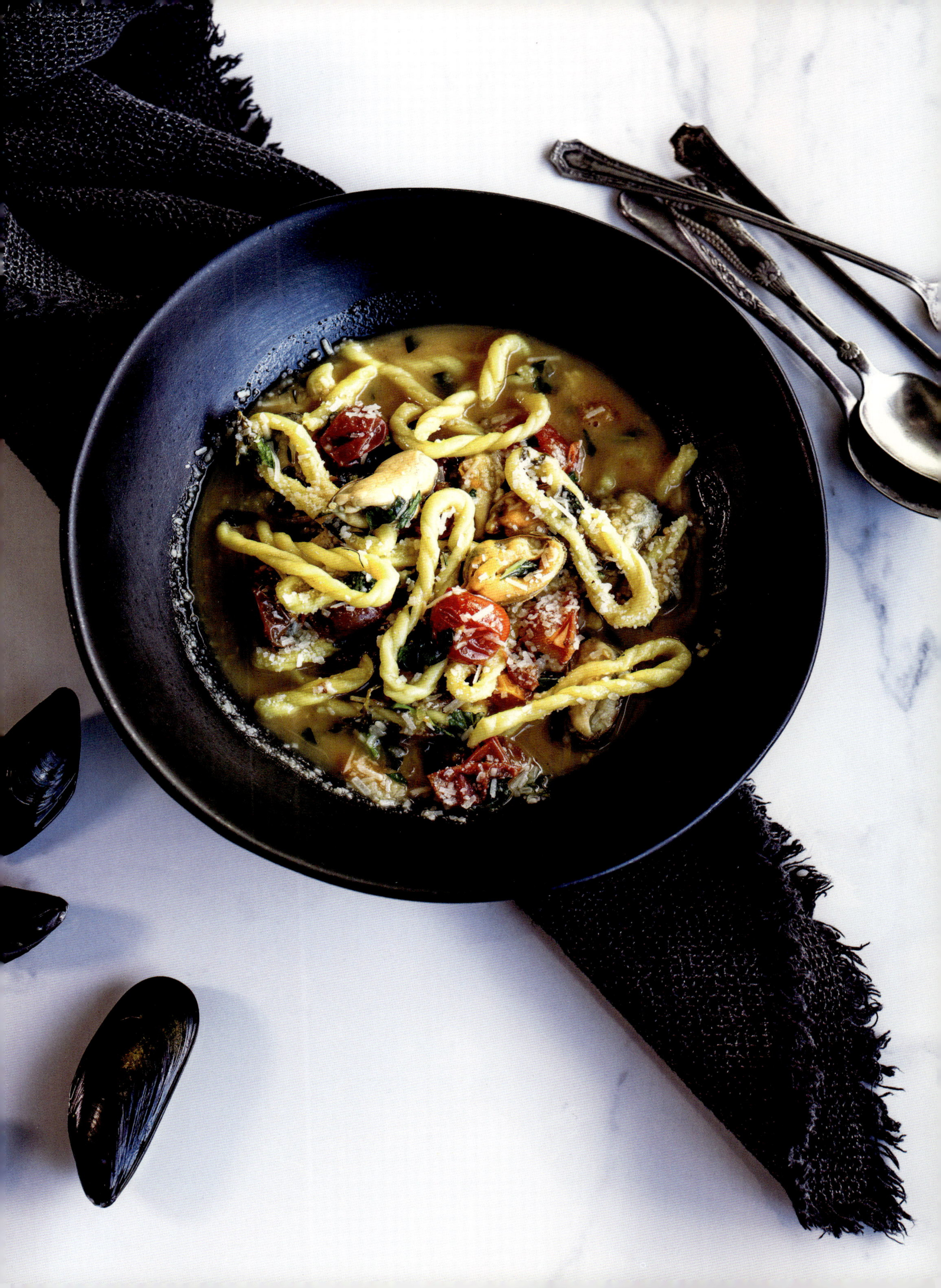

SARDINIAN LORIGHITTAS
continued from page 120

> It takes lots of practice to create a uniform batch of lorighittas, but don't let the challenge discourage you. Gather your friends to make the work quicker, and feel free to laugh at how ugly your first lorighittas turn out. The pasta dough, blistered tomatoes and shucked mussels can all be prepared in advance, so your friends' hard work can be quickly rewarded and enjoyed.

In a large stockpot, bring 6 quarts water and 2 tablespoons salt to a boil over high heat. While the water is heating, place mussels in a large skillet over high heat and add wine, shallot, garlic and thyme. Cover and steam until mussels open, about 4 minutes. Uncover and remove from heat. (Cook mussels in 2 batches if necessary, removing cooked mussels and adding the second batch to the same liquid.) When cool enough to handle, pick mussels from the shells. Discard shells and place mussels in a small bowl. Strain pan liquid into a small bowl for the pasta sauce. Reserve the skillet.

Cook lorighittas in boiling water until al dente, approximately 12 to 14 minutes, stirring from the bottom of the pot to prevent sticking. (Semolina pasta takes a little longer to cook than egg pasta; pull one out to start tasting for doneness at about the 10-minute mark.) Before draining the cooked pasta, reserve ½ cup cooking water and set aside.

While pasta is cooking, return mussel liquid to the skillet, leaving any sediment that has settled in the bottom behind, and bring to a simmer over medium-high heat. Add saffron threads and cook for 1 minute. Add blistered tomatoes and mussels to the pan and simmer for 1 minute. Add drained lorighittas to the skillet along with butter and basil. Using tongs or a wooden spoon, gently toss and fold to mix the ingredients well. Add the remaining teaspoon of salt if necessary and the reserved pasta water to emulsify the sauce. Divide the pasta among 4 bowls and drizzle with extra-virgin olive oil.

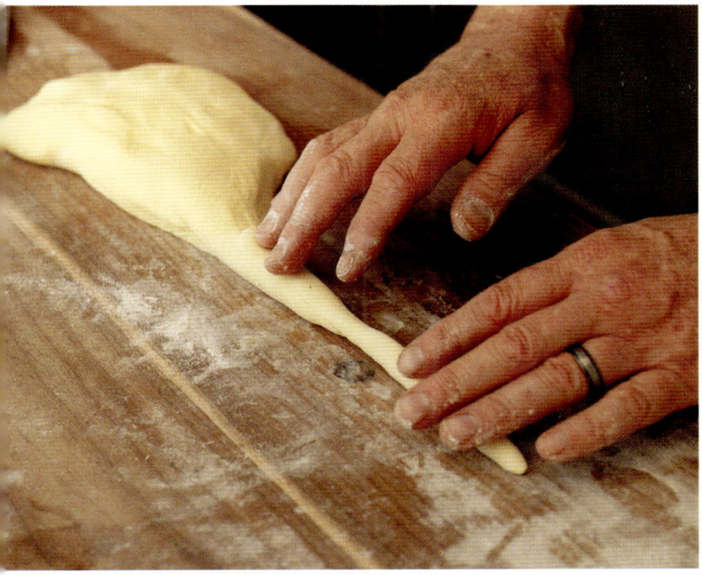
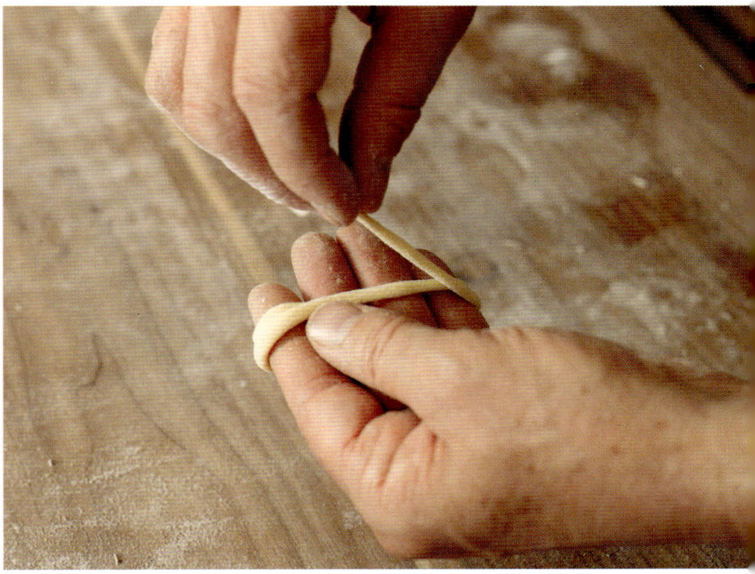
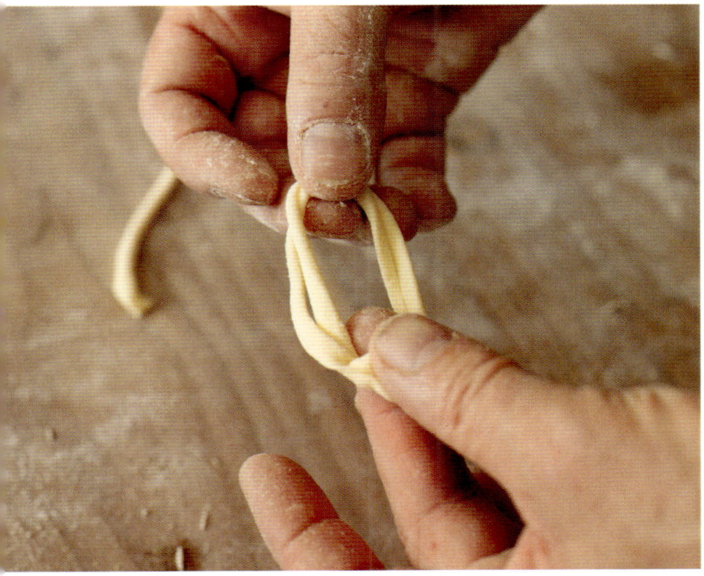
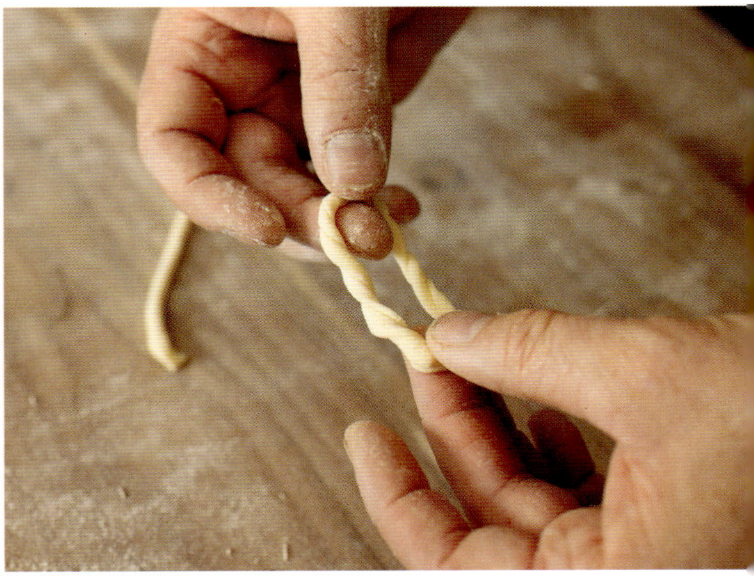

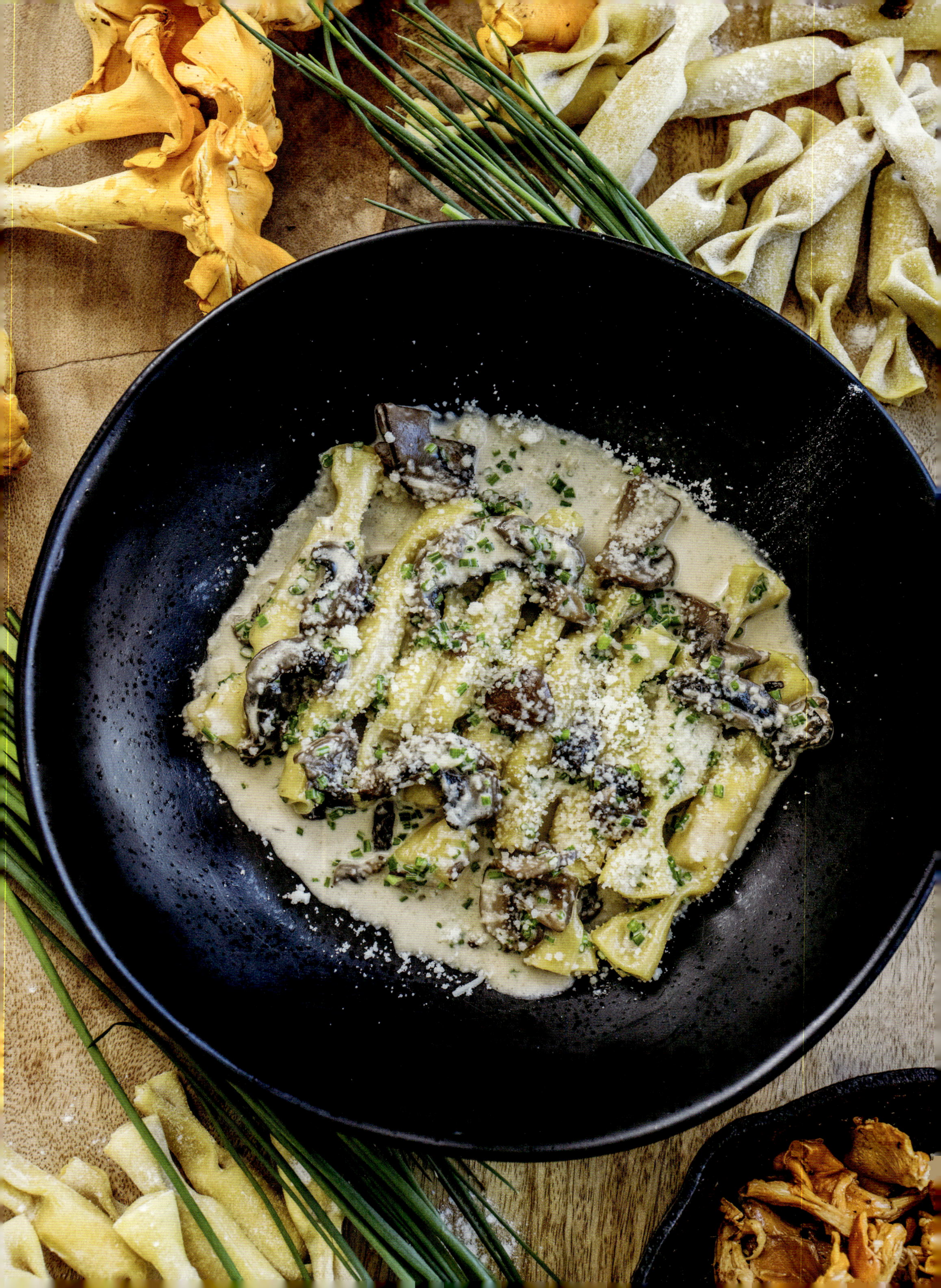

CARAMELLE PASTA
with CHEESE FILLING

CHEESE FILLING
Makes approximately 1⅔ cups

1 cup heavy cream

8 ounces fresh mozzarella, cut into ½-inch cubes

½ cup (2 ounces) shredded sharp provolone

CARAMELLE PASTA
Makes approximately 80 pieces, or 8 appetizer portions

All-purpose flour, for dusting

Egg Pasta Dough (page 90), room temperature

2 tablespoons kosher salt

Mushroom Marsala Sauce (page 253)

Parmesan cheese, for serving

Special equipment: Spray bottle filled with water, disposable plastic piping bag (substitute a small spoon)

We make these adorable Tootsie Roll–shaped packages of warm, cheesy goodness by hand daily. I made the mistake of taking them off the menu once during our first summer and I had a revolt on my hands. So, they are on it forever. Not only will they impress your dinner guests, but they are a fun pasta shape to make with kids of all ages. // **SERVES 8**

MAKE FILLING

Bring heavy cream to a boil in a small saucepan. Reduce heat to a simmer and cook until reduced to ⅔ cup, about 8 to 10 minutes.

Transfer hot cream to a high-speed blender. With the machine running on low, slowly add both cheeses in small batches. Gradually increase the speed to high until the mixture is emulsified. Cool to room temperature, then refrigerate in an airtight container.

When it's time to fill pasta, let filling stand at room temperature 30 minutes before transferring to a disposable piping bag.

The cheese filling will keep, refrigerated in an airtight container, for up to 4 days.

MAKE PASTA

Dust a large baking sheet with all-purpose flour and set aside.

Follow directions for rolling and sheeting egg pasta dough (page 86). Try to form sheets at least 3 inches wide by 3 feet long. (Since the width may vary as you roll, 3 inches will ensure that the entire sheet is wide enough to form the 2-inch-wide rectangles needed for caramelles.) Place the sheets of dough on a lightly floured work surface as they are done, and cover with plastic wrap or a damp (not wet) kitchen towel.

Position 1 pasta sheet on the work surface with a long side closest to you. Using a small knife or pastry cutter, measure and cut the entire length to a 2-inch width. (Save scraps to reroll.) Cut the sheet crosswise at 3½-inch intervals to create rectangles. Repeat with the remaining pasta sheets for a total of approximately 80 rectangles. Gently stack the rectangles in groups of 8. Cover the dough with plastic wrap or a damp (not wet) kitchen towel.

continues on page 126

PASTA

CARAMELLE PASTA WITH CHEESE FILLING
continued from page 125

As your pasta proficiency increases, you can stack the sheets together and cut the rectangles more efficiently. Be careful that the sheets don't stick together, or the dough will have to be rerolled.

Lay 8 rectangles (or as many as you have room to work with at a time) side by side on the work surface with the long sides closest to you. Pipe a 1-inch log of cheese in the center of the bottom half of each rectangle. (Alternatively, use a small spoon to place a 1-inch log of cheese on the dough.)

Lightly mist the rectangles with water from a spray bottle. One at a time, fold the edge closest to you over the filling and tuck it gently into the opposite side. Keep rolling until cheese is fully enclosed and the seam is on the bottom, forming a semi-round tube. Repeat with the remaining 7 rectangles.

To seal the filling inside, place both index fingers on top of the tube, just beyond each end of the cheese log. Press down gently to flatten the dough, sealing in the cheese. Then, pinch each flattened area between a thumb and index finger, sealing the tube in the opposite direction and creating a little frill at each end to resemble a wrapped candy, or *caramelle*. Set the piece on the prepared baking sheet and repeat until all the pasta is shaped. Place the baking sheet in the freezer for at least an hour, until ready to cook.

Bring 6 quarts water and 2 tablespoons salt to a boil in a large stockpot. While water is heating, heat mushroom Marsala sauce to serving temperature. Add frozen caramelles to boiling water and cook just until soft in the center, about 2 minutes; the pasta should remain al dente. Drain well, and immediately (and gently) toss with sauce. The pasta should be lightly sauced, not "buried in soup." Divide equally among bowls or transfer to a large serving platter and serve with a sprinkle of Parmesan cheese.

Uncooked caramelles will keep frozen in an airtight container for up to 6 months.

> Most home pasta machines roll sheets about 5 to 6 inches wide. I may be creating confusion by trying to dictate widths of pasta throughout the pasta section of this book. What you want to do is practice getting the most width you can from each sheet in order to be efficient. With each dough ball needing 4 passes through the machine to laminate, then another 4 or 5 passes to achieve the correct thickness, each sheet of pasta could be 10 passes through or more if nothing crazy happens like sticking and tearing. Proficiency and efficiency in rolling the sheets will minimize your frustration. Making fresh pasta should be enjoyable, not a hassle.

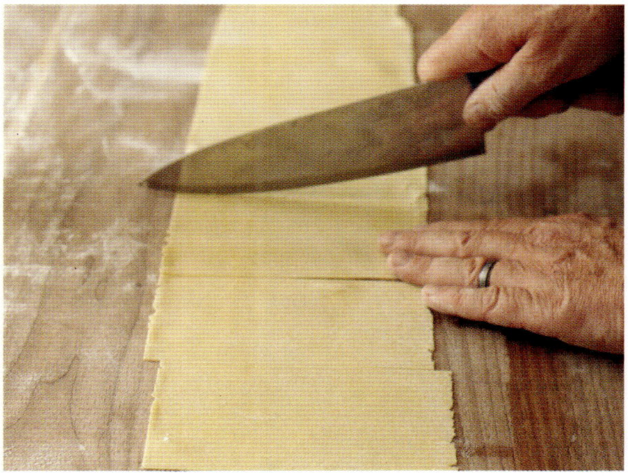
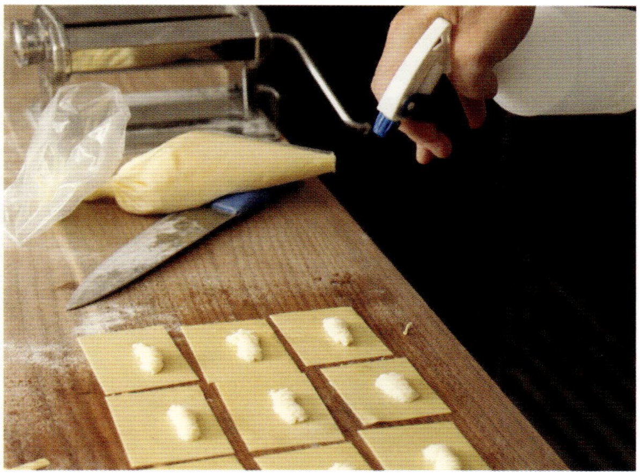
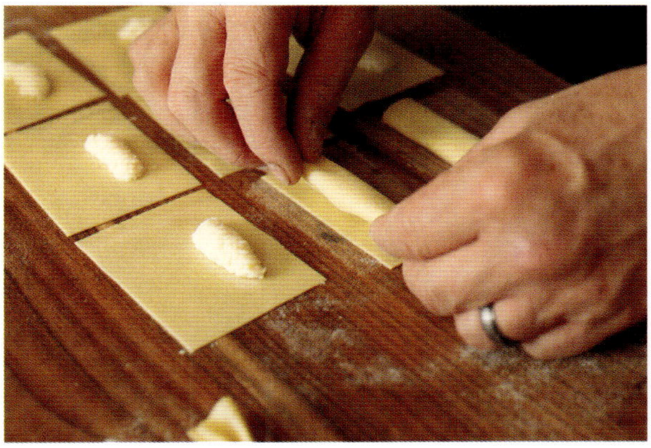
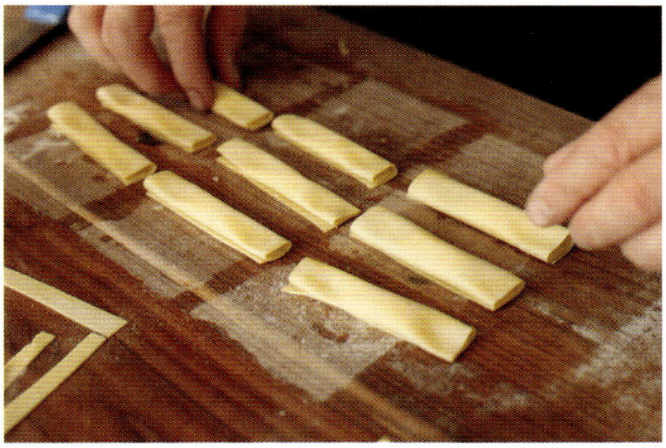
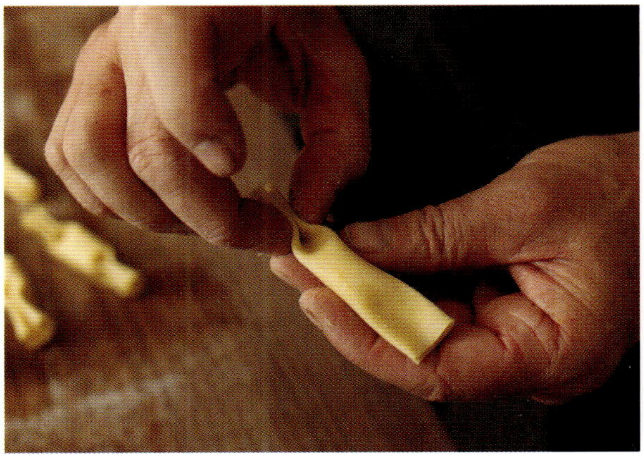
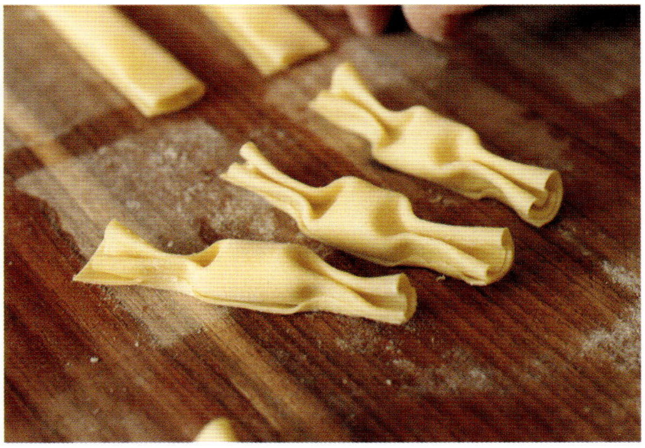

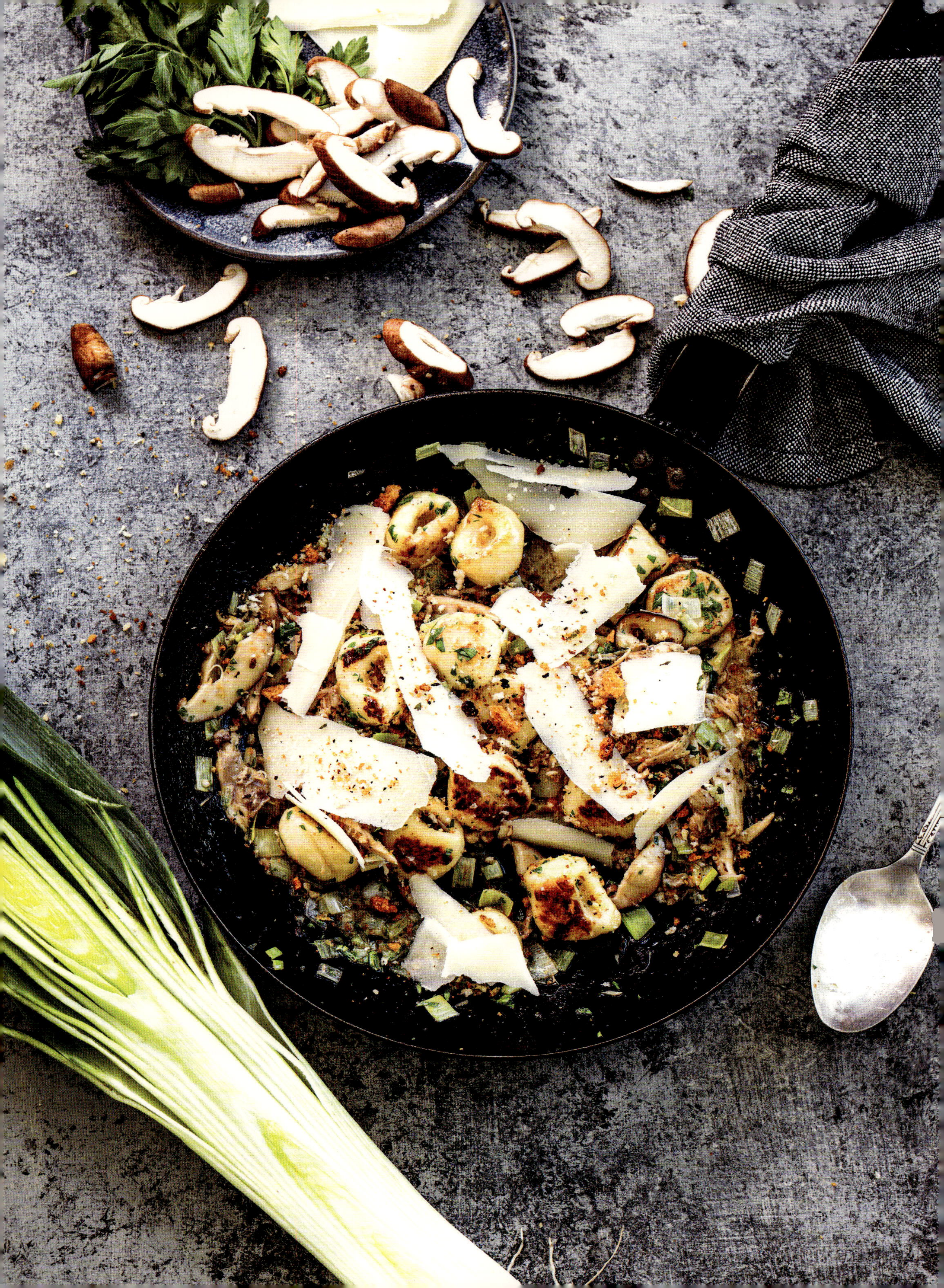

RABBIT GNOCCHI

POACHED RABBIT

3-pound whole rabbit, cut crosswise in half between back and legs

1 yellow onion, cut into 4 to 6 chunks

1 large carrot, cut into 4 to 6 chunks

1 rib celery, cut into 4 to 6 chunks

1 leek, dark green leaves only, washed well and roughly chopped

1 garlic bulb, halved horizontally

1 cup dry white wine

3 sprigs fresh rosemary

1 bay leaf

2 tablespoons kosher salt

1 tablespoon black peppercorns

GNOCCHI AND SAUCE

2 tablespoons canola oil

1¼ pounds cooked Potato Gnocchi (page 93)

2 cups fresh shiitake mushrooms, sliced

1 cup leeks, thinly sliced (white section only)

3 cups rabbit broth

3 tablespoons soft butter

2 cups shredded rabbit

½ cup fresh cut chives

1 teaspoon kosher salt

2 tablespoons Pangrattato (page 267)

Shaved Grana Padano, for garnish

I've always strived to push the envelope at my restaurants with regard to ingredients. I'd like to think there have been many more hits than misses, but sometimes we must pull an unusual dish from the menu simply because it doesn't sell. I thought this dish would suffer that fate when my former chef de cuisine, Carl Thorne-Thomsen, introduced it at Michael Smith Restaurant in 2007. Turns out, I was wrong. Our guests are wild about rabbit, and this hearty entrée has been a mainstay on the Farina menu since day one. // **SERVES 4**

TO POACH RABBIT

Combine rabbit, 6 quarts water and remaining ingredients for Poached Rabbit in a large stockpot. Bring to a boil, then lower heat and let simmer for 2 hours, or until meat easily pulls from bones. Let rabbit cool in the liquid, then remove and coarsely shred the meat into evenly sized pieces. Strain the broth, discarding vegetables. Set broth and meat aside in separate containers.

TO FINISH THE DISH

Heat a large, heavy-bottomed skillet over high heat. Add oil. When it begins to smoke, carefully add gnocchi, stirring constantly until gnocchi turns slightly brown, about 1 minute. Add shiitakes and leeks, continuing to stir until vegetables soften, about 1 minute. Stir in broth and bring to a boil. Add butter, stirring until sauce thickens and emulsifies. Fold in rabbit, chives and salt.

TO SERVE

Divide Rabbit Gnocchi among 4 bowls. Sprinkle with breadcrumbs and cheese.

PASTA

AGNOLOTTI *dal* PLIN

3 cups spinach leaves

1 cup fresh Italian parsley leaves

½ cup yellow onion, peeled and roughly chopped

½ cup carrot, roughly chopped

1 celery rib, roughly chopped

1½ teaspoons fresh rosemary leaves, roughly chopped

1½ teaspoons fresh thyme leaves

1 garlic clove, peeled

2 fresh sage leaves

1 tablespoon butter

4 ounces ground pork

4 ounces ground beef

4 ounces ground veal

½ cup Poultry Broth (page 237)

2 teaspoons kosher salt, plus more to taste

1½ teaspoons ground black pepper, plus more to taste

¼ teaspoon ground nutmeg

1 cup grated Grana Padano cheese

2 large eggs

Egg Pasta Dough (page 90)

All-purpose flour, for dusting

Sage Brown Butter Sauce (page 267)

Parmesan cheese, for garnish

Special Equipment: Spray bottle filled with water, crimped pastry wheel and bench scraper

This iconic Piedmont dish can be found on every menu in that region of Italy. There are stories about its origin stemming from an extravagant king's banquet after staving off conquering invaders. But the down and dirty is—it's a stuffed pasta that uses leftover braised meats and vegetables. Always one of the most in-demand offerings at Farina when it's on the menu, this dish can be a little daunting to make at home. I've lost count of how many times over the years guests have asked me how I make it. So, ask and you shall receive. But don't say I didn't warn you.

// MAKES ABOUT 125 AGNOLOTTI

Combine spinach, parsley, onion, carrot, celery, rosemary, thyme, garlic and sage in a food processor and process until finely minced. Set aside.

Melt butter in a large, heavy-bottomed skillet over high heat. When it is hot but not smoking, work in batches to brown half the pork, beef and veal together. Use a slotted spoon to transfer the cooked meat to a bowl and repeat with remaining meats, leaving fat in the pan. Add spinach and vegetable mixture to the pan and cook until lightly browned, 5 to 7 minutes. Return cooked meat to the pan and add chicken broth. Season with salt, pepper and nutmeg; stir, scraping up any residue from the bottom of the pan, until ingredients are well incorporated. Cook until liquid evaporates, then remove from heat and set aside to cool completely.

Add half the mixture to the food processor along with ½ cup Grana Padano cheese and 1 egg. Pulse until it forms a loose paste, about 10 seconds. Transfer to a bowl and repeat with remaining filling, cheese and egg. Mix batches together and correct the seasoning with salt and pepper.

To shape the agnolotti, follow directions for rolling and sheeting the pasta dough (page 86). Working with a quarter of the dough at a time, try to form sheets at least 3 inches wide by about 3 feet long. Place the sheets of dough on a work surface lightly dusted with all-purpose flour and cover with plastic wrap or a damp towel.

Dust a large baking sheet with all-purpose flour and set aside.

Position 1 pasta sheet on the work surface with a long side closest to you. Use the backside of a butter knife to lightly mark a 1-inch border along the bottom edge of the dough without cutting through. Using a small spoon, scoop small dollops of filling (the size of a peanut M&M) onto the dough, so they sit just above the border line and are spaced ¾ inch to 1 inch apart.

continues on page 132

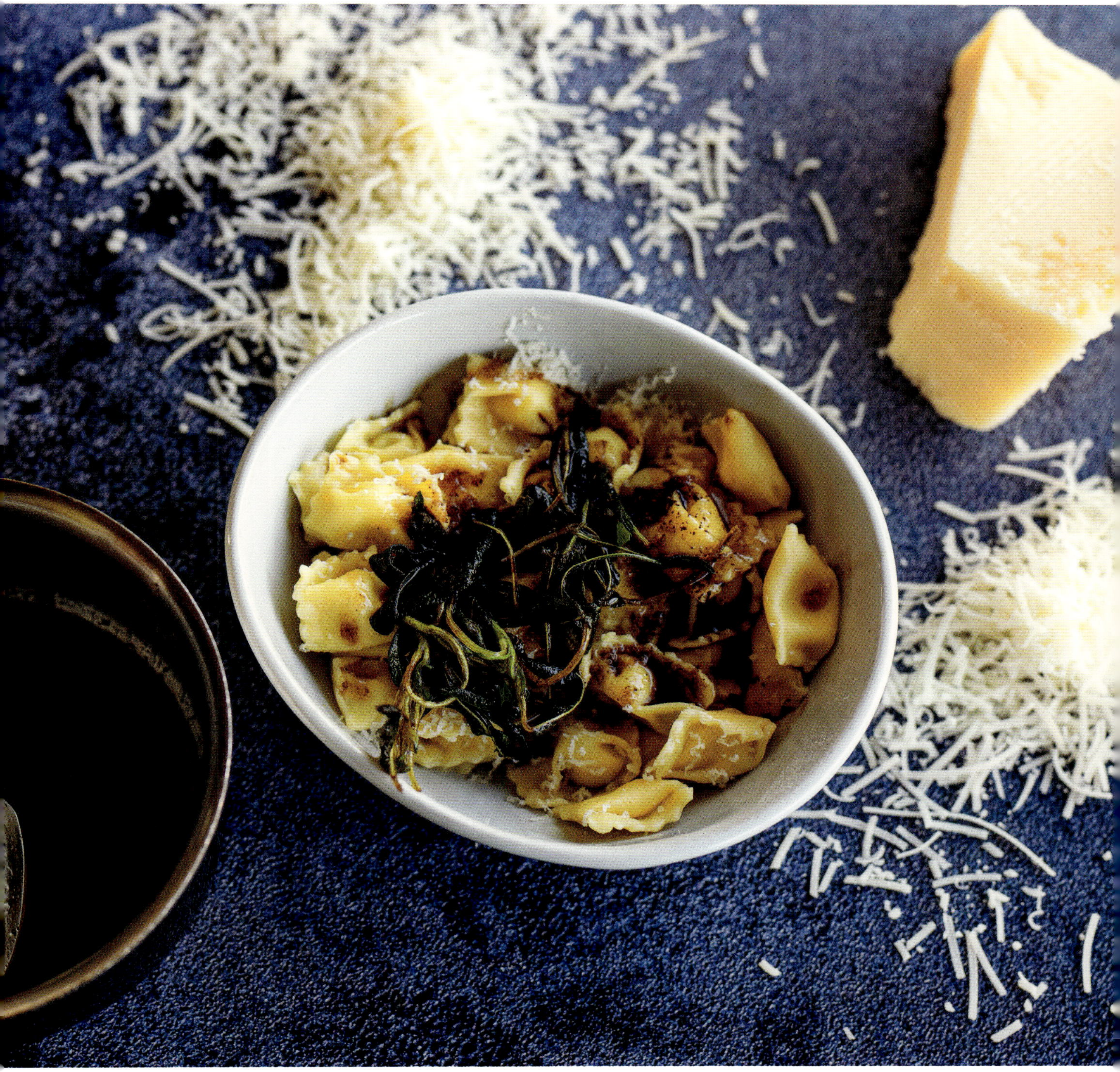

AGNOLOTTI *dal* PLIN
continued from page 130

When the full length of the dough has been topped with filling, spray the entire sheet with a fine mist of water from a spray bottle. Lift and fold the bottom edge of dough up and over to enclose the filling, creating about an inch of folded-over pasta.

The folded-over pasta sheet will form a long, wide lump over the dollops of filling. Gently slide your index finger along the doubled-up pasta edge so it lightly sticks together. Don't press between the mounds yet.

Starting at one end of the filled log, place the thumb and forefinger of one hand between 2 dollops of filling, and pinch the dough so it forms an upright seal between them. Use both hands to repeat pinching and sealing down the length of the dough sheet. If large air bubbles form, gently separate the doubled-up pasta edge to release them. If the dough will not separate easily, use a pin or toothpick in the next spot to be pinched.

Slide your index finger along the doubled-up edge again, this time to form a tight seal. Separate the pinched strip of filled dough from the unused portion of the pastry sheet by running a crimped pastry wheel or sharp knife along the length of the doubled-up edge, about ¾ inch away from the filling.

Lightly mist the strip of filled dough with the water bottle. To separate the individual agnolotti, cut between the vertical pinches, rolling the pastry wheel away from you. This movement will roll each cut piece away from you, sealing its edges at the same time. When the entire strip has been cut, use a bench scraper to lift agnolotti onto the prepared baking sheet. Keep them separated so they don't stick together. Place the pan in the freezer for at least an hour, until ready to cook. (For longer storage, place solidly frozen agnolotti in an airtight container and freeze until needed, up to 6 months.)

Bring 6 quarts water and 2 tablespoons salt to a boil in a large stockpot. While the water is heating, prepare sage brown butter sauce to serving temperature. Add frozen agnolotti to boiling water, and cook just until soft in the center, 2 to 5 minutes. The pasta should remain al dente. Drain well, and immediately (and gently) toss in the sauce. The pasta should be lightly sauced, not "buried in soup." Divide equally among bowls or transfer to a large serving platter and serve with a sprinkle of Parmesan cheese.

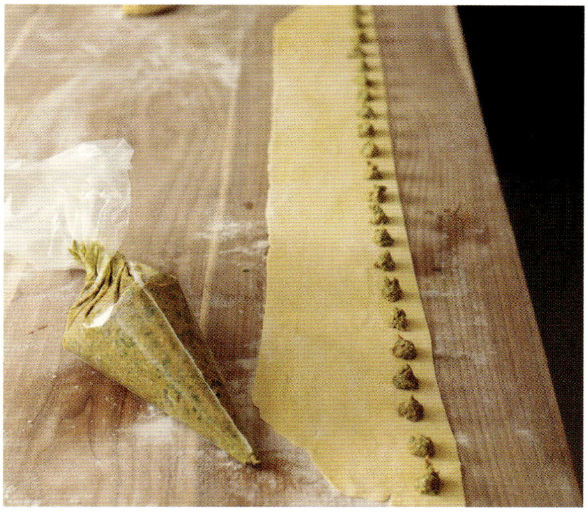
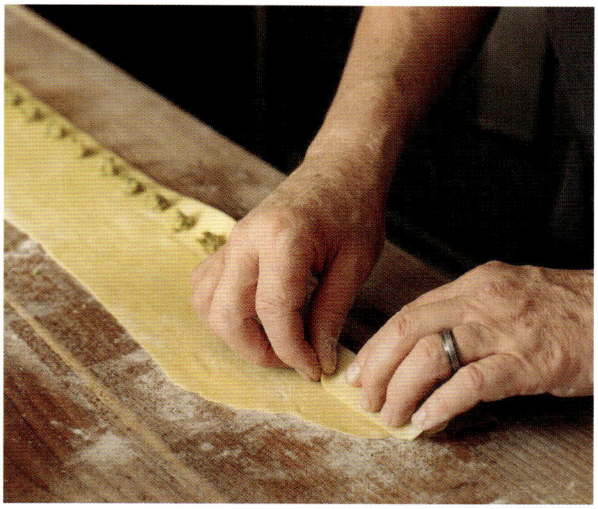
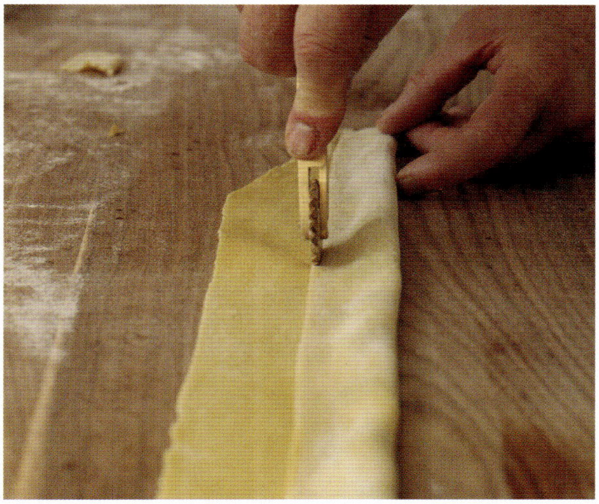
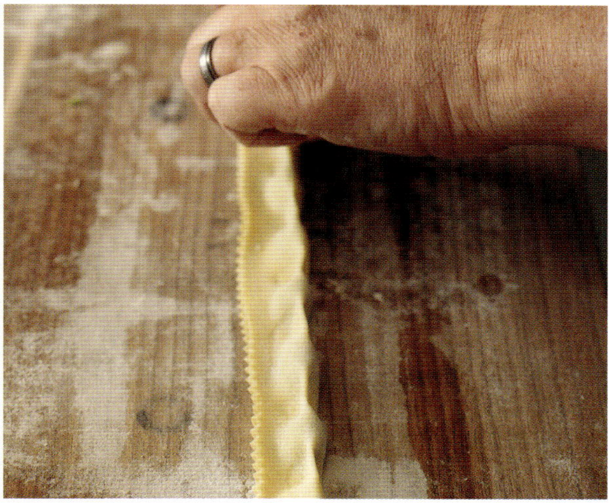
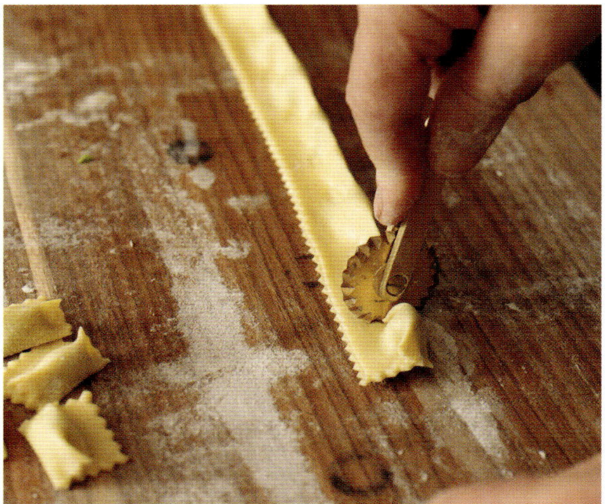
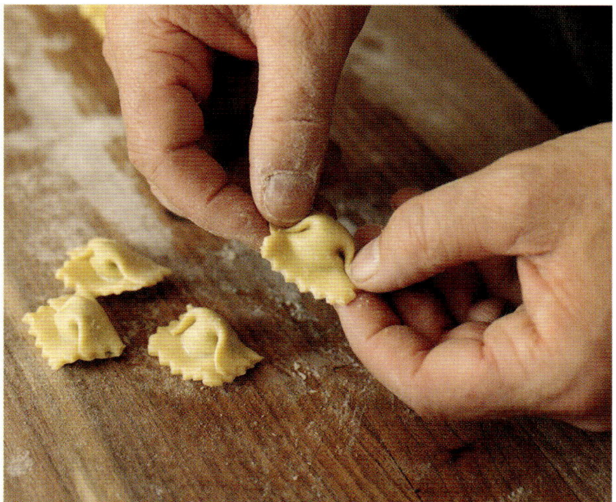

PASTA

SQUID INK SPAGHETTI
with KING CRAB and PESTO CALABRESE

Squid Ink Pasta Dough (page 92), room temperature

1 cup all-purpose flour, for dusting

2 tablespoons plus 1 teaspoon kosher salt, divided

1½ cups Pesto Calabrese (page 248)

8 ounces king crab meat from about 1 pound crab legs, lightly shredded

½ cup roughly chopped fresh basil

3 tablespoons fresh lemon juice

1 cup grated Grana Padano cheese, divided

3 tablespoons unsalted butter

½ cup Pangrattato (page 267)

High-quality extra-virgin olive oil, for drizzling

In 1985, Chef Alain Culaud at La Presqu'île in Cassis would tell me I'd become rich someday by making squid ink pasta in America. At that point in my career, I had no idea what lay ahead of me as a chef, other than being tasked with making squid ink pasta every day after we ate the family meal. On a big old wooden door in the driveway of the restaurant, I would crank out 2 kilos of those lovely black ribbons.

On New Year's Eve in 1987 at Charlie Trotter's, the pasta would again help shape my culinary future. Through some mishap, the squid ink fettuccine that was prepared for an entrée that evening fell apart upon hitting the pasta water. Charlie demanded wildly, "Does anyone in this fucking kitchen know how to make pasta?" I had only been on board about 5 months, but I carefully raised my hand. In short, I made the same pasta that I knew so well from Cassis and saved New Year's Eve. Charlie promoted me to sous chef not long after that. // SERVES 4 to 6

Follow directions for rolling and sheeting pasta dough (page 86). Place the sheets of dough on a work surface lightly dusted with flour as they are done, and allow them to dry for 15 minutes, or just long enough so pasta strands will not stick together when cut.

Dust a large baking sheet with all-purpose flour and set aside.

Use a knife or bench scraper to square off the ends of the dough sheets, reserving trim. Cut each pasta sheet crosswise into thirds. Stack the trimmed pieces and repeat the rolling process to make a final sheet of dough. Run the sheets through the spaghetti cutter on a pasta machine, dusting with flour if necessary to prevent sticking. Lay each portion of cut pasta on the floured baking sheet and cover with a damp towel.

In a large stockpot, bring 6 quarts water and 2 tablespoons salt to a boil. Drop pasta into the water and stir to prevent sticking. Cook for 3 to 4 minutes, until chewy and toothsome. Before draining the cooked pasta, reserve 1 cup cooking water and set aside.

While pasta is cooking, stir together pesto, crab and basil in a large skillet and bring to a low simmer over medium heat. Drain pasta and transfer to the skillet. Increase heat to medium-high and add ¾ cup reserved pasta water and lemon juice, using tongs or a wooden spoon to toss and mix ingredients well. Add ½ cup Grana Padano, butter and remaining 1 teaspoon salt, tossing and mixing until sauce looks emulsified. Add more reserved pasta water as needed to create a saucier pasta if desired.

Divide pasta among shallow bowls. Sprinkle each with pangrattato and remaining cheese. Finish with a generous drizzle of high-quality extra-virgin olive oil.

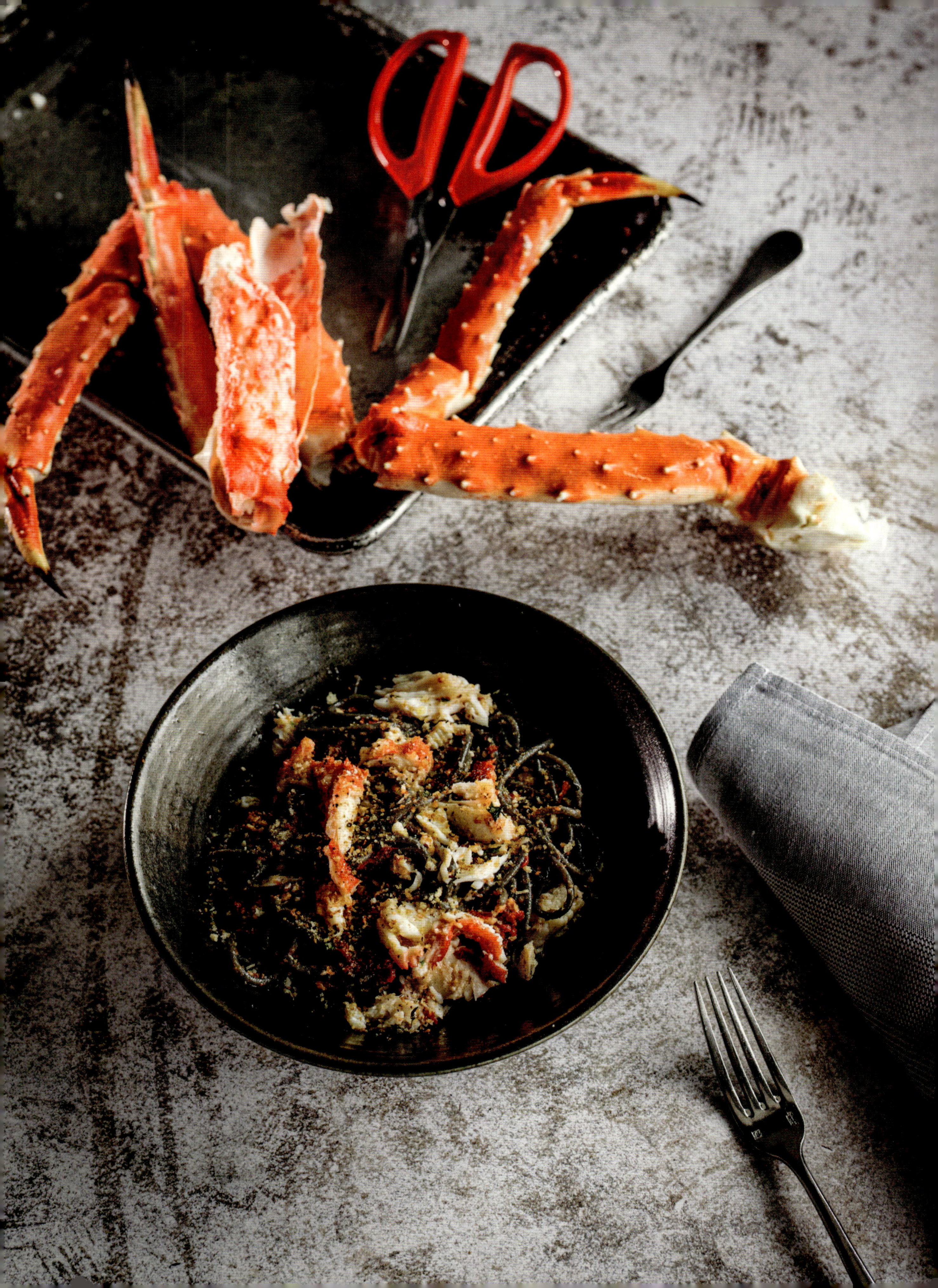

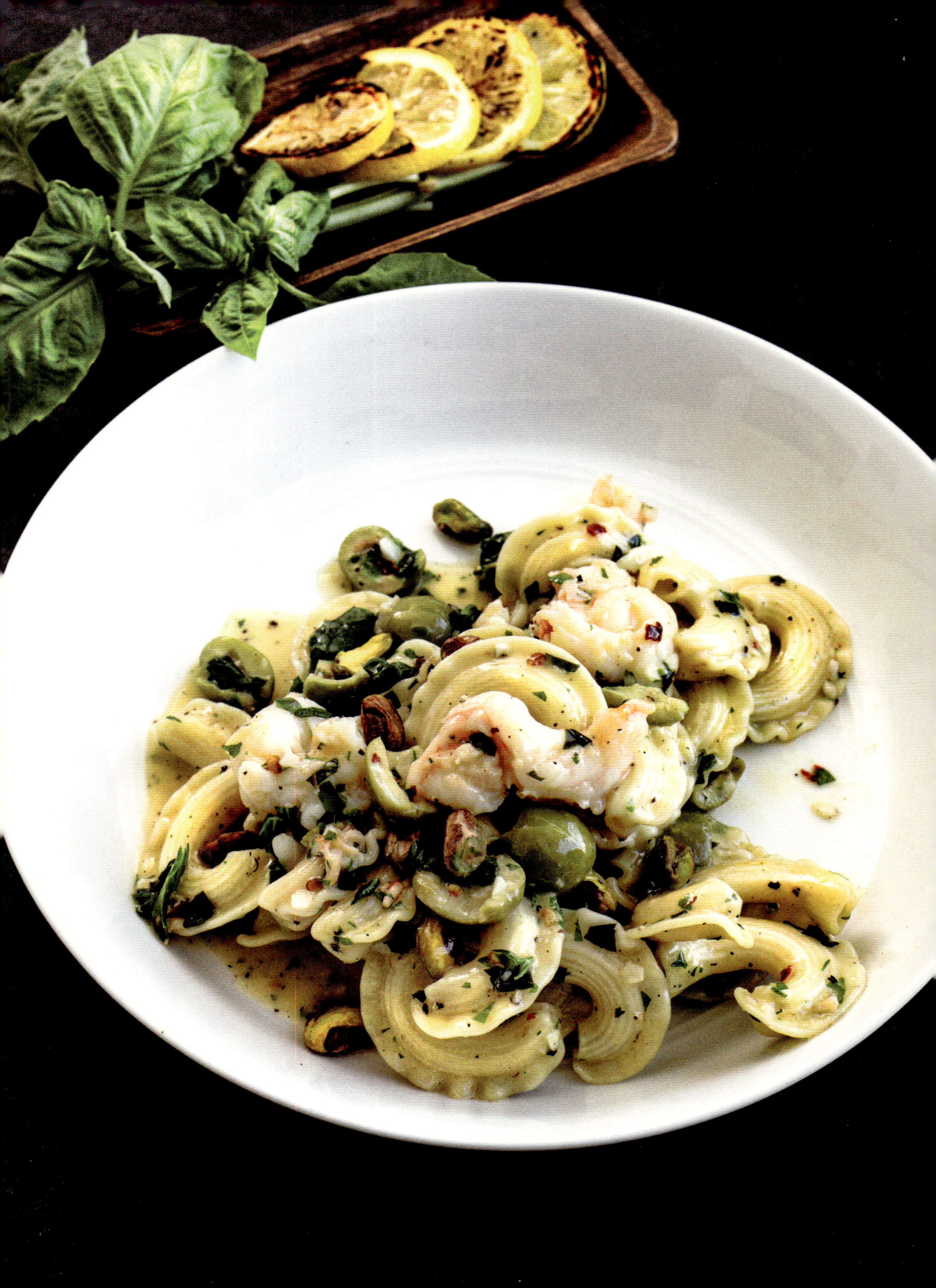

CRESTE DI GALLO
with SHRIMP, CASTELVETRANO OLIVES and PISTACHIOS

1 pound (26/30) raw shrimp, peeled and deveined, tails removed

4 tablespoons roasted pistachios

2 tablespoons plus 1 teaspoon kosher salt, divided

2 tablespoons extra-virgin olive oil

1½ cups pitted Castelvetrano olives, halved lengthwise

4 Calabrian chilies, drained and minced

2 garlic cloves, peeled and minced

16-ounce package creste di gallo dried pasta (or radiatore or fusilli)

3 tablespoons fresh lemon juice

1 tablespoon freshly grated lemon zest

¼ cup roughly chopped fresh basil, or more to taste

4 tablespoons unsalted butter

4 tablespoons Grana Padano cheese, divided

2 tablespoons Pangrattato (page 267)

High-quality extra-virgin olive oil, for drizzling

The shape of creste di gallo refers to the cockscomb on a rooster's head. This pasta has generated feverish reactions when I take it off the menu, and rightly so—it's really tasty. The combination of Castelvetrano olives, sweet shrimp and pistachios works so well. Finish the dish with a little nugget of butter, fresh basil and a spark of heat from the Calabrian chilies. // **SERVES 4 to 6**

Halve shrimp lengthwise (this is easier to do if shrimp are slightly frozen). Set aside.

Lightly crush pistachios and set aside.

In a large stockpot, bring 6 quarts water and 2 tablespoons salt to a boil. While water is heating, swirl olive oil in a large, deep-sided skillet over medium heat. Add shrimp, olives and chilies and cook for 2 minutes, stirring well. Add garlic and cook 1 more minute, then turn off the heat and set aside.

Cook pasta al dente, according to package directions. Before draining pasta, reserve 1 cup cooking water and set aside. Drain pasta and add to the skillet with the shrimp. Return the skillet to medium-high heat and add ¾ cup reserved pasta water, lemon juice, zest, pistachios, basil and remaining 1 teaspoon salt. Use tongs or a wooden spoon to toss and mix ingredients well. Add butter and half the cheese. Keep tossing and mixing the pasta until the sauce looks emulsified. Add more pasta water as needed to create a saucier pasta if desired.

Divide pasta equally among bowls or transfer to a serving platter and sprinkle with pangrattato and the remaining Grana Padano. Finish with a generous drizzle of extra-virgin olive oil.

PASTA

CHILLED ANGEL HAIR PASTA
with OSETRA CAVIAR, PONZU and FURIKAKE

- 2 tablespoons kosher salt
- 8 ounces dried angel hair pasta
- 1 ounce Amur osetra caviar
- 1 tablespoon chives, finely minced
- 4 tablespoons Ponzu
- 2 ounces raw ahi tuna, finely diced (optional)
- Nori kome furikake seasoning (available at an Asian grocery)
- 2 tablespoons high-quality extra-virgin olive oil, for drizzling

I have always been intrigued by pasta with caviar and have prepared many different versions over the years. At Farina we make nori-flavored spaghetti, much like this recipe. On a recent summer trip to the Outer Banks with Nancy's family, I had these ingredients in the house for upcoming dinners during the week. Naturally, I am the resident chef on these vacations! One morning I was hungry for chilled soba noodles tossed with ponzu and furikake. I didn't have soba noodles on hand, but I did have angel hair pasta. I went about cooking my pasta breakfast while the rest of the family was cooking eggs and bacon and other requisite breakfast foods and looking skeptically at my choice of breakfast ingredients. As my finished pasta came together, they all wanted to peek into my bowl. It smelled delicious and now they pleaded for a taste. What was exceptionally weird 2 minutes before was now delicious. Within minutes, I was cooking another round of breakfast for 8 others! // SERVES 2

Bring 6 quarts water and salt to a boil in a large stockpot. Drop the angel hair into the water, stirring to keep it from sticking. Cook pasta for 6 minutes or follow the directions on the box.

In a medium-size prep bowl, combine caviar, chives, ponzu and tuna (if using).

When pasta is cooked al dente, pour into a strainer and run cold water over the noodles until they are chilled. When sufficiently chilled, let noodles drain for 1 minute so they don't drag unnecessary water into the prepared prep bowl. Add noodles to the bowl and use tongs or a fork to toss and mix pasta with the other ingredients.

Divide pasta into 2 bowls and generously sprinkle furikake on top. Drizzle with olive oil and enjoy your breakfast!

INGREDIENTS: TROUT ROE AND SEA SALT • PERISHABLE: KEEP REFRIGERATED BETWEEN 26°F & 38°F (-3° TO 3°C)
Caviar Star
RAINBOW TROUT
NET WT. 7 OZ (200g)
PACKAGED BY GREAT ATLANTIC TRADING INC • OCEAN ISLE BEACH, NC 28469

SPINACH HANDKERCHIEF PASTA
with BASIL PESTO and POMODORO

Spinach Pasta Dough (page 90), at room temperature

1 cup all-purpose flour, for dusting

2 tablespoons plus 1 teaspoon kosher salt, divided

2 cups Pomodoro Sauce (page 255)

½ cup pesto at room temperature

4 tablespoons grated Grana Padano cheese

Summertime brings ripe, juicy tomatoes and fresh basil. They put me in my happy place. For this dish we use a version of maltagliati, which in Italian means "badly cut." We don't actually use badly cut pasta sheets, but rustic is okay here—we don't require that the rectangles be perfectly shaped. We call it handkerchief pasta at Farina. The pesto in this preparation should be smooth as silk to coat the pasta sheets, according to tradition. // **SERVES 4**

Prepare spinach dough recipe and follow the directions for rolling and sheeting (page 86). Cut the rolled pasta sheets into 3 x 5-inch rectangles, ending up with at least 24 handkerchiefs.

Lay the finished pasta rectangles on a lightly floured baking pan. Lightly dust pasta rectangles with flour and set them flat on the work surface to dry for 20 minutes. They won't be dry enough to crumble and break, but dry enough to stack together like a deck of cards before cooking.

While pasta sheets dry, bring 6 quarts water and 2 tablespoons salt to a boil in a large stockpot.

In a small saucepan, bring pomodoro sauce to a boil, then set aside. Add pistou to a large stainless steel mixing bowl and set aside.

Drop half the pasta into the boiling water (stir well to keep it from sticking) for 2 to 3 minutes or until al dente. Lift cooked pasta out of the water with a long-handled mesh strainer and toss it into the reserved bowl of pesto (it's okay to drag a tiny bit of pasta water into the bowl, it will loosen and warm the pesto). Repeat with remaining pasta. Sprinkle remaining 1 teaspoon salt into the pesto bowl, then use tongs or a wooden spoon to mix and toss the cooked sheets around in the bowl to fully coat with pesto.

Divide handkerchief pasta between 4 pasta bowls and spoon a generous dollop of warm pomodoro sauce on top of the pasta. Sprinkle with Grana Padano.

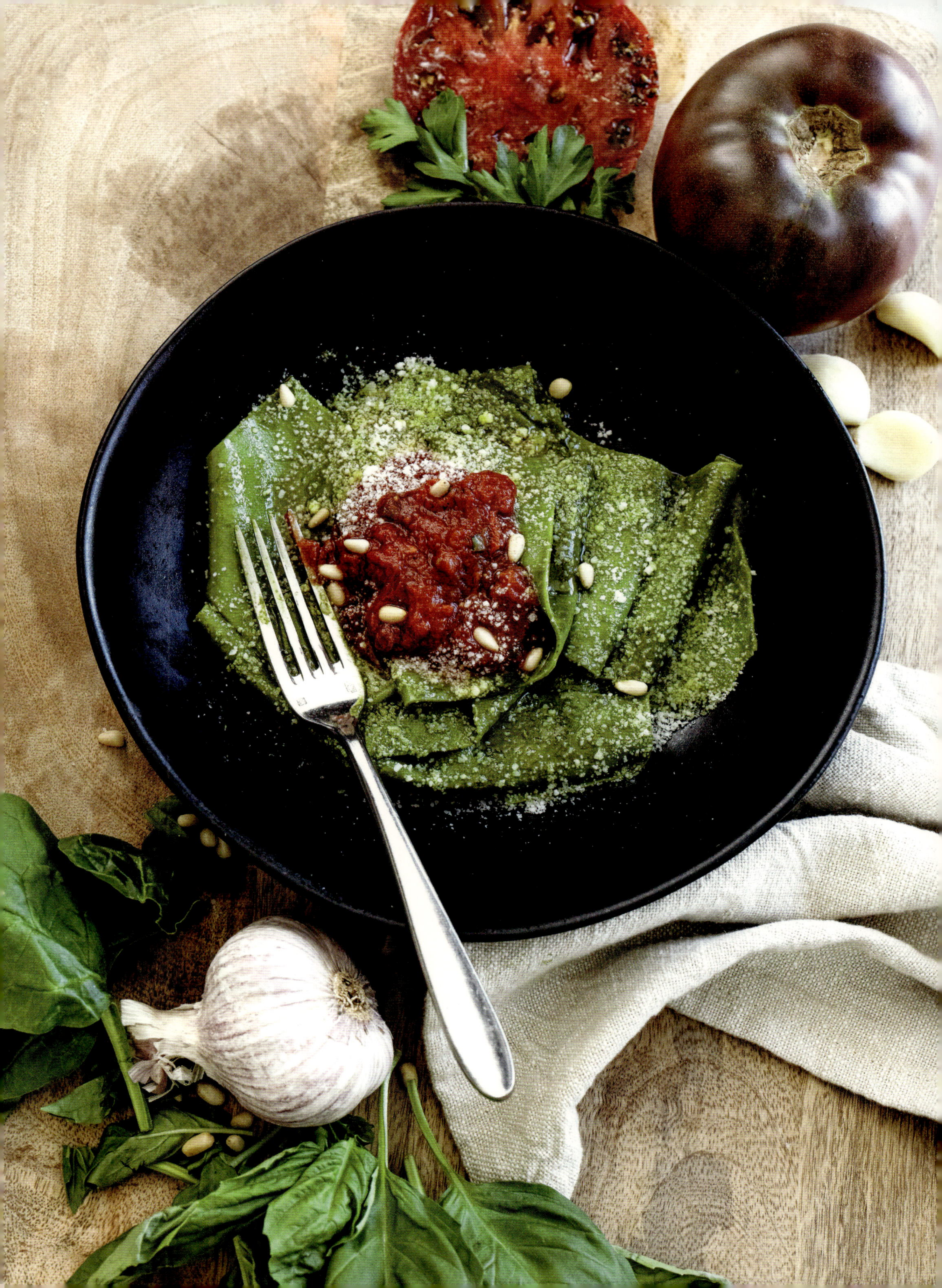

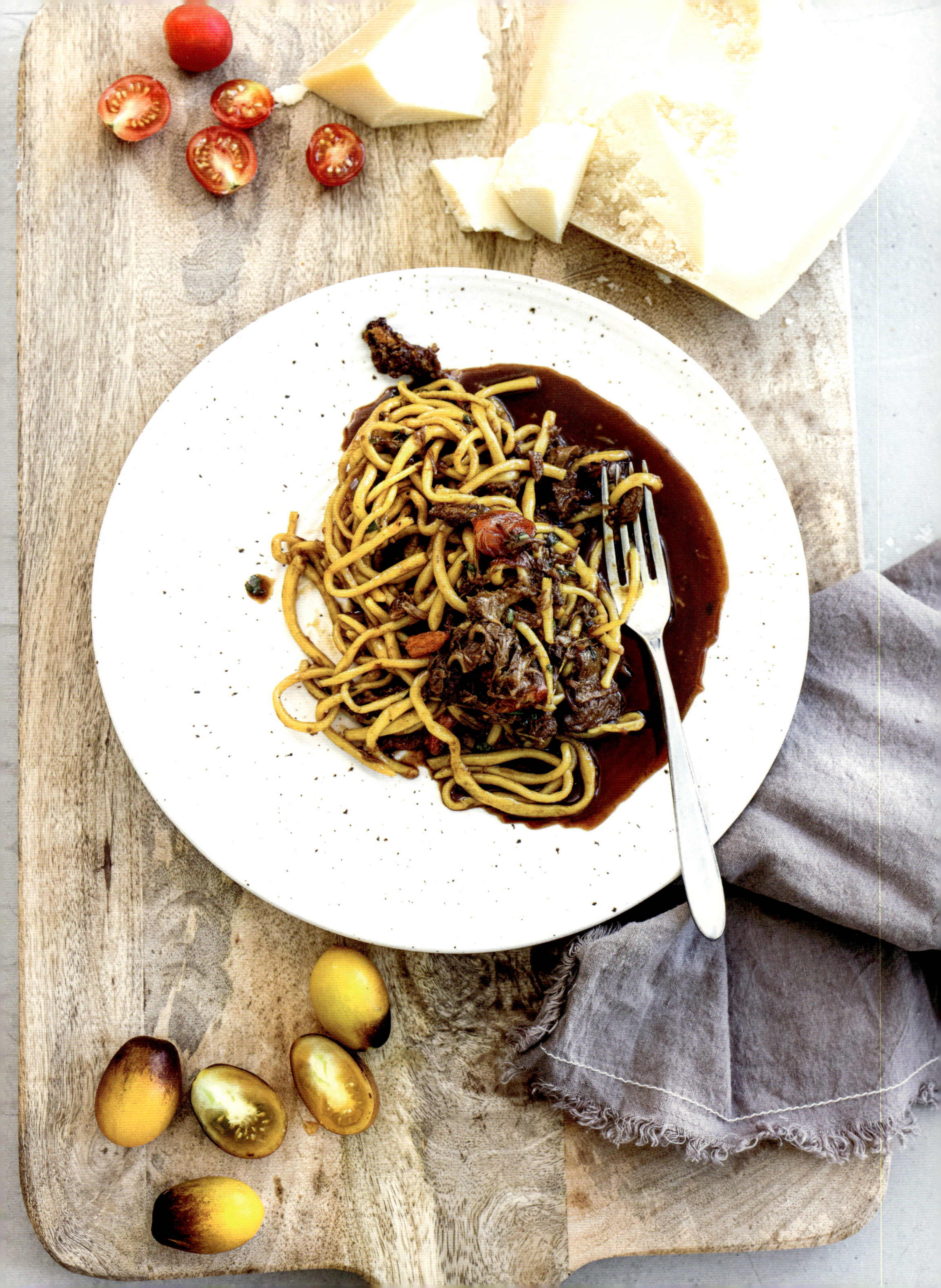

TUSCAN PICI NOODLES
with BRAISED SHORT RIBS and ROASTED CHERRY TOMATOES

Semolina Dough (page 92) at room temperature

½ cup all-purpose flour, for dusting

2 tablespoons kosher salt

3 tablespoons extra-virgin olive oil

1 tablespoon minced garlic

2 cups shredded meat from leftover Braised Beef Short Ribs (page 163)

1 cup leftover short rib sauce

1 cup Blistered Cherry Tomatoes (page 243)

4 tablespoons grated Grana Padano cheese

2 tablespoons diced fresh basil

High-quality extra-virgin olive oil, for drizzling

Pici is a rustic fat spaghetti from Tuscany. I have eaten this wormy-looking noodle many times in Florence, and I just love the toothiness of it. It looks perfectly imperfect and is always rolled by hand. This recipe makes use of leftover pot roast, and pici noodles are one of the easiest pastas to make at home. You won't need a pasta machine or a rolling pin. In fact, this eggless dough is also used for the Sardinian Lorighittas (page 120). // SERVES 4

ROLLING THE PICI

Prepare semolina dough recipe.

Pinch off a small portion of pasta dough about the size of a golf ball. Cover the remaining dough with a damp towel to prevent it from drying out. Flatten the dough ball into an oval. Then with both open palms, move your hands back and forth in front of you, rolling the oval into a log until it stretches and forms into a thin rope about ⅛ inch thick. Cut each strand into 8-inch sections. As you form and cut each pici strand, lay it on an all-purpose-flour-dusted baking sheet. You'll need about 20 pici strands per portion of pasta. Repeat the rolling technique until you have about 80 pici pasta strands.

MAKE THE PASTA DISH

Bring 6 quarts water and salt to a boil in a large stockpot.

While water is coming to a boil, swirl olive oil in a large skillet (with deep sides) over medium heat and add garlic. Cook until garlic is lightly golden. Add short rib meat, sauce and blistered tomatoes. Bring to a gentle boil and cook for 3 minutes. Turn heat off and keep warm.

Drop pici into the boiling water and cook for 6 to 8 minutes or until al dente (semolina dough makes a hearty and toothsome pasta and it takes longer to cook than other handmade pasta shapes). Before draining the cooked pasta, reserve 1 cup cooking water and set aside.

Drain pasta and toss into the skillet with the meat. Return skillet to medium-high heat and add half the reserved pasta water. Use tongs or a wooden spoon to toss and mix the pasta ingredients well. Add half of the Grana Padano cheese and all of the basil and keep tossing and mixing the pasta until the sauce looks emulsified. Add more reserved pasta water as needed to create a saucier pasta if desired.

Divide pasta between 4 warm bowls and sprinkle with remaining Grana Padano. Finish with a drizzle of olive oil.

3
ENTRÉES

We work with the seasons when determining what seafoods and meats go on the Farina menu, just like we do with our seasonal farm vegetables. While I support the whole locavore idea, one of the main responsibilities I have in my restaurants is teaching young culinarians. And for them to become skilled cooks, they need to work with seafood and meats from all over the world. Indeed, one of the greatest memories of my cooking life was working at Charlie Trotter's in Chicago. Food came in our back door from every region of the planet, and I saw more cool stuff there than I had ever seen before, like Spanish *percebes* (gooseneck barnacles in English), Buddha's hand citrus, live king crab, black truffles and Wagyu beef. Those experiences helped make me the chef I am today.

Our menu runs the culinary gamut, from dishes baked in casseroles and fish broiled under a salamander, to chops and steaks cooked over a wood-fired grill and seafood simply sautéed. I use these different cooking techniques along the kitchen hot line so our cooks can produce large volumes of food at a high level of execution.

Historically, entrées in the French tradition (what I trained in) usually come with a vegetable garnish and a starch component. The Italian table tends to be much simpler. The main protein might be all alone on the plate, with side dishes placed on the table, much like the steakhouse model. That's what I love about Italian cooking: It's rustic and naked at times, so the product had better be of high quality. I've spent much of my career looking to anoint a dish with the perfect dainty garnish or to meticulously cut the vegetables into impossibly tiny brunoise. In my Italian kitchen I need to remind myself to "let it go." Season the food correctly, cook it correctly and drizzle it with its own glorious juices. That should be enough, most of the time.

I've left some of these recipes open to interpretation as to what to serve with them. Everyone has their favorite standbys, so match them up with something I have provided in these pages, however you choose. But mostly, enjoy the cooking process, prep a few things in advance and then enjoy the meal you've just cooked with friends and family.

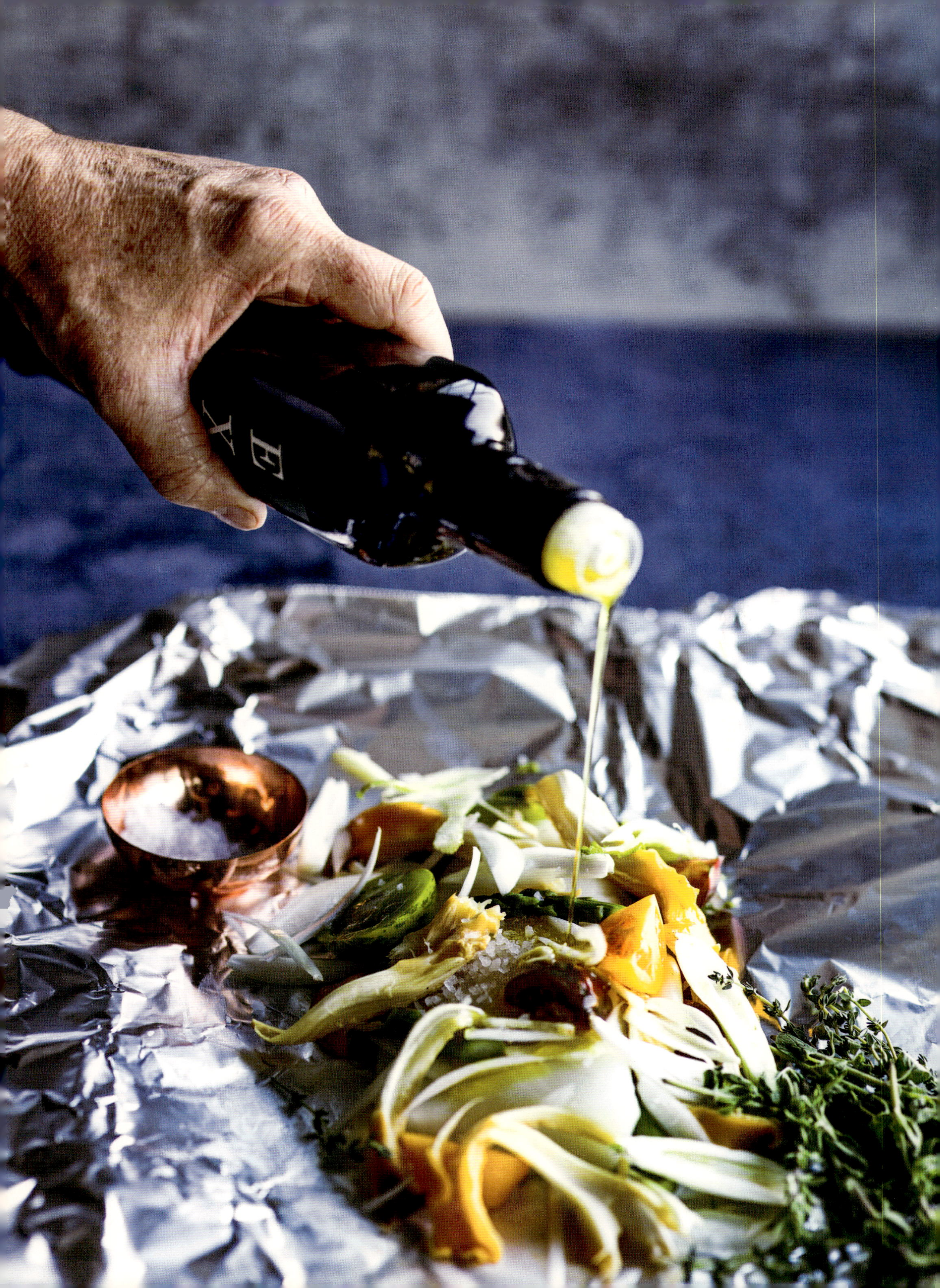

BAKED HALIBUT
with SUMMER VEGETABLES

4 halibut fillets (5 ounces each)

Kosher salt

2 shallots, peeled and thickly sliced

3 cloves garlic, peeled and thinly sliced

1 small green zucchini, diced large

1 small gold zucchini, diced large

1 large summer heirloom tomato, cut into thick wedges

1 bulb fennel, sliced very thin

1 cup fresh chanterelle mushrooms, cleaned and pulled into thin strips

¼ cup high-quality extra-virgin olive oil, plus more for foil

2 sprigs fresh thyme

1 tablespoon fresh chopped parsley

3 sprigs fresh oregano

½ cup Marsala wine

8 leaves fresh basil, stacked and diced

4 pieces tin foil (12" x 12")

I love grilling in the summer months, but halibut can be finicky on the grill because it easily sticks to the grates. To combat that, I build cooking vessels (papillotes) out of tin foil, allowing the fish to sit on the grill and cook through. So, it winds up being more baked than grilled, but the dish inevitably picks up the grill aromas, adding a nice finishing touch. To appease my family's insatiable appetite for vegetables (me, not so much), I also pack each vessel with seasonal vegetables, fresh herbs and great olive oil. // **SERVES 4**

Prepare an outdoor grill. Season halibut fillets on all sides with salt. Set aside.

Combine remaining ingredients except Marsala and basil in a large prep bowl and season with 2 teaspoons kosher salt. Toss well to coat. Set aside.

Lay foil pieces on a clean work surface. Use a pastry brush to smear olive oil on foil. Sprinkle foil lightly with salt. Place a halibut fillet in the middle of each piece of foil. Evenly divide the vegetable mixture on and around the halibut. Drizzle Marsala evenly over halibut and vegetables.

For each papillote, raise two opposite edges of foil, press them together and fold them to seal at the top, then fold the sides of the foil packet to seal completely.

Place foil packs on prepared grill and cook for 12 minutes. Remove the halibut packets onto a large baking tray. Open foil packets and sprinkle basil evenly over the contents.

To serve, place the cooked foil fish boats on platters on the table as is. The aroma is awesome!

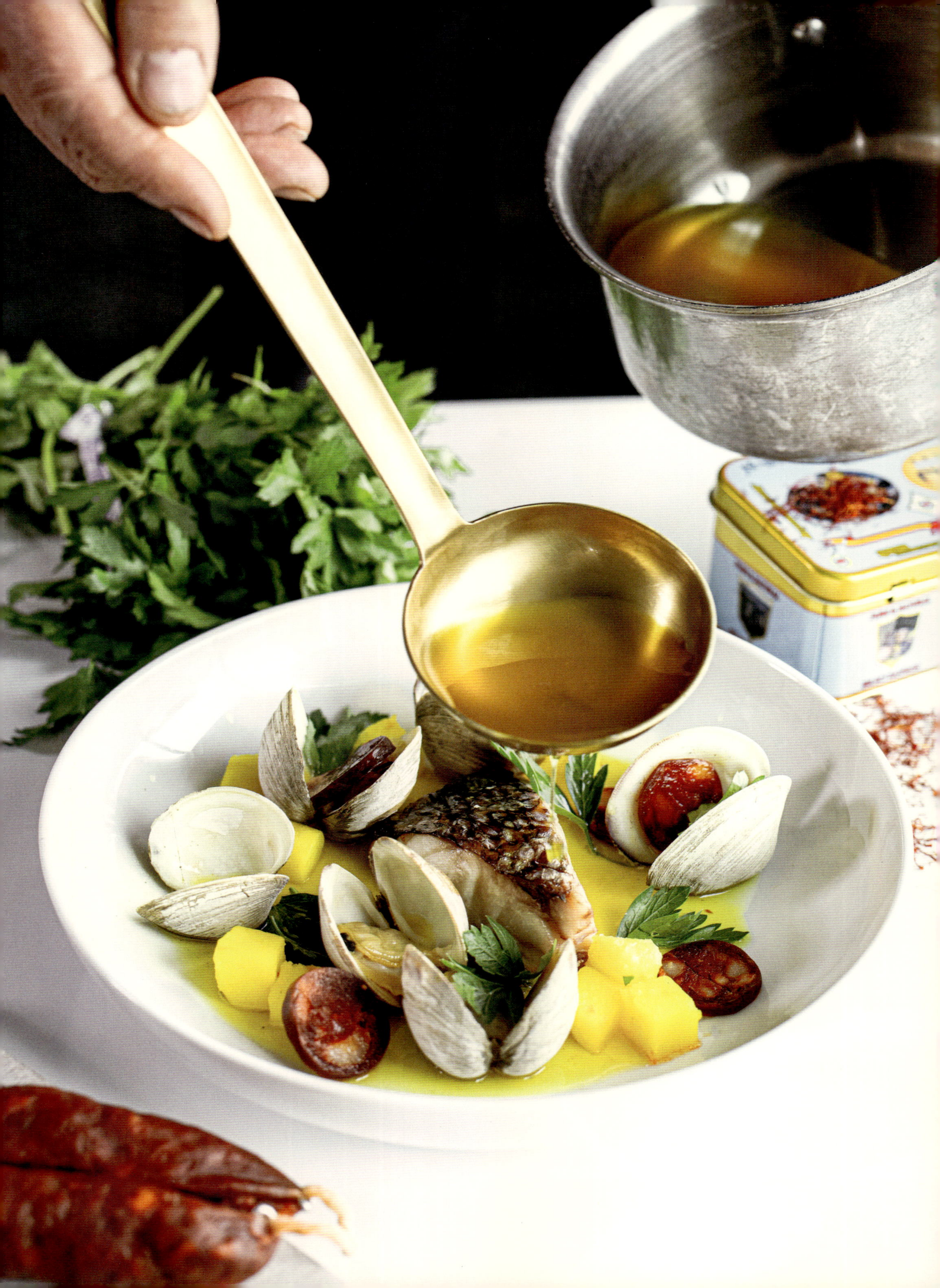

STRIPED BASS
with SAFFRON BROTH, CLAMS and CHORIZO

4 skin-on striped bass fillets (4 ounces each; or substitute branzino)

3 teaspoons kosher salt, divided

1 teaspoon Spanish smoked paprika

2 dozen Manila clams

2 cups Poultry Broth (page 237; or substitute water)

½ cup dry white wine

1 shallot, sliced

1 clove garlic, mashed

1 bay leaf

2 sprigs fresh thyme

6 small Yukon gold potatoes, cut in half

1 pinch saffron threads

1 Spanish chorizo (6 inches long), cut into thin coins (do not substitute Mexican chorizo)

½ cup chopped fresh parsley

2 tablespoons extra-virgin olive oil

I fell in love with American sea bass (stripers) in 1991 when there was a teachers' strike on the East Coast and some educators began fishing commercially for stripers to make up for lost wages. I was working at Carlo's Restaurant in Chicago at the time, and we received weekly shipments of the "schoolteacher striped bass." They're majestic (and well-educated) creatures. // SERVES 4

Using a paper towel, pat fish fillets dry on both sides, then sprinkle both sides with 2 teaspoons salt and smoked paprika. Place fillets skin side up in the refrigerator for 1 to 2 hours to dry out the skin.

Combine clams with poultry broth (or water), white wine, shallot, garlic, bay leaf and thyme in a large skillet. Cover and place over high heat to steam open the clams, approximately 5 minutes. Strain liquid from clams into a separate sauce pot and discard the aromatics. Remove clams to a prep bowl and cover with plastic wrap; keep warm.

Heat clam liquid over low heat and add potatoes, remaining 1 teaspoon salt and saffron. Simmer slowly over low heat until potatoes are cooked through, approximately 12 minutes. Add chorizo and parsley for 1 minute and then turn off heat. Set aside.

Heat a large nonstick sauté pan over medium-high heat and add olive oil. Add 4 fish fillets, skin side down, and cook for 4 minutes. Press lightly on the flesh with a metal spatula to ensure the skin is flat. Reduce heat to medium low and continue to cook from the bottom up for another 4 minutes. Flip the fish over and cook for 1 minute to finish cooking the flesh side. Remove fillets to a paper towel-lined baking sheet.

Have on hand 4 shallow entrée bowls. Place a fillet in the center of each bowl. Divide warm clams evenly between bowls. Spoon potatoes and chorizo into each bowl, then pour warm broth over everything in each bowl.

SEAFOOD

LAKE SUPERIOR WHITEFISH
with MUJADARA

4 6-ounce skin-on whitefish fillets (or substitute any white, flaky fish with skin)

2 large Spanish onions, halved lengthwise

2 tablespoons kosher salt, divided, plus more to taste

2 tablespoons ground cumin, divided

4 pinches cinnamon, divided

4 pinches ground coriander, divided

1 cup jasmine rice

½ cup green lentils

½ cup red lentils

½ cup extra-virgin olive oil, divided

1 tablespoon unsalted butter

4 garlic cloves, thinly sliced

1 bay leaf

½ cup fresh parsley, roughly chopped

½ cup fresh cilantro, roughly chopped

High-quality extra-virgin olive oil, for drizzling

4 lemon wedges, for garnish

Summer heirloom tomatoes, sliced, as accompaniment

I have always liked bringing unfamiliar or uncommon ingredients into my cooking, and I love the flavors of Sicily and Sardinia. Those Italian island cuisines incorporate many spices, fruits and berries from the Arab food lexicon. Mujadara is a wonderfully aromatic rice and lentil dish from Lebanon that works perfectly with the mild and flaky whitefish from the icy waters of the Great Lakes. Don't forget to plan ahead for this recipe, to allow the fish to dry in the refrigerator for a few hours before frying.

// SERVES 4

TO PREP THE FISH

About 4 to 5 hours before serving, pat the fish dry with a paper towel. Refrigerate it uncovered, skin-side up, on a baking sheet to dry before frying.

TO MAKE THE MUJADARA

Thinly slice 3 onion halves into half-moons. Mince the fourth onion half and set all the onions aside, keeping minced onions separate.

Combine 3 cups water, 1 teaspoon salt, 1 teaspoon cumin, 1 pinch cinnamon and 1 pinch coriander in a small saucepan over medium-high heat. When water boils, stir in rice, return to a boil, cover the pan and adjust heat so rice simmers until al dente, 11 to 13 minutes. Strain rice if necessary, and transfer to a bowl. Set aside.

In a second small saucepan, combine 3 cups water, 1 tablespoon salt, 2 teaspoons cumin, 1 pinch cinnamon and 1 pinch coriander over medium-high heat. When water boils, stir in green lentils, return to a boil, then adjust heat so lentils simmer until al dente, about 25 to 30 minutes. Strain lentils, rinsing for a minute under cold water to stop the cooking. Drain well and transfer to a second bowl. Set aside.

To cook red lentils, combine 3 cups water, 2 teaspoons salt, 1½ teaspoons cumin, 1 pinch cinnamon and 1 pinch coriander in a small saucepan over medium-high heat. When water boils, stir in red lentils, return to a boil, then adjust heat so lentils simmer until al dente, about 10 to 12 minutes. Strain lentils, reserving 1 cup cooking liquid, and rinse lentils for a minute under cold water to stop the cooking. Drain well and add to the bowl of green lentils.

Heat 2 tablespoons olive oil and butter in a large skillet over medium-high heat. When butter melts, stir in minced onions and cook until onions soften and lightly caramelize, about 6 minutes. Add garlic, bay leaf, remaining 1½ teaspoons cumin, and remaining pinches cinnamon and coriander. Cook, stirring until spices are fragrant, about 2 minutes more, being careful not to burn the garlic or spices. Add ½ cup red lentil liquid and bring to a simmer. Stir the rice and lentils into the skillet, stirring well to mix in onions and spices. Remove from heat and set mujadara aside, keeping it warm.

Heat a wide, heavy-bottomed skillet on high heat. When the pan is hot, add 2 tablespoons olive oil, and when oil is hot enough that a slice of onion sizzles on contact, very carefully add just enough sliced onions to cover the surface of the pan completely (too many will cause onions to steam instead of fry). Allow to cook untouched for 1 minute. Stir onions, loosening any bits stuck to the pan. Stir occasionally at first, so onions continue to fry and brown but don't burn, then stir more often, adjusting the heat as necessary, until onions are deeply browned and crisp at the edges, 6 to 10 minutes. Turn them out onto a paper towel–lined plate. Add 2 tablespoons more olive oil to the pan and repeat the process until all the onions have been fried crisp and dark golden brown. Fold two-thirds of the onions into the mujadara, reserving the rest to garnish the fish.

TO MAKE THE FISH

Place a large nonstick pan over high heat and swirl 1 tablespoon olive oil around the pan. Sprinkle fillets generously on both sides with salt and lay fish in the pan, skin side down. Press gently on flesh side with a metal spatula so skin is flat against the pan. Turn the heat down to medium and cook for about 3 minutes. (Pressing the fillet firmly into the pan helps keep the skin flat and crisps it more completely.) Continue to cook for another 5 to 7 minutes, until skin is crisp and flesh has mostly cooked through from the bottom up. Flip fillets and cook just until opaque all the way through, about 1 minute more. Use a spatula to turn fish fillets out onto a paper towel, skin side up, to drain.

When fish is ready to serve, add cilantro and parsley to the mujadara and toss lightly until evenly distributed. Correct with salt as needed.

TO SERVE

Spoon mujadara onto a large serving platter. Arrange whitefish fillets skin side up over the top and garnish the crispy fish skins with remaining fried onions. Drizzle extra-virgin olive oil on and around the fillets and serve with fresh lemon wedges.

The finished dish is full of enticing warm, herbaceous spice on the palate, and the acid of the lemon brightens and lifts it to another level. For more Mediterranean verve, serve the mujadara with a side plate of sliced and seasoned summer heirloom tomatoes.

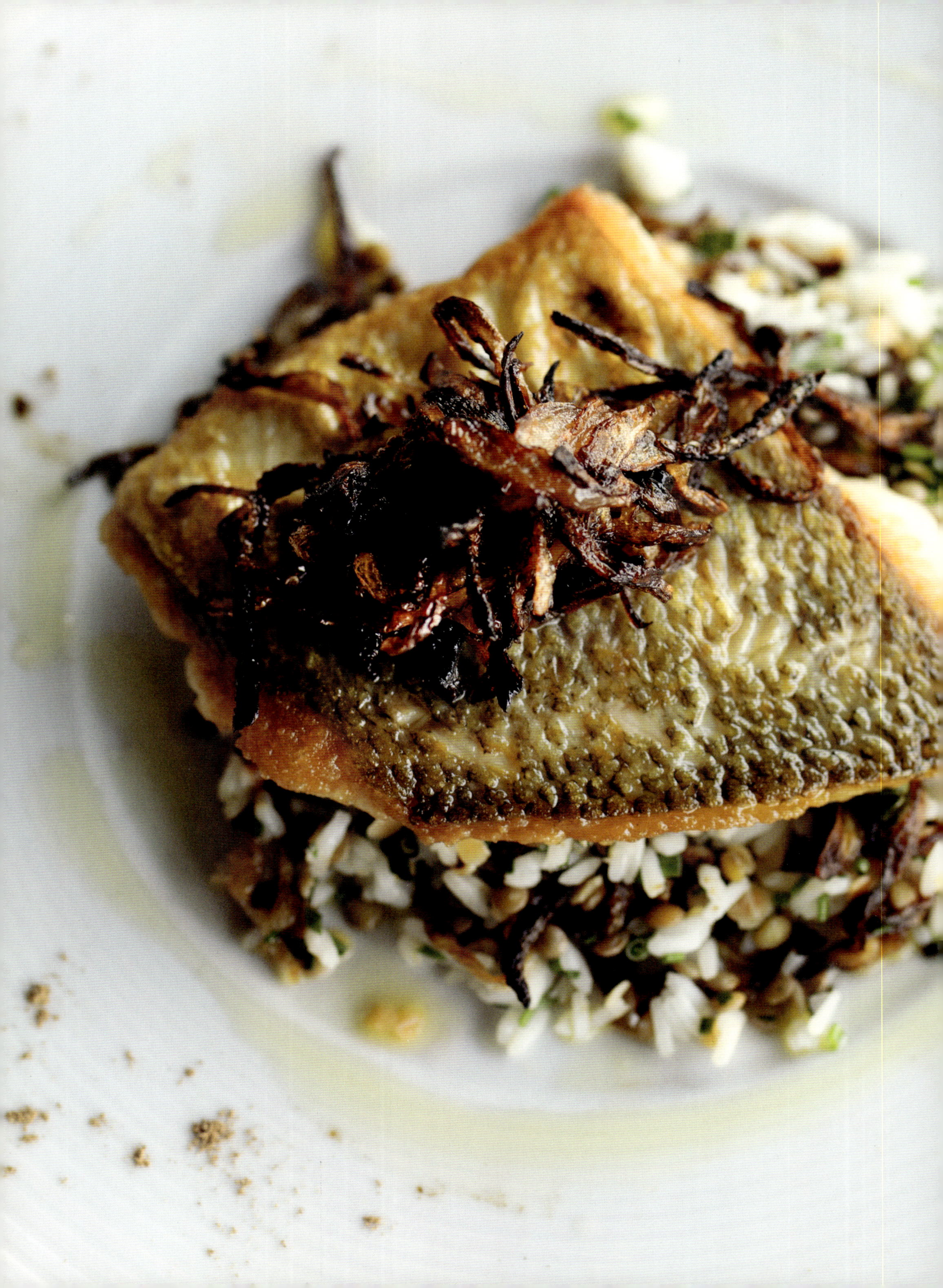

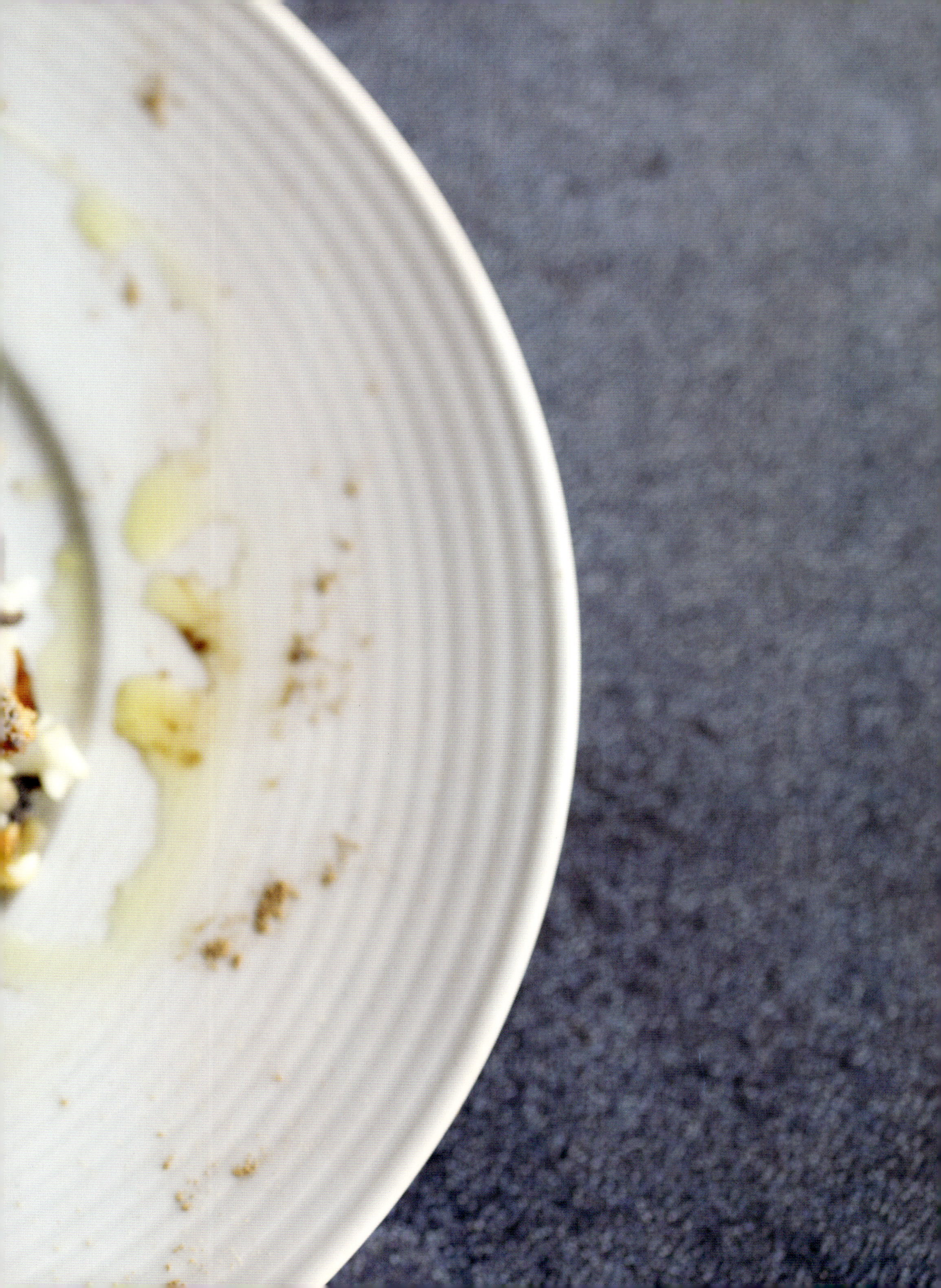

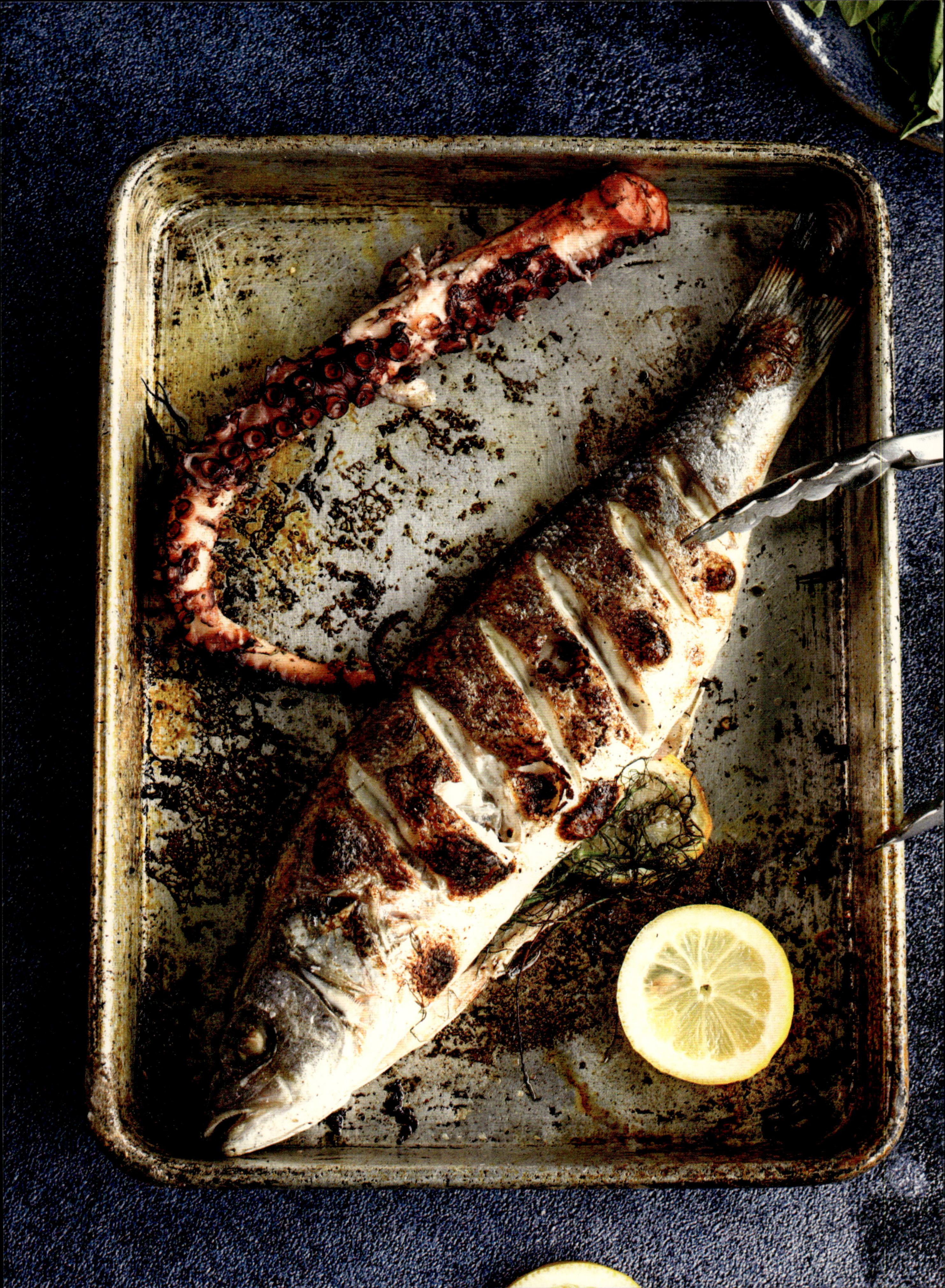

WHOLE OVEN ROASTED BRANZINO
with ARUGULA, FENNEL and LEMON

1 small bulb fennel, halved then sliced very thin with a sharp mandoline

2 cups arugula

2 shallots, thinly sliced

2 medium garlic cloves, thinly sliced

2 tablespoons fresh oregano leaves

1 tablespoon fresh thyme leaves

1 lemon, halved, one half cut into 10 slices

1/3 cup high-quality extra-virgin olive oil, divided

1 whole branzino (3 pounds), head and tail on

Kosher salt

Freshly ground black pepper

We get our whole branzino (European sea bass) from the waters of the Ionian and Mediterranean seas. And of course, we whole-roast them over a wood fire with all their friends like fennel, garlic and lemons. Just like they do along the Mediterranean coastline.
// **MAKES 1 WHOLE FISH**

Preheat an outdoor grill to high heat or preheat oven to 400°F.

Divide sliced fennel into 2 prep bowls. Add arugula to 1 bowl then refrigerate.

Add shallots, garlic, herbs and sliced lemons to second bowl of fennel and mix well with your hands or tongs. This bowl of fennel will be divided into thirds. Set aside.

Prepare a parchment paper–lined baking sheet large enough to hold the branzino. Use a pastry brush to cover the paper with a thin layer of olive oil. Scatter one-third of the fennel blend on the baking sheet, concentrating on the area where the fish will lie, then set aside.

Wash branzino under cold water, making sure to rinse the cavity of the branzino belly. Use scissors to clip the fins from each side of the fish. There are fins on either side of the head, two on the top ridge of the back and one below, near the tail. Cut the fins off as close to the body as possible and discard. With the fish lying on its side and the head to your right, make 5 slits into the flesh with a sharp knife. Start at the top and angle left as you slice into the flesh. Flip the branzino over and repeat cutting 5 slits on this side.

Sprinkle the fish cavity and both sides of the branzino flesh with salt and pepper. Fill the cavity lightly with a third of the fennel blend, then press it closed and lay the fish on the fennel-covered baking sheet. Scatter remaining third of fennel blend on top of branzino and drizzle a little olive oil over the flesh.

If using an outdoor grill, oil the grill grates and place fish directly on the grill; cook for 6 minutes on each side. If you think the fish might stick to the grill grates, use a sheet of tin foil under the fish.

If using an oven, bake branzino on the fennel-prepared baking sheet, uncovered, for 10 to 12 minutes or until fish is cooked through. Transfer cooked branzino to a serving platter. For an extra boost of deliciousness, scrape the blistered and charred aromatic vegetables onto the platter.

Squeeze lemon juice and drizzle olive oil into the reserved bowl of fennel and arugula. Season lightly with salt and pepper. Mix well, then lay the arugula salad on the platter next to the branzino. Finish the dish with one last squeeze of lemon juice and a sturdy drizzle of exceptional extra-virgin olive oil.

SEAFOOD

SEARED ARCTIC CHAR
and SAUCE VIERGE

SAUCE VIERGE

3 large ripe red tomatoes

½ cup fresh lemon juice

½ cup high-quality extra-virgin olive oil

1 shallot, minced

1 tablespoon coriander seeds

1 teaspoon fresh thyme leaves

1 teaspoon fresh mint, chiffonade

1 tablespoon fresh chives, minced

2 tablespoons fresh basil, diced

1 teaspoon kosher salt

Freshly ground black pepper

ARCTIC CHAR AND SERVING

1 tablespoon extra-virgin olive oil

4 arctic char fillets, refrigerated skin side up to stay dry

Kosher salt

2 cups arugula

1 cup purslane

Freshly ground black pepper

When I first arrived in Cassis, France, to work at La Presqu'île, I learned to make two items pretty quickly. One was sauce vierge and the other was rouille, the rusty red cousin of aioli (see Note). Sauce vierge is on menus throughout the south of France and it embodies everything a delicious tomato sauce should be. The sauce was developed in 1976 by Chef Michel Guérard as he was introducing nouvelle cuisine to the world, along with other chefs like Alain Chapel and Michel Troigros. It means "virgin sauce" and is an uncooked, chunky tomato vinaigrette. Olive oil plus fresh tomatoes plus herbs . . . bingo! // SERVES 4

MAKE SAUCE VIERGE

Bring a medium-size pot of water to a boil.

Prepare a prep bowl with an ice bath. Drop tomatoes in the boiling water for 30 seconds. Transfer tomatoes to the ice bath with a long-handled skimmer. Remove from ice after 5 minutes and dry off. Discard the ice bath.

Peel tomatoes, discard skin and dice tomatoes into small cubes. In a medium prep bowl, combine diced tomatoes, lemon juice, olive oil, shallot, coriander seeds and all herbs. Add salt and sprinkle with freshly ground black pepper; stir to mix well. Set aside.

MAKE ARCTIC CHAR

Place a large nonstick pan over high heat and swirl olive oil around the pan. Sprinkle fish fillets generously on both sides with salt and lay them skin side down in the pan. Press gently on the flesh side with a metal spatula so the skin is flat against the pan. Reduce heat to medium and cook for 8 to 10 minutes, until skin is crisp and flesh is mostly cooked through from the bottom up. Flip fillets and cook until the flesh is opaque all the way through, approximately 1 minute. Use a spatula to transfer fish fillets to a paper towel to absorb excess oil.

TO SERVE

Combine arugula and purslane in a salad bowl and sprinkle lightly with salt and pepper. Lay a bouquet of greens on each of 4 dinner plates and place cooked char next to the salad. Spoon a generous amount of sauce vierge on the char and around the plate.

The first time I made rouille (saffron and tomato aioli to garnish bouillabaisse) in Cassis, I asked the chef where I should store it. He said, "Put it over on the windowsill." I was shocked but did as I was told. What surprised me was the fact that rouille, which is basically a raw egg mayonnaise, would be stored in the refrigerator in America. Not on a sunny windowsill, in the south of France, by the sea, in the dead heat of summer! But things are different in the old country.

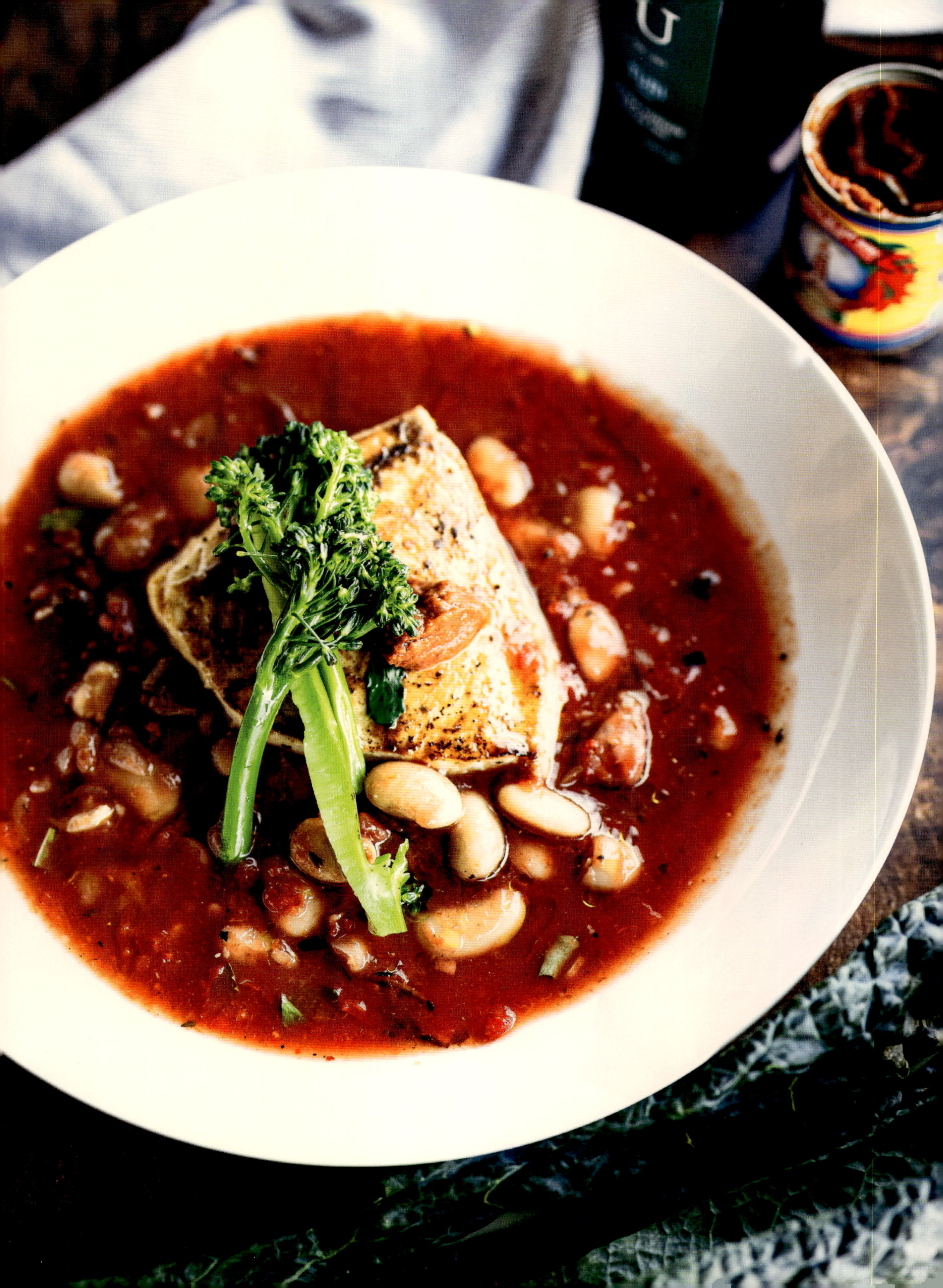

SEAFOOD

SWORDFISH
with BROCCOLINI, OLIVES and WHITE BEANS

4 center-cut swordfish steaks (6 ounces each and 1 inch thick)

½ cup high-quality extra-virgin olive oil, divided

1 tablespoon fresh thyme leaves, divided

2 teaspoons fresh marjoram or oregano leaves

1 tablespoon plus 1 teaspoon kosher salt, divided, plus more to season fish

½ teaspoon ground black pepper, plus more to season fish

1 Spanish onion, minced

4 large garlic cloves, minced

28-ounce can San Marzano crushed tomatoes

12-ounce jar cooked corona beans, drained and rinsed (or substitute lupini beans)

16 Taggiasca olives (or substitute Kalamata olives)

1 bay leaf

8 broccolini stalks, ends trimmed

4 teaspoons harissa paste

½ cup fresh Italian parsley leaves (for garnish)

At Farina we cook swordfish steaks over a wood-fired grill and serve them alongside Taggiasca olives and corona beans. I also like to use northern African spices to accentuate this dish, because I think they are easily identifiable with Sicilian cooking due to Sicily's proximity to the African continent. Don't fret if wood-fire grilling isn't your thing; the swordfish also flourishes in a cast-iron skillet. // **SERVES 4**

Drizzle fish with a light coating of olive oil, smearing on both sides. Rub half the thyme leaves and all the marjoram between the palms of your hands, then sprinkle on the oiled fish. Season with salt and pepper and refrigerate, covered, until ready to grill, up to 1 day in advance.

To cook beans, heat 2 tablespoons olive oil in a saucepan over medium-high heat. Add onions and sweat for 2 minutes, then add garlic. Stir and cook for another minute. Add tomatoes, beans, olives, ¼ cup olive oil, remaining thyme, bay leaf, 1 teaspoon salt and black pepper to the pan. Bring to a boil then reduce heat to a simmer. Cook over low heat for about 10 minutes, stirring occasionally.

While beans are cooking, bring 2 quarts water and remaining 1 tablespoon salt to a boil in a medium saucepan. Blanch broccolini for 6 minutes. Drain and keep warm.

Prepare a very hot (400 to 500°F) fire in an outdoor grill. Grill fish for 3 to 4 minutes on each side, until opaque throughout. (Alternatively, place a large cast-iron skillet on the stove over high heat until it starts to smoke. Swirl in 1 tablespoon olive oil, and carefully arrange fish steaks in the pan so they are not touching. Sear for 3 minutes on each side, until opaque throughout.)

To serve, divide bean stew among 4 shallow bowls and top each with a swordfish steak. Lay 2 stalks of broccolini on top of each steak, then spoon a teaspoon-size dollop of harissa onto each steak. Drizzle it all with a bit more olive oil, and sprinkle parsley leaves randomly over each finished bowl.

> The bean stew can be cooked several days ahead and stored in an airtight container in the refrigerator. The fish can be marinated overnight or for several days if it is very fresh.

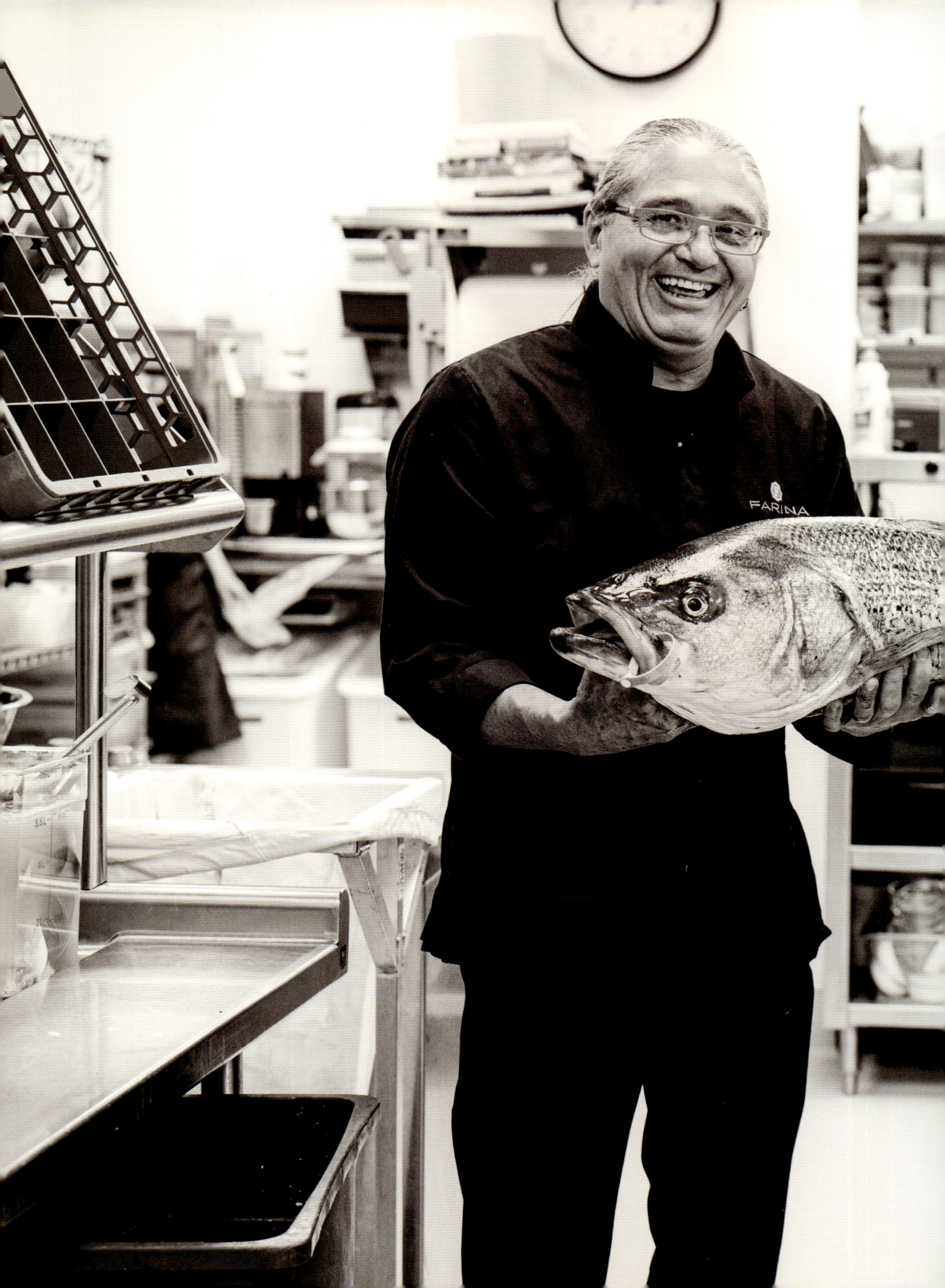
FARINA

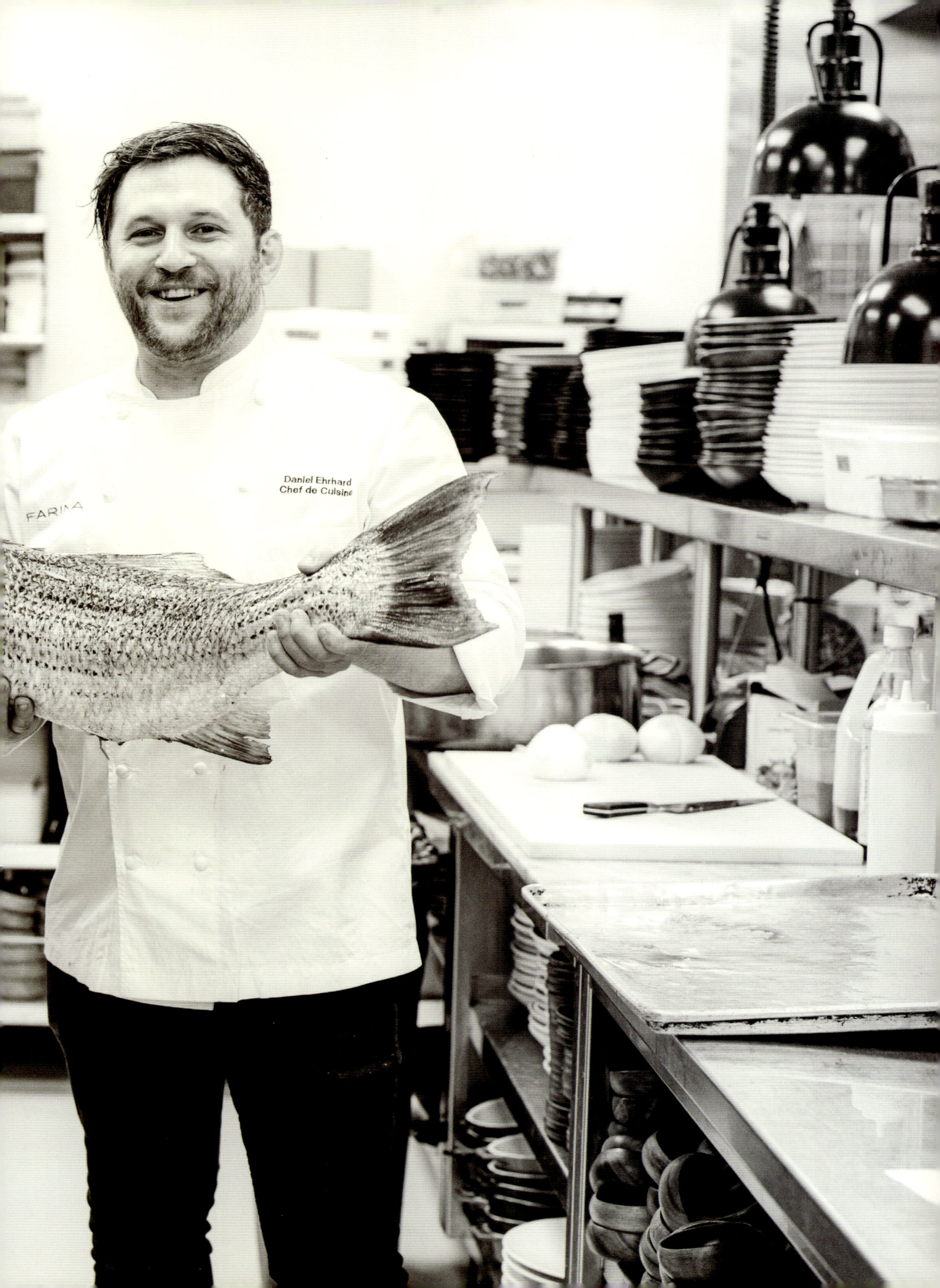
Daniel Ehrhard
Chef de Cuisine
FARINA

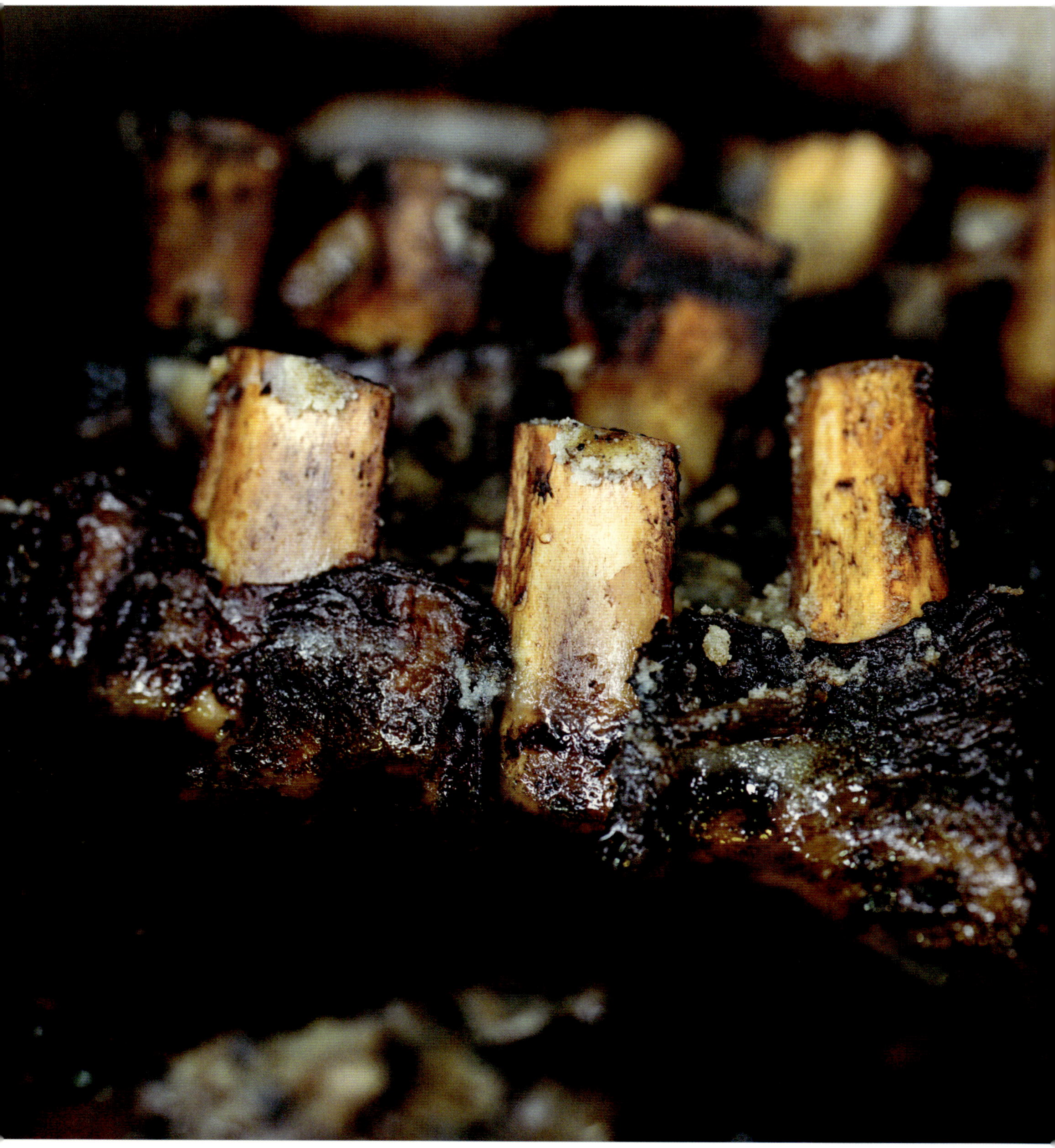

BRAISED BEEF SHORT RIBS

5 pounds boneless short ribs

1 tablespoon salt

1 tablespoon ground black pepper

½ cup canola oil

1 cup carrots, roughly chopped

1 cup Spanish onions, diced large

1 cup celery, roughly chopped

12 cloves garlic, mashed

2 Calabrian chili peppers, chopped

1 bay leaf

4 sprigs fresh thyme

4 sprigs fresh oregano

4 sprigs fresh Italian parsley

1 cup pomegranate molasses

½ cup tomato paste

2 cups red wine

2 tablespoons all-purpose flour

3 quarts Bone Broth (page 236)

Nancy is always insisting that I put these on the menu. They certainly have a well-deserved spot in our collection of dishes, but I only have a finite number of entrée slots on the menu. So, I generally wait until winter to offer these, because the short ribs are so rich and deeply flavorful. Winter also gives Nancy plenty of time to search far and wide for the perfect big red wine to match. Recent favorites include Gianni Gagliardo Barolo or Chappellet Mountain Cuvée. // SERVES 4

Preheat oven to 300°F.

Liberally season short ribs with salt and pepper. Heat canola oil in a large braising pan over high heat. Working in batches, sear short ribs on all sides, about 5 minutes per batch. Transfer short ribs to a plate.

Add carrots, onions, celery, garlic, chili peppers and herbs to the same braising pan. (Use a paper towel to wipe away any darkly burnt spots; deep brown glazing is fine and helps develop the sauce.) Cook over medium-high heat, stirring often, until vegetables are lightly browned, about 5 minutes. Reduce heat to medium-low and stir in pomegranate molasses and tomato paste. Stir constantly for 2 minutes. Add red wine, reduce heat to a low simmer and cook for 5 minutes. Put flour in a small fine strainer, then work with a wooden spoon in one hand and the strainer of flour in the other. Shake a little bit of flour over the syrupy liquid and stir well with the wooden spoon. Repeat until the flour is gone. Next, add bone broth to the braising pan and bring to a boil. Add short ribs back to the pan of boiling sauce, cover the pan with a lid or foil and transfer to the oven. Cook until short ribs are tender, about 3 hours.

Remove from oven and let cool in sauce for 20 minutes. Transfer short ribs to a platter.

Separate the braising vegetables and herbs from the meat. Save them for another recipe such as soup or bone broth. Strain the liquid into a stainless steel bowl. Let the sauce sit for 10 minutes and the fat will rise to the top. Spoon fat from the surface of the sauce and discard. Correct the sauce with salt if necessary and more broth if it is too thick.

Serve short ribs in the braising pan directly on the table, or on a family-style platter, or portion the short ribs individually and serve in shallow entrée bowls.

> At Farina we serve short ribs with many different garnishes, depending on the season, with heavier accompaniments in the fall and winter and lighter accompaniments in the summer and spring. In the fall we like to serve the ribs with mashed potatoes or polenta; braised winter root vegetables are delicious as well. In spring or summer, you can't go wrong with fresh peas, fava beans and asparagus.

MEATS

POMEGRANATE MOLASSES MARINATED
TOMAHAWK PORK CHOPS

1 cup Pomegranate Molasses Marinade (page 249)

3 sprigs fresh thyme

3 sprigs fresh oregano

6 cloves garlic, crushed

2 tomahawk pork chops (25 ounces each)

Kosher salt

Freshly cracked black pepper

Who doesn't love caramelized pork chops? And tomahawk chops at that. After the chops are done cooking, give them one last brush of the pomegranate molasses. Also, I highly recommend accompanying this recipe with an Heirloom Tomato and Missouri Peach Salad (page 47) and our Mashed Potatoes (page 239). // **SERVES 2**

Combine marinade, thyme, oregano and garlic in a prep bowl and mix well.

Massage the marinade into both sides of the pork chops, then sprinkle generously with salt and pepper on both sides. Place on a large baking sheet, cover with plastic wrap and marinate for at least 24 hours in the refrigerator.

Prepare an outdoor grill to 400°F.

Grill chops for 3 minutes on each side (pomegranate molasses is very sticky and will burn quickly, so you may need to flip chops multiple times to prevent over-charring).

> If the grill is too hot and aggressive, transfer chops to a large baking sheet and finish them in a preheated 375°F oven, for approximately 8 minutes. I like to cook my pork chops to a little over medium in temperature, heading toward medium-well.

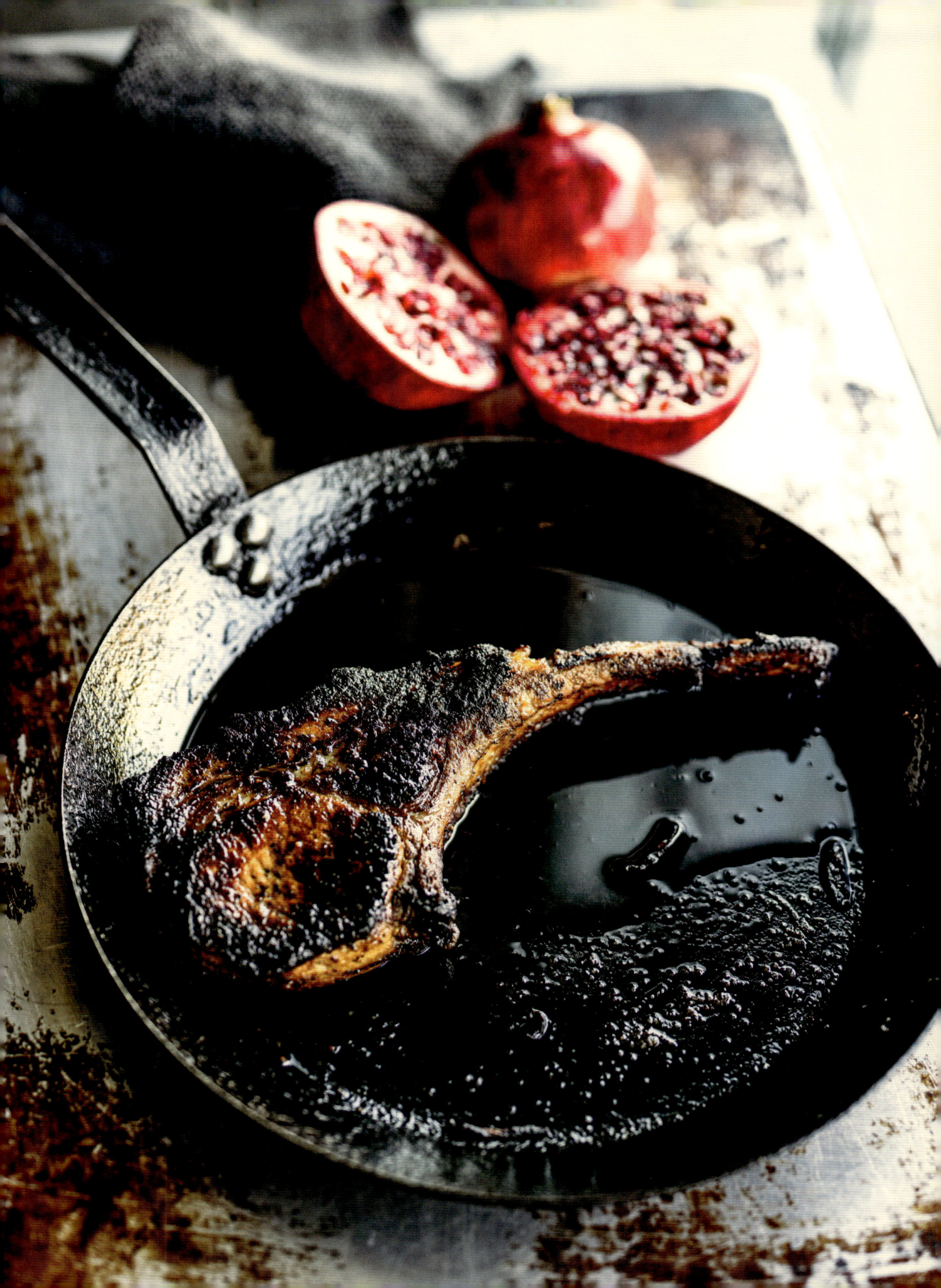

MEATS

DUCK BREAST APICIUS
with FOIE GRAS

4 duck breasts (8 ounces each, skin on)

Kosher salt

½ cup Apicius Spice Mix (page 248)

1 ¼ cup Madeira wine, divided

2 tablespoons light honey

1 tablespoon fresh thyme leaves, divided

2 large shallots, finely diced, divided into 3 portions

2 cloves garlic, smashed

2 tablespoons unsalted butter, divided

1 tablespoon black peppercorns

1 cup demi-glace (store-bought)

2 bunches Tuscan black kale, leaves picked from stems and washed (see Chef's Tip, below)

Freshly ground black pepper

1 cup fresh chanterelles, washed and cleaned of debris

4 foie gras medallions (2 ounces each, ½ inch thick)

John Starr, a gastronome and longtime Farina regular, has traveled the world multiple times over and often sends me photos of noteworthy dishes. Upon returning from one of his culinary conquests, he requested that I cook him Roast Duck Apicius, a classic preparation from the early days of French cookery based on a beloved recipe by the first-century Roman gourmet Marcus Gavius Apicius, to whom the ancient cookbook *Apicius* is attributed. The mélange of spices wafting through your kitchen will be warm and familiar yet exotic and provocative when you're preparing this marvelous duck dish.   // **SERVES 4**

Set each duck breast skin side down on a work surface. Trim any excess skin that protrudes from the natural shape of the breast. Turn the breasts over, skin side up. Using a sharp boning knife, score the skin in a crosshatch pattern, making the crosshatches in ¼-inch intervals across the skin (this helps the fat render and will yield crispier skin). Place scored breasts on a baking sheet and sprinkle generously with salt and Apicius spice mix.

In a small bowl, combine ¼ cup Madeira, honey and half the thyme leaves and mix well. Pour honey mixture over duck breasts and massage the marinade and spices into the flesh and skin. Set aside at room temperature for 45 minutes.

While duck is marinating, sweat 1 portion of shallot and 1 garlic clove in a small sauce pot with 1 tablespoon butter for 2 minutes. Add remaining thyme, peppercorns and ½ cup Madeira to the sauce pot and bring to a boil. Reduce the liquid by half, then add demi-glace and bring to a boil. Reduce the heat and simmer on low heat for 5 minutes without stirring. Strain demi-glace into a clean sauce pot and add remaining ½ cup Madeira. Set aside and keep warm.

Roughly chop kale leaves and combine in a small saucepan over low heat with remaining 1 tablespoon butter, ½ cup water and a second portion of minced shallots. Cook kale for 25 minutes or until leaves are tender. If kale turns dry during cooking, add ¼ cup water to moisten. Repeat if necessary. Remove from heat, season with a pinch of salt and pepper. Keep warm.

Remove duck breasts from marinade and pat dry with a paper towel. Place breasts skin side down in a cold, large, nonstick sauté pan. Place pan on the stove on the lowest heat setting (the skin of the breasts needs to cook very slowly in order to render the most fat out of the skin, resulting in a crispier texture).

> To clean any variety of kale or Swiss chard, hold the end of the stalk in one hand and with your other hand put a light but full grasp around the end where the leaves start. Squeeze and pull your hand along the stalk firmly and the leaves will release from the stalk on both sides. Discard the stalk or, alternatively, peel the stalk with a vegetable peeler, then dice it finely and sauté it along with the leaves.

Continue cooking the breasts in their fat on low heat for 15 minutes, then transfer to a plate to rest. Strain seeds and spices out of the rendered duck fat. Pour the clean duck fat back into the sauté pan and adjust to medium-high heat. When the fat is almost smoking, add breasts back to the pan, skin side down. Sear them in the hot rendered duck fat for 1 minute to caramelize the skin. When breasts are ready to come out of the pan, turn the heat off and add remaining smashed garlic for a quick splash through the pan. Use tongs to lather the breasts in the caramelized garlic. Transfer breasts to a plate and let rest for 10 minutes to relax the meat.

With the duck pan still hot and the duck fat still in the pan, add chanterelles to the pan and cook for 3 minutes or until soft. Add the final portion of shallot at the end of cooking time and adjust the seasoning on the chanterelles with salt and pepper. Remove chanterelles to a small bowl and keep warm.

Discard any remaining duck fat and wipe the pan clean with a cloth. With no oil or butter in the pan, turn the heat on high, wait 1 minute, then sear foie gras slices for 1 minute on each side (foie gras will release quite a bit of fat during the cooking process). Transfer foie gras to a paper towel–lined plate. Save foie gras fat (in the pan) for another use.

To serve, place a small mound of kale in the middle of each of 4 warm dinner plates. Slice each duck breast in half lengthwise and nestle both halves of duck into the kale so that the beautiful pink flesh is visible. Place a seared slice of foie gras on top of each serving. Sprinkle chanterelles around the edges of the kale and finally, spoon Madeira sauce over the top of the foie gras and around the edge of the chanterelles.

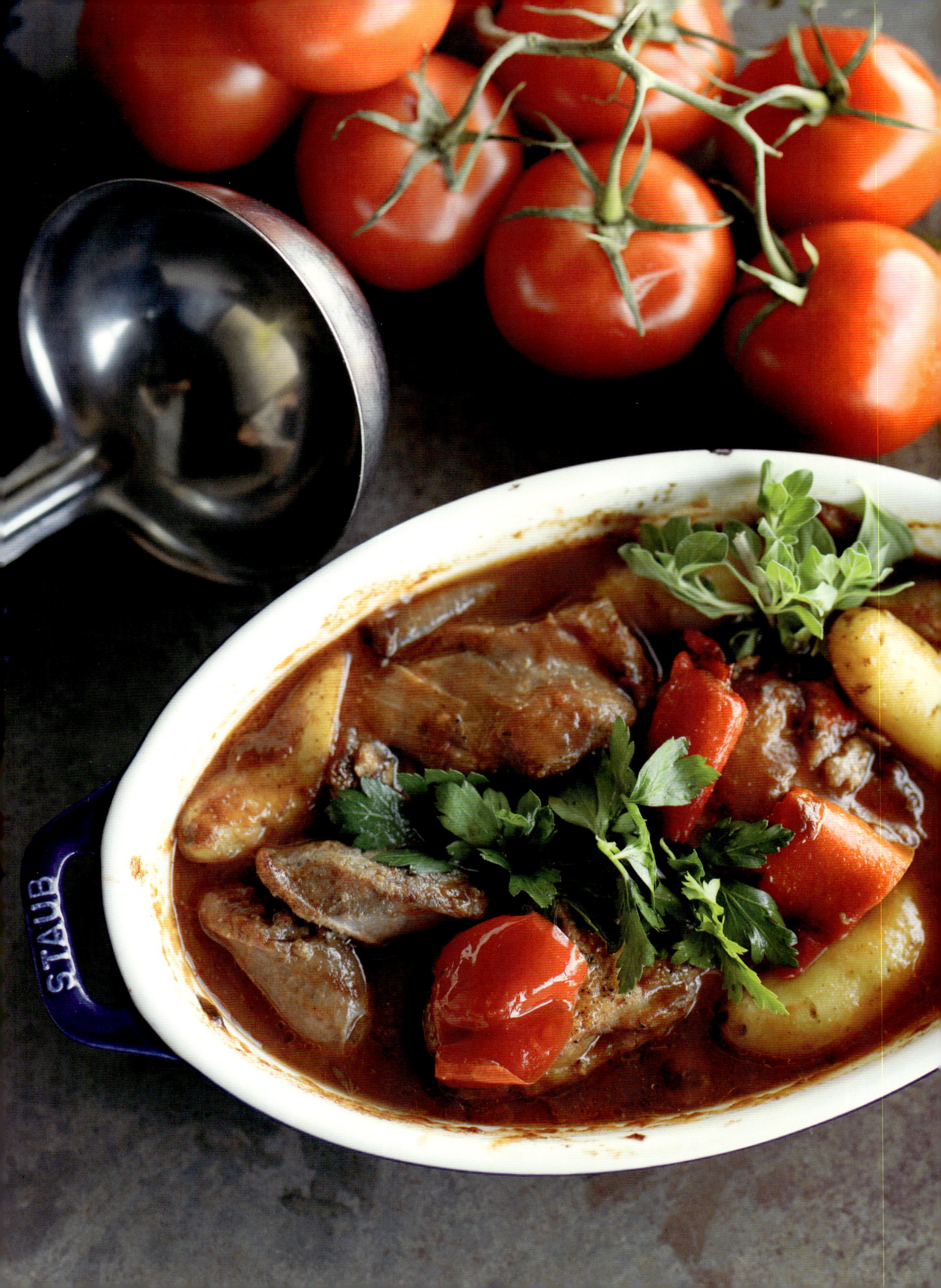
STAUB

CHICKEN SCARPARIELLO

This classic Italian-American dish, also known as shoemaker's chicken, usually goes on the Farina winter menu because the spicy tomato broth provides warmth from the cold Kansas City climate. This recipe calls for sliced potatoes, but I often eat mine with mashed potatoes to soak up the crazy-good chicken sauce.
// SERVES 4

Ingredients

- ¼ cup apple cider vinegar
- 1 cup white wine
- ¼ cup pickled cherry pepper juice
- 3 tablespoons extra-virgin olive oil
- 8 chicken thighs
- 4 mild Italian sausage links
- 4 large shallots, sliced in half lengthwise
- 10 whole garlic cloves
- 2 red bell peppers, seeds and stems discarded, each cut into 4 large squares
- 2 pickled hot cherry peppers, drained and chopped
- 2 sprigs fresh thyme
- 4 sprigs fresh oregano
- 3 bay leaves
- 3 tablespoons tomato paste
- 4 small Yukon gold potatoes (about the size of a golf ball), sliced in half
- 1½ quarts Poultry Broth (page 237)
- Kosher salt
- Chopped fresh parsley, for serving

Instructions

Combine vinegar, wine and pickled pepper juice in a container. Mix well and set aside.

Heat a large, deep skillet over medium-high heat. Add olive oil, then lay chicken thighs skin side down and cook until skin is crisp, approximately 5 minutes. Flip thighs over and lightly brown the flesh side, for 2 minutes. Transfer chicken to a plate. Add Italian sausages to the skillet and brown on at least 2 sides. Transfer sausages to plate with chicken thighs. Reduce heat to medium-low and add shallots, garlic, bell peppers, cherry peppers, thyme, oregano and bay leaves. Cook, stirring continuously, for 3 minutes.

Stir in tomato paste and add potatoes. Stack chicken thighs, skin side up, and sausages on top of vegetables. Holding the skillet lid in one hand, use the other hand to deglaze the skillet with white wine juice. Quickly cover the skillet with the lid. As the pan deglazes and steams, the acid of the vinegar and wine will penetrate the chicken thighs. When the liquid is almost completely reduced, after about 2 minutes, add enough poultry broth to reach the bottom edges of the chicken skin. Cover again and bring to a boil. Adjust the broth seasoning with salt to taste, then reduce heat to low and simmer until chicken and potatoes are cooked through, approximately 15 minutes.

Serve the dish family-style from the same skillet directly at the table or divide among 4 shallow bowls—each bowl gets 2 chicken thighs and 1 Italian sausage. Divide vegetables evenly between the bowls. Ladle plenty of broth into each bowl, then sprinkle with fresh chopped parsley. Serve with warm, crusty French bread or a ciabatta loaf.

MEATS

VEAL MILANESE

- 3 large eggs
- 1 cup milk
- 1 tablespoon kosher salt, plus more for seasoning
- ½ tablespoon freshly ground black pepper, plus more for seasoning
- 2 cups all-purpose flour
- 4 cups panko breadcrumbs
- 2 tablespoons fresh parsley, chopped
- 1 tablespoon fresh thyme leaves
- 1 tablespoon fresh oregano leaves
- 4 pieces veal scaloppine (5 ounces each), thinly sliced or pounded
- 4 cups Pomodoro Sauce (page 255)
- 1 cup Lemon-Caper Butter Sauce (page 252)
- 1½ cups canola oil
- 1 boule fresh ovolini mozzarella, sliced into 4 pieces

I hesitate to put traditional dishes on the menu. Guests have so many memories and ideas of how they should be prepared that I'm afraid I won't meet expectations. At Farina, we serve our veal Milanese with pomodoro sauce and melted mozzarella, then we drizzle the whole plate with lemon caper butter. I couldn't choose between the two sauces, so we do both. Perhaps it's gilding the lily, but it is *magnifico!* // **SERVES 4**

Arrange 3 large, shallow casserole pans and 1 baking sheet on a prep area.

Combine eggs and milk in a casserole pan, season with a pinch of salt and pepper, then whisk to mix well.

Measure flour into another casserole pan.

In a third pan, combine panko, parsley, thyme, oregano, 1 tablespoon salt and ½ tablespoon pepper. Rub panko mixture with your hands to release the aromas and flavors of the fresh herbs.

Working with 1 veal cutlet at a time, sprinkle a pinch of salt and pepper on each side, then dip it in flour, shaking off excess. Place floured veal into the egg wash, covering it completely on both sides. Lay veal in panko and press the crumbs into the wet veal; flip and repeat, making certain crumbs completely cover both sides of veal. Set aside on the baking sheet and continue breading the 3 remaining veal cutlets (this step can be done several hours in advance). Refrigerate veal until ready to cook.

PREPARE THE SAUCES

Heat pomodoro sauce in a small pan until it boils, then set aside and keep warm. In a separate saucepan, make lemon-caper butter sauce and set aside to keep warm.

FRY THE VEAL

Preheat broiler.

Heat a sauté pan (with sides) large enough to safely hold the canola oil, over high heat. Heat oil to the smoking point and gently place 2 pieces of breaded veal in the hot oil and fry until golden brown, approximately 3 minutes on each side. Transfer cooked veal to a paper towel–lined baking sheet and sprinkle with salt and pepper. Repeat with remaining veal. Remove paper towels from the baking sheet (they will catch fire in the broiler), then spoon a generous amount of pomodoro sauce onto the middle of each piece of fried veal. Place a slice of mozzarella on the pomodoro sauce. Place the baking sheet of veal under the broiler on the middle rack for 1 to 2 minutes or until mozzarella melts.

TO SERVE

Divide remaining pomodoro sauce on 4 warm entrée plates. Place a piece of veal on top of the sauce and then use a spoon to drizzle warm lemon-caper butter sauce on and around veal.

Serve veal with a simple green salad, a favorite pasta or grilled summer vegetables, such as asparagus or broccolini.

> The same process used in this recipe can be replicated to make Pork Milanese and Chicken Milanese. They both can be prepared in advance and froze for up to 1 month.

MEATS

PORCHETTA
(INSPIRED *by* DARIO CECCHINI)

1 boneless pork belly (8 pounds) with loin attached (rectangular cut with skin on)

3 tablespoons kosher salt

2 tablespoons coarsely ground black pepper

4 tablespoons fennel pollen (or substitute crushed toasted fennel seeds)

8 large leaves fresh sage, finely chopped

3 tablespoons fresh rosemary, finely chopped

15 large cloves garlic, thinly sliced

1 cup dry white wine

2 cups Poultry Broth (page 237)

Special equipment: Butcher twine

I've been fortunate to have Dario Cecchini (and his wife, Kim), the world's most acclaimed butcher, cook with me in Kansas City on two occasions, once in 2010 and again in 2014. The renowned Italian meat maestro is an incredibly generous chef with a huge heart, massive butcher hands and wealth of talent and knowledge gleaned from working at his 250-year-old family butcher shop in Panzano, in Italy's Chianti region. I learned quite a few things when he cooked for us, making the perfect porchetta being one of them. Some argue that this is the quintessential Italian dish—not pizza, not pasta, not prosciutto. I'm not sure I would go that far, but this porchetta is absolutely *delicioso*! // SERVES 8

Preheat oven to 300°F.

Place pork belly skin side up on a clean work surface. Use a sharp boning knife to score (cut) shallow diagonal slits in each direction of the skin. Cut through the skin but not all the way through the flesh. Cut the slits all the way down the length and all the way to the sides. When finished scoring the skin, it will resemble a grid pattern like the exterior of a pineapple.

Turn the belly over to expose the flesh. Position the belly horizontally from left to right. Generously sprinkle salt and pepper on the flesh side, making sure to cover every part of the meat. Sprinkle fennel pollen over the meat and follow with chopped sage and rosemary, rubbing firmly to penetrate the flesh. Spread sliced garlic evenly over the flesh.

Roll pork belly into a tube, starting with the edge closest to you; pinch and press the first 2 inches of belly into itself, then continue to roll it as tight as possible. It is okay that it may not roll into a full-on spiral—you are simply trying to roll it as tight as possible. Use butcher twine to tie the belly closed at every inch down the length of the roll. Sprinkle the exterior of the belly generously with salt. (The pork roll can be prepared to this point and refrigerated, uncovered, several hours or up to a day in advance.)

Place porchetta on a roasting rack in a deep roasting pan. Roast in the preheated oven, uncovered, for 4 hours. When meat is easily pierced with a paring knife and the juices run clear (not pink), the porchetta is done cooking.

> Bring the porchetta to room temperature before roasting if it has been prepared well in advance and refrigerated. A significant amount of pork fat will render out of the porchetta as it is cooking.

Let porchetta rest at room temperature for 30 minutes. While porchetta is resting, turn oven heat up to 425°F. Put porchetta back in the oven and roast for another 10 minutes or until the skin turns a deep golden brown and is crackling crisp. Remove from the oven and let it rest for 20 minutes, lightly covered with foil.

To make gravy, remove rack from the roasting pan and skim off the fat. Add white wine and use a metal spatula to scrape the caramelized residue and crunchy bits off the bottom of the pan. Transfer the wine and pan juices to a small sauce pot and add poultry broth, then bring to a boil. Stir well and correct the seasoning with salt and pepper if necessary.

Carve the pork into thick slices and serve with gravy and your favorite side dishes.

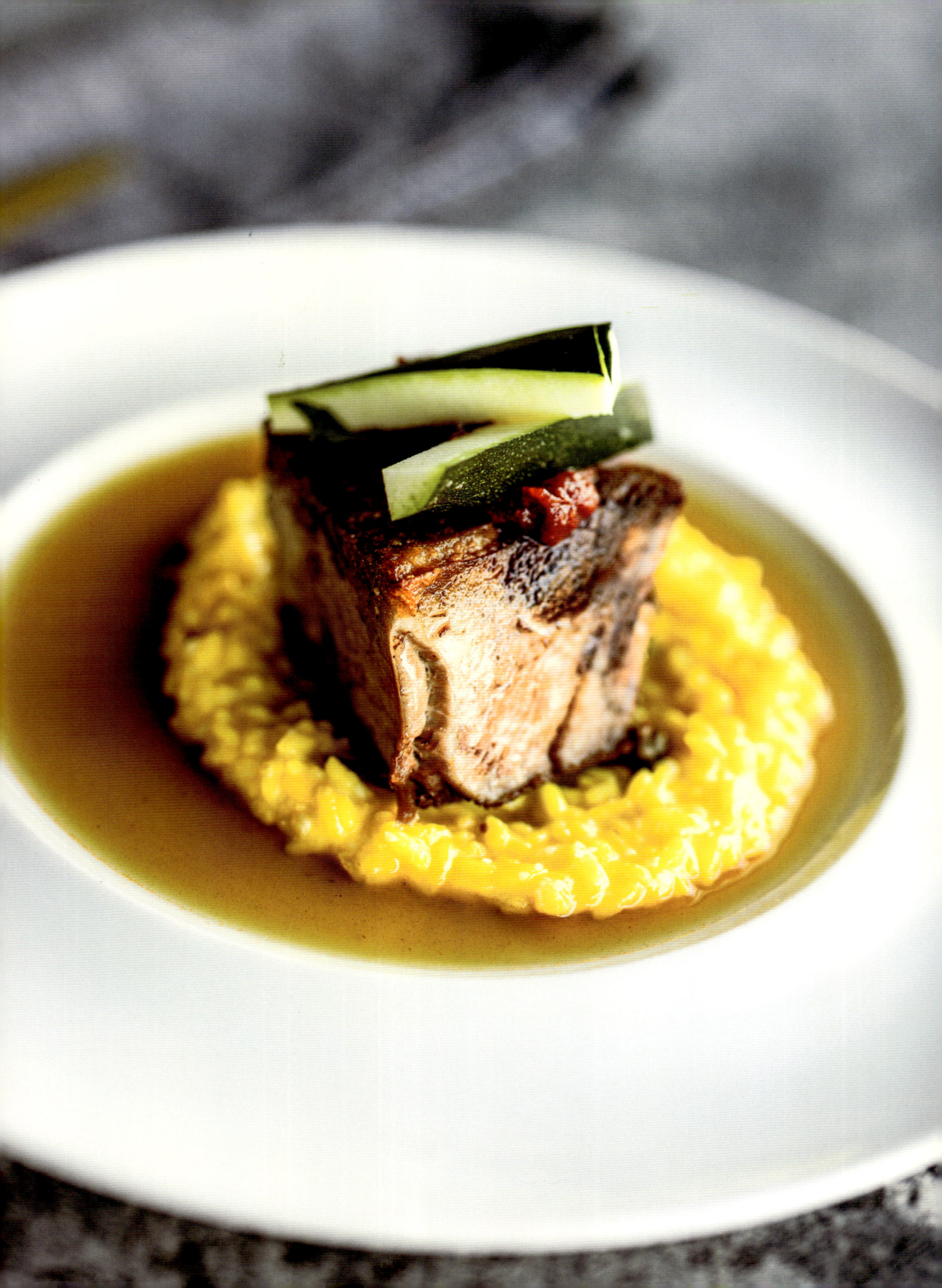

EIGHT-HOUR PORK ROAST

1 boneless pork butt (approximately 6 pounds)

1 tablespoon salt

1 teaspoon freshly ground black pepper

2 yellow onions, thinly sliced

2 bay leaves, torn into several pieces

1 tablespoon rosemary leaves

1 cup dry white wine

2 cups Poultry Broth (page 237)

¼ cup canola oil

A creation of Carl Thorne-Thomsen, a former chef de cuisine at Michael Smith, this pork roast slow cooks in the oven for a minimum of 8 hours. It originally appeared on the menu at Michael Smith Restaurant in 2007, and now it's a permanent Farina fixture. I make the occasional garnish change, but essentially, it's the same wonderful, tender piece of pork that debuted 15 years ago. I recommend serving it alongside starches such as polenta, mushroom risotto or mashed potatoes and a medley of roasted root vegetables. // **SERVES 4**

Preheat oven to 275°F.

Rub pork all over with salt and pepper, then place it in a baking dish and spread onions, bay leaves and rosemary on top. Pour wine and broth into the pan and cover the dish with aluminum foil. Bake in the oven for 8 hours. Remove the braised pork from the oven and set aside to cool at room temperature for 1 hour in the braising liquid. Separate the pork from the braising liquid and chill the pork in the refrigerator for at least 12 hours. Pass the braising liquid through a fine strainer into a small container and refrigerate. When the braised pork is fully chilled and very firm, portion it into equal-size 1½-inch steaks.

Shortly before serving time, preheat oven to 350°F.

Reheat the braising liquid and bring to a boil. Keep warm and set aside.

Sprinkle both sides of the pork steaks generously with salt and pepper. Heat a large heavy-bottomed skillet over medium-high heat and swirl in canola oil. Sear pork steaks until deep golden brown and crispy on both sides, approximately 3 minutes per side. Place skillet in the oven and bake pork steaks for 10 to 12 minutes. When pork is heated through, remove from the oven and serve with the natural roasting juices and your favorite side dishes.

LAMB WELLINGTON

- 2 pieces boneless lamb loins cut from the rack
- Kosher salt
- Freshly ground black pepper
- 1 tablespoon fresh tarragon leaves, chopped
- 3 whole large carrots, peeled and rough chopped
- 1 cup dry red wine
- 1 whole shallot, peeled and sliced
- 1 tablespoon whole black peppercorns
- 1 cup meat demi-glace (store-bought)
- 2 tablespoons canola oil
- 8 cups fresh spinach
- 2 pieces frozen puff pastry (10" x 10"), thawed
- ½ cup egg wash (1 egg whisked with ½ cup milk)

Why is everything baked in a pastry so damn good? You can put literally any meat or fish in a puff pastry and it will be delicious! And the best part, Wellingtons are simple to make, and you can prepare them well ahead of your next dinner party. // **SERVES 4**

Preheat oven to 400°F.

Season lamb fillets generously with 1 tablespoon each of salt, pepper and chopped tarragon. Set aside.

Place carrots in a sauce pot and cover with water. Add 1 teaspoon salt and bring to a boil. Reduce heat and cook carrots until very soft. Drain, reserving a few tablespoons of cooking liquid for the blender if needed. Add cooked carrots to a blender and mix on high speed until silky smooth. Keep warm and set aside. (Carrot puree can be prepared several days in advance and kept in the refrigerator.)

Combine red wine, shallot and peppercorns in a small sauce pot and bring to a boil. Continue to cook at a high simmer until red wine reduces to a syrup. Add demi-glace and return to a boil. Reduce heat and simmer for 5 minutes. Strain, set aside and keep warm.

Heat a large sauté pan over high heat and swirl in 2 tablespoons canola oil. When oil has almost reached the smoking point, place lamb loins in the pan and sear for 45 seconds on each side. Remove and set aside to cool.

In the same pan, sauté spinach with a pinch of salt and pepper until wilted. Transfer spinach to a small pan and allow spinach to cool, then squeeze to expel excess water. Chop roughly and set aside.

continues on page 178

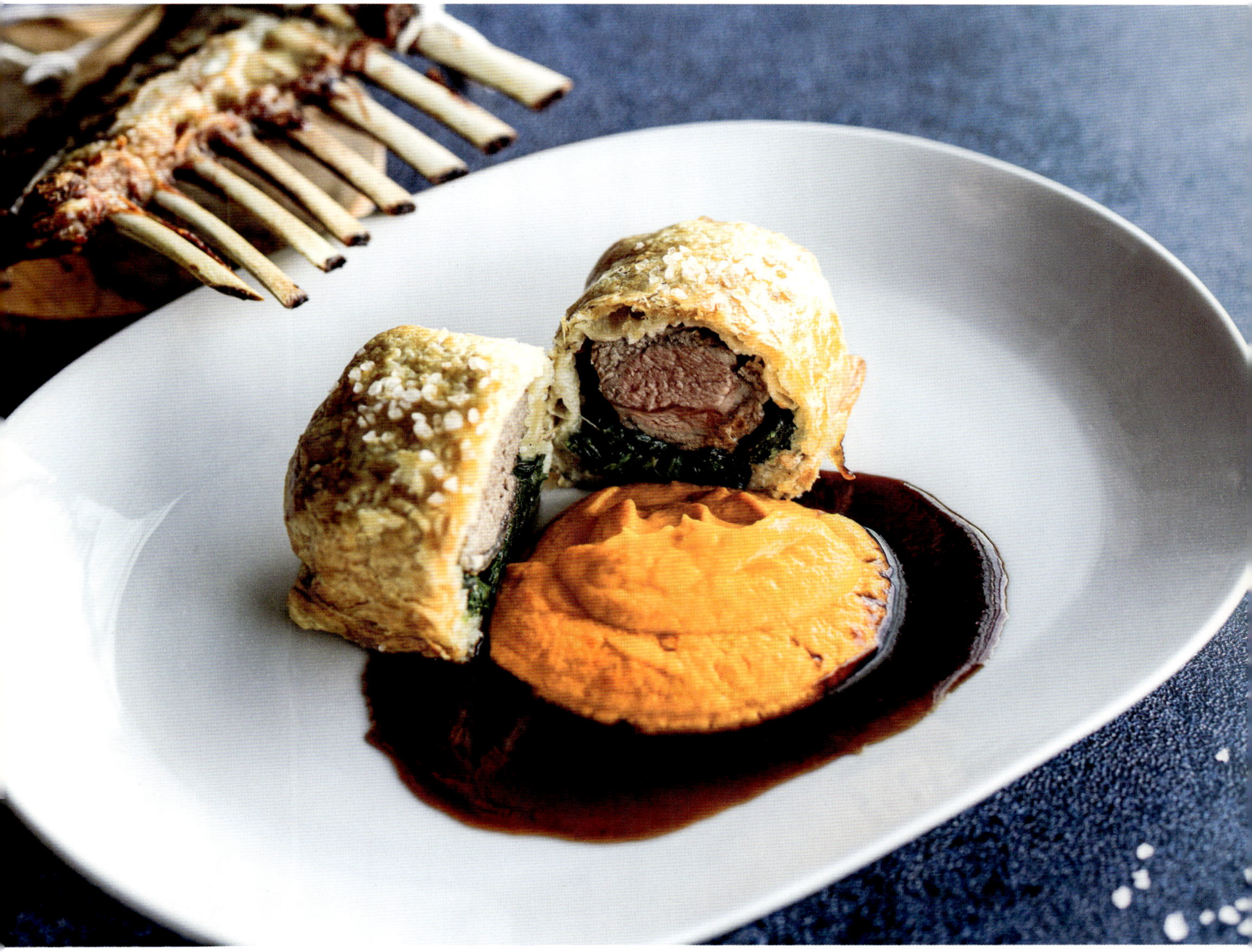

LAMB WELLINGTON

continued from page 176

TO ASSEMBLE LAMB WELLINGTON

Place both puff pastry sheets on a lightly floured work surface. Make sure the length of the puff pastry is longer than the loins of lamb.

Lay a ½-inch-thick mound of spinach (same length and width as the lamb) on the puff pastry. Then set 1 lamb loin on top of the spinach. Repeat for the second Wellington. Cut a small square notch out of each corner of the pastry sheets. Brush all exposed pastry areas with egg wash. Fold both ends of the pastry onto lamb loin. Gently, but tightly, pull the pastry flap closest to you over onto the loin, sealing the flap onto the folded ends. Continue to firmly roll the loin away from you to enclose the loin entirely in the pastry. The seam edge should land in the middle and bottom of the loin. Cut the excess dough if this is not the case. After flipping the loin over the seam, the top of the pastry should be clean and smooth, and the loin should be completely encased in the pastry with no holes or exposed corners. Repeat with the other pastry sheet, lamb and spinach. Brush each pastry packet generously with remaining egg wash and sprinkle with salt. Place both on a large, parchment-lined baking sheet, 6 inches apart. (The Lamb Wellingtons can be prepared up to this point hours in advance and kept in the refrigerator.)

Bake Lamb Wellingtons in the preheated oven for 12 minutes. The pastry will turn a deep golden brown and the lamb will be at medium-rare temperature. While lamb is baking, reheat pureed carrots.

Remove lamb from oven and let rest for 10 minutes.

TO SERVE

Slice each Lamb Wellington into 4 equal pieces. Spoon a dollop of carrot puree onto the middle of each warm dinner plate. Place 2 pieces of lamb on either side of the puree and then spoon demi-glace just in front of the puree and Wellington.

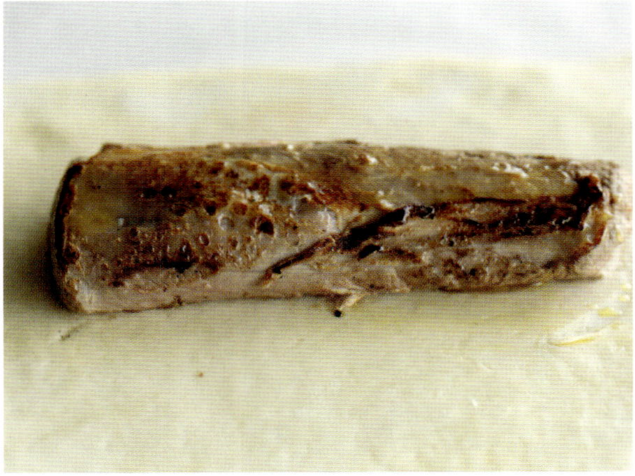
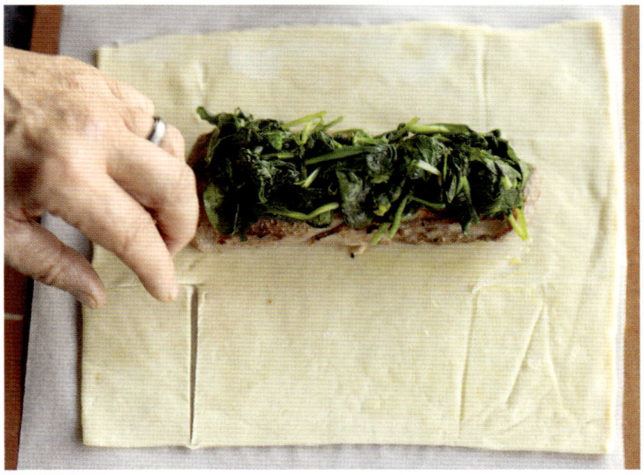
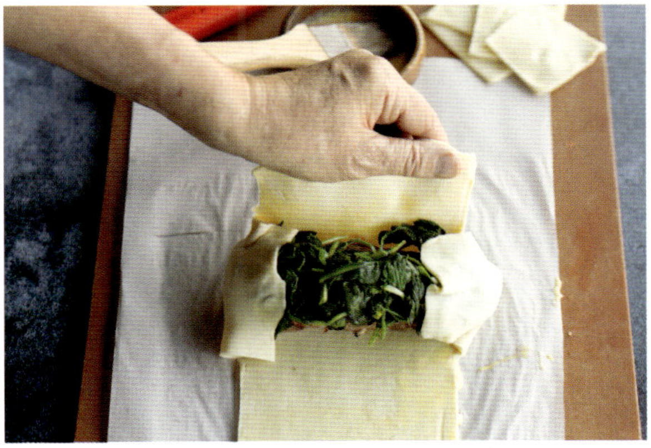
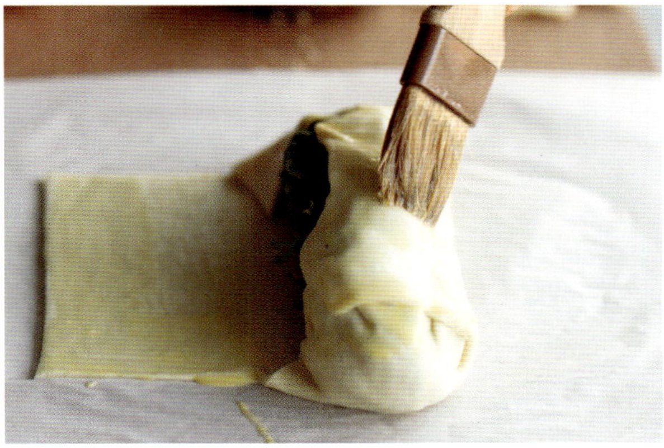
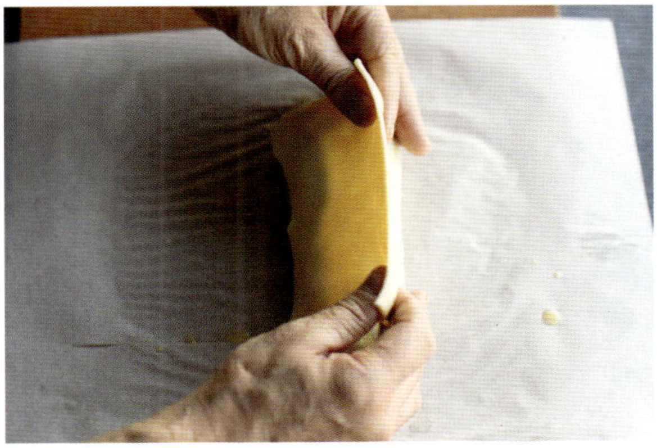
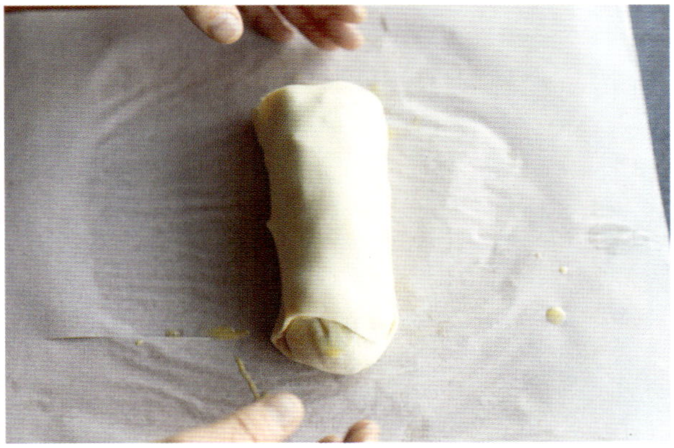
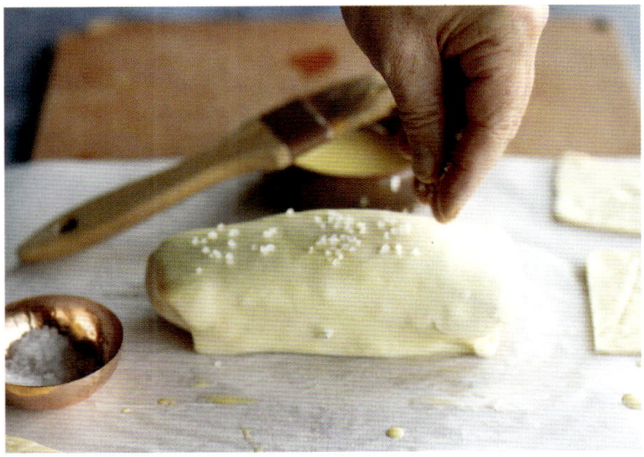

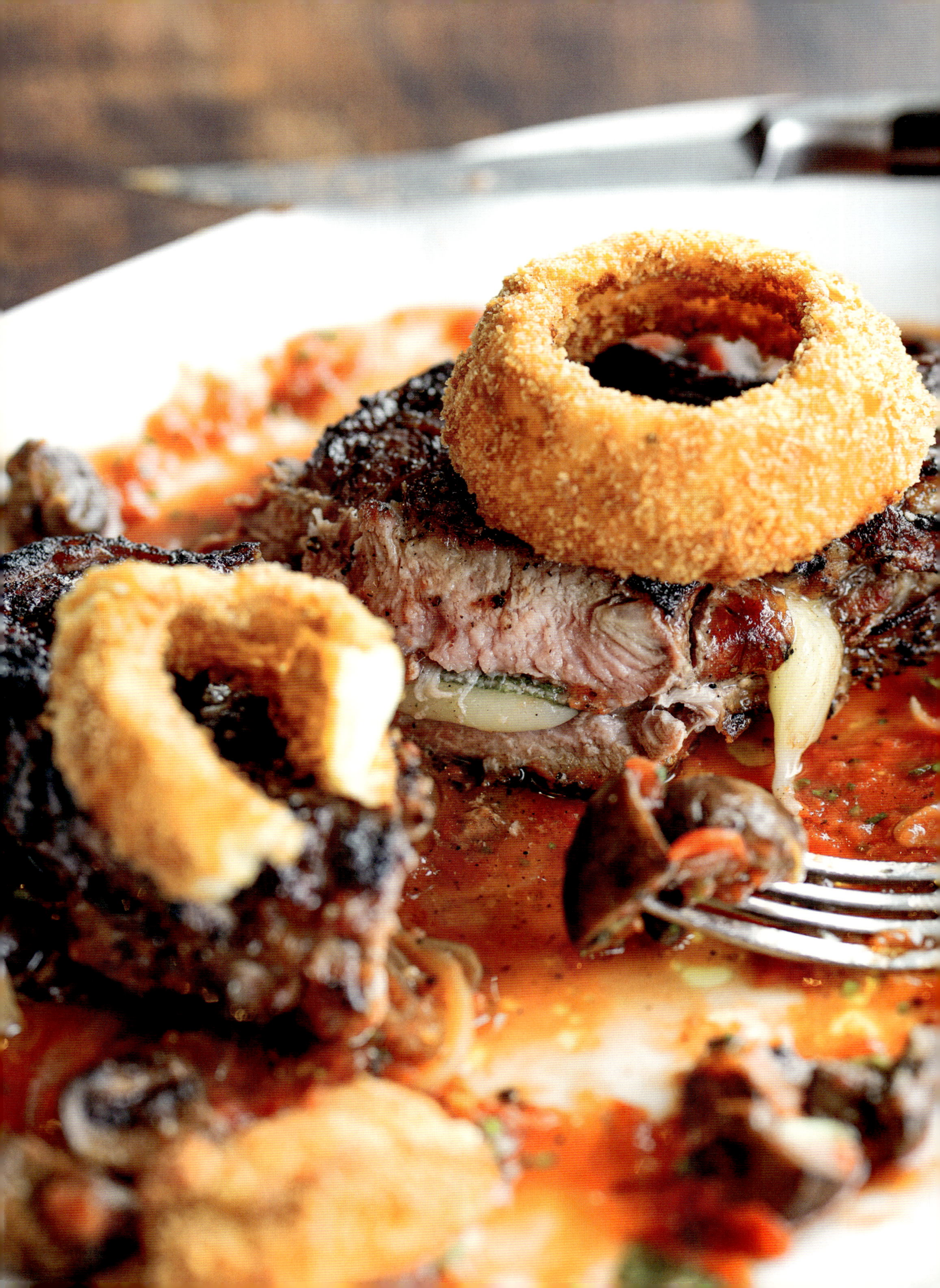

VEAL CHOPS
STUFFED *with* SMOKED MOZZARELLA *and* PROSCIUTTO

4 slices prosciutto

8 leaves fresh sage

6 ounces scamorza (smoked mozzarella), cut into 4 logs, ¾ inch by 3 inches

4 bone-in veal chops (22 ounces each)

Kosher salt

Fresh cracked black pepper

1 quart Pizzaiola Sauce (page 251)

Special equipment: Butcher twine

Steve Westhead has become a good friend of Farina and his first time eating with us he asked if I could stuff his veal chop with mozzarella. He was surprised that I agreed to do it. Some chefs get too protective of their food and refuse such requests. I modified it a bit with smoked mozzarella, adding sage and prosciutto.

// SERVES 4

Prepare an outdoor grill to 400°F.

Lay out prosciutto slices vertically on a work surface. Lay 2 sage leaves on each prosciutto slice. Place 1 mozzarella log horizontally on each prosciutto slice and roll them up. Set aside.

Lay veal chops on a work surface with the bone positioned up and away from you and on the left side of the thick medallion of meat. Use a sharp boning knife and, starting at the outer edge of the medallion of veal, insert the knife toward the bone to make a deep slit into the center of the meat (it's okay to touch the bone). Work the knife horizontally along the edge of the meat to create a wide opening. Gently spread the 2 flaps of meat apart and sprinkle with a pinch of salt and pepper. Stuff a mozzarella log into the opening. Press the veal flaps together to enclose the cheese. Repeat with the remaining 3 chops. Use butcher twine and tie each chop closed in 2 spots along the medallion and around the bone. Set aside.

Grill chops for 8 to 10 minutes on each side, flipping every couple of minutes to keep them from charring too dark on either side.

Heat pizzaiola sauce to a boil in a medium sauce pot. Divide sauce between 4 warm plates.

Use scissors to cut the butcher twine from each chop, then set a chop in the middle of each plate. I like to serve this veal dish with seasonal grilled vegetables, such as asparagus, broccolini or young carrots.

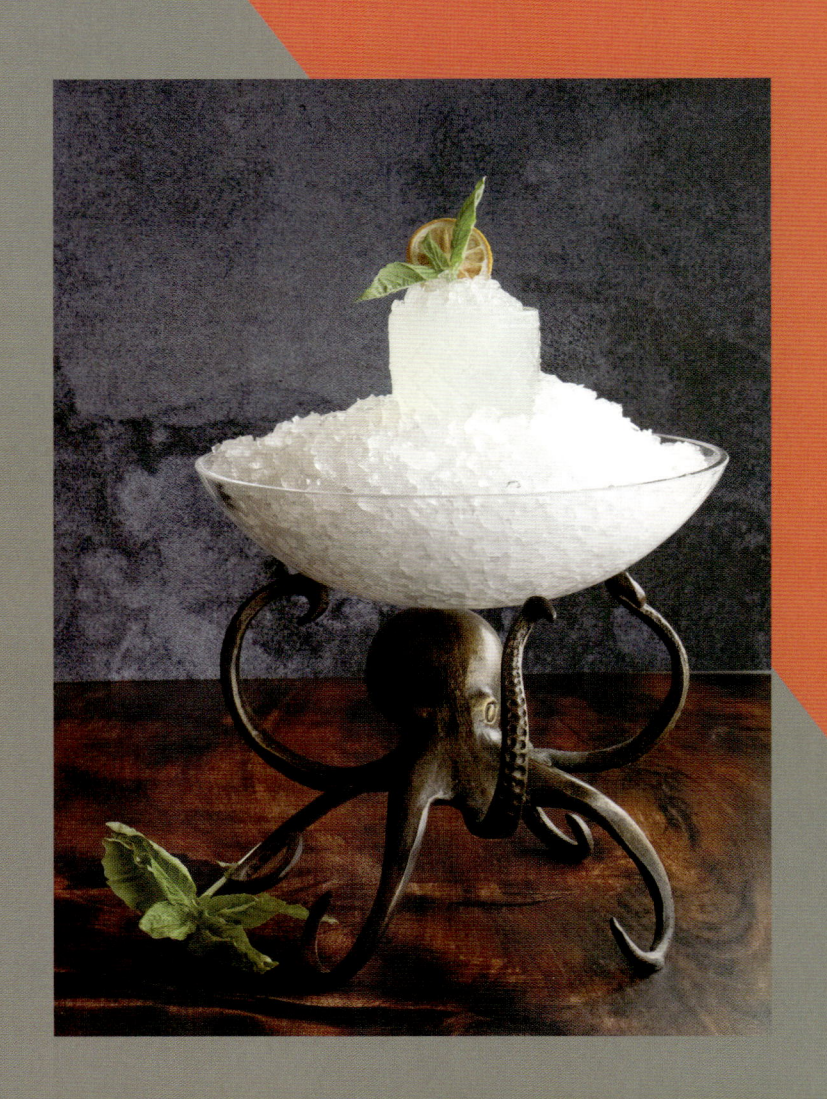

4
COCKTAILS

What a great time to be a bartender. We're enjoying a renaissance in cocktails, and innovative bartenders are serving modern concoctions with fascinating ingredients, artistic garnishes and antique glassware. We look to the past in reimagining tradition, and we look to chefs' kitchens to inspire new and seasonal flavor profiles.

Farina's beverage director, Alberto "Berto" Santoro, joined the Unites States Bartenders' Guild (USBG) in 2010 and has traveled to some of the world's best spirits and liquors destinations—researching cognac in France, sherry in Jerez and agave in Oaxaca. With each visit, he brings those experiences home to Kansas City to curate our cocktail program.

The modern cocktail movement has created curious and sophisticated drinkers in Kansas City, and this allows us the freedom to experiment and use some of the same seasonal ingredients in the bar as we use in the kitchen. Berto's philosophy of running a bar is like how a chef runs a kitchen. He sources local ingredients wherever possible and has daily orders and prep lists for our fresh ingredients and booze. His team regularly discusses flavor combinations, flavor extractions, mixing methods and ice quality to maintain a high-level program. Some people think bartending is just slinging drinks, but our goal is precision in color, aroma and taste. The Farina bar team measures pours for the simple reason of consistency. You'll often see Berto and his team hand-cutting 2-inch ice blocks into jewels or rocks that will be served with an old fashioned, a Negroni or a Boulevardier.

The Farina bartenders know how to shake the hell out of a drink! Not just to chill and mix, but to achieve gorgeously aerated cocktails with a silky texture. They can stir it up, too, especially if your cocktail is in an oversize, stemmed mixing glass with a long-handled spoon. Why? Because it's sexy, that's why. And because your drink needs a stir. We fine strain all "up" drinks so they are clear, clean and refined. All these elements are extremely important in good bartending.

Sure, a well-made drink is the reason you're at our bar, but hospitality is paramount to all of us at Farina. Warm, familiar surroundings and friendly, knowledgeable bar staff make it a special experience. If you don't see a drink on our menu that interests you, simply tell us what booze you like, answer a few other questions and we'll make you a drink. Just don't ask us to make you "something fun!" You're an adult. At a bar. So act like that.

We're proud to have a lot of regulars at Farina. Sometimes they want to chat about a crappy day and other times they simply want to sip a drink in peace. Being a regular is such a personal thing. There is a level of comfort that is hard to describe. Chatting up our guests creates interesting conversations and sometimes provides inspiration for cocktail names. Berto has a lot of fun naming our cocktails with witty pop culture references like "You Apricotta Be Kidding Me," "Go Home and Get Your Shine Box," "Macho Man Brandy Savage" and "Da Two Yoots." Now you can make some of these Farina favorites at home. Cheers!

ARTISANAL COCKTAIL NUANCES

ICE

It's kind of a big deal. Using the correct ice influences how you sip and enjoy a great cocktail. At Farina we use clear oversize block ice that we carve into jewel-shaped cubes. Oversize spheres are popular and work well in a variety of cocktails like Negronis and old fashioneds, along with straight pours of spirits you wouldn't want to over-dilute, like premium whiskey and tequila. Crushed ice is great for refreshing, seasonal spritzy-type cocktails like juleps, swizzles and tiki-style drinks. We use 1-inch cubes for drinks that are shaken or stirred then strained over ice. If you are really serious about your home bar program, keep your drink ice separated from your main freezer to avoid it picking up the flavors of the freezer. You probably don't want your "Da Two Yoots" to taste like Oaxacan mole sauce!

INGREDIENTS

Using fresh juices, herbs and quality spirits is key to making the perfect drink. We prepare all our citrus juices fresh each day using an industrial Sunkist juicer. For at-home cocktails, a small hand-press juicer will work fine. Everyone has their personal favorite booze brands, but look around your city or region for small craft distilleries that are cranking out unique spirits. There are so many on the market right now. Experiment and see what you like. You can certainly stay with the tried-and-true brands that you are accustomed to, but if you want to build a unique and premium home bar program, consider trying some new spirits.

BALANCE

Balancing a cocktail correctly is very important, and harmony is the goal. A well-balanced cocktail is pleasing and keeps you going back for another sip. Two parts strong, one part sweet and one part sour is generally a good rule of thumb for making a balanced drink. To balance one flavor with another means to offset the first flavor because it is too dominant. For example, a classic whiskey sour is 2 ounces whiskey, 1 ounce simple syrup and 1 ounce fresh lemon juice. Everyone's palate is a bit different, so play around with the proportions until your drink tastes how you want it to. Maybe you like a more citrusy drink, or perhaps you prefer your cocktails a little sweeter. Keep a notebook near your bar so you can jot down your first impression and other thoughts about the cocktail.

GLASSWARE

The shape of a glass affects how intensely a drink's aroma can hit your nose. Certain drinks require specific glassware like a Nick & Nora tulip shape or an old fashioned glass. But you'll also use tall Collins glasses and coupes for many cocktails. There has been a movement recently toward antique cocktail glassware. These glasses are sexy and really put the elegance back into cocktail drinking. They tend to be smaller in size, which is better overall when you start geeking out and want to try multiple cocktails during the evening. Downing several martinis from 10-ounce glasses will get you smashed in a hurry! Lastly, keep your glasses cold so you'll be ready to craft a satisfying cocktail at a moment's notice.

GARNISHES

Our general philosophy about drink garnishes is to keep it simple. For example, with strained drinks, don't leave too many fragments of a crushed and shaken cocktail in the glass. Stuff gets stuck in the straw or in your teeth. The sipping process should be clean. You should use seasonal fruits, herbs and vegetables whenever you can. Otherwise, it's up to you how simple or complicated the garnish is. Overall, the garnish should echo, either visually or aromatically, the ingredients in a drink. And the garnish should complement the intended balance of flavors.

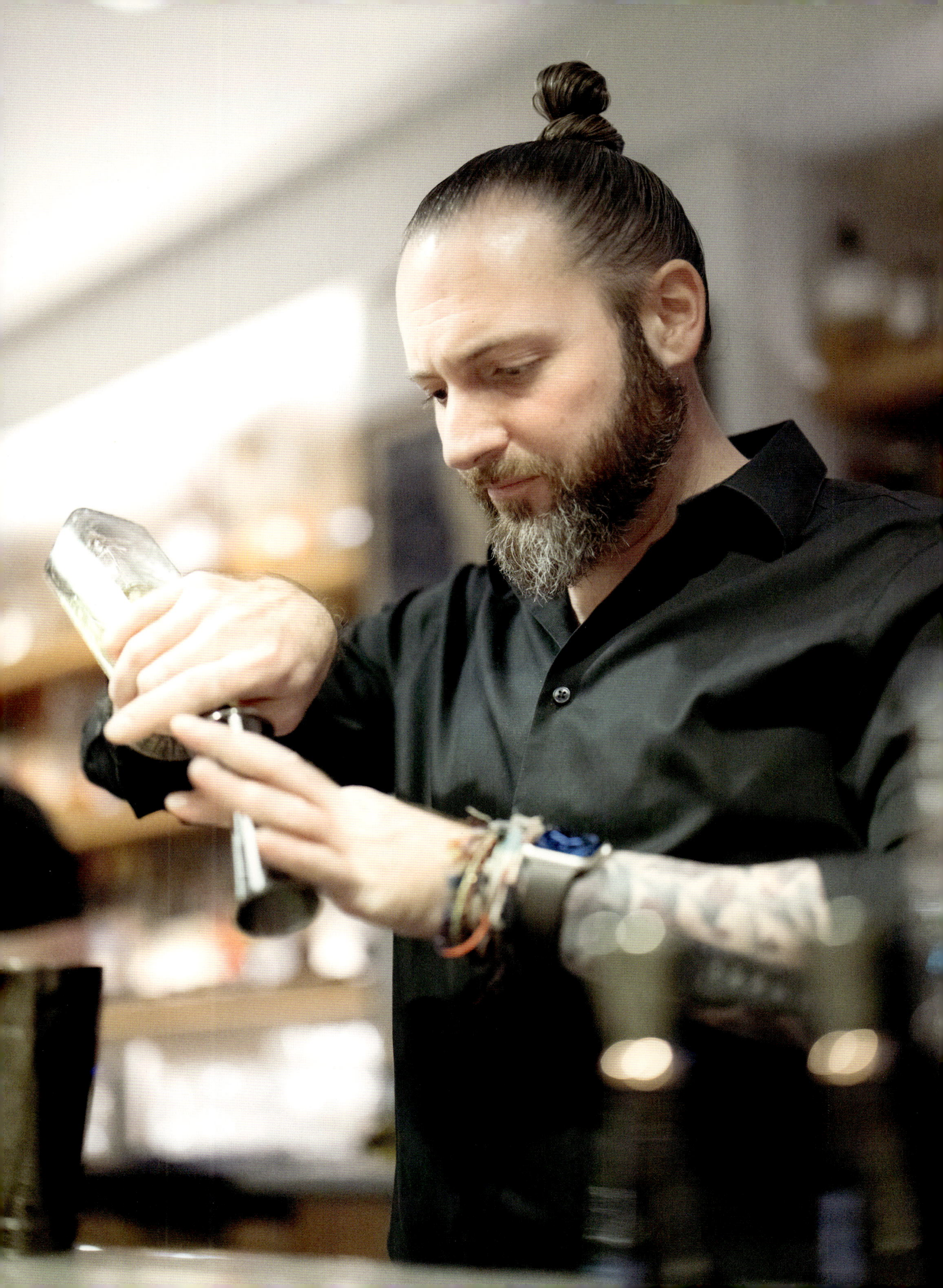

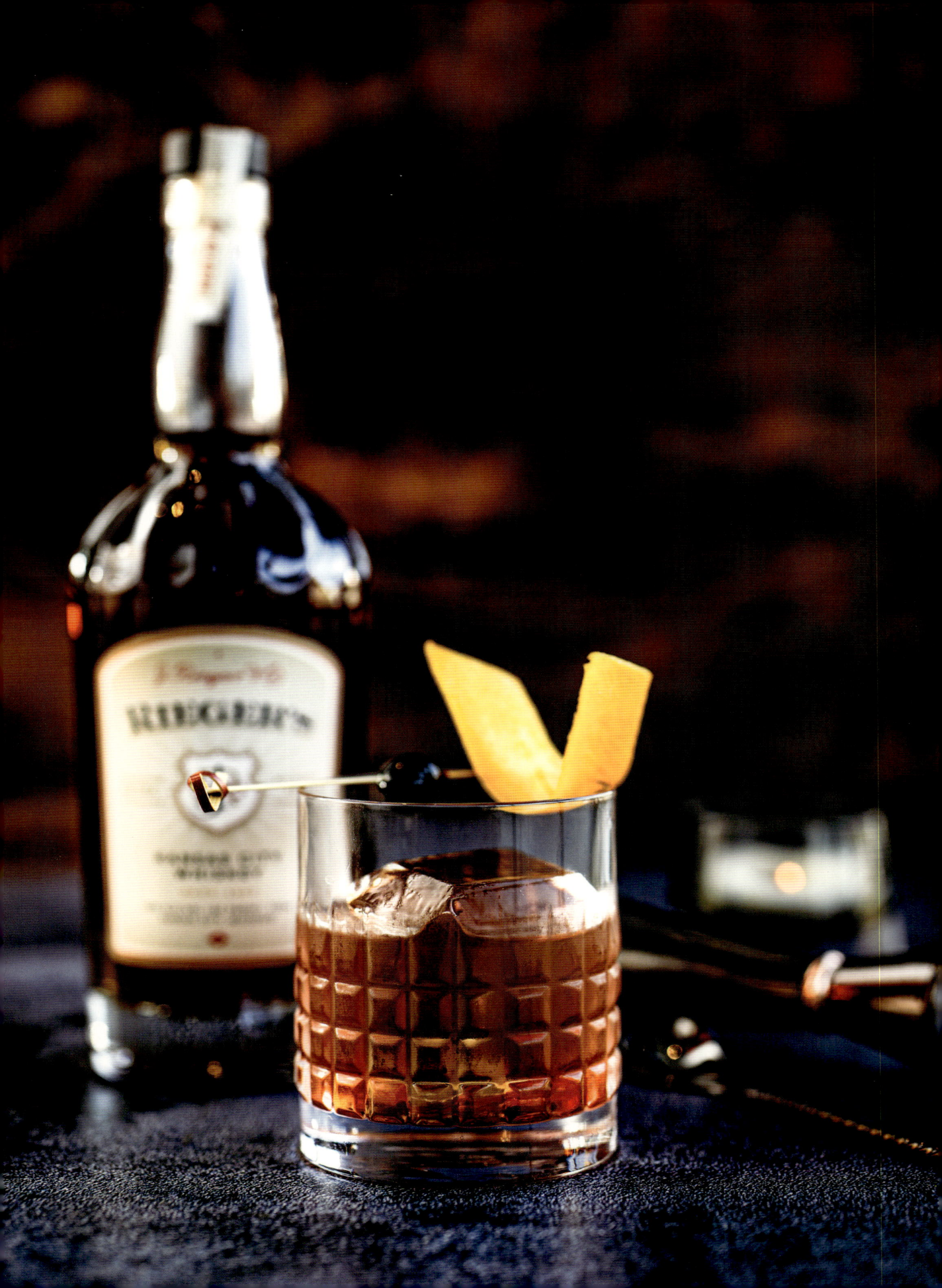

FARINA OLD FASHIONED

- 2 ounces J. Rieger's Kansas City whiskey
- ½ ounce simple syrup
- 2 dashes Angostura aromatic bitters
- 2 dashes Regans' Orange Bitters No. 6
- 2 dashes Fee Brothers Old Fashion Aromatic Bitters
- 1 orange peel
- 1 Amarena cherry

Until fairly recently, there was only one way to make an old fashioned—muddle bourbon with an orange slice, sugar, bitters and a Maraschino cherry. In recent years, the cocktail has returned to its pre-Prohibition glory in the form of a stirred cocktail with elevated ingredients. At Farina it's our best-selling cocktail and we make it using a local whiskey, a blend of bitters and an Amarena cherry. **// MAKES 1 COCKTAIL**

Combine all ingredients except orange peel and cherry in a mixing glass with cubed ice and stir gently for 20 seconds. Place an oversize ice cube or sphere in a rocks glass, then strain the drink over the ice. Use a vegetable peeler or sharp paring knife to peel a wide ribbon from the orange peel while avoiding the bitter white pith just under the citrus skin. Express (twist and squeeze) the orange peel over the top of the cocktail, letting the natural oils spray over the finished drink. Garnish with an Amarena cherry skewered on a pick.

COCKTAILS

OLD DOG, NEW TRICKS

APPLE FENNEL HONEY SYRUP
Makes 2 cups

⅓ cup honeycrisp apple juice

3 tablespoons fresh fennel, diced

6 ounces amber honey

6 ounces water

OLD DOG, NEW TRICKS
Makes 1 cocktail

1½ ounces Citadelle gin

½ ounce La Miraja Ruche Vino Aromatizzato alla China

½ ounce St. George Pear Brandy

½ ounce fresh lime juice

¾ ounce Apple Fennel Honey Syrup

2 dashes Peychaud's Aromatic Cocktail Bitters

1 honeycrisp apple

Sometimes we all feel like an old dog, but we can still learn new tricks. Like this cocktail that was birthed after Berto's trip to the motherland (Italy) that spawned his obsession with aromatized wines like Barolo Chinato, along with other wines fortified with cinchona bark. The spirits are typically served as a digestif after dinner, but the cocktail applications are endless.

MAKE APPLE FENNEL HONEY SYRUP

Combine all ingredients in a small saucepan and bring to a boil. Reduce heat to simmer and cook for 5 minutes. Remove from heat and let syrup cool for 10 minutes. Strain the syrup, discarding fennel, into a small container. Cover and store in the refrigerator for up to 2 months.

MAKE OLD DOG, NEW TRICKS

Combine all ingredients except apple in a cocktail shaker with cubed ice. Shake aggressively for 20 seconds. Fill a tall Collins glass with cubed ice and strain the drink over the ice. Garnish with fan-shaped thin apple slices to serve.

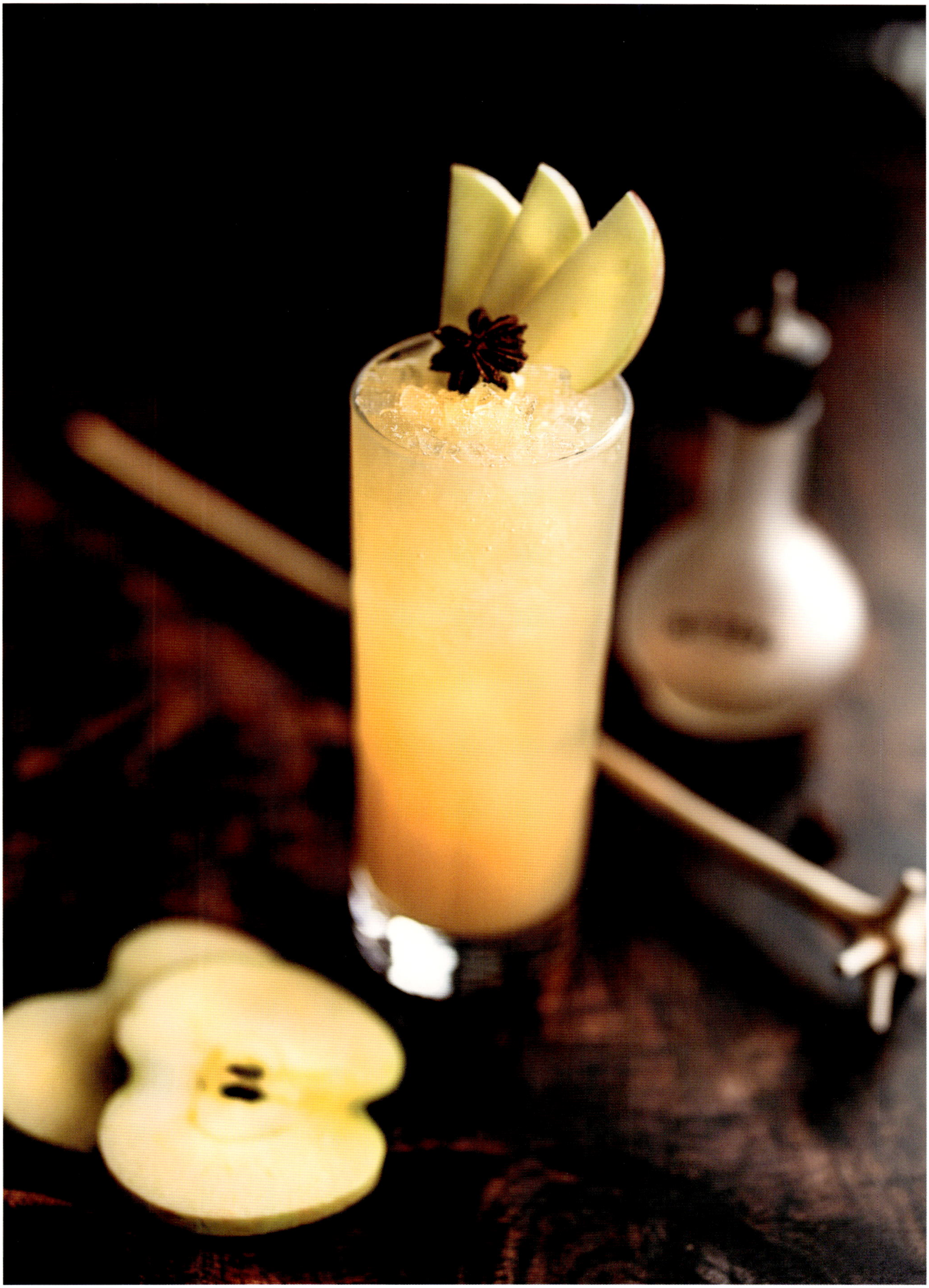

COCKTAILS

GO HOME *and* GET YOUR SHINE BOX

CALABRIAN CHILI HONEY SYRUP
Makes 1 cup

4 ounces amber honey

4 ounces water

½ ounce sliced Calabrian chili peppers

GO HOME AND GET YOUR SHINE BOX
Makes 1 cocktail

1 ounce Del Maguey Vida mezcal

½ ounce Amaro Montenegro

¼ ounce fresh lime juice

½ ounce fresh grapefruit juice

½ ounce Calabrian Chili Honey Syrup

3 dashes Bittermens Hellfire Habanero Shrub Bitters

1 fresh sage leaf

Berto has been on a bit of a mezcal crusade the past few years, earning his level 1 and level 2 mezcalier certifications. It's a polarizing spirit. Some people think it tastes like an ashtray. Others absolutely love its smoky nuances. This cocktail is one of Berto's many attempts to convert all non-lovers of mezcal. The Amaro Montenegro gives it an Italian twist, and the cocktail's name is an ode to Berto's favorite gangster movie, *Goodfellas*.

MAKE CALABRIAN CHILI HONEY SYRUP

Combine all ingredients in a medium saucepan and bring to a boil. Reduce heat to a simmer for 5 minutes. Remove from the stove and let cool. Strain out the chilies and store in an airtight container for up to 1 month in the refrigerator.

MAKE GO HOME AND GET YOUR SHINE BOX

Have on hand a chilled coupe glass. Combine all ingredients except sage in a cocktail shaker with cubed ice. Shake aggressively for 30 seconds. Strain the drink into the chilled coupe glass and garnish with a sage leaf to serve.

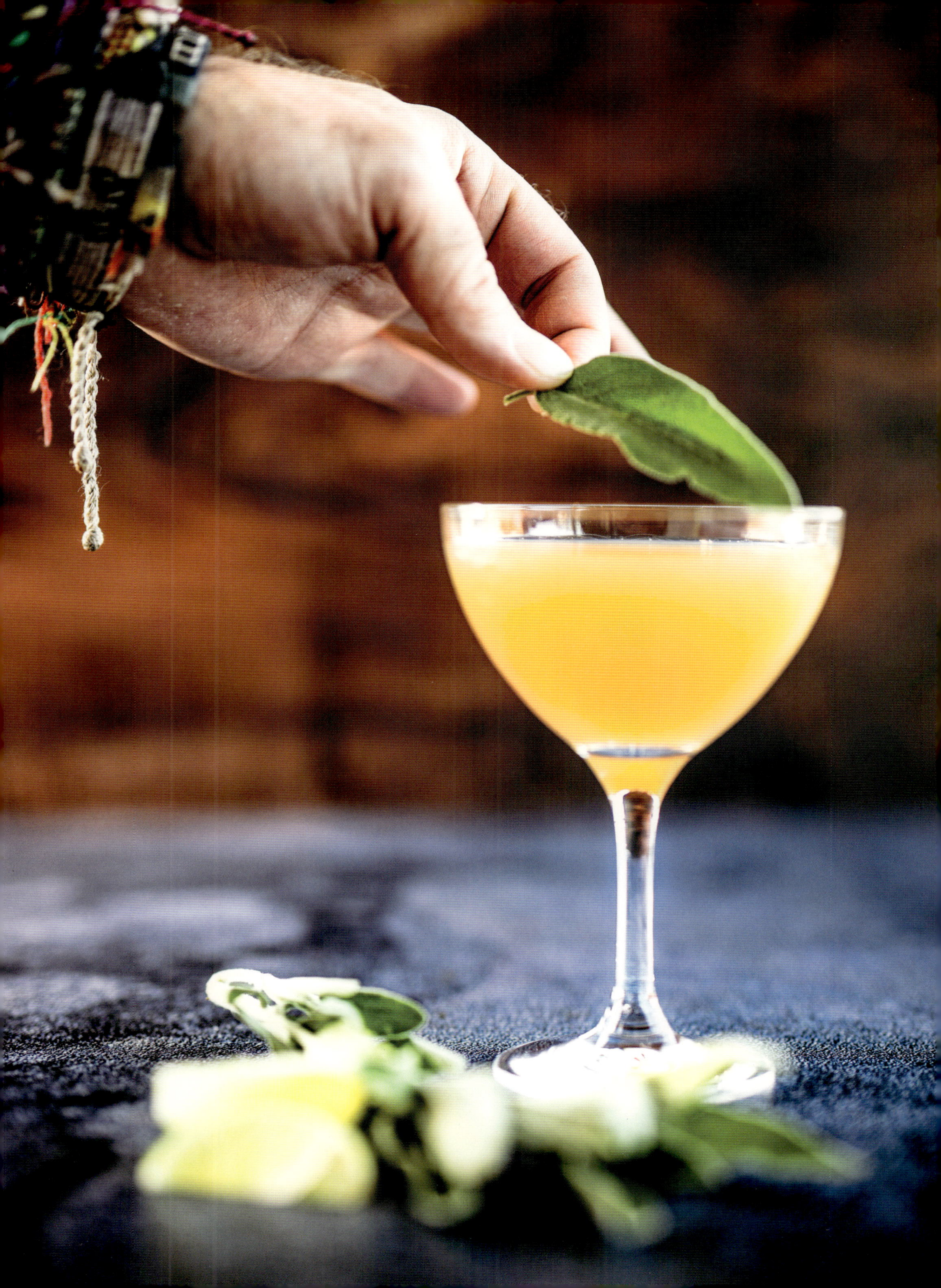

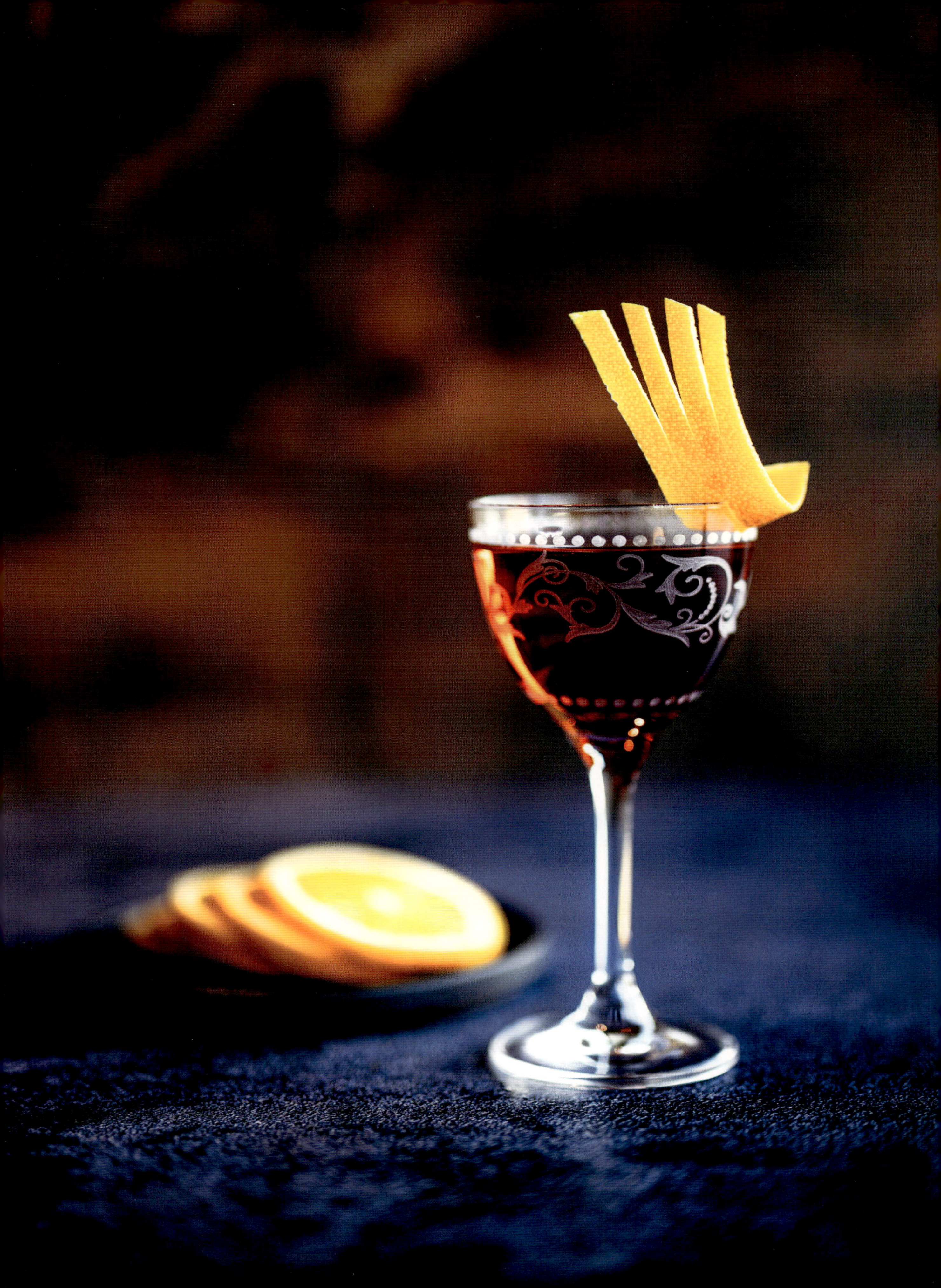

FARINA BARREL-AGED NEGRONI

4 cups J. Rieger's Midwestern Dry Gin

4 cups Aperol

4 cups Dolin Rouge sweet vermouth

1 cup Carpano Antica Formula Vermouth

Orange peel, for cocktail garnish

Special equipment:
1 gallon-size oak bourbon barrel (available online)

We started aging cocktails in used bourbon barrels in 2009, a trend begun a few years earlier by Jeffrey Morgenthaler, the legendary Portland barman at the now defunct Clyde Common restaurant. We use Aperol to make our Negroni riff a little more approachable and we balance it with two types of vermouth. It's a crowd pleaser for sure. // **MAKES 1 BARREL**

In a large stainless prep bowl, combine all liquid ingredients and stir gently until mixed well. Use a funnel to transfer the liquid to the barrel. Seal the barrel with the bung and let the alcohol age for at least 4 weeks.

After the aging process is complete, to make 1 cocktail, place an oversize ice cube or sphere in a rocks glass. Pour aged Negroni over the large ice. Use a vegetable peeler or sharp paring knife to peel a wide ribbon of orange peel. Express (twist and squeeze) the orange peel over the top of the drink, letting the natural oils spray over the finished cocktail.

> You don't need to empty the barrel completely after aging. Simply drain a preferred amount into a clean, empty wine bottle. Seal the wine bottle with a used cork and store in the refrigerator until you are ready for a cold Negroni. The remaining alcohol in the barrel can be topped off with a new batch. The continuation of the process will only enhance the overall flavor of the Negroni as it ages. You can maintain this process for years to come.

COCKTAILS

ESPRESSO MARTINI

1½ ounces vanilla vodka (or reposado tequila)

1½ ounces Caffè Borghetti liqueur

¾ ounce espresso

¼ ounce heavy cream

3 espresso beans

We've noticed a huge resurgence in the popularity of this cocktail. On weekend nights it has often accounted for about 30 percent of our beverage service. Perhaps it's all the folks leaving Red Bull and vodka behind and replacing it with espresso martinis. Either way, it'll get you caffeinated for the second half of your night!

// MAKES 1 COCKTAIL

Combine all liquid ingredients in a cocktail shaker with cubed ice. Shake aggressively for 30 seconds. Strain the drink into a chilled coupe glass and garnish with espresso beans.

> It's great with vanilla vodka, but try it with reposado tequila sometime.

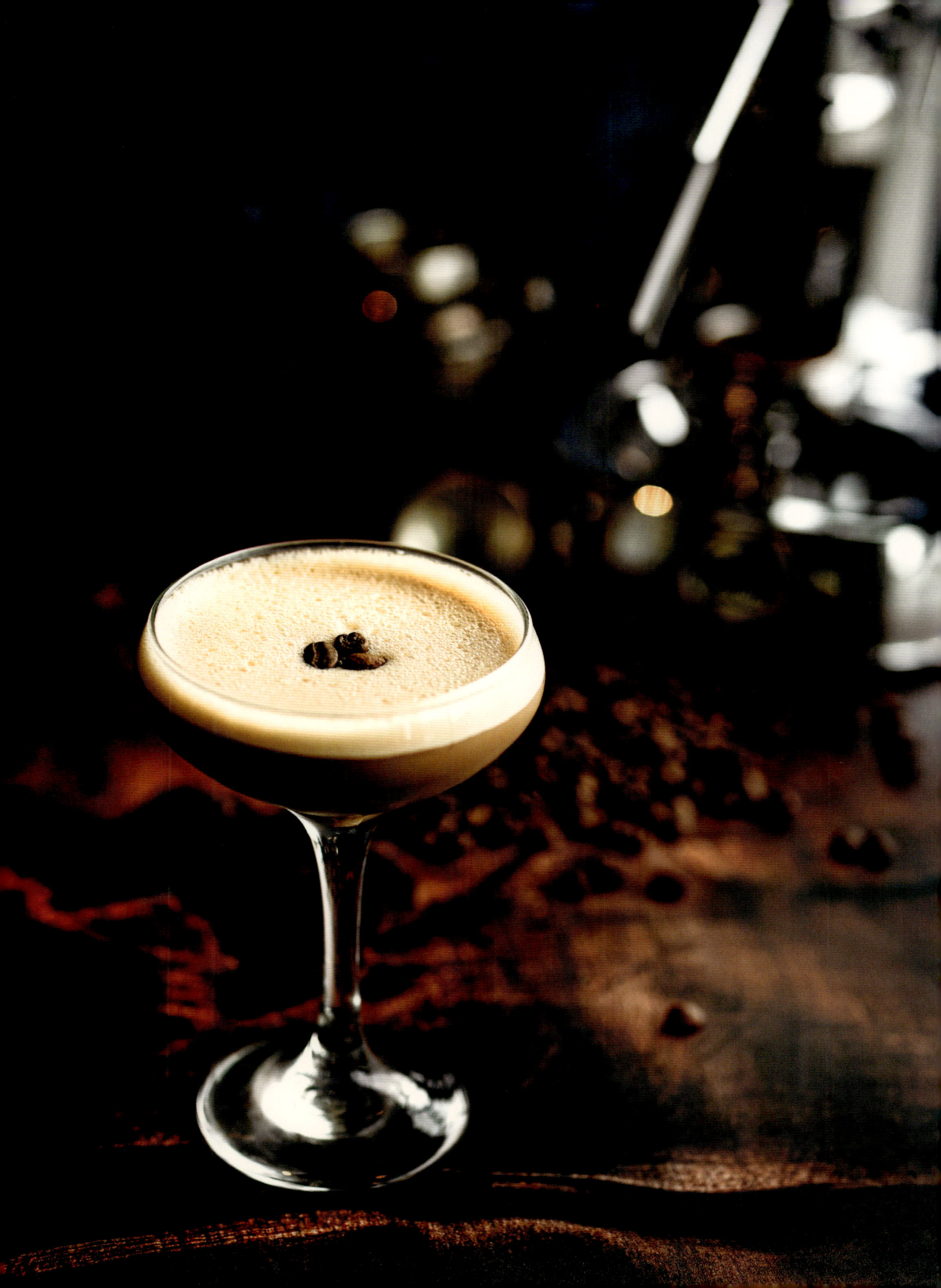

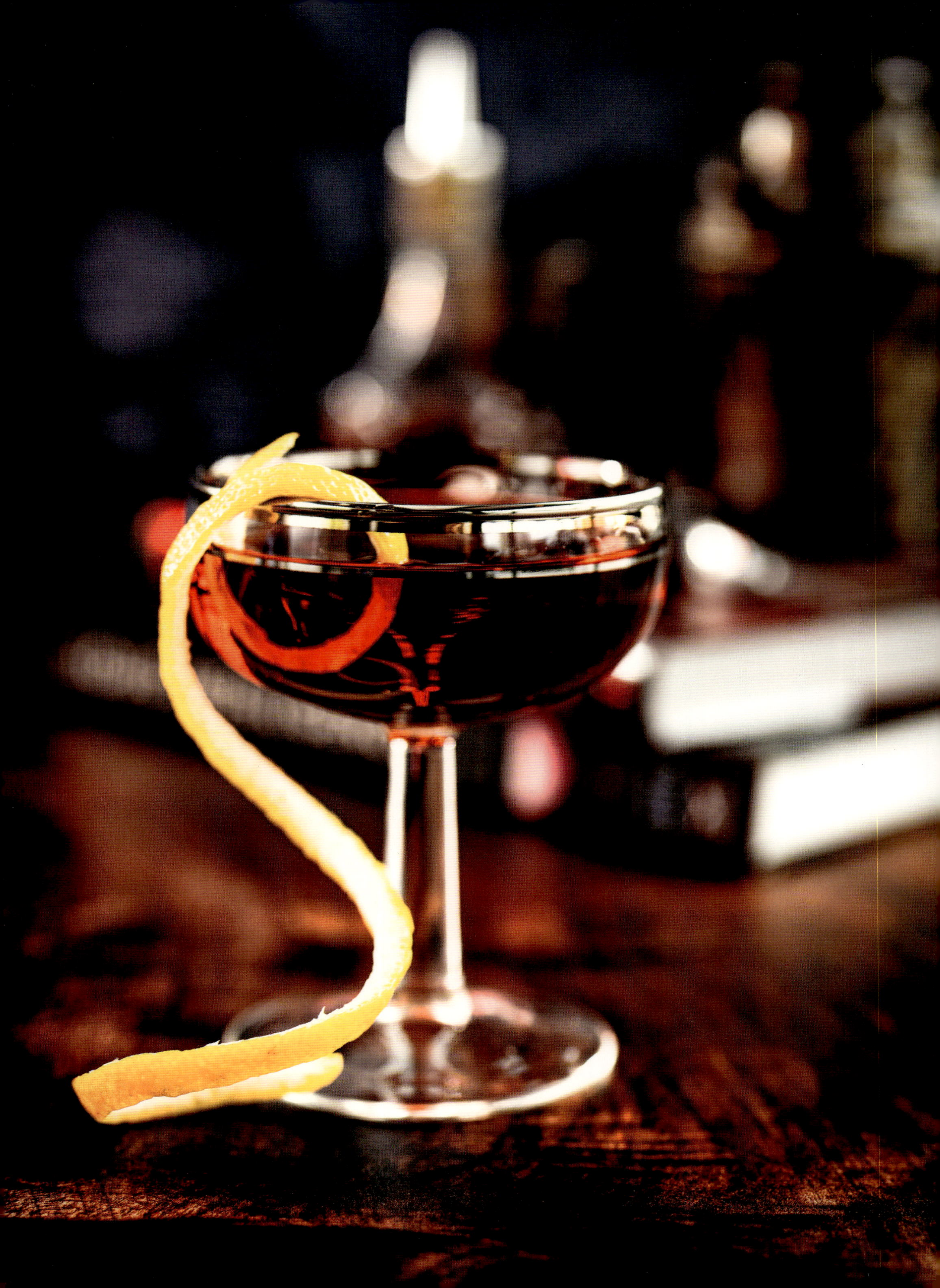

1977 LIVE *from* FLORENCE

1 ounce Angel's Envy port-finished bourbon

½ ounce Amaro Casoni

¾ ounce G.D. Vajra Barolo Chinato

1 fresh grapefruit peel

Sometimes the crazy stories you concoct while traveling also inspire mighty fine concoctions for imbibing. Such is the case with the name of this cocktail, inspired by Berto's experience on a train ride from Paris to Florence with a group of other tattoo-covered bartenders from the United States. A passenger asked the group if they were a rock band, which made them feel really damn cool, so they went with it. The late Ryan Junior, a bartender from Portland, Oregon, was wearing a hat that simply said "1977," so that became the band's name for the remainder of the train ride to Florence, where they were "scheduled to perform" that evening.
// **MAKES 1 COCKTAIL**

Combine all liquid ingredients in a mixing glass with cubed ice and stir gently for 20 seconds. Strain the drink into a chilled coupe glass.

Use a vegetable peeler or sharp paring knife to peel a wide grapefruit-peel ribbon. Express (twist and squeeze) the grapefruit peel over the top of the drink, letting the natural oils spray over the finished cocktail.

DA TWO YOOTS

BASIL-INFUSED COCCHI AMERICANO BIANCO
Makes 1 cup

10 basil leaves

1 cup Cocchi Americano Bianco

DA TWO YOOTS
Makes 1 cocktail

¾ ounce Finocchietto

¾ ounce Malfy Gin Con Limone

¾ ounce Basil-Infused Cocchi Americano Bianco

¾ ounce fresh lemon juice

1 fresh basil leaf, for garnish

The name of this cocktail is a nod to the famous courtroom scene in the movie *My Cousin Vinny*, and the drink itself stems from when Berto discovered Finocchietto while visiting Piedmont. This fennel liqueur is a great after-dinner digestif on its own, but Berto knew when he first tasted it that he wanted to use it in a refreshing cocktail. He experimented pairing it with Malfy lemon-flavored Italian gin and basil-infused Cocchi Americano Bianco and the cocktail came together pretty quickly. Finocchietto can be hard to find in Kansas City, so Berto makes his own using a method similar to making limoncello, by soaking fennel fronds in vodka or grain alcohol.

MAKE BASIL-INFUSED COCCHI AMERICANO BIANCO

Lightly crush basil leaves in the palms of your hands. Combine them with Cocchi American Bianco in a small container. Seal with a lid, then shake for 20 seconds. Leave it to infuse for at least 24 hours. Strain out basil leaves and store the Cocchi in an airtight container for up to 2 weeks, refrigerated.

MAKE DA TWO YOOTS

Combine all liquid ingredients in a cocktail shaker with cubed ice and shake aggressively for 30 seconds. Fill a tall Collins glass with crushed ice and strain the drink over the ice. Garnish with a fresh basil leaf to serve.

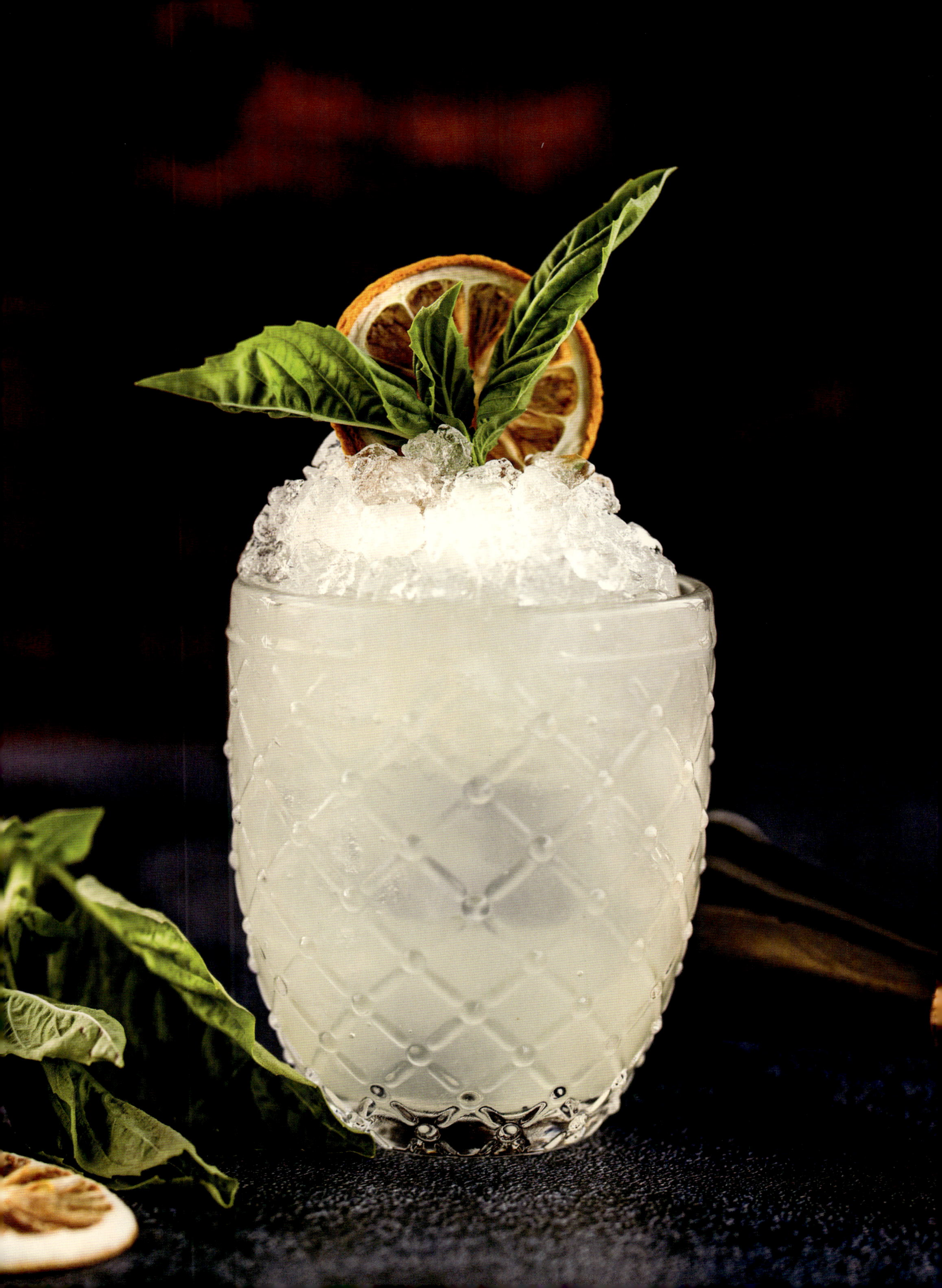

5
DESSERT

While I have made a lot of desserts over the years —I even worked in a French bakery in Denver back in 1984—I knew from the beginning that I was not going to be a pastry chef. Most pastry chefs I've known are laser-focused, highly talented artists. They have to start work at 4 a.m., which is a tad early for me. Plus, pastry chefs work with a limited range of ingredients—flour, butter, sugar, eggs, chocolate and fruit. I needed a lot more food at my disposal than that.

Ali Woody is our pastry chef at Farina. She's young, talented, wildly creative and, like so many pastry chefs, just a little wacky. I simply guide her wackiness onto the plate.

I am a huge fan of fresh fruit, especially in spring and summer when the choices seem endless: peaches, apricots, nectarines, melons, plums, and berries of every color. Fruit, fruit and more fruit. Ripe summer fruit has all the flavor bomb (read: umami) you need for deliciousness. Just add a touch of pastry and you've got everything you need.

While we love fresh fruit at Farina and try to incorporate it into our desserts as much as we can, winter and fall can present challenges on this front and require true talent. You'll see more cakes, tarts and budinos on our menu during those colder months, more extensive use of chocolate, hazelnut pastes and custards. Ali is a whiz at all of this, and the following pages represent her vision of our dessert program at Farina.

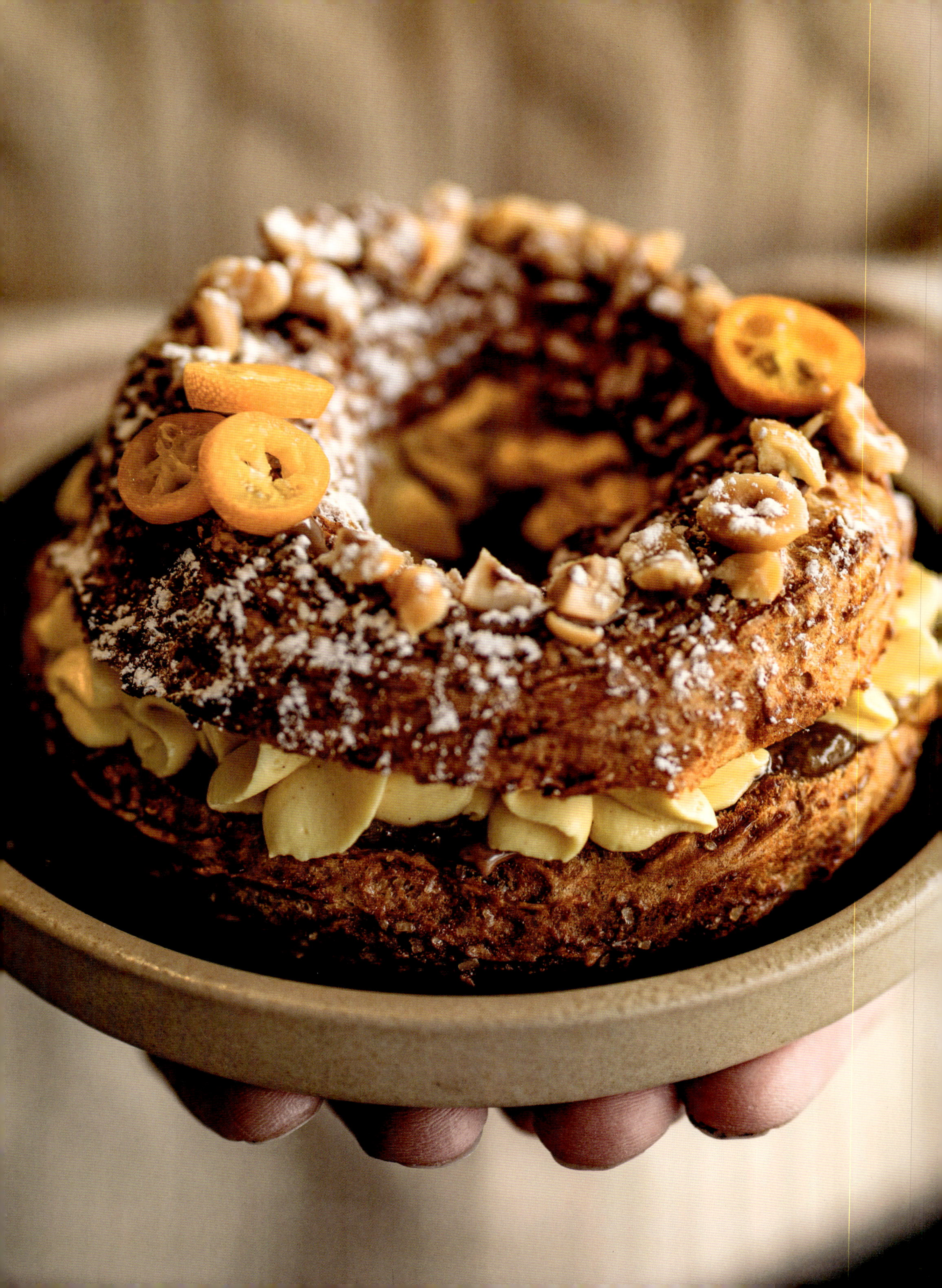

BLOOD ORANGE PARIS-BREST

PÂTE-À-CHOUX

8 large eggs

1 cup (2 sticks) butter

2 tablespoons sugar

1 teaspoon kosher salt

2 cups all-purpose flour

BLOOD ORANGE MASCARPONE CREAM

1 cup heavy cream

8 ounces mascarpone cheese, softened at room temperature

½ cup blood orange puree

½ cup powdered sugar

1 teaspoon kosher salt

½ teaspoon vanilla extract

¼ teaspoon orange extract

CRUNCHY HAZELNUT-PRALINE CREAM

2 ounces milk chocolate, chopped

½ cup hazelnut paste

1 tablespoon butter

2 tablespoons pralines, chopped

1 ounce feuilletine

GARNISHES

1 cup orange marmalade

½ cup fresh kumquat slices

¼ cup hazelnuts, finely crushed

½ cup powdered sugar

Chef Ali created this dessert for the annual Farina Tomato Dinner. We've never put it on our daily menu, but it was so well received that I'm including it here. We also happened to have a photo shoot scheduled that day and the dessert was too gorgeous not to shoot. Paris-Brest is a classic French dessert, and Ali created her version of it to rave reviews! // **MAKES 12 SERVINGS**

MAKE PÂTE-À-CHOUX

Preheat oven to 400°F.

Line a baking sheet with parchment paper and use a 3-inch round cookie cutter to trace 12 circles across the sheet, leaving 2 inches of space around each circle. Set aside.

Crack eggs into a measuring cup and set aside. Combine 2 cups water, butter, sugar and salt in a large saucepan over medium-high heat and bring to a boil. Once it's boiling, add flour all at once. Use a wooden spoon to stir the mixture vigorously until it has turned to a thick paste. Reduce heat to medium and continue stirring until smooth, approximately 3 minutes. Use a rubber spatula to scrape the warm paste into a mixing bowl fitted to a stand mixer. Mix on medium speed for about 30 seconds to allow steam to escape. Next, with mixer still running, add eggs one at a time until fully incorporated. Batter should appear smooth and creamy. Chill batter for 35 minutes, then transfer it into a piping bag fitted with a medium star-shaped tip.

Place the parchment-lined baking sheet on the countertop and pipe batter over the previously traced circles, forming rings of dough. Make sure the ends are slightly overlapping to complete a circle. Bake for 20 to 30 minutes or until pastry has puffed and reached a deep golden brown. Remove the pâte-à-choux from the oven and set on a cooling rack for at least 30 minutes. When cooled completely, use a serrated knife to gently slice the pastries in half horizontally. Separate the halves, keeping the tops aside.

continues on page 204

DESSERT

BLOOD ORANGE PARIS-BREST
continued from page 203

MAKE BLOOD ORANGE MASCARPONE CREAM

Using a stand mixer, whip heavy cream on high speed until stiff peaks form. In a separate mixing bowl, use a rubber spatula to stir mascarpone until slightly softened and supple. Fold blood orange puree, powdered sugar, salt and extracts into mascarpone until smooth. Gently fold whipped cream into mascarpone mixture. Transfer to a piping bag fitted with a large, star-shaped tip and refrigerate for 1 hour.

MAKE CRUNCHY HAZELNUT-PRALINE CREAM

Heat water in the bottom of a medium sauce pot to create a double boiler. Combine milk chocolate, hazelnut paste and butter in a medium bowl and place it on the double boiler. Stir ingredients together until melted and smooth, 4 to 5 minutes. Remove chocolate mixture from heat and use a rubber spatula to fold in noisettes and feuilletine. Let cool at room temperature for 15 to 20 minutes.

ASSEMBLE PARIS-BREST

Arrange bottom halves of pâte-à-choux side by side on a baking sheet. Use a small offset spatula to spread crunchy hazelnut-praline cream on the cut pâte-à-choux bottoms. Then, spread a thin layer of orange marmalade on top of the hazelnut-praline cream. Next, pipe blood orange mascarpone cream in a fluffy ring around the pâte-à-choux bottoms. Place pâte-à-choux tops (or crowns) on the mascarpone cream and press lightly to secure them. Use a small offset spatula to spread a thin, narrow layer of orange marmalade around the center of the tops. (The marmalade will help the garnishes stick to the tops.) Sprinkle crushed hazelnuts on the marmalade, then arrange several kumquat slices over each top. To finish, use a small, fine-mesh strainer to dust each of the crowns with powdered sugar.

DESSERT

FARINA TIRAMISU

MASCARPONE CUSTARD

2 cups heavy cream

2 packets powdered gelatin

¾ cup Marsala wine, slightly warmed

10 large egg yolks

¾ cup sugar

1 teaspoon kosher salt, divided

16 ounces mascarpone cheese, room temperature

Juice and zest from 1 orange

1 teaspoon vanilla extract

ESPRESSO SYRUP

3 cups granulated sugar

3 cups water

½ cup instant espresso granules

1 ounce J. Rieger's Caffè Amaro (or substitute your favorite amaro cordial)

1 ounce dark rum

Juice and zest from 1 orange

2 tablespoons cocoa powder

1 teaspoon vanilla extract

1 cinnamon stick

TIRAMISU CAKE

Cooking spray, to grease pan

60 ladyfinger cookies, store bought

½ cup cocoa powder, for final garnish

This coffee-flavored, no-bake sponge cake is a forever favorite at Farina and Italian restaurants everywhere. To ensure success when serving, the parchment paper lining the bottom of the pan and sides is essential to slice and lift out tiramisu portions after it has been refrigerated. If you are spooning out the tiramisu straight from the pan, this step is not necessary.

// **MAKES A 13-BY-9-INCH CAKE**

MAKE MASCARPONE CUSTARD

In the bowl of a stand mixer, whip cream until soft peaks form. Set aside.

In a small separate bowl, stir gelatin into warm Marsala to bloom for 5 minutes; keep warm.

Set up a double boiler by filling a large soup pot with 3 inches water, making sure that the bowl of a stand mixer will fit snugly into the pot without touching the water. Bring water to a boil.

Combine egg yolks, sugar, Marsala–gelatin mixture and ½ teaspoon salt in the bowl of a stand mixer and set it over the double boiler. Whisk the mixture continuously until sugar and gelatin have dissolved, approximately 3 to 4 minutes. The mixture will thicken slightly and become lighter in color. Remove from heat, transfer the bowl to the stand mixer and mix on high speed until the outside of the bowl is cool to the touch, approximately 5 to 6 minutes.

While egg mixture is cooling, combine mascarpone, orange juice and zest, remaining ½ teaspoon salt and vanilla extract in a small bowl. Use a spoon to stir until cheese has softened and the ingredients are well incorporated. When egg mixture is cool and with the mixer running on low speed, add cheese mixture to the mixing bowl a little at a time. Then, increase the speed to medium and whisk just until cheese and egg are well combined and a soft, creamy mixture forms, approximately 1 to 2 minutes. Be careful not to curdle or break the cheese mixture. Remove bowl from the mixer and fold in whipped cream. Keep at room temperature until ready to assemble tiramisu.

continues on page 207

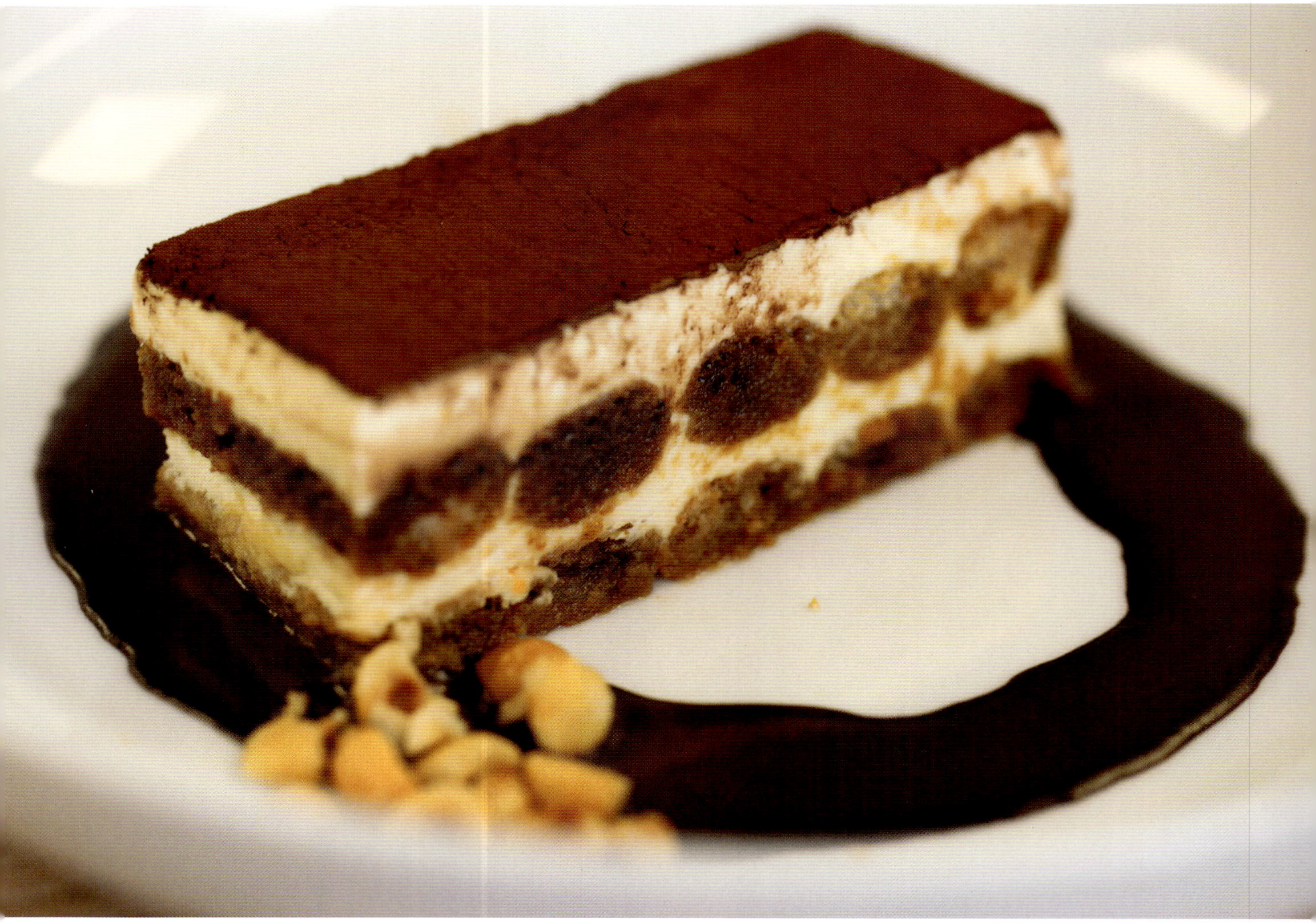

FARINA TIRAMISU

continued from page 205

MAKE ESPRESSO SYRUP

Bring syrup ingredients to a boil for 3 minutes, stirring frequently, then strain, cool and set aside.

MAKE TIRAMISU CAKE

Use cooking spray to coat the bottom and sides of a 9-by-13-inch baking dish. Then cut a piece of parchment paper to line the bottom and sides.

Soak each lady finger in cooled espresso syrup for a couple of seconds at a time, until completely saturated. Arrange cookies side by side to fill the bottom of the prepared baking dish. If necessary, cut ladyfingers to the size needed to fill the bottom entirely. Next, use an offset spatula to spread half of the mascarpone mixture over the cookie layer, then repeat the previous step of soaking and arranging cookies to create a second layer on top of the mascarpone. Press cookies lightly into the cream. Spread remaining mascarpone cream on the soaked cookies.

Lay a thick towel down on a clean countertop. Lift the baking dish 2 to 3 inches off the counter and drop it down on the towel. Repeat several times. This helps the overall cake layers settle and attach to each other, firming up. Finally, dust the top generously and evenly with cocoa powder. Refrigerate for at least 2 hours, or until gelatin has fully set.

DESSERT

CARAMELIZED BRIOCHE
with FALL PEARS and FIGS

BRIOCHE

2 teaspoons active dry yeast

3 tablespoons granulated sugar

⅓ cup slightly warm water

3½ cups all-purpose flour

1 teaspoon kosher salt

6 large eggs, room temperature

1½ cups (3 sticks) butter, softened

Egg wash (1 egg beaten with 1 tablespoon milk)

POACHED FRUIT

4 ripe Bartlett pears

1 cup Marsala wine

½ teaspoon vanilla extract

4 cups granulated sugar

TO FINISH

2 tablespoons butter, softened

4 tablespoons granulated sugar

8-ounce jar apricot marmalade

1 quart vanilla ice cream

2 cups fresh figs

½ cup toasted almonds, crushed

This is a wonderful and very popular dessert at Farina. Making it is a two-day process, so prepare the brioche a day ahead of time. Once you've assembled the dessert the next day, you can freeze the rest of the brioche for multiple uses. The sugar crust on the brioche plays an integral role in forming the dessert's layers of texture. // SERVES 4

MAKE BRIOCHE

Combine yeast, sugar and water in a small bowl and let bloom, approximately 5 minutes.

In the bowl of a stand mixer fitted with a dough hook, combine flour, salt and yeast mixture; mix on low speed. Add eggs one at a time, then increase mixer speed to medium-high and knead the dough until it looks smooth and elastic, approximately 3 to 5 minutes. The dough will pull away from the sides of the bowl.

Decrease speed to low and add butter, 1 tablespoon at a time, allowing butter to completely incorporate before adding the next tablespoon. Once all butter has been incorporated, increase speed to medium and mix well for 20 minutes. Scrape down the sides of the bowl as needed. The dough will look shiny, and the texture will be smooth and supple.

Give dough the "windowpane test" to check if sufficiently kneaded (elastic): Take a small nugget of dough and, using your fingers, stretch it out into a thin "window" about 4 to 5 inches wide. If it doesn't break and you can see light through it, then the dough is ready. If not, continue to mix the dough for another 8 to 10 minutes. Remove dough from the bowl and shape it into a firm ball. Place it in a greased bowl and cover with plastic wrap. Refrigerate overnight.

The next day, remove dough from refrigerator and let it proof (double in size) in the bowl at room temperature for 1 hour.

Butter an 8-by-5-inch loaf pan, or coat the inside with cooking spray, then line the bottom with parchment paper.

continues on page 210

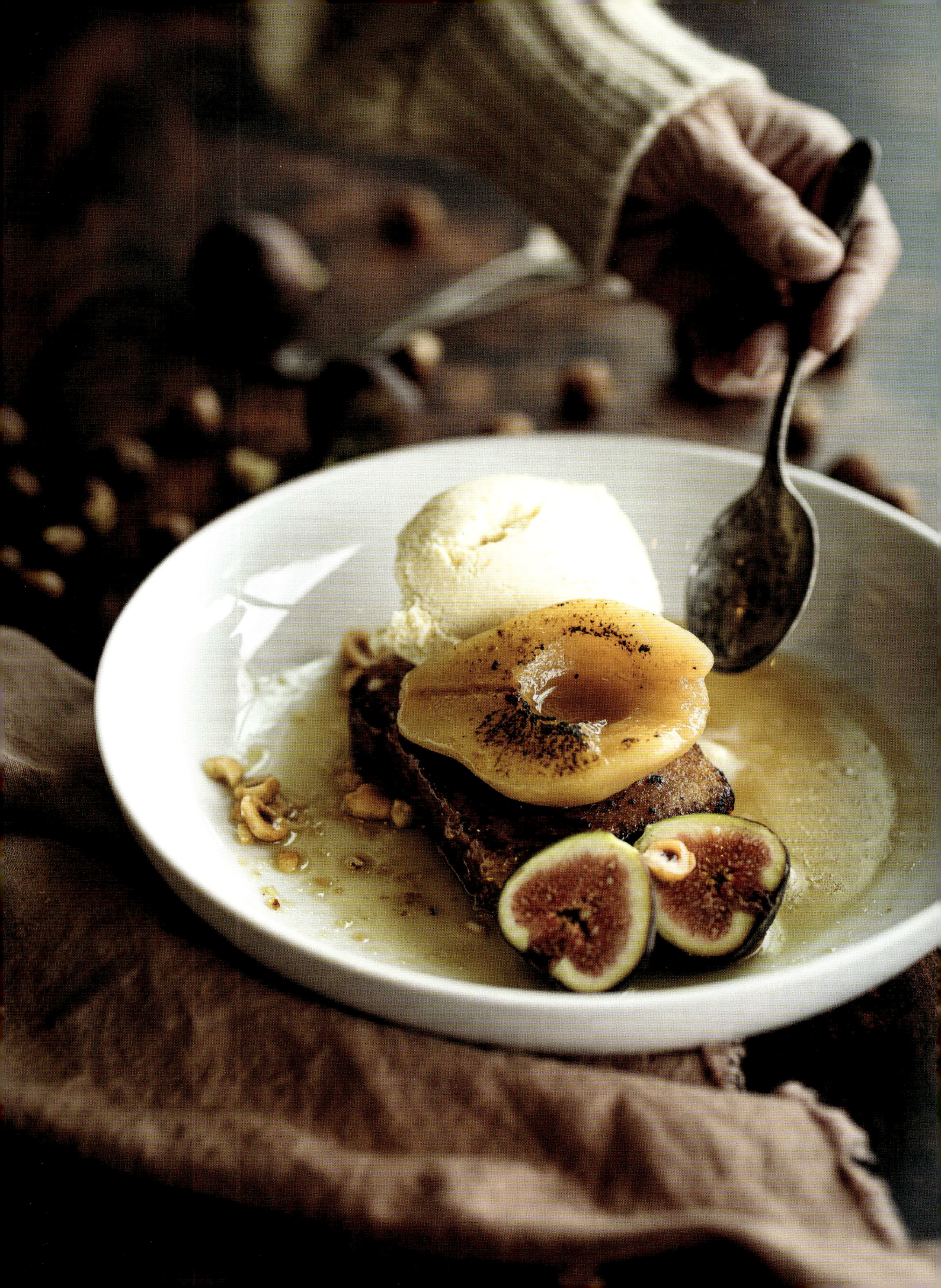

DESSERT

CARAMELIZED BRIOCHE with FALL PEARS and FIGS
continued from page 208

Turn dough out from the bowl onto a lightly greased work surface and shape it into a log. Place the log in the prepared loaf pan. Allow to proof for 1½ to 2 hours or until dough has doubled in size inside the loaf pan.

Preheat oven to 350°F.

Brush the top of brioche dough with egg wash. Bake at 350°F for 45 minutes or until outer crust is a deep brown color and interior is cooked through. Test the interior doneness with a cake tester probe. It should come out without any uncooked dough clinging to it.

Remove brioche from oven and let cool for 5 minutes. Turn out loaf onto a cooling rack. Don't let the brioche cool completely inside the pan or the crust will sweat and become soggy.

MAKE POACHED FRUIT

Cut pears in half and remove stems and cores. Set aside.

Combine 3 cups water, Marsala, vanilla extract and sugar in a medium pot and bring to a boil over high heat, then reduce to a simmer for 5 minutes. Place pears into the syrup and allow to poach gently for 3 to 5 minutes depending on their ripeness. Remove pot from heat and allow pears and syrup to cool. Store pears in the poaching liquid until ready to serve.

TO SERVE

Once brioche has fully cooled, cut 4 1-inch-thick slices from the loaf. Wrap remaining brioche in plastic wrap and reserve for another use. Arrange the 4 brioche slices on a baking sheet, not touching each other. Spread a thin layer of soft butter on each slice of bread and apply an even, generous coating of granulated sugar over the top. Chill the prepared brioche slices for 15 minutes in the refrigerator. Use a blowtorch or the oven broiler to caramelize the sugar on the brioche slices, as with a crème brûlée. Carefully, allow sugar to bubble and caramelize, then let toasts cool. The sugar will harden to create a deep golden crust on each slice.

Spread a generous spoonful of apricot marmalade across the bottom of 4 dessert plates. Place a caramelized brioche toast on top of the marmalade. Then, place 2 poached pear halves on top of the brioche. Finish with a scoop of ice cream, fresh figs and crushed almonds. Drizzle a small amount of poaching liquid over the fruit and around the plate.

> The fruit garnish on this dessert can change with the seasons. Plums, peaches and apricots are wonderful in the summer, pears and apples work well in the fall and winter months.

PEACH and BLACKBERRY CROSTATA
with LEMON CURD ICE CREAM

LEMON CURD ICE CREAM

1 cup fresh lemon juice

Zest from 2 lemons

1 cup granulated sugar

1 teaspoon kosher salt

6 large eggs

8 egg yolks

1 cup cold butter, cut into cubes

PIE DOUGH

3 cups all-purpose flour

1 tablespoon granulated sugar

1 teaspoon kosher salt

2½ sticks cold butter, diced into pea-size morsels

1 large egg, beaten

4 to 6 tablespoons ice cold water

A crostata is a rustic Italian fruit pie. Italians typically use fruit marmalade as the filling for crostata, with little or no fresh fruit added. They also tend to bake it much flatter. We like to pack ours with peak-season peaches and blackberries and pair it with a heaping scoop of lemon curd ice cream. Sometimes we add a smear of our own marmalade on the dough before piling on the fruit. // **MAKES 6 CROSTATAS**

MAKE LEMON CURD ICE CREAM

Set up a double boiler by filling a large soup pot with 3 inches water, making sure that a medium mixing bowl will fit snugly into the pot without touching the water. Bring water to a boil.

Combine all ingredients except butter in a medium mixing bowl. Place the bowl over double boiler on the stove and whisk ingredients vigorously to combine. Continue whisking (gently and steady now) until mixture has paled in color and thickened enough to coat the back of a spoon, like a custard. Remove the curd from the double boiler and whisk in cold butter. Cool the finished curd in an ice bath or let it cool down naturally. When fully cold, churn the curd in the canister of an ice cream machine, following the manufacturer's instructions.

MAKE PIE DOUGH

Combine flour, sugar, and salt in a mixing bowl. Pour it into a pile on a clean work surface. Add cold butter on top of the flour, then use your hands to rub butter into flour for about a minute. Drizzle beaten egg over the flour mixture along with 4 tablespoons water. Gradually mix egg and water into flour just until a shaggy dough forms, about 3 to 4 minutes. Add remaining water if necessary.

The dough for crostatas and pies is like biscuit dough. Don't overwork the dough or it will be tough, not crisp and flaky. Continue to knead dough lightly until the shagginess turns smooth. You might still see small chunks of butter in the dough and that is okay. Wrap the dough in plastic wrap and chill for at least 1 hour before rolling out.

continues on page 213

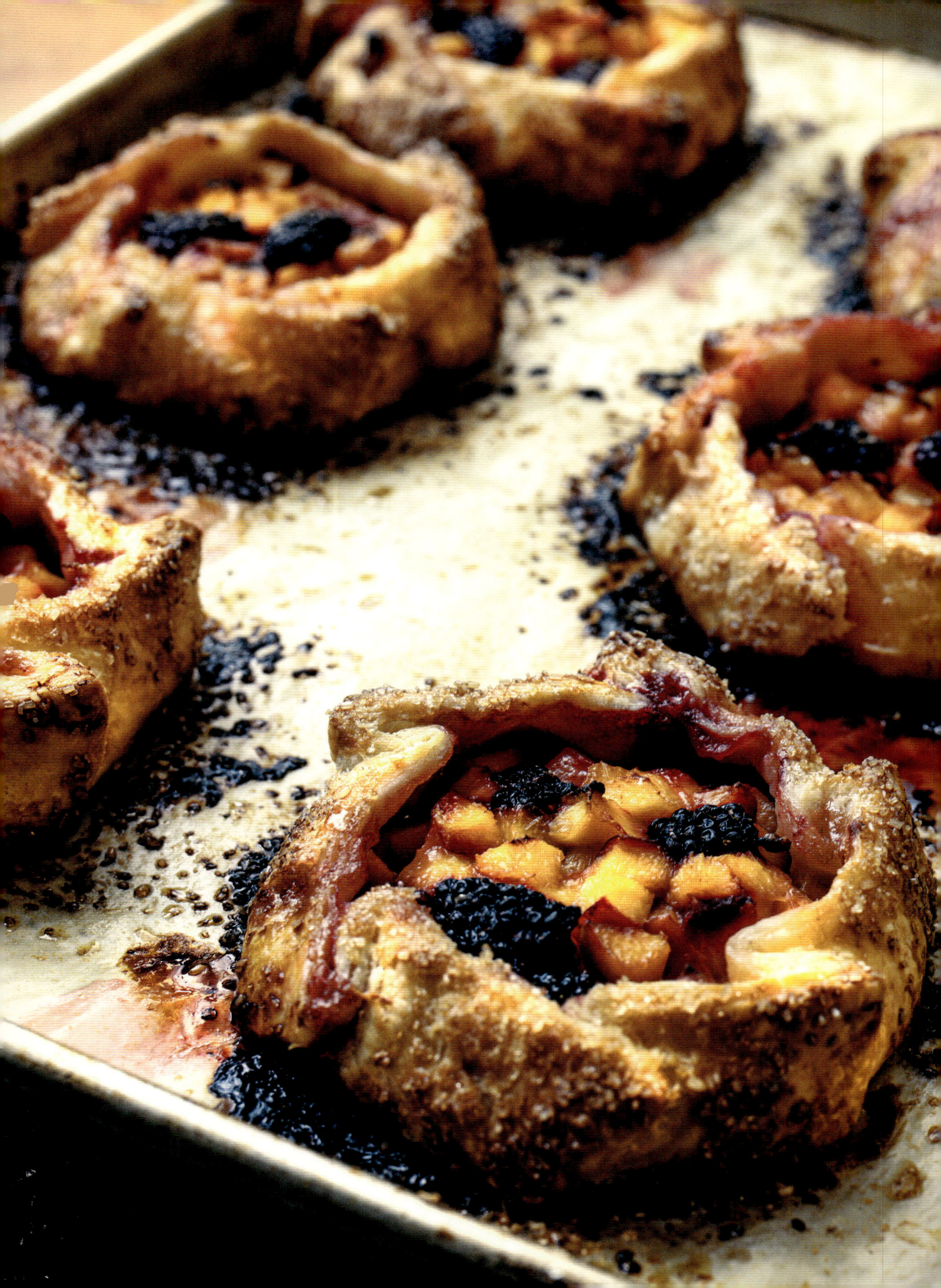

DESSERT

PEACH and BLACKBERRY CROSTATA with LEMON CURD ICE CREAM

continued from page 211

PEACH AND BLACKBERRY CROSTATA

2 tablespoons cornstarch

1 lemon, juiced and zested

½ cup granulated sugar, plus more for dusting

1½ quarts ripe summer peaches (unpeeled), diced large

½ quart whole blackberries, halved

6 pie dough circles, 6 inches in diameter and ⅛ inch thick

Egg wash (1 egg beaten with 1 tablespoon milk)

½ cup apricot jelly (optional)

4 tablespoons powdered sugar, for dusting

MAKE CROSTATAS

Preheat oven to 400°F.

Combine cornstarch, lemon zest and granulated sugar in a small bowl. In a larger mixing bowl, combine fruits with sugar mixture and lemon juice. Lay the dough circles on a work surface. Scoop a large handful of peaches and blackberries onto the center of each dough circle, leaving a 1-inch border of pastry around the fruit. Pinch and fold the pastry border, pleating it over the edges of the fruit, leaving the center fruit exposed. Brush pastry with egg wash and sprinkle granulated sugar around the edges.

Bake for 35 to 40 minutes, until crust is a deep golden-brown color and filling has started to bubble. Remove crostatas from the oven and let cool on a baking rack. If desired, heat apricot jelly in a small saucepan until melted, then brush over the top of the cooled fruit to glaze.

When ready to serve, dust crostatas with powdered sugar and serve with a healthy scoop of lemon curd ice cream.

DESSERT

SUMMER BERRY COBBLER
with PEACH ICE CREAM

Summer is the sweetest season for Missouri berries. This cobbler stars three of the Show-Me State's favorites—raspberries, blueberries and blackberries. Of course, it would be a sin to serve this without a scoop of homemade peach ice cream. **// SERVES 4**

PEACH ICE CREAM

3 cups heavy cream

1 cup peach jam or marmalade

½ cup granulated sugar

½ teaspoon kosher salt

½ teaspoon vanilla extract

¼ teaspoon almond extract

8 egg yolks

BERRY FILLING

1 cup granulated sugar

2 tablespoons cornstarch

1 cup summer blackberries

1 cup summer raspberries

1 cup summer blueberries

Juice and zest of 1 lemon

COBBLER CRUMB

2 cups all-purpose flour

1½ cups brown sugar

1 cup (2 sticks) cold butter, diced small

½ cup pecan pieces

½ cup toasted almonds, finely crushed

½ teaspoon kosher salt

2 tablespoons buttermilk

MAKE PEACH ICE CREAM

In a saucepan, combine heavy cream, jam, sugar, salt and extracts and bring to a boil over high heat. Stir often until sugar has dissolved, to keep the marmalade from sticking to the bottom of the pan and burning the ice cream base. Turn off heat as soon as the cream comes to a boil.

While cream is heating, whisk egg yolks in a separate large mixing bowl. Temper the egg yolks by slowly pouring a thin stream of the heated cream mixture into the egg yolks while whisking constantly.

Allow ice cream base to chill completely in the refrigerator. Then, churn the batter in an ice cream machine according to the manufacturer's instructions. Store in the freezer for at least 1 hour before serving.

MAKE BERRY FILLING

Whisk together sugar and cornstarch in a medium-size mixing bowl. Add fruit and toss to coat with sugar. Gently stir in lemon juice and zest. Set aside.

MAKE COBBLER CRUMB

In a separate mixing bowl, combine flour, brown sugar, butter, nuts and salt. Using your hands, crush the butter into the flour and nut mixture until it resembles a mealy consistency. Add buttermilk to moisten, being careful not to overmix. Cobbler topping should still be crumbly.

ASSEMBLE COBBLERS

Preheat oven to 375°F.

Evenly divide macerated berries and juice into 4 individual-size, shallow custard dishes. Top each dish of berries with a generous heap of crumble mixture, making sure to cover berries. Bake cobblers on a baking sheet until sauce bubbles and thickens, and crust is a deep golden-brown, approximately 25 minutes. Remove cobblers from oven and let cool for 10 minutes. Serve warm with a scoop of peach ice cream.

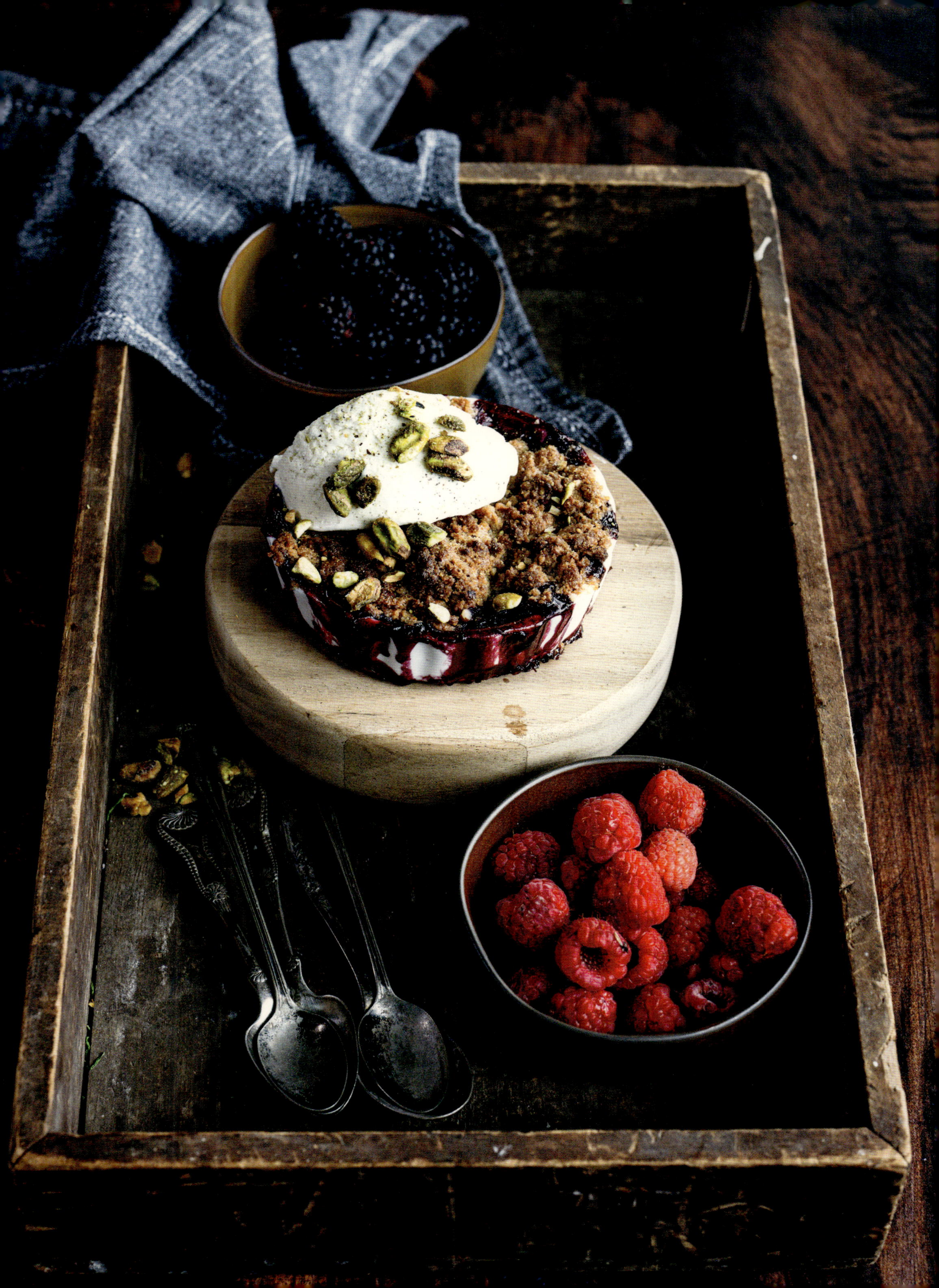

DESSERT

TORTA NOCCIOLA

1 tablespoon butter or pan spray (for greasing the pan)

2¼ cups toasted hazelnuts

2 tablespoons cocoa powder

2 tablespoons ground espresso

4 teaspoons baking powder

¼ cup unsalted butter, melted to warm

2 teaspoons vanilla extract

8 egg yolks

1¼ cups powdered sugar (for cake mix)

8 egg whites

1 tablespoon powdered sugar (for egg whites)

2 cups Frangelico syrup (2 parts simple syrup, 1 part Frangelico)

This quintessential Italian cake originates from the Langhe region of Piedmont, an area renowned for its superb hazelnuts. The cake is best served slightly warm with a dollop of whipped cream or your favorite ice cream. A seasonal fresh fruit compote is also a wonderful addition. // **MAKES 1 CAKE**

Preheat oven to 325°F.

Butter or spray a 10-inch springform pan and set aside.

Combine hazelnuts, cocoa powder, espresso and baking powder in a food processor and process until mixture is fine and powdery. Set aside.

Combine melted butter and vanilla; set aside.

Using a stand mixer with a whisk attachment, whip egg yolks and 1¼ cups powdered sugar until pale and fluffy, about 5 minutes. Transfer the mixture to a mixing bowl and set aside. Wash and dry the mixer bowl thoroughly, then combine egg whites and 1 tablespoon powdered sugar and whip the egg whites to stiff peaks, about 2 minutes.

Using a rubber spatula, slowly fold nut mixture into the fluffy egg yolks, alternating with melted butter mixture, until everything is fully combined. The batter should be thick like dough. Use a rubber spatula to fold egg whites into the batter in 3 parts. Batter will become looser with each addition.

Pour batter into greased springform pan and bake until center is just set, 30 to 40 minutes. Remove cake from the oven. Using a pastry brush, generously soak the hot cake with Frangelico syrup. Remove detachable ring from the springform pan and allow cake to fully cool before slicing.

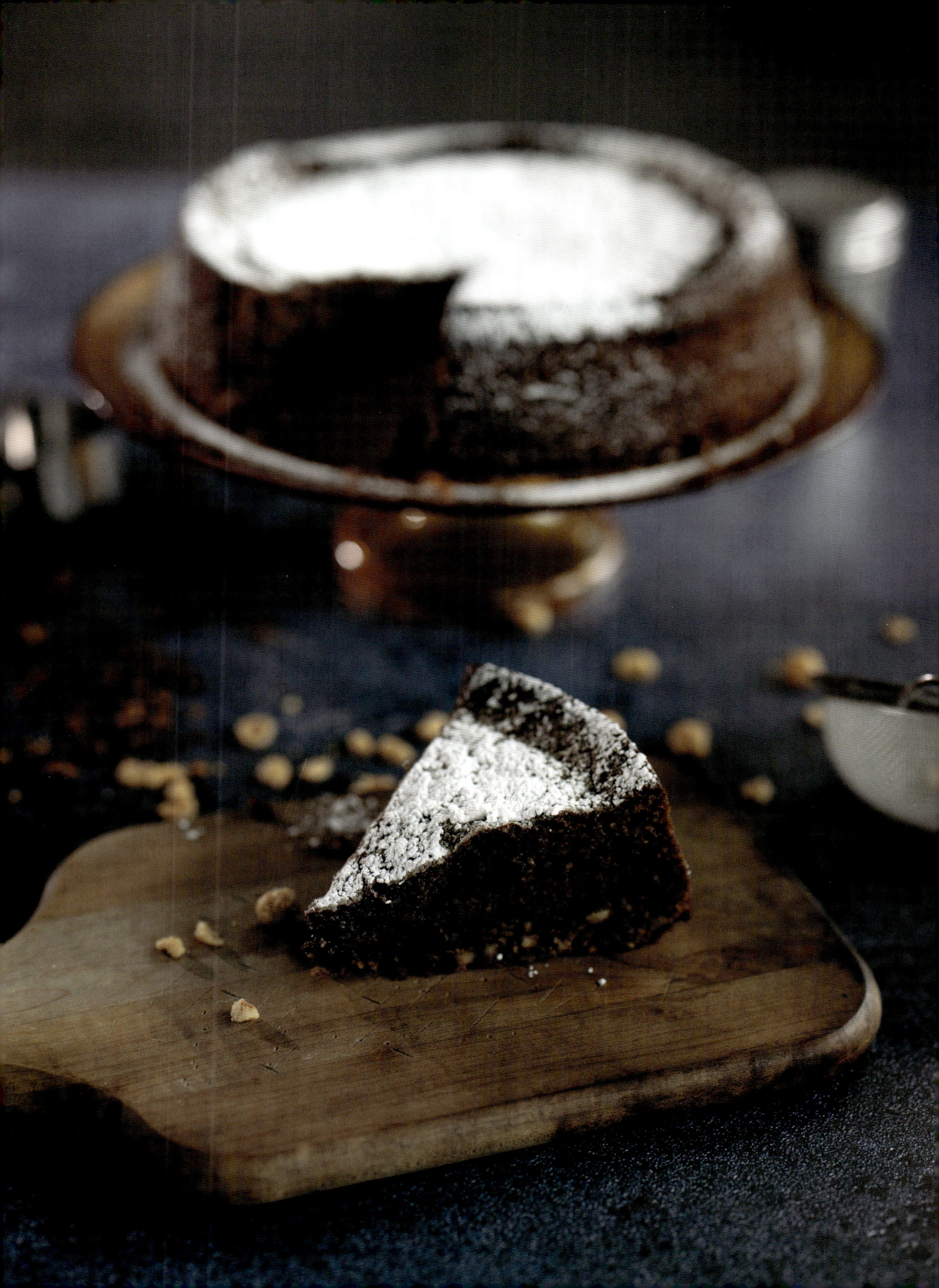

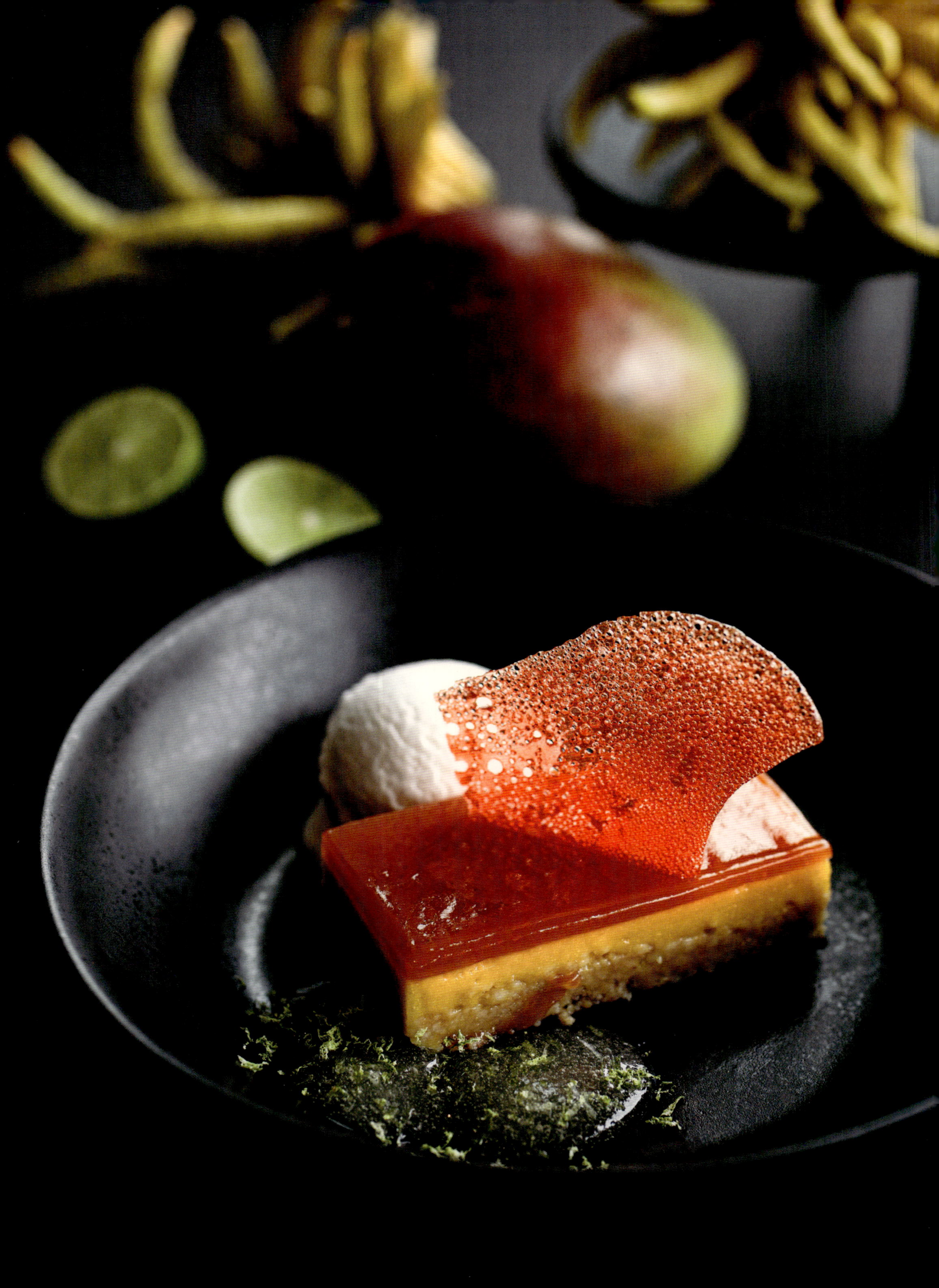

DESSERT

GUAVA–PASSION FRUIT BAR
with COCONUT-MAKRUT SORBET

COCONUT-MAKRUT (KAFFIR LIME) SORBET

1 cup granulated sugar

½ teaspoon kosher salt

3 makrut (kaffir) lime leaves, torn into pieces

1 16-ounce can coconut milk

BUTTER COOKIE CRUST

1½ cups cold butter, cubed

2 teaspoons vanilla extract

2 cups sugar

3 cups all-purpose flour

1 teaspoon kosher salt

¼ cup melted butter

PASSION FRUIT CURD

1 cup passion fruit puree or juice

1 cup granulated sugar

6 large eggs

6 egg yolks

½ teaspoon kosher salt

1 pound butter, cubed

GUAVA GELÉE

8 gelatin sheets

1 cup granulated sugar

3 makrut lime leaves (or substitute key limes)

2 cups guava puree or juice

When you need to liven up your Italian kitchen with some fresh tropical flavors, this island-inspired dessert does the trick. I absolutely love guava and passion fruit, separately and together. They may not be traditional Italian flavors, but here they are, matched up in a delicious dessert. Kaffir lime leaves can be found online or at Asian markets. I have a 4-foot-tall kaffir lime tree in my dining room that produces leaves at a prolific pace. // **SERVES 12**

MAKE COCONUT-MAKRUT SORBET

In a small saucepan, combine 1 cup water, sugar, salt and lime leaves and bring to a boil, stirring to dissolve sugar, for about 5 minutes. Remove syrup from heat and mix in coconut milk. Strain the sorbet mixture into a small container and set the container in an ice bath to chill or refrigerate until completely chilled, 1 to 2 hours.

Churn the sorbet in an ice cream machine according to the manufacturer's instructions. When ready, transfer sorbet to a small container and freeze for at least 1 hour before serving.

MAKE BUTTER COOKIE CRUST

Preheat oven to 375°F.

Using a stand mixer on medium-high speed, cream together cubed butter, vanilla and sugar until mixture turns a pale yellow color. Combine flour and salt in a small bowl. Reduce mixer speed and gradually pour flour mixture into the butter-and-sugar mixture. When thoroughly combined, scoop cookie dough out onto a small baking sheet. Using an offset spatula, spread dough evenly across the baking sheet. Bake for 8 to 10 minutes or until cookie reaches a golden-brown color and is cooked through. Remove baking sheet from oven and allow it to cool at room temperature, then break cookie into pieces. Keep oven heated at 375°F.

Using a food processor, crush cookie pieces into a fine crumb. Transfer to a mixing bowl, add melted butter and mix well. Press the mixture evenly, about 1¼ inch thick, across the bottom of a 13-by-9-inch baking pan lined with parchment paper. Put the baking pan in the oven for 3 to 5 more minutes, until crumb has baked to a deeper golden-brown color. Remove and set aside to cool.

continues on page 220

GUAVA-PASSION FRUIT BAR
with COCONUT-MAKRUT SORBET

continued from page 219

MAKE PASSION FRUIT CURD

Set up a double boiler by filling a large soup pot with 3 inches water, making sure that a medium mixing bowl will fit snugly into the pot without touching the water. Bring water to a boil.

Whisk together all ingredients except butter in a large mixing bowl over the double boiler. Continuously whisk until mixture has thickened to a pudding-like consistency and lightened in color, approximately 10 minutes. Remove the curd bowl from heat and quickly whisk butter cubes into the curd, a few pieces at a time, until fully incorporated. When butter is incorporated, pour the curd over the previously made cookie crust, using an offset spatula to evenly distribute the curd. It should be about 1 inch thick. Refrigerate until curd has set completely, at least 1 hour.

MAKE GUAVA GELÉE

Bloom (soften) gelatin sheets in enough cold water to cover, for approximately 5 minutes, until softened completely. Gather the gelatin with your hands and gently squeeze out excess water. Set aside.

Bring 1 cup water, sugar and makrut (kaffir) leaves to a boil in a medium sauce pot. When water boils, remove pot from heat and whisk in gelatin and guava puree. Pass the guava mixture through a fine strainer into a medium mixing bowl.

Use a ladle to evenly pour guava gelée over the top of the chilled passion fruit curd. The gelée should be about ½ inch thick. Refrigerate until gelée has fully set, at least 1 hour.

TO SERVE

Once the guava gelée has set up completely, remove the baking pan from the refrigerator and use a hot knife to cut the tart into squares. An efficient portion size for the dimensions of this pan is 12 pieces, 4 cuts across the length and 3 cuts across the width. Serve with a scoop of coconut-makrut sorbet.

DESSERT

WHITE COCONUT LAYER CAKE

COCONUT CAKE

1 tablespoon butter or cooking spray, to grease cake pans

2 cups all-purpose flour

1½ cups granulated sugar

1 cup finely shredded coconut, plus extra for garnishing the cake

3 teaspoons baking powder

1 teaspoon kosher salt

½ cup warm water

1 cup canola oil

1 cup buttermilk

2 eggs

1 teaspoon coconut extract

1 teaspoon vanilla extract

½ teaspoon almond extract

ALMOND BUTTERCREAM

2 cups (4 sticks) butter, softened

1 teaspoon vanilla extract

½ teaspoon almond extract

2 pounds powdered sugar

4 tablespoons heavy cream

This is a delicious version of the classic coconut cake. When filling and frosting the cake, remember that you will be dividing the amount of frosting onto 2 cake layers and spreading enough on the exterior of the finished cake to hold the shredded coconut in place. When spreading the frosting, the spatula can become tacky quickly. To prevent that, dip the spatula in hot running water, wipe it dry, then resume spreading. You'll be pleasantly surprised at the smoothness of this procedure.

// MAKES 1 DOUBLE-LAYER CAKE

MAKE COCONUT CAKE

Grease 2 8-inch round cake pans and set aside.

Preheat oven to 325°F.

Combine flour, sugar, 1 cup coconut, baking powder and salt in the bowl of a stand mixer. Whisk together remaining wet ingredients in a separate mixing bowl. With the mixer running on low speed, gradually pour wet ingredients into dry ingredients and mix until barely combined, approximately 1 minute (over-mixing the batter will make the cake crumb tough). Divide batter between the cake pans and bake on the middle oven rack for 20 to 25 minutes, or until a toothpick inserted in the center comes out clean. Allow cakes to cool for 30 minutes before inverting pans over cooling racks.

MAKE ALMOND BUTTERCREAM

Combine butter and extracts in the bowl of a stand mixer. Using the whisk attachment, whip at medium-high speed for 2 minutes. Reduce speed to low and gradually spoon in powdered sugar, adding cream a little at a time as needed to moisten. When all the sugar and cream have been added, increase speed to high and whip until frosting has lightened in color and has almost doubled in volume, approximately 2 to 3 minutes. Transfer the buttercream frosting to 1 or more piping bags and set aside.

continues on page 223

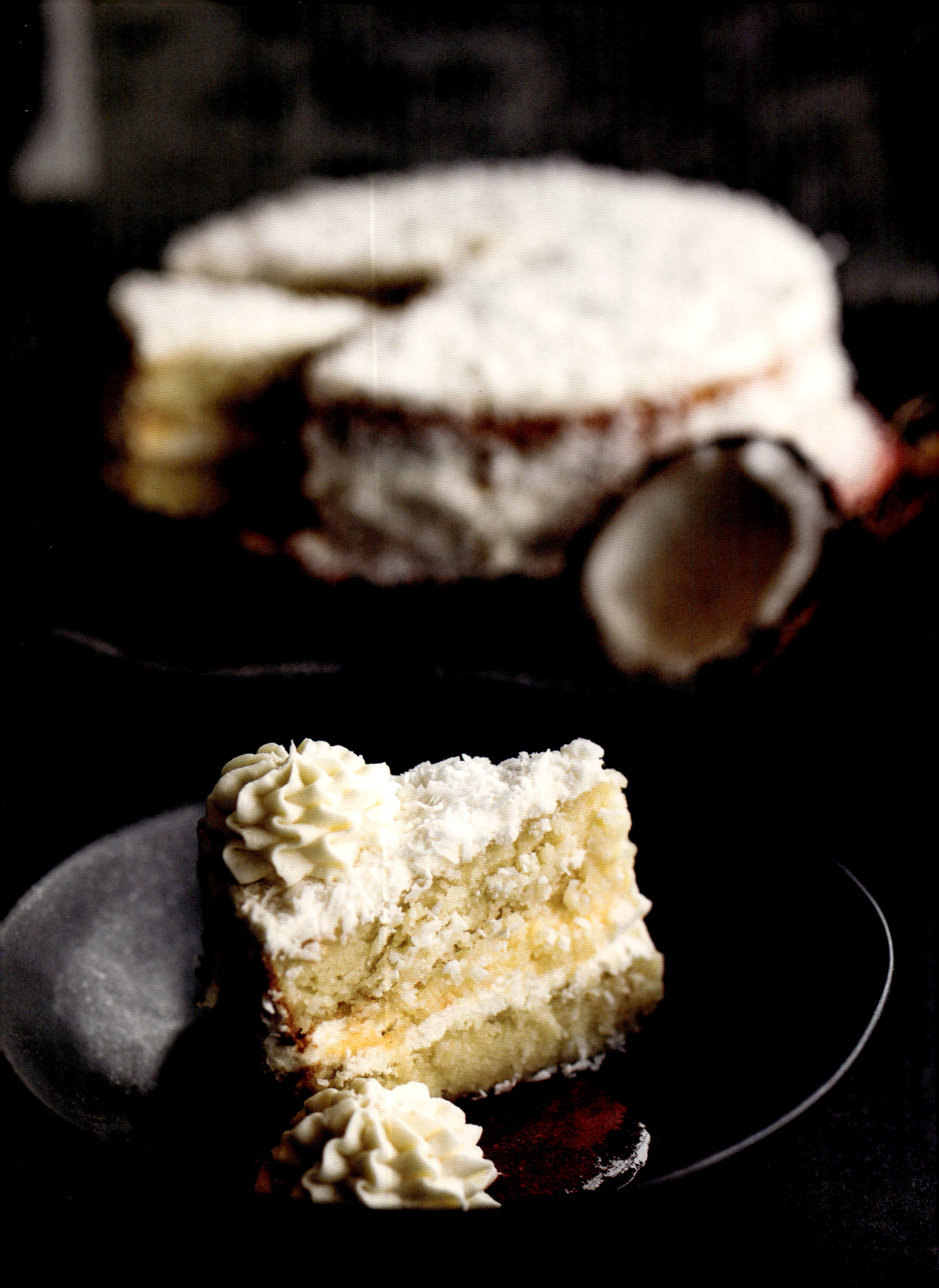

WHITE COCONUT LAYER CAKE

continued from page 221

FROST THE CAKE

When the cakes are fully cooled, use a long, serrated knife to level off the raised cake tops so that both top and bottom are flat. Place 1 layer on a round platter or large dinner plate.

Cut the end off the filled piping bag at a ¾-inch width and pipe an even layer of buttercream over the bottom layer of cake. Use an offset metal spatula to smooth the frosting evenly and just to the edges of the cake. Next, place the second cake layer on top of the buttercream and repeat the previous step by spreading the frosting evenly on the top cake layer. Reserve enough buttercream to cover the cake sides lightly. Again, use the metal spatula to spread the frosting around the outside edges of the cake. Press shredded coconut onto the top of the cake. To coat the sides, fill your hand with shredded coconut and by slightly cupping your hand, press the coconut onto the sides of the cake, turning as needed.

DESSERT

SUMMER PEACH TRIFLE

This recipe showcases one of the many ways we make the most of Missouri peach season. Sweet, light and just right, this dessert is always a summertime standout. // MAKES 6 TO 8 TRIFLES

CRUMB

- 1 cup butter, cold and cubed
- ½ cup brown sugar
- ¼ cup granulated sugar
- 1 teaspoon vanilla extract
- 2 cups all-purpose flour
- ½ cup hazelnuts, roasted and finely chopped
- ½ teaspoon kosher salt
- 4 ounces hard chocolate bar, crushed into small pieces

CREAM

- 1 cup mascarpone cheese
- ½ cup powdered sugar
- ½ teaspoon kosher salt
- ½ teaspoon vanilla extract
- ¼ teaspoon almond extract
- 2 cups heavy cream

PEACHES

- 1 cup Marsala wine
- 1 cup sugar
- 4 peaches, diced

SAUCE

- ¼ cup warm water
- 1 cup raspberry jam

GARNISH

- 2 fresh ripe peaches, cut into slices, skin on
- 16 fresh raspberries

MAKE CRUMB

Preheat oven to 350°F.

In a stand mixer fitted with a paddle attachment, cream together butter, sugars and vanilla extract, starting on low speed and gradually increasing to medium-high speed. In a separate bowl, combine flour, nuts and salt. With mixer on low speed, gradually add dry ingredients to butter mixture until fully incorporated. Fold in chocolate pieces until evenly distributed. Dough will be dry and crumbly. Sprinkle dough across a parchment-lined cookie sheet and bake for 8 to 10 minutes or until crumb is a dark brown color. Remove crumb from the oven and allow to cool. Transfer baked cooled crumble to a bowl and break into ¼-inch chunks with your hands.

MAKE CREAM

In the bowl of a stand mixer fitted with a whisk attachment, combine mascarpone, powdered sugar, salt, vanilla and almond extracts on low speed, until sugar has dissolved, approximately 3 minutes. Pour in cream and gradually increase speed to high. Allow cream to whip just until stiff peaks form, being careful not to overmix, about 1 minute. Transfer mascarpone cream into a piping bag fitted with a medium-size star attachment.

MAKE PEACHES

Combine Marsala and sugar in a small saucepan over high heat. Bring to a boil, then remove from heat and allow to cool until syrup is warm to the touch. Pour syrup over diced peaches and allow them to soak until syrup has cooled to room temperature, approximately 20 minutes.

MAKE SAUCE

In a small bowl, whisk warm water into raspberry jam to thin it to a sauce-like consistency.

MAKE TRIFLES

Set out 8 individual trifle glasses and spoon in 2 to 3 tablespoons raspberry sauce to cover the bottom of each. Scoop a layer of crumb, about ½ inch high, over top of sauce. Use a spoon to gently level out the top of the crumb layers. Pipe a layer of cream around the edges in each glass. Fill glasses with diced peaches, leaving about ½ inch of room at the top of the trifle. Finish trifles by piping 2 to 3 stars of cream on top of peaches, then sprinkle with remaining crumb.

Garnish with fresh peach slices and raspberries.

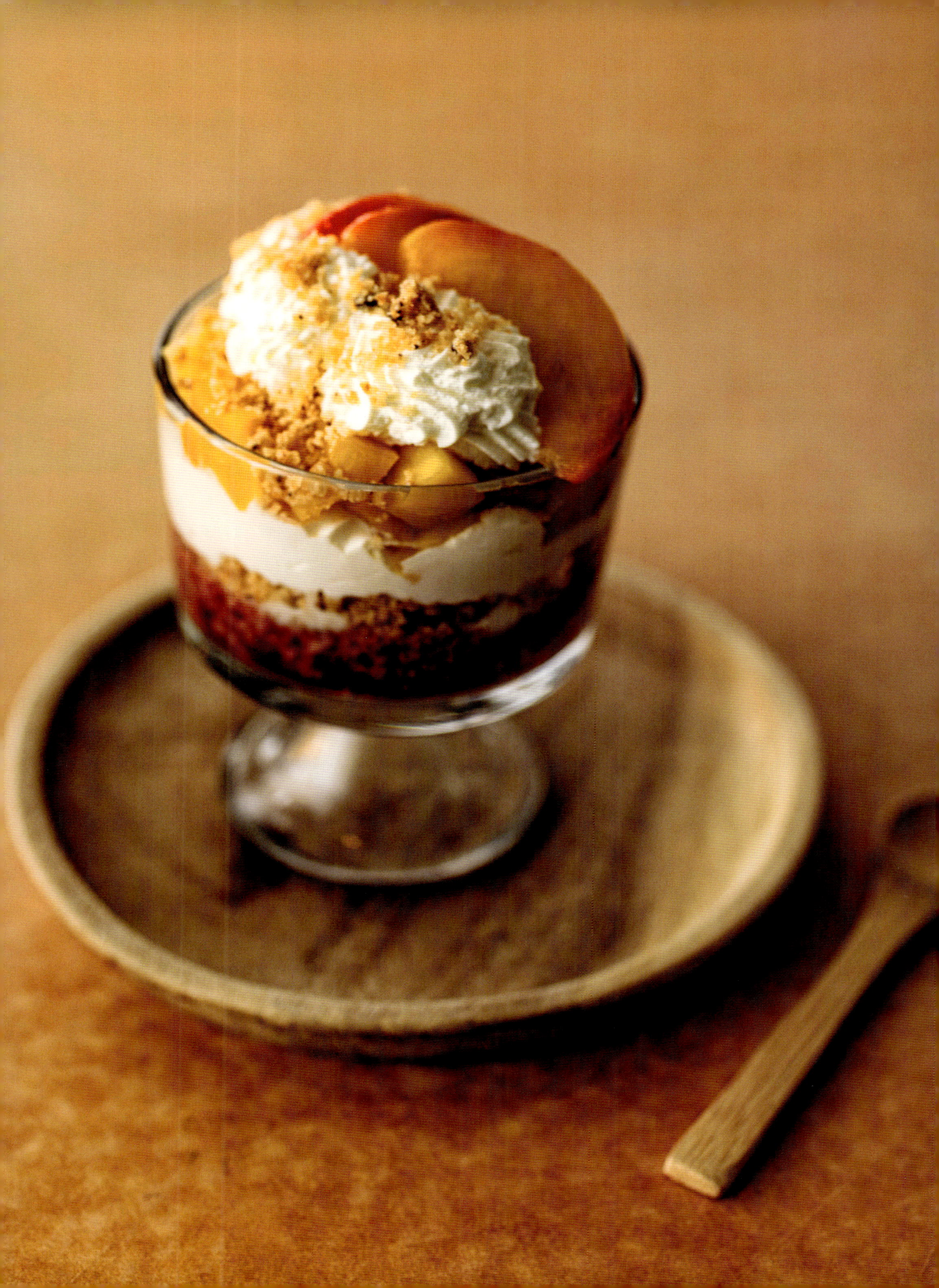

6

THE MODERN PANTRY

To help you feel more comfortable cooking the recipes in this book, I've created a list of ingredients we rely on at Farina. If you cook often at home, you probably already have some of these ingredients, along with many more of your own favorites. By keeping a well-stocked pantry, you're keeping a kitchen full of possibilities so you can create a variety of meals out of basic core ingredients. In general, I like to define a pantry as the refrigerator, freezer and dry storage area.

To cook more efficiently and successfully at home, let your ingredients multitask. For example, if you buy whole baby carrots at the farmers market, make pesto from the leafy carrot tops, and cook the remaining carrots to garnish meat stews or salads. Save the ends of onions and celery to flavor your soups and stocks. Trim your tenderloin into steak filets, then roast the silver skin in the oven to add to bone broth. Trim excess tenderloin parts (we call it "the chain") into pieces to braise with red wine for a delicious pasta sauce. In short, use your pantry ingredients (and imagination) in multiple ways to create a variety of meals.

What kind of pantry do you keep? Basic? Advanced? Expert? Admittedly, this cookbook leans more toward the advanced and expert pantry and cook. And I'm sorry about that! The photos of our dishes can make preparation look simple, but many of the final recipes have sub-recipes. I tend (read: NEED) to use interesting ingredients from all over the world, and that makes your shopping more cumbersome. My repertoire of essential ingredients makes sense for my own Italian vision but maybe you need a nudge to try some of them. Luckily, those ingredients are available through many different online stores. You may or may not cook many recipes from this book, but once you stock some of these ingredients in your pantry you will discover and create new ways to use them based on foods you love to eat.

EXTRA-VIRGIN OLIVE OIL

I first learned about extra-virgin olive oil while working at Chateau Pyrenees in Denver in the early 1980s. My mentor chef, Jean-Pierre Lelievre, had recently returned to Nice, France (where I would join him in 1985), and after two interim chefs, George Mavrothalassitas, or Mavro, took the executive chef job and reconceptualized the restaurant toward the Mediterranean style that I love so much today. I didn't know a thing about this style of cooking at the time, but many of the components were delicious. Olive oil and raw tuna!

I have no idea what brand of olive oil he was able to get in Denver back then. I'm sure it wasn't what Mavro really wanted, but he made do with what he had. When I arrived in Nice in 1985, I saw that olive oil was used in and on everything, or so I thought, and was an integral part of the many ingredients making up the "cuisine of the sun."

We used to go to Nicolas Alziari for our olive oil. It was a small shop in old Nice near Cours Saleya, the largest and oldest flower market in France, that has been producing olive oil since 1868. Olive oil has been produced in Europe since 3000 B.C.

Although I love their oil and many others, I use Italian oils almost exclusively nowadays. In this book, I often say, "drizzle with high-quality extra-virgin olive oil." What does that mean? It's a bewildering proposition, with so many olive oils available in stores. I like to keep a few styles around my home kitchen, two that I can drizzle on finished dishes and an all-purpose oil that I can cook with regularly. Of the two oils that I drizzle, one is fruity and sweet from Umbria or Lebanon and one is prickly and peppery on the back of the throat, like a Tuscan or Sicilian oil.

At home, I finish almost all pasta dishes with extra-virgin olive oil. That's probably not very Italian in most cases, but I love the extra boost—it's absolutely delicious! For big-flavor pastas, grilled foods and cheese, I go with spicy oils from Sicily, Tuscany and Puglia. I use the softer oils for salads, light pasta, fish and even ice cream.

HOW DO YOU KNOW WHAT TO BUY?

The quality of extra-virgin olive oil is really determined by you and your taste buds. You taste olive oil in a similar way to tasting wine. Pour the oil into a small wineglass, swirl, inhale, slurp and swallow. Smack your lips together multiple times, circulating it throughout your mouth and sucking as if pulling it through a straw. Swish the oil around so that it coats your tongue. Essentially, you want your tongue to detect different flavors and your brain to consider the characteristics of each oil. Sweetness, fruit, richness will show on the tip of your tongue, acidity will provoke the sides of the tongue and finally, peppery bitterness will be the sensation on the back of your palate.

SOME OF MY FAVORITE OLIVE OILS

CAPEZZANA (Tuscany) On the palate the flavors and texture are very clean, redolent of mild, delicate herbs such as fennel fronds, dill and watercress.

OLIO VERDE (Sicily) This extraordinary extra-virgin olive oil is unusually green but also has a wonderful, full and intricate flavor, with strong hints of almond, apricot, tomato and lime.

VILLELLA (Umbria) Fragrant hints of green fruit initially, developing into a distinct aroma of ripe almond. Elegant with a particular flavor of sweet artichoke. Bitterness and pungency are present and balanced.

EXAU TURI (Calabria) Herbaceous fragrances of freshly cut grass and vegetables, walnut and clear pungent sensations of green pepper.

ENZO BOLD (California) Organic oil that we use as everyday oil at Farina. A robust and well-balanced oil featuring nutty, grassy green notes with a spicy bold and peppery finish.

PLANETA (Sicily) The bright green hue means you'll find a pleasant tang in the tasting notes, along with herbs like sage and juniper with scents of citrus and green tomatoes.

TITONE (Sicily) A robust oil with bright, herbaceous notes of arugula and hints of tomato leaf. A pleasing finish of black pepper lingers on the palate.

TENUTA LENZINI (Lucca) This rich, buttery and fruity olive oil is low in acidity with notes of grass and has a mild peppery finish. The buttery profile is unusual for Tuscan oils, but prevalent in Lucca.

MAALOUF (Lebanon) This is primarily an early-harvest oil with intense green color. It possesses a buttery and grassy character, accompanied by a peppery finish with an almond aftertaste. Soft and subtle.

NICOLAS ALZIARI (Nice, France) Velvety and silky on the palate with delicate overtones of almonds and hazelnuts. Light and flowery.

TAGGIASCA MONOCULTIVAR (Liguria) Made with 100 percent Taggiasca olives. Sweet with delicate aromas, with a dense and persistent presence in the mouth.

A L'OLIVIER (France) Arbequina olive oil with notes of freshly cut herbs, salad leaves, artichoke, tomato and sorrel. Distinctly sweet, ripe tropical fruit and mild olive flavor.

O-MED (Spain) The aroma of the Arbequina oil is reminiscent of green banana with hints of green apple. A soft finish, but it still hits at the end with a bit of white pepper.

LAVI (Israel) The oils from Galilee are very low in acidity, with artichoke leaf nuances. Lavi is soft and fruity and tastes of mild ripe black olives.

FRANCESCO PEPE EREDE (Italy) This oil is beautiful on the palate. Intense grassy notes and a very long finish. I love this oil.

WHAT DO THE VARIOUS DESIGNATIONS MEAN?

PDO — Protected Designation of Origin
PGI — Protected Geographical Indication
AOP — Appellation d'Origine Protégée
DOC — Designation of Controlled Origin

Extra-virgin olive oil is treated with the same standards of classifications as wines and other artisanal products. To earn a designation, the producer must apply for and pass certification standards that control the origin of the oil.

GRANA PADANO *versus* PARMIGIANA-REGGIANO

At Farina we use a Parmesan-style cheese called Grana Padano. Many people are not aware of Grana Padano, and those who are might think of it as a cheap version of Parmigiano-Reggiano. But there is nothing inferior about it. Both are extraordinarily good cheeses that were first made by Cistercian monks more than 1,000 years ago. Grana Padano and Parmigiano-Reggiano are produced in different areas of northern Italy, and both have earned the Protected Designation of Origin (PDO) label, which requires adhering to a strict set of rules as well as being produced in a specific geographic region. Essentially, they have been made using the same artisan craftsmanship and production techniques that have undergone very few changes over the centuries. Both cheeses are versatile, in that they can both be enjoyed in chunks on a cheese board, grated over foods and melted into sauce. Another little-known fact is that the extensive maturation process, coupled with specific production methods, results in a lactose-free cheese.

WHAT IS GRANA PADANO?

Grana Padano is indeed less expensive than Parmigiano-Reggiano for several reasons, primarily because about a million more wheels of Grana Padano are produced annually. Grana Padano is made only with partially skimmed cow's milk, and the cows are restricted to grazing only on grasses in the northern Po River Valley regions of Piedmont, Trentino–Alto Adige, Emilia-Romagna, Lombardy and Veneto. This region of land is quite a bit larger than allowed by the rules for Reggiano production. Grana Padano is the best-selling PDO cheese in the world, and about 25 percent of all the milk in Italy is used to make it.

WHAT IS PARMIGIANO-REGGIANO?

Parmigiano-Reggiano, the "King of Cheeses," falls under a stricter set of rules. The cheese can be made with whole and skimmed milk from the regions of Parma, Reggio Emilia, Modena, Mantua, and Bologna, which is a smaller grazing area than Grana Padano's. The name protection laws are so strict that Reggiano must be made and packaged in the region of origin in order to retain the label of Parmigiano-Reggiano. The term "Parmesan" can only be used if the cheese is PDO. The steps required to produce Grana Padano and Parmigiano-Reggiano are virtually the same, except for the specific bylaws associated with Parmigiano-Reggiano. Parmigiano must age longer, from a minimum of 12 months up to 48 months or longer, and will also be fire branded with the Parmigiano-Reggiano logo after passing the PDO quality-control tests that confirm the wheel as authentic.

STEPS OF GRANA PADANO AND PARMIGIANO-REGGIANO CHEESE PRODUCTION

UNPASTEURIZED COW'S MILK The partially skimmed milk comes from local farms in the geographical area specified by PDO, and from cows milked twice a day.

COPPER CAULDRONS Two hundred ninety gallons of partially skimmed milk go into each traditional bell-shaped copper cooking cauldron, yielding two wheels of cheese, called "twin wheels."

WHEY Whey is the liquid remaining after milk has been curdled and strained. It is full of lactic acid bacteria and triggers the transformation of milk into cheese.

HEAT Once whey has been added, the milk is brought to a temperature of 88º to 91ºF.

RENNET Calf rennet is added, once the milk mixture reaches 88º to 91ºF.

BREAKING OF THE CURD The curd is then broken with a giant whisk (*spino*) into pieces that are as small as grains of rice.

HEATING The broken curd is then heated to a maximum temperature of 136ºF to complete the cooking process. The curd granules settle at the bottom of the copper cauldron.

RESTING The curd granules are left to rest in the copper cauldron, immersed in the whey, for a maximum of 70 minutes from the end of the heating phase, so that they combine to form a compact mass.

LIFTING Using a sort of a wooden shovel (*pala*) and a linen cloth (*schiavino*), the curd mass is raised from the bottom of the cauldron and cut into two equal parts, in order to create two wheels.

EXTRACTION Each of the two wheels is removed from the copper cauldron, wrapped in linen cloths and placed on a shelf—the *spersola*.

FIRST MOLDING Each wheel is placed into a special mold, the *fascera*, made of plastic. A heavy object of the same material is then placed on top of the cheese to press.

MARKS OF ORIGIN After about 12 hours, another piece of *fascera*, engraved with the marks of origin, is inserted.

CASEIN PLATE A casein plate with a specific ID code is placed on the top face of the wheel; this is crucial for the traceability of each wheel.

SALTING Two days later, the process of salting starts: the cheese wheels are soaked in brine—a solution of water and salt. This step can take from 14 to 30 days, depending on the saline solution and the size of the wheel.

DRYING Once the salting is finished, the wheels are taken into a "hot room" (*camera calda*) where they will dry for a few hours.

AGING Finally, the 80-pound cheese wheels will be taken to a specific maturing warehouse, where they will be left to age for a minimum of nine months and up to two years. At the nine-month mark, multiple tests are conducted. A ball-pein hammer test is used to detect signs of abnormal fermentation, a needle test is used to determine if the scent is up to par, and finally a chunk of cheese is extracted for a probe test to evaluate the color and texture. After passing each of these tests, the wheel will be fire branded with a logo to confirm the wheel as authentic PDO.

(information sourced from www.granapadano.it)

PANTRY

SALAD DRESSINGS

The key to successful salad dressings is the acid-to-oil ratio. All other components are for flavor. The general rule is one-third vinegar (any acid) to two-thirds oil. To properly season your dressings, dissolve the salt in vinegar first before mixing with oil. Salt does not easily dissolve in oil. For light and delicate lettuces, you want a light but flavorful dressing. For a heartier salad with roasted vegetables, tomatoes or cucumbers, use a heavier-style dressing like tzatziki or Caesar. These Farina favorites complement a variety of salad styles and can be made on short notice using easy-to-find ingredients.

DIJON RED WINE DRESSING

1 cup red wine vinegar

2½ cups canola oil

½ cup extra-virgin olive oil

1 shallot, finely minced

1 tablespoon Dijon mustard

2 teaspoons kosher salt

1 teaspoon ground black pepper

MAKES 3 CUPS

Whisk all ingredients together in a mixing bowl. Store in refrigerator for up to 2 weeks.

FARINA ITALIAN DRESSING

1 cup red wine vinegar

2½ cups canola oil

½ cup extra-virgin olive oil

2 teaspoons kosher salt

1 teaspoon ground black pepper

4 sprigs fresh thyme, hard stems removed

4 sprigs fresh oregano, hard stems removed

1 clove garlic

1 tablespoon tomato paste

MAKES 3 CUPS

Combine all ingredients in a blender and blend until smooth. Store in the refrigerator for up to 2 weeks.

POMEGRANATE VINAIGRETTE

1 cup red wine vinegar

¾ cup pomegranate molasses

2½ cups canola oil

½ cup extra-virgin olive oil

1 shallot, cut in half

4 sprigs fresh thyme, hard stems removed

2 teaspoons kosher salt

1 teaspoon ground black pepper

MAKES 3 CUPS

Combine all ingredients in a blender and blend until smooth. Store in refrigerator for up to 2 weeks.

CAESAR DRESSING

2 egg yolks

¼ cup Parmesan cheese

2 teaspoons anchovy paste

3 cloves garlic, thinly sliced

2 tablespoons Worcestershire sauce

¼ cup fresh lemon juice

1 tablespoon Dijon mustard

1 teaspoon kosher salt

1 teaspoon ground black pepper

1 cup canola oil

1 cup extra-virgin olive oil

MAKES 3 CUPS

Combine all ingredients except oils in a small food processor. Blend well, then slowly add canola oil followed by olive oil. The dressing will be the consistency of mayonnaise or aioli.

ORANGE-FENNEL POLLEN DRESSING

½ cup apple cider vinegar

1 cup fresh lemon juice

1 cup orange juice

2½ cups canola oil

½ cup extra-virgin olive oil

2 teaspoons kosher salt

1 teaspoon ground black pepper

1 tablespoon fennel pollen

MAKES 5½ CUPS

Whisk all ingredients together in a mixing bowl. Store in refrigerator for up to 2 weeks.

TZATZIKI DRESSING

1 cup thick Greek yogurt

½ cup cucumber, finely grated

½ cup fresh lemon juice

1 tablespoon fresh dill, chopped

1 tablespoon fresh mint, chopped

1 clove garlic, finely minced

1 cup water

2 tablespoons extra-virgin olive oil

2 teaspoons kosher salt

1 pinch cayenne pepper

MAKES ABOUT 2 CUPS

Place all ingredients in a medium mixing bowl. Whisk vigorously to combine well. Check seasoning and acid balance, add salt or more lemon juice as needed. Refrigerate until ready to use.

SICILIAN HARISSA VINAIGRETTE

1 tablespoon harissa (available in Middle Eastern grocery stores)

⅓ cup apple cider vinegar

1 teaspoon tomato paste

1 pinch fennel pollen

1 teaspoon lemon zest

1 cup canola oil

1 pinch kosher salt

I was first introduced to harissa in Nice in the mid-1980s. I was living in a one-bedroom apartment on a street called Rue Pertinax, which could just as well have been named Little Morocco or Little Tunisia. The aromas of strong coffee, couscous cooking on the stoves and alas, dog poop, were pervasive (not many grassy areas in Nice to run pets!). Harissa is a spicy condiment most closely associated with couscous royale, the classic Tunisian dish. However, it has also found its way into some Sicilian recipes as the result of hundreds of years of Arab rule over the island, which influenced Sicilian cuisine with ingredients like cumin, cinnamon, pomegranates, semolina, citrus, dried fruits, saffron, pistachios and almonds. This vinaigrette is a thrilling marinade for charred lamb and pizza as well as a spicy, but very tasty, salad dressing.

// MAKES 1 CUP

Combine all ingredients in a small bowl and whisk together. The dressing is best used right away but can be refrigerated. Shake well before using.

BONE BROTH

- 5 pounds meaty beef bones, marrow bones or shanks (cut in half)
- 6 tablespoons tomato paste, divided
- 1 whole pig's foot (have your butcher cut it lengthwise in half)
- 1 yellow onion, cut into 4 to 6 chunks
- 2 medium to large carrots, cut into 4 to 6 chunks
- 2 celery ribs, cut into 4 to 6 chunks
- Dark green leaves from 1 leek, washed well and roughly chopped
- 1 head garlic, cut in half horizontally
- 2 tablespoons black peppercorns
- 3 large fresh oregano sprigs
- 3 large fresh thyme sprigs
- 2 bay leaves
- 1 teaspoon kosher salt

Bone broth has numerous health benefits, a result of the slow cooking process that releases valuable nutrients. A good homemade bone broth yields much richer and more flavorful soups, sauces and gravies. The wonderful aroma drifting through the kitchen will undoubtedly make you crave a cup of hot, hearty bone broth when snow is on the ground. So make friends with your butcher and don't ever toss those bones in the trash before roasting and simmering them. // **MAKES 2 TO 3 QUARTS**

Preheat oven to 350°F.

Place all bones (except pig's foot) on a rimmed baking sheet. Smear 3 tablespoons tomato paste on bones. Roast for 45 minutes or until dark golden brown.

As bones are roasting, smear remaining 3 tablespoons tomato paste around the inside of an 8-quart stockpot, about halfway down. Add pig's foot, vegetables, garlic, peppercorns, herbs and salt to pot, and cover with 5 quarts water. Place pot over high heat and bring to a boil.

Add roasted bones to the pot. Pour 1 cup of boiling broth water (or plain water) onto the hot baking sheet; let stand for 5 minutes. Scrape up the caramelized bits and pieces with a metal spatula and add residue and water back to cooking broth. There should be about 1 inch of space between liquid and the rim; if not, fill pot to that capacity. Return to a boil, skim off foam rising to the top of the pot, then reduce heat to a simmer and let simmer very gently for 8 hours, stirring occasionally. If water level dips below bones at any time during cooking process, add enough additional water to re-cover them by 1 inch.

After 8 hours, remove from heat and allow broth to cool. Remove the big pieces of meat with a large, slotted spoon, then strain broth into a large bowl. Refrigerate until the fat rises to the top and solidifies, so you can remove it easily.

Transfer the defatted broth to airtight containers and refrigerate up to 4 days or freeze up to 6 months.

POULTRY BROTH

2 pounds bone-in and skin-on chicken thighs

2 pounds whole chicken wings

1 pound turkey necks

1 yellow onion, peeled and cut into 4 to 6 chunks

1 large carrot, cut into 4 to 6 chunks

1 celery rib, cut into 4 to 6 chunks

Dark green leaves of 1 leek, washed well and roughly chopped

1 head garlic, cut in half horizontally

3 large fresh oregano sprigs

3 large fresh thyme sprigs

2 tablespoons black peppercorns

2 bay leaves

1 teaspoon kosher salt

Making your own stocks at home with animal bones is more of a hassle than using store-bought broths, but they are deeper in flavor and taste much better. Find a local butcher and ask for chicken and turkey parts. Meat with bones or bones with meat, it doesn't matter. This recipe calls for a combination of thighs, wings and necks, but if you aren't "chicken," don't be scared to throw some feet in the pot too. // **MAKES 4 QUARTS**

Combine all ingredients in a large stockpot and add 6 quarts cold water. If ingredients are not fully immersed, add more water to cover by 1 inch. Place the pot over high heat and bring to a boil. As broth boils, skim off the foam rising to the top, then reduce the heat and simmer very gently for 3 hours. If liquid level dips below solids at any time during the cooking process, add enough additional water to re-cover by 1 inch.

Allow broth to cool. Remove large pieces of meat with a large, slotted spoon, then strain broth into a large bowl. Refrigerate until the fat rises to the top and solidifies, so it can be removed easily. Transfer broth to airtight containers and refrigerate for up to 4 days or freeze for up to 6 months.

CHUNKY PROSCIUTTO BROTH

3 quarts water

2 pounds various prosciutto scraps (skin, fat, meat, knuckles and slices)

I love this broth and always keep it in the freezer or refrigerator. It will enhance any soup, ragu or pasta. Restaurant kitchens produce a lot of scrap foods left over from various recipes, and I am always developing new ways to use perfectly good scraps. The Italians have a long history of adding prosciutto pieces to soups and ragus, and for our purposes, it is easier to add scraps of prosciutto to recipes after it's already cooked and softened. So I created this incredible umami bomb using just 2 ingredients: prosciutto and water. **// MAKES 2 QUARTS**

Combine both ingredients in a large stock pot and bring to a boil. Reduce to a simmer and cook for 3 hours. If the water dips below the meat at any time, top off with more water. The broth is done when prosciutto scraps are very soft and gelatinous. Remove from heat and let cool for several hours.

Transfer cooked prosciutto scraps to small individual plastic containers. Break up any large chunks into smaller pieces. Pour liquid over the meat to cover. When cold, the broth is very firm, like gelatin, and can be covered and refrigerated for up to 2 weeks or stored in the freezer for up to 6 months.

GRANA PADANO CHEESE BROTH

8 ounces Grana Padano rinds

5 cups water

We grind all our cheese fresh every day, so we always have rinds in our kitchen cooler that we use to make cheese broth. This broth is great for vegetarian pasta dishes, as liquid for making fresh breads, and in the sauces for our Carbonara and Cacio e Pepe. **// MAKES 1 QUART**

Combine both ingredients in a sauce pot and bring to a boil. Reduce heat and gently simmer on low heat for 1 hour. Stir often, as the rinds will stick to the bottom of the pot. Strain and discard rinds. The broth can be kept in the refrigerator for up to 5 days or frozen for up to 6 months.

MASHED POTATOES

4 large russet potatoes, washed

2 cups heavy cream

½ pound (1 stick) cold butter, cut into ½-inch cubes

¼ cup extra-virgin olive oil

1 tablespoon kosher salt

1 tiny pinch cayenne pepper

Special equipment:
Fine-sieve food mill

We like our mashed potatoes to be creamy and buttery! This recipe definitely accomplishes that. Serve them with our Eight Hour Pork Roast (page 175) or Braised Beef Short Ribs (page 163). You will not regret it. // **SERVES 4**

Preheat oven to 400°F.

Place washed potatoes in a roasting pan and bake for 90 minutes or until soft inside, then let cool for 10 minutes. While potatoes are cooking, heat heavy cream in a wide braising pan and bring to nearly boiling. Turn off heat and keep warm.

Set food mill on the edge of the braising pan with cream. Peel potatoes (discard skin) and put through the food mill so the potato pulp falls into the warm cream. Remove food mill and use a whisk to beat in cold cubed butter. Stir in olive oil, salt and cayenne pepper.

Cover the pan of potatoes with plastic wrap and keep warm near the stove or in a low warming oven. The potatoes can be prepared and kept warm up to 2 hours in advance. Stir vigorously when ready to serve.

> We bake the potatoes in the skin instead of peeling and boiling in water. Our intention is to infuse as much creamy goodness into the potatoes as possible. Dry potatoes achieve that better than wet potatoes. However, if you insist on boiling, dry them on a tray for about 15 minutes in a 300°F oven after they have been riced.

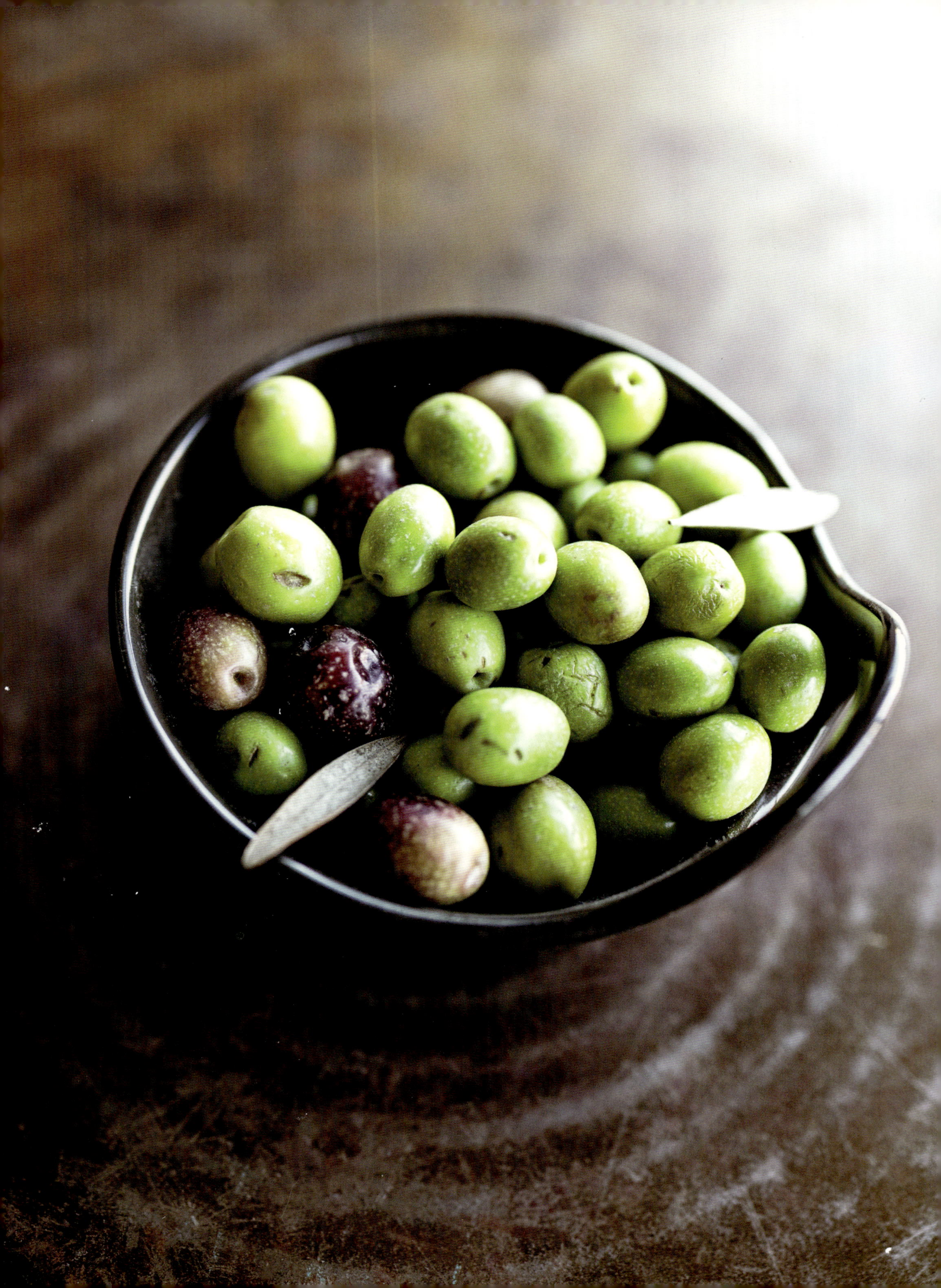

MARINATED OLIVES

1 to 2 jars (19 ounces) Castelvetrano olives

2 cups grapeseed oil

½ cup extra-virgin olive oil

2 cloves garlic, smashed with a knife

2 shallots, sliced thinly

1 small orange, cut into 8 thin slices

½ teaspoon ground cinnamon

1 teaspoon red pepper flakes

2 teaspoons fennel seeds, crushed

2 tablespoons fresh thyme leaves

2 tablespoons fresh oregano leaves

1 bay leaf, torn into 3 pieces

1 teaspoon paprika

1 teaspoon coriander seeds

These olives come from the town of Castelvetrano in Sicily. They are a nice green color and sweeter than a typical olive. We bring a small bowl of these olives to every table at Farina and guests often ask what is in the marinade. We even sell them by the quart upon request. It's a failproof recipe that will be gobbled up quickly when served on a charcuterie board or as an hors d'oeuvre. Just remember to marinate the olives for at least one day prior to serving. // **MAKES ABOUT 5 CUPS**

Combine all ingredients in a large mixing bowl and stir well. Refrigerate in an airtight container for up to a month.

PANTRY

RED BELL PEPPER SYRUP

7 red bell peppers (deep red is best), stemmed, seeded and cut into narrow strips

1 teaspoon sugar

1 tablespoon fresh lemon juice

Special equipment:
1 vegetable juicer (masticating type)

This syrup will keep in the refrigerator for a few weeks, and it's a great flavor enhancer when finishing various dishes. You can drizzle it on soups, add it to salad dressings, squirt it on pizza and use it in beef tartare. It's a bit sweet when reduced, so adjust the acid level to create a balance that's just right for you. If you're feeling extra ambitious after making this syrup, the extracted pulp can be put in a food dehydrator for 8 hours to dry. When the pulp is crispy dry, puree it in a blender to a fine powder as another flavor-enhancing garnish on savory dishes. We try not to discard anything at Farina that can be used as a food ingredient.

// **MAKES ABOUT ⅓ CUP**

In front of a juicer, set up a small container to catch the discharged vegetable debris and a different container to catch the juice. Feed bell pepper strips through juicer. Feed the discharged pulp through juicer a second time to extract any remaining juice.

Pass juice through a fine sieve into a sauce pot. Place pot on stove, add sugar and simmer for 40 minutes or until it reduces to a very bright red syrup. Stir in lemon juice and transfer to a container to cool. Refrigerate in an airtight container for up to 2 weeks or freeze for up to 6 months.

> I know it sounds weird to add sugar and then announce that it's too sweet. We add it to help the juice turn into syrup sooner; otherwise, the juice will eventually turn into a syrupy liquid but there will much less of it. So in order to increase the volume a bit, we add sugar and then balance it with lemon juice or apple cider vinegar.

PICKLED CHERRIES

- 3 cups red wine vinegar
- 3 cups water
- 1 cup sugar
- 2 bay leaves
- 2 sprigs fresh thyme
- ¼ cup black peppercorns
- 1½ tablespoons kosher salt
- 1 stick cinnamon
- 1 pinch red pepper flakes
- 3 pounds fresh red cherries, stems attached

The art of pickling and preserving food has been done for centuries. In the chef world, we are always looking to preserve vegetables and fruits to prolong their use after the growing season is over. We use these cherries to garnish our prosciutto plates at Farina. At home, after these delectable cherries have all been eaten—and they quickly will be—save the pickling juice for deglazing pan-fried pork chops or making cherry–red wine salad dressing. // **MAKES ABOUT 1 GALLON**

Combine all ingredients except cherries in a stainless steel sauce pot and bring to a boil. Reduce heat and simmer for 15 minutes. While pickling liquid is simmering, examine cherries to make sure they are full and plump. Discard any bruised or crushed cherries.

Divide cherries evenly among 6 medium-size canning jars and pour hot pickling liquid over cherries. Let cool at room temperature, then cover with a tight lid and store in the refrigerator for up to 3 months.

BLISTERED CHERRY TOMATOES

- 2 quarts ripe, mixed-color cherry tomatoes
- 3 cloves garlic, crushed into a paste
- 3 sprigs fresh thyme
- 3 sprigs fresh oregano
- 1 tablespoon kosher salt (or to taste)
- 2 teaspoons ground black pepper
- ¼ cup extra-virgin olive oil
- ¼ cup fresh basil leaves, chopped

Perfect for pastas, salads, bruschetta or just about anything else you would ever crave a tomato on, this is a wonderful way to make the most of a prolific garden harvest. These blistered tomatoes are a great condiment to have at your fingertips all summer. Even better, stock some in the freezer for those winter nights when you crave tomatoes and summer is nowhere in sight.
// **MAKES ABOUT 2 QUARTS**

Preheat oven to 350°F.

Combine all ingredients except basil in a mixing bowl. Toss until tomatoes are well coated.

Pour tomatoes onto a baking sheet and roast for 25 to 30 minutes, until they soften and begin to slightly burst. Remove from oven. When tomatoes are cool, add basil and gently combine.

APRICOT MOSTARDA

- ¼ cup olive oil
- 2 shallots, finely minced
- ½ cup fennel, finely minced
- 1 pound dried apricots, each cut into quarters
- 1 cup dry white wine
- ⅓ cup mustard seeds
- ¼ cup fennel seeds, crushed
- 1 cup water
- ¾ cup granulated sugar
- 4 tablespoons Chinese yellow mustard powder

Mostarda is an Italian condiment frequently used to garnish cheese plates and salumi platters on antipasto tables. You can use many different dried fruits—cherries, figs, apples and cranberries—to make mostardas. They also pair very well with meats off a wood-burning grill. // **MAKES APPROXIMATELY 1 QUART**

Add olive oil, shallots and fennel to a medium shallow sauce pot and set over medium-high heat. Sauté shallots and fennel until translucent, approximately 10 minutes. Add remaining ingredients except mustard powder and bring a boil. Reduce heat to low and let apricots simmer slowly for 35 minutes. The apricots will be very soft and most of the liquid will have been absorbed. If the sauce pot gets dry during the cooking process, add an additional ¾ cup water.

Transfer apricot mixture to a medium bowl and let cool for 10 minutes. While apricots are cooling, measure mustard powder into a medium bowl. Stir in 3 to 4 tablespoons water and mix the powder into paste. Set aside. When apricots have cooled for 10 minutes, fold in mustard paste and check for seasoning. Add a pinch of salt if necessary.

> Mostarda can be smooth like a thick paste, or it can be chunky. The taste profile is sweet and fruity but also has a fairly strong aroma and mustard flavor. Store the mostarda in a tightly sealed container for up to 1 month in the refrigerator.

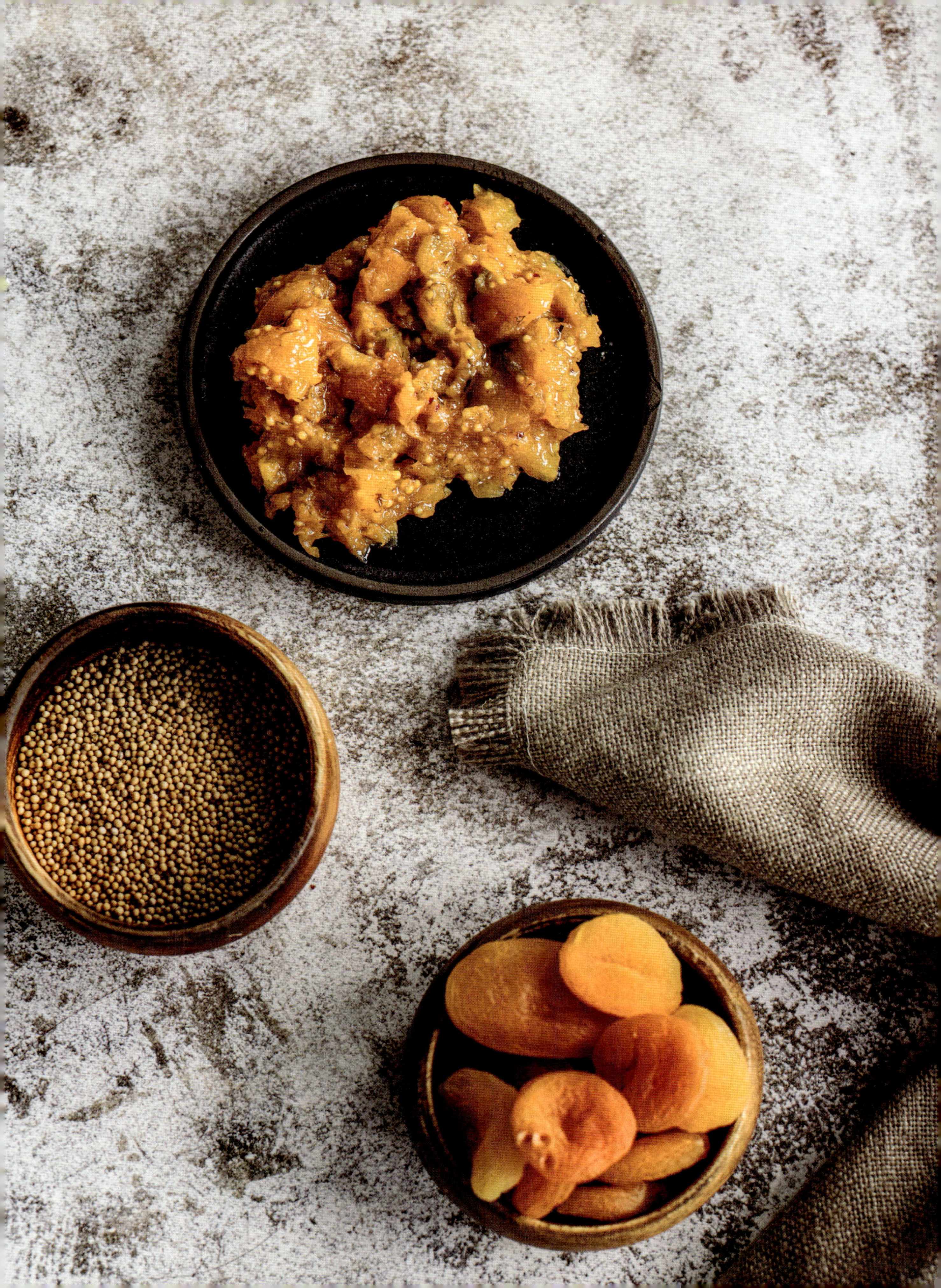

PEACH TRUFFLE RELISH

- 1 large ripe summer peach, halved, pit removed, skin on
- 1 tablespoon chopped black truffle
- ½ shallot, minced
- 1 teaspoon chopped chives
- ½ teaspoon pomegranate molasses
- ½ teaspoon sherry vinegar
- 1 teaspoon extra-virgin olive oil
- ½ teaspoon kosher salt
- 1 pinch Aleppo chili pepper

I created this relish as a garnish on roasted racks of veal for our annual dinner with Kurlbaum Tomato Farm. Until fairly recently, fresh black truffles were not available in the summer because they were harvested only in the winter in a few select regions of the world. Luckily, that changed when the first Australian truffles were harvested in 1999. Their quality has improved every harvest since, and they are now on par with the prized Périgord black truffles and Norcia black truffles from Italy. The expanded truffle production allows American restaurants to pair summer produce with black truffles, resulting in more creative uses for the fungi than ever before. This recipe calls for a real black truffle to create an authentic flavor profile. The result: a summer relish that is perfect with grilled meats or beef carpaccio. // **MAKES ABOUT 1 CUP**

Dice peach into small cubes about the size of a pea. In a small bowl, gently mix peach cubes with remaining ingredients using a rubber spatula. Keep chilled in refrigerator.

CROSTINI *and* BRUSCHETTA

CROSTINI

1 French baguette

¼ cup extra-virgin olive oil

2 teaspoons kosher salt

BRUSCHETTA

1 Italian ciabatta loaf, sliced at ¾-inch intervals

¼ cup extra-virgin olive oil

2 teaspoons kosher salt

Crostini and bruschetta are common breads used in Italian antipasti. Both are crucial and versatile components that provide a crispy and chewy vehicle for exploring a variety of flavors, seasonal vegetables, meats, cheeses and olives.

The difference between bruschetta and crostini lies in the type of bread used and the preparation. The word bruschetta, or *bruscare*, means "to roast over coals." Bruschetta are made by toasting or grilling thick slices of rustic Italian-style loaves like ciabatta. At Farina, we grill the slices on our wood-fired grill, giving the bread a dark brooding char that stands up to bold toppings. Crostini, on the other hand, are sliced from smaller, tight-crumbed loaves like French baguettes. They are usually brushed with olive oil or butter and toasted to a golden color. We use crostini at Farina as side components for soups and various spreads. In Italy, you'll often see an antipasti table offering crostini topped with a variety of spreads or savory jams and a few intensely flavored vegetables. Bruschetta and crostini are equally wonderful to have in your pantry for snacking on a moment's notice. // **CROSTINI MAKES ABOUT 35 SLICES // BRUSCHETTA MAKES ABOUT 15 SLICES**

MAKE CROSTINI

Preheat broiler to high heat.

Slice baguette on a slight angle at ½-inch intervals. Arrange the slices on a baking sheet and brush with olive oil. Sprinkle lightly with salt. Place the pan 6 inches from the broiler element and toast until golden brown, 1 to 2 minutes, watching carefully to prevent burning. Remove the pan from the oven, carefully flip each slice over and toast again on the second side. Allow crostini to cool completely.

Store crostini in an airtight container for up to 1 week.

MAKE BRUSCHETTA

Preheat broiler to high heat.

Arrange ciabatta slices on a baking sheet and brush with olive oil. Sprinkle lightly with salt. Place pan 6 inches from broiler element and toast until golden brown, 1 to 2 minutes, watching carefully to prevent burning. Remove the baking sheet from the oven, carefully flip each slice and toast for another 1 to 2 minutes, until golden brown. Toasted bruschetta can be topped right away with your favorite garnishes or cooled completely and used later.

Store bruschetta in an airtight container for up to 1 week.

PANTRY

PESTO CALABRESE

1 cup sun-dried tomatoes (preferably the variety soaked in olive oil)

½ cup toasted almonds

5 cloves garlic

4 pieces Calabrian chilis, drained and stemmed

2 tablespoons Tuttu Calabria rose marina sauce (available online)

¾ cup fresh basil leaves

1 cup extra-virgin olive oil

½ cup pecorino cheese

This quick and easy red pesto is excellent as a bruschetta topping or sauce for your favorite pasta. I love almonds, and Sicily grows some of the best. For this recipe, the almonds are slightly chunky and the crunch of the pesto has a wonderful hint of spiciness. The rose marina sauce is optional but give it a try; its an umami bomb in a jar that takes your Italian pantry to the next level.
// **MAKES 2 CUPS**

Combine all ingredients except pecorino cheese in a high-speed blender and pulse on and off multiple times to mix the ingredients into a chunky paste (it should resemble a regular basil pesto, except red). Use a rubber spatula to scrape the pesto into a small bowl, then fold in pecorino cheese. If not using right away, store in an airtight container for up to 1 week in the refrigerator.

> If the packaged sun-dried tomatoes are stiff and dry, sprinkle them with a little water and heat in the microwave for 20 to 30 seconds to soften.

APICIUS SPICE MIX

1 tablespoon fennel seeds

2 tablespoons coriander seeds

2 teaspoons cumin seeds

1 teaspoon celery seeds

1 tablespoon allspice berries

1 tablespoon Sichuan peppercorns

1 tablespoon black peppercorns

8 pieces star anise

½ teaspoon ground cinnamon

¾ tablespoon ground ginger

1 teaspoon ground cloves

Apicius spice is a fascinating blend that dates to the first century A.D., when Roman cooks did not always have access to sugar for seasoning. In modern times, the spice mix is commonly associated with Roast Duck Apicius, a menu item that has been featured at many Michelin-starred restaurants in Paris. // **MAKES ½ CUP**

Place all seeds, berries, peppercorns and star anise in a nonstick sauté pan over medium-high heat. Move the pan around the heat continuously for 3 to 4 minutes to lightly toast the spices. It's important to keep the spices moving or they will quickly burn and taste bitter.

Transfer spices to a high-speed blender and pulse on medium-high multiple times to crush them fine but not ground to a powder. Transfer blended spice mix to a small prep bowl and stir in cinnamon, ginger and cloves; mix well. Store in an airtight container for up to 1 month.

BURNT ONION ASH

6 large yellow onions

One of my pasta cooks, Andrew, asked me if we could flavor a pasta dough with burnt onion. So we created this burnt onion powder. It's absolutely terrific! We use it in our cracker dough, sprinkle it on salads and sometimes we dust it on steamed halibut. But you can be creative and sprinkle this fine powder over meats, vegetables and fish for a flavorful finisher.

// **MAKES ABOUT 1 CUP**

Preheat oven to 200°F.

Cut each onion in half, then cut each half into very thin slices. Spread onion slices in a thin layer on 2 cookie sheets. Place in oven for 24 hours, or until onions are dry and chocolate brown. Let rest at room temperature for 1 hour. Put burnt onions in a blender and grind to a fine powder.

POMEGRANATE MOLASSES MARINADE

1 cup pomegranate molasses

½ cup fresh lemon juice

2 tablespoons Aleppo chile flakes

5 cloves garlic

4 sprigs fresh thyme

4 sprigs fresh oregano

1 cup fresh parsley leaves

¼ cup fennel seeds

My friend Norman Van Aken turned me on to this condiment in 1994 while I was a chef at the American Restaurant, and it's been a love affair ever since. It's a great addition to braised meats and also makes for a tangy all-purpose marinade that works well with grilled meats or broiled hearty fish fillets. The molasses will burn quickly, so keep the grill or broiler on moderate heat and let the marinade do its job of creating a sticky, gooey goodness.

// **MAKES 1½ CUPS**

Place all ingredients in a blender and blend on high until mixture is smooth.

Scrape marinade into a plastic storage container and refrigerate for up to 2 weeks.

ROMESCO SAUCE

4 large red tomatoes, cored and halved

8 cloves garlic

6 fire-roasted piquillo peppers

1 Spanish onion, sliced

4 sprigs fresh thyme

½ cup almonds

¼ cup hazelnuts

¼ cup pistachios

2 cups extra-virgin olive oil

6 ½-inch-thick slices French baguette

1 ancho chili, stemmed and soaked in scalding water 20 minutes to soften

4 tablespoons sherry vinegar

1 tablespoon kosher salt

This delicious sauce is a traditional condiment from the Tarragona region of Spain and dates back to the Romans. Even though it's not an Italian recipe, it embodies all that makes Italian cooking so appetizing. This is a convenient sauce to have on standby for grilled fish and roasted vegetables. Work in 3 small batches to puree the roasted vegetables and avoid overpacking the blender.
// MAKES 1 QUART

Preheat oven to 325°F.

In a large roasting pan, combine tomatoes, garlic, piquillo peppers, onion, thyme and all nuts. Toss together to mix well, then spread out evenly in the pan. Roast for 1 hour. Remove from oven and add 1 cup water. Stir to mix well, scraping and loosening the charred and sticky bits stuck to the bottom of the pan.

Add a third of the roasted vegetables to a blender, plus a third of the olive oil, 2 slices of bread and a third of the softened ancho chili. Pulse on low to start, then gradually increase the speed to continue processing until the mixture turns a ruddy red color, emulsified and creamy but still coarse with nuts. Scrape contents into a large bowl and repeat the process 2 more times.

When finished, whisk together the 3 batches so the final romesco is balanced. Whisk in sherry vinegar and salt. Let cool, then store in airtight containers in the refrigerator for up to 1 week.

PIZZAIOLA SAUCE

4 tablespoons extra-virgin olive oil

2 cups button mushrooms, quartered

1 cup Spanish onions, sliced thick

1 teaspoon garlic, minced

½ teaspoon red pepper flakes

1 tablespoon fresh oregano leaves

1 tablespoon fresh thyme leaves

2 tablespoons diced fresh basil

½ cup dry white wine

4 cups Pomodoro Sauce (page 255)

2 teaspoons kosher salt

1 teaspoon ground black pepper

Originating in Naples in the 1800s, pizzaiola sauce implies "in the manner of the pizza maker." Typically, leftover pizza toppings were tossed in with red sauce and then used on meats. Here, caramelized onions and mushrooms in a spicy pomodoro make a great addition to our grilled stuffed veal chops (page 181). I recommend making a big batch of this sauce to store in the refrigerator to enhance a quick pasta, sauce an arctic char, or deglaze roasted potatoes that are hot out of the oven. // **MAKES 1½ QUARTS**

Heat a large, deep, heavy skillet over medium-high heat. Swirl in olive oil and when it is almost smoking, add mushrooms and onions and let them sit without disturbing for 1 minute. After a minute, stir mushrooms and onions and cook for 5 minutes more. Add garlic, red pepper flakes, oregano, thyme and basil and continue to stir for 1 minute. Add wine and let it boil and reduce, approximately 8 to 10 minutes. Add pomodoro sauce, salt and pepper and simmer for 20 minutes. Serve when ready or store in an airtight container in the refrigerator for up to 5 days.

PANTRY

LEMON-CAPER BUTTER SAUCE

- 1 shallot, minced
- 1 sprig fresh thyme
- 1 bay leaf
- ¼ cup white wine vinegar
- ¼ cup dry white wine
- ¼ cup heavy cream
- ½ pound butter, cut into small cubes and room temperature
- ¼ cup fresh lemon juice
- 1 teaspoon kosher salt
- 2 tablespoons capers

This recipe is a little more involved than simply melting butter in a saucepan after frying a piece of fish. Yes, it's easier to do that, but too often the butter separates and can become oily. This lemon butter is rich and velvety and won't separate. It's also versatile, so you can add many different flavor components like dill, lemongrass, garlic, olives or diced tomatoes. // **MAKES 1 CUP**

In a small saucepan, combine shallot, thyme, bay leaf, vinegar and wine and bring to a boil. Reduce the wine until it is nearly evaporated and looks syrupy. Add heavy cream and bring to a boil over medium-high heat and cook for 5 to 6 minutes or until reduced by half or very thick. Turn off the heat and whisk in the cubed butter. As butter melts, the sauce will turn smooth. Strain sauce into another small sauce pot. Stir in lemon juice, salt and capers. Keep in a warm spot on the stove while the remaining components of dinner are being prepared.

> The secret here is the heavy cream. Once it reduces and thickens, it holds the whisked butter in place without breaking. This sauce can be made well in advance, then reheated. Just keep it warm, stirring occasionally, as you make dinner.

MARSALA MUSHROOM SAUCE

1 tablespoon unsalted butter

3 cups cremini mushrooms, thinly sliced

1 shallot, minced

2 fresh thyme sprigs

1 bay leaf

2 cups Marsala wine, divided

1 cup dry white wine

1 cup Poultry Broth (page 237) (or vegetable stock)

4 cups heavy cream

1½ teaspoons kosher salt

A perfect caramelle companion, this sauce gets a big flavor pop from the Marsala added at the end. The poultry broth can be omitted, making it a nice vegetarian option. This is also used as a traditional sauce for veal and pork piccata, as well as for many fish preparations. // **MAKES 1 QUART**

Heat a large skillet over medium-high heat and add butter. When butter foams, spread mushrooms over the bottom of the skillet and let sit without stirring for 2 minutes. Give mushrooms a quick stir to release juices.

Add shallot, thyme and bay leaf, then cook while stirring for 5 minutes. Add 1½ cups Marsala, white wine and poultry broth (substitute vegetable broth if using). Boil gently to reduce until liquid looks syrupy, 15 to 20 minutes. Add heavy cream and continue to boil gently until thickened, approximately 15 to 20 minutes more, stirring occasionally and adjusting heat if cream threatens to boil over. Stir in remaining ½ cup Marsala and salt and remove from heat. Remove thyme sprigs and bay leaf before serving.

Transfer sauce to an airtight container and refrigerate for up to 4 days.

BUTTERNUT SQUASH AGNOLOTTI FILLING

1 medium butternut squash, cut in half lengthwise, seeds removed

2 teaspoons kosher salt, plus more to taste

2 teaspoons ground black pepper

¼ cup honey

6 garlic cloves

5 fresh sage leaves

2 teaspoons roughly chopped fresh rosemary leaves

½ cup walnut halves

1 cup Grana Padano cheese

I have been "burning" squash this way for 30 years. The deep, dark sweetness of the caramelized honey creates a nice complexity and several levels of flavor when the roasted herbs and garlic mingle together. This also makes a great substitute for the meat filling in the Agnolotti dal Plin recipe (page 130).

// **MAKES 3½ CUPS FILLING**

Preheat oven to 425°F.

Use a paring knife to carefully score the cut surface of the squash in a crosshatch pattern, and lay squash halves cut side up on a foil-lined baking sheet.

Sprinkle squash generously with salt and pepper. Brush honey over the scored surface and add the rest to the cavities. Tuck garlic into the cavities with honey. Roast squash for about 40 minutes. The honey and the surface of the squash will turn very dark, almost burnt. At this point, reduce oven temperature to 350°F and spread sage and rosemary on top of squash. Cover squash loosely with foil and continue roasting until very soft, about 30 minutes. Maintain oven temperature.

Let squash cool on the baking sheet for 30 minutes. While squash cools, spread walnuts on a small baking sheet and bake at 350°F until fragrant and just starting to color, 5 to 8 minutes. Set aside to cool.

Scrape squash flesh from the skin, and place flesh, along with garlic and herbs, into the bowl of a food processor fitted with a steel blade. Add walnuts and cheese; process until mixture is smooth and well blended. Adjust salt if necessary. Scrape mixture into a medium bowl and set aside until needed.

Refrigerate unused filling in an airtight container for up to 5 days or freeze for up to 6 months.

MEATBALL SAUCE

3 tablespoons extra-virgin olive oil

1 Spanish onion, roughly chopped

5 cloves garlic

1 bay leaf

3 sprigs fresh thyme

3 sprigs fresh oregano

2 28-ounce cans peeled plum tomatoes

1 cup Chunky Prosciutto Broth (page 238)

1 teaspoon kosher salt

1 teaspoon ground black pepper

1 cup water

This was the first sauce ever to feature my Chunky Prosciutto Broth when it debuted on the menu at Farina's sister restaurant, Extra Virgin, in 2008. The flavor from the cooked prosciutto is deep and wonderfully rich. It really enhances an otherwise simple meatball sauce. // **MAKES 2 QUARTS**

Heat olive oil in a 4-quart saucepan over medium-high heat. Add onions and garlic cloves and cook for 4 minutes. When onions begin to turn golden, add remaining ingredients and bring to a boil. Reduce heat and simmer for 30 minutes.

Working in batches, puree the sauce in a blender until it is velvety smooth. Pass each blended batch through a fine strainer into a large prep bowl. When all the sauce has been pureed and passed through the strainer, whisk the batches together to combine. Adjust the seasoning with more salt if necessary. Let cool. Store meatball sauce in an airtight container in the refrigerator for up to 5 days or freeze for up to 6 months.

POMODORO SAUCE

2 cans (28 ounces each) San Marzano peeled plum tomatoes

1 tablespoon tomato paste

1 tablespoon kosher salt

½ cup fresh basil leaves, diced

½ cup extra-virgin olive oil

A quick tomato sauce is something that should always be in your arsenal. At Farina, we don't cook the pomodoro until just before using it on a plate of spaghetti or gnocchi. Even then, we simply heat the sauce quickly, correct the seasoning and add pasta, gnocchi or other finishing ingredients. // **MAKES 2 QUARTS**

Strain juice from canned tomatoes, keeping both separate. Add strained tomatoes and tomato paste to a food processor and pulse very slowly on and off for 5 seconds at a time to crush the tomatoes into a lumpy textured puree.

Pour crushed tomatoes into a medium stainless steel bowl and add strained tomato juice, salt, basil and olive oil and mix well. The pomodoro should have a beautiful sheen from the olive oil and a cravingly delicious flavor intensified by the salt and fresh basil.

COMPOUND BUTTERS

Flavored butters: that's what compound butters are. You can blend almost anything (except, perhaps, old tennis shoes!) into butter, and it will taste delicious. These flavorful butters are very useful to keep on hand in your freezer or refrigerator. Use a nugget here or there to finish a pan sauce for chops, top a grilled steak, or broil fish and seafood. The secret to success here is to make sure the butter is very soft, and work in 2 batches to avoid overcrowding the food processor.

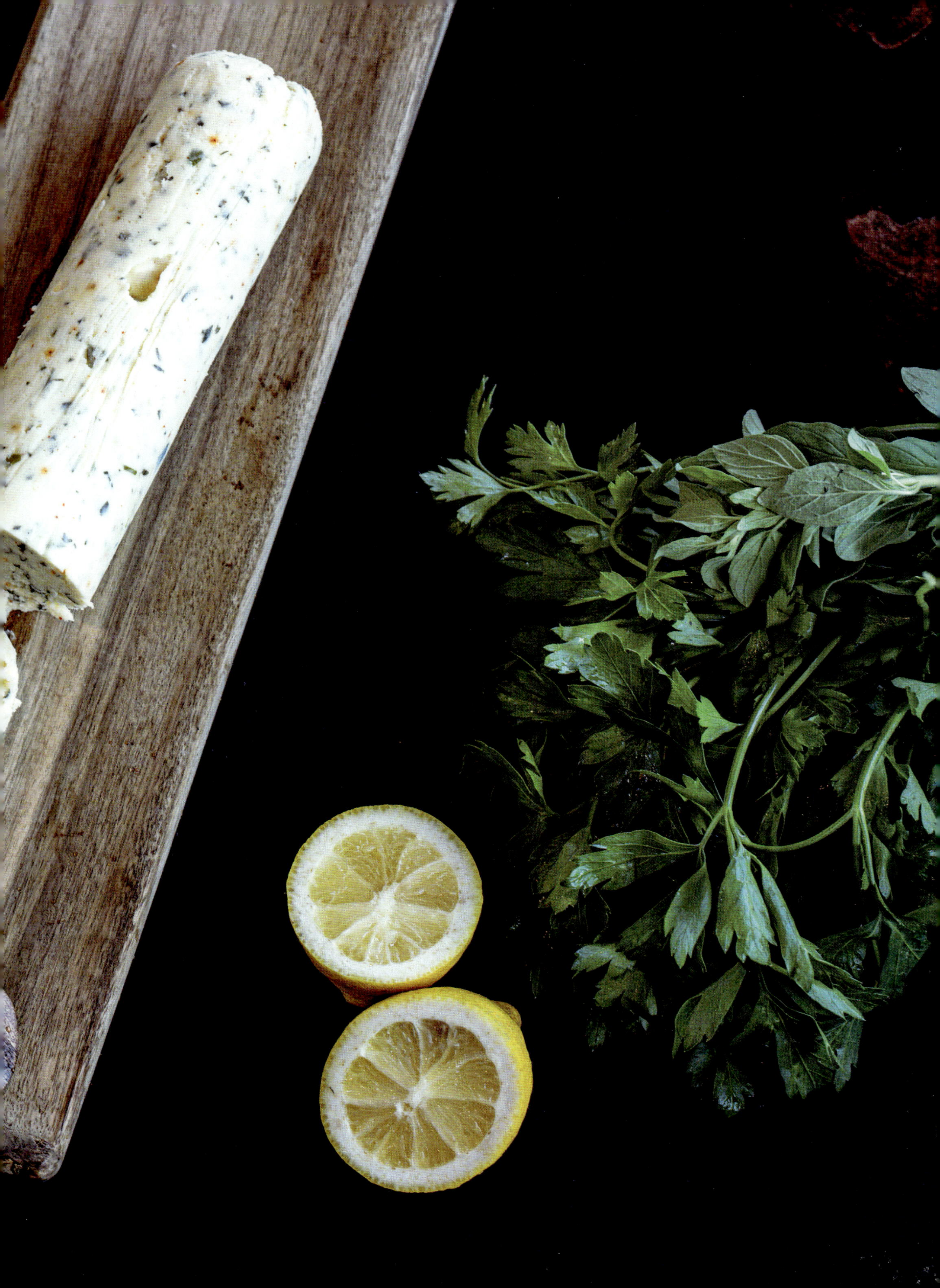

FARINA STEAK BUTTER

- 2 cups dried mixed mushrooms
- 1 pound unsalted butter, softened
- 4 cloves garlic, roughly chopped
- 1 cup fresh parsley leaves
- 1 shallot, roughly chopped
- 2 tablespoons white miso
- 5 sprigs fresh thyme
- 4 sprigs fresh oregano
- 1 tablespoon kosher salt
- 1 tablespoon ground black pepper
- ¼ cup Worcestershire sauce
- ¼ cup fresh lemon juice

We melt this butter on every wood-grilled ribeye at Farina. It's an umami bomb full of mushroom flavor that brings steak to a new level, and it also goes well with fish, vegetables and other meats. Add a nugget of this butter to a pan of sauteed Missouri morels or to finish a nice fall risotto. // **MAKES ABOUT 3 CUPS**

Heat 5 cups of water to a boil. Place mushrooms in a large stainless steel prep bowl. Pour boiling water over mushrooms and let them soak for 1 hour. Drain mushrooms from water and let cool for about 20 minutes. (Reserve mushroom liquid for soup recipes or as a substitute for bone broth.)

Place half of the butter in a food processor, then add half of the mushrooms and half amounts of the remaining ingredients, mixing until everything is well chopped and blended smoothly into the butter. Scrape butter into a large mixing bowl. Repeat with remaining ingredients, then add this batch to the mixing bowl. Use a rubber spatula to blend the 2 batches together. Taste for seasoning and adjust with more salt or lemon juice, if desired.

Using the rubber spatula, scrape butter onto a sheet of plastic wrap and roll into a log. Twist the ends of the plastic tight to firm up the roll. Chill in refrigerator for at least 1 hour.

SEAFOOD BROILING BUTTER

1 pound unsalted butter, softened

4 garlic cloves, roughly chopped

1 cup fresh parsley leaves

1 shallot, roughly chopped

5 sprigs fresh thyme

5 sprigs fresh oregano

¼ cup fresh lemon juice

2 tablespoons white miso paste

1 tablespoon kosher salt

1 tablespoon ground black pepper

This is an all-purpose butter that we use for broiled oysters, broiled sea bass and clams casino. For oysters and clams we stuff the half shells with the powerful butter and zesty breadcrumbs and then place them under a broiler. // **MAKES ABOUT 3 CUPS**

Place half of the butter in a food processor, then add half of each of the remaining ingredients and mix until everything is well chopped and blended smoothly into the butter. Scrape butter into a large mixing bowl. Repeat with remaining ingredients and add this batch to the mixing bowl. Use a rubber spatula to blend the 2 batches together. Taste for seasoning and adjust with more salt or lemon juice, if desired.

Using a rubber spatula, scrape butter onto a sheet of plastic wrap and roll into a log. Twist the ends of the plastic tight to firm up the roll. Chill in refrigerator for at least 1 hour.

CLAM BUTTER

- 1 pound unsalted butter, softened
- 4 garlic cloves, roughly chopped
- 1 cup fresh parsley leaves
- 1 shallot, minced
- 5 sprigs fresh thyme
- 5 sprigs fresh oregano
- ¼ cup fresh lemon juice
- 2 tablespoons white miso paste
- 1 teaspoon kosher salt
- 1 tablespoon ground black pepper
- 1 cup chopped sun-dried tomatoes
- 1½ cups chopped clams
- 1 tablespoon tomato paste
- 1 tablespoon red pepper flakes
- 1 cup Parmesan cheese

Our Clam Toast appetizer (page 40) features this flavored butter; it's also a great all-around butter to use with all types of seafood. For more versatility, you can omit the clams because it works wonderfully when added to pasta, risotto or a pan sauce for baked salmon. // **MAKES ABOUT 6 CUPS**

Place half of the butter in a food processor, then add half of each of the remaining ingredients and mix until everything is well chopped and blended smoothly into the butter. Scrape butter into a large mixing bowl. Repeat with remaining ingredients and add this batch to the mixing bowl. Use a rubber spatula to blend the 2 batches together. Taste for seasoning and adjust with more salt or lemon, if desired.

Using a rubber spatula, scrape butter onto a sheet of plastic wrap and roll into a log. Twist the ends of the plastic tight to firm up the roll. Chill in the refrigerator for at least 1 hour.

BLACK PEPPERCORN BUTTER

1 cup whole black peppercorns

1 bay leaf

1 pound unsalted butter

2 tablespoons fresh lemon juice

2 tablespoons kosher salt

As a young cook I would often see "braised" black peppercorns left behind in slow-cooked stews and stockpots. The soft peppercorns were tasty like a peppercorn should be, but the harsh bite was cooked out. I always thought they would be good if mashed into something else and it occurred to me that they would be perfect in a compound butter. An excellent addition to grilled pork chops, halibut steaks or freshly baked focaccia, this versatile butter enhances everything it graces with a gentle spice and extra richness. // **MAKES 3 CUPS**

Combine 4 cups water, peppercorns and bay leaf in a soup pot. Bring to a boil, then reduce to a simmer and cook for 3 to 4 hours (or, after bringing to a boil, transfer mixture to a crockpot and cook on medium for 6 hours). Drain peppercorns and discard liquid.

Place butter, cooked peppercorns and lemon juice in a food processor and blend until peppercorns are fully chopped and combined with butter. Add salt and taste for seasoning, adjusting with more salt or lemon juice, according to preference.

Using a rubber spatula, scrape butter onto a sheet of plastic wrap and roll into a log. Twist both ends of the plastic tight to firm the roll. Place in refrigerator to cool for at least 1 hour.

PANTRY

CRISPY FARRO

- 1 cup dry farro
- 3 teaspoons kosher salt, divided
- 2 sprigs fresh thyme
- 2 garlic cloves, smashed
- 1 bay leaf
- 4 cups grapeseed oil

We like crunchy things in our salads at Farina and anything is fair game, from grains like farro and quinoa to onion, chicharrones, croutons and red rice. Crunchy things just seem to satisfy my palate and I think most people agree. Enhance just about any type of salad with this grainy goodness that provides a perfect crunch and an added layer of texture. // **MAKES 1 CUP**

Combine farro, 6 cups water, 1 teaspoon salt, thyme, garlic and bay leaf in a medium stockpot and bring to a boil over medium-high heat. Reduce heat to simmer for 20 minutes or until farro is chewy but cooked through. Strain farro and save the liquid for soups and other recipes. Dry cooked farro on a kitchen towel.

Heat grapeseed oil in a large, deep skillet over high heat until temperature reaches 375°F. Carefully add cooked farro and fry for 4 minutes until crispy. Scoop farro out of hot oil with a long-handled skimmer and transfer to a towel-lined baking sheet to absorb excess oil and cool. When farro is cool to the touch, transfer to a prep bowl with 2 teaspoons salt and mix well.

Store in an airtight container at room temperature for up to 2 weeks.

CRISPY QUINOA

1 cup tricolor quinoa

2 cloves garlic, smashed

4 teaspoons kosher salt, divided

3 cups grapeseed oil

I have made heaps of quinoa in my career, and it can be a tricky grain to cook. Often it comes out mushy. This recipe is foolproof and calls for frying the cooked quinoa, which results in salty, crunchy grains that can garnish seafood ceviche, cooked fish entrées, salads and even pasta. // **MAKES 1 CUP**

Combine quinoa, 2½ cups water, garlic and 2 teaspoons salt in a sauce pot and bring to a boil over medium-high heat, then reduce to a gentle simmer, uncovered. Cook until quinoa has absorbed the water, approximately 15 minutes. Remove pot from heat and cover with a tight-fitting lid for 5 minutes. Fluff quinoa with a fork. (If it has not absorbed all the water, drain it in a fine-mesh strainer. If the quinoa is still moist, transfer it onto a heavy kitchen towel to absorb any other moisture.)

Heat grapeseed oil in a large deep skillet over high heat until temperature reaches 375°F. Carefully add cooked quinoa and fry until quinoa is crispy, approximately 4 minutes. Scoop quinoa out of the oil with a long-handled skimmer onto a towel-lined baking sheet to cool. When quinoa is cool to the touch, transfer to a prep bowl with 2 teaspoons salt and mix well.

Store in an airtight container at room temperature for up to 2 weeks.

FARINA FOCACCIA

- Extra-virgin olive oil
- 1½ tablespoons kosher salt
- ½ cup sourdough starter
- 1 tablespoon active dry yeast
- 2 cups bread flour
- ½ cup semolina flour
- 1 tablespoon malt powder
- Cooking spray
- ½ cup fresh oregano, finely chopped
- ½ cup grated Grana Padano cheese
- 2 tablespoons large-grain sea salt (or kosher salt)

When making focaccia, never punch down the dough during the folding and rising period. Many bread recipes will call for doing so, but the secret to developing beautiful air pockets is the technique of folding the dough many times onto itself. You'll notice during the folding process that big air pockets develop and will sometimes puncture as you fold. No worries. You are creating many more by the repeating technique.

// **MAKES AN 11-BY-17-INCH SHEET OF BREAD**

Grease an 11-by-17-inch baking sheet with 3 tablespoons extra-virgin olive oil. Prepare a large plastic container (with lid) by rubbing the interior with 3 tablespoons olive oil.

In a bowl, whisk together ¼ cup olive oil, kosher salt and ⅓ cup tepid-to-warm water. Set aside.

In a separate bowl, whisk together 2 cups tepid-to-warm water with sourdough starter and yeast. Set aside.

Combine both flours and malt powder in the bowl of a stand mixer and whisk with a dough hook attachment. With the mixer running on low, pour the 2-cups-water/starter mixture into the dry ingredients and mix for exactly 25 seconds. Turn off the mixer. The dough will be a shaggy mass and look nothing like a bread dough—that is perfectly fine. Let this dough mass rest for 30 minutes. After 30 minutes, turn the mixer on low again and add the second, ⅓-cup-water/oil mixture into the dough. When the water is incorporated into the dough, increase the speed to medium-high. Knead dough for 20 minutes or until it pulls from the sides and passes the "windowpane test": Take a small nugget of dough and, using your fingers, stretch it out into a thin "window" about 4 to 5 inches wide. If it doesn't break and you can see light through it, then the dough is ready. If not, continue to mix the dough for another 8 to 10 minutes.

Turn dough out onto a floured surface and shape it into an oval. Place dough in the oiled plastic container and seal with the lid. Allow dough to proof for 25 minutes. Turn dough out onto the floured surface with the longer length of oval perpendicular to you. Without punching down the dough, take the far end and fold it halfway to the center of the dough, pressing lightly to seal. Gently pull to fold the nearest end toward and over the other fold. Once the folds are complete, turn the dough over and return it to the container and seal it. Let dough proof for another 25 minutes. Repeat the folding and rising process 3 more times for a total of 4 times.

> At the beginning of the dough recipe, the dough is mixed for only 25 seconds. In the bread world this is called autolyse ("oh-toe-lease"). This is the practice of combining the flour and some of the water for a very short time (seconds), and then leaving the shaggy dough mixture to rest for a long period, typically 20 to 30 minutes. During the resting time, gluten bonds begin forming, the dough takes on a smoother texture and the dough structure is strengthened overall. Then the technique of folding and rising multiple times creates air pockets and structure.

After the last rise, gently transfer dough to the prepared baking sheet. Let dough rest on the baking sheet for 2 minutes. Then, with lightly oiled hands (to prevent sticking), press dough from the center, outward, toward each side of the baking sheet, essentially spreading the dough to fit the pan. Don't worry if the dough does not completely cover the sheet at this point. Spray top of dough with cooking spray and cover lightly with plastic wrap. Let dough rise to double its current size, about 45 minutes, depending on how warm your kitchen is.

When dough has doubled in size, remove plastic wrap and use your fingers (spread out) to poke dimples all over the dough. Before baking, combine ½ cup extra-virgin olive oil and ½ cup water in a small bowl and brush top of dough lightly with the mixture. Sprinkle the top generously with oregano and Grana Padano cheese. Cover lightly with plastic wrap and let rise for another 20 minutes.

Preheat oven to 450°F. Remove plastic wrap and sprinkle dough with sea salt.

Bake focaccia for about 15 to 20 minutes. Turn the bread around and bake for another 15 to 20 minutes. The bread will puff up again and develop a hard crust. Be sure to bake the bread beyond golden brown; a deep, dark brown crust is important for the overall flavor of the bread. Remove bread from the oven and cool on a baking rack.

COCKTAIL SAUCE

1 medium carrot, peeled, roughly chopped

2 stalks celery, roughly chopped

1 shallot, roughly chopped

1 cup ice cubes

3 cups ketchup

1 cup chili sauce

2 heaping tablespoons prepared horseradish

3 tablespoons Worcestershire sauce

2 tablespoons lemon juice

1 teaspoon black pepper

2 teaspoons kosher salt

Textural contrast is important in cooking, and I really like the crunch of raw vegetables in this sauce. It's important that the vegetables are finely minced. As the sauce sits for a few hours, or even a day, the vegetables enhance its overall flavor. You can simplify this recipe by using store-bought cocktail sauce, then just add the minced vegetables and adjust the horseradish to suit your taste. // **MAKES 1 QUART**

Place carrot, celery and shallot in a small food processor with ice and process on high speed until finely minced. Drain vegetables from the water produced during processing. Scrape vegetables into a medium-size stainless steel bowl and add all remaining ingredients. Stir to mix well.

> When I want to mince large quantities of garlic or to finely mince mirepoix vegetables, I add 1 cup ice to the food processor as it spins. This technique reduces the heat created by the speed of the machine and keeps the product loose and free to spin easily. Then strain the vegetables or garlic through a fine mesh strainer, discarding the liquid.

PANGRATTATO

4 to 5 slices sourdough bread (5 ounces), crusts removed (or substitute a different artisanal bread)

2½ tablespoons extra-virgin olive oil

1 tablespoon unsalted butter, softened

1 tablespoon fresh oregano leaves

1 tablespoon fresh thyme leaves

1 tablespoon roughly chopped fresh parsley

2 teaspoons minced garlic

1 bay leaf, crumbled

1 teaspoon kosher salt

1 teaspoon freshly ground black pepper

½ teaspoon red pepper flakes

Panko works fine, but homemade pangrattato yields distinctly superior breadcrumbs. We typically don't use the bread crust for this recipe, but a little crust can provide added texture if needed.
// **MAKES 2 CUPS**

Place bread in the bowl of a food processor and process to coarse crumbs. Transfer to a mixing bowl.

Add remaining ingredients to crumbs. Mix and crush crumbs together well until evenly blended.

Transfer seasoned breadcrumbs to a nonstick skillet over medium-low heat. Cook, stirring occasionally, until crumbs are crunchy and deep golden brown, about 30 minutes. Watch closely and stir often near the end of cooking to avoid overbrowning. Cool completely.

Store pangrattato in an airtight container for up to 2 weeks.

SAGE BROWN BUTTER SAUCE

1 cup unsalted butter

1 shallot, finely minced

6 large fresh sage leaves, chiffonade

3 tablespoons balsamic vinegar

1 tablespoon fresh lemon juice

½ teaspoon kosher salt

½ teaspoon fresh ground black pepper

Essentially, this is a vinaigrette with butter acting as the oil. Try it on homemade butternut agnolotti for a flavorful fall pasta.
// **MAKES 1¼ CUPS**

Melt butter in a small saucepan over medium-high heat. Cook until it turns a dark golden brown and gives off a nutty scent, approximately 5 to 7 minutes. Scrape the bottom of the pan occasionally to loosen any caramelized bits that form during browning. As soon as butter browns, remove from heat to avoid burning.

Carefully add shallot and sage to hot butter, stirring for 30 seconds. Stir in vinegar, lemon juice, salt and pepper; set aside.

Rewarm the sauce and whisk to emulsify right before serving.

CONSERVA DI POMODORI
(TOMATO PASTE)

I first read about homemade tomato paste in *My Calabria*, by Rosetta Costantino and Janet Fletcher. They describe drying fresh pureed tomato sauce in the hot Mediterranean sun until it turns into tomato paste or *conserva di pomodori*. We have great tomatoes in Missouri, so I was inspired to start making my own tomato paste in the summer. I only do it once a year, in preparation for our annual Kurlbaum Tomato Dinner. I use the sun-dried tomato paste for tomato butter to accompany our bread service that night. It can be a long, precarious process for sure, but you may end up feeling like you're in the old country. The depth of color is intense, and the flavor of the sun-dried paste is wonderful. Beware, the weather has to be hot and dry because rain will ruin all your hard work! // **MAKES 1 QUART**

10 pounds ripe, meaty tomatoes, stems and cores removed, cut into quarters

¼ cup kosher salt

Special equipment:
1 fine-mesh strainer

1 mesh food tent

Place tomatoes in a stockpot large enough to hold them. Add 1 cup water and bring to a boil over high heat. Continue boiling tomatoes, stirring occasionally, for 30 minutes to soften and render them juicy.

Transfer hot tomatoes 3 cups at a time into the canister of a high-speed blender. Place a thickly folded kitchen towel over the blender top, and carefully pulse tomatoes on low speed until the pressure (created by the heat) diminishes. Next, with the towel still covering the blender top, pulse on high for 30 seconds to fully puree the tomatoes. Transfer tomatoes into a large prep bowl. Repeat until all tomatoes have been pureed. Then, set up a fine-mesh strainer and pass the pureed tomatoes into the previously used stockpot.

Return the stockpot to the stove and bring tomato puree to a boil. Add salt and, stirring occasionally, reduce the puree to 1 quart, approximately 1 hour of cooking time. Toward the end of the cooking time, stir often to prevent scorching and reduce heat to prevent intense splattering. When puree is ready, you can dry the tomato puree in the oven or in the sun, as follows.

OVEN METHOD

Preheat oven to 200°F.

Spread tomato puree evenly onto a large baking sheet with sides. Place baking sheet in the center of the oven and bake puree for approximately 3 hours to dry out. Every 30 minutes or so, use a rubber spatula to spread puree around and distribute it evenly on the baking sheet. Be meticulous about spreading it thin and evenly, mixing the dry edges into the moist center part. Smears on the edges that are too thin will burn. After about 2 hours the puree will dry significantly and start to become sticky and thick. Continue to monitor closely and fold any edges into the middle that are drying too fast, to prevent burning. After about 3 hours, the puree will resemble what you would recognize as tomato paste. If it still seems too runny or moist, return the baking sheet to the oven and cook it longer. When the paste is ready, remove from oven and let it cool completely. When cool, transfer paste to a clean jar, tamping it down to make sure there are no air pockets. Cover the top completely with a thin layer of olive oil. Cover and refrigerate for up to 1 year. After each use, level the surface and top with olive oil.

SUN-DRIED METHOD

Pour tomato puree onto a large baking sheet with sides and set it out in the sunniest, hottest part of your yard or deck. Following the sun during the day, move the baking sheet to keep it in the direct sun for as many hours as possible. Bring the baking sheet inside overnight. You may need to do this multiple days to dry the puree long enough to become tomato paste. Use a mesh food tent to cover it, preventing insects from getting into the puree as it is drying outside.

> This method of making your own tomato paste is old school and pretty cool, I think. But it is a long process and the recipe won't make very much; admittedly, you may not think it's worth the time and effort. But after making it the first time, go for it! Make it a bigger project and perhaps triple or quadruple the tomato amount to yield a significantly larger amount of tomato paste.

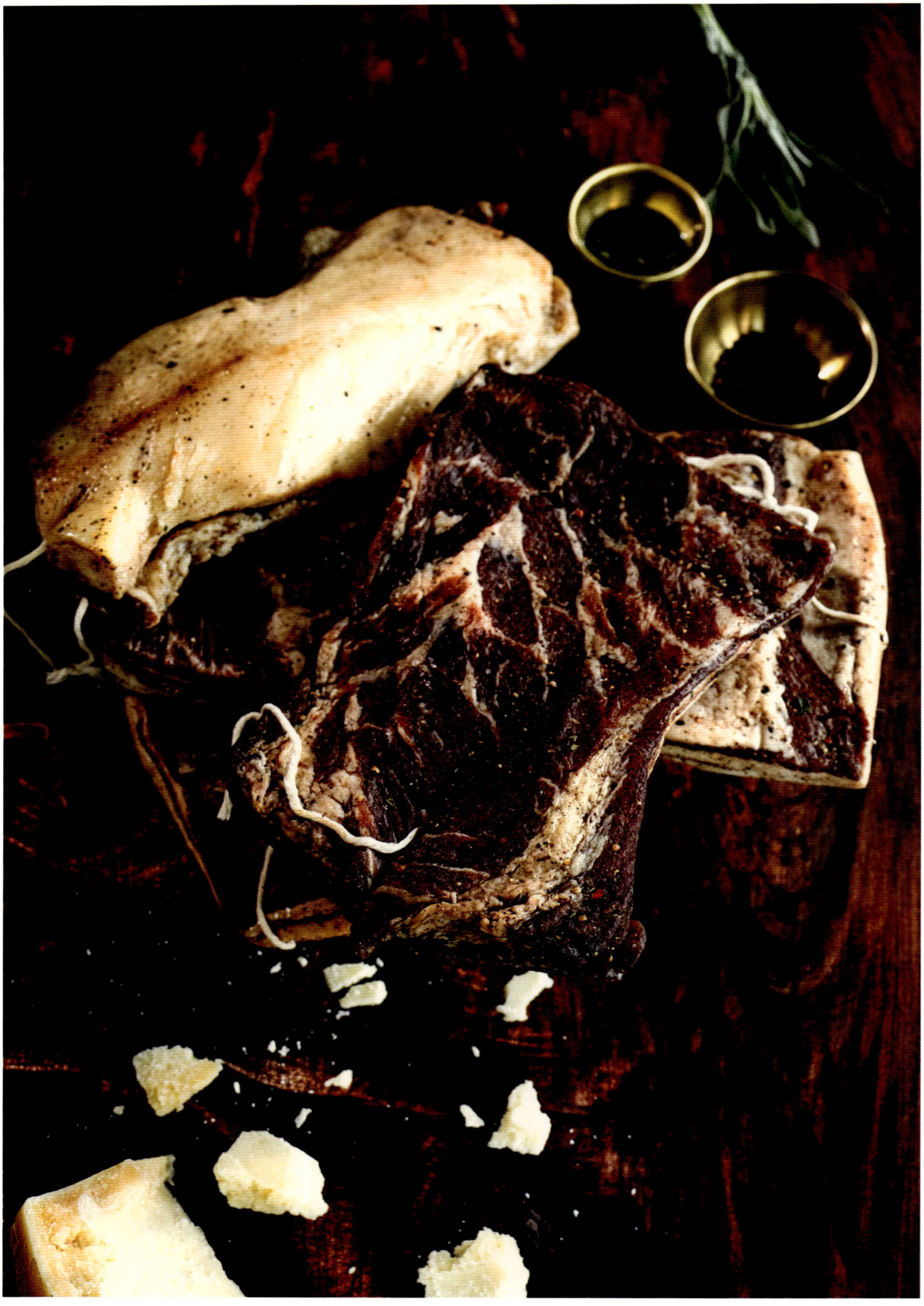

HOME-CURED PANCETTA

1 cup kosher salt or sea salt

2 teaspoons cure #2 or pink salt

¼ cup brown sugar

1 cup black peppercorns, crushed

2 tablespoons juniper berries, crushed

3 tablespoons fennel seeds, crushed

3 whole cloves, crushed

1 tablespoon celery seeds

2 tablespoons red pepper flakes

10 cloves garlic, thinly sliced

2 tablespoons fresh rosemary leaves

½ cup fresh thyme sprigs, roughly chopped

10 bay leaves, crumbled

1 piece fresh pork belly (10 pounds), skin removed

Special equipment: Butcher twine

This salt rub can also be used to cure pork jowls (aka guanciale).

We cure our own pancetta and guanciale at Farina to use in pasta dishes like Bucatini Carbonara and Rigatoni all'Amatriciana, as well as salads and hearty entrées. Pancetta is the easiest of all the cured salumi to make at home. After the requisite curing salts, you can spice the flavor up any way you desire. This recipe is adapted from a book my longtime chef friend Brian Polcyn cowrote with Michael Ruhlman, titled *Salumi: The Craft of Italian Dry Curing*.
// **MAKES APPROXIMATELY 8 POUNDS**

Using a large, nonreactive prep bowl, combine salt, cure #2 or pink salt, and brown sugar; set aside.

In a blender or food processor, combine peppercorns, juniper berries, fennel seeds, cloves, celery seeds and red pepper flakes. Pulse on medium-high speed until spices are crushed but not powdered. Transfer crushed spices to a sauté pan and place over medium heat. Toast for 40 seconds, stirring continuously with a wooden spoon to warm and release the aroma. Transfer toasted spices to the prep bowl with salt mixture. Add sliced garlic, rosemary, thyme and bay leaves to prep bowl. Using a latex glove on one hand, abrasively mix and crush together the herbs, spices and garlic.

Hold pork belly over a stainless-steel food pan or food-grade plastic container and vigorously rub the salt cure into the flesh of the meat on all sides. Next, scatter a solid layer of the salt cure on the bottom of the container, then lay the belly on the layer of salt. Finish by distributing the remainder of the salt cure over the top and along the sides of the belly.

Cover the container with a lid or plastic wrap and refrigerate for 7 days. After day 3, flip the belly over and distribute the salt cure on and around the belly again. After day 7, rinse the belly under cold water to remove the curing salt. Poke a hole in one corner of the belly and insert a piece of butcher twine through the hole. Tie a knot, creating a loop about 6 inches long, then hang the belly to dry in a refrigerator or in any environment where the temperature will remain between 45° and 55°F. A cool basement, a modified refrigerator or a wine cellar are all good options.

Disclaimer: Curing raw meats in a non-professional environment can be dangerous. Don't eat any cured meats that smell sour or have unidentified mold growing.

UNUSUAL *and* HIGHLY RECOMMENDED PANTRY STAPLES

POMEGRANATE MOLASSES
This is made from the juice of sour pomegranates, which is reduced until it is a deep purple syrup. We use it in marinades, salad dressings and glazes. It's wonderful on roasted rack of lamb and anything coming off an open wood-fired grill.

BARBERRIES
Garnet-colored barberries have a strikingly tart flavor that is prized throughout the Middle East. Similar in flavor to unsweetened dried cranberries, they are tiny and easy to scatter around dishes. The barberry is a favorite dried fruit of mine, and I use it everywhere I can. It adds a pop of bright flavor and a brilliant color to rice and grains as well as rich meat braises and vegetable dishes.

SQUID INK
Squid ink, also known as cuttlefish ink, is a black liquid that squid, cuttlefish and octopuses produce to protect themselves from predators. It is an inky black pigment that chefs use to color and flavor pasta, rice and sauces. It tastes salty like the sea and is prevalent in Mediterranean and Japanese cooking.

NEONATA / ROSAMARINA SAUCE
Neonata means "newborn" in Italian. It's the name of a condiment (also referred to as rose marina sauce) that originated from the coast of southern Calabria. It is made from anchovies that are preserved with salt, a mix of sweet and hot peppers, and olive oil, then left to cure. Essentially it becomes a chunky Italian version of fish sauce. In Calabria, the condiment is spread on crostini and added to pastas and vegetables. It's a flavorful ingredient in our popular Sardinian black rice dish at Farina.

ALEPPO CHILE FLAKES
Named after the Syrian city of Aleppo, this chili pepper has a relatively mild flavor profile with a sweet undertone on the palate. We like to use the flakes on our raw meat and fish dishes as well as for garnishes on pasta and seafood.

HARISSA
Originally from Tunisia, this is a salty and fiery chile condiment typically used as a garnish for the country's celebrated Couscous Royale. It's made of dry red chiles, garlic, citrus, extra-virgin olive oil and warm spices like cumin, coriander and caraway seeds.

DEMI-GLACE
Chef Auguste Escoffier standardized a recipe for demi-glace in his *Le Guide Culinaire* published in 1903. Demi-glace is a richly concentrated brown stock that is reduced until it forms a deeply flavored, gelatinous meat sauce. Demi-glace is the base sauce used in many other flavored sauces in the French cooking canon.

GIGANTE BEANS
Gigantes are large, flat, cream-colored beans popular in the Mediterranean and common in Greek cuisine. They need a long soak before cooking and have a sweet, mild taste and meaty texture. We use them for salads and stews because they hold their shape well after cooking. The name Gigante comes from the Greek word for giant. Corona beans can be used as a substitute.

LUPINI BEANS
Lupini beans are the seeds of the *Lupinus albus*, a plant belonging to the Leguminosae family. The round, mustard-colored beans are popular throughout Italy and the Mediterranean, where they are commonly eaten pickled, as a garnish on meat and cheese boards. They are an excellent source of protein and are a nutritional powerhouse, full of fiber and containing all 9 amino acids.

BLACK GARLIC
Black garlic is a soft-sticky garlic clove (bulb) that has been aged at about 160°F in high humidity for at least 3 weeks and sometimes longer. It has been used for flavor and medicinal purposes and in a variety of Asian cuisines for centuries. It imparts a mild garlic flavor to cooking, and its black color is

bold and inspiring. It is similar in texture to a dried fig but will puree into sauces very easily.

CALABRIAN CHILI PEPPERS

Originating from Calabria on the southern coast of Italy, these appealing chili peppers are a long and slender variety. They have a salty, smoky and even fruity taste, although they are predominantly spicy. They typically come in jars and are cooked and stored in oil. Save the oil as a tasty condiment to drizzle on pizza, eggs, or pasta.

CRESCENZA CHEESE

Part of the family of stracchino cheeses, Crescenza is a fresh, creamy, spreadable and rindless cheese from the regions of Lombardy, Veneto and Piedmont. We use it as filling for stuffed pasta and to stir into risottos.

FARRO

Farro is a wheat product, an ancient grain similar to barley, with which it can be used interchangeably in pilafs. High in protein and fiber, it has long been a staple in Italian cookery. Farro retains a significant amount of chew when cooked. We use it in winter, when our menu reflects heartier dishes. We also fry farro and use it as a crunchy garnish for salads and carpaccio.

QUINOA

Quinoa was originally cultivated by pre-Columbian civilizations in Peru and Bolivia. It is a high-altitude plant and, like lupini beans, a nutritional powerhouse. It is a seed that's high in plant protein and fiber, having all 9 essential amino acids. That makes quinoa one of the best non-animal food sources of complete protein.

BURRATA CHEESE

A relatively recent innovation, Burrata may date back to about 1900, when brothers Lorenzo and Vincenzo Bianchini created it on their farm in Italy's Puglia region. When making Burrata, the still-hot cheese is formed into a pouch, which is then filled with scraps of leftover mozzarella and topped off with fresh cream before closing. We use Burrata with osetra caviar and on top of salads.

PECORINO ROMANO

Pecorino is a hard cheese made from 100 percent sheep's milk. Pecorino Romano is one of the most ancient types of cheese. Its production is protected by the Italian government and it is allowed to be made only in Lazio, in the Tuscan province of Grosseto, and on the islands of Sardinia. The sheep's milk is made into chalky white 50-pound drums and typically aged about 8 months. The taste profile is salty and nutty.

MOZZARELLA DI BUFULA

Another in a long line of great Italian cheeses, buffalo mozzarella is a shimmering, porcelain-white ball of creamy cheese, made from the milk of Italian Mediterranean buffalo. It is a traditional cheese of Campania and is considerably more delicate than regular mozzarella. The flavors of the grazing fields are reflected in the taste of the cheese. Craig Ramini, a Silicon Valley software consultant who died in 2015, had a crazy dream to produce Italian-worthy American mozzarella di bufula. His Ramini Mozzarella company lives on and continues to make an incredible cheese.

PANGRATTATO

Pangrattato means "grated bread." Chefs could simply use the term "breadcrumbs," but pangrattato sounds so much fancier to Americans. History tells us that poor Italians, mostly in the south, would grate stale bread over pasta in place of the Parmesan cheese they could not afford. We toast the breadcrumbs slowly over very low heat with lots of herbs, garlic and olive oil. It provides a great texture of crunch on pasta and soups.

FENNEL POLLEN

Found throughout the Mediterranean, fennel pollen is a powder made from the tiny blossoms at the end of the fennel plant. It is one of the most important ingredients when making porchetta, and we also use it in vinaigrettes and sprinkle it on carpaccio. It's generally sold in small amounts, but a little goes a long way.

WHERE TO FIND FOODS

AMAZON
- Pasta shapes
- Tutto Calabria condiments
- Calabrian chili peppers
- Cookbooks

D'ARTAGNAN
- Demi-glace
- Game meats
- Sausages
- Beans

IGOURMET
- Cheeses
- Gourmet meats
- Olive oils
- Olives

OLIO2GO
- High-quality olive oils

MANICARETTI
- Artisanal pasta
- Olive oils
- Olives
- Anchovies

WILLIAMS SONOMA
- Chocolates
- Vinegars
- Gourmet sauces
- Demi-glace
- Meat boards

MARKY'S
- Tutto Calabria condiments
- Artisanal cheese

EATALY
- Selections of everything Italian

BEMKA
- All selections of caviar
- Winter truffles

WULF'S FISH
- Fresh seafood

ISLAND CREEK OYSTERS
- East Coast oyster selections

FORTUNE FISH & GOURMET
- Fresh seafood
- Spanish gourmet foods

FOODS IN SEASON
- Wild mushrooms
- Seafood
- Wagyu beef
- Seasonal foraged ingredients

WEBSTAURANTSTORE
- Cooking equipment

FANTE'S
- Pasta tools
- Other pasta-making supplies

BUON'ITALIA
- Tipo 00 flour
- Semolina
- Rose marina sauce
- Olive oils

LOCAL KANSAS CITY MARKETS

Shahrazad Market
Al Habashi
Hung Vuong Market
888 Int'l Market
Oriental Supermarket
Carollo's Italian Grocery
Bella Napoli
Cupini's

COOKBOOKS I LOVE TO READ

Pasta. Missy Robbins, New York, Ten Speed Press, 2021

Mastering Pasta. Marc Vetri and David Joachim, Berkeley, Ten Speed Press, 2015

American Sfoglino. Evan Funke, San Francisco, Chronicle Books, 2019

The Mozza Cookbook. Nancy Silverton, New York, Knopf Doubleday, 2011

My Calabria. Rosetta Costantino and Janet Fletcher, London, W.W. Norton, 2010

Salt Fat Acid Heat. Samin Nosrat, New York, Simon & Schuster, 2017

The Flavor Matrix. James Briscione and Brooke Parkhurst, New York, HMH, 2018

Falastin. Sami Tamimi and Tara Wigley, New York, Ten Speed Press, 2020

Bestia. Ori Menashe and Genevieve Gergis, New York, Ten Speed Press, 2018

Cooking by Hand. Paul Bertolli, New York, Clarkson Potter, 2003

Essentials of Classic Italian Cooking. Marcella Hazan, New York, Knopf, 1992

Bugialli on Pasta. Giuliano Bugialli, New York, Harry N. Abrams, 2000

Pasta, Pane, Vino. Matt Goulding, New York, Harper Collins, 2018

The Essential Oyster. Rowan Jacobson, New York, Bloomsbury, 2016

Tasting Rome. Katie Parla and Kristina Gill, New York, Clarkson Potter, 2016

The Truffle Underground. Ryan Jacobs, New York, Clarkson Potter, 2019

Friuli Food and Wine. Bobby Stuckey, Lachlan Mackinnon-Patterson, Meredith Erickson, New York, Ten Speed Press, 2020

Pok Pok. Andy Ricker and JJ Goode, Berkeley, Ten Speed Press, 2013

PANTRY

LEFTOVERS *and* FOOD SCRAPS

Not all trash is trash. If you buy a brand-new *trash can* and bring it home, is it dirty? Just because it's labeled a trash can doesn't mean it's dirty . . . until it is. I apply this logic to foods as well. Just because we have always thrown away the ends of onions or carrots or even meat bones, that doesn't make them trash. The European way of cooking is to use every part of the animal or vegetable, and that has stuck with me as I moved through my career in kitchens. I save food scraps of many kinds to use as a base for soups or to flavor stocks and broths. Keep a bag in the freezer and add to it as you can. When it fills up, it's probably time to make a new meat or vegetable broth. Here are some helpful hints on how to make the most of your food scraps.

VEGETABLE SCRAPS

AT FARINA:

I save most of my herb and vegetable scraps at Farina and Extra Virgin to make stocks and broths. I use the ends, peels, roots and stalks from vegetables such as carrots, shallots, onions, celery, garlic, fennel and leeks. We keep them in the cooler until needed, and after flavoring the stocks, they are strained and discarded. Of course, you should always wash any dirt from scraps before cooking.

AT HOME:

If you do a lot of home cooking, you can use scraps to create something new like soup, stew or flavored stock. Cauliflower cores (no leaves) make a great cauliflower soup with heavy cream and leftover mashed potatoes. And the same is true with broccoli stems! Boil heavy cream, potatoes and stems (cores) until soft, then emulsify it all to a silky smooth texture in your blender. If you start saving scrap vegetables (btw … my wife, Nancy, hates that—fridge clutter!), you can substitute them in recipes where they are a flavoring component, as with braised meats and stews. Also, save the stems from any fresh herbs (except dill and mint) that you cook with and put them in your soups and braises. Fresh herbs cost enough as is, so you'll want to get one more use out of them if possible. I don't use dill or mint in basic stocks and broths because their flavors are too distinct and strong.

MEAT SCRAPS

AT FARINA:

We cut steaks and chops every day in our restaurants, so we save every single scrap of meat that doesn't make it to the main entrée cut. We roast the stringy, sinewy pieces for stocks. We grind the tiny morsels of meat scraps for hamburgers or Bolognese sauce. And we braise the heftier lean meat scraps for stews and soups. Finally, we save all bones, from pork and beef to chicken and veal. They are roasted and added to our weekly meat stocks.

AT HOME:

Maybe you have leftover ribs from pork chops or scraps of grilled steak or chops from last night's dinner. Save those to go with your vegetable scraps to use in broths. Often, butcher shops or meat markets have inexpensive off cuts of meat and bones that are wonderful in a stock after a long simmering. You can freeze anything raw right away. And leftover scraps that are already cooked will keep for about 4 days in the refrigerator.

SOUP BONES: Soup bones (chicken, turkey or pork necks) from your local butcher shop or farmers' market are usually inexpensive and they become soft after hours of cooking, releasing lots of great flavors. Beef bones, knuckles, shanks and marrow bones are some of my other favorites. Try to find bones that still have chunks of meat on them. That really pumps up the flavor!

HERBS: All broths are flexible with regard to herbs. Discover which herbs you like best. You can't go wrong with adding fresh thyme, oregano, bay leaf or savory. I personally don't like to use dry herbs because they are too strong. If you use them, use tiny amounts.

Note: When your bone broth is finished cooking, the meats will fall off the bones. Those tender meats are great to stir into soups or pasta noodles as a simple lunch or light dinner.

ACKNOWLEDGMENTS

FIRST AND FOREMOST, TO BILL AND PEGGY LYONS: Thank you for making this book and Farina Ristorante & Oyster Bar possible. Without you, there would be no restaurant or book.

Many chefs dream of someday having their own restaurant. Bill, as my business partner for more than 20 years, you gave Nancy and me the support to realize those dreams several times over.

TO MY BEAUTIFUL WIFE AND TALENTED BUSINESS PARTNER, NANCY SMITH: I never would have realized my potential without you by my side every step of the way. You are a wonderful life partner and the fearless general manager of our restaurants. Your growth and development as our wine director has been extraordinary to behold. Thank you for tolerating my propensity for adventure and sharing in our travels throughout the world, specifically Italy. From Pantelleria and Sicily to the Veneto and Piedmont, through Tuscany and Rome and down to Naples and Calabria, you've created some of the greatest Italian food and travel experiences of my life.

TO MY MOTHER, DONNA COMEAU: You worked your ass off to raise Nathelle and I by yourself. One day when I was about 12 or 13 you told me, "You'll get a job one day and it'll probably be in the restaurant business." Yes, ma'am, you were right about that! Thank you for being a tough mom and showing me that hard work can pay off. We moved every year for a while when I was growing up and that gave me the courage to travel the world. I wasn't sure how to find the world back then, but I knew it was out there for me. And Nathelle, thank you for putting up with me. Even though I was a pain-in-the-butt little brother.

TO THE SERVICE TEAM AT FARINA AND EXTRA VIRGIN RESTAURANT: You have become family over the years, and you are simply the best servers in Kansas City. A special shoutout to Angie and Ben, you are food superheroes!

THANK YOU, TOO, TO THE KITCHEN TEAM AT FARINA: You have been on point (most of the time, anyway), and together we have learned how to run an Italian kitchen. You are all talented young cooks. May you have great futures in the hospitality business.

TO MY TEACHERS: Jean-Pierre Lelievre, George Mavrothalassitis, Charlie Trotter, Gordon Sinclair, Jim and Bob Fredregill, Tom Johnson, Michael Tracy, Carl Thorne-Thomsen, Doug Frost, Solomon Melesse and, again, Bill Lyons. You have been chefs, business mentors and experts sharing your knowledge with me. The restaurant business is filled to the brim with so many improbable characters, and I have tried to learn something from all the restaurants where I have worked. So many incredible people have intersected the roads of my journey, and when I needed energy, inspiration and coaching, I found it from you. Thank you all.

TO JENNY WHEAT: Your photography makes my food look *delicioso*! We had a vision of what we wanted the food to look like for this book, and you nailed it. You took on a big project and we made deadlines with long, fast and furious photoshoots. I love that you live and work in the Crossroads Arts District. It's been exciting and gritty down here and you just glide through and share your friendship and talent. And a big high-five to Janie Jones for bringing food props, making us laugh and helping drive our look.

TO OUR PUBLISHER, STORY FARM AND BOB MORRIS: You read my short story and wanted to publish a book with us here at Farina. Many thanks to Bo Morris and Jason Farmand for guiding the editing and design ideas. Its helps when you like what we like. Thank you for giving me the confidence to pull it off.

TO NANCY BOYCE, who tested the recipes and taught me how to properly write a recipe. You listened suspiciously as I fibbed about testing the recipes before emailing them to you. And upon receiving them, you said, "WE NEED TO TALK!" Thank you for putting up with my nonsense.

TO BERTO: It's been a fun ride with you. Thank you for driving the bar programs and introducing us to spirits of all kinds. Your travels and my travels bring depth and authenticity to what we are doing at Farina.

TO MY CHEF DE CUISINE, DANIEL ERHARDT: Your talent in the kitchen is immense and I cannot do it without you. Thank you for working with me all these years.

TO MY FORMER CHEF DE CUISINE, DAVID PADBERG: You opened Farina with me. And we managed to pull it off with only a few bumps. It was fun and rewarding!

TO DIEGO: Thank you for continuing to grow with us. You are a huge help to Nancy and she appreciates your attention to detail. It seems you are both married to Open Table and I'm sorry about that. You are always impeccably dressed and our guests and staff love you!

TO MY DAUGHTERS, MISHA AND SOPHIE, WHO GREW UP IN AND AROUND ALL OF MY RESTAURANTS: I hope I inspired you to be passionate about food and travel. Sharing that generosity and hospitality with your friends will come back to you in spades. You both decided to be chefs. I want the best and most success for you!

TO CRAIG NEUMAN: Thank you for always listening to my crazy stories about guests and my far-flung food adventures, and for designing a great Farina logo! All of our brand identities are modern and smart. You have great taste in design.

TO K-SQUARED: Thank you, Katie and Kimberly, for relentlessly promoting our restaurants and continuously brainstorming food and wine ideas and stories, from fun parties to serious writing and everything in between. When the Covid pandemic hit Kansas City, you were instrumental in helping us navigate and communicate in the new and ever-changing world.

AND TO EVERYONE IN KANSAS CITY: You welcomed me to your city when I arrived at The American Restaurant in 1994. I was uncertain how long I would stay in Kansas City because I wanted to be in the "big" city. But I came to love it here and have enjoyed my fair share of success. I appreciate your support. Thank you to everyone who has stuck with me. The Michael Smith and Extra Virgin restaurants stumbled along in an up-and-coming neighborhood but eventually succeeded, providing the steppingstone to Farina.

INDEX

Page numbers in italics indicate photos.

1977 Live from Florence (cocktail), *196*, 197

A
agnolotti
　Agnolotti dal Plin, 130–32, *131*, *133*
　Butternut Squash Agnolotti Filling, 254
Aleppo chile flakes, 272
All'Amatriciana, Rigatoni, *102*, 103
almonds
　Pesto Calabrese, 248
　Romesco Sauce, 250
anchovies
　Treviso and Bartlett Pear Salad with Gorgonzola, *56*, 57
Angel Hair Pasta with Osetra Caviar, Ponzu and Furikake, Chilled, *138*, *139*
Aperol
　Farina Barrel-Aged Negroni, *192*, 193
Apicius Spice Mix, 248
　Duck Breast Apicius with Foie Gras, 166–67, *167*
Apricot Mostarda, 244, *245*
Arctic char
　Seared Arctic Char and Sauce Vierge, *156*, 157
arugula
　Persimmon Salad with Carrots, Pomegranate Seeds and Kumquats, *52*, 53
　Seared Arctic Char and Sauce Vierge, *156*, 157
　Whole Oven Roasted Branzino with Arugula, Fennel and Lemon, *154*, 155
Ash, Burnt Onion, 249
asparagus
　King Crab and Asparagus Bruschetta, *36*, 37
avocados
　Cucumber Salad, *58*, 59
　King Crab and Asparagus Bruschetta, *36*, 37

B
Baked Halibut with Summer Vegetables, *146*, 147
barberries, 272
basil
　Pesto Calabrese, 248
　Pistou, *60*, 64–65
　Provençal Pistou Soup, *60*, 64–65
　Spinach Handkerchief Pasta with Basil Pesto and Pomodoro, *140*, *141*
　Tuna Crudo with Eggplant, Blistered Tomatoes, Lemon and Basil, *38*, 39
bass, striped
　Striped Bass with Saffron Broth, Clams and Chorizo, *148*, 149
beans
　gigante, 272
　lupini, 272
　Minestrone, *60*, 61
　Provençal Pistou Soup, *60*, 64–65
　Swordfish with Broccolini, Olives and White Beans, *158*, 159
　Watercress, Hearts of Palm and Crispy Farro Salad, *50*, 51
beef
　Agnolotti dal Plin, 130–32, *131*, *133*
　Bone Broth, 236
　Braised Beef Short Ribs, *162*, 163
　Duck Meatballs, *42*, 43
　Ragù alla Bolognese, 106–07, *107*
　Tuscan Pici Noodles with Braised Short Ribs and Roasted Cherry Tomatoes, *142*, 143
beets
　Roasted Carrot and Beet Salad, *48*, 49
blackberries
　Peach and Blackberry Crostata with Lemon Curd Ice Cream, 211–13, *212*
　Summer Berry Cobbler with Peach Ice Cream, 214, *215*
black garlic, 272–73
black pepper
　Black Peppercorn Butter, 261
　Cacio e Pepe, *100*, 101
Black Truffle Omelet, *68*, 69
Blistered Cherry Tomatoes, 243
　Grilled Octopus with Potatoes and Blistered Tomatoes, *44*, 45
　Sardinian Lorighittas with Mussels, Saffron and Blistered Tomatoes, 120–22, *121*, *123*
　Tuna Crudo with Eggplant, Blistered Tomatoes, Lemon and Basil, *38*, 39
Blood Orange Paris-Brest, *202*, 203–04
blueberries
　Summer Berry Cobbler with Peach Ice Cream, 214, *215*
Bolognese, Ragù alla, 106–07, *107*
Bone Broth, 236
bourbon
　1977 Live from Florence, *196*, 197
Braised Beef Short Ribs, *162*, 163
　Tuscan Pici Noodles with Braised Short Ribs and Roasted Cherry Tomatoes, *142*, 143
branzino
　Whole Oven Roasted Branzino with Arugula, Fennel and Lemon, *154*, 155
bread. *See also* sandwiches
　autolyse method, 265
　Caramelized Brioche with Fall Pears and Figs, 208–10, *209*
　Clam Toast, *40*, 41
　Crostini and Bruschetta, 247
　Farina Focaccia, 264–65, *265*
　Pangrattato, 267
　Romesco Sauce, 250

INDEX

Summer Tomato Gazpacho (Salmorejo), 60, 62
broccolini
- Bucatini All'Ubriaco with Broccolini and Walnuts, 116, 117
- Ricotta Pincenelle with Sausage and Broccoli, 114, 115
- Swordfish with Broccolini, Olives and White Beans, 158, 159

Broiled Cotuit Oysters, 34, 35
broth, homemade
- Bone Broth, 236
- Chunky Prosciutto Broth, 238
- Grana Padano Cheese Broth, 238
- Poultry Broth, 237

bruschetta
- Crostini and Bruschetta, 247
- King Crab and Asparagus Bruschetta, 36, 37

bucatini
- Bucatini All'Ubriaco with Broccolini and Walnuts, 116, 117
- Bucatini Carbonara, 104–05, 105

buffalo mozzarella cheese (mozzarella di bufala)
- about, 273
- Heirloom Tomato and Missouri Peach Salad with Buffalo Mozzarella and Pomegranate Vinaigrette, 46, 47

Burnt Onion Ash, 249
- Burnt Onion Linguini with Shaved Tuna Heart and Egg Yolk, 118, 119
- Burnt Onion Pasta Dough, 90

burrata cheese
- about, 273
- Burrata and Osetra Caviar, 32, 33
- Persimmon Salad with Carrots, Pomegranate Seeds and Kumquats, 52, 53

butter, compound. See compound butters
butternut squash
- Butternut Squash Agnolotti Filling, 254
- Minestrone, 60, 61
- Provençal Pistou Soup, 60, 64–65

butter sauces
- Lemon-Caper Butter Sauce, 252
- Sage Brown Butter Sauce, 267

C

Cacio e Pepe, 100, 101
Caesar Dressing, 234
Caffè Borghetti liqueur
- Espresso Martini, 194, 195

cake
- Torta Nocciola, 216, 217
- White Coconut Layer Cake, 221–23, 222

Calabrian chiles, 273
capers
- Lemon-Caper Butter Sauce, 252

Caramelized Brioche with Fall Pears and Figs, 208–10, 209
Caramelle Pasta with Cheese Filling, 124, 125–26, 127
Carbonara, Bucatini, 104–05, 105
carrots
- Lamb Wellington, 176–78, 177, 179
- Minestrone, 60, 61
- Persimmon Salad with Carrots, Pomegranate Seeds and Kumquats, 52, 53
- Roasted Carrot and Beet Salad, 48, 49

Castelfranco lettuce
- Treviso and Bartlett Pear Salad with Gorgonzola, 56, 57

caviar
- about, 26
- Burrata and Osetra Caviar, 32, 33
- Caviar Beggar's Purses, 28, 29
- Caviar Sandwich, 30, 31
- Chilled Angel Hair Pasta with Osetra Caviar, Ponzu and Furikake, 138, 139

champagne
- Champagne and Black Truffle Risotto, 72, 73

chanterelles. See also mushrooms
- Baked Halibut with Summer Vegetables, 146, 147
- Duck Breast Apicius with Foie Gras, 166–67, 167

cheese. See also specific types of cheese
- Bucatini Carbonara, 104–05, 105
- Burrata and Osetra Caviar, 32, 33
- Cacio e Pepe, 100, 101
- Caramelle Pasta with Cheese Filling, 124, 125–26, 127
- Heirloom Tomato and Missouri Peach Salad with Buffalo Mozzarella and Pomegranate Vinaigrette, 46, 47
- Italian Black Truffle and Cheese Sandwich, 70, 71

Cherries, Pickled, 243
Chianti
- Bucatini All'Ubriaco with Broccolini and Walnuts, 116, 117

chicken
- Chicken Scarpariello, 168, 169
- Poultry Broth, 237

Chilled Angel Hair Pasta with Osetra Caviar, Ponzu and Furikake, 138, 139
chorizo, Spanish
- Striped Bass with Saffron Broth, Clams and Chorizo, 148, 149

Chunky Prosciutto Broth, 238
clams
- Clam Toast, 40, 41
- Clam Toast Butter, 260
- Striped Bass with Saffron Broth, Clams and Chorizo, 148, 149

cobbler
- Summer Berry Cobbler with Peach Ice Cream, 214, 215

Cocchi Americano Bianco
- Da Two Yoots, 198, 199

cocktails
- artisanal cocktail nuances, 184
- Bert Santoro's bartending team, 183
- 1977 Live from Florence, 196, 197
- Da Two Yoots, 198, 199
- Espresso Martini, 194, 195
- Farina Barrel-Aged Negroni, 192, 193
- Farina Old Fashioned, 186, 187
- Go Home and Get Your Shine Box, 190, 191
- Old Dog, New Tricks, 188, 189

Cocktail Sauce, 266
coconut
- White Coconut Layer Cake, 221–23, 222

coconut milk
- Guava-Passion Fruit Bar with Coconut-Makrut Sorbet, 218, 219–20

compound butters
- about, 256
- Black Peppercorn Butter, 261
- Clam Toast Butter, 260
- Farina Steak Butter, 258
- Seafood Broiling Butter, 259

Conserva di Pomodori (Tomato Paste), 268, 268–69
Cotuit Oysters, Broiled, 34, 35
crab
- King Crab and Asparagus Bruschetta, 36, 37
- Squid Ink Spaghetti with King Crab and Pesto Calabrese, 134, 135

crepes and crespelle
- Caviar Beggar's Purses, 28, 29

INDEX

Crespelle and Black Winter Truffles, 74, 74–75
Crescenza cheese
  about, 273
  Crespelle and Black Winter Truffles, 74, 74–75
  Italian Black Truffle and Cheese Sandwich, 70, 71
Crespelle and Black Winter Truffles, 74, 74–75
Creste di Gallo with Shrimp, Castelvetrano Olives and Pistachios, 136, 137
Crispy Farro, 262
  Watercress, Hearts of Palm and Crispy Farro Salad, 50, 51
Crispy Quinoa, 263
Crostini and Bruschetta, 247
cucumbers
  Cucumber Salad, 58, 59
  Summer Tomato Gazpacho (Salmorejo), 60, 62
  Tzatziki Dressing, 235

D
dandelion leaves
  Fava Bean and Dandelion Salad with Lemon Dressing, 54, 55
Da Two Yoots (cocktail), 198, 199
demi-glace, 272
dessert
  Blood Orange Paris-Brest, 202, 203–04
  Caramelized Brioche with Fall Pears and Figs, 208–10, 209
  Farina Tiramisu, 205–07, 206
  Guava-Passion Fruit Bar with Coconut-Makrut Sorbet, 218, 219–20
  Peach and Blackberry Crostata with Lemon Curd Ice Cream, 211–13, 212
  Summer Berry Cobbler with Peach Ice Cream, 214, 215
  Summer Peach Trifle, 224, 225
  Torta Nocciola, 216, 217
  White Coconut Layer Cake, 221–23, 222
Dijon Red Wine Dressing, 232
dough, fresh pasta
  Burnt Onion Pasta Dough, 90
  Egg Pasta Dough, 90
  Pincenelle Pasta Dough, 95
  Semolina Pasta Dough, 92
  Spinach Pasta Dough, 90
  Squid Ink Pasta Dough, 92
dressings, salad. *See* salad dressings
duck
  Duck Breast Apicius with Foie Gras, 166–67, 167
  Duck Meatballs, 42, 43

E
Egg Pasta Dough, 90
eggplant
  Tuna Crudo with Eggplant, Blistered Tomatoes, Lemon and Basil, 38, 39
eggs
  Black Truffle Omelet, 68, 69
  Bucatini Carbonara, 104–05, 105
  Burnt Onion Linguini with Shaved Tuna Heart and Egg Yolk, 118, 119
  Burnt Onion Pasta Dough, 90
  Egg Pasta Dough, 90
  Spinach Pasta Dough, 90
  Squid Ink Pasta Dough, 92
Eight-Hour Pork Roast, 174, 175
escargots
  Lumache with Spinach, Garlic and Escargots, 110, 111
espresso
  Espresso Martini, 194, 195
  Farina Tiramisu, 205–07, 206
  Torta Nocciola, 216, 217

F
Farina
  history of, 14
  reimagining leftovers and food scraps, 276–77
  wine service, 18–19
Farina Barrel-Aged Negroni, 192, 193
Farina Focaccia, 264–65, 265
Farina Italian Dressing, 233
Farina Old Fashioned, 186, 187
Farina Steak Butter, 258
Farina Tiramisu, 205–07, 206
farro
  about, 273
  Crispy Farro, 262
  Watercress, Hearts of Palm and Crispy Farro Salad, 50, 51
fava beans
  Fava Bean and Dandelion Salad with Lemon Dressing, 54, 55
fennel
  Baked Halibut with Summer Vegetables, 146, 147
  Grilled Octopus with Potatoes and Blistered Tomatoes, 44, 45
  Minestrone, 60, 61
  Whole Oven Roasted Branzino with Arugula, Fennel and Lemon, 154, 155
fennel pollen
  about, 273
  Orange-Fennel Pollen Dressing, 234
  Porchetta, 172–73, 173
  Sicilian Harissa Vinaigrette, 235
figs
  Caramelized Brioche with Fall Pears and Figs, 208–10, 209
Finocchietto
  Da Two Yoots, 199
fish and seafood
  Arctic Char and Sauce Vierge, Seared, 156, 157
  Burnt Onion Linguini with Shaved Tuna Heart and Egg Yolk, 118, 119
  Clam Toast, 40, 41
  Clam Toast Butter, 260
  Creste di Gallo with Shrimp, Castelvetrano Olives and Pistachios, 136, 137
  Halibut with Summer Vegetables, Baked, 146, 147
  King Crab and Asparagus Bruschetta, 36, 37
  Lake Superior Whitefish with Mujadara, 150–51, 152
  Octopus with Potatoes and Blistered Tomatoes, Grilled, 44, 45
  Oysters, Broiled Cotuit, 34, 35
  Sardinian Lorighittas with Mussels, Saffron and Blistered Tomatoes, 120–22, 121, 123
  Seafood Broiling Butter, 259
  Squid Ink Pasta Dough, 92
  Squid Ink Spaghetti with King Crab and Pesto Calabrese, 134, 135
  Striped Bass with Saffron Broth, Clams and Chorizo, 148, 149
  Swordfish with Broccolini, Olives and White Beans, 158, 159
  Tuna Crudo with Eggplant, Blistered Tomatoes, Lemon and Basil, 38, 39
  Whole Oven Roasted Branzino with Arugula, Fennel and Lemon, 154, 155
Focaccia, Farina, 264–65, 265

INDEX

foie gras
    Duck Breast Apicius with Foie Gras, 166–67, *167*
fontina cheese
    Italian Black Truffle and Cheese Sandwich, 70, *71*
food scraps and leftovers, 276–77
Frangelico
    Torta Nocciola, 216, *217*
frisée lettuce
    Fava Bean and Dandelion Salad with Lemon Dressing, 54, *55*
furikake seasoning
    Chilled Angel Hair Pasta with Osetra Caviar, Ponzu and Furikake, 138, *139*

G

garlic
    black garlic, 272–73
    Lumache with Spinach, Garlic and Escargots, 110, *111*
    Spaghetti Aglio e Olio, 108, *109*
Gazpacho, Summer Tomato (Salmorejo), *60*, 62
gigante beans, 272
gin
    Farina Barrel-Aged Negroni, *192*, 193
    Old Dog, New Tricks, 188, *189*
Gnocchi, Rabbit, *128*, 129
goat cheese
    Roasted Carrot and Beet Salad, 48, *49*
Go Home and Get Your Shine Box (cocktail), 190, *191*
Gorgonzola cheese
    Treviso and Bartlett Pear Salad with Gorgonzola, 56, *57*
Grana Padano cheese
    vs. Parmigiano-Reggiano cheese, 230, *230*
    steps of cheese production, 231
    Broiled Cotuit Oysters, 34, *35*
    Butternut Squash Agnolotti Filling, 254
    Cacio e Pepe, 100, *101*
    Champagne and Black Truffle Risotto, 72, *73*
    Crespelle and Black Winter Truffles, 74, *74–75*
    Duck Meatballs, 42, *43*
    Fava Bean and Dandelion Salad with Lemon Dressing, 54, *55*
    Grana Padano Cheese Broth, 238
    Pistou, *60*, 64–65
    Provençal Pistou Soup, *60*, 64–65

Ricotta Pincenelle with Sausage and Broccoli, 114, *115*
Rigatoni All'Amatriciana, *102*, 103
Squid Ink Spaghetti with King Crab and Pesto Calabrese, 134, *135*
Watercress, Hearts of Palm and Crispy Farro Salad, 50, *51*
green beans
    Provençal Pistou Soup, *60*, 64–65
Grilled Octopus with Potatoes and Blistered Tomatoes, 44, *45*
guanciale
    Rigatoni All'Amatriciana, *102*, 103
guava puree
    Guava-Passion Fruit Bar with Coconut-Makrut Sorbet, *218*, 219–20

H

halibut
    Baked Halibut with Summer Vegetables, 147
harissa
    about, 272
    Sicilian Harissa Vinaigrette, 235
hazelnuts
    Roasted Carrot and Beet Salad, 48, *49*
    Romesco Sauce, 250
    Summer Peach Trifle, 224, *225*
    Torta Nocciola, 216, *217*
hearts of palm
    Watercress, Hearts of Palm and Crispy Farro Salad, 50, *51*
Heirloom Tomato and Missouri Peach Salad with Buffalo Mozzarella and Pomegranate Vinaigrette, 46, *47*
Home-Cured Pancetta, *270*, 271

I

ice cream
    Guava-Passion Fruit Bar with Coconut-Makrut Sorbet, *218*, 219–20
    Peach and Blackberry Crostata with Lemon Curd Ice Cream, 211–13, *212*
    Summer Berry Cobbler with Peach Ice Cream, 214, *215*
Italian Black Truffle and Cheese Sandwich, 70, *71*

K

kaffir lime leaves

Guava-Passion Fruit Bar with Coconut-Makrut Sorbet, *218*, 219–20
kale
    cleaning, 167
    Duck Breast Apicius with Foie Gras, 166–67, *167*
king crab
    King Crab and Asparagus Bruschetta, 36, *37*
    Squid Ink Spaghetti with King Crab and Pesto Calabrese, 134, *135*
kumquats
    Persimmon Salad with Carrots, Pomegranate Seeds and Kumquats, 52, *53*

L

Lake Superior Whitefish with Mujadara, 150–51, *152*
lamb
    Lamb Wellington, 176–78, *177*, *179*
leeks
    Rabbit Gnocchi, *128*, 129
leftovers and food scraps, 276–77
lemons
    Fava Bean and Dandelion Salad with Lemon Dressing, 54, *55*
    Lemon-Caper Butter Sauce, 252
    Peach and Blackberry Crostata with Lemon Curd Ice Cream, 211–13, *212*
    Tuna Crudo with Eggplant, Blistered Tomatoes, Lemon and Basil, 38, *39*
    Veal Milanese, 170–71, *171*
    Whole Oven Roasted Branzino with Arugula, Fennel and Lemon, 154, *155*
lentils
    Lake Superior Whitefish with Mujadara, 150–51, *152*
    Lumache with Spinach, Garlic and Escargots, 110, *111*
lupini beans, 272

M

Madeira
    Duck Breast Apicius with Foie Gras, 166–67, *167*
Marinade, Pomegranate Molasses, 249
Marinated Olives, 240, *241*
Marsala wine
    Caramelized Brioche with Fall Pears and Figs, 208–10, *209*

FARINA 283

INDEX

Marsala Mushroom Sauce, 253
Summer Peach Trifle, 224, *225*
mascarpone cheese
    Blood Orange Paris-Brest, *202*, 203–04
    Farina Tiramisu, 205–07, *206*
    Summer Peach Trifle, 224, *225*
Mashed Potatoes, 239
Meatballs, Duck, 42, *43*
Meatball Sauce, 255
mezcal
    Go Home and Get Your Shine Box, 190, *191*
Milanese, Veal, 170–71, *171*
miso paste, white
    Clam Toast Butter, 260
    Seafood Broiling Butter, 259
mortadella
    Ragù alla Bolognese, 106–07, *107*
Mostarda, Apricot, 244, *245*
mozzarella cheese. *See also* scamorza cheese
    Caramelle Pasta with Cheese Filling, *124*, 125–26, *127*
    Veal Milanese, 170–71, *171*
mushrooms. *See also* chanterelles
    Champagne and Black Truffle Risotto, 72, *73*
    Marsala Mushroom Sauce, 253
    Pizzaiola Sauce, 251
    Rabbit Gnocchi, *128*, 129
mushrooms, dried
    Farina Steak Butter, 258
mussels
    Sardinian Lorighittas with Mussels, Saffron and Blistered Tomatoes, 120–22, *121*, *123*

N

neonata/rosamarina sauce, 272

O

octopus
    Grilled Octopus with Potatoes and Blistered Tomatoes, 44, *45*
Old Dog, New Tricks (cocktail), 188, *189*
olive oil, extra-virgin
    designations, 229
    Michael Smith's favorite olive oils, 229
    tasting, 228
    Spaghetti Aglio e Olio, 108, *109*
olives
    Creste di Gallo with Shrimp, Castelvetrano Olives and Pistachios, *136*, 137
    Marinated Olives, 240, *241*
    Swordfish with Broccolini, Olives and White Beans, *158*, 159
Omelet, Black Truffle, 68, *69*
onions
    Burnt Onion Ash, 249
    Burnt Onion Linguini with Shaved Tuna Heart and Egg Yolk, 118, *119*
    Burnt Onion Pasta Dough, 90
    Pizzaiola Sauce, 251
Orange-Fennel Pollen Dressing, 234
oysters
    Broiled Cotuit Oysters, 34, *35*

P

pancetta
    Bucatini Carbonara, 104–05, *105*
    Home-Cured Pancetta, 270, *271*
    Minestrone, 60, *61*
    Ragù alla Bolognese, 106–07, *107*
    Treviso and Bartlett Pear Salad with Gorgonzola, 56, *57*
    Watercress, Hearts of Palm and Crispy Farro Salad, 50, *51*
Pangrattato, 267
    about, 273
    Broiled Cotuit Oysters, 34, *35*
pantry ingredients
    extra-virgin olive oil, 228–29
    Grana Padano *vs.* Parmigiana-Reggiano, 230–31
    ingredients that multitask, 227
    sourcing, 274
    unusual and highly recommended pantry staples, 272–73
Paris-Brest, Blood Orange, *202*, 203–04
Parmesan cheese
    vs. Grana Padano cheese, 230
    steps of cheese production, 231
    Clam Toast, 40, *41*
    Clam Toast Butter, 260
    Minestrone, 60, *61*
parsley
    Pomegranate Molasses Marinade, 249
    Roasted Carrot and Beet Salad, 48, *49*
    Treviso and Bartlett Pear Salad with Gorgonzola, 56, *57*
passion fruit puree
    Guava-Passion Fruit Bar with Coconut-Makrut Sorbet, *218*, 219–20
pasta
    about, 81
    cooking, 96

"Four Kings of Rome," 98
"Lola" the pasta machine, 11, 14
making fresh pasta dough
    by hand, 84
    by machine, 84
    laminating the dough, 84, *85*, 126
    rolling the dough, 86, 126
    rerolling excess dough scraps, 86
    cutting and shaping the dough, 86
    Burnt Onion Pasta Dough, 90
    Egg Pasta Dough, 90
    Pincenelle Pasta Dough, 95
    Semolina Pasta Dough, 92
    Spinach Pasta Dough, 90
    Squid Ink Pasta Dough, 92
Pasta Atipica seasonal offerings, 89
Agnolotti dal Plin, 130–32, *131*, *133*
Bucatini All'Ubriaco with Broccolini and Walnuts, 116, *117*
Bucatini Carbonara, 104–05, *105*
Burnt Onion Linguini with Shaved Tuna Heart and Egg Yolk, 118, *119*
Cacio e Pepe, *100*, 101
Caramelle Pasta with Cheese Filling, *124*, 125–26, *127*
Chilled Angel Hair Pasta with Osetra Caviar, Ponzu and Furikake, 138, *139*
Creste di Gallo with Shrimp, Castelvetrano Olives and Pistachios, *136*, 137
Lumache with Spinach, Garlic and Escargots, *110*, 111
Minestrone, 60, *61*
Potato Gnocchi, *93*, 93
Provençal Pistou Soup, 60, 64–65
Rabbit Gnocchi, *128*, 129
Ragù alla Bolognese, 106–07, *107*
Ricotta Pincenelle with Sausage and Broccoli, 114, *115*
Rigatoni All'Amatriciana, *102*, 103
Sardinian Lorighittas with Mussels, Saffron and Blistered Tomatoes, 120–22, *121*, *123*
Sorpresine with Poultry Broth and Black Truffles, 76, 77
Spaghetti Aglio e Olio, 108, *109*
Spinach Cappelletti Filled with Spring Peas, 112, *113*
Spinach Handkerchief Pasta with Basil Pesto and Pomodoro, 140, *141*

INDEX

Squid Ink Spaghetti with King Crab and Pesto Calabrese, 134, *135*
Tagliatelle with Italian White Truffles, 78, *79*
Tuscan Pici Noodles with Braised Short Ribs and Roasted Cherry Tomatoes, *142, 143*
pastry, puff. *See* puff pastry
peaches
    Heirloom Tomato and Missouri Peach Salad with Buffalo Mozzarella and Pomegranate Vinaigrette, *46, 47*
    Peach and Blackberry Crostata with Lemon Curd Ice Cream, 211–13, *212*
    Peach Truffle Relish, 246
    Summer Peach Trifle, *224, 225*
peach jam
    Summer Berry Cobbler with Peach Ice Cream, *214, 215*
pears
    Caramelized Brioche with Fall Pears and Figs, 208–10, *209*
    Treviso and Bartlett Pear Salad with Gorgonzola, *56, 57*
peas
    Spinach Cappelletti Filled with Spring Peas, *112, 113*
Pecorino Romano cheese
    Cacio e Pepe, *100, 101*
    Spaghetti Aglio e Olio, *108, 109*
peppers, bell
    Chicken Scarpariello, *168, 169*
    Red Bell Pepper Syrup, 242
peppers, hot cherry
    Chicken Scarpariello, *168, 169*
peppers, piquillo
    Romesco Sauce, 250
peppers, roasted red
    Summer Tomato Gazpacho (Salmorejo), *60, 62*
persimmons
    Persimmon Salad with Carrots, Pomegranate Seeds and Kumquats, *52, 53*
pesto
    Pesto Calabrese, 248
    Pistou, *60*, 64–65
Pesto Calabrese, 248
Pici Noodles with Braised Short Ribs and Roasted Cherry Tomatoes, Tuscan, *142, 143*
Pickled Cherries, 243

pie
    Peach and Blackberry Crostata with Lemon Curd Ice Cream, 211–13, *212*
pig's foot
    Bone Broth, 236
Pincenelle Pasta Dough, 95
pistachios
    Creste di Gallo with Shrimp, Castelvetrano Olives and Pistachios, *136, 137*
    Romesco Sauce, 250
Pistou, *60*, 64–65
Pizzaiola Sauce, 251
pomegranate molasses
    about, 272
    Heirloom Tomato and Missouri Peach Salad with Buffalo Mozzarella and Pomegranate Vinaigrette, *46, 47*
    Pomegranate Molasses Marinade, 249
    Pomegranate Molasses Marinated Tomahawk Pork Chops, *165*
    Pomegranate Vinaigrette, 233
pomegranates
    Persimmon Salad with Carrots, Pomegranate Seeds and Kumquats, *52, 53*
Pomodoro Sauce, Tomato, 255
ponzu sauce
    Chilled Angel Hair Pasta with Osetra Caviar, Ponzu and Furikake, *138, 139*
Porchetta, 172–73, *173*
pork
    Agnolotti dal Plin, 130–32, *131, 133*
    Eight-Hour Pork Roast, *174, 175*
    Home-Cured Pancetta, *270, 271*
    Pomegranate Molasses Marinated Tomahawk Pork Chops, *164, 165*
    Porchetta, 172–73, *173*
    Ragù alla Bolognese, 106–07, *107*
potatoes
    Chicken Scarpariello, *168, 169*
    Grilled Octopus with Potatoes and Blistered Tomatoes, *44, 45*
    Mashed Potatoes, 239
    Minestrone, *60, 61*
    Striped Bass with Saffron Broth, Clams and Chorizo, *148, 149*
Poultry Broth, 237
prosciutto
    Chunky Prosciutto Broth, 238

    Veal Chops Stuffed with Smoked Mozzarella and Prosciutto, *180*, 181
provolone cheese
    Caramelle Pasta with Cheese Filling, *124, 125*–26, *127*
puff pastry
    Lamb Wellington, 176–78, *177, 179*

Q
quinoa
    about, 273
    Crispy Quinoa, 263

R
Rabbit Gnocchi, *128, 129*
Ragù alla Bolognese, 106–07, *107*
raspberries
    Summer Berry Cobbler with Peach Ice Cream, *214, 215*
    Summer Peach Trifle, *224, 225*
raspberry jam
    Summer Peach Trifle, *224, 225*
Red Bell Pepper Syrup, 242
Relish, Peach Truffle, 246
resources
    Michael Smith's favorite cookbooks, 275
    unusual and highly recommended pantry staples, 272–73
    where to find specialty foods, 274
rice
    Champagne and Black Truffle Risotto, 72, *73*
    Lake Superior Whitefish with Mujadara, 150–51, *152*
ricotta cheese
    Pincenelle Pasta Dough, 95
    Ricotta Pincenelle with Sausage and Broccoli, *114*, 115
    Spinach Cappelletti Filled with Spring Peas, *112, 113*
Rigatoni All'Amatriciana, *102, 103*
Risotto, Champagne and Black Truffle, 72, *73*
Roasted Carrot and Beet Salad, *48, 49*
Romesco Sauce, 250

S
saffron
    Sardinian Lorighittas with Mussels, Saffron and Blistered Tomatoes, 120–22, *121, 123*
    Striped Bass with Saffron Broth, Clams and Chorizo, *148, 149*
Sage Brown Butter Sauce, 267

FARINA 285

INDEX

salad dressings
    acid-to-oil ratio, 232
    choosing the right dressing, 232
    Caesar Dressing, 234
    Dijon Red Wine Dressing, 232
    Farina Italian Dressing, 233
    Orange-Fennel Pollen Dressing, 234
    Pomegranate Vinaigrette, 233
    Sicilian Harissa Vinaigrette, 235
    Tzatziki Dressing, 235
salads
    Cucumber Salad, 58, 59
    Fava Bean and Dandelion Salad with Lemon Dressing, 54, 55
    Heirloom Tomato and Missouri Peach Salad with Buffalo Mozzarella and Pomegranate Vinaigrette, 46, 47
    Persimmon Salad with Carrots, Pomegranate Seeds and Kumquats, 52, 53
    Roasted Carrot and Beet Salad, 48, 49
    Treviso and Bartlett Pear Salad with Gorgonzola, 56, 57
    Watercress, Hearts of Palm and Crispy Farro Salad, 50, 51
sandwiches. See also bread
    Caviar Sandwich, 30, 31
    Italian Black Truffle and Cheese Sandwich, 70, 71
Santoro, Alberto ("Berto"), 183
Sardinian Lorighittas with Mussels, Saffron and Blistered Tomatoes, 120–22, 121, 123
sauces
    Cocktail Sauce, 266
    Lemon-Caper Butter Sauce, 252
    Marsala Mushroom Sauce, 253
    Meatball Sauce, 255
    Pizzaiola Sauce, 251
    Romesco Sauce, 250
    Sage Brown Butter Sauce, 267
    Seared Arctic Char and Sauce Vierge, 156, 157
    Tomato Pomodoro Sauce, 255
sausage
    Chicken Scarpariello, 168, 169
    Ricotta Pincenelle with Sausage and Broccoli, 114, 115
scamorza cheese. See also mozzarella cheese
    Veal Chops Stuffed with Smoked Mozzarella and Prosciutto, 180, 181

Seafood Broiling Butter, 259
    Broiled Cotuit Oysters, 34, 35
Seared Arctic Char and Sauce Vierge, 156, 157
semolina flour
    Farina Focaccia, 264–65, 265
    Semolina Pasta Dough, 92
Semolina Pasta Dough, 92
    Sardinian Lorighittas with Mussels, Saffron and Blistered Tomatoes, 120–22, 121, 123
    Tuscan Pici Noodles with Braised Short Ribs and Roasted Cherry Tomatoes, 142, 143
Short Ribs, Braised Beef, 162, 163
shrimp
    Creste di Gallo with Shrimp, Castelvetrano Olives and Pistachios, 136, 137
Sicilian Harissa Vinaigrette, 235
Smith, Michael
    childhood, 11
    culinary school, 12–13
    early kitchen experiences, 11–12
    Farina, 14
    favorite cookbooks, 275
    James Beard Awards, 13
    Michael Smith Restaurant, 13–14, 18
    Truffle Knighthood, 66, 67
Smith, Nancy, 18–19, 19
Sorpresine with Poultry Broth and Black Truffles, 76, 77
soups
    Minestrone, 60, 61
    Provençal Pistou Soup, 60, 64–65
    Summer Tomato Gazpacho (Salmorejo), 60, 62
sourcing ingredients, 274
Spaghetti Aglio e Olio, 108, 109
Spice Mix, Apicius, 248
spinach
    Agnolotti dal Plin, 130–32, 131, 133
    Lamb Wellington, 176–78, 177, 179
    Lumache with Spinach, Garlic and Escargots, 110, 111
    Spinach Pasta Dough, 90
Spinach Pasta Dough, 90
    Spinach Cappelletti Filled with Spring Peas, 112, 113
    Spinach Handkerchief Pasta with Basil Pesto and Pomodoro, 140, 141
squid ink
    about, 272
    Squid Ink Pasta Dough, 92

Squid Ink Spaghetti with King Crab and Pesto Calabrese, 134, 135
Striped Bass with Saffron Broth, Clams and Chorizo, 148, 149
Summer Berry Cobbler with Peach Ice Cream, 214, 215
Summer Peach Trifle, 224, 225
Summer Tomato Gazpacho (Salmorejo), 60, 62
Swiss cheese
    Italian Black Truffle and Cheese Sandwich, 70, 71
Swordfish with Broccolini, Olives and White Beans, 159

T

Tagliatelle with Italian White Truffles, 78, 79
terminology
    list of designations, 229
    Protected Designation of Origin (PDO), 230
Tiramisu, Farina, 205–07, 206
Tomahawk Pork Chops, Pomegranate Molasses Marinated, 164, 165
tomatoes
    Baked Halibut with Summer Vegetables, 146, 147
    Blistered Cherry Tomatoes, 243
    Burrata and Osetra Caviar, 32, 33
    Conserva di Pomodori (Tomato Paste), 268, 268–69
    Grilled Octopus with Potatoes and Blistered Tomatoes, 44, 45
    Heirloom Tomato and Missouri Peach Salad with Buffalo Mozzarella and Pomegranate Vinaigrette, 46, 47
    Minestrone, 60, 61
    Romesco Sauce, 250
    Sardinian Lorighittas with Mussels, Saffron and Blistered Tomatoes, 120–22, 121, 123
    Seared Arctic Char and Sauce Vierge, 156, 157
    Summer Tomato Gazpacho (Salmorejo), 60, 62
    Tuna Crudo with Eggplant, Blistered Tomatoes, Lemon and Basil, 38, 39
    Tuscan Pici Noodles with Braised Short Ribs and Roasted Cherry Tomatoes, 142, 143

INDEX

tomatoes, canned
- Meatball Sauce, 255
- Pizzaiola Sauce, 251
- Rigatoni All'Amatriciana, *102*, 103
- Spinach Handkerchief Pasta with Basil Pesto and Pomodoro, *140*, *141*
- Swordfish with Broccolini, Olives and White Beans, *158*, 159
- Tomato Pomodoro Sauce, 255
- Veal Chops Stuffed with Smoked Mozzarella and Prosciutto, *180*, 181
- Veal Milanese, 170–71, *171*

tomatoes, sun-dried
- Clam Toast Butter, 260
- Pesto Calabrese, 248

Tomato Paste (Conserva di Pomodori), *268*, 269

Torta Nocciola, *216*, *217*

Treviso and Bartlett Pear Salad with Gorgonzola, *56*, 57

Trifle, Summer Peach, *224*, *225*

truffles
- about, 66, *67*
- Black Truffle Omelet, *68*, 69
- Champagne and Black Truffle Risotto, *72*, *73*
- Crespelle and Black Winter Truffles, 74, *74–75*
- Italian Black Truffle and Cheese Sandwich, *70*, 71
- Peach Truffle Relish, 246
- Sorpresine with Poultry Broth and Black Truffles, 76, *77*
- Tagliatelle with Italian White Truffles, *78*, *79*

tuna
- Tuna Crudo with Eggplant, Blistered Tomatoes, Lemon and Basil, *38*, 39

tuna hearts, cured
- Burnt Onion Linguini with Shaved Tuna Heart and Egg Yolk, 118, *119*

turkey
- Poultry Broth, 237

Tuscan Pici Noodles with Braised Short Ribs and Roasted Cherry Tomatoes, *142*, 143

Tzatziki Dressing, 235

V

veal
- Agnolotti dal Plin, 130–32, *131*, *133*
- Veal Chops Stuffed with Smoked Mozzarella and Prosciutto, *180*, 181
- Veal Milanese, 170–71, *171*

vermouth, sweet
- Farina Barrel-Aged Negroni, *192*, 193

vodka, vanilla
- Espresso Martini, *194*, *195*

W

walnuts
- Bucatini All'Ubriaco with Broccolini and Walnuts, 116, *117*
- Butternut Squash Agnolotti Filling, 254

Watercress, Hearts of Palm and Crispy Farro Salad, *50*, 51

Wellington, Lamb, 176–78, *177*, *179*

whiskey
- Farina Old Fashioned, *186*, 187

White Coconut Layer Cake, 221–23, *222*

whitefish
- Lake Superior Whitefish with Mujadara, 150–51, *152*

Whole Oven Roasted Branzino with Arugula, Fennel and Lemon, *154*, 155

wine. *See also* specific types of wine
- pairing, 18–19
- wine service at Farina, 18–19

Woody, Ali, 201

Y

yogurt
- Cucumber Salad, *58*, *59*
- Tzatziki Dressing, 235

Z

zucchini
- Baked Halibut with Summer Vegetables, *146*, *147*
- Provençal Pistou Soup, *60*, 64–65

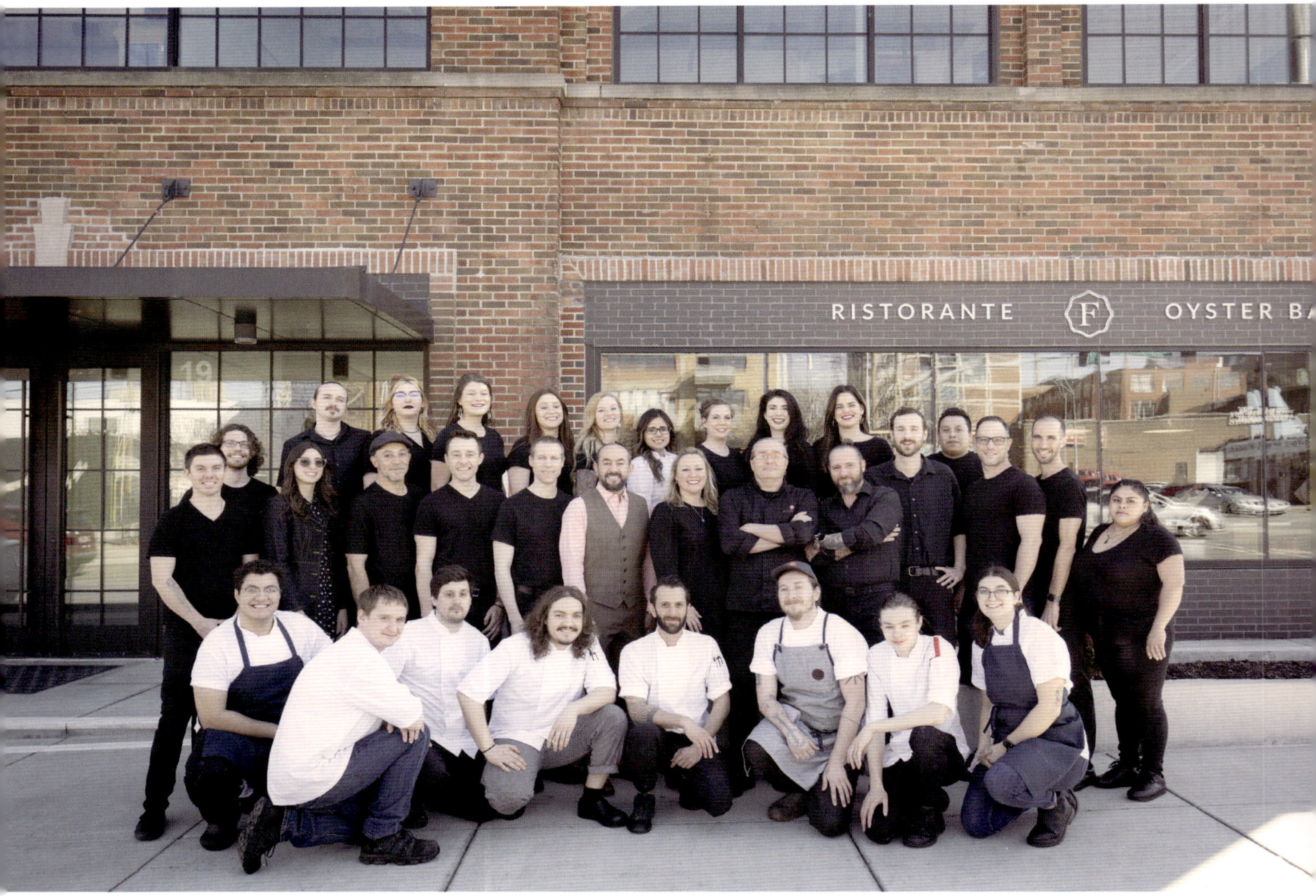
RISTORANTE
F
OYSTER BA
19

Chef Michael Smith (right) and Alberto "Berto" Santoro, Farina beverage director

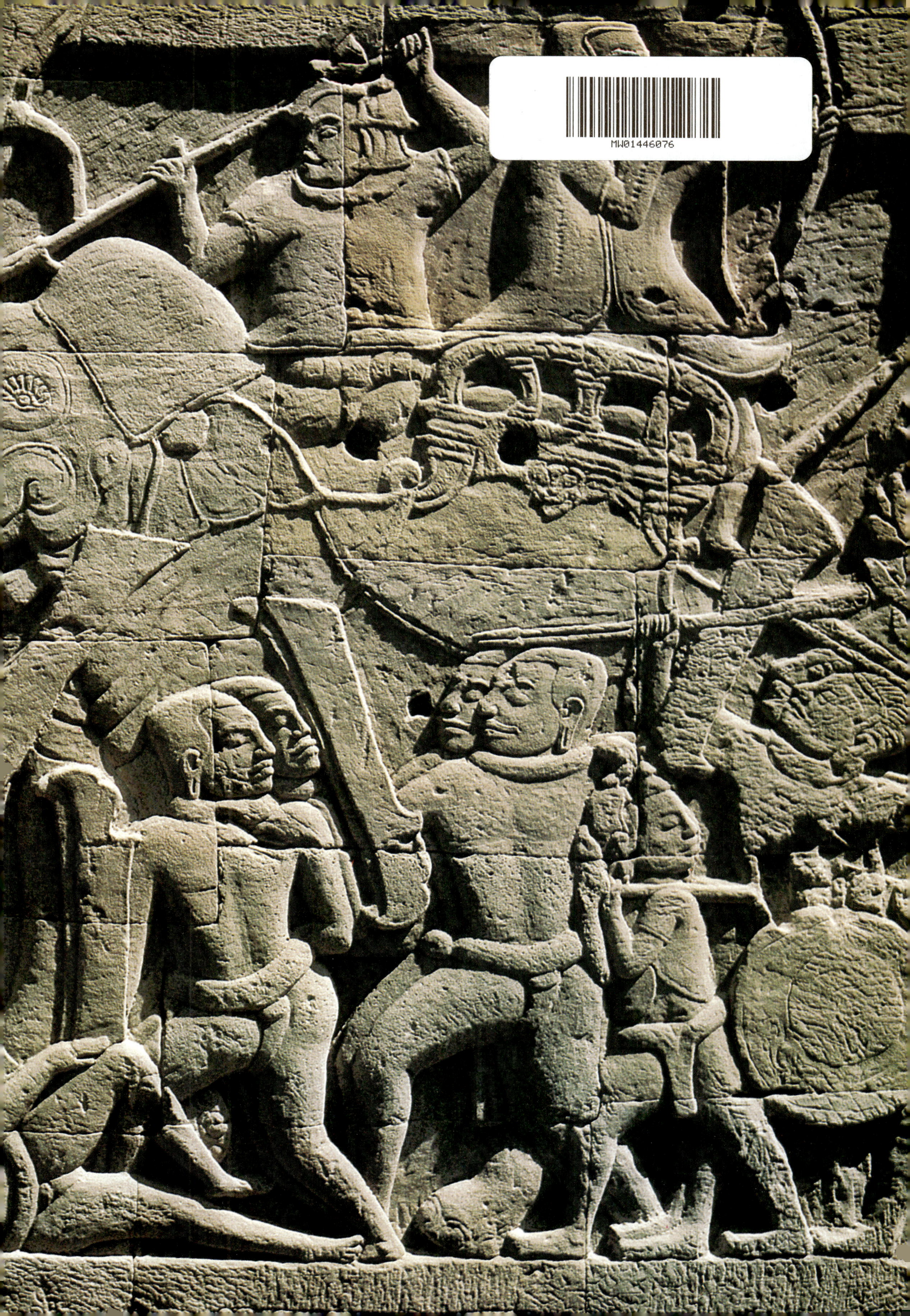

ANGKOR
and Khmer Art

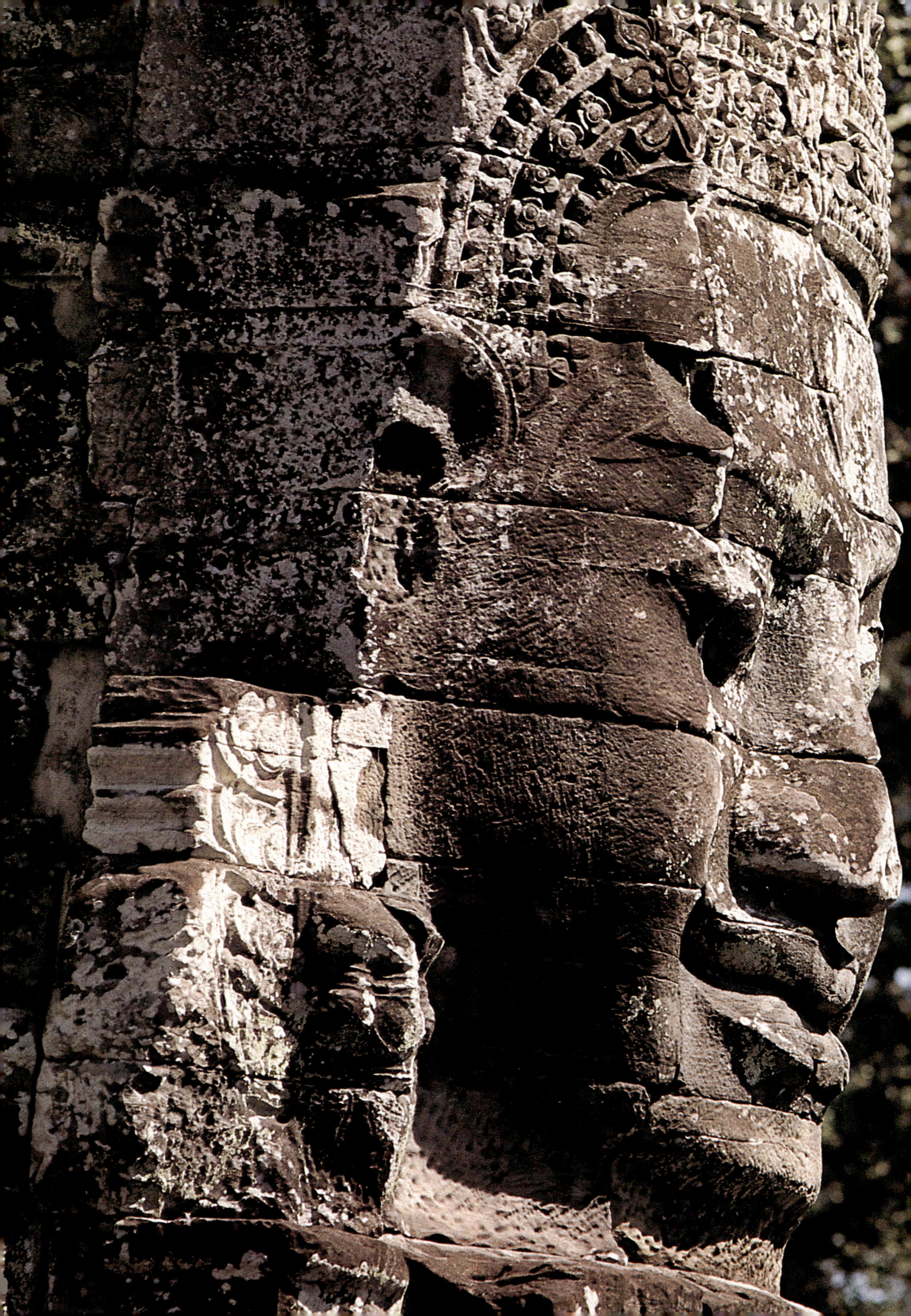

ANGKOR
and Khmer Art

Text and photographs
by Henri STIERLIN

PARKSTONE

Cover

Posthumous effigy of the wife of King Jayavarman VII. Late 12th/early 13th century. Stoneware (H. 110cm./44 in.). Musée Guimet, Paris.

View of Angkor Vat from the west.

Endpapers

Low reliefs portraying a combat between the Khmers and the Chams on the outer gallery of the Bayon at Angkor. The art of the Bayon which dates back to the reign of Jayavarman VII (about 1200) is characterized by its liveliness and spontaneity. We here see a carnac leading his war elephant through the ranks of infuriated warriors while an archer seated on the elephant's back bends his bow.

Title page

One of the gigantic Lokesvara masks carved at the summit of the towers of the Bayon at Angkor. Jayavarman VII identified himself with the Buddha and was portrayed with his features: compassionate smile and half-closed eyes suggesting meditation. The Bayon rises in the centre of the city of Angkor Thom and is crowned by 216 of these enormous images looking in all four directions.

Photo credits

The 140 colour photographs that illustrate this work devoted to the «World of Angkor and Southeast Asia» were all provided by Henri STIERLIN, Geneva, except for the following documents:
G. MELIN (Ziolo, Paris), p. 6, 8 bottom and left, 9 top and right.
Christiane DEROY (Ziolo, Paris), p. 7, 8-9 bottom.
Yvan BUTLER, Geneva, p. 11 bottom.
Rudolph MENTHONNEX, Geneva, p. 12, 17, 20 right, 26 left, 56-57, 72-73 bottom.
Hans HINZ, Basel (Office du Livre, Fribourg), pp. 14, 15, 33, 59, 68, 69, 80, 81, 82, 83, 84, 85, 86 bottom, 87, 89 right (Extracts from *The Khmers* and *Thai Sculpture*), back cover (Artephot, Paris).
René PERCHERON (Artephot, Paris), p. 86 top, 88, 89 left.
Olga BAENNINGER (Colorama Studio, Lausanne), p. 90, 91.
Nigel CAMERON (Robert Harding Ass., London), p. 92, 94, 95.
Bernard JOLIAT, Geneva, p. 93.
R. ROLLAND, (Artephot, Paris), front cover.

© *This edition : Agence Internationale d'Edition Jean-François Gonthier, 1997, Paudex (Switzerland)*

ISBN 1 85995 308 5

Printed in France by Sager, La Loupe (28)

Contents

Indian Influence on Java	6
Birth of the Khmer Culture	10
The Classic Age: Bantéay Srei	22
Angkor Wat and the "Rice Factory"	34
The Decline and Renaissance of Angkor	58
Angkor Thom: Zenith and Decay of Khmer Art	68
The Arts of Champa, Thailand and Burma	80

Indian Influence on Java

Situated between India and China, Southeast Asia has been the birthplace of several cultures, some of which rank among the world's greatest civilizations. In this work, we intend to survey the entire spectrum of Greater Indian art, from Burma to Java via the Indochinese peninsula. Among the Indianized kingdoms which sprang up in Southeast Asia since the beginning of the Christian era, we shall especially emphasize the great Khmer civilization and its capital, Angkor, in modern-day Cambodia. Angkor indeed deserves to play the leading part not only because of its exceptional artistic and architectural achievements but also on account of the hydrological, agricultural and ecological problems solved there.

Except North Vietnam which as early as the third century B. C. was actually a province of the Chinese empire, most of the countries of Southeast Asia came under the cultural and religious influence of India. The various States established in this region can therefore be called Indianized kingdoms. There were many reasons for the spread of Indian thought. People are too often inclined to ascribe it exclusively to the activity of Buddhist missionaries. In fact, the process of Indianization usually began by Hinduizing the population, the rulers and their court. Buddhism became widespread several hundred years later.

Proselytism was actually by no means the main factor in the process of Indianization which took place in both Indo-China and the islands of the Indian Archipelago. As a matter of fact, international trade was much more important. In order to meet the demand for exotic goods issuing from the Roman Empire at the height of its glory, Indian traders had to lay in stocks of spices. They scoured the seas and made stops in the archipelagoes. They brought back precious goods which were then dispatched towards Rome via the Gulf of Oman and the Red Sea. About 30 or 40 B. C., a certain Hippalus discovered that the monsoon made it possible to reach the Indian Malabar Coast by crossing straight over the open sea instead of coasting. Ships left the West from June to September and made the return trip after the wind shifted, from November to April. Indian eastward expansion also took advantage of the monsoon winds. Traders set out from Bengal or the Coromandel Coast, crossed the Indian Ocean, doubled the Malacca peninsula — or crossed the isthmus by caravans — and sailed north towards Indo-China or south towards the islands. On account of the seasonal rhythm of the monsoon winds, the daring Indian navigators were obliged to spend several months in the countries they traded with. Just as the Romans established warehouses in southern India, Indian traders also founded colonies to which they imported their dwellings, temples and customs. At the beginning of the Christian era, India went through a period of intense creative activity which resulted in the birth of a highly developed culture and dynamic religious trends among both Buddhists and Brahmins, encouraged by the strong Hindu revival; influence on the less developed regions visited by Indian traders was therefore considerable.

Javanese Architecture

While the earliest works discovered on the island of Java betray the influence of the Hindu Pallava dynasty which produced an admirable art style at the site of Mamallapuram in India, the most outstanding monument is a Buddhist temple: the Great Stupa at Borobudur, erected in the eighth and ninth centuries in the plains of central Java.

Seventy-two small latticed stupas containing seated Buddhas adorn the three circular platforms surrounding the huge central stupa at Borobudur (Central Java).

Facing page, top:
The temple-stupa at Borobudur (Central Java) was built to honour Gautama Buddha. The monument dates back to the eighth or ninth century. The Enlightened Being is here shown in the yoga position.

Facing page, bottom:
The Great Stupa at Borobudur is actually a hill that has been terraced and clothed in stone. The platforms rise up to a height of 45 m (150 ft.). The entire structure covers an area of 1½ hectares (3¾ acres) and is studded with chapels housing images of the Buddha. This edifice, the largest Buddhist monument in the world, is now being restored. More than one million stone blocks will have to go through chemical processing.

Built under the Sailendra dynasty (the so-called "kings of the mountain"), this colossal edifice, 123 m (404 ft.) square at its base, rises up to a height of 45 m (148 ft.). The terraces culminate in a stupa which symbolizes the tomb of Gautama Buddha. The monument is actually a terraced mound faced with stone. The square ground-plan includes four median stairways. The various terraces are studded with "chapels" and stupas.

The edifice as a whole takes on cosmic symbolism. Its ordonnance was believed to account for the organic structure of the Cosmos. Five square galleries of decreasing dimensions lead up to four concentric circular terraces culminating in the great central stupa. The monument's original foundations have been hidden by supports which conceal 160 low reliefs depicting the joys and sorrows of this world. Above the world of desires, according to Mahayana Buddhism, is the world of forms, represented by the four square galleries containing 360 niches, each one of which houses a statue of the Buddha, as well as more than one thousand low reliefs relating part of the Enlightened Being's life story. The upper level with its circular terraces symbolizes the world of ecstatic visions. It is decorated with latticed stupas, each containing a seated Buddha shown in the yoga position. Seventy-two such small stupas surround the great Buddha hidden in the central stupa.

The edifice was intended for the rite of circumambulation: worshippers walked around the structure according to a formula already in use at Sanchi in India in the third century B. C.

The Prambanam Complex

About A. D. 930, the Great Stupa at Borobudur was abandoned when the seat of government was shifted to the east. At the beginning of the tenth century, however, a Hindu site dedicated to Shiva was flourishing not far from Borobudur. The Prambanam complex, built by the princes of Mataram, contains remarkable artistic creations influenced markedly by Indian art. The complex consists of three main shrines rising within a walled enclosure 110 m (360 ft.) on each side. It is surrounded by 224 minor temples and another concentric surrounding wall, 220 m (720 ft.) on each side. Admirable carvings similar to the ones seen at Borobudur portray scenes from the great Indian epic known as the Ramayana.

Detail of a kala, or guardian-spirit, at the temple of Prambanam (Java). Tenth century.

Small temple belonging to the Lara Djonggrang complex at Prambanam, Java. This Hindu monument exhibits analogies with Indian temples.

The great temple of Shiva, Lara Djonggrang, at Prambanam, is the most imposing Hindu monument on the island of Java. The sanctuary dates from the early tenth century. It is 47 m (154 ft.) high and 30 m (99 ft.) square at its base.

Low relief decorating the gallery of the Lara Djonggrang temple at Prambanam. This is a good example of Javanese sculpture inspired by the Ramayana: a dancing-girl, armed with sword and shield, is dancing a war dance.

Buddhist low relief from the temple of Tandji Mendut at Magelang (Central Java). This temple not far from Borobudur was built in the ninth century. We here see an ogre converted to Buddhism playing with children.

Birth of the Khmer Culture

The most important of the Indianized civilizations of Southeast Asia is unquestionably that of the Khmers which developed in modern-day Cambodia. In the heart of Indo-China, Cambodia partakes of the twofold influence which accounts for the peninsula's name: India and China. The historic period began only when these two great powers came on the scene. The first name given the lower Mekong basin, heartland of the Khmer culture, was in fact Chinese. As early as the first century B.C., the kingdom of Founan, mentioned in Chinese texts as extending from the Bassac to the Gulf of Siam, created its own distinctive culture, many features of which betray Indian influence. This is particularly true of farming methods; the irrigated rice plantations created in the delta testify to Indian connections. This method of growing rice, perfected in India hundreds of years before, was responsible for the

Detail of the Prah Ko temple at Roluos: parapets consisting of lions run along the stairways leading to the prasats. There is a sandstone lintel above the doorway. Guardians, or Dvarapalas, stand on either side of the entrance.

Facing page, top:
Group of six prasats crowning the sanctuary of Prah Ko at Roluos near Angkor. These brick towers erected in 879 are Jayavarman II's funerary temple.

Facing page, bottom:
On the bank of the Siemreap river near Angkor, a traditional Cambodian hut built on piles.

Aerial view of Cambodian straw huts on the bank of the Siemreap river near the Great Lake.

prosperity which enabled Founan, as early as the second century, to extend its influence over most of Indo-China, from southern Burma to Malaya.

In the sixth century, the Founan empire broke up. A new kingdom known as Tchen-la rose out of the disorder on the ruins of the old empire. Governed by the Kambujas, or Khmers, it inherited Indianized art and technology from Founan. The capital, Sambor Prei Kuk, founded in 616, marked the beginnings of Khmer architecture. Similar in many respects to the art of Champa, examples of which can be seen in the eastern part of the peninsula, it gradually departed from the Indian models copied by Founan artists and local features began to appear. The eighth century, however, was a period of instability and disorder in Cambodia; the rulers of Java assumed dominion over Tchen-la. In fact, the Sailendra dynasty was ruling over the whole of the China Sea. The Khmer kings did not manage to consolidate their power until the eleventh century. Yet both the Khmer temple-palaces and the conception of royalty shared by the rulers of Angkor bear witness to Javanese influence.

The Setting

Flying over Cambodia, especially over the enormous plain of the lower Mekong, one is impressed by the perfectly flat surface stretching out before one's eyes. These lowlands covered in some places by a compact network of rice-fields, completely surround the Tonle-Sap, the "Great Lake" on the shore of which one can see villages of straw huts built on piles. In the jungle clearings, hamlets alternate with the great temples; their rectilinear surrounding walls form geometric designs in the landscape.

Facing page, top left:
The Bakong at Roluos. The sanctuary at the summit of the pyramidal structure dates back to the twelfth century and was built more than two hundred years after the monument raised by Indravarman.

Facing page, top right:
Detail of a sandstone Apsara decorating one of the satellite-prasats at the Bakong.

Aerial view of the Bakong, at Roluos. This sandstone pyramid was erected in 881 at the centre of the city of Hariharalaya, founded by King Indravarman. A series of satellite-prasats surround the temple-mountain.

A lowland country covered with dense vegetation where earth and water mix and mingle and go to make up an inextricable network of rivers, canals and flooded rice-fields, Cambodia is deluged by the monsoon rains which periodically give way to a long dry season. The country has a subtropical climate and a very peculiar river regime: when the flood waters of the Mekong flow down from the Himalayas, swollen by melting snow and the first monsoon rains, the two arms of the delta are no longer sufficient to drain off the enormous seasonal overflow. The water then flows back towards Tonle-Sap, fighting its way upstream until it reaches the Great Lake which triples or quadruples in size in a few weeks. The lake which thus serves as a spillway releases the excess water as soon as the rate of flow of the Mekong comes back down to normal.

This peculiarity of the Cambodian Great Lake has influenced both farming and building techniques in the surrounding area. The water level can vary from 10 to 12 m (33 to 39 ft.) between its lowest point and flood level. This pulsation — almost like a beating heart — inspired the earliest known form of Khmer agriculture, based on floating rice which was the country's main food crop before the introduction of irrigated rice plantations. Surprisingly enough, this plant has stems which can grow up to 10 cm (4 in.) a day and reach a length of 9 to 10 m (30 to 33 ft.). The wild rice can thus keep up with the rising and falling water level.

Furthermore, when the lake quadruples its area, the countless fish swarming in it have an opportunity to go spawn in the flooded forests. When the water subsides, fishermen have but to lay their traps made of bamboo curtains several hundred metres long: they catch tons and tons of fish. Dried fish is in fact the main source of protein in the Cambodian diet. Last but not least, the populations living on the shores of the lake were obliged to adapt themselves to the changing water level. They created a kind of lacustrian architecture, built on piles, recalling the civilization of prehistoric lake dwellers in Europe. Certain features of this lacustrian architecture, copied in stone, were to remain

Below:
One of the minor prasats at the Bakong at Roluos. This brick tower has lost its roof and much of its ornamentation.

characteristic of the great classic Khmer architecture at Angkor Wat, often derived from primitive structures built on piles. Traditional straw huts built on piles can still be seen nowadays...

Thanks to the Mekong, fish and rice are the main resources of the Cambodian lowlands. The exotic goods and precious wood found in the tropical rain forest also attracted Indian traders who sailed up the Mekong to the Great Lake during the floods.

India's Contributions

Even before the arrival of Indian merchants, the Cambodians had their own religion. An animistic religion in which water played the leading part. The Water Spirits, or Dragons similar to the ones seen in southern China, so often portrayed during the classic period, derived from this primitive religion; under the influence of India, they became Nagas. The Naga king, a mythical serpent living on the floor of the primordial ocean, is one of the fundamental figures in the Khmer religion. Quite a few other native Cambodian deities were probably similarly assimilated to gods imported from India.

The Khmers adopted Indian religions in a very free way. Hinduism was of course still based on the worship of Shiva, Vishnu and Brahma, Buddhism on the adoration of the Enlightened Being, Gautama Buddha the merciful. Yet, no matter what gods they were dedicated to, the temples testify above all to a specific ordonnance of the universe of which they are a symbol. Both Hindu and Buddhist monuments are built according to the same cosmological principles. These basic postulates which control Khmer architecture indicate a rigorously structuralized view of the world. Mount Meru, the World Mountain, dwelling-place of the gods, forms the axis round which the cosmos revolves; a primordial ocean surrounds inhabited land just as the moat surrounds the temple;

Facing page, top left:
This standing Bodhisattva dates from the seventh century. The bronze statue is 35 cm (14 in.) high and is meant to represent a future Buddha on the path to Awakening.

Facing page, top right:
This 24 cm (9.6 in.) high seventh century bronze represents a Bodhisattva with an oval halo making a reassuring gesture.

Facing page, bottom:
After the small pre-Khmer bronze statues inspired by the Buddhist religion, this bust of Vishnu dating from the eleventh century and found in the Western Mébon is one of the most remarkable surviving Khmer bronzes. This 217 cm (87 in.) long fragment of a colossal statue shows the god reclining in a relaxed pose.

Beautiful Buddhist statues rank among the earliest examples of Khmer bronze sculpture. This Buddha dating from the seventh century is 27 cm (11 in.) high.

15

space is partitioned by axes meeting at right angles, marked off by gateways and causeways which account for the arrangement of both the sanctuaries and the surrounding universe.

In Cambodian religion, the personality of the gods seems to have been of only minor importance. Though the various monarchs who built the temples may have had a partiality for Vishnu, Shiva, Brahma or any one of their countless avatars in the Hindu pantheon, though some may even have worshipped the Buddha, the architecture remains basically the same. A kind of osmosis takes place among the various deities of Indian mythology. Khmer syncretism will see no difference. It almost seems as if the various religions imported from India were all looked upon as equivalent.

Besides religion, India's chief contribution was probably the Sanskrit alphabet used for holy texts such as the Ramayana or the Mahabharata, great verse-chronicles of the heroic exploits of the gods and goddesses. In addition to the alphabet and the learned tongue, Khmer culture adopted Indian mathematics, astronomy and technology.

Yet India made its most striking contribution in the fields of art and architecture: the Khmer world derives from Indian art traditions. If anyone has any doubts about this, all he has to do is take a look at Khmer temples and monasteries. The basic sculptural and architectural vocabulary was directly inspired by Buddhist or Hindu models. Like Indian temples, Khmer shrines are laid out round a high tower, or prasat, the roof of which is corbeled inwards so as to symbolize the abode of the gods at the summit of the World Mountain; the groundplan is based on a magic diagram, the mandala, which includes a cella, or tiny chamber housing the statue of the deity; the cella is always square, on account of the symbolic meaning attached to this geometric figure which was believed to represent perfection. Since the ritual did not require the presence of the worshippers, this holy of holies was usually quite tiny; in the Hindu religion, the high priest alone waited on the idol, anointing his image with offerings of milk and melted butter.

In front of the tower, or prasat, the temple sometimes includes a porch-like structure or pronaos, known as the mandapa, generally built facing east. This is especially true of the flat temples, as opposed to the Mount Meru-type structures. The eastward orientation is probably a relic of ancient forms of sun-worship: the sun's first beams were supposed to wake the idol up at dawn.

The Earliest Monuments near Angkor

The Founan temples, no doubt constructed in light and perishable materials (wood and straw), have not been preserved. The earliest known samples of Khmer architecture date back to the Tchen-la kingdom and are located at Sambor Prei Kuk, 140 km (87 mi.) southeast of Angkor. This capital, named after its founder, Isanavarman, who ruled from 616 to 635, was then known as Isanapura. The basic groundplan is square. Several temple complexes stand within two square surrounding walls, the largest of which is 2 km (1.2 mi.) long on each side. The prasats face east. These brick towers have corbeled roofs usually constructed in several storeys decorated with miniature pavilions meant, needless to say, to symbolize the dwellings of the gods on Mount Meru.

A pavilion dedicated to the sacred bull Nandi leads to the temple of Shiva, a square structure with recess-panelling, pilasters and bold ornamental moulding on each level. The doorways, cantoned by colonnettes, have sandstone lintels and are crowned by projecting pediments. A footbridge built on piles, recalling prehistoric Khmer traditions, connects the tower with the pavilion dedicated to Nandi.

After this first flourishing period, the disturbances which marked the eighth century put a temporary stop to Cambodian development. The Javanese occupation which followed, enriched authentically Khmer art

Lion standing watch at the foot of the huge stairway leading up to the Phnom Bakheng temple at Angkor.

traditions with new ideas and architectural techniques characteristic of the temples built on the Dieng Plateau on the island of Java. Hindu carvers at Angkor were inspired by Buddhist architecture at Borobudur. Java's main contribution to Khmer art was in fact the temple-mountain.

The earliest Mount Meru-type structures in Cambodia date back to A.D. 800 and can be seen at Rong Chen near Kulen and Prasat Ak Yom in the plain of Angkor. However the great period of Khmer art actually began with the temple-palaces erected at Roluos. This town south of Angkor was founded by King Indravarman who reigned from 877 to 889. The first Khmer capital was known as Hariharalaya, the name being derived from that of the god Harihara, a kind of synthesis of Shiva and Vishnu. It contains two extremely interesting complexes: Prah Ko and Bakong. Prah Ko is the funerary temple of King Jayavarman II, Indravarman's grand-father. It was erected in 879 and dedicated to the god Shiva. Like the temples at Sambor Prei Kuk, this temple consists of two square surrounding walls and a single terrace on which six brick prasats are arranged in two rows. These towers exhibit sandstone window-frames and blank doors. Monolithic niches contain beautiful deities carved in high relief. Lions recalling Chinese felines stand watch at the top of the stairways leading up to the terrace. In front of each prasat, we can see an image of the sacred bull Nandi carved in the round.

The monumental complex also includes long structures used as vestries and libraries, as well as a cruciform gateway, or gopura, which gives access to the sacred enclosure. Dimensions however are by no means overwhelming: none of the prasats exceeds 15 m (49 ft.) in height. The true genius of Khmer architecture is more faithfully embodied by the Bakong temple-mountain at Roluos.

Built in 881 by Indravarman, the Bakong temple was the centre of the town of Hariharalaya, capital of the realm. The king here created an artificial mountain crowned by a cella dedicated to the god Shiva. The edifice proper consists of five square sandstone terraces, the first of

Aerial view of Phnom Bakheng with its five-storeyed pyramid erected by Yasovarman in 893 at the centre of his capital, Yasodharapura. A sanctuary consisting of five towers in a quincuncial arrangement originally stood on a small terrace at the summit. These structures have fallen into ruins, but the 60 minor prasats have been partially preserved.

which is 67 m (220 ft.) long on each side. The upper terrace is located 15 m (49 ft.) above the ground. The entire structure called for 60,000 metric tons of building materials. Four median stairways make for twofold orthogonal symmetry. Monumental gateways, or gopuras, give access to these stairways flanked by lion-parapets. The next to last terrace contains twelve small prasats. Stone elephants on the corners of the three lower levels were supposed to symbolize the stability of the universe. The sanctuary at the summit of the edifice was added when the monument was restored in the twelfth century and is probably loftier than the original prasat.

The pyramid itself is surrounded by eight brick towers housing minor shrines. The complex rises within a square surrounding wall. In the middle of each side of the wall is a gateway crowned by a cruciform gopura. Long buildings used as vestries and libraries crowd round about the wall.

The Bakong temple marks the firm establishment of classical Khmer architecture as opposed to its Javanese prototypes. The temple complex is surrounded by an enormous moat, 60 m (197 ft.) wide, which transforms the sanctuary into an island. The dimensions of this moat filled with water are quite imposing: 340 × 360 m (1116 × 1182 ft.). Causeways leading over the moat on all four sides give access to the gopuras. In Hindu symbolism, this moat was supposed to represent the cosmic ocean. It was itself surrounded by a 140 m (460 ft.) wide ring of land which was the site of the city proper, made up of straw huts built on piles similar to the ones that can still be seen in modern Cambodia. None of these buildings constructed in perishable materials has been preserved. Another moat, 22 m (72 ft.) wide, surrounded the residential area and

The pyramid of Phnom Bakheng as seen from the ground with its narrow stairway, string walls bearing effigies of lions and rows of small minor prasats.

formed a boundary to the urban centre, the whole of which was 700 m (2300 ft.) wide and 800 m (2625 ft.) long.

At Roluos in the ninth century Khmer city-planners created a grandiose complex remarkable for its central pyramid, concentric moats and median causeways with their monumental stone Naga-parapets. The idea of temple-cities was beginning to take shape. Bakong was not only a sanctuary for the god-king worshipped as an earthly incarnation of Shiva. This work of architecture was actually a synthesis of religion, housing and agriculture. It was a symbol of the complete and rigorously structuralized organic system which governed Cambodian society as a whole.

Bronze Statues

While the temples at Sambor and Roluos were dedicated to Hindu gods, most of the bronze statues which have been preserved (some of them dating back to the seventh century) are Buddhist images. Hindu rites were in fact associated with royal pomp and Brahmanism was maintained at the court, whereas Buddhism appealed to the lower classes of society. These bronzes are remarkable for their hieratical style, their elegance, their fine feeling for sculptural form and their surprisingly high quality.

These statues, contemporaneous with the great Indian masterpieces, recall the masterly creations of the Chola dynasty (ninth to twelfth centuries). Few examples of earlier Buddhist images in India have come down to us.

The Phnom Bakheng Temple

Throughout Khmer history, great reigns were marked by the creation of royal cities. Indravarman's successor, Yasovarman, who became king in 889, left Roluos and founded his own capital, Yasodharapura. The town is surrounded by a wall the perimeter of which measures 12 km (7.5 mi.). A natural hill rises in the centre. The king built his great temple, Phnom Bakheng, on this hill. A wall 650 m (2133 ft.) long and 440 m (1444 ft.) wide, running from east to west, surrounds the sanctuary at the foot of the hill. A median causeway leads up to the hill-top on which the temple-palace rises 60 m (197 ft.) above the city. The edifice itself is a six-storeyed square structure, 76 m (250 ft.) on each side. The sanctuary, located on the upper terrace, consists of five prasats in a quincuncial arrangement. The five lower levels each contain 12 sandstone prasats, i.e. 60 towers all in all. The temple-mountain itself is surrounded by 44

A natural hill serves as a base for Phnom Bakheng. The temple's upper terrace rises up 75 m (246 ft.) above the plain of Angkor.

Above:
Four median stairways lead up to the brick sanctuary crowning the temple of Baksey Chamkrong, a four-storeyed laterite pyramid built at Angkor in 920.

minor brick prasats. The median stairways are flanked by string walls decorated with images of lions.

The Phnom Bakheng temple with its 109 towers is a replica of Mount Meru, believed to have five peaks and seven different levels. If we count the ground level, the five storeys and the upper terrace, the pyramid does indeed have seven steps. On each side of the pyramid, we can see 33 towers symbolizing the 33 deities who live at the summit of Mount Meru in Indian mythology. In addition, the temple is a veritable stone calendar: the 108 prasats surrounding the main sanctuary symbolize the four phases of the moon which have twenty-seven days each.

The Koh Ker Interlude

Since the foundation of Angkor in 802, preclassical Khmer architecture had already created an extremely expressive artistic language. The vocabulary of the plastic arts was renewed only in 921 when Jayavarman IV usurped the throne and founded a new capital at Koh Ker where he erected the great Prasat Thom temple complex. One can notice a transition here from square to cruciform ground-plans. The Prang, a tremendous 36 m (118 ft.) high seven-storeyed pyramid rises above the complex. The sanctuary reaches a height of 60 m (197 ft.).

Sandstone lion-parapet running along the edge of the first terrace of the temple of Prè-Rup, built at Angkor in 961.

Right:
Aerial view of the Prè-Rup temple-mountain with its concentric enclosures. The three-storeyed laterite pyramid is crowned by five brick towers in a quincuncial arrangement.

Prè-Rup: a Step towards Classicism

Under Rajendravarman, Jayavarman IV's successor, the seat of power was shifted back to Angkor. Rajendravarman's architectural ventures at first displayed a rather diffident style. A good example is the flat temple known as the Eastern Mébon. Later on, however, the ruler erected more ambitious edifices such as the Prè-Rup temple, an artificial mountain constructed in laterite with brick prasats. With Prè-Rup, the Khmer temple-mountain assumed its true dimensions.

Yet Khmer architecture had yet to go through a long evolution before the beginning of the classic period which was to culminate in the twelfth century with the construction of Angkor Wat, the great temple of the Khmers, comparable, as an architectural entity, to the Taj Mahal.

Built on a double base, the main sanctuary at Prè-Rup marks the centre of a royal city built east of Yasodharapura by King Rajendravarman when the court came back to Angkor after the Koh Ker interlude.

Detail of a small octagonal column in the Eastern Mébon, built at Angkor in 952.

Beautiful, delicately carved sandstone lintel above one of the prasats in the Eastern Mébon, dedicated to the god Shiva.

The Classic Age: Bantéay Srei

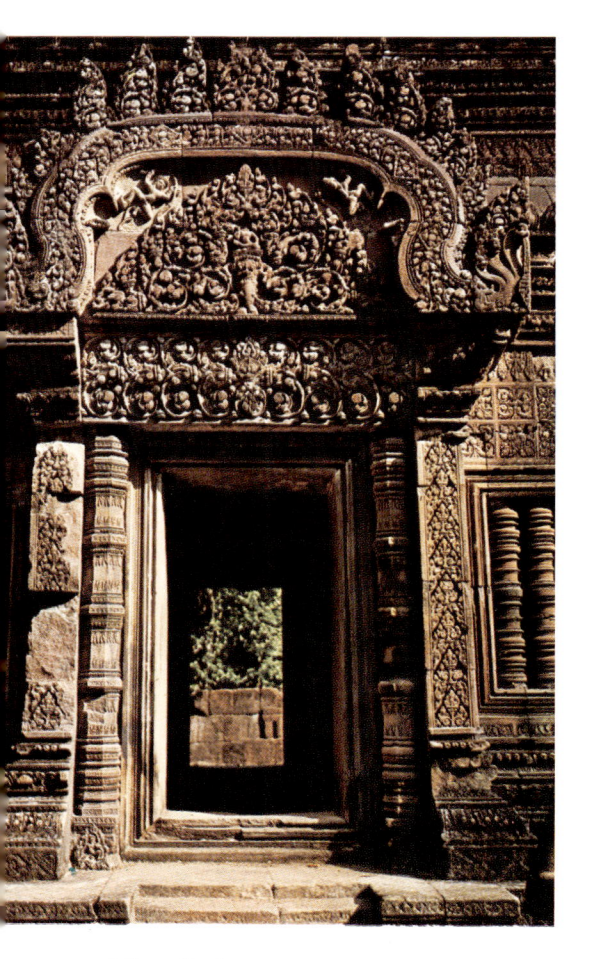

Like all features of the small temple of Ishvarapura, a genuine masterpiece built at Bantéay Srei in 967, this doorway leading into the mandapa in front of the main sanctuary is remarkable for its delicate ornamentation. Both the lintel and the spandrel are magnificently carved.

Facing page:
Detail of one of the admirable Apsaras, or heavenly maidens, adorning the temple at Bantéay Srei. Tenth century Khmer sculpture reached a peak of perfection here. This graceful and charming figure is carved in gorgeous pink sandstone.

The classical style in Khmer art has its birthplace at Bantéay Srei, 25 km (16 mi.) north of Angkor. As it is often the case in the world of art, classical features were at first purely decorative and had no influence on the over-all structure or ground-plans of the buildings. This is true of the small Ishvarapura temple at Bantéay Srei. While the lay-out is inspired by the Prasat Thom temple at Koh Ker, the sculptural ornamentation is an example of pure classicism.

The temple at Bantéay Srei is an unrivalled masterpiece of Cambodian art. Oddly enough, it was not built by a king. Unlike other Khmer temple-palaces serving simultaneously as monuments to a glorious reign and funerary temples for the ruler, Bantéay Srei was erected by a Brahmin, Yajnavaraha, grand-son of Harshavarman (900-921). He founded the temple in 967 and dedicated it to the god Shiva. The fact that the edifice was not intended for a king, accounts for its diminutive dimensions. The entire monument is indeed built on a reduced scale. For example, the temple doorways do not exceed 1.3 m (4.3 ft.) in height.

The 200 m (660 ft.) long complex displays a central walk with porticoes flanked by galleries. This 55 m (180 ft.) long walk leads to a gopura in front of the moat surrounding the temple complex. A second gopura on the other side of the moat gives access to the temple which consists of a single terrace supporting three prasats. As at Prah Ko, the prasats are arranged side by side. In front of the central prasat we can see a long mandapa, or assembly hall, henceforth characteristic of all flat temples as opposed to the Mount Meru-type structures. The towers have four storeys decorated with miniature prasats symbolizing the dwellings of the gods on Mount Meru. They do not exceed 10 m (33 ft.) in height.

However, as stated above, the quality which marks the temple at Bantéay Srei is the incredible perfection of its sculptural ornamentation. All the buildings are covered with sculptural carvings in high and low relief. The jambs, the lintels, the spandrels, the balustered windows, the mouldings running along the terrace are all decorated with delicately carved sculptures. The most splendid of all are the guardian spirits and heavenly maidens adorning the façades of the prasats. Unbelievably graceful Apsaras and Devatas inhabit this divine world. Charming, youthful and smiling Dvarapalas stand watch on the threshold of the sanctuaries. Delicate sensuality pervades these miniature sculptures which almost seem to have been made by a goldsmith.

Latticed stone garlands and foliated scrolls half hide backgrounds imitating ornamental tiles. The plinths are covered with luxuriant foliage; the small octagonal columns display an abundance of lavish superposed bands; the sharp outlines of the pedestals create rhythmic patterns of light and dark; the edges of the roofs, reproducing

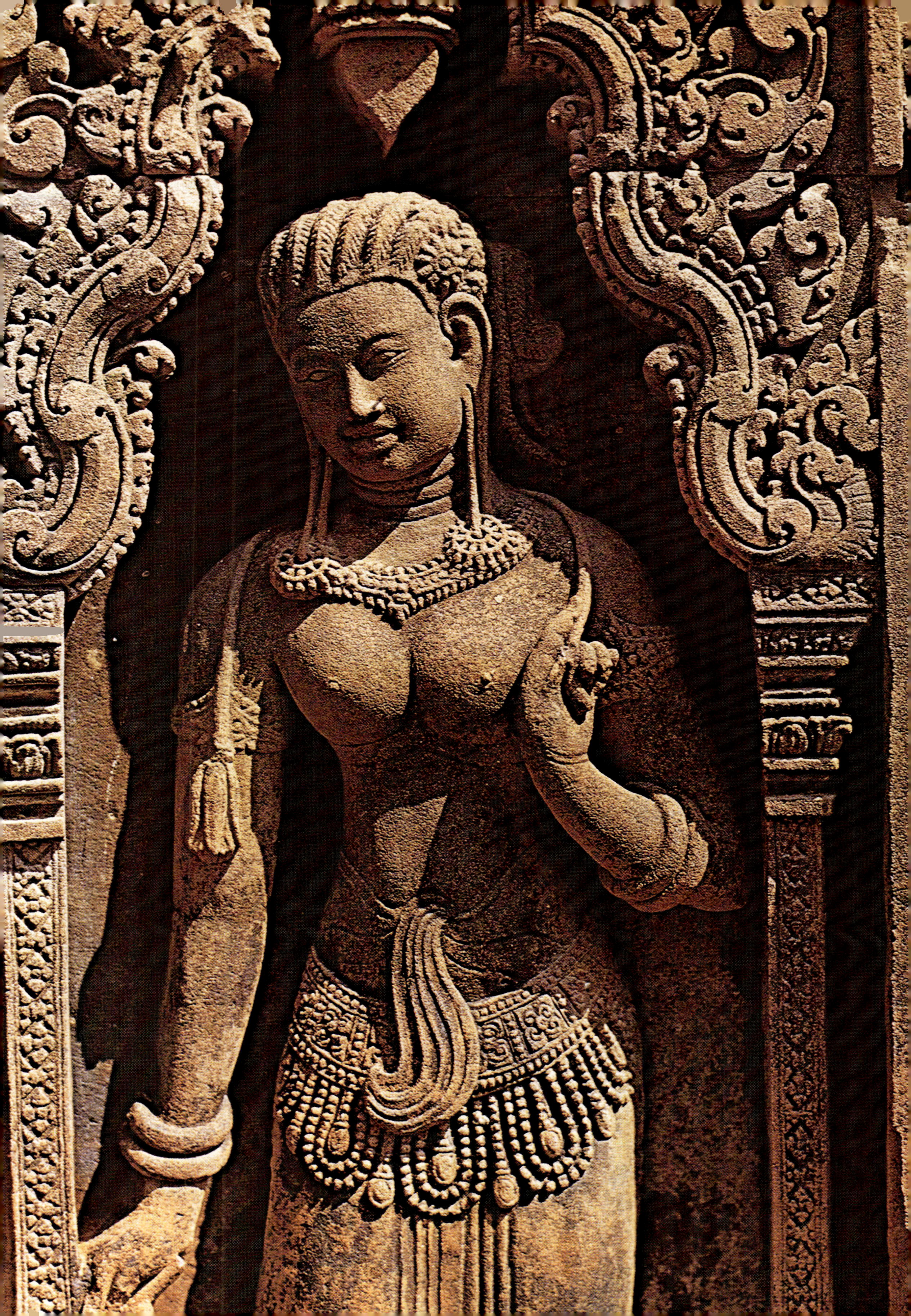

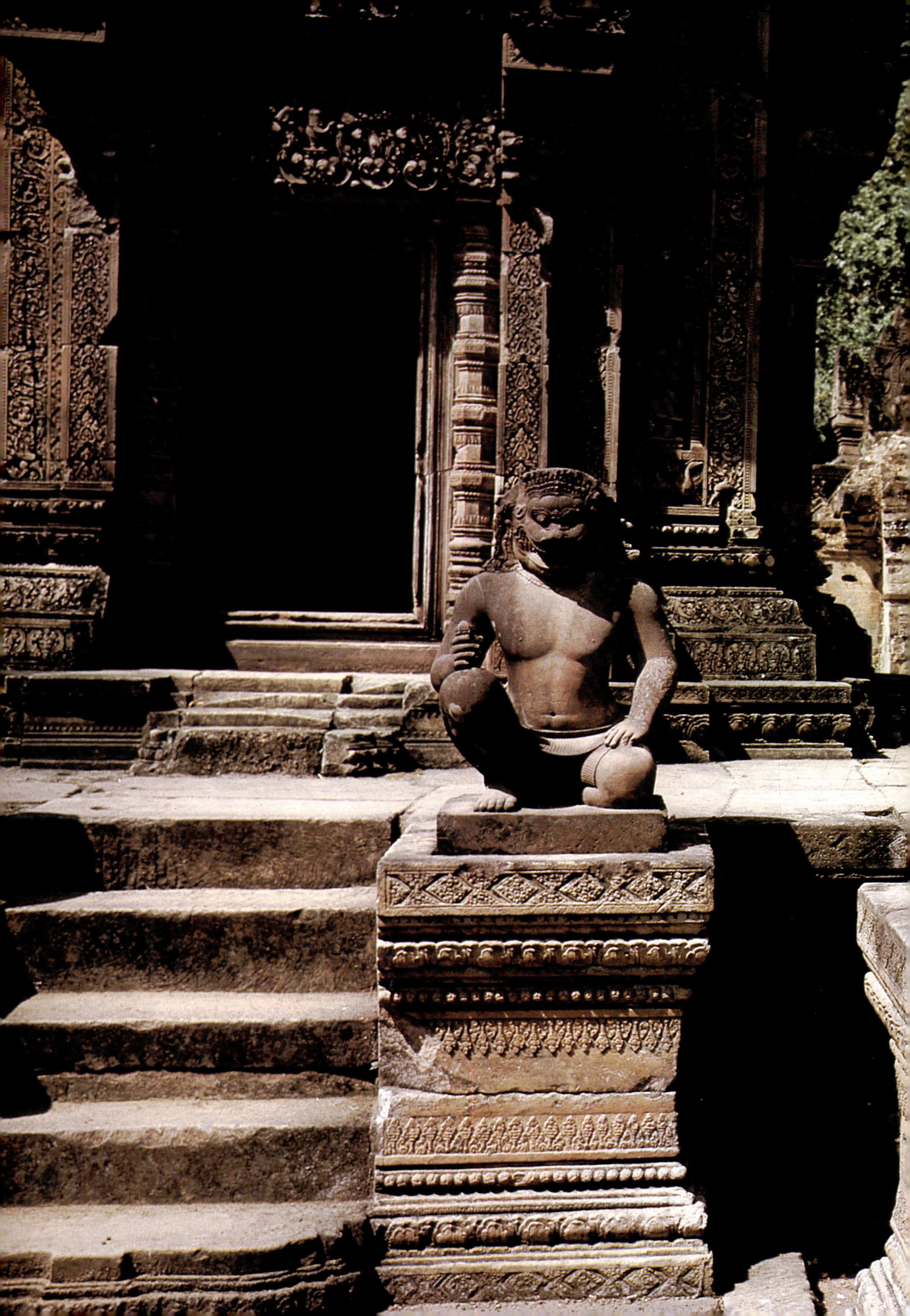

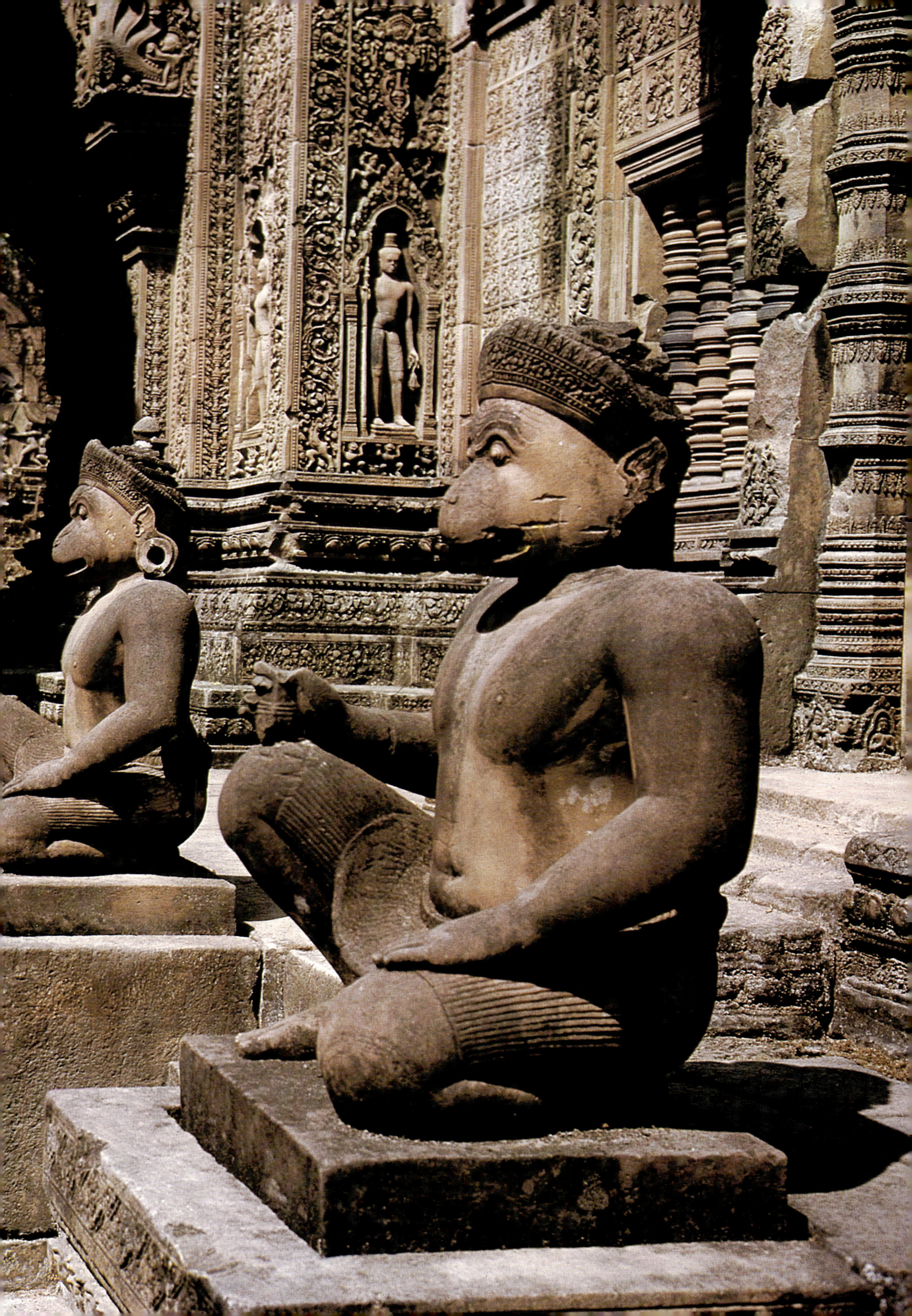

Detail of a presiding genius standing watch in front of the prasats at Bantéay Srei. This fantastic being with a bird's beak is the Brahmani kite Garuda which Vishnu rides.

Minor prasat at Bantéay Srei. The roof with its four storeys decorated with miniature pavilions is supposed to be a replica of Mount Meru.

Overleaf:
The temple at Bantéay Srei near Angkor is chiselled like a piece of jewellery. Squatting figures with human bodies and monkey's or monster's heads are carved in the round on either side of the stairway leading up to the sanctuaries decorated with low reliefs.

ornamental tiles in the shape of lotus leaves, smooth off the angles. In front of the prasats, monkey-headed guardian spirits carved in the round crown the string walls. Other similar statues bear the effigy of the Brahmani kite Garuda.

This lavishness, this overt luxuriance which seems to be an integral part of the architecture make Bantéay Srei an unrivalled jewel of Southeast Asian art. And when one examines the spandrels of the prasats, one discovers, beneath the multifoil arches, superb low reliefs depicting mythological scenes inspired by the heroic exploits related in the Ramayana.

It is no wonder that this marvel lost in the Cambodian jungle, hemmed in by tropical vegetation, has aroused the cupidity of vandals. It inspired Malraux's famous novel, *The Royal Way*, the story of a luckily unsuccessful attempt at stealing some of the most remarkable carvings at Bantéay Srei.

The temple is constructed entirely in pink sandstone, which is very hard to come by in the Angkor area. It has been remarkably restored by the archaeological service of the Preservation of Angkor, formerly directed by the French school of the far east.

The Cambodian Monarchy

As stated above, Bantéay Srei is an exception insofar as it was erected by a Brahmin who, though he may have been of royal descent, never came to the throne of Angkor. As a rule, the great temple-palaces were erected by the rulers in order to commemorate their reign and give their subjects a holy place capable of calling the gods' blessings down upon them. This idea was derived from a formula probably borrowed by Jayavarman II, the first great Khmer builder, from the Sailendra rulers of Java where he had sojourned. The king of the Khmers looked upon as an intercessor with the gods on behalf of mankind, was more or less deified.

The image of the god-king was defined in connection with the Mount Meru-type temple-palaces, also imported from Java. The god was believed to reside in the prasat at the summit of the pyramid which contained his statue. The king mounted the terraces of the sanctuary and approached the god in order to perform the rites which enabled him to communicate with the divinity and, consequently, gave him some power over the god. These rites obliged the god to guarantee the kingdom's prosperity.

The king interceded with the gods who controlled the regular recurrence of the monsoons. (Similar primitive agrarian rites were still per-

Detail of the sculptural carvings decorating a door jamb at Bantéay Srei.

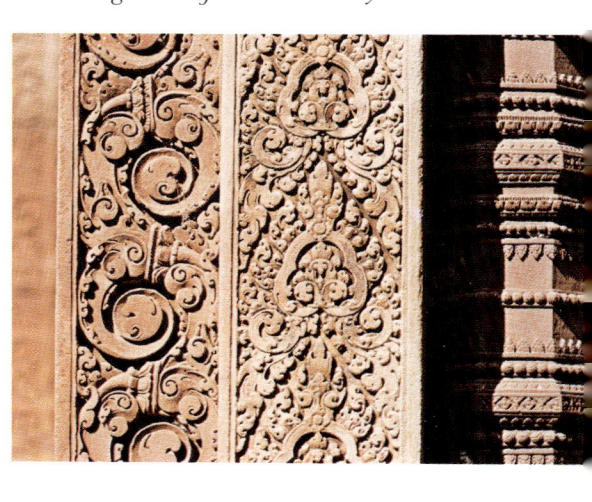

formed in Cambodia not long ago.) The ruler was therefore responsible for maintaining order in the universe. He meted out the gifts and blessings human life was dependent on. He was the god's representative on earth. He was the god's anointed; as soon as he came to the throne, he was consecrated by the priests. He embodied supreme authority. He was the life and soul of the country, the guide who decided upon the construction of not only temples but also the irrigation systems which account for the realm's prosperity. The king called on both technical knowledge and magico-religious remedies in order to enrich his empire and exalt the power of the gods in whose paradise he was to dwell after death. This is why the dead ruler was worshipped in the temple he had built; the funeral ceremonies identified him with the god he had honoured during his lifetime.

The Khmer kingdom was a hereditary monarchy. Not only did the king have complete power over his subjects but he was also the supreme magistrate. The Chinese traveler Tcheou Ta-Kouan who sojourned at the court of Angkor in the thirteenth century wrote: "Even insignificant disputes are always judged by the ruler". Moreover, the king was not altogether cut off from the masses: "The ruler holds audience twice a

Scene from the Ramayana decorating a lintel at Bantéay Srei: Ravana the giant is carrying off Rama's wife, Sita.

Above left:
Three geese form the pedestal of an Apsara at Bantéay Srei.

day for affairs of State. Officials and common people who wish to see him sit on the ground and wait for him".

Priests and courtiers enjoyed privileges which were denied the great mass of peasants, fishermen, merchants, craftsmen and workmen in the building trade. The Cambodian social system was rigorously hierarchical. There was a very powerful water police, an army and a corps of civil servants for maintaining order in the world of Angkor. However, there were no castes in Khmer society. This fact explains the vitality of the social system peculiar to ancient Cambodia. Public offices were not hereditary. High officials never became feudal lords. Khmer society was an open society: anyone could accede to the highest offices. A peasant was thus free to become a warrior or a technician. But a high official could also lose his job and become a mere peasant. According to the doctrine of metempsychosis, nothing can ever be definitively acquired. Both society and religion go through cycles of never-ending reversals.

All this was made possible by the collectivist character of the Khmer civilization: private ownership of capital goods was unknown in ancient Cambodia. Land belonged to those who tilled it. When a peasant had sown rice in a field for five years, he had the right to claim the land. But when the owner died, his succession reverted to the king. Inscriptions state that the king actually owned all the land. The rice-fields were periodically re-allocated; no peasant went without land.

One of the terrifying demons standing watch in front of the prasats at Bantéay Srei.

Torso of one of the beautiful Apsaras at Bantéay Srei: adorned with sumptuous jewellery and wearing a gauzy pagne and a wide wrought metal belt round her hips, the nymph is holding a water lily.

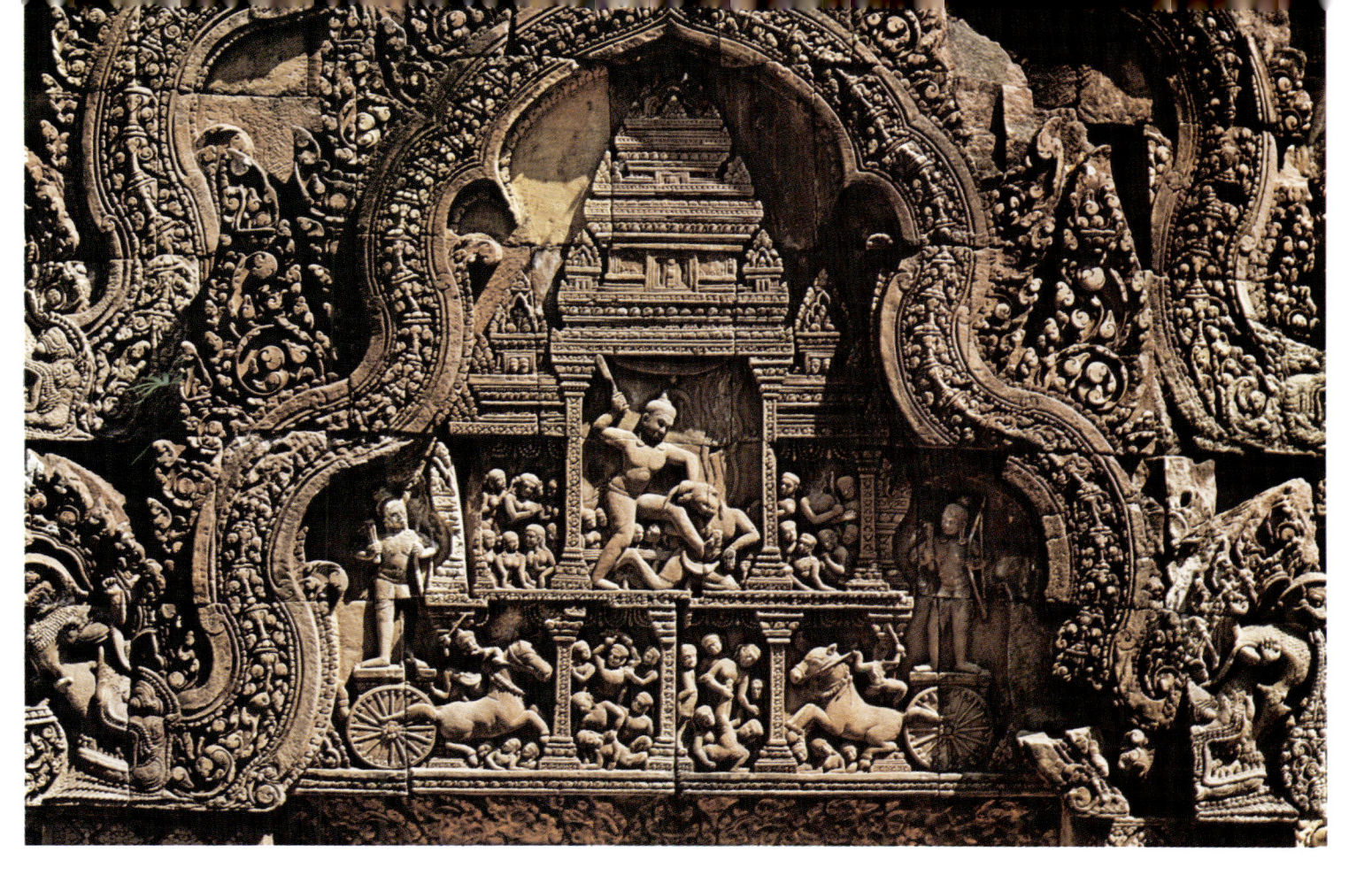

The Creation of Surrounding Galleries

Early Khmer temples are characterized by the presence of long buildings — used as vestries and libraries — which completely surround both pyramids and flat temples outside the sacred enclosure. Tenth century monuments from Koh Ker and the Eastern Mébon to Prè-Rup and Bantéay Srei provide stunning examples of this phenomenon. With occasional gaps at the corners or where the structures are connected with the gopuras, these long halls almost completely encircle the sanctuaries.

The Phimeanakas temple-palace, erected between 978 and the dawn of the eleventh century in the centre of the capital conceived by Jayavarman V in the Angkor area, represented a genuine architectural revolution. The Phimeanakas, or "Aerial Palace", near the royal palace, is a three-storeyed step-pyramid constructed in laterite. It is not square but rectangular: 35 m (115 ft.) long and 28 m (92 ft.) wide. The upper platform is 12 m (39 ft.) high. On all four sides, wide stairways lead up the steep slope of the pyramid. On this rectangular base, King Suryavarman I (1002-1050) erected a central cruciform tower. The four stairways lead to projecting entrance halls at the foot of the prasat. On the edge of the upper terrace, surrounding the prasat, the ruler had a veritable ring gallery constructed in sandstone with corbeled vaults instead of the usual long halls.

This gallery displays traceried windows opening on both sides of the platform. The windows' stone balusters let through a softened light. Henceforth, the function of the buildings surrounding the sanctuary was completely changed. The long halls were formerly used as vestries, libraries and store-rooms for offerings and sacred objects. The ring galleries, on the contrary, were mere passageways. Was this evolution undergone by religious architecture connected with changed rites? Was it the result of Buddhist influence, a copy of structures intended for the rite of circumambulation? In India, ring galleries first appeared at the Kailasa temple at Ellora, which dates back to the eighth century. The tradition continued at Tanjore (eleventh century), Somnathpur (thirteenth century) and even at Madura (sixteenth century)... The phenomenon actually seems to represent an interpenetration of Bud-

Detail of the scrolls carved in pink sandstone on one of the jambs of a prasat at Bantéay Srei.

Above:
Krishna getting ready to kill his uncle Kamsa in his magnificent palace. This low relief carved on a spandrel in one of the libraries at Bantéay Srei gives us a good idea of what the wooden palaces of the Khmer rulers may have looked like.

The aspect of Phiméanakas' pyramid, according to a picture by Louis Delaporte done in 1968.

One of the basins faced with sandstone which supplied the Angkor Thom palace district with water. This work dates back to the tenth century.

Side view of the temple-mountain of Phimeanakas built at Angkor in 978. The three stages constructed in laterite are crowned by a sandstone gallery, probably added at the very beginning of the eleventh century.

dhist and Hindu rites. At Angkor this syncretism went so far that, without iconographic information, it would often be well nigh impossible to tell Buddhist shrines apart from Hindu ones.

Be that as it may, the ring gallery at Phimeanakas marked a turning point in the history of Khmer architecture. As a matter of fact, a gallery had already been built several years earlier at the temple of Ta Kèo. At Ta Kèo, however, the windows open only on the inside; on the outside they are replaced by blank traceried windows. The sloping roofs at Ta Kèo also differ from the corbeled vaults characteristic of classic period creations.

The temple-palace at Ta Kèo renewed the traditions of preclassical Khmer architecture prior to the foundation of Koh Ker. There developed a period of conscious archaism. After a whole series of monuments characterized by the use of laterite — Baksei Chamkrong,

Flight of stairs climbing the top stage of the pyramid of Ta Kèo. This temple-mountain, under construction from 980 to 1013, was never finished.

Eastern Mébon, Prè-Rup, Phimeanakas — Khmer architects went back to using sandstone, the traditional building material which had been used only at Bantéay Srei since the beginning of the tenth century.

Though it is hard to be sure, the edifice was probably built between 980 and 1013. Work may well have been begun by Jayavarman V; as at Phimeanakas, laterite was used in the construction of the lower levels. It was continued by Suryavarman I, the inventor of surrounding galleries, who prefered sandstone. Construction took place during a period of domestic conflicts; the edifice remained unfinished. Ornamentation is lacking. Rough hewn blocks give the temple a harsh, cubistic appearance.

Not counting the sanctuaries, the five steps rise up to a height of 22 m (72 ft.). The five upper sanctuaries, or prasats, form a quincunx. The central prasat has a cruciform ground-plan with four projecting porches. The main tower rises up to a height of 45 m (148 ft.).

Monuments like Ta Kèo, Bantéay Samre and the Baphuon testify to the originality and technical mastery of tenth and eleventh century Khmer architects. At the same time, statuary too was improving and becoming more ambitious. Colossal works of art, much larger than the sculptures decorating Bantéay Srei, were executed in bronze. The only surviving specimen is the admirable reclining Vishnu found in the Western Mébon which dates back to the late eleventh century. Tcheou Ta-Kouan thought this statue was a reclining Buddha. Such a mistake is by no means surprising when dealing with the syncretist Khmer civilization. A yet better proof: at Bantéay Samre, which is a Hindu temple dedicated to Vishnu, low reliefs decorating some spandrels portray Buddhist scenes.

The Baphuon, a five-storeyed sandstone step-pyramid 100 m (330 ft.) wide and 120 m (394 ft.) long at its base, had a single sanctuary, surrounded by two ring galleries, which probably reached a height of over 50 m (164 ft.). Though such undertakings may seem a bit too venturesome when one considers the technological possibilities of the eleventh century, the fact is that by that time Khmer architecture had solved most of its technical problems. It is true that the temple built by Udayadityavarman II, who came to the throne of Angkor in 1050, suffered on account of its builder's ambition: given up to the jungle, whipped by the torrential monsoon rains, the sandstone walls burst asunder. A team led by Bernard-Philippe Groslier was restoring this colossal edifice when the dramatic events which recently steeped Cambodia in blood put a stop to the rescue operation...

The tremendous capital of the Khmer kingdom came to full maturity in the eleventh century. Everything was ready for the birth of the masterpiece which represents the zenith of the classic period: the great temple of Angkor Wat which has given the site a title to world fame.

Naga-parapets in the courtyard of the flat temple of Bantéay Samre at Angkor. This temple, dedicated to Vishnu, was built about the mid-twelfth century.

This twelfth century bronze from the Angkor area probably held a mirror on its head and gracefully upraised hands. It is 30 cm (12 in.) high.

Angkor Wat and the "Rice Factory"

Silhouette of the temple of Angkor Wat standing out against the sky at sunrise: the towers rising in a quincuncial arrangement ressembling a tiara mingle with the trees. The temple was built by Suryavarman II.

Visitors catch their first glimpse of Angkor Wat when they fly over the enormous temple before landing at Siemreap. Angkor Wat beheld from this point of view — the point of view of the gods the sanctuary is dedicated to — looks like a gigantic diagram made up of squares, lines and interlocking enclosures recalling a nest of Russian dolls. The ordonnance of the temple complex, surrounded by a wide moat filled with water, is rigorous, orthogonal, almost despotic. At the centre of a series of ring galleries encircling the sanctuary, five tremendous towers soar up in a quincuncial arrangement like a genuine jungle cathedral. This colossal work of architecture is in fact contemporaneous with the great Gothic naves of Chartres, Sens or Notre-Dame.

Even when the site of Angkor was abandoned after the decline of the Khmer kingdom, the temple itself has always been kept in repair. Though dedicated to Vishnu, as early as the fourteenth century it housed a bonze monastery. This fact accounts for its present name: in Cambodian, Angkor Wat means "the capital which has become a Buddhist monastery". Protected by the piety of the faithful, the temple buildings were constantly revered. And when the first European — a Portuguese missionary — made his way to Angkor about 1580-1590, the complex was just being restored. Later on, in the seventeenth and eighteenth centuries, Portuguese, Spanish and French travellers visited the ancient capital. There was even one Japanese who went on a pilgrimage to Indo-China; when he arrived at Angkor, he thought he had reached the heartland of the Buddhist religion in India. He was the first to draw a map of Angkor Wat. In 1860 the Frenchman Henri Mouhot wrote a description of Angkor Wat and attracted public attention to the Khmer monuments. The Mekong mission led by Douart de Lagrée in 1866 and Louis Delaporte's explorations made it possible to carry out the first scientific research on Cambodian works of art. The engravings made by Delaporte during Lagrée's expedition, published in 1868, rank among the main causes of the interest aroused by the discovery of Khmer civilization.

Two Predecessors: Prah Vihear and Wat Phu

Among the great monuments erected during the classic period shortly before the colossal temple of Angkor Wat, we should briefly mention, outside the site of Angkor itself, the Prah Vihear and Wat Phu. These great temples were the result of the affluence Cambodia had been living in since the eleventh century. The country was at the peak of its power, though the government was often obliged to subdue revolts and follow a policy of repression, to say nothing of the border conflicts with the

Angkor Wat as seen from the summit of Phnom Bakheng. The complex, built between 1113 and 1150, is surrounded by the tropical forest.

Detail of an engraving made by Louis Delaporte during Lagrée's expedition and published in 1868. Imaginary, though quite accurate aerial view of the temple of Angkor Wat.

Chams on the east who made several bloody raids into the Khmer empire.

The enormous Prah Vihear temple built at the summit of a spur of the Dangrek range facing north is over 800 m (2625 ft.) long at its base. The culmination of the monument is a sanctuary located on the edge of a steep cliff, 80 m (263 ft.) high. While the earliest elements of this monumental complex date back to the reign of Yasovarman, who founded this "temple of Shiva at the summit" about A. D. 900, most of the buildings were erected under Suryavarman I (prior to 1050) and Suryavarman II (1113-1150), the builder of Angkor Wat.

The Khmer architectonic vocabulary reveals itself here in all its splendour. The third gopura with its galleries spread out over a width of more than 100 m (330 ft.) foretells the magnificent propylaea which can still be seen at Angkor Wat. The two cruciform courtyards flanking the sanctuary on the east and on the west, though they are not organically connected with the temple complex, also inspired the architects of Angkor Wat.

The main difference between Prah Vihear and Angkor Wat consists in the generalized use of stone vaults in the latter, while the galleries at Prah Vihear generally have tiled roofs with timber frameworks.

Wat Phu was erected by Jayavarman VI (1080-1107) only shortly before the construction of the masterpiece known as Angkor Wat. It was built in northeastern Cambodia on the bank of the Mekong. Unlike Prah Vihear perched on the summit of a mountain, Wat Phu is backed by a hill which overlooks the monument. The 1400 m (4945 ft.) long complex, facing east, displays a processional causeway, lined here and there with platforms, which leads to an enormous stairway. The stairway

Propylaea at Angkor Wat viewed from the entrance to the causeway crossing over the 200 m (660 ft.) wide moat. One should take note of the colossal Naga-parapets.

climbs seven storeys and leads to an enormous sanctuary 25 m (82 ft.) above the base of the monument. In front of the prasat there is a mandapa. A U-shaped gallery completes this tremendous complex.

However, as beautiful as they may be, these great temple-palaces are far from equalling the perfection and serenity of Angkor Wat. Cambodian architects profited by the teachings of experience. The temple-mountain of Angkor Wat represents the apotheosis of classical Khmer architecture.

Angkor Wat: a City within a City

Erected by Suryavarman II (1113-1150), the most famous and most glorious of all Khmer rulers, Angkor Wat is indeed the largest and the most beautiful of all the temples built on the Indochinese peninsula. Remarkable for its quality and its perfect feeling for form and volume, its over-all lay-out and the arrangement of its various components, this magnificent monument is the masterpiece of classical Khmer aesthetics and city-planning.

Angkor Wat lies in the southeast sector of the ancient city of Yasodharapura, built in the late ninth century and surrounded by an enormous moat the perimeter of which measures 16 km (10 mi.). This part of the urban complex had to be wholly reorganized in order to make room for Suryavarman II's gigantic creation. The temple complex takes up almost all the available space. The temple itself is surrounded by a moat almost 200 m (660 ft.) wide contained within a rectangular enclosure 1500 m (4925 ft.) long and 1300 m (4270 ft.) wide covering an area of about two square kilometres (0.8 sq. mi.). The park surrounding

Graceful dancing Apsara carved in low relief on the pillars of the gallery in front of the temple of Angkor Wat.

View of the propylaea at Angkor Wat: the northern portico at sunset.

The penetration in Angkor Vat, according to a picture by Louis Delaporte, published in 1868.

Apsaras carved in low relief on the walls behind the propylaea at Angkor Wat. The nymphs are wearing brocade skirts and high jewelled crowns.

the temple covers an area of one million square metres (1,200,000 sq. yd.), minus 100,000 square metres (120,000 sq. yd.) occupied by the various buildings and galleries which divide the park into four square basins. What can we conclude from these colossal dimensions? They bear witness to the fact that the great temple-palaces were the centres of urban complexes of which the stone structures alone have survived. The entire area contained within the enclosure was probably covered with dwellings for the high dignitaries, palace officials, courtiers and priests. This explains the name given the complex after the Siamese invasions: "the royal city which has become a Buddhist monastery". After the defeat of the Khmer rulers by the Chams in the late twelfth century, Cambodia experienced a Buddhist revival and the temple dedicated to Vishnu was transformed into a bonze monastery. Nonetheless, the inhabited area was originally the royal city, the capital of the Khmer kingdom. And Angkor Wat was not only a gigantic temple but also a great urban centre, the seat of executive and religious power.

Angkor Wat was actually a city within the city of Yasodharapura, situated as it was in the southeast sector. This fact also explains the temple's orientation facing west. Unlike most Cambodian sanctuaries, it is entered from west to east. If the temple had been built facing east, as it was usually the case, the entrance would have been located on the outskirts of the ancient city of Yasodharapura. This would have been ridiculous. According to a traditional precept of the sthapatis, or Hindu priest-architects, a sanctuary should never "turn its back" on the city in which it stands.

Entering the Holy City

On account of this arrangement of space characteristic of most Khmer temples, it is extremely important to enter the right door when visiting.

Below:
Sandstone Apsaras from Angkor Wat. No less than 1500 of these heavenly maidens are carved on the temple walls.

Façade of the temple of Angkor Wat seen from the great causeway with its Naga-parapets: a genuine jungle cathedral.

In order to perceive space as the creator intended, one must in fact follow in the priests' footsteps. This is why Angkor Wat should be visited from west to east, just as the ordonnance of the whole complex seemingly suggests doing.

Drawing near the monument, one first comes upon a very wide moat filled with water, on the edge of which extends a cruciform terrace. The moat is crossed by a wide causeway, 250 m (820 ft.) long, proceeding from the terrace. Magnificent parapets consisting of gods holding the body of a Naga run along the causeway which is supported by columns standing on either side of the sustaining wall. These columns recall the wooden footbridges built on piles which are a traditional feature of Khmer architecture. The presence of the giant snake deity on the edge of the moat stresses the close connection between the Naga king and water.

As for the moat itself, the rectilinear banks of which are faced with stone tiers, its perimeter measures 5.5 km (3.4 mi.). Facing the great entrance causeway, a vast gallery, 235 m (770 ft.) long, runs along the moat forming the temple's majestic propylaea. The causeway leads to a triple gopura in the middle of the gallery. Towers rise at both ends of the propylaea. This monumental entrance jutting out into the park is a miniature replica of the temple's façade which spreads out before our

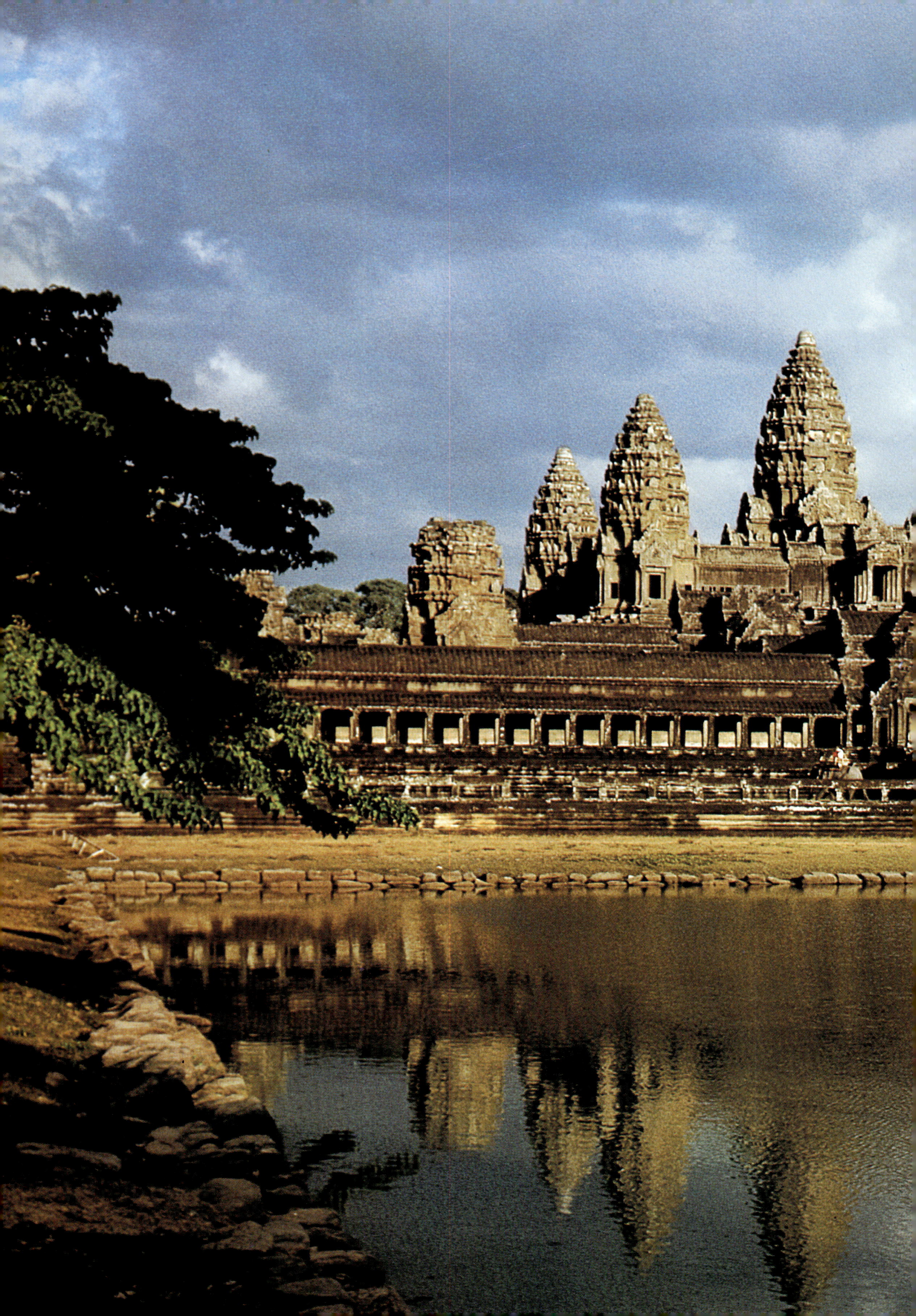

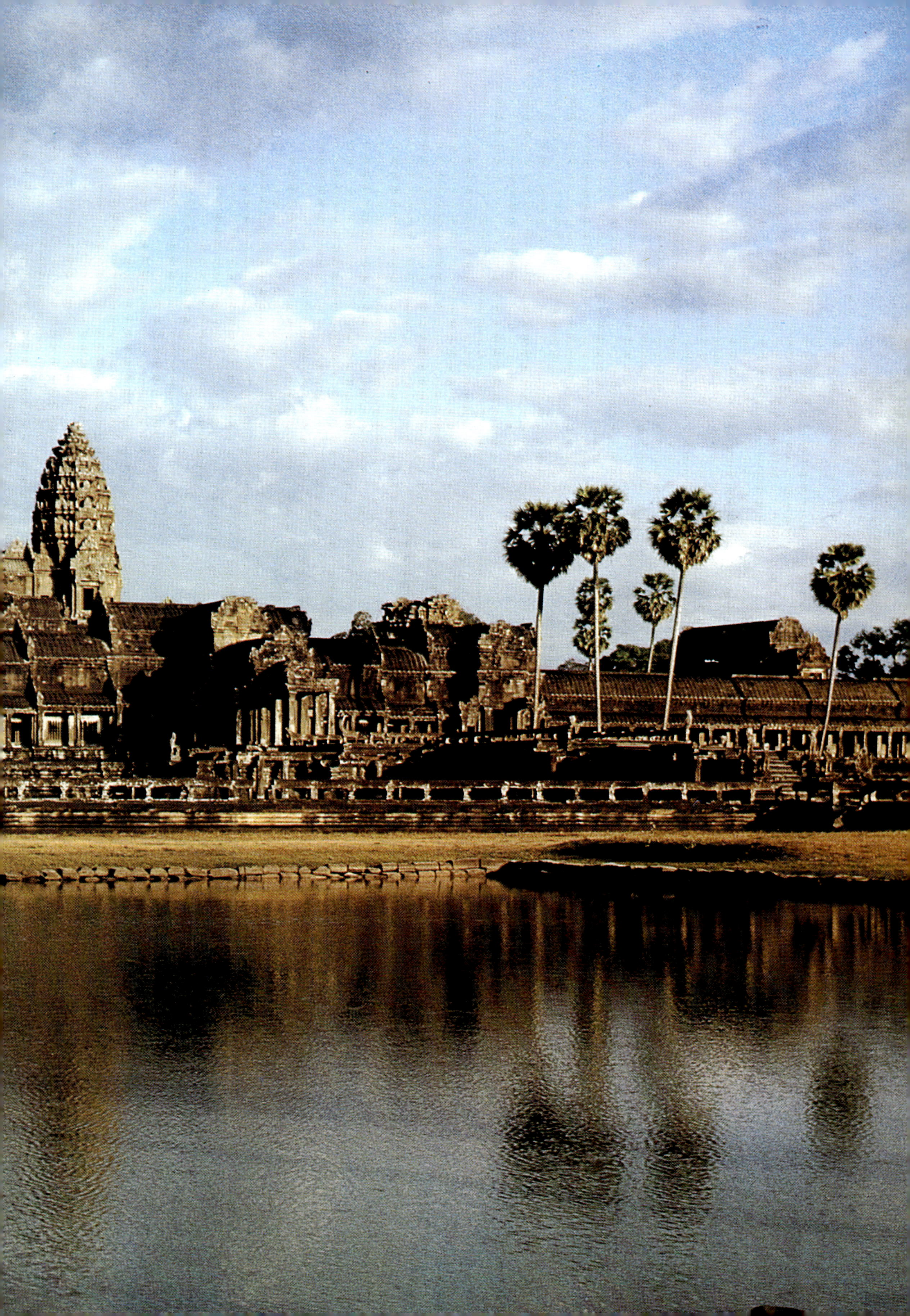

View of the façade of the outer gallery on the south side of Angkor Wat. The square pillars supporting the roof of the side-aisle buttress the main gallery. The curved sandstone sloping roof imitating tiles is a typical feature of Khmer architecture.

Overleaf:
Over-all view of the temple of Angkor Wat mirrored in the northwest basin. At sunset a golden glow lights up the towers of the splendid funerary temple of Angkor's most glorious king, Suryavarman II, who ruled in the early twelfth century.

eyes when we cross the threshold. The outer wall of the gallery running along the moat consists of porches supported by square pillars. Looking towards the temple, blind walls screen the central monument. These galleries built entirely in sandstone with half-vaulted curved sloping roofs are perfect examples of classical Khmer architecture.

Angkor Wat attests its architect's feeling for sculptural form and arrangement. Crossing the threshold of the propylaea, one gets a sensational view of the façade of the main temple culminating in five towers, the quincuncial arrangement of which ressembles a tiara. One is truly struck with astonishment at this amazing and enrapturing sight. The size and magnificence of the monument by no means detract from its refinement. As a whole, it bears witness to an authentically dynamic perception of space. Khmer art reaches one of its peaks here.

Like a rectilinear vista, the raised paved causeway with its Naga-parapets leads to the foot of the temple-mountain, 350 m (1150 ft.) from the triple gateway. Halfway between the propylaea and the main monument, beautiful libraries, 40 m (130 ft.) long, stand on either side of the causeway. These buildings have cruciform ground-plans. Median stairways lead up to porches jutting out on all four sides. When one passes the libraries, one catches sight of two vast rectangular basins, 65 m

(215 ft.) long and 50 m (165 ft.) wide. The lofty mountain composing the holy city of Angkor Wat is mirrored in the water.

The temple itself is built on a platform 340 m (1115 ft.) long and 215 m (705 ft.) wide. In front of the temple, the causeway leads to a cruciform terrace supported by columns, a petrified relic of primitive lake dweller-type architecture. Public rejoicings connected with the worship of the god-king probably took place on the two-storeyed terrace outside the temple precincts. Young girls dressed as Apsaras and Devatas (heavenly maidens living in the city of the gods) danced the famous ritual ballets here...

The Great Temple of Angkor Wat

The edifice stands on a lofty pedestal decorated with ornamental mouldings. The main entrance is flanked by two side entrances hidden behind high porches remarkable for their pediments and carved spandrels. The wings of the enormous surrounding gallery with its open porches supported on square pillars proceed symmetrically from the entrance. From one corner tower to the other, the façade extends over a width of 187 m (614 ft.). The complex is 215 m (705 ft.) from front to back.

On the inside, the vaulted sandstone gallery is supported by a blind wall, while on the outside it is shored up by a side-aisle surmounted by a half-vault which serves the purpose of a flying buttress. The perimeter of the surrounding gallery measures 800 m (2625 ft.). The inner wall is decorated with magnificent low reliefs. This vast storied frieze is interrupted only by the entrance gopuras and corner towers. A kind of pictorial chronicle of the Khmer empire embellished with legendary scenes from the Ramayana and the Mahabharata portraying all the fabulous beings in Hindu mythology unfolds here before our eyes. These enormous "frescoes" carved in fine sandstone display an extraordinary feeling for monumental composition. Common people admitted into the gallery where they performed the rite of circumambulation could read a genuine "Paupers' Bible", in the mediaeval sense of the word. Readers of the low reliefs kept the temple on their left, as they did for rites performed at funerals: the edifice was in fact intended as a funerary temple in which the god-king was worshipped after his death.

The sculptural carvings cover an area of almost 1200 square metres (1440 sq. yd.). We see the judgment of the dead and the rewards promised the just, the heavenly palaces in which they will enjoy eternal

Corner pavilion in the outer gallery at Angkor Wat. A tower originally crowned this cruciform structure with projecting porches.

Detail of the low reliefs decorating the outer gallery at Angkor Wat on the west side of the temple complex. The entire inner wall of this porch's southern face illustrates a scene from the Mahabharata: the battle of Kuruksetra. A 40 m (130 ft.) long low relief shows a rough-and-tumble of warriors and chariots.

Facing page:
The low relief at Angkor Wat showing scenes from the battle of Kuruksetra dates back to the early twelfth century. The fine-grained sandstone used in construction enabled Khmer carvers to reproduce the most minute details of the clothing and equipment of the troops clashing in these scenes inspired by the Hindu epics.

bliss in the company of charming Apsaras; but we also behold the wicked and the appalling tortures that will be inflicted on them by terrifying demons. Another low relief portrays a famous scene from Hindu mythology, "The Churning of the Sea of Milk": in order to give his subjects happiness and bliss, the king is beating the Ocean of Fortune to get the ambrosia out of it. Not all the scenes depicted have something to do with religion. For example, we can see Suryavarman II reviewing a parade of his troops. Siamese scouts, infantry, horses and chariots make up a picturesque and teeming throng arranged in distinct groups bearing insignia and carrying parasols.

These relief sculptures testify to Khmer carvers' remarkable feeling for composition. The reliefs cover vast areas: some scenes are 100 m (330 ft.) long and only 2 m (6.6 ft.) high. The continuous sequence is subdivided by hardly perceptible pauses and repetitions. The great scenes unfold before our eyes like a row of pictures lined up side by side.

The temple consists of three stages. On the first level is a remarkable cruciform courtyard facing west. This structure is the very heart of Angkor Wat. It consists of a quadrilateral in which two galleries supported on square pillars cross at right angles. This courtyard integrates the terrace decorated with reliefs to the temple's second enclosure. The galleries divide the structure into four small yards which may originally

Parading troops at the battle of Kuruksetra: low relief in the western gallery at Angkor Wat.

Right:
Troops celebrating their victory after the battle of Kuruksetra.

have been filled with water for the ablutions which are a fundamental part of Hindu ritual. This cruciform structure made up of a quadruple row of pillars supporting a nave buttressed by side-aisles is surrounded by galleries decorated with a veritable garland of Apsaras carved in high relief. These nymphs created for the delight of the gods and the blessed form a genuine ballet. The graceful deities dance alone or in groups. They are wearing long brocade skirts and high jewelled diadems. An impression of refined sensuality emanates from these smiling images which invite us to rejoice.

The quadrilateral formed by this cruciform courtyard opens on the side onto the vast spaces which encircle the first stage of the monument and separate it from the second stage. On either side of the courtyard there are two libraries, smaller than the ones we have already seen along the entrance causeway. To go to the second stage, one keeps following the same west-east line which now starts going up. Vaulted galleries proceeding from the cruciform courtyard climb gradually upwards, concurrently with exterior staircases. They display a series of interlocking pediments which have their prototypes at Bantéay Srei.

No one is allowed on the second stage except the priests who have retired from the world in order to devote themselves to meditation. This

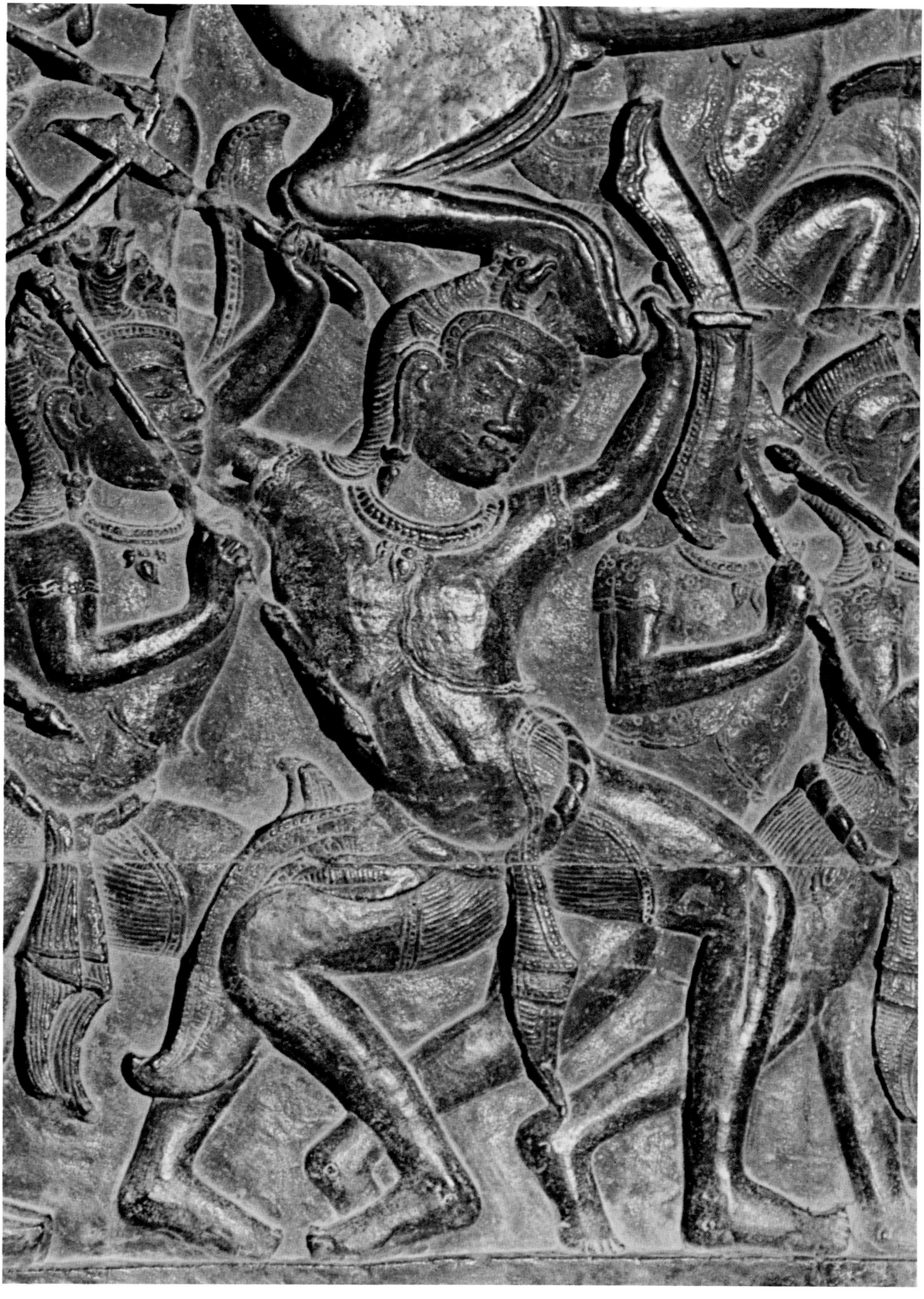

explains why the gallery encircling this stage is closed off from the outside world by a windowless surrounding wall. In this austere cloister, man, hoping to attain true wisdom, indulges in serious reflexions on his conduct. He cuts himself off from the world and its temptations. The architecture is therefore severe, reduced to the essentials: neither Apsaras nor Devatas adorn this gallery with its single nave supported on a row of traceried windows with turned stone balusters. This second gallery is 100 m (330 ft.) wide and 115 m (377 ft.) long. It contains the tremendous foundation mass for the monument's five towers. The ring courtyard is reduced here to a narrow alley crushed beneath the overwhelming mass of the pyramid's third stage, 13 m (43 ft.) above. Steep stairways lead up to this 60 m (197 ft.) square structure.

The Quintuple Tower

Only the king and the high priest were allowed on the third stage which supports the quincunx consisting of the sanctuary and the four towers surrounding it. This is where the god resided, in the form of his statue. This is where the rites identifying the ruler with the god were performed.

The third stage is surrounded by a gallery open on both sides. Traceried windows with stone balusters let through a softened light and a distant image of the surrounding world. Those who have access here are free from all temptation. Vaulted passageways supported by quadruple rows of pillars proceeding from the middle of each side of the

Corner of the cruciform courtyard at Angkor Wat with its double row of pillars.

Central gallery in the cruciform courtyard at Angkor Wat: pillars support a corbeled vault buttressed by side-aisles. This light and airy structure is probably a replica of wooden prototypes.

Detail of the Apsaras decorating the cruciform courtyard at Angkor Wat.

Group of Apsaras dancing beneath the galleries of the cruciform courtyard at Angkor Wat. These lively carvings sheltered from the elements were meant for the gods' delight.

gallery lead to the central sanctuary. The over-all arrangement is similar to that of the cruciform courtyard. The main difference lies in the presence of the spiring central sanctuary with its four attendant towers, or prasats.

Twelve stairways — three on each side — climb the massive pedestal to the upper level. Nonetheless the structure seems to be hovering in the air, as if its soaring towers were just so many "rockets" pulling it along. This structure with its airy, transparent galleries is simultaneously the most lyrical and the most original creation of Khmer architecture. The prasats seem transfigured as compared with their pre-Khmer prototypes. And the great central tower overlooking the plain of Angkor, buttressed by four porches and exposed to the four winds, rises up to a height of 65 m (213 ft.), 42 m (138 ft.) above the upper level.

This lofty soaring invites us to go beyond our human horizon, get on a helicopter and take a look at the monument from the gods' aerial point of view. This is in fact the best way to view the Khmer temple, built for "those above". And this sight alone enables us to clearly make out the gigantic mandala drawn on the ground by the temple complex, reflecting the image of the gods' heavenly palace at the summit of Mount Meru. Angkor Wat was created in the image of both the macrocosm and the microcosm. It combines a feeling for boundless space and attention to minute detail. It symbolizes the perfect beauty of the work of art man wishes to offer up to the gods.

The Wealth of Angkor

Yet this stupendous achievement makes us ask one meanly materialistic question: what did the Khmer kings owe their wealth to? What enabled them to produce such an enormous monument? Even in an absolute monarchy, even in a theocracy wholly centred on the worship of the gods, such things surely had to be "paid for". The construction of the temple of Angkor Wat called for 350,000 cubic metres (455,000 cu. yd.) of building materials, i.e. almost one million metric tons of rock which had to be brought from the far-off sandstone quarries situated near Kulen, 40 km (25 mi.) north of Angkor. When the rivers swelled, the rough hewn blocks were conveyed on rafts down the streams which feed the Great Lake, through the canals of the urban complex and the temple moat. The moat made it possible to bring building materials on the site on all four sides of the edifice simultaneously.

But, once again, how was it possible to support the tens of thousands of workmen employed in this tremendous undertaking: quarrymen, cart and raft-makers, stone cutters, masons, sculptors, etc.? Where could they get the raw materials for the bronze statues, so few of which have survived, the doors set off with gold and silver inlays, the brocade and gauze adorning the altars where offerings were placed? How did they pay the artists and craftsmen who worked on this marvellous temple for decades and decades?

These questions prompt us to investigate the causes of Khmer prosperity. In order to understand the "miracle of Angkor", one must trace Cambodian history to its origin.

The Birth of Rice Plantations

The Indian traders who settled on the southern coast of Indo-China first introduced advanced farming methods into Southeast Asia. Thanks to them, the first rice plantations appeared on the peninsula at the beginning of the Christian era. The variety of rice grown was obtained by selection. It was already sown in India in the third millenium B.C. To ripen, this rice requires constant care and a well regulated irrigation system.

In Founan, the Mekong delta was the centre of this agricultural system based on irrigated rice-fields. This technique, constantly improved, accounts for Khmer prosperity during the classic period. Rice needs lots of water: its bushy roots must be submerged. However, stagnant water is of no help. The plant has such a great need for oxygen that it dies if the water is not constantly changed. Only complicated hydrological techniques can create the imperceptible circulation of water indispensable for rice growing.

Two ballerinas from the Cambodian Royal Ballet dancing in front of the galleries at Angkor Wat. They are wearing traditional costumes.

The traditional orchestra which plays for the ritual dances includes percussion instruments and only one flute.

As far back as the third century A. D., rice plantations were established in the Bassac area and along the coast of the Gulf of Siam. Canals brought water from the Mekong or Menam to flood the chequer-board fields consisting of compartments separated by small embankments. The water flowed downhill from one compartment to the next until it finally reached a canal which drained off the excess. This system made it possible to till relatively unfertile soil without impoverishing it. The moving water constantly fertilized the soil and the yield was phenomenally high. Whereas one hectare (2.5 a.) of wheat yielded about 500 kg (1100 lbs.) in the Middle Ages, one hectare of irrigated rice-fields could yield two or three crops a year and produce 2000 kg (4400 lbs.) of rice. And when we compare the yield per hectare for pasture land, wheat and rice fields, we discover that cattle yield 340,000 calories per hectare, wheat 1,500,000 calories and rice 7,300,000 calories per hectare. This explains rice's popularity in regions with a high population density. From a nutritional standpoint, the yield is more than twenty times higher!

Of course, these enormous figures have nothing much to do with the Founan period. Irrigation was still dependent on flooding caused by the monsoons. The rainy season, however, is not very long. The dry season which follows lasts from six to eight months, during which time the water level in the rivers is too low to irrigate all the rice-fields. During the pre-Khmer period, there was usually only one crop a year and the Cambodians grew leguminous plants such as beans on the side.

The development of the Khmer civilization was the by-product of a genuine technological revolution based on methods of artificial irrigation introduced in the ninth century. When Jayavarman II founded his capital in the plain of Angkor, he realized right away what advantages the location had. Situated north of the Great Lake, the alluvial plain of Angkor appears to be absolutely flat. In actual fact, it slopes gently down from north-northeast to south-southwest. Three permanent streams flow down from the Kulen range and feed the lake.

Cambodian Royal Ballet performing on the terrace leading to the temple of Angkor Wat.

Above:
Khmer dancing-girl wearing ritual head-dress and ornaments.

49

The north wing of the cruciform courtyard at Angkor Wat consists of a gallery with vaulting supported on columns leading from the lower level to the second stage. Spandrels decorate the roofs of these exterior staircases. At the base of the edifice, horizontal moulding runs along the edges of the open patios.

Carvings decorating a door jamb at Angkor Wat : tiny praying figures amidst foliage.

The Creation of Artificial Lakes, or Barays

To go from simply cultivating rice-fields yielding one crop a year to conceiving the desire to make them produce two or three, a very important step must be taken. This progress implies the will to free human communities from their subservience to the rhythm of nature. This step was taken by the Khmer rulers at Angkor when they decided to create enormous artificial reservoirs, known as barays. The main purpose of these reservoirs was a better distribution of the region's water resources, above all rainfall which some months is extremely abundant but more often wholly lacking.

However there is a fundamental difference between the Cambodian barays and the "tanks" adjacent to Indian temples. While the reservoirs created in India were bored like gigantic wells, the barays were constructed by means of dykes raised above the level of the surrounding land. The body of water was kept in reserve at a height. And this is precisely the clever thing about barays : thanks to gravity feed, there is no need for pumping, Persian wheels or Archimedean screws. When one wants to flood the rice-fields, it suffices to open a gap in the Cambodian baray.

The water stored in the barays is supplied by the abundant monsoon rains (there is 1.60 m — 5.25 ft. of annual precipitation) and by "forced" canals, i.e. canals which bring water from upstream since, on account of the dykes, their gradient is lower than that of the surrounding plain. These canals run into the barays at a height of two, three or even four metres (6.6-13 ft.) above ground level.

The enormous quantities of water the Khmers managed to stock in the plain of Angkor thanks to the barays and their canals made possible non-stop irrigation of the rice plantations during the seven or eight month long dry season. When a hole was made in the dykes, the force of gravity drew the precious liquid through a network of canals, drains, trenches and arterioles all the way to the most distant rice-fields planted on either side of the barays.

National Development

The irrigation system which, between the eighth and twelfth centuries, transformed Angkor into a genuine rice factory, was basically organized according to these simple principles. We shall now go over the various phases of this fantastic national development programme.

The first extensive irrigation works we know of in the Angkor area date back to the reign of Indravarman, the creator of the monuments at Roluos (Prah Ko, Bakong, etc.). We mean to speak of the baray at Lolei, the size of which is already quite impressive. It forms an artificial lake 3800 m (12,470 ft.) long and 800 m (2625 ft.) wide. If the mean depth of the head of water stored in the reservoir was only 2 m (6.6 ft.), the total volume must have been about six million cubic metres (7,800,000 cu. yd.). Such a tremendous achievement was certainly not a trial shot: previous attempts must have been made under Jayavarman II and Jayavarman III. Though much less ambitious, they made it possible to perfect the technique. We have found no trace of these early ventures on the spot.

Be that as it may, the first baray we know of already has perfect proportions: it is almost four times longer than it is wide. It has been constructed perpendicular to the slight gradient of the surrounding plain. This is quite clever. If the artificial lake had been square, the southern dyke would have to have been much higher than the northern one, so as to make up for the slope of the ground. On the other hand, the rectangular structure created an optimum balance between the

View of the traceried windows in the second gallery at Angkor Wat. The structure stands on a base outlined by ornamental moulding.

Cruciform gopuras at Angkor Wat as seen from the temple's raised terrace. The roofs exhibit crossed gables.

Angkor Wat was originally a Hindu temple dedicated to Shiva. When it was consecrated to the worship of Buddha after the decline of the Khmer empire, Buddha images were set out in the galleries.

The gallery encircling the second stage of the temple of Angkor Wat has only one opening on to the outside world. At sunset, balustered windows above the cruciform courtyard let through a softened light.

volume of earth used in the construction of the dykes and the volume of water kept in reserve.

The Lolei baray was however merely the first link in a chain of similar constructions, all of which were built according to the same principles. The water stored at Lolei was used not only for irrigation purposes but also to feed the moat surrounding the temple of Prah Ko as well as the double moat surrounding the city of Hariharalaya with its centre at Bakong. It then flowed through the sanctuary of Prasat Prei Monti and discharged into the Great Lake.

Water, indispensable for agriculture, was also one of the fundamental factors taken into account by architects and city-planners. Canals proceeding from the baray brought fresh drinking water to the town's inhabitants. Waste water was carried away by the current. The water in the moats traced the town boundaries and also served to defend Khmer urban centres.

Indravarman's achievement was an organic whole which could be neither perfected nor modified. The ruler's successors introduced the same system in other regions, thus making their contribution to the humanized environment in which the Khmer culture developed. For example, Yasovarman, Indravarman's successor, had the idea of creating an even bigger baray 20 km (12 mi.) upstream. He drew bold plans for an artificial lake no less than 7000 m (22,975 ft.) long and 1800 m (5910 ft.) wide. The result was the Eastern Baray at Angkor, estimated capable of holding thirty million cubic metres (39,000,000 cu. yd.). It is worthy of note that while the dimensions were doubled as compared with Lolei, the volume was quintupled.

As stated above, Yasovarman also created, about A. D. 900, the great city of Yasodharapura with its centre at Phnom Bakheng. This square city, 4 km (2.5 mi.) on each side, was entirely surrounded by water: on the east by the canalized Siemreap river and on the other three sides by a moat almost 200 m (660 ft.) wide.

This tremendous collective effort made it possible to devote thousands of hectares to the intensive cultivation of rice. Yet one hundred and fifty years later, about 1050, the irrigation system was expanded once again by the construction of the Western Baray under Udayadityavarman II. The king created an artificial lake even bigger than the one built by Yasovarman. The Western Baray is 8000 m (26,260 ft.) long and 2200 m (7,220 ft.) wide. When full, it must have held about forty million cubic metres (52,000,000 cu. yd.) of water.

In 250 years, Angkor was thus transformed into a tremendous complex of reservoirs and canals which made possible the intensive cultivation of rice. The three barays could hold a total of 75 million cubic metres (97,500,000 cu. yd.) of water. Thanks to these enormous reservoirs, rice plantations covering an area of almost 1000 square kilometres (400 sq. mi.) yielded three crops a year. The result was the most extensive high-yield agriculture in Southeast Asia.

"Scientific" Agriculture

How can one obtain three crops a year, knowing that rice takes about five months to ripen and must necessarily be harvested before the monsoon? Khmer cultivators did their best to answer this question and make the most of the twelve months in the year.

They gave up rule-of-thumb methods for rice growing and adopted a kind of "scientific" agriculture in which rice was looked upon as a bedding plant. Instead of going through the whole process consisting of plowing, sowing, irrigating and reaping on the spot in the flooded fields, the Khmers realized that it would be advantageous to sow the rice in beds where the shoots come up very thick; when they reach a height of

Stone balusters ressembling woodwork subdue the light in the second gallery at Angkor Wat.

Detail of the balusters at Angkor Wat showing the interplay of light and shadows on the window frames.

Detail of a pillar with its capital supporting a carved lintel on the third stage of the temple of Angkor Wat.

View from the second ring courtyard at Angkor Wat. We here see the upper level with its five lofty towers, or prasats. Three stairways lead up to three projecting porches.

Facing page:
Soaring sanctuary of the temple of Angkor Wat. This is a cruciform structure consisting of a prasat with four projecting porches. The tower develops by a reduplication of vertically compressed storeys.

20-25 cm (8-10 in.), these shoots are transplanted in the freshly harvested, plowed and submerged fields. These beds take up only one tenth of the land under cultivation. They make it possible to sow a second time before reaping the first crop. By transplanting, one can gain up to 40 or 50 days. This method alone was capable of transforming Angkor into the tremendous rice factory which was the main cause of its rulers' wealth and power and made it possible for them to erect their admirable temples.

The district supplied by the Khmer irrigation system covered an area of some 1000 square kilometres (400 sq. mi.), i.e. 25 × 40 km (16 × 25 mi.). Allowing for the space taken up by the barays, canals, cities and plots reserved for other crops, rice was probably grown on at least half of this total area, i.e. some 60,000 hectares (150,000 a.). The annual yield per hectare was from 2 to 2.5 metric tons of rice. During the classic period, from 130,000 to 150,000 metric tons of rice were produced each year.

When dealing with the population of Angkor, we shall see that this production was quite sufficient to meet the country's needs. There was even a rather large food surplus. Rice farming actually made possible the creation of the great works of architecture which overlook the canals and barays like mediaeval chapels rising above the bridges in European cities. An unbroken logical and organic connection linked up the small embankments separating the rice paddies and the lofty spires, or prasats, in which the statues of the gods stood watch, the rigorous organization of the capitals and urban centres built in the plains and the alignment of the dykes and causeways which covered the country with a gigantic network of coordinate axes.

The term "environment" is nowhere more meaningful than at Angkor. The capital of the Khmer kingdom is indeed a perfect example of how man can give nature a helping hand. Without the irrigation system, the birth of an important civilization would have been altogether impossible in the heart of the hostile Indochinese jungle. Angkor is actually a miracle, an agreement entered into by earth, water, men and gods. The uniting of these four factors thoroughly changed the appearance of the plain in the Angkor area. The rice plantations make it ressemble a chequer-board. Thanks to them, this part of the world has become an ecological masterpiece. Rice and religion link up a whole series of phenomenons controlling national development.

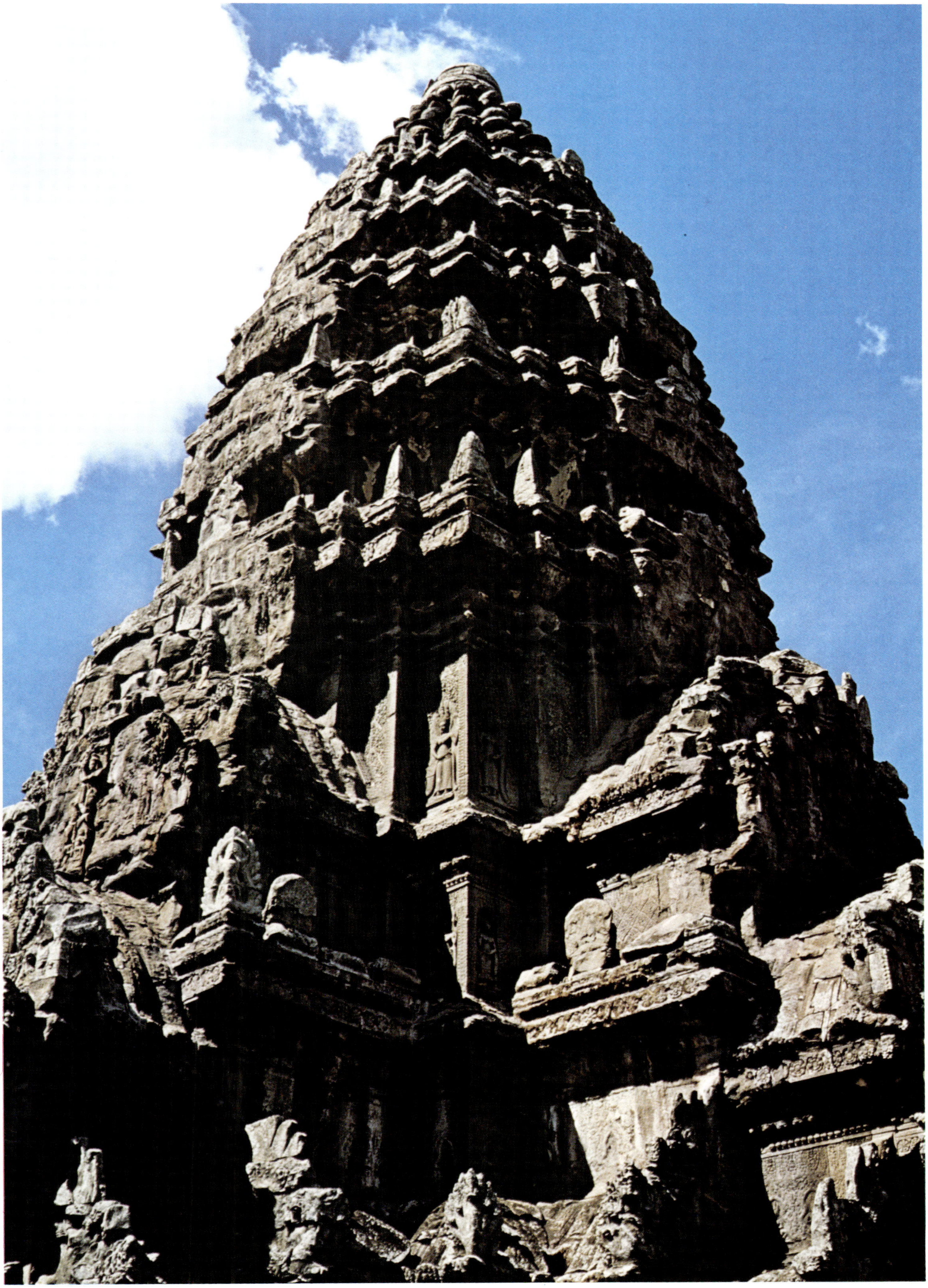

Over-all aerial view of the great temple of Angkor Wat. We here see the mandala which was the basis for the ground-plan of the complex with its concentric enclosures. Twelve steep stairways lead to the central platform on which five towers rise up in a quincuncial arrangement. On the second level the narrow ring courtyard is enclosed within the second gallery bristling with corner towers and cruciform gopuras. A large ring courtyard separates this second level from the outer gallery which can be only partially seen here. To the right, the cruciform courtyard at the end of the median causeway connecting the temple with the outer moat.

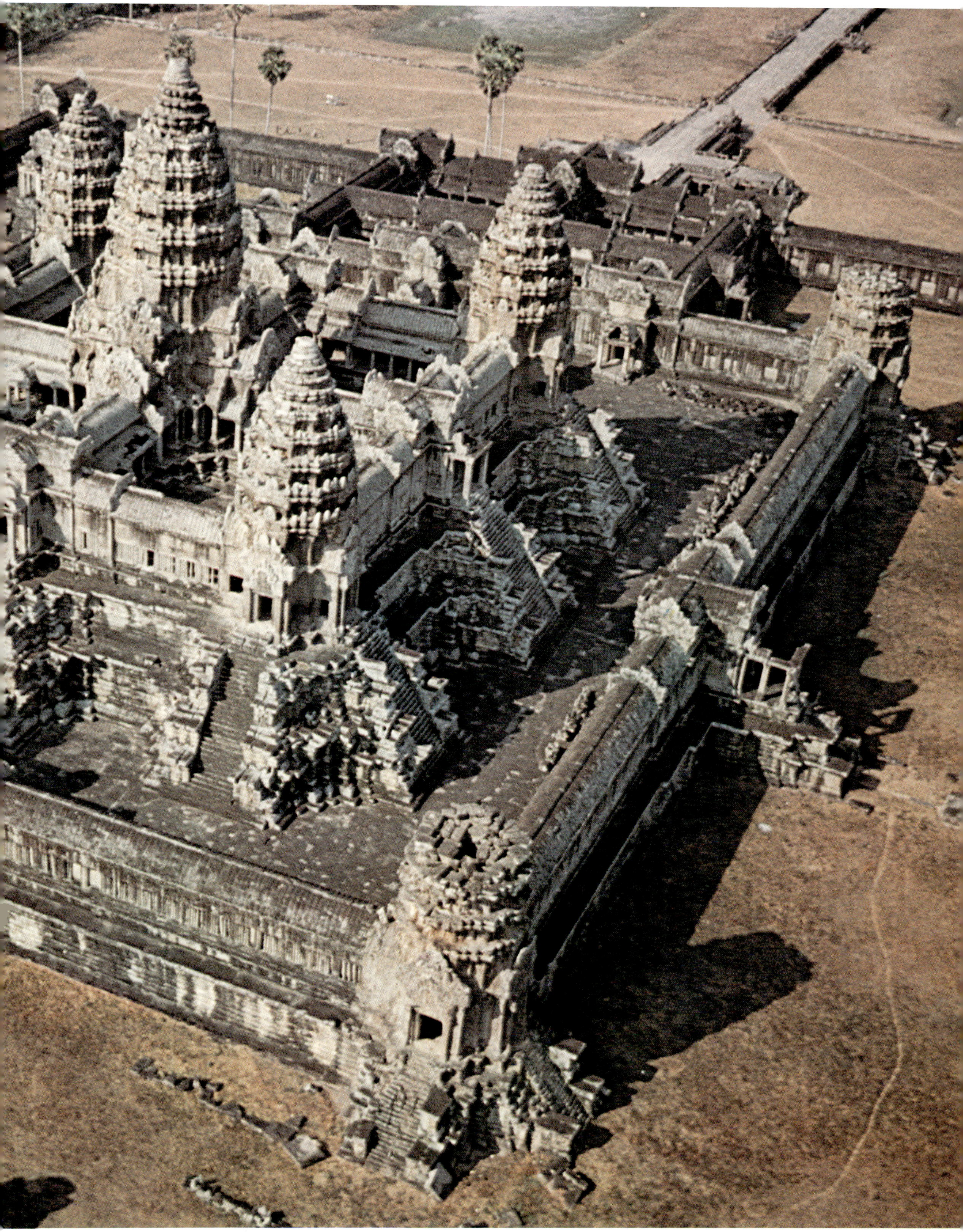

The Decline and Renaissance of Angkor

Under Suryavarman II, the Khmer empire reached the peak of its power. A period of dynastic instability followed his reign. About 1150, the country, disunited and steeped in blood by the quarrels of rival factions, was on the brink of anarchy. The Tarpeian Rock is not far from the Capitol. The ruler who had successfully governed almost the whole of Indo-China had forgotten to make arrangements for his succession. Regions formerly under Khmer suzerainty took advantage of the disorder and revolted. The Chams made a daring raid into Angkor. They sailed up the Mekong to the Great Lake, surprised the Khmer capital and burned it to the ground in 1177.

The situation was disastrous: for four years, Cambodia was, in the words of Khmer chroniclers, "plunged into a sea of misfortune". The strict order which had governed the society, the irrigation system, the cities and the army gave way to total anarchy. The entire country was ravaged. The statues of the gods were overthrown or stolen, the treasury plundered, the palaces reduced to ashes.

Royal authority was re-established by Jayavarman VII. He defeated the Cham invaders in naval combat, seized the capital and, in 1181, had himself crowned king of Angkor. Jayavarman directly undertook to rebuild the ruined city and restore the kingdom to its former splendour. His reign marked a period of glory for the Khmer world. It was a most brilliant swan song.

The Rise of Buddhism

This resurgence had consequences not only in the political and military fields (an especially important one being the conquest of Champa, the Khmer rulers' most dreaded enemy) but also in the sphere of religion. Whereas the king's court was traditionally Hindu, Jayavarman VII chose the Buddhist faith in order to come closer to his subjects (he used to fraternize with his soldiers in the "Resistance" during the Cham occupation), breach the gap between the government and the masses and consolidate the social hierarchy.

This reign is noteworthy for its architectural achievements. The period was characterized by a kind of building fever, hitherto unheard of in Cambodian history. Jayavarman VII alone erected or laid the foundations for almost as many monuments as all his predecessors since the beginning of the classic period. It looks almost as if he wanted to eradicate at one fell swoop all traces of the humiliation caused by Cham depredation. Hurling defiance at his enemies, he rebuilt the capital and brought Khmer civilization to the acme of its glory.

The odd thing about this architectural flourish which followed the

Several temples constructed at Angkor under Jayavarman VII have yet to be freed from their jungle shrouds. Here we see graceful Apsaras, hugged by tropical creepers, sleeping in the shade.

court's conversion to Buddhism is that the building principles and the ground-plans of the temples remained more or less the same. The Buddha was worshipped in sanctuaries which look almost like replicas of Hindu shrines dedicated to Shiva or Vishnu. The over-all architectural concepts hardly changed. Most of the temples erected by Jayavarman VII are flat temples similar to many built during the classic period. The ground-plans are not cruciform, as at Koh Ker, Bantéay Srei or Prah Vihear, but square as it was generally the case for the Mount Meru-type structures. Similar monuments had already been erected in the capital at Bantéay Samre. However the most amazing specimen is doubtless the temple of Bing Mealea, built 40 km (25 mi.) east of the royal city at about the same time as the temple of Angkor Wat. Its dimensions are almost identical with those of Suryavarman II's masterpiece. The outer gallery is 180 m (590 ft.) long and 150 m (490 ft.) wide. Bing Mealea was a Hindu temple. It has no central pyramid. A mandapa, or assembly hall, stands in front of the sanctuary. Most of the Buddhist temples built under Jayavarman VII, such as Prah Khan, Bantéay Kdei, Ta Som and Ta Prohm, were modeled after this complex.

Jayavarman VII defeated the Cham invaders, liberated Angkor and converted to Buddhism. This portrait of the ruler dates back to the late twelfth century and was found at Prah Khan. The half-closed eyes are suggestive of blissful meditation.

Facing page:
Romantic view of Angkor as described by Pierre Loti at the dawn of the twentieth century: a gopura at Ta Prohm overrun with tropical creepers. Sculptural carvings portraying frail Apsaras decorate what remains of the walls.

Temple of Ta Prohm at Angkor, consecrated in 1186. The powerful roots of the silk-cotton trees have played havoc with the monument. Archaeologists have intentionally left the temple as it was discovered in the nineteenth century.

Dvarapala armed with a bludgeon standing watch at the entrance to a temple built under Jayavarman VII. The very flamboyant style is typical of the Bayon period.

During the classic period, galleries were built round the various stages of the step-pyramid temples. In the flat temples, the galleries seem to replace the missing stages. Under Jayavarman VII, Buddhist temples are characterized by a series of concentric galleries. Seen from a bird's-eye view, they look like two-dimensional graphic symbols of Mount Meru's seven levels. Instead of emphasizing the central spire, this arrangement symbolizes the protective mountain ranges encircling the universe. After the Cham invasion, the Khmer world became awake to the danger threatening its borders. Architecture is revealing of this anxiety.

Though no important innovations have been made as far as groundplans are concerned, on the other hand the sculptural ornamentation belongs to a new style, characterized by a peculiar flamboyancy. The strict, classical style of Angkor Wat where sculptural decoration is subordinated to architectural form, gives way to an art which abolishes the dividing line between sculpture and structure. The walls, roofs and pillars are completely covered with carvings. The faces of the Buddha-King, or the Blessed One, surrounded by luxuriant decorative motifs, can be seen everywhere. Jayavarman VII identified himself with the popular Buddhist deity, Lokesvara.

Monuments amidst Jungle Overgrowth

In actual fact, this building fever which seized hold of the Khmer kingdom after the Cham invasion led to hasty and often sloppy work. When the tropical forest took possession of the site abandoned in the fifteenth century, the monuments more or less fell to pieces. The roots of the big trees — cedars, mahogany trees, silk-cotton trees, etc. — split the walls, broke up the paving on the terraces, overturned the balusters, cracked the corbeled vaults and tore the roofs asunder. Unlike Angkor Wat which was never surrendered to the invading jungle, the countless creations of Jayavarman VII disappeared under tropical creepers and overgrowth, their walls collapsed, their sculptural carvings were shattered by the green tentacles. In the romantic semi-darkness of the rain forest, only birds and monkeys dwell in the ruins. The setting is in perfect harmony with this luxuriant art. The surrounding jungle seems to reproduce on a larger scale the wealth of sculptural detail decorating the façades of the temples.

On account of the dilapidated state of Jayavarman II's monuments, they were long believed to be more ancient than the classical temples. Finally in 1927 the edifices were assigned to their true dates. The temples of Jayavarman VII, thought to have been built about A.D. 900, actually belong to the period between 1181 and 1219.

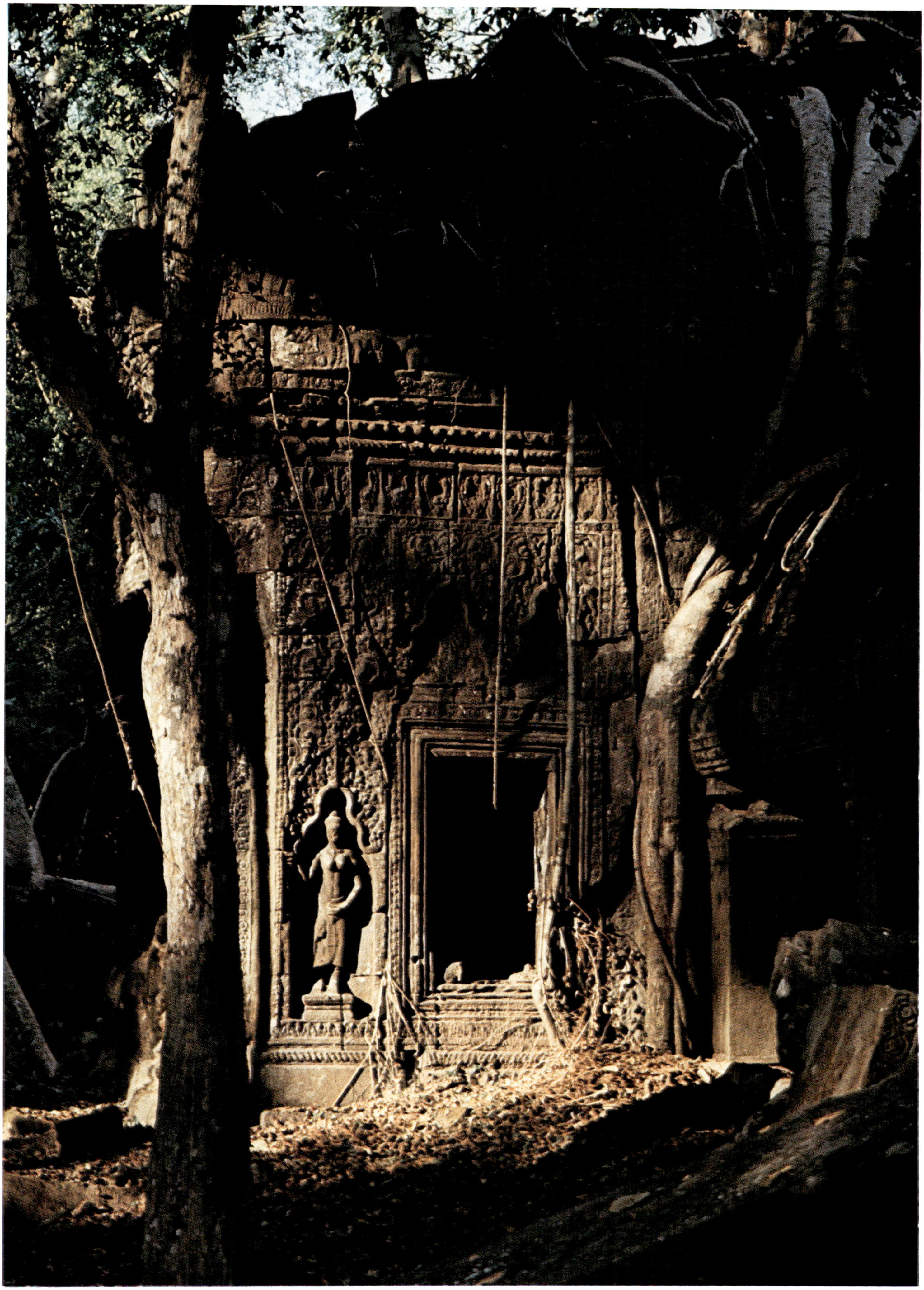

Jayavarman VII's Temples

Thanks to Jayavarman VII, the defeat of the Chams was followed by a period of intense architectural activity in the Angkor area. On the ruins of the old city, the victorious king laid the foundations for a throng of grandiose temples. The invaders had played havoc with the capital. The king first felt the need for a base of operations from which he would be able to supervise the rebuilding. He therefore erected a temple-city on the southeast corner of the Eastern Baray. This complex is known as Ta Prohm. The temple was consecrated in 1186, only five years after Jayavarman VII seized power in the country. The enclosure is 1000 m (3300 ft.) long and 600 m (1970 ft.) wide. One can now see the buildings just as they were discovered by explorers in the nineteenth century. The temple is completely overgrown. It looks magnificent and dramatic in this untamed wilderness.

Ta Prohm consists of three concentric enclosures. Most late Buddhist monasteries were indeed modeled after Bing Mealea. The first enclosure contains a prasat and a large mandapa, or assembly hall, the roof of which is supported on pillars. Covered passageways lead to the second enclosure. These connecting corridors constantly increase in number and complexity. The rigorous arrangement characteristic of classical architecture finally gives way to a jumble of halls, a confused network of galleries and passageways. The original plan was actually more restrained, but the monument underwent many transformations during its construction. It looks almost as if the Buddhist priests had modified the king's orders, adding all kinds of extras and outbuildings within the temple walls. The result is entangled baroque flamboyancy. An inscription at Ta Prohm indicates that the complex contained 39 sanctuaries, or prasats, 566 stone dwellings and 288 brick dwellings.

Lion standing watch on the edge of the Srah Srang basin at Angkor. There may have been some Chinese influence on Khmer art.

Right:
Like a "wharf", these terraces at Srah Srang with their Naga-parapets lead to the temple of Bantéay Kdei built by Jayavarman VII.

Inner Space

The temple was no longer exclusively a place of worship to which the king and the high priest alone had access: henceforth it was a Buddhist monastery inhabited by thousands of bonzes under the supervision of a fatherabbot.

Traditional forms were adapted to suit the special requirements of the Buddhist religion. Accent was shifted to inner space. The temples contained an increasing number of roofed halls. The ritual of the Hindu religion was very simple: the priest anointed the lingam or statue of the god with offerings of milk and butter. Buddha's Doctrine, however, calls for assemblies of the faithful who live together in religious communities. This explains the changes. These practical requirements gave birth to the jumbled, swarming mass of buildings crowded together in the courtyards of the various enclosures in which the bonzes dwelt. The cruciform courtyard was gradually changed into a kind of hypostyle hall. This trend implied new building techniques. However it was impossible to go beyond the technical limits inherent in the use of corbeled vaults: long spans without supports were out of the question. The traditional patios were not eliminated, but they became narrow shafts through which light came in and rain water was drained off. These light wells break the monotony of the hypostyle-type structures. After the thirteenth century, the same communal requirements caused a return to primitive building materials like wood and thatch...

Jayavarman VII did not build temples alone. Like his predecessors,

Gopura crowned by a tower at the temple of Bantéay Kdei built under Jayavarman VII. The mask carved on the tower is typical of the Bayon period. At the dawn of the thirteenth century, colossal masks were carved on the towers surmounting Angkor Thom's monumental gateways.

Jungle invaders still occupy the temple of Prah Khan at Angkor, built between 1184 and 1191. Are the roots of these enormous silk-cotton trees breaking or supporting the walls?

Vaulted halls in the temple of Prah Khan at Angkor. Henceforth temples were also used as monasteries and comprised an increasing number of buildings.

though on a smaller scale, he continued work on the irrigation system. He was probably first obliged to restore the entire network, repair the dykes, clean out the canals and renew the water supply in the barays. In front of the temple of Bantéay Kdei, begun at about the same time as Ta Prohm, he dug a vast rectangular ornamental lake, 750 m (2460 ft.) long and 400 m (1315 ft.) wide, known as Srah Srang. The temple itself consists of two enclosures surrounded by a double moat.

At the western end of Srah Srang is a structure recalling a "wharf". This cruciform terrace with steps going down to the water's edge exhibits beautiful Naga-parapets. Here once again, the Nagas are closely connected with water. In fact, the Nagas play an important part in all Cambodian religions, among both Hindus and Buddhists, to say nothing of pre-Khmer animists and water-worshippers. A wooden structure was probably built on the terrace overlooking the wharf.

North of Angkor, on the eastern bank of the new Neak Pean baray (3300 m — 10,870 ft. long and 1000 m — 3300 ft. wide) which runs along the side of the Eastern Baray, Jayavarman VII erected the great temple of Prah Khan. Under construction from 1184 to 1191, this temple ressembles Ta Prohm as far as the ground-plan goes. The monastery proper is contained within an inner enclosure 220 m (720 ft.) long and 170 m (560 ft.) wide. However the complex as a whole is no less than 960 m (3150 ft.) long and 700 m (2300 ft.) wide. It is surrounded by a moat and exhibits the four traditional median gopuras. Besides these gateways, the complex contains 102 towers, 485 stone buildings and 439 cells for the monks. In the centre of the temple complex is a large cruciform sanctuary with a mandapa. Four median connecting corridors lead to the sanctuary.

The cruciform courtyard has now become a hypostyle hall, similar to Indian ranga mandapas, intended for temple dancing-girls. North of this hall we see an astonishing structure consisting of two components: a terrace which probably supported a wooden construction and a pillared structure made up of columns arranged in rows of four supporting an upper level with windows but no stairway leading up to it. This minor structure, the purpose of which has not been ascertained, recalls provincial architecture from the Lower Empire, characterized by its massive cylindrical columns with bands round the base and the capital. Real columns are a brand new phenomenon in Khmer architecture. Previously the only cylindrical supports were piles supporting raised causeways which can be looked upon as petrifications of primitive footbridges.

At Prah Khan, instead of the several-storeyed roofs decorated with miniature pavilions which usually crown the prasats, the monks' cells exhibit dome-shaped roofs. They look like fleecy clouds that have come down and settled on the tree-tops. New requirements gradually changed the arrangement of space, mass and volume. But these complexes were built hastily and often carelessly. They foretell the rapid decay of Khmer architecture. Stone is not well bonded and the sculptural ornamentation is often dull and lifeless.

Classical galleries (broken on the corners) give way to genuine ring porticoes for the rite of circumambulation. The increasing importance of inner space calls for new kinds of roofing. Nevertheless, quantity has priority over quality. All the temples erected under Jayavarman VII are examples of quick and careless building. It seems as if the Khmers needed to feel reassured, as if they had a premonition of the impending and unrelenting decline of their civilization.

The Bayon

The most extraordinary monument raised by Jayavarman VII is the one he built in the centre of the new capital he founded about 1200. We mean to speak of the Bayon, the most important temple in the city of Angkor Thom. This creation is just the opposite of Angkor Wat. It is an intricate, bewildering and awe-inspiring complex that underwent many transformations during its construction. The Bayon represents the apotheosis of baroque architecture in Cambodia.

The Bayon's outer gallery, 130 m (430 ft.) wide and 140 m (460 ft.) long, consists of an open portico, as at Angkor Wat. The inner walls are blind and lavishly decorated with low reliefs. These carvings exhibit a noticeable trend towards naturalism. Unlike the official and hieratical scenes depicted at Angkor Wat, they more ressemble statues from the life. We shall say more about this astounding portrayal of everyday life in thirteenth century Cambodia later...

From an architectural standpoint, the accent is on inner space. This

Apsara carved on a jamb at Prah Khan.

Above:
In the jungle of Prah Khan at Angkor, an amazing pillared structure, the purpose of which has not been ascertained.

Left:
Massive columns made up of cylindrical drums support an upper level with square windows. The bases and capitals of the columns exhibit broad carved bands. No stairway leads to the upper level of this peculiar pillared structure at Prah Khan.

applies to both the median gopuras and the corner towers in the outer gallery of the Bayon. Both gopuras and towers have cruciform ground-plans. They recall the pillared structures first seen at Prah Khan. By means of twelve supports (the four central pillars are much thicker than the eight ones on the edges) architects created a roofed structure 20 m (66 ft.) long on each side. These dimensions are quite impressive, considering the use of corbeled vaults.

A ring courtyard leads to the second gallery which is only 70 m (230 ft.) wide and 80 m (263 ft.) long. Towers are built at intervals upon the gallery, one on each corner and three above each of the gopuras: sixteen towers all in all. Enormous masks representing Lokesvara are carved on each face of these towers. With their kind features, closed eyes and meditative expression, these masks are meant to portray not only the Buddha but also the divine king. Other towers on the corners of the cruciform structure surrounding the second gallery also exhibit these enormous masks looking in all four directions.

These smiling effigies of the god-king deep in meditation crown each and every one of the Bayon's 54 towers. The complex displays a total of 216 masks looking north, south, east and west as if to say that both religion and government are ubiquous. Yet this constellation of masked towers also represents a map of time, a gigantic materialization of lasting and passing time. Each of the four masks symbolizes one of the sun's positions on its course overhead: one of the heads is always in the sun, another in the shade, the other two half in the sun and half in the shade. The Bayon is a kind of symphony in light and dark consisting of variations on the theme of the sun moving across the sky beating time for the universe.

At the centre of the complex a huge tower rises on a circular base calling to mind traditional Buddhist stupas intended for the rite of circumambulation. The ground-plan is based on a magic diagram, or mandala, which here is round, in harmony with the spirit of Buddhist teachings. The Bayon was originally intended to be a flat temple. The central tower is the result of a transformation. Thanks to it, the complex became a genuine temple-mountain 42 m (138 ft.) high. Eight chapels radiate from the central sanctuary, forming a structure recalling the Wheel of the Doctrine. Four halls, one of which is a square pillared mandapa, stand in front of the circular sanctuary.

Sculptural Ornamentation

The relief sculptures decorating the outer gallery give us precious information about life in Angkor under the last great Khmer ruler. We

View of the galleries in the temple of Prah Khan at Angkor. A series of halls and doorways lead to the central sanctuary.

The ring galleries and gopuras in the Buddhist monastery of Prah Khan contain stone dwellings for the monks.

can see here all the events that took place during the war against the Chams, the great battles won by Jayavarman VII, the infantry, the war elephants and the long pirogues with their bronze prows. These vast compositions actually recount all the outstanding events that took place during the king's reign. The quality that marks them is a feeling for picturesque detail and keen observation. They show us wounded warriors at their last gasp, sailors devoured by crocodiles, infuriated enemies fighting tooth and nail. Besides the great military frescoes, we can also see quiet scenes: merchants argue in front of their stalls, cock-fights draw bettors, cooks prepare skewered meat and rice cakes, a Chinese trader gets off his junk and palavers on the wharf, hunters track wild animals in the forest, fishermen catch fish in the Great Lake.

This is an intimist art closely related to the joys and sorrows of everyday life. Buddha the Merciful One has toned down the pomp and ostentation of the king's court. These lively carvings form a vivid contrast to the grandiose hieratical style characteristic of Angkor Wat where we beheld portrayals of ceremonial etiquette, troops arrayed in meticulous order and the stiff and starchy elect enjoying themselves in a somewhat academic paradise...

At the Bayon an entire spiritual itinerary has been materialized in stone: by way of the moving universe symbolized by the masked towers, one can go from everyday life with its wars and quarrels, its peaceable customs and humble tasks to the motionless and unchanging embodiment of meditation and divine perfection.

Such is the pathetic message left us by Jayavarman VII, the last of the great Khmer rulers. During his reign, architecture went beyond its boundaries. It renounced the hieratical manner and abolished the dividing line between sculpture and structure. Mystic diagram and way of initiation all in one, it gave man a key to the universe and the heavenly world.

Below:
A wooden building probably stood on this laterite terrace facing the pillared structure at Prah Khan. String walls run along the stairways.

Frieze of dancing-girls decorating a lintel above a doorway in the temple of Prah Khan. During the Bayon period, the royal ballet played an increasingly important part in religious life. Some temples contain special halls for the dancing-girls.

Angkor Thom: Zenith and Decay of Khmer Art

The new trend in Khmer architecture reached its zenith at Angkor Thom, "the great royal city", founded by Jayavarman VII about 1200. In order to replace the cities devastated by the Chams, the king decided to build a new capital bigger and more beautiful than all those built before. City-planning was given broader symbolic meaning than ever before. The monuments are unbelievably bold and flamboyant. In fact, the creations at Angkor Thom rank among the most original in the history of Khmer art.

Angkor Thom is a fortified city. A moat 100 m (330 ft.) wide runs along the surrounding wall which forms an enormous quadrilateral 3 km (1.9 mi.) square. The perimeter of the moat measures 12 km (7.5 mi.). At the top of the wall there is a parapet walk. On the inside the wall is buttressed by a sloping glacis at the foot of which is a canal which runs all the way around the city. The moat is crossed over by median causeways on all four sides. These causeways go under huge arched gateways crowned with towers, or gopuras, bearing the effigy of Lokesvara, the Buddhist deity whose image also adorns the towers of the Bayon. The causeways then lead to the Bayon situated in the heart of the city. As stated above, Jayavarman VII looked upon himself as an earthly incarnation of the Buddha. The Bayon symbolized the ruler's apotheosis. The median causeways divide the city into four equal districts. In the northeastern sector yet a fifth causeway parallel to the one leading to the Bayon's main entrance, proceeds from the west face of the surrounding wall to the Gate of Victories and the royal palace. It is the only unsymmetrical feature in the complex.

The Giants' Causeway

On the five dykes which cross over the 100 m (330 ft.) wide moat faced with laterite blocks we find an extremely interesting work of art: the Giants' Causeway. The five causeways leading over the moat to the entrance gopuras have enormous carved stone parapets which may well have been inspired by Prah Khan. These parapets consist of 54 giants on each side holding the body of a colossal Naga.

The giants on the right when entering the city portray the guardian spirits of the underworld, the ones on the left the presiding genii of the heavens. The former are terrifying with their grimacing faces and protruding eyes; the latter have calm, haughty and serene expressions. The two Nagas held by these giants lift their heads and look one square in the eye when one approaches the city. Actually, seven open-fanged mouths ready to bite peep from under their swollen hoods. The mythical serpent's tail frames the entrance gopura.

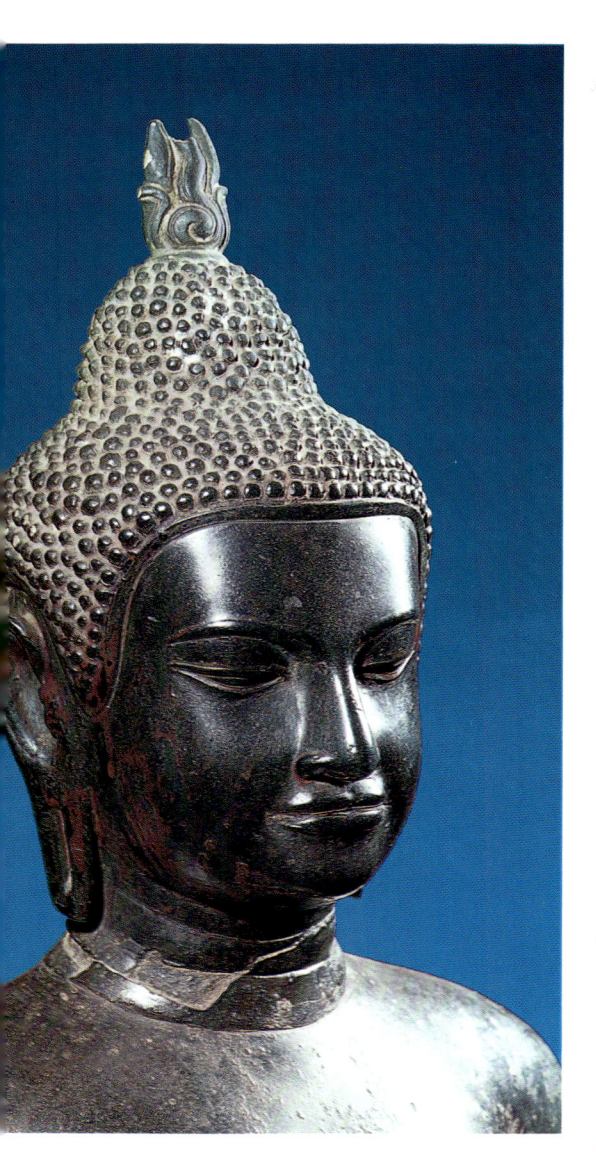

Bronze head of a standing Buddha which dates from the thirteenth century.

Facing page:
Meditating Buddha sitting on the coils of the Naga king in the shade of the serpent-deity's hood. This thirteenth century work of art found in the central sanctuary of the Bayon was originally decorated in several colours.

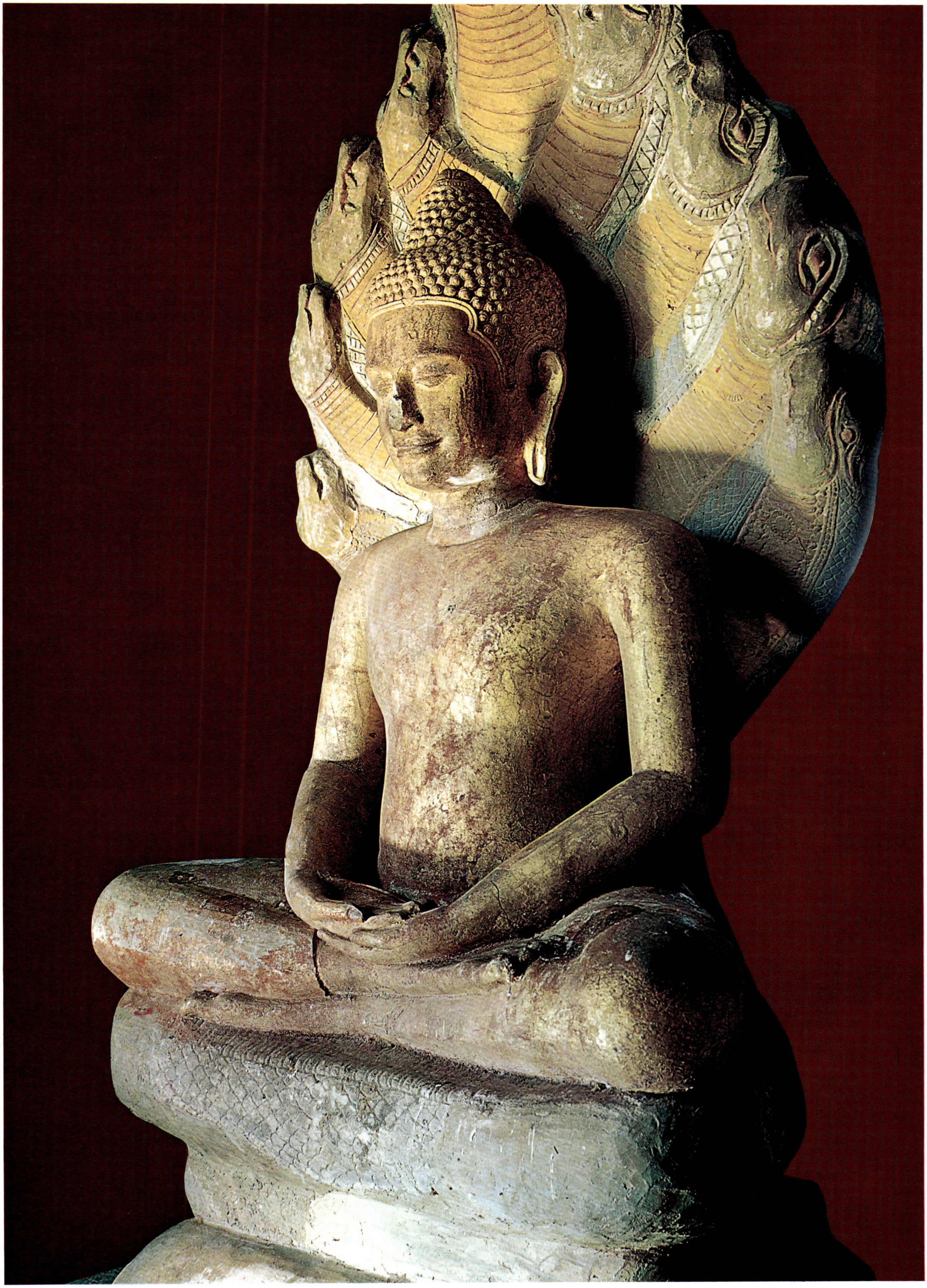

Below:
Causeway crossing over the moat at Angkor Thom. Parapets consisting of 54 giants on each side represent the Churning of the Sea of Milk: the creation of the universe as seen by Indian cosmology. In the background, a gopura gives access to the southern part of the city. The great Buddha heads carved on the towers portray the king as Lokesvara.

Detail of the face of a god adorning the Giants' Causeway leading to the royal city of Angkor Thom built in 1200 by Jayavarman VII.

This stupendous allegory carved in the round is several metres high and 100 m (330 ft.) long. It leads up to the colossal Lokesvara mask crowning the gateway. The theme portrayed is one of the great favourites in Indian mythology, the Churning of the Sea of Milk, which is supposed to symbolize the creation of the world. This Hindu theme, also portrayed in a remarkable low relief decorating the outer gallery at Angkor Wat, continued to inspire Buddhist carvers even after Jayavarman VII converted to the Buddhist faith. The Angkor Thom version is an unrivalled sculptural masterpiece.

The universe created by the gods is compared to the pat of butter that appears when cream is churned. The Asuras and Devas take turns pulling on the Nagas in order to get the ambrosia the ruler wishes to give to his subjects so as to guarantee them happiness and good fortune. But the Nagas are also the guardians of the treasure. This is why their fearsome heads rise up on the threshold of the causeway which crosses over the moat. Both gods and demons take part in the creation of the universe. This dualism accounts for the nature of the universe and results in the immortality of the elect.

Under the masked towers crowning the gopuras, in the re-entrant angles of the cruciform structure we find low reliefs portraying the three-headed elephant which the god Indra rides. In Hindu mythology, Indra is the thunder-bearer, master of the heavens inhabited by the Thirty-three gods. Though the ruler adopted the Buddhist faith, he by no means renounced the symbolic language derived from Hindu mythology. The result is an imposing syncretism combining the two religions imported from India.

Principles of Khmer City-Planning

We have already mentioned several Khmer capitals such as Yasodharapura with its centre at Phnom Bakheng, and Udayadityavarman's capital built round the Baphuon. Like Angkor Thom, these cities had a square layout. One may be wondering what the guiding principles of Khmer city-planning actually were.

As in all fields, Indian influence was decisive. Indian city-planning followed strict rules. The founding of a city was an extremely important event. All kinds of magical and religious precautions had to be taken in order to guarantee the success of the undertaking and the well-being of

Causeway crossing over the moat at Angkor Thom, viewed from the top of the wall surrounding the city. Some of the giants lining the causeway are heavenly genii, others are demons. The moat is dry.

Smiling god adorning the Giants' causeway at Angkor Thom.

the inhabitants. Indian cities had square layouts, since this geometric figure was supposed to symbolize stability and absolute perfection. The layout was based on a magic diagram known as a mandala: a circular figure inscribed in a square itself subdivided into a chequer-board comprising a given number of units, or padas. Mandalas of increasing complexity were employed as cities grew bigger. A city with two units on each side contained four padas. If each side was subdivided in three, there were nine padas, and so forth: the resulting chequer-board could comprise 16, 25, 36, 64, 100 or even 144 padas... Indian cities usually had a symmetrical layout with an equal number of padas on either side of the main axis. When the sum was an even number, the figure was known as a manduka. The square city was also divided into four equal parts by median causeways meeting at right angles. Khmer city-planning employed a similar arrangement, recalling the Romans with their "cardo" and "decumanus". The temple was situated at the intersection of the median causeways and the perpendicular connecting heaven and earth at the summit of Mount Meru, the sacred mountain on which the gods built their heavenly dwellings. Man communicated with the gods by climbing the World Mountain which was believed to be the earth's axis. The city itself was a replica of the cosmos. The moat represented the primordial ocean encircling the universe.

The enormous city of Angkor Thom (it covers an area of 9 square kilometres — 3.6 sq. mi.) was also laid out according to a mandala which we have attempted to reconstruct. How many padas did Jayavarman VII's city comprise? In order to answer this question, we have examined the city's subdivisions, taking into account the asymmetrical causeway leading through the Gate of Victories to the royal palace. One of the main subdivisions is located in the northeastern sector between the eastern causeway and the northern moat and comprises one third of this sector. In addition, a perpendicular canal in the southwestern sector cuts the area comprised between the moat and the southern causeway in half. Each side of the square should consequently be divided into fourths and sixths, the pada being a common multiple of these two fractions ($1/4$ and $1/6$), i.e. one twelfth. The city of Angkor Thom contains 144 padas, twelve on each side. Each pada is about 250 m (820 ft.) square and covers an area of 62,500 square metres (75,000 sq. yd.).

As for Angkor Thom's hydrological system, the moat, 100 m (330 ft.) wide and 5-6 m (16-20 ft.) deep, was broken into four sections by the median causeways. It brought fresh water to the city on the northeast. Waste water was drained off on the southwest. Within the city itself, canals run along either side of the causeways. These canals lead to

Engraving by Louis Delaporte showing the Bayon restored as the artist imagined it in 1868.

Aerial view of the Bayon at the centre of Angkor Thom. This monument erected at the dawn of the thirteenth century is the most intricate and fascinating creation of Khmer architecture. Each and every one of its 54 towers is decorated with four huge Buddha heads portraying Jayavarman VII for a total of 216 enormous masks looking in all four directions.

another large canal which runs along the inner perimeter of the surrounding wall. Since the ground sloped down gradually from north to south, it was possible to keep the circulation of fresh drinking water apart from the discharge of waste water which flowed into a basin at the southeast corner of the city. This basin called Beng Thom was 400 m (1300 ft.) long and 200 m (660 ft.) wide. Proceeding from the basin, vaulted canals 60 m (197 ft.) long and 10 m (33 ft.) wide emptied into the outer moat.

This network also made water transport possible within the city of Angkor Thom. Jayavarman VII's capital with its canals running along raised causeways was in fact a kind of Southeast Asian Venice. A compact network of canals divided the residential areas into padas. Straw huts with thatched roofs were built on these padas. The Chinese traveller Tcheou Ta-Kouan who visited Angkor Thom when the city was at the peak of its glory, states that tiles were used only for the temples and the king's palace. He adds that the size of the dwellings varied according to their owner's social status. This rule was also followed by Indian, Chinese and Japanese city-planners during the mediaeval period. The palace, all the official buildings and the noblemen's dwellings were built facing east. Wooden constructions were oriented along the same line as the Bayon.

The Population of Angkor

How many people actually lived in Greater Angkor in the twelfth and thirteenth centuries when the Khmer capital was in the hey-day of its splendour? We can make one estimate based on the amount of land under cultivation and another one based on the housing density. With the help of ancient texts, we shall then attempt to corroborate these estimates.

Aerial photography has enabled us to reestablish the Khmer land register. As stated above, rice was probably grown on about 60,000 hectares (150,000 a.). The cities and villages, barays, roads, canals, pasture

Detail of a mask carved on a tower of the Bayon: a smiling Buddha watching over the city of Angkor Thom.

Detail of a low relief decorating the Bayon. These carvings which date back to the thirteenth century show Khmer warriors armed with javelins launching an attack.

Right:
Work of a tower cleaning, having the faces of Bayon, according to a picture by Louis Delaporte.

lands and fields devoted to other less important crops such as fruit and leguminous plants occupied about 40,000 hectares (100,000 a.). The 60,000 hectares of rice plantations were divided up among smallholders. Each family cultivated about two hectares (5 a.), provided they had enough hands to accomplish the complicated tasks involved in growing rice: plowing, sowing in beds, flooding, transplanting, irrigating, reaping, threshing, hulling, etc. The average Khmer family had about ten members all of whom lived in a straw hut built on piles. Four or five members were of an age to work in the fields. At least two working hands were needed to cultivate one hectare of rice, three counting the women who helped with the wearisome task of transplanting.

A first estimate based on the amount of land devoted to the intensive cultivation of rice by the Khmers of Angkor shows that there must have been at least 150,000 farm workers. Counting their families, they made up a population of 300,000 or 400,000 people. If we add to this number the fishermen, stock breeders and their families, we obtain a total of half a million people who made up the rural class and lived outside the city walls.

We can attempt to make a second estimate on the basis of what we know about Khmer urban centres. Supposing half of the walled city of Angkor Thom (9 sq. km — 3.6 sq. mi.) was taken up by the temples, palace complex, streets and canals, we are left with a remainder of some 5 square kilometres (2 sq. mi.) on which the straw huts of the common people — the most important class of Khmer society, numerically speaking — were built. These straw huts, identical with the ones the peasants lived in, were about 8 m (26 ft.) long and 4 m (13 ft.) wide. They were built in small gardens shaded by sugar palms. The lots covered an area of no more than 400-500 square metres (480-600 sq. yd.). The city of Angkor Thom alone may well have contained from 10,000 to 12,000 straw huts housing about ten people each for a total of 120,000 inhabitants.

Facing page, top:
The Bayon viewed from the ground. In the foreground, the outer gallery decorated with remarkable low reliefs illustrating battle scenes and everyday life at Angkor Thom. The structure has lost its roof.

Taking into account the various older urban centres which had not yet been abandoned (such as Roluos and Angkor Wat), as well as the countless towns founded by Jayavarman VII himself on the outskirts of Angkor Thom, the Khmer capital in its hey-day probably had a population of about 200,000-250,000 inhabitants including merchants and craftsmen as well as the army, water police, government employees and courtiers.

Adding the rural population and the urban population, it would seem that Angkor must have had from 700,000 to 750,000 inhabitants in the twelfth and thirteenth centuries. One may be inclined to be sceptical about such a dense population, but the fact remains that though

Unfinished battle scene carved in low relief on a wall of the Bayon: Jayavarman VII is about to take the Chams by surprise and drive them out of Angkor. Elephants support the infantry's advance.

thirteenth century Paris had only 100,000 inhabitants, on the other hand Changan, the capital of China from the seventh through the twelfth century, had over one million inhabitants living within its walls (the walls were 10 km — 6 mi. long and 8 km — 5 mi. wide). In China, as in the Khmer kingdom, the intensive cultivation of rice made this possible. The irrigated rice-fields were a necessary source of food supply for a great population. Rice alone was responsible for these large urban concentrations in mediaeval Asia.

We have mentioned a text corroborating our estimates. An inscription carved on a wall of the Ta Prohm temple at Angkor, erected in 1186, clearly states that "12,640 people dwelt within the temple walls." The outer surrounding wall is 1000 m (3300 ft.) long and 600 m (1970 ft.) wide. The total area comprised within the temple walls is therefore about 600,000 square metres (720,000 sq. yd.). The temple proper, along with its basins and causeways, covers an area of about 100,000 square metres (120,000 sq. yd.). The remaining area (500,000 square metres — 600,000 sq. yd.) was divided into lots of 500 square metres (600 sq. yd.) each, on which straw huts were built. According to our

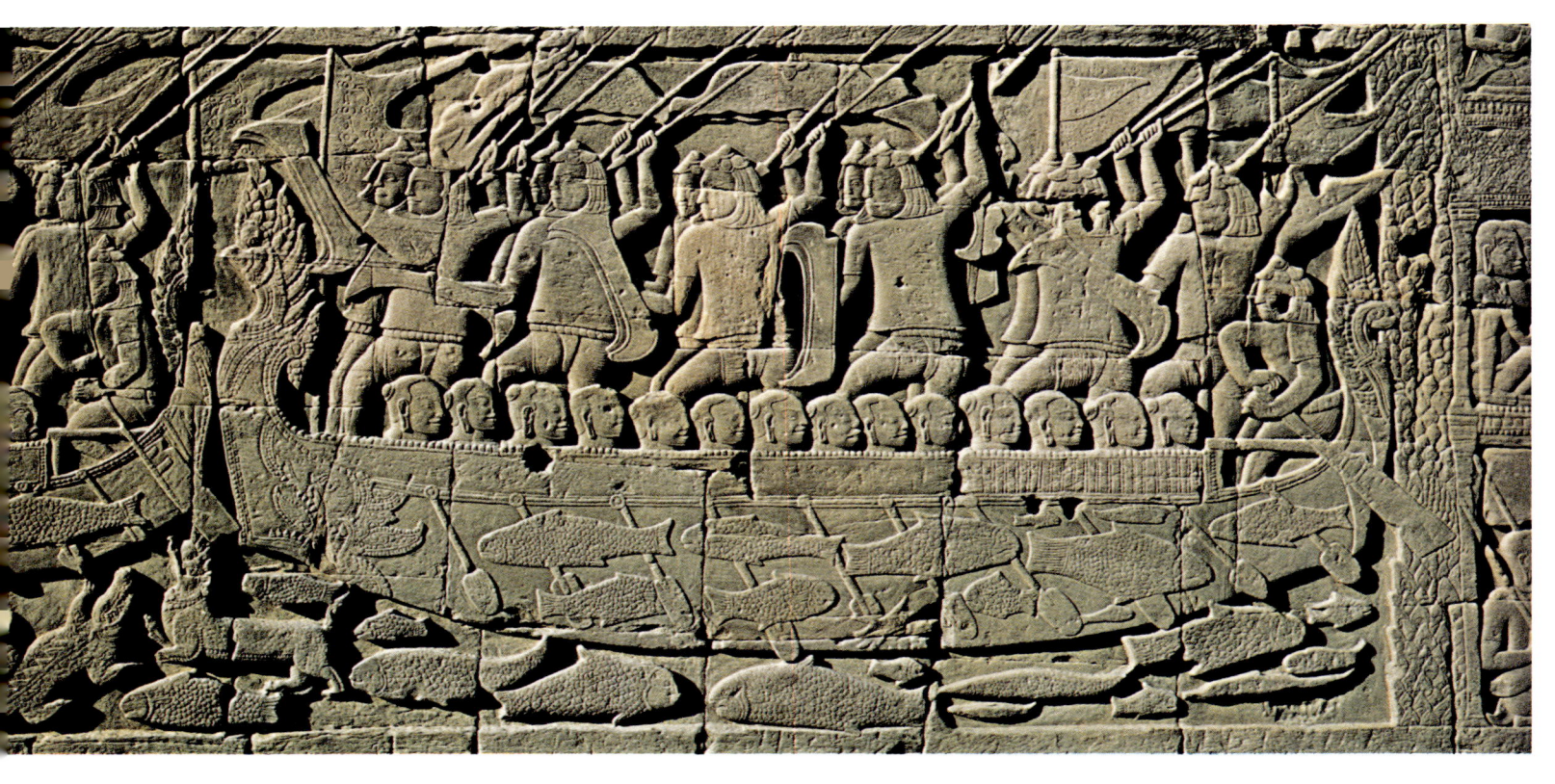

Low relief decorating a wall of the Bayon: Cham naval forces attacking Angkor. We can make out the landing troops armed with lances and shields, the oarsmen's heads, the boats' bronze prows and the fish swimming in the river.

Hunters on the look-out for storks in the Cambodian forest. Low relief decorating the Bayon at Angkor.

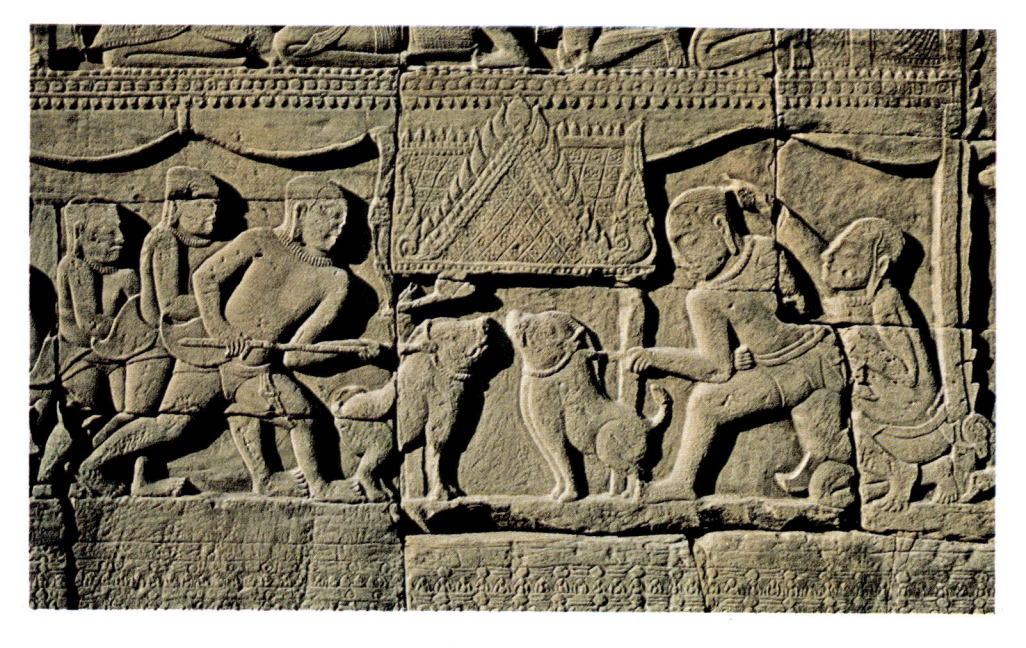

Jayavarman VII's soldiers just loved wild boar fights. The ring is in the shade of a lavishly decorated porch roof. Low relief at the Bayon.

estimate, 1000 straw huts housing from 10 to 12 people each do indeed give us a total of 12,000 inhabitants. The inscription seems therefore to confirm our estimate of the total urban population of Angkor.

As stated above, the intensive cultivation of rice in the Angkor area yielded from 130,000 to 150,000 metric tons per year. If each Khmer citizen ate from 250 to 300 gr (8.75-9.5 oz.) of rice daily (i.e. over 3000 calories), the population of Angkor consumed, for its own needs, about 80,000 metric tons of rice per year. We are left with a surplus of 60,000-70,000 metric tons, accounting for about 40% of the total production. Angkor owed its prosperity to this tremendous food surplus. The Khmer kingdom was the main rice-producing area of Southeast Asia. The sale of rice to Chinese and Indian traders made possible the construction of the great irrigation works and magnificent temple-palaces of the Khmer empire.

Rice enabled the Khmer rulers to finance their great architectural undertakings and support the thousands of artists and craftsmen in their employ.

The Downfall of Angkor

Under Jayavarman VII, Khmer civilization reached a new peak after the collapse caused by the Cham invasion. At the dawn of the thirteenth century, Angkor experienced an extraordinary renaissance attested by the creation of a new art style and the founding of a magnificent capital. Only a short time later, the Khmer kingdom was struck down by sudden death. The population, weakened by work on the countless building sites of Jayavarman VII, was no longer strong enough to hold out against the attacks of new invaders. The main danger was no longer Champa, situated east of Angkor. The new threat lay on the western frontier. Driven south by the Mongols who were descending upon Indo-China by way of the Burmese valleys, the Thais were penetrating deeper and deeper into the Menam basin. The Chams took advantage of the situation and threw off the Khmer yoke. About the same time, in the late thirteenth century, Tcheou Ta-Kouan came to Angkor as an ambassador and admired the last radiance of this glorious civilization which had ruled over the whole of Southeast Asia. Shortly after his visit, the Khmers lost all their influence in Indo-China.

During the fourteenth century, a few insignificant kings came to the throne of Angkor. In the mid-fifteenth century, the city was abandoned. Though the ancient capital was temporarily reoccupied by Satha about 1570 after a king named Ang Chan "rediscovered" it while on a hunting expedition, though the temple of Angkor Wat was kept in repair until

The masked towers of the Bayon may well be the most fascinating creation of thirteenth century Khmer architecture.

Facing page:
View of the Bayon in the midst of the Cambodian jungle. The masks carved on the temple towers portray Jayavarman VII as the Buddha.

The masked towers as seen from the terraces of the Bayon. There is no dividing line here between sculpture and architecture.

1587 or 1593, the fact remains that the decay of Angkor was incredibly rapid. How can this sudden downfall be explained?

In 1353, 1393 and 1431 the royal city of Angkor was seized, plundered and laid waste by Siamese invaders from the Thai kingdom which had been established west of Cambodia. After these reverses, the central government was no longer strong enough to prevent the barays and canals from silting up. The last kings of Angkor failed to keep the irrigation system working simply because they did not have enough manpower to clean out the canals and artificial lakes. The failure of the irrigation system put the food supply in jeopardy.

Nevertheless, Angkor was abandoned quite abruptly. Why? Some archaeologists presume that a dyke broke, causing calamitous flooding. In some places diggings have revealed a layer of alluvial deposits.

All of these factors doubtless helped bring about the country's downfall. However we believe there was yet another determining cause. During the Siamese invasions, the irrigation system was certainly badly damaged. The precarious balance man had created artificially by means of canals and barays was disturbed. The water flow changed. In the canals clear river water replaced the muddy water which had kept the fields fertile for such a long time. The flow was no longer strong enough to carry along sediment torn from the banks. As soon as the water cleared up, malaria became a problem. Anopheles mosquitoes do not lay eggs in muddy water. Both the adults and the larvae show a marked preference for clear water. The population of Angkor was probably decimated by fevers and malaria before the enormous city was abandoned. An ecological catastrophe brought the incredible irrigation system to a standstill. As a result, the Khmers lost their wealth, prosperity and power. Rice production ceased as if it had been under a curse. The survivors went back to the sites where their ancestors had lived before the rise of Khmer civilization and the creation of the rice factory which had been the main cause of their splendour and glory.

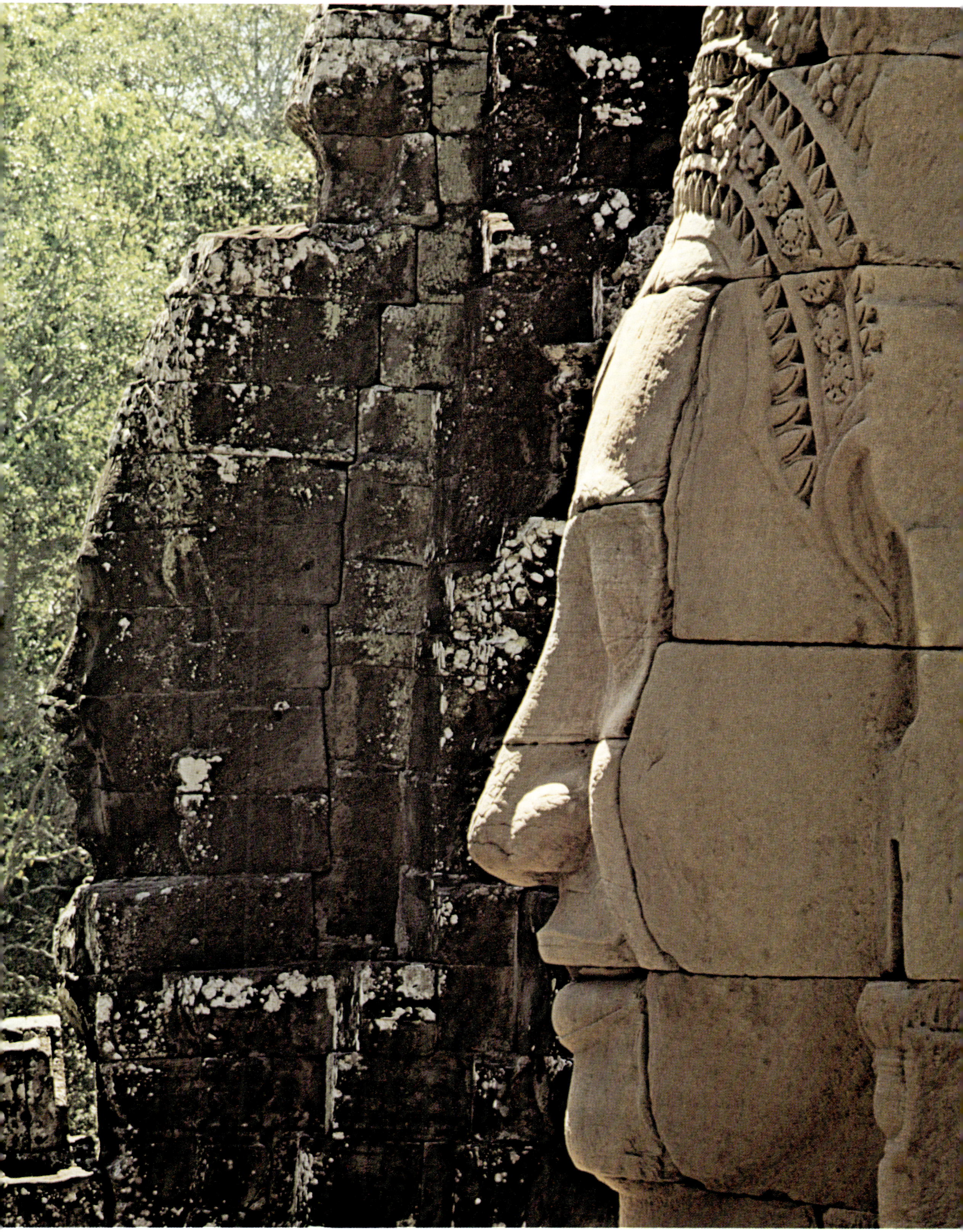

The Arts of Champa, Thailand and Burma

The neighbours of the Khmer kingdom in Indo-China were Hinduized at an early date. Subdued by the Khmers, they then came under Cambodian influence and their art traditions went through about the same evolution. This is especially true of Champa, situated east of Cambodia.

The Chams defeated Angkor for the first time and brought about the first collapse of Khmer civilization during the period of dynastic instability following the reign of Suryavarman II. Their cultural development followed a parallel course.

The earliest monuments, generally constructed in brick, are quite similar to Khmer sanctuaries at Sambor Prei Kuk and Kulen. The roofs of the prasats are constructed in storeys of decreasing dimensions decorated with miniature pavilions symbolizing the dwellings of the gods at the summit of Mount Meru. Stone is seldom used and only for ornamental features such as lintels and relief sculptures.

The Chams were traditionally a sea-faring people. The early period of Cham architecture, dating back to the seventh and eighth centuries, was characterized by a marked Indonesian influence. This first Mi-son period was followed by a Buddhist transition style, a good example of which is the important monastery erected at Dong-Duong in the ninth century. A Hindu revival took place in Champa in the twelfth and thirteenth centuries. The result was the second Mi-son style and the striking Binh-dinh complexes, remarkable for their colossal towers the quincuncial arrangement of which is derived from Angkor.

However the Annamites were continually encroaching on the northern frontiers. The Chams were pushed south until their kingdom finally disappeared in the fourteenth century.

The last Cham monuments mark the end of Hindu dominion in Indo-China. About the same time, the Khmer ruler converted to the Buddhist faith. While the cult of Sakyamuni was losing ground in India, the Southeast Asian followers of the Blessed One kept up the ancient traditions of Buddhist architecture as conceived at Sanchi more than one thousand years before.

Birth of the Thai State

As stated in the preceding chapter, the Thais were the people who succeeded in destroying the highly developed Khmer civilization and ruining the majestic city of Angkor with its fabulous irrigation system. The Thai kingdom was situated in the Menam basin west of Cambodia in a region which had long been under Khmer suzerainty. Other cultures had developed in the country, formerly known as Siam, before the Thais settled there.

This female deity found at Aranya Pratet on the Cambodian border shows great affinities with Khmer art. It dates from the seventh century.

Facing page:
This small bronze standing Buddha dating from the fifth or sixth century was found at Nakhon Pathom in the Menam delta.

As far back as the seventh century, the Buddhist kingdom of Dvaravati which had its capital at Nakhon Pathom in the Menam delta asserted its influence in western Founan. Founan was the cultural forefather of the Khmer civilization. This early period was characterized by Indian influence, particularly on the Malay peninsula where works of architecture have direct connections with Indian originals, among others the monuments erected by the Hindu Pallava dynasty on the Coromandel Coast. Hindu art traditions gained ground in the eighth century when the Srivijaya dynasty from Sumatra took hold of the Malacca peninsula. Both Buddhist and Hindu monuments so much ressemble their Indian prototypes that it is hard to say whether they were imported by Indian traders and missionaries or copied on the spot by Siamese artists.

In the eleventh century, the Khmers occupied the Lopburi region and the Korat plateau situated northwest of Angkor. Cambodian art exerted a very strong influence on art traditions in these two regions. Even before the eleventh century, Khmer art forms had penetrated into Siam: one of the most beautiful statues of the female deity made in the seventh century (Sambor Prei Kuk period) has been found at Aranya Pratet in the frontier province of Battambang, a traditional cause of conflicts between Siamese and Cambodians.

Classic Khmer temples such as those at Phimai and Lopburi bear witness to the fact that Khmer expansion was not merely a political matter. When Jayavarman VII seized almost the whole of Siam, he also exported Cambodian art traditions.

The Wat Chet Yot at Xieng Mai in northern Thailand is a Buddhist temple erected in the fifteenth century. This edifice constructed in laterite, brick and stucco owes something to Burma. The inner chambers exhibit barrel-vaults. This monument was raised for the 2000th anniversary of Buddha's death. It was modeled after the Indian temple at Bodhgaya, a copy of which had already been built at Pagan in the thirteenth century.

After a whole series of revolts against their suzerains, the Thais finally threw off the Khmer yoke in the thirteenth century and founded a kingdom with its capital at Sukhothai. The Lopburi region remained independent until the establishment of the kingdom of U Thong in 1350. With the founding of Ayuthia, the country was finally united.

Origin of the Thais

Who were the Thais and where did they come from? They were a highland people driven out of the Blue River valley by the Chinese advance. They fled southwards and crossed the mountainous regions of Laos and Upper Burma before reaching the Indochinese lowlands about the tenth century. They were a tribal society and had no religion, culture or alphabet of their own. They often went into the service of the Khmer

The Chai Mongkon within the walls of the Temple of the Supreme Patriarch built at Ayuthia in the fourteenth century. It was constructed entirely in brick. The small stuccoed stupa crowning the main tower was added in the late sixteenth century. The tiny minor shrines surmounted by cone-shaped spires are typical of the Ayuthia school.

This reclining Buddha symbolizing Guatama on the threshold of death was carved at Sukhothai in the fifteenth century. The painted ornamentation and disciples were added in the nineteenth century when the statue was moved to Bangkok.

Facing page:
This colossal Buddha head was cast in bronze and gilded at Ayuthia in the late fifteenth century. It is 170 cm (68 in.) high and exhibits all the main characteristics of Thai sculpture: conventionalized features, sharp lines, clear volumes. It is truly a masterpiece of Southeast Asian bronze sculpture.

rulers of Angkor. Low reliefs at Angkor Wat show Thai scouts reconnoitring for the Cambodian troops. When the decline of the Khmer empire began, the Thai vassals attacked their former masters and threw off the cambodian yoke.

When they settled in the Menam basin, they converted to Buddhism under the influence of the Dvaravati kingdom. When the Mongol invasions convulsed northern Indo-China, they set about carving out an independent Thai realm, encroaching upon the territory of both Burma and Siam. In a series of daring raids they subdued Cambodia and seized Angkor. The kingdom of Sukhothai was established in 1287, the same year the Mongols destroyed the enormous city of Pagan, capital of Burma.

Unlike the Khmer world which drew inspiration from both Hindu and Buddhist traditions, the Thais remained faithful to Sakyamuni. However, even after the triumph of Buddhist doctrine, the Brahminic "idols" were not wholly repudiated. The thirty-three deities dwelling at the summit of Mount Meru were still honoured by the Thais. Furthermore, in the kingdoms of Ayuthia and Bangkok, Hindu rites were performed at the king's court. All the Indianized realms in Southeast Asia were indeed characterized by this syncretism, combining the great religious systems born in India. The same is true of Thai art, in which Indian and Khmer features were united with truly national art forms.

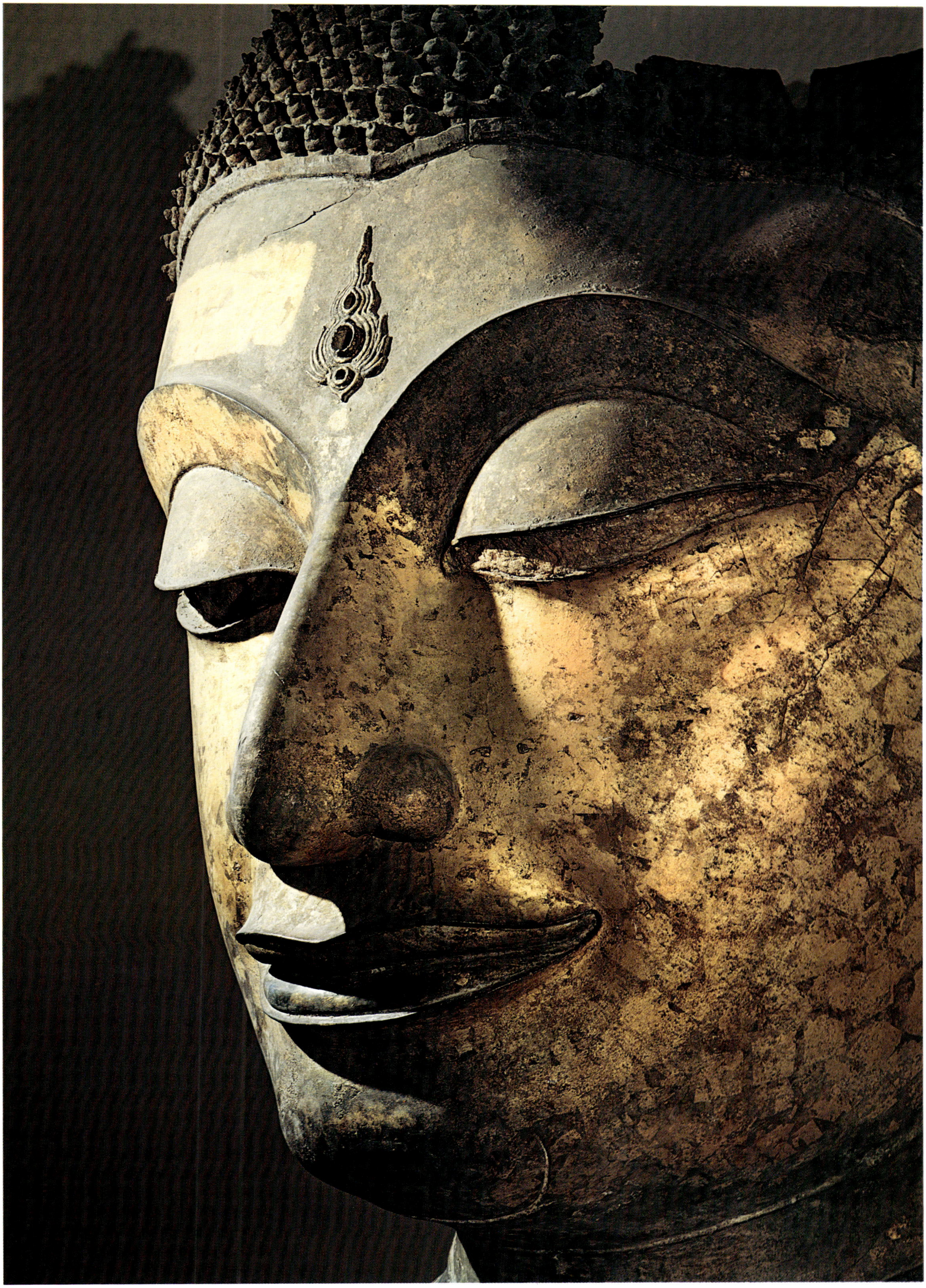

Below:
This carved wooden footprint of the Buddha is 220 cm (88 in.) long. It is stylized. All the toes have the same length. This specimen of the Ayuthia school dates from the fifteenth century. It can be seen at the Wat Pra Rup at Suphanburi in the Menam delta.

The Wat Pra That Haripunchai stupa at Lamphun, the ancient city of Haripunjaya, was built in 1447. Most Buddhist stupas in northern Thailand looked about the same.

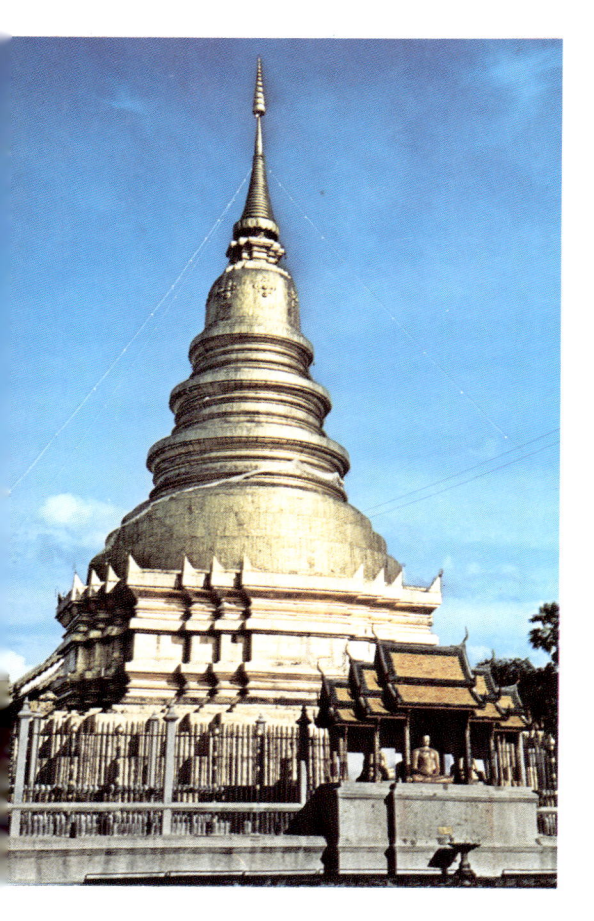

Siamese Modes of Expression

In the eleventh, twelfth and thirteenth centuries, the architecture of the Menam basin was unmistakably Khmer. The temples were constructed in stone, as at Angkor. During the Thai period, however, stone as a building material was replaced by brick and stucco. The Sukhothai temple consists of a tower, or prang, in front of which is a pillared mandapa. It has obvious connections with both Hindu sanctuaries and bell-shaped Burmese Buddhist stupas. These traditional forms were gradually departed from. Accent was shifted from over-all architectural structure to formal and decorative symbolism. Khmer features were "caricatured". Thai art also came under Burmese influence. The prangs (the Siamese equivalents to the Khmer prasats) became loftier, more slender and aspiring. As a rule, these towers culminate in stupa-like structures crowned by spires. The walls, formerly characterized by the set-backs inherent in cruciform ground-plans, are decorated with a series of stucco carvings in low relief. They exhibit reduplications of the ring of Buddhas running along the walls of the sanctuary and the prayer room.

As early as the Sukhothai period, but even more so after the foundation of Ayuthia, there developed a distinctively Siamese sculpture. Khmer, Burmese, Himalayan and South Chinese contributions somewhat modified the legacy of India, Java and Sumatra. All these trends were assimilated. Thai sculpture is characterized by its beautiful forms. Thailand's most important artistical contribution is indeed in the field of sculpture.

Thai Buddha images are highly stylized: an aquiline nose with a sharp bridge joining the curve of the eyebrows, half-closed eyes with sinuous slits suggesting meditation, full lips lit up by a slight smile of bliss, severe and restrained forms. Particularly in the art of bronzes, Ayuthia statues are characterized by their extraordinary expressiveness and purity of line.

From Sukhothai to Ayuthia

Founded by King Rama Kamheng who reformed the country's laws and religion and gave the Thais their alphabet (derived from the Khmer alphabet), the kingdom of Sukhtothai extended from the Menam basin to Ligore in the southern part of the Malay peninsula. After sixty-six years of existence, Sukhothai was annexed in 1353 by the new-born kingdom of Ayuthia with its capital of the same name, founded in 1347.

In the far north, however, the kingdom of Lan-na with its capital at Xieng Mai remained independent through the eighteenth century. As

Detail of a gilded bronze Buddha (153 cm — 61 in. high) dating back to the seventeenth century. Though made during the Ayuthia period, the head-dress and jewelled diadem recall the Sukhothai school.

Under the influence of Siamese Arts the Lao architecture of Wat Pra Khao at Vieng Chan, according to a picture by Louis Delaporte (1873).

Facing page, left:
The great Wat Phu Khao Thong cetiya, erected in 1569 north of Ayuthia, is a good example of the Mon style. It was built by the Burmese in order to commemorate their victory over the Thais.

Facing page, right:
Sixteenth century bronze from the Xieng Mai area. It is 74 cm (29.6 in.) high and represents a Buddhist deity at prayers. The figure is wearing lavish attire and a gilt diadem.

This reclining Buddha waiting for death is 28 m (92 ft.) long. It dates from the mid-eighteenth century and can be seen at Ayuthia. The Pra Buddha Sai-Yat, as it is called, is constructed in brick and stuccoed. The forms and clothing are simplified.

far as art and culture are concerend, this district belonged to Burma's sphere of influence.

After the decisive victories gained against the Khmers and the influx of riches from the plundering of their capital, Angkor, the city of Ayuthia became one of the most important urban centres in Indo-China. Angkor could no longer compete with the Thai realm which thus had plenty of room to expand and soon became the major power in Southeast Asia. During this period of prosperity, countless Buddhist monasteries were built. The city constantly expanded. Artistic production was considerable. Thousands of statues of standing, walking, squatting and seated Buddhas were cast in bronze. The stupas took on slender forms and were crowned by needle-shaped spires which give them a very elegant appearance. Some of them contained royal burial chambers where votive offerings were made. These chambers were decorated with beautiful murals.

However this period of prosperity came to a sudden end in 1767 when the Burmese took Ayuthia. The invaders set fire to the city, reduced it to ashes and then withdrew.

Bangkok and Light Architecture

When the Siamese shifted their capital to Bangkok, architecture also changed. There was a return to the forms typical of wooden architecture

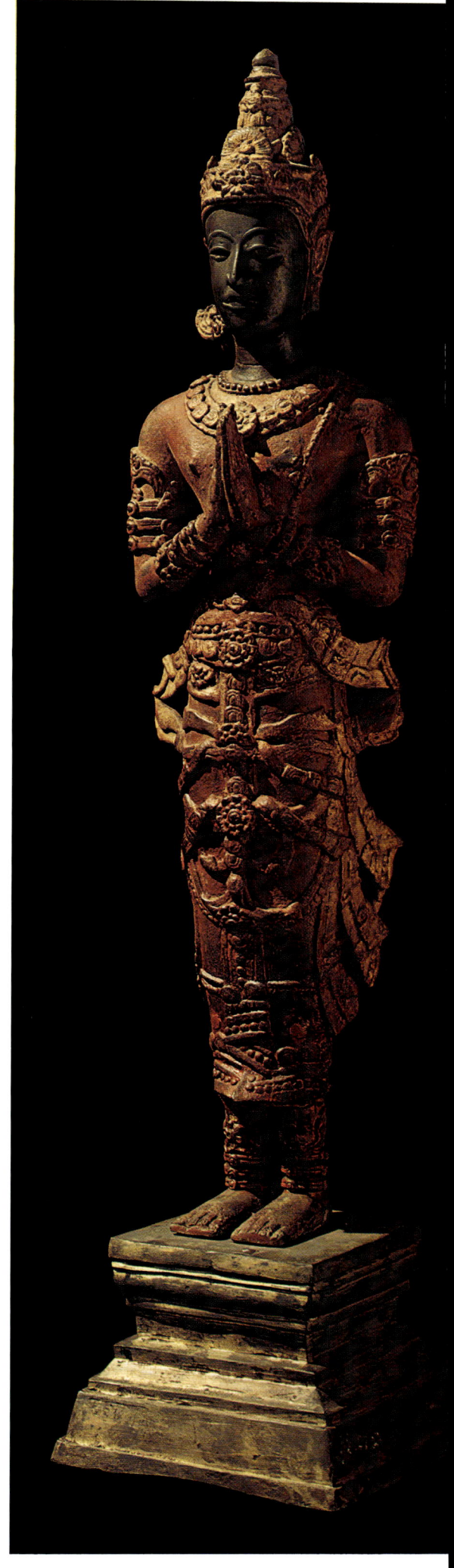

Detail of a Garuda mural at the Wat Po, at Bangkok. These gilded stucco sculptures date from 1793. The Garuda bird is holding two Nagas by their tails.

The "Temple of Marble" at Bangkok, built in the nineteenth century. Its real name is the Wat Benchamabopit-Viharn. The structure owes something to China as witness the lacquered tiles and slightly curved sloping roofs.

with sloping tiled roofs. Khmer palaces portrayed in the low reliefs decorating Angkor Wat and the Bayon exhibit similar features, derived from traditional wood and straw constructions dating from before the use of stone as a building material. When stone came into use, the forms and structures characteristic of these wooden prototypes were simply "petrified". The raised footbridges built on piles found at most Khmer temples as well as the traceried windows with their stone balusters seen at Angkor are good examples of this phenomenon.

This light architecture was in favour at Angkor under Jayavarman VII. The Buddhists prefered it for their monasteries, pagodas and vast assembly halls. It was probably widespread in Thailand in both the Sukhothai and Ayuthia kingdoms. However some of these buildings were destroyed by the tropical climate, others by the terrible Burmese invasion. None have survived. The only examples that can now be seen date from the Bangkok period (late eighteenth and nineteenth centuries).

The general contour of these buildings consists of straight lines meeting at right angles. The roofs are supported on pillars standing at regular intervals. Every set-back in the façade — porch or penthouse — is topped by a saddle-back roof perpendicular to the main ridge, making for a system of crossed gables. The roofs are arranged in recessed tiers recalling classical Khmer architecture at Bantéay Srei and Angkor Wat where each tier displays a carved pediment. The over-all design displays the same feeling for elegant forms which marks Thai sculptures.

The buildings constructed in perishable materials at Bangkok are actually not particularly original from an architectural point of view. Similar structures can be seen throughout the Indochinese peninsula. The most interesting thing about the ones at Bangkok is their polychrome decoration. The gilt statues, colourful lacquered roof tiles and ornamental motifs give us an idea of what the stone monuments at Angkor may originally have looked like. These Thai buildings with their slender, aspiring and slightly curved roofs also somewhat recall Chinese architecture...

Indochinese art was already on the decline during this period. The Bangkok style is characterized by stereotyped forms and superfluous, overwrought ornamentation. These buildings, genuine "living fossils", can nevertheless be looked upon as the last echoes of the grandiose Indochinese civilizations.

Burmese Art and Architecture

Burma is situated in the northwestern part of the Indochinese peninsula. It is a hilly and mountainous region crossed by the great Irrawaddy river which flows down from the Himalayan ranges. The country comprises two areas, both of which came under the cultural influence of India: Upper Burma in the sun-scorched plain surrounding the city of Pagan, and Lower Burma, situated in the Irrawaddy delta.

As early as the third century B. C., the Buddhist doctrine was brought to Burma by a missionary sent out by King Asoka, the first Indian ruler to convert to Buddhism and devote himself to the promotion of the new faith. Later on, Hindu missionaries also settled in Burma, but Buddhism has remained the country's main religion. Burmese royal temples were mostly dedicated to Hindu gods. The king was the patron of the Brahmins who served him as counsellors and ministers. The majority of the population, however, embraced the Buddhist faith.

The inhabitants of Burma comprised two main types living in the two main areas. The Mons held the Irrawaddy delta in the south and the land extending to the northern border of Siam. The Pyu held the Irrawaddy valley in Upper Burma. At Prome in the fifth to seventh centuries the Pyu erected brick stupas on circular bases with cylindrical towers surmounted by cone-shaped roofs. Unlike the Khmers who used

Bangkok stucco sculpture with its gilt inlays is like a distant echo of the splendour of Angkor before the plundering of the Khmer capital.

only corbeled arches, the Pyu (who spoke a Tibeto-Burman language and had come into direct contact with China) knew how to raise true arches and vaults with keystones. This contribution, unknown in India until the Muslim conquerors established the sultanate of Delhi in the eleventh century, is a distinctive feature of Burmese architecture as seen at Pagan. It puts it in a class apart from the other monuments of Indo-China and the Indian Archipelago.

In the ninth century, Upper Burma was invaded by another people: the Burmese, like their predecessors, the Pyu, came from the Tibeto-Chinese region. They took the city of Pagan, situated on the west bank of the Irrawaddy. At first they continued to practise their primitive religion, worshipping the "Nats" on the "Gold Mountain", an extinct volcano 50 km (30 mi.) from the capital. However they soon began to absorb the Buddhist religion. About A.D. 1000, a Burmese king of Pagan had an ordination hall built, indicating that the court had adopted the teachings of the Enlightened Being. The golden age of Buddhist art in Burma continued through the thirteenth century.

King Aniruddha who ruled from 1044 to 1077 conquered the kingdom of Thaton in Lower Burma, the centre of Mon civilization. He deported the Mon rulers to Pagan along with 30,000 monks, artists and craftsmen. The Mon civilization was more highly developed than that of the northern highlanders, since they had been in touch with Indian traders and missionaries for several hundred years. Pagan then became the "city of four million pagodas", as inscriptions call it. It was the capital of the united kingdom of Burma.

Pagan: a Reminder of Past Glories

The city of Pagan covered an area of about 250-300 square kilometres (100-120 sq. mi.). It had 20 km (12.5 mi.) of frontage on the Irrawaddy. Until its defeat in 1287 by Mongol troops led by Kublai Khan, more than 5000 monuments, pagodas, stupas and monasteries were erected at Pagan. In the heart of the urban centre was a walled city surrounded by a square wall, the left side of which ran along the river bank.

As at Angkor and in the rest of Southeast Asia, the dwellings, palaces and most of the monasteries were built in wood and straw. Some had brick walls with stucco ornamentation and tiled roofs. The only monuments constructed in stone were those intended as monuments to Buddha's glory. Hindu temples were few and far between.

Most of the large stone buildings in the city of Pagan can be divided into two main groups: on the one hand, the stupas consisting of a solid foundation on which several storeys rise in tiers and culminate in a circular or octagonal bell-shaped structure crowned by a lofty spire, and on the other hand the temples with their emphasis on inner space. These

Relief sculpture in the Nan-paya temple at Pagan. Eleventh century. This Buddhist figure has three heads like Brahma in Hindu iconography.

The great Minnanthu temple at Pagan built in 1183 is a pyramidal structure consisting of a central core and a ring gallery with openings on all four sides. At its base the edifice is 50 m (164 ft.) square. One should take note of the vaulted doorways.

temples could exhibit one of two arrangements: some contain a central chamber housing a statue of the Buddha; others, more obviously intended for the rite of circumambulation, have a vaulted corridor running round a solid core. One or four Buddhas can be contained in the niches contrived in this central core which supports a lofty spire. The stupas, built as memorials to Buddha's tomb, usually contain no inner space apart from a tiny reliquary. Median stairways lead up to the terraces which were sometimes used for the rite of circumambulation, as for example at Borobudur. In its final phase of evolution, the Burmese stupa is circular with a bell-shaped profile. The soaring spire tapers off towards the top. The very slender silhouette of these Burmese temples probably reflects the influence of the Sikharas, or towers, the most impressive features of the temples of Hindu India.

Most temples at Pagan are built in the shape of reliquaries. In fact, the polychrome stucco ornamentation is an enlarged copy of goldsmiths' works. However, though they do contain inner spaces, these temples are actually enormous artificial mountains provided with chapels and galleries in their mass. In comparison to the mass of solid brick, the empty spaces are minute. These constructions do indeed resemble rock-cut shrines, though the building techniques employed are by no means primitive. Pointed and Tudor arches support the vaulted ceilings of the inner chambers. Why didn't the Burmese use their knowledge and skills to construct brick assembly halls? Quite simply because, according to their traditions imported from India, stone was used only for building temples; as a rule, halls used for group meditation and ordination ceremonies were wooden with thatched or tiled roofs.

Most of the temples at Pagan have cruciform ground-plans. The corridors in colossal edifices like the Ananda pagoda make up genuine labyrinths with passageways crossing at right angles hollowed out of the artificial mountain.

View of the plain round Pagan: the site is studded with monuments as far as the eye can see. Remains of no less than 5000 monuments, mostly Buddhist, can be traced in the ancient Burmese capital. To the left, the Thatbinnyu pagoda built in 1144 rises up to a height of nearly 70 m (230 ft.). The temple contains a vaulted hall housing a statue of the Buddha. In the foreground, a small shrine.

A good many frescoes, glazed terra-cottas and stone relief sculptures portraying scenes from the life of the Buddha decorate the temples at Pagan. The edifice was a holy place, a kind of "Paupers' Bible" made in stone where pilgrims came to read the Blessed One's life story.

The Mongol invasion which put the city of Pagan to fire and sword also put an end to the work of Burmese artists and architects. The enormous holy city was abandoned. A minor Burmese renaissance took place at other urban centres such as Pegu, Mingun, Mandalay and Rangoon. Late Burmese architects were often inspired by the art of Tibet and Ceylon.

Conclusion

The cultural gifts which India lavished on the whole of Southeast Asia had a strange fate. Missionaries imported both the ageless mythology of Hindu polytheism and the more "rationalistic" philosophy taught by Buddhist doctrine. Via Southeast Asia, the teachings of the Merciful One penetrated into the Far East where the doctrine survived, like the light of a dying star which takes thousands of years to reach us. When Buddhism vanished from the Indian subcontinent — save for the high valleys of the Himalayas — it found a new home in the east where the Buddhist religion is still practised from the Burmese mountains to the shores of Bali and from the Malay Archipelago to Japan.

This is indeed India's paradox. India was the homeland of a religion which, on the eve of its decline only ten centuries after its birth, spread throughout the whole of Asia, inspired millions of people and developed new schools such as the Great and Little Vehicle, the Mahayana and the Theravadins. At the same time, India itself was experiencing a Hindu renaissance. This Hindu resurgence reinforced the caste system which, along with religious taboos, paralysed Indian society. These fundamental customs of ancient India were never accepted by Buddhist neophytes in Indo-China and Indonesia who valued Indian thought as a means of meditation and deliverance.

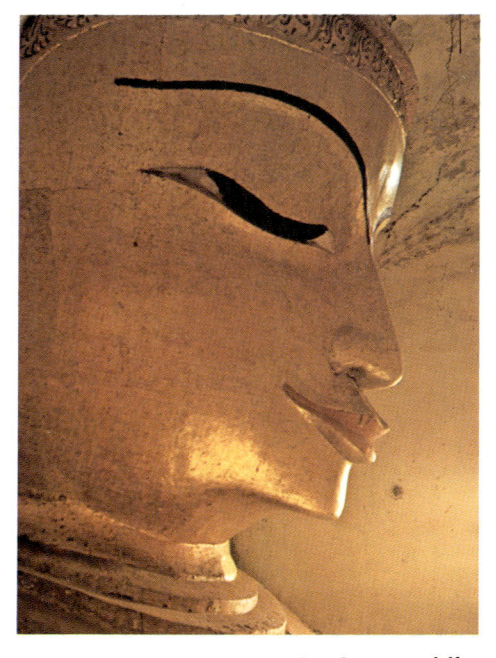

Amazing stylization of the Buddha image at Pagan.

Above:
The Kuthodaw pagodas in the town of Mandalay date from the nineteenth century.

Facing page:
Bupaya stupa at Pagan: this Buddhist stupa standing on a cliff overlooking the Irrawaddy was built in the eighth or ninth century. It ranks among the oldest and most venerated holy places in Burma.

MANDALAY
PAGAN
Irrawaddy
PROME
PEGU
RANGOON
THATON
CHIENG MAI
LAMPUN (LAMPHUN)
SUKHODAYA (SUKHOTHAI)
PIMÂI (BIMAYA)
Phanom Dang Raek
PRAH VIHAR
PRASAT
LOPBURI
KÓRÂT
BANTEAY CHMAR
SUBARNAPURI
(SUPHAN BURI)
AYUDHYÂ
Phanom Kulen
KOH KER
NAGARA PATHAMA
(NAKHON
PATHOM)
ARANYAPRATET
BANGKOK
ANGKOR
(Yasodharapura)
BANTEAY SREN
BENG MEALEA
SIEM-REAP
PRAH KHAN
Mè Nâm
ROHIOS (Hariharâlaya)
SAMBOR PREI KUK
(Isanapura)
BATTAMBANG
KOMPONG THOM
Tonle Sap
Mekong
BA PHNOM
GULF OF SIAM
TA PROHM
TAKEO
JAVA
MAGELANG
BOROBUDUR
PRAMBANAM